University Technology Transfer

Universities have become essential players in the generation of knowledge and innovation. Through the commercialization of technology, they have developed the ability to influence regional economic growth. By examining different commercialization models this book analyses technology transfer at universities as part of a national and regional system. It provides insight as to why certain models work better than others, and reaffirms that technology transfer programs must be linked to their regional and commercial environments.

Using a global perspective on technology commercialization, this book divides the discussion between developed and developing countries according to the level of university commercialization capability. Case studies examine policies and culture of university involvement in economic development, relationships between university and industry, and the commercialization of technology first developed at universities. In addition, each chapter provides examples from specific universities in each country from a regional, national and international comparative perspective.

This book will be highly relevant to all those with an interest in innovation studies, organizational studies, regional economics, higher education, public policy and business entrepreneurship.

Shiri M. Breznitz is Assistant Professor at the Munk School of Global Affairs at the University of Toronto, Canada.

Henry Etzkowitz is Senior Researcher at the Human Sciences and Technologies Advanced Research Institute, Stanford University, USA, and Visiting Professor at School of Management, Birkbeck College, London University and Edinburgh University Business School, UK.

Routledge Studies in Global Competition
Edited by John Cantwell, Rutgers
The State University of New Jersey, USA
and
David Mowery
University of California, Berkeley, USA

For a complete list of titles in this series, please visit www.routledge.com.

University Technology Transfer

The globalization of academic innovation

Edited by
Shiri M. Breznitz and Henry Etzkowitz

LONDON AND NEW YORK

First published 2016 by Routledge

2 Park Square, Milton Park, Abingdon, Oxfordshire OX14 4RN

52 Vanderbilt Avenue, New York, NY 10017

Routledge is an imprint of the Taylor & Francis Group, an informa business

First issued in paperback 2019

British Library Cataloguing in Publication Data
A catalogue record for this book is available from the British Library

Library of Congress Cataloging in Publication Data
University technology transfer : the globalization of academic innovation / edited by Shiri Breznitz and Henry Etzkowitz.
pages cm
Includes bibliographical references and index.
1. Academic-industrial collaboration. 2. Technology transfer. I. Breznitz, Shiri M. II. Etzkowitz, Henry, 1940-
LC1085.U57 2015
378.1'035--dc23
2015010691

ISBN: 978-0-415-71468-6 (hbk)
ISBN: 978-0-367-86874-1 (pbk)

Typeset in Times New Roman
by Saxon Graphics Limited, Derby

Contents

PART VI
Conclusion   461

Figures

Tables

Graphs

Contributors

Joaquín M. Azagra-Caro is a Tenured Scientist at INGENIO (CSIC-UPV), which is a joint research institute of the Spanish National Research Council (CSIC) and the Polytechnic University of Valencia (UPV), Spain.

Shiri M. Breznitz is an Assistant Professor at the Munk School of Global Affairs at the University of Toronto, Canada.

Elena Castro-Martínez is a Tenured Scientist working at INGENIO (CSIC-UPV), which is a joint research institute of the Spanish National Research Council (CSIC) and the Polytechnic University of Valencia (UPV), Spain.

Sabarni K. Chatterjee is a Senior Licensing and Patenting Manager at the Office of Technology Transfer, National Institutes of Health and Human Services, Rockville, MD. He is also the Deputy Regional Coordinator of the Federal Laboratory Consortium for Technology Transfer, Mid-Atlantic Region.

Paige Clayton is a Doctoral Student in the Department of Public Policy at the University of North Carolina, Chapel Hill, U.S.A.

Thiago J. C. C. Soares is a Researcher in the Technology and Innovation Management Group at the Federal University of São Paulo, Brazil.

Pablo D'Este is a Tenured Scientist at INGENIO (CSIC-UPV), which is a joint research institute of the Spanish National Research Council (CSIC) and the Polytechnic University of Valencia (UPV), Spain.

Henry Etzkowitz is President of the Triple Helix Association; Editor-in-Chief of *Triple Helix* (a journal of university–industry–government innovation and entrepreneurship); and author of the book *The Triple Helix* (Routledge 2008). He is also Visiting Professor Birkbeck and University of London, and Advisor to the Shandong Academy of Sciences, P.R. China.

Claudio Fassio is a Post-Doctorate fellow at the School of European Political Economy (SEP), LUISS Guido Carli, Rome, and research fellow at BRICK, Collegio Carlo Alberto, Italy.

Maryann Feldman is the Heninger Distinguished Professor in the Department of Public Policy at the University of North Carolina, Chapel Hill and Program Director at Science of Science and Innovation Policy (SciSIP) at the National Science Foundation (NSF), U.S.A.

Ignacio Fernández de Lucio is Research Professor at the Spanish Council for Scientific Research (CSIC) working on INGENIO (CSIC-UPV), which is a joint research institute of the Spanish National Research Council (CSIC) and the Polytechnic University of Valencia (UPV), Spain.

Ciara Fitzgerald is a Lecturer in the Department of Accounting, Finance and Information Systems at the University College Dublin, Ireland.

Adela García-Aracil is a Tenured Scientist of CSIC at INGENIO), which is a joint research institute of the Spanish National Research Council (CSIC) and the Polytechnic University of Valencia (UPV), Spain.

Christiane Gebhardt is the Vice President Head Global Initiatives at Malik Management Institute in St. Gallen, Switzerland.

Lodewijk L. Gelauff is Project Manager at ScienceWorks in The Hague, Netherlands.

Aldo Geuna is Full Professor at the Department of Economics and Statistics Cognetti De Martiis, University of Torino and Fellow of the Collegio Carlo Alberto, Italy.

John Glasson is Professor Emeritus of Planning in the Department of Planning, Oxford Brookes University, U.K.

Devrim Göktepe-Hultén is an Assistant Professor at the Department of Business Administration, Lund University, Sweden.

Nicola Hepburn is Manager, Policy & Research at a major financial institution in Toronto, Canada.

Jonathan J. Jensen is a Senior Licensing Manager at Partners HealthCare, Boston, MA, U.S.A.

Martin Kenney is a Professor in Community and Regional Development in the College of Agriculture and Environmental Sciences at the University of California, Davis (U.S.A.); a Senior Project Director at the Berkeley Roundtable on the International Economy; and Senior Fellow at the Research Institute for the Finnish Economy, Helsinki, Finland.

Patrick C. Kilgore is a registered patent attorney in private practice in Chicago, Illinois, focusing on representing clients in patent litigation concerning small molecule and biologic pharmaceuticals.

Helen Lawton Smith is Professor of Entrepreneurship, Department of Management, Birkbeck, and University of London, U.K.

Eric London is Senior Director at W.L. Ross & Co. LLC in New York, NY, U.S.A.

Lita Nelsen is the Director of the Technology Licensing Office M.I.T., Cambridge, MA, U.S.A.

Tran Ngoc Ca is Director of Secretariat for the National Council for Science and Technology Policy, Personal Assistant to S&T Minister and Deputy Director, National Institute for Science and Technology Policy and Strategy Studies, Hanoi, Vietnam.

Rory P. O'Shea is a faculty member at the University College Dublin (UCD) School of Business, Ireland.

Donald Patton is a research associate with Community and Regional Development at the University of California, Davis, U.S.A.

Guilherme Ary Plonski is a Professor at the University of São Paulo (USP; Brazil). He is affiliated with both the Business School and the Engineering School, and is the Research Director of the Center for Technology Policy and Management.

Tatiana Pospelova is a PhD student at the School of Economics, Lomonosov Moscow State University, Russia.

M. Elizabeth R. dos Santos is Head of the Technology Transfer Office of the Pontifical Catholic University of Rio Grande do Sul (PUCRS), Brazil.

Mark L. Rohrbaugh is Special Advisor for Technology Transfer, Office of the Director, National Institutes of Health, Department of Health and Human Services, Bethesda, MD, U.S.A.

Federica Rossi is Lecturer at the Department of Management, Birkbeck, University of London, U.K.

Ashley J. Stevens is a Lecturer at Boston University's Strategy and Innovation Department, School of Management, Boston, MA, U.S.A. and is also President of Focus IP Group, an IP consulting company. Previously, he was Director of the Office of Technology Transfer of Boston University and Director of the Office of Technology Transfer of the Dana-Farber Cancer Institute, a teaching affiliate of the Harvard Medical School, U.S.A.

Robert J.W. Tijssen is Professor at Leiden University (Netherlands), Stellenbosch University (South Africa) and one of U-Multirank's project managers.

Ana L. V. Torkomian is a Professor in the Department of Production Engineering, Federal University of São Carlos (DEP/UFSCar), Brazil.

David A. Wolfe is Professor of Political Science at UTM and Co-Director of the Innovation Policy Lab at the Munk School of Global Affairs in Toronto, Canada.

Jarunee Wonglimpiyarat is a Member in the College of Innovation, Thammasat University, Thailand.

Katrine Wyller works with early phase governmental support for business development at the Research Council of Norway, Oslo.

Qingzhi Zhang is an Assistant Professor at the University of the Chinese Academy of Sciences, Beijing, P.R. China.

Chunyan Zhou is the Director and senior researcher for the International Triple Helix Institute (ITHI), U.S.A. She is also the Co-Director and leading researcher for the Regional Innovation & Entrepreneurship Center at Shandong Academy of Science, P.R. China.

Frank J.M. Zwetsloot is CEO of ScienceWorks, The Hague, Netherlands.

Part I
Introduction

1 The evolution of technology transfer

Henry Etzkowitz

Three questions

Why do universities transfer technology? Is not technology transfer a business far removed from traditional academic missions of education and research? Nevertheless, how did interface between academia and industry become an academic pursuit, despite divergent institutional logics? Evolving from an informal professorial avocation to a professional administrative office and from a legal to marketing to an entrepreneurial approach, technology transfer has spread across academia. As the transfer of technology has shifted from marginal to mainstream, a host of questions have been raised over the purpose of the university, the nature of knowledge and the role of the university in society. Serendipitous discoveries, whose beneficial consequences also subjected the university and populace to risk, drove the initial direction of policy discourse.

The origins of formal university technology transfer may not surprisingly be traced to events at the University of Wisconsin, a land grant school with a practical orientation strongly focused on the state's agricultural dairy industry and more intriguingly to the University of Toronto, a liberal arts research university whose practical orientation was largely confined to its medical school where research was carried out to cure disease. A successful diabetes research project generated significant intellectual property in the early twentieth century (Bliss 1982). Both cases generated issues of ethical manufacture that required formal intellectual property protection to resolve (Apple 1989). In subsequent decades, the economic spillover from early instances of university technology transfer moved front and center as a significant, if not primary, motivation for stakeholders, inside and outside of academia. These developments have raised fundamental epistemological, ethical and normative issues.

In the Faust legend there is a bargain with the devil and an exchange of a soul for arcane, highly desired, knowledge. Some critics argue that the university has made a similar arrangement by involving itself in technology transfer in the first place (Washburn 2005). In the following sections we discuss the expansion of technology transfer from its traditional meaning of movement across national borders (still an important and even primary mode in many countries) to movement among units within and among firms and between university and industry. The rise of university technology transfer is part of a second academic revolution, making contribution to economic and social development an accepted academic mission that is interwoven with education and research.

Technology transfer and the academic mission

Extending beyond well-accepted service tasks, technology transfer is conventionally viewed as an expression of the so-called linear model, proceeding from research to invention and innovation (Bush 1945). However, technology transfer may also be viewed within a broader non-linear framework that also includes feedback mechanisms proceeding from societal needs and invention back to blue sky research. The supposedly discrete categories of basic and applied research, never watertight, with handovers between them along a linear path, are superseded by "polyvalent knowledge" with theoretical and practical implications inherent in the same research finding. In a classic instance of polyvalence, agricultural researchers at U.S. land grant universities in the 1930s discovered hybrid corn by extending their government funded research programs, designed to solve immediate crop problems, to address fundamental questions in genetics (Griliches 1960).

The inclusion of technology transfer in the academic mission is part of a broader paradigm shift from a research to an entrepreneurial academic mode superseding the dyadic Humboldtian paradigm, combining research and education. However, research and a mindset to translate research into practice, if not personal economic reward, is the prerequisite to technology transfer Research was typically an add-on to the classical academic mission of education that included preservation and dissemination of high culture and training for legal, ecclesiastical and medical professions. A research mission, however, is a prerequisite to a technology transfer mission, if not an entrepreneurial remit that can be built upon a teaching as well as a research base.

Most important to academics: students, faculty and administrators and university stakeholders is the question of which academic model to follow: the now traditional research university model, focused on education and research, with technology transfer and innovation an adjunct activity or an emerging entrepreneurial university model in which the two academic missions that converged into an integrated format in the late nineteenth century are joined with a third mission of contribution to economic and social development that is of equal status. The dual Humboldtian paradigm is transmogrifying into a Triple Helix University, paradoxically both more closely linked to industry and government, while expanding its independence as a more salient institutional sphere (Etzkowitz 2008).

The choice between the research and entrepreneurial models suggests different roles and status for technology transfer in the university. Answers to the following questions will indicate preference for one model or the other: Should academic knowledge be conceptualized as a meandering stream of fundamental research from which practical implications emerge as an occasional serendipitous byproduct? Or has a normative revolution occurred in which polyvalent knowledge, with simultaneous theoretical and practical import, publishable and patentable attributes? Spin-offs may be generated and discoveries are disseminated in the media as well as academic journals. Heretofore, between discovery and utilization one or two generations intervened whereas more recently these phenomena occur within the same generation, simultaneously or even in reverse order.

Pasteur's Quadrant denotes research that is of both theoretical and practical import (Stokes 1997). It is accompanied by two additional eponomyzed quadrants, Edison and Bohr representing each side of a traditional theoretical practical divide. However, Indeed, the exemplary exponents of these quadrants Niels Bohr and Thomas Edison do not entirely fit their respective quadrants. Bohr took the practical consequences of research in nuclear physics into account and lobbied politicians to influence its utilization. Edison, the consummate "cut and try" inventor was also the discoverer of the "Edison effect."

In contrast to the concept of Pasteur's Quadrant in which basic knowledge with practical implications is confined to a delimited sphere, we expect polyvalent knowledge to envelop the traditional quadrants of basic and applied research. Researchers may pursue a variety of crosscutting objectives simultaneously rather than operating according to either/or motivations that separate advancement of fundamental understanding from solution of practical problems.

Second, the polyvalent knowledge position indicates that transfer should be embedded in the educational and research missions as well as vice versa, with incubators as well as labs an integral part of academic physical structures, with representatives of transfer offices present at research group meetings to identify potential IP and technology transfer part of the academic degree program as well as economic development mission.

Third, the Pastuer's quadrant model suggests that various formats of knowledge production and utilization may co-exist peacefully, likely located in different parts of the university, with the engineering and medical schools taking a polyvalent approach while the arts and sciences follow the meandering stream. These theoretical perspectives have implications for the course and direction as well as location, of technology transfer in an academic setting. First, the meandering stream position suggests that technology transfer should be carried out in isolation from education and research, with technology transfer professionals available to assist transfer of inventions disclosed to them but that they not take a pro-active stance to suggest lines of investigation out of concern that such steering would violate the purity of academic knowledge.

The nature of knowledge is also at issue. If a constructivist position is taken science is seen as socially shaped with knowledge claims malleable and subject to social control. On the other hand, if scientific knowledge is viewed as containing an irreducible empirical core that social factors to not influence, then alternative policy implications may be drawn. Social factors may drive topic selection, influence perception and non-perception of results, e.g. difficulties anomalies have in disrupting paradigms. Thus, recognition of a discovery may lag until a build-up of results or the passing of adherents (Kuhn 1962, Ventner 2013).

Nevertheless, social factors do not ultimately determine the nature of scientific knowledge. They explain as much as 75% of variance but there is an irreducible empirical core (Fleck [1935] 1976). Indeed, attempts to produce fraudulent knowledge claims will be more quickly discovered if they are expected to produce commercializable results as well. A pragmatic test of the claims will quickly ensue and the validity will be ascertained. On the other hand, most academic papers are not read, let alone cited and a fraudulent paper may reside in the scientific literature indefinitely, while still driving tenure and promotion decisions. Thus university technology transfer has become central to debates over academic mission, the nature of the science and innovation.

Technology transfer and innovation

Technology transfer is the movement of particular inventions, entire technological systems or knowledge of how to construct them across national or organizational boundaries. The processes of technology transfer have been noted to occur across time and space, during the medieval period in the diffusion of such basic technologies as the waterwheel, windmill and heavy plough, and in the relations among civilizations such as China and the West, in which both organizational technologies such as bureaucracy and physical technologies such as gunpowder moved westward. Technology transfer is a key element of economic growth, perhaps even more important than the invention and development of technology.

Technology transfer is a complex process that requires appropriate organizational and cultural "software" as well as technical "hardware" to be accomplished in its most productive form. More than the relocation of a physical artifact, technology transfer also involves entrepreneurship, specific skills, even government finance or patronage as well as commercial demand. According to Misa (1995) technology transfer, in its most developed form, is the ability to obtain knowledge and skills from an originating source, adapt them to use in a different economic and social structure and then diffuse them into new technical applications in other industrial sectors.

Equal partners freely entering into agreements, the contemporary positive image of technology transfer has a reverse mirror image. Headrick (1988) shows how colonial powers have used technology transfer as a means to increase their economic and political influence, without necessarily having to use military force. In this inherently unequal patron/client relationship the "sender" typically restricted the transfer process to a narrow domain and limited access to the knowledge transferred by having its nationals operate the relocated technology. For example, British engineers operated locomotives for as long as three-quarters of a century after the construction of the first railroad in India, keeping this skill out of the hands of the "receivers" for as long as possible.

The purpose of colonial technology transfer was to draw the less developed country more fully into the colonizer's economic and political orbit. Thus, colonizers in India and Africa put transportation technologies, such as rail and road, in place to assist in the extraction of resources and the movement of troops.

Communication technologies such as telegraph and telephone systems were installed to help a few colonial administrators maintain political control over vast regions and large populations. Nevertheless, once installed these technologies became a double-edged sword, used by indigenous peoples for their own purposes, including creation of networks and organizations to displace their colonial rulers. When Tata built steel mills with technology imported from the U.S.: British officials viewed them as a bulwark of empire while nationalist Indian entrepreneurs saw the groundwork for an independent economy.

After independence, technology transfer as an economic development strategy becomes clear to both sides, as the former colonizer and newly independent nation, struggle to assert their opposing interests. David (1981) delineates the workings of this process as overall favorable to the emerging nation, at least in the growth of the U.S. textile in the early nineteenth century. American manufacturers sought to obtain knowledge and devices from Britain through socially mobile individuals willing to leave their home country and recreate devices upon their arrival in the U.S. Although it could not prevent the movement of technology the British government was able to exact an additional cost on its transfer through export and immigration controls.

On the U.S. side, technology transfer was facilitated and magnified by the availability of technologically knowledgeable individuals who adapted the technology to local circumstances. Knowledge embodied in persons, whether laborers or factory owners, was far more important to successful transfer of technology than the artifacts themselves. In this analysis particular bits of technology were moved by specific individuals across national boundaries within the same industrial sector.

David's (1981) case study of textile technology exemplifies Inkster's category of narrow technology transfer. In this mode a particular technology is transferred from its place of origin as a technological process in a particular industry to another geographical site within the same industrial context. On the other hand, in broad technology transfer a technology is moved from its place of origin to a variety of applications across several industries. For the latter to be more likely to take place a local R&D capacity is required.

What are the preconditions for successful technology transfer? Landes (1972) emphasizes conditions at the receptor site as a prerequisite for successful technology transfer: the importance of a stable political and legal environment, with reliable contracts replacing force as the guarantor of relationships. Tar and Dupuy (1988) also emphasize the importance of the unique physical, economic and social context into which technology is transferred. If technology is not appropriately modified to fit local circumstances it may well fail to take hold. Thus, British "destructor" technology for incinerating urban wastes that was economical in a dense urban setting, where even outlying land was too costly to be devoted to a dump, worked less well in the U.S. in the late nineteenth and early twentieth centuries, where burying wastes was a viable alternative.

There are fascinating anomalies in technology transfer. The movement of technology across national borders has been found to be more rapid than diffusion within them. For example, Watt's steam engine patented in Britain in 1776, came into use in France in 1779 and Germany in 1788, yet its use was not widespread until the 1830s and 40s. Kenwood and Lougheed's (1982) finding suggests the salience of regional disparities to the potential for technology transfer and the greater likelihood for transfer among "high-tech" areas, wherever they are located. Tod (1995) focuses on the question: Can technology transfer generate a capacity for innovation (in the Australian context)? The answer is at least in part dependent upon the ability to move newly acquired technical capabilities more broadly across the economy.

With the decline of colonialism and protectionism technology transfer has taken on a new meaning, denoting the movement of technology across institutional spheres such as between academia and industry (Gibbons et al. 1994). Beginning with the contractual sale of specific pieces of intellectual property between firms, technology transfer becomes a way of integrating inventors and manufacturers, producers and users of technology. Beyond a unidirectional flow of rights to artifacts between organizations in different places, technology transfer can grow into a two-way flow of ideas and techniques among a variety of partners who may come to see themselves as participants in a virtual joint enterprise. Alternatively, universities and their faculty may become adversaries in tough negotiations and find themselves, on opposite sides of court battles over patents as in Madey v. Duke in which a university claimed the intellectual property rights of a faculty member, including rights generated while employed at another university.

The sources of university technology transfer

Entrepreneurs hanging around MIT's laboratories, acting like vultures by seeking commercializable technology to take without recompense, inspired the university to protect its intellectual property. University technology transfer originated at MIT in the form of a joint faculty/administration committee to evaluate inventions and encourage their protection and development. Faculty can reasonably extend their professional capacities to evaluate the commercial potential of colleagues' research, especially if they have participated in spin-off creation, but protection of IP requires specialized legal expertise that if carried out by a university requires a home. Thus, the technology transfer office (TTO) was invented at the University of Wisconsin, first in the form of a foundation, a quasi-independent organization, to establish distance from traditional academic missions,

Teachers with only limited formal higher training early laid the groundwork for informal technology transfer. Alexander Graham Bell, whose training in audiology largely occurred within an intergenerational "family business" of teaching the deaf, for example, developed the telephone as a teacher at Boston University, in facilities provided by the university receiving release time from teaching to carry out the project and spun out a firm. On the other hand, Princeton physicist Joseph Henry, who had worked out the theory of the invention of the telegraph felt inhibited from taking the next steps to reduce his ideas to practice. From his later vantage point as the Director of the Smithsonian Institution, having missed out on the invention of the telegraph, he ruefully advised Bell not to make the same mistake with telephony (Moyer 1997).

A special class of institutions of higher learning—the so-called land grant universities in the U.S., e.g. University of Connecticut and MIT, and polytechnic universities in Europe, ETH Zurich and Polytechnico Milan—focused on supporting regional mechanical and agricultural industries (Artz 1966, Rossiter 1975). This practical orientation spread to a broader group of universities, hybrids of the polytechnic/land grant mode and the liberal arts College, New York University, focused on commerce, and Stanford on engineering are prototypical examples of universities that combine practical with theoretical academic pursuits. MIT expanded its purview into the humanities and social sciences to facilitate students ascent to corporate leadership positions that might otherwise be occupied by Harvard graduates whose liberal arts curriculum was presumed to better prepare them for leadership.

There are multiple pathways to an entrepreneurial academic mode. Entrepreneurial universities have arisen from diverse academic traditions. MIT derived an entrepreneurial academic model from a synthesis of the U.S. Land Grant and European Polytechnic traditions. Nevertheless, MIT also incorporated specific elements of the liberal arts tradition in order to give its technical students a broader purview. Stanford, like New York University, originated as a synthesis of the liberal arts university tradition and a private university model oriented respectively to technological and commercial local economic development. The Pontifical Catholic University of Rio de Janeiro took an entrepreneurial turn in the face of loss of research funding from Brazil's former military regime. At many universities, an entrepreneurial initiative is encapsulated in a particular organizational mechanism like an incubator facility or TTO that, at least initially, is segregated from the rest of the university.

A technology transfer regime may be instituted directly by a national government, as in Japan, through a funding program replete with benchmarks and qualification procedures, or indirectly as in the U.S., through legal changes incentivizing universities to develop transfer capabilities. The Amendment to U.S. patent law of 1980, better known eponymously after its sponsors Senators Birch Bayh and Robert Dole, gave universities ownership of intellectual property rights to federally funded research, an explicit role in technology transfer and included inventors in the reward scheme (Stevens 2004).

Heretofore uninterested universities established a TTO, showing an interest in putting research to use and thus meeting the criteria for continued receipt of federal research funding. Despite low expectations these new offices sometimes achieved a highly successful patent, as at Columbia University, thus gaining support of the university's administration for expansion of their activities. Other offices, less lucky or lacking a prolific faculty adopted a "pump priming" strategy, encouraging researchers to explore the commercial potential of their research (Etzkowitz and Goktepe 2010). In yet other cases, offices remained dormant (Feldman and Desrochers 2004) until reorganized, for example, as part of a strategy to develop a biotech industry next to Johns Hopkins University.

Integrating the transfer process in an entrepreneurial academic culture has become a virtually universal goal in divergent academic systems. Organizational capabilities are enhanced in systems that leave intellectual property rights in the hands of the inventor as in "the Professor's exemption" in Sweden. Following medieval European practice the professoriate was exempt from many of the obligations of the ordinary citizen, like the requirement to quarter soldiers in ones house in times of emergency and were also sometimes entitled to special emoluments such as public provision of wine. Similarly professors were allowed to retain control of the intellectual property that they generated during their university employment. Thus Swedish tech transfer office negotiates with faculty to gain the rights to their discoveries for purposes of commercialization. Faculties are not required to disclose. On the other hand, the office has the ability to offer support such as covering patent fees and otherwise supporting research commercialization as an incentive for faculty to wish the university's participation. The Bayh-Dole Act of 1980 laid the groundwork for universities to construct policies that encourage professors to treat disclosure of intellectual property as the quid pro quo for receiving federal research funds.

Differences are often less than perceived as the U.S. system guarantees the faculty member a significant share of the results, in contrast to corporate inventors who are entirely dependent upon the generosity of their employers to receive anything beyond a commendation or possibly a promotion but not a direct share of profits from their invention. The U.S. Bayh-Dole Act, in effect, created a "partial professor's privilege," guaranteeing university inventors a significant share of rewards in contrast to firm employees, dependent upon employer's generosity. Thus, the inventor is granted a significant interest even as formal rights are placed under the control of the university. In the former instance, the university may negotiate to acquire intellectual property rights; in the latter, the university is strongly dependent upon inventor cooperation to realize value from formal rights.

Tech transfer: legal mode

The legal format is characterized by the university's recognition of the necessity to patent in order to protect the university's reputation and ensure user safety, was recognized at Toronto and Wisconsin, respectively, through the insulin and milk purity test experiences (Bliss 1984, Apple 1989). A marketing format transformed the arm's length intellectual property protection approach into a more pro-active regime in which the university actively sought out prospective licensees, beyond the purview of the inventor. This phase included brainstorming to simultaneously extend patent claims and identify additional markets. Entrepreneurial faculty at Stanford and MIT translated inventions into firms before the development of formal technology transfer. Aspiring schools created an incubation and entrepreneurial training process designed to replicate, in a collapsed time frame, the early informal developments at Stanford and MIT (Hatakenaka 2004).

These evolutionary phases are also instantiated in actually existing TTO's as their institutional logics. Thus a TTO, typically led by an attorney, may follow the legal approach, protecting the discoveries but making little effort to actively seek out licensees beyond the basic announcement on the TTO's website. The marketing model is the next step, with the TTO making an active effort to seek out potential licensees by developing and extending relationships in industry, especially those relevant to its main source of inventors. The following step is an entrepreneurial approach in which the TTO actively support the formation of a firm, providing entrepreneurial talent and even financing to support the early stages of firm formation. At this point the TTO typically becomes part of a broader innovation unit within the universities, supporting a variety of entrepreneurial activities that include but extend beyond technology transfer

University technology transfer in the U.S. innovation system

The theoretical framework for U.S. technology transfer was created in the context of the Second World War when basic researchers combined forces with engineers to produce new weapons as an extension of basic research (e.g. the atomic bomb) as well as from military requirements to detect hostile aircraft (e.g. radar). Although the scientists expected that they were putting aside their theoretical pursuits for the duration of the wartime emergency they found, to their surprise, that new ideas for investigation were arising from their involvement with practical problems.

The efflorescence of theory from practice was a phenomenon earlier noted by a young engineering professor at MIT, Vannevar Bush, who brought back ideas from his consulting practice for elucidation with his students. Later, as a high level wartime science and technology administrator, looking towards peacetime and operating in an ideological environment in which a role for government is highly suspect (cf. the recent U.S. health care debate), Bush disentangled science from its social context and placed it on a metaphorical plane to attain his broader objective: government support of research for a variety of purposes in the post-war, superseding the narrower wartime focus that had provided temporary large-scale funding for scientific research (Baxter 1946).

Bush's post-war linear model is the partial revival of the wartime non-linear "triple helix" that the U.S. has since more fully recuperated through the Bayh-Dole Act and other measures. In the "game of legitimation" that Bush was playing, he had to, with one hand, place research on a neutral ground ("the frontier") while with the other, execute a sleight of hand and link its benefits back to the housing, military, health and other impetuses to research with practical goals that each received their special chapter in the Endless Frontier Report (Bush 1945).

A "linear model" served that purpose well although Bush was likely not a believer and certainly not a practitioner of linearity (Balconi, Brusoni and Orsenigo 2009). Vannevar Bush was an engineer, consultant, entrepreneur, teacher and researcher, in other words, the prototypical MIT professor. Bush was a student of the "consulting engineers" who had been recruited to MIT to introduce research in the late nineteenth and early twentieth centuries. They also brought their consulting practices with them into academe and synthesized a new academic entrepreneurial model (Etzkowitz 2002). As noted earlier, Bush made a practice of bringing back to his MIT graduate students theoretical issues arising from his industrial consulting projects and working them out together (Bush 1970).

One of these students was Fred Terman, who brought the model back with him to Stanford as a young professor where he expanded upon it in his own work, with students such as Hewlett and Packard, and later as an academic administrator in forming new research groups and then departments with conjoint theoretical and practical objectives. Bush and Terman are implicit exponents of "polyvalent knowledge" that is simultaneously theoretical and practical, publishable and patentable, rather than flowing through a constricted linear pipeline. Bush made a step-change in the academic entrepreneurial model, in the run-up to the Second World War, when he went to Washington D.C. to head the Carnegie Institution and led an effort that gave academia a central place in wartime research, with industry and the military. Academic scientists, especially those who led these labs, lost their fear of government funding, as inevitably leading to government control of science. Wartime experience in a collaborative leadership role, with industry and government, provided grounds for acceptance of state research support and an entrepreneurial role for the university in society as the engine of innovation, the implicit thrust of the Endless Frontier Report.

Government has since found it necessary to revise its role and play a more active part "downstream," by crafting innovation policies and programs to insure that research results, however generated, are actually put into practice. Indeed, even in a country with multiple research agencies like the U.S., this has been the approach as NSF's remit was extended into engineering and then to the provision of public venture capital (Etzkowitz, Gulbrandsen and Levitt 2000). Behind the laissez-faire presumption of the linear model that academic research results would seamlessly pass to industry through graduated students taking employment and industrial researchers following the journal literature, a more focused organizational approach to technology transfer, utilizing the patent system, had grown from its origins at MIT in the early twentieth century According to a university official, "The national innovation strategy is to put federally funded R&D on a conveyer belt that gets the R&D commercialized either by tech transfer to established companies or by wrapping the R&D into a university start-up..."[1]

Technology transfer and regional absorptive capacity

The confluence between public benefit and revenue models focuses attention on the region surrounding the university. A TTO director said that, "our mission is to promote technology to benefit the public; to the extent it results in revenue it is a good thing." In a region without previous high tech development, the TTO director may be the first person with an official responsibility for this topic. Even though his or her remit is focused on the university, an entrepreneurial director will soon expand it to include helping create the conditions for high-tech development in the area. Once local economic development considerations are taken into account, the issue broadens from the difficult enough one of finding a licensee to one of identifying a local source to develop the technology.

As one director put it, the objective is "to not just license technology but to capture and keep it in … [the state]." A TTO director in a peripheral region said that, "We now have a situation where faculty can do pre-incubation in their labs, we lease them space and sublicense equipment. The next step is either have a research bay or small lab that their company can rent and then graduate them out to incubator and other facilities run by the community." Another director described various sources of funding to explore commercial potential, including the university's own resources, "a small internal fund that can fund projects like that 50k per project" as well as external sources such as angel and state government funding.

In contrast to firm absorptive capacity that is held to be a function of prior related knowledge (Cohen and Levinthal 1990), developing regional absorptive capacity often entails breaking with previous practice (Saxenian 1994, Huffman and Quigley 2002). Regional absorptive capacity is operationalized as an entrepreneurial support structure of angel networks, venture capital opportunities, public relations and law firms oriented to support firm formation and cluster development but may take various forms. (Cooke 2001, Norrman 2005). Stanford faculty and students had the advantage not only of the location of largest proportion of the U.S. venture capital industry adjacent to the campus but also of colleagues with earnings from their previous ventures who could also afford to invest, as MIT entrepreneurs had long done.

On the other hand, when capacities are weak, new organizational formats may be invented such as the venture firm in early post-war New England or the "Courtyard for Agro-experts" in contemporary China (Tu, Gu and Wu 2005). In a region lacking a university, regional authorities developed a model of joint living and lab spaces to allow academics to visit for a limited time period, conduct research and consult on local agricultural problems.

University technology transfer must adapt to regional circumstances. A relatively low-key approach can work in a "thick" region, with strong entrepreneurial support capabilities while a more pro-active approach is indicated in a "thin" region, where absorptive capacity is weak. In the latter case, a TTO may take a leadership role to promote the creation of an external support structure and may also have to fill internal gaps when inventor interest is limited. Conversely an office may take a relatively passive stance when regional absorptive capacity and inventor interest is strong. However, this may result in untapped potential among moderately entrepreneurially oriented faculty, suggesting the applicability of support structures that are commonplace in aspiring universities to success cases as well.

The technology transfer gap has been filled by measures offering varying types and levels of support. Two approaches are typical: (1) intensified search to enhance the disclosure rate; and (2) entrepreneurial assistance to improve innovation chances. A half-time position in technology transfer and an academic department has been instituted in the Columbia University Medical School as a unique arrangement for an individual faculty member. This "dual-life" scheme formalized the "scouting function" of ARD, the original venture capital firm that served as an informal TTO and incubator for MIT in the early post-war. A serial entrepreneur, working at Stanford's Office of Technology Licensing (OTL) as a part-time licensing officer in between start-ups, frustrated with the paucity of licensing opportunities for a technology that he strongly believed in, formed a firm with special permission.

This "one-off" instance of a de-facto "entrepreneur in residence program" may regularly be found in Swedish university incubators. The two modes may also be combined. Thus, the "Chalmers Innovation System" includes a masters program in innovation and entrepreneurship to which student teams apply with commercialization ideas that they often source in academic research groups (Jacob et al. 2003). A Swedish hospital encourages nurses to be aware of the commercialization potential of devices they have invented and pairs them with "idea Pilots" and advisors to speed the innovation process (Nählinder 2010).

These experiments may be synthesized into an intensive transfer regime, to encourage a higher proportion of staff to become involved, including those not traditionally thought of as innovators, as well as raise the innovation rate. Aspiring schools typically view institutions they wish to emulate after success has already been achieved. They view the current policies, arrangements and procedures in place and assume that their replication will induce a similar result in their own institutions. However, what has been worked out at this later time may not be appropriate to an initiation phase. In the early stages of developing technology transfer, aggressive steps were taken. In a mature phase, once successful relations were developed, policies mandated strong boundaries. In an earlier era a Stanford administrator noted that it was, "not uncommon for a post-doc working in a Stanford lab to be spending a couple of days a week at a faculty start-up before it dawned that this was not consistent with the basic principles of the institution. What we are trying to avoid is the kinds of connections between a Stanford faculty member's academic program, resources, facilities, people and their outside entity. We are trying to keep a barrier between those."

The director of technology transfer at MIT, Lita Nelson, states that there is a "Chinese Wall" between academia and industry at her university strict rules are in place forbidding faculty members from playing an active role in firm formation. Decades earlier, the original venture capital firm, ARD, used underutilized space at MIT as an "incubator" for the firms that it was assisting MIT faculty members to establish. Currently, it is said that Ms Nelson merely turns the next card on her Rolodex to notify an area venture capitalist of the latest campus invention with start-up potential. The paradox is that if an aspiring entrepreneurial university adopts Stanford's and MIT's current practices, it may impede their chances of success. The precursor era of a success case is likely more relevant to the current situation of a follow-on region. Moreover, the best practices of an aspiring entrepreneurial university may be relevant to improving the practice of an international success case. In between mind and market, lab and Wall Street (or the City), a "permeable zone" emerges where two cultures intermingle (Kohler 2002:11).

A panoply of organizational hybrids to transfer scientific projects with economic potential have been invented such as incubator facilities, venture capital firms, science parks and TTOs. Many persons who work in these venues embody qualities drawn from both cultures. A meta-innovation system comprising bottom up, top down and lateral initiatives, from university, industry and government, individually and collectively, increasingly translates research into use and foster social as well as technological innovation (Etzkowitz et al. 2005).

The future of university technology transfer

Does this pecuniary interest in research represent a fundamental mission shift or is it a temporary aberration? It has been suggested that interest in intellectual property rights is receding and that universities are recovering from their "corporate fling" and returning to traditional tasks, motivated by international rating schemes that privilege article production. On the basis of a few years' modest downturn in the Association of University Technology Managers (AUTM) survey of U.S. academic patenting and cognate data, Leydesdorff and Meyer (2010) concluded that the end of university tech transfer is nigh. They drew this inference without seriously considering alternative explanations for a down-tick such as tighter criteria for patenting—e.g. protecting only what is identified as commercializable in advance rather than patenting in the expectation that a future

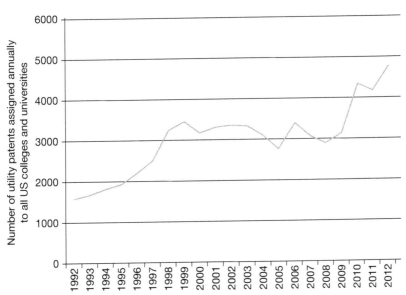

Source: USPTO official website: www.uspto.gov/web/offices/ac/ido/oeip/taf/univ/org_gr/all_univ_ag.htm

Figure 1.1 Number of utility patents assigned annually, to all U.S. colleges and universities

pecuniary use may be identified. The U.K., on the other hand, showed a continuous up-tick (Lawton-Smith 2014). Indeed, the most recent AUTM survey data has shown an uptick in university patenting, continuing a two-year trend suggesting that, with U.S. academic patenting on the rise again, the downturn was only a temporary blip.[2] The slowdown and leveling off of U.S. university patenting, prematurely interpreted as the end of the Bayh-Dole era was disconfirmed as university patenting resumed its steady rise.

Others note a general slowdown in patenting as an artifact of changes in U.S. PTO practice and personnel to process applications. The institution of a preliminary patenting procedure, allowing a year of protection to explore the viability of a full application, has allowed offices to be more selective in their patent applications. Perhaps more significant is the continuing rise of university originated start-ups (AUTM 2010) and the expansion of technology transfer to an integrated model that supplies faculty inventors with entrepreneurial partners and seed funding from internal university resources, in effect, packaging start-ups (Tedeschi 2010). In any event, patents are, at best, an indirect proxy for commercialization of university research, as many sit on the shelf, or website, of their TTO while other innovations rely on trade secrecy for protection and may never be disclosed.

Even in a highly academic science oriented firm like Cetus, Kary Mullis, the inventor of polymerase, a major biotechnology innovation, received a payment of only $10,000. On the other hand, he received broader rewards as part of his employment contract (Rabinow 1997) signify regime change from a marketing to entrepreneurial mode of technology transfer in which patenting is a significant but less important part of university technology transfer success than firm formation and growth. Or, it may simply be an artifact of resource stringency induced by the Great Recession of 2008 in which case we may expect an uptick as its effects recede.

Rather than a diminution of technology transfer activities, an expansion is underway as an increasing number of universities shift from a relatively narrow focus on licensing intellectual property to a broader focus on facilitating translational research and investing in start-up formation from campus inventions. For example, the University of Virginia has significantly broadened the remit of its office, and restructured its capabilities, to focus on firm formation and contribution to regional economic development (Cadwalader 2103). Indeed, the Obama Administration has recently made university technology transfer a centerpiece of its economic renewal strategy but is limited by financial constraints in its implementation. The Administration encourages experienced universities to disseminate their expertise through President Obama's Webinar series. Universities also use their endowments to create venture funds and state and local governments, e.g. New York City, are committing resources to stimulate university innovation performance (Henton and Held 2013).

Columbia University has expanded the focus of its TTO from licensing to the creation of new ventures. In pursuit of this objective, universities are increasingly willing to act as angels in funding the early stages of firm-formation. New York recently realized that it lacked an MIT, as a necessary element of its hoped-for transition from a financial, real estate and corporate headquarters city to a Silicon-

Valley-like start-up center. To realize this objective quickly Mayor Bloomberg developed a competitive scheme to attract such an institution to New York, offering land, money, and a New York venue as the attractor. Cornell University, wishing to expand its presence in the city, teamed with Technion, an experienced entrepreneurial university and won the competition. Future economic growth is expected from societal investment in research and new ways are being sought to transfer technology from research institutes to the economy.[3] Traditional measures do not capture the full extent of these developments.

The analysis of university patenting and technology transfer has suffered from a misplaced focus on numbers without context, a phenomenon that Ptirim Sorokin, the founder of Harvard's Sociology Department, identified as "Quantrophrenia" in his classic work *Fads and Foibles in Modern Sociology* (Sorokin 1956). Statistics themselves, not merely unreliable data, contribute to creating misplaced objectives. This is the principle that "every measure which becomes a target becomes a bad measure" (Hoskin 1996) by inducing "a fixation on the metric rather than on the creativity and initiative that any practice requires" (Paquet 2009). Quantrophrenia is the competitive tendency inherent in statistics to become a basis of rating comparisons that may counterproductively skew activity.

More than a half-century later, a phenomenon identified as counterproductive to sociological analysis has moved beyond academia into public policy through the uncritical use of university ranking systems. For example, the former version of the U.K. Research Assessment Exercise (RAE) evaluation of universities placed great weight on publications but did not credit contribution to economic development, even though it was becoming increasingly important as an academic mission. Thus, the evaluation exercise worked against objectives set by the study's government sponsors. Making the formerly left out activity into its own indicator may solve one problem while creating another. Once patenting became a criterion of academic success in Italy, a TTO Director reported that faculty members pressured him to patent discoveries, irrespective of whether a commercial potential could be discerned.[4] Thus, a numerical criterion may drive inappropriate activity unless strong safeguards are put into place.

Moreover, not all outputs are included in the official statistics. For example, AUTM spin-off data includes what is reported by TTO's but misses those start-ups that have gone out under the radar of the TTO or were begun by undergraduates, or others, who are not employees required to disclose. Some universities keep close watch but others do not consider themselves to be "intellectual property police." The problem is not only with quality of data—"the garbage in; garbage out" phenomenon and with the reification of quantification, the misguided application of scientistic methods from the physical sciences to the social world—but also with the shortening of time frames that may cut off significant potential results that have a long gestation period. Nevertheless, tech transfer has generated an increase in revenues from $7.3 million in 1981 to $3.4 billion in 2008 (Loise and Stevens 2010:188) and from 390 patents in 1980 to 3088 by 2009 (Schacht 2012).[5]

Although most universities do not yet earn from patent licensing and technology transfer, a few have gained significantly. The Axel patents were so financially rewarding to Columbia University that it made an attempt, which ultimately failed, to change the law and extend their life. The Cohen-Boyer patent around the same time produced more than 200 million dollars in royalties for the University of California and Stanford, the home institutions of the researchers. The techniques were broadly introduced to a wide variety of firms, with the academic institutions requesting relatively modest payments from each firm (Feldman, Colaianni and Liu 2007).

Due to the early stage nature of most academic originated technology, transfer often takes place to a new firm that the university may play a key role in founding. The Cohn Boyer patents for recombinant DNA were a notable exception to this rule; the technology had obvious utility (Feldman, et al. 2005). Some firms immediately realized its potential and could be induced to license merely by making the fee reasonable; others could be convinced that the technology was relevant to their objectives. Although Niels Reimers, Stanford's Director of Technology Transfer, retrospectively viewed the license fee as a "tax," the value added by the university's TTO was the demonstration to firms that the invention was relevant to their business.

A decade or so later, Rockefeller University announced the receipt of $20 million in payment for a patent license for the "obesity gene" from Amgen, a biotechnology company, "with an agreement to pay many times that amount if the protein proves useful in treating fat people." (Kolata 1995) In this case the result did not prove useful in the end and no further funds were transferred. In the above instances, despite the pecuniary interest of the universities and the researchers in the discoveries, the traditional university industry relationship of two entities, with a gap in between, held fast. Nevertheless, despite difficulties, the gap is narrowing as institutional boundaries are broken, bridged, moved and reconfigured.

Conclusion: technology transfer and the university of the future

University technology transfer is a salient part of a broader realignment of academic mission to more fully encompass contribution to economic and social development. Especially, when considering the amounts of public funding invested in university research, it is reasonable to expect societal benefit beyond advancement of knowledge and accomplishments worthy for their own sake such as elucidation of intriguing physical phenomenon like the Higgs Boson or the reattribution of a Renaissance bronze to Michelangelo.

It is early days and a plethora of transfer innovations instituted in recent years, from Brazil's interface foundations (Plonski 2015, this volume), China's university run enterprises (UREs) (Zhou 2015, this volume) augur further innovation in transfer as, like the U.S. Bayh-Dole Act of 1980, they are globalized and reinterpreted. Stanford's Innovation system, articulated by its users if not by an official framework, distributed across and without campus, comprises immanent elements with names like StartX, MediaX, Biodesign, Spark, Ignite, D-School, ME310, Radicand, Epicenter and OTL, offer entrepreneurial mentoring, translational research funding and links to Silicon Valley networks.

These "innovations in innovation" promise to transform university technology transfer from an arm's length relationship to an element integrated into the university's teaching and research missions. The proliferation of innovation initiatives, going well beyond the TTO and the licensing of intellectual property, is an indicator of mission change. The nineteenth-century Humboldtian dual mission university is becoming a twenty-first-century Triple Helix University.

Notes

1 T. Stanco (2004) George Washington University techno-l, 180604, Start-up discussions.
2 Loet Leydesdorff, Personal Communication 22 August 2012 "University patenting after declining during the period 1999–2008 began to increase again as strongly as before. The 2011 data confirm the previously signaled trend [2010]." Chart I is credited to Professor Leydesdorff, its creator.
3 The growing literature on the drivers, dynamics and consequences of academic entrepreneurship shows the global diffusion of the entrepreneurial university model. See, for example, Barry Bozeman (2000), Technology Transfer and Public Policy: A Review of Research and Theory, *Research Policy*, 29 (4–5): 627–655; and Frank Rothaermel, Shanti D. Agung and Lin Jiang (2007) University Entrepreneurship: A Taxonomy of the Literature, *Industrial and Corporate Change*, 16 (4): 691–791.
4 Personal communication to the author.
5 These may be considered "low-ball" estimates as they are taken from results reported to AUTM, that does not include all players nor are all entrepreneurial activities on campus reported to the office. A high-end estimate may be extrapolated from studies of the entrepreneurial activities of alumni of leading universities like MIT and Stanford. See Bank of Boston (1997) The Impact of Innovation, Bank of Boston study, Boston: Federal Reserve Bank; and Charles Eesely and William Miller (2012) Stanford University's Economic Impact via Innovation and Entrepreneurship. Available online: http:// engineering.stanford.edu/sites/default/files/Stanford_Innovation_Survey_Executive_ Summary_Oct2012.pdf (accessed 6 May 2015).

References

Apple, R. (1989) *Patenting University Research*, Harry Steenbock and the Wisconsin Alumni Research Foundation, 80 ISIS 375, 378
Artz, F. (1966) *The Development of Technical Education in France. 1500–1850*, Cambridge: MIT Press
AUTM (Association of University Technology Managers) (2010) Licensing Survey
Balconi, M., Brusoni, S. and Orsenigo, L. (2009) In Defense of the Linear Model: An Essay, *Research Policy*, 39 (1): 1–13
Baxter, J. (1946) *Scientists Against Time*, Cambridge, MA: MIT Press
Bliss, M. (1982) *The Discovery of Insulin*, Chicago, IL: University of Chicago Press
Bush, V. (1945) *Science: The Endless Frontier*. Washington DC: U.S. Government Printing Office
Bush, V. (1970) *Pieces of the Action*, New York: Morrow
Cadwalader, E. (2013) Technology Transfer: Fueling America's Innovation Pipeline, Helice, 1/4. Available online: www.triplehelixassociation.org/helice. Accessed 12 February 2015
Cohen, W. and Levinthal, D. (1990) Absorptive Capacity: A New Perspective on Learning and Innovation, *Administrative Science Quarterly*, 35 (1): 128–152

Cooke, P. (2001) Regional Innovation Systems, Clusters and the Knowledge Economy, *Industrial and Corporate Change*, 10 (4): 945–974

David, Jeremy (1981) *Transatlantic Industrial Revolution: The Diffusion of Textile Technologies Between Britain and America, 1790–1830s*, Cambridge: MIT Press

Etzkowitz, H. (2002) *MIT and the Rise of Entrepreneurial Science*, London: Routledge

Etzkowitz, H. (2008) *The Triple Helix: University-Industry-Government Innovation In Action*, London: Routledge

Etzkowitz, H. (2013) Mistaking Dawn for Dusk: Quantophrenia and the Cult of Numerology in Technology Transfer Analysis, *Scientometrics*, 52 (4): 515–538

Etzkowitz, H. (2014) The Entrepreneurial University Wave: From Ivory Tower to Global Economic Engine, *Industry and Higher Education*, 28 (4): 223–232

Etzkowitz, H. and Goktepe, D. (2010) Maybe They Can? University Technology Transfer Offices as Regional Growth Engines, *International Journal of Technology Transfer and Commercialisation*, 9 (1–2): 166–181

Etzkowitz, H., Gulbrandsen, M. and Levitt, J. (2000) *Public Venture Capital*, New York: Harcourt

Etzkowitz, H., Mello, J. and Almeida, M. (2005) Towards "meta-innovation" in Brazil: The Evolution of the Incubator and the Emergence of a Triple Helix, *Research Policy*, 34 (4): 411–424

Feldman, M., Colaianni, A. and Liu, K. (2005) Commercializing Cohen Boyer: 1980–1997, Copenhagen Business School/Aalborg University DRUID, Working Paper, 05–21

Feldman, M., Colaianni, A. and Liu, K. (2007) Lessons from the Commercialization of the Cohen-Boyer Patents: The Stanford University Licensing Program. In Anatole Krattiger et al. (eds) *Intellectual Property Management in Health and Agricultural Innovation: A Handbook of Best Practices*, MIHR: Oxford, U.K. and PIPRA: Davis, U.S.A. Available online: www.ipHandbook.org

Feldman, A. and Desrochers, M. and P. (2004) Truth for Its Own Sake: Academic Culture and Technology Transfer at the Johns Hopkins University, *Minerva*, 42 (2): 1573–1871

Fleck, L. ([1935] 1976) *Genesis and Development of a Scientific Fact*, Chicago: University of Chicago Press

Gibbons, Michael, Limoges, C., Nowotny, H., Schwartzman, S., Scott, P. and Trow, M. (1994) *The New Production of Knowledge: The Dynamics of Science and Research in Contemporary Societies*, Beverly Hills: Sage

Griliches, Z. (1960) Hybrid Corn and the Economics of Innovation, *Science*, 132, 29 July

Hatakenaka, S. (2004) *University–Industry Partnerships in MIT*, Cambridge and Tokyo, London: Routledge

Headrick, D. (1988) *The Tentacles of Progress: Technology Transfer in the Age of Imperialism 1850–1940*. New York: Oxford University Press

Henton, D. and Held, K. (2013) The Dynamics of Silicon Valley: Creative Destruction and the Evolution of the Innovation Habitat, *Social Science Information*, 52 (4): 539

Hoskin, K. (1996) The "Awful Idea of Accountability": Inscribing People into the Measurement of Objects. In R. Munro and J. Mouritsen (eds), *Accountability: Power, Ethos and the Technologies of Managing*, London: International Thomson Business Press, 265–282

Huffman, D. and Quigley, J. (2002) The Role of the University in Attracting High Tech Entrepreneurship: A Silicon Valley Tale, *Annals of Regional Science*, 36 (3): 403–419

Jacob, M., Lundquist, M. and Hellsmark, H. (2003) Entrepreneurial Transformations in the Swedish University System: The Case of Chalmers University of Technology, *Research Policy*, 32, 1555–1568

Kenwood, A.G. and Lougheed, A.L. (1982) *Technological Diffusion and Industrialization Before 1914*, New York: St. Martins

Kohler, R. (2002) *Landscapes and Labscapes*, Chicago: University of Chicago Press

Kolata, G. (1995) Researchers Find Hormone Causes a Loss of Weight, *New York Times*, 27 August 1995: 1, 20

Kuhn, T. (1962) *The Structure of Scientific Revolutions*, Chicago: The University of Chicago Press

Leydesdorff, L. and Mayer, M. (2010) The Decline of University Patenting and the End of the Bayh-Dole Effect, *Scientometrics*, 83(2): 355–362

Landes, D. (1972) *The Unbound Prometheus: Technological Change and Industrial Development in Western Europe from 1750 to the Present*, Cambridge: Cambridge University Press

Lawton-Smith, H. (2014) Innovation Module Lecture, Birkbeck College, University of London, June

Loise, V. and Stevens, A. (2010) The Bayh-Dole Act Turns 30, *Les Nouvelles*, p. 188

Misa, T.J. (1995) *A Nation of Steel: The Making of Modern America 1865–1925*, Baltimore: Johns Hopkins University Press

Moyer, A. (1997) *Joseph Henry: The Rise of an American Scientist*, Washington, D.C.: Smithsonian Institution Press

Nählinder, J. (2010) Where are All the Female Innovators? Nurses as Innovators in a Public Sector, *Innovation Journal of Technology Management and Innovation*. 5 (1): 13–29

Norrman, C. (2005) Publicly Funded Support of Technology-Based Ventures. Studies in Science and Technology Thesis. No. 1219. Department of Management and Economic Linkoping: Linkoping University

Paquet, G. (2009) *Crippling Epistemologies and Governance Failures – A Plea for Experimentalism*, Ottawa: The University of Ottawa Press.

Plonski, G. (2015) University Technology Transfer in Brazil: A Comprehensive Picture, this volume (Chapter 20)

Rabinow, P. (1997) *Making PCR: A Story of Biotechnology*, Chicago: University of Chicago Press

Rossiter, M. (1975). *The Emergence of Agricultural Science—Justus Liebig and the Americans, 1840–1880*, New Haven, CT: Yale University Press, 1975

Saxenian, A. (1994) *Regional Advantage*, Cambridge: Harvard University Press

Schacht, W. (2012) The Bayh-Dole Act: Selected Issues in Patent Policy and Commercialization of Technology, Congressional Research Service, 7-5700, p. 9. Accessed 12 February 2015

Sorokin, P. (1956) *Fads and Foibles in Modern Sociology*, Chicago: Henry Regnery & Co.

Stevens, A. (2004) The Enactment of Bayh-Dole, *Journal of Technology Transfer*, 29 (1): 93–99

Stokes, D. (1997) *Pasteur's Quadrant—Basic Science and Technological Innovation*, Washington DC: Brookings Institution Press

Tarr, J. and Dupuy, G. (eds) (1988) *Technology and the Rise of the Networked City in Europe and America*, Philadelphia: Temple University Press

Tedeschi, B. (2010) The Idea Incubator Goes to Campus, *New York Times* (Business Section), 20 June

Tod, J. (1995) *Colonial Technology: Science and the Transfer of Innovation to Australia*, Cambridge: Cambridge University Press

Tu. J., Gu, S. and Wu, G. (2005) A New Pattern of Technology Transfer in Rural China: Triple Helix of Academy-Agriculture-Government Relations in Baoji City, *Asian Journal of Technology Innovation,* 13 (2): 157–178

U.S. Patent Office (2014) Number of Utility Patents Assigned Annually to all U.S. Colleges and Universities. Available online: www.upso.gov/web/offices/ac/ido/oeip/taf/univ/org_gr/all_univ_ag.htm (last accessed 4 March 2015)

Ventner, C. (2013) *Life at the Speed of Light: From the Double Helix to the Dawn of Digital Life*, New York: Viking

Vise, D. (2005) *Google*, New York: Delacorte

Washburn, J. (2005) *University Inc.: The Corporate Corruption of Higher Education*, New York: Basic Books

Zhou, C. (2015) China's University Technology Transfer System: Political Mobilization of Academy for Economic Growth, this volume (Chapter 16)

2 The globalization of academic innovation

Shiri M. Breznitz

Universities, acknowledged as centers of knowledge and symbols of technological frontiers, have become essential players in the generation of new knowledge and innovation. Through the commercialization of technology—the dissemination and commercialization of their ideas to the private market—universities have the ability to directly influence regional economic growth. Different commercialization models and specific universities have dominated the perception of what makes up a successful technology transfer process. These models and universities have been intensively studied, with conflicting conclusions. By extending our view from a specific commercialization model to analyze technology transfer at universities as part of a national and regional system, this edited book provides a better understanding of why certain models work better than others. Even more important is the reaffirmation that technology transfer programs need to be linked to the region and commercialization environments in which they are located.

Historically, universities were the domain of the upper classes who studied such subjects as literature and philosophy. Over time, universities began to serve the general public, offering more practical subjects, such as applied research, and training students for professions like medicine and law. By the early 1900s, universities had become recognized as regional and national engines of growth. Today's university model has a public service component, offering a wider basis for research and teaching—both of which have the power to promote social change. The university service component was influenced by a neoliberal economic perspective, which holds that universities are evaluated on the basis of their contribution to the economy. Therefore, in most countries, universities that rely heavily on public funding are pressured to "pay back the community" and act as responsible citizens (Russell, 1993). To prove their contribution to society, many universities turned to metrics. Research commercialization happens to be one of the easier activities to measure. Most universities' annual reports these days contain many pages of data describing patents, licenses, and university spinouts even though these activities represent a very small part of the university's output and its contribution to society.

The United States was one of the first countries to seize the potential of university research. If we examine the history of the country, we find close relationships between university research and the government as well as private enterprises (Breznitz, 2014). Interestingly, the United States used university research and academic faculty early on and through both world wars. Moreover, academia has been an important source of new products and processes in fields such as aerospace and leisure, from radar to Google. As has been evident in studies of the role of government in technological development such as Mariana Mazzucato's *The Entrepreneurial State*, we find that government-funded research in the United States at universities and government labs has led to the development of some of the world leading products and processes (Mazzucato, 2013).

The Bayh-Dole Act of 1980 plays an important role in grounding the university's role in technology commercialization. The Bayh-Dole Act gave universities the rights to federally funded inventions (1981, Cornell University Law Department, 2005). As several studies point out, the impact of this legislation is questionable (Mowery, 2004; Mowery et al., 1999; Nelson R, 2001; Thursby and Thursby, 2003). Some claim that it was beneficial, and others that these changes were a natural result of relationships between university and industry as well as technological changes. Increasingly, we find more indication of complications created by the law. Authors who believe that commercialization of technology should be achieved by a professional service or that ownership should be transferred to the inventor for commercialization purposes claim that TTOs have become bureaucratic and have not been providing "enough service" or "the correct service" for industry (Kenney and Patton, 2009; Litan and Mitchell, 2010; Litan et al., 2007). Litan and Mitchell describe university technology transfer offices (TTOs) as "bottlenecks of technology." Adding market freedom to the discussion, Litan and Mitchell argue that professors should be allowed to choose the agency with which they would like to commercialize their technology. They believe that university licensing offices should strive to improve service and commercialization output or perhaps dismantle TTOs (Litan et al., 2007). Kenney and Patton (2009) support Litan and Mitchell regarding the influence of the Bayh-Dole Act on the commercialization of technology, claiming that the existing university technology commercialization model is not optimal. While the Bayh-Dole Act's purpose was to promote knowledge transfer and commercialization of technology from institutions of higher education to industry, the actual result is a bureaucratic system that delays technology diffusion through ineffective incentives and revenue-maximization goals (Kenney and Patton, 2009).

Universities around the world have attempted to adopt the "ultimate model of successful technology transfer," which many consider the model adopted in the United States. This approach, however, has both positive and negative aspects. This book focuses on both aspects. On the one hand, the U.S. model pushes universities to transfer technologies to the market. It encourages university–industry relationships and dissemination of new ideas both of universities at firms and vice versa. On the other hand, the U.S. model is not without fault (Kenney and Patton, 2009; Litan and Mitchell, 2010; Litan et al., 2007). Most universities do not possess the funding or the skills to commercialize technology, follow patents, or even to engage in proper due diligence. Moreover, by copying the U.S. or similar models, most universities ignored their own regional and environmental factors, which have consistently proven to affect university technology commercialization (Lawton Smith and Bagchi-Sen, 2012; Breznitz, 2014). Thus, in many cases, the adaptation failed and even had a negative effect on commercialization (Breznitz, 2011).

We now turn to a review of the university technology commercialization literature. In particular, we review the impact of the history and environment of the region in which universities locate, as well as the specific commercialization mechanisms established at different institutions of higher education.

Review of the literature

Existing studies show that universities' commercialization ability is affected by both external and internal factors (Lawton Smith and Ho, 2006; Mowery et al., 1999; Pike, 2002; Rahm et al., 2000; O'Shea et al., 2005). The external factors refer to the region's history and entrepreneurial environment. The history of a region in which a university operates has a direct impact on its ability to transfer technology from the public to the private domain. Did the region have an industrial base, such as Detroit? Or is it more a university town, such as Cambridge, UK? How good was the relationship between the university and industry over time? What was the regional culture? Is industry or entrepreneurship acceptable? This kind of a history and environment lead to actual policies in the form of intellectual property rights laws and tax incentives, which play an important role in the ability of universities to succeed in technology transfer and have a good university–industry relationship. In the United States, the federal Bayh-Dole Act has influenced regions in general and university–industry relationships in particular (Mowery and Sampat, 2001). The Bayh-Dole Act stipulates that the university owns the intellectual property rights for inventions that originated from a federal research grant. In Europe, each country created its own legislative incentives that formed a climate for university technology transfer. Inspired by the changes in the United States and the success of a few regions such as Silicon Valley, many European countries have attempted to implement similar policies in their regions (Lawton Smith, 2006). As we can see from the chapters about Ireland (Fitzgerald and O'Shea), Italy (Rossi, Fassio, and Geuna), Spain (García-Aracil, Castro-Martínez, Azagra-Caro, D'Este, and Fernández de Lucio), Switzerland (Gebhardt), and the UK (Lawton Smith and Glasson), they all have very different legislation with regard to university technology commercialization.

Environmental factors are also relevant to the relationship among institutions at the national and regional level. The ability of a group of local institutions to transfer knowledge and hence to affect the ability of a locality to innovate depends on their number, strength, and collaboration efforts. Sharing of information and collaboration among institutions drives innovation. According to innovation systems theory, the environment in which universities operate—the relationships between nonfirm institutions and organizations in the region, such as government, trade associations, universities, and research institutes—influences their ability to innovate (Nelson, 1993).

Moreover, universities, as part of a system of innovation, do not operate in a void; they are influenced by the networks and relationships in their specific locality (Freeman, 1995). These are symbiotic relationships, in which technology transfer influences innovation, and relationships in the system of innovation influence the ability to transfer technology. According to innovations systems theory, some regions possess a particular infrastructure that allows them to realize maximum regional learning. The learning and knowledge creation process is accomplished through a set of institutions that promote knowledge creation and learning by the local firms. Firms, institutions, and individuals share a basis of trust and understanding that differs from region to region and allows some regions to perform in a way that promotes their economic development.

As it is evident in the chapter about Switzerland, it is vital to understand that innovation results from the combined work of both public and private institutions. The public sector provides support to the private sector by enhancing production and distribution of technology and by reducing transaction costs (Lundvall et al., 2002). Consequently, universities and research institutes play an important part in the national and regional innovation process. This point can be effectively analyzed using Etzkowitz's (1995) "Triple Helix" model, which, with its focus on the communication networks among university, industry, and government, provides an argument for commercializing scientific knowledge. Etzkowitz and Leydesdorff (2000) argue that universities, industries, and governments increasingly find themselves working together, understanding that economic development can be achieved by creating and fostering innovative environments.

Developing an innovative environment at a national or regional level can be achieved through the incorporation of university spinouts, specific policies, networking among firms and government laboratories, and basic research conducted at universities. With globalization, corporations have increasingly discovered the advantages of tapping into the best research and practices in many places around the world. In other words, knowledge and top-quality research have geographical characteristics (Etzkowitz and Leydesdorff, 2000). As such, they are concentrated in specific locations and are based on regional learning, networking, and technology transfer. Not all countries or regions possess the best knowledge, and while globalization allows them to import and export this knowledge, corporations still need to tap into the particular endowments of specific localities.

Internal factors, such as university technology transfer culture, policy, and organization have been shown in previous studies to have an impact on the ability of universities to commercialize technology (Shane, 2004; Roberts, 1991; Zucker et al., 1998; Clark, 1998; Lockett and Wright, 2005; Kenney and Goe, 2004). The first is the university's entrepreneurial culture, which is formed to support risk-taking, innovation, new business creation, and a willingness to collaborate with industry (Bercovitz and Feldman, 2007; Clark, 1998; James, 2005; Kenney and Goe, 2004; Schoenberger, 1997). Studies that focus both on organizational change and university culture emphasize the organization and individual view toward commercialization and entrepreneurship as the basis of university technology transfer success (Bercovitz et al., 2001; Clark, 1998; Kenney and Goe, 2004).

Creating an entrepreneurial culture affects the university and its researchers in multiple ways: it allows faculty to work on applied research and to accept the ability of academic research to make profit and a public impact, as well as creating opportunities for founding new companies based on university research.

The second internal factor is technology transfer policy, which affects the university's ability to patent, license, and spin out companies (Lawton Smith, 2006; Link and Siegel, 2005; Shane, 2002; Siegal and Phan, 2005; Thursby and Thursby, 2005; Zucker et al., 2002). Studies find that policy plays an integral part in universities' success in technology transfer, particularly in commercialization of university-developed technology. One such policy is intellectual property rights (IPR), which at universities refers to copyrighting academic publications—that is, journals and books—and patents filed by the university for an invention that was the result of university research. The chapters on Canada (Hepburn and Wolfe) and Italy (Fassio, Geuna, and Rossi) indicate to what extent IPR regulations differ from one country to another. According to these studies, in Italy, faculty and staff own their IPR, while Canada has a mixed-used policy in which each institution has its rules with regard to ownership of intellectual property (IP). But individual ownership of IP can be problematic. In Italy, while individual researchers own the IPR of their inventions, most universities lack the managerial experience and the commercial orientation to assist them with the commercialization process.

Incentives are an important policy that has been showed to impact commercialization. According to Di Gregorio and Shane (2003) and Link and Siegel (2005), changes in faculty incentives change their behavior. If a higher share of royalties is allocated to the inventor (the faculty member), universities will license more inventions to existing companies. Furthermore, Shane (2004) claims that when a lower share of royalties is distributed to inventors more spinouts will result. Since the royalty share is low, the only way for inventors to increase their return on an invention is by founding a company and becoming a major shareholder. Another aspect of technology transfer policy that influences a university's spinout capability is the extent to which research collaboration is permitted. Faculty collaboration with industry through consulting or research projects affects industry-sponsored research as well as the university's culture and view of applied research. University–industry research collaboration promotes financial support from industry, which supports students or provides grants for particular research. Moreover, if the research results in an invention, industry will purchase the invention equity or license the technology from the university (Blumenthal et al., 1996; Thursby and Thursby, 2005; Zucker et al., 2002). Shane adds that the proportion of industry's contribution to research funding is a predictor of the level of university spinouts. Spinout formation grows with the proportion of industry funding (Shane, 2004).

The third internal factor is the TTO. Depending on its policy, staff, mission statement, and even its "position" within the organization, the university's TTO has the ability to influence technology commercialization (Bercovitz et al., 2001; Clarysse B. et al., 2005; Link and Siegel, 2005; O'Shea et al., 2005; Owen-Smith and Powell, 2004; Siegel et al., 2004). TTOs at universities have four main purposes: (1) to evaluate inventions and determine whether they are patentable; (2) to patent the inventions; (3) to license the technology; and (4) in some cases, to assist in the creation of spinout companies. A TTO's responsibilities are flexible and open to interpretation, however, and they differ significantly between universities. Some universities will patent only a technology for which there is market demand. For many, the spinout of companies is not a priority; their goal is to secure income from licensing their patents. Increasingly, most universities, regardless of their research capabilities, have established a TTO (Feldman and Breznitz, 2009; Sampat, 2006), and they have become an indicator of university commercialization and entrepreneurship. Vietnam, where universities still harbor a negative view of the establishment of TTOs, is a good example of a lack of engagement in commercialization.

The level of resources associated with the TTO affects its commercialization ability. Several studies show that TTOs that have personnel with higher levels of education and business experience tend to have a better understanding of the technology and negotiation processes at firms (Lockett and Wright, 2005; Shane, 2004; O'Shea et al., 2005). Since university and industry have different perspectives, highly educated TTO employees who have knowledge of both the technical and business jargon reassure both inventors and investors that their product is getting the best available treatment. Other factors that relate to the availability of resources are the use of outside lawyers and the compensation of technology transfer officers (Siegel et al., 2003; O'Shea et al., 2005; Owen-Smith and Powell, 2001; Shane, 2004). A study by O'Shea et al. (2005) found that the historical background and past technology transfer success of each university is related to future capabilities and options for the university with regard to spinout capability. When a TTO successfully had an invention go through the commercialization process and receives returns in the form of royalties, the office is strengthened and motivated to continue with the commercialization process. Yale University, for example, has had success in technology commercialization via its patenting of Zerit™, one of the drugs used in the treatment of HIV/AIDS.

Organization of this book

The literature reviewed above indicates how both external and internal factors affect the ability of a university to commercialize technology. In the individual chapters of this book, we explore this process in twelve countries, using a country-centric approach as well as analysis of specific universities.

Following the two introductory chapters in Part I, where Chapter 1, by Henry Etzkowitz, describes the evolution of university technology transfer, we offer four chapters in Part II on the less discussed faults of the U.S. model. In Chapter 3, Maryann Feldman and Paige Clayton follow the increasing litigation in which universities are involved, indicating how early such litigation started. Many of the TTOs are dealing with legal filings and defending themselves from litigation rather than commercializing university technology. Chapter 4, by Henry

Etzkowitz, examines how the perception of a successful TTO like the one at Stanford University changed from enabling some of the most disruptive technology to becoming a gatekeeper that is holding technology back in exchange for financial gains. Chapter 5, by Henry Etzkowitz and Devrim Göktepe-Hultén, demonstrates that best practices used in some of the most successful TTOs do not fit all universities. Moreover, using the conventional metrics of patents and licenses, while not taking into consideration regional and historical factors, leads to misrepresentation of less established TTOs. Chapter 6, by Ashley J. Stevens, Jonathan J. Jensen, Katrine Wyller, Patrick C. Kilgore, Eric London, Sabarni K. Chatterjee, and Mark L. Rohrbaugh, documents the shift in roles between the public and the private sector in the U.S., where the public sector now plays a more direct role in the applied research part of drug discovery.

In Part III, we turn to a global perspective on technology commercialization, dividing our discussion between developed and developing counties according to the level of university commercialization capability. These case studies examine policies and culture of university involvement in economic development, relationships between university and industry, and the commercialization of technology first developed at universities. In addition, each chapter provides examples from specific universities in each country from a regional, national, and international comparative perspective.

The terms "developed" and "developing" as used here distinguish between countries that adopted a more U.S.-centric commercialization model and those that have not. The "developed" ones include those in which there is a focus on university technology commercialization, whether through a collaboration, state involvement, or industry leadership. "Developing" countries, addressed in Part IV, are those in which there is still no particular policy toward university technology commercialization or the policy is in place, but the current conditions do not allow for progressive commercialization or university–industry collaboration.

The "developed" countries include Switzerland, the UK, Ireland, and Canada. These countries are very different in their approach to the commercialization of university research but are highly focused and driven by technology spinning out of universities. Chapter 7, on Switzerland, by Christiane Gebhardt, describes the strong push by the federal government and collaboration between industry and academia. Chapter 8, on the UK, written by Helen Lawton Smith and John Glasson, demonstrates eloquently how regional differences affect universities' ability to commercialize technology. Although the British government implemented many different policies to support university commercialization of technology, the regional impact was the result of the different universities' abilities to commercialize technology as well as the demand side from the region itself. The four universities described in this chapter are leaders with regard to technology transfer. However, they vary widely in the extent of their success with commercialization. The chapter shows how important regional history and environment are to the success or failure of technology transfer models. Chapter 9, on Ireland, by Ciara Fitzgerald and Rory P. O'Shea, demonstrates the systematic push by the Irish government starting in the 1980s to build up research and technology transfer infrastructure. Irish universities chose to adapt to the commercialization push, though, as the authors claim, they still face many roadblocks in employing transparent policies regarding the share of royalties, leave of absence, length of IP negotiation, and equity investment policy. Chapter 10, on Canada, by Nicola Hepburn and David A. Wolfe, provides excellent evidence of the power that specific institutional characteristics have on technology commercialization. Unlike in the United States, Canadian universities each establish their own intellectual property regimes, as seen in the universities studied in this chapter. Even though the universities discussed are all active in technology commercialization, they use different models and policies to achieve their goals, which developed out of their different histories.

Then, in Part IV, we consider "developing" countries, where we find some efforts to develop technology commercialization. However, either these countries have not been able to embrace this push toward university research or their academic system is not well equipped to allow for commercialization and a relationship between universities and industry. Chapter 11, on Spain, by Adela García-Aracil, Elena Castro-Martínez, Joaquín M. Azagra-Caro, Pablo D'Este, and Ignacio Fernández de Lucio, indicates that in the early 1990s the country gradually changed its policy toward university commercialization. Spanish universities have become more research oriented and have experienced a substantial increase in their knowledge and technology transfer activities. However, the social and economic impact of university–industry relations remains at a nascent stage. Chapter 12, on Thailand, by Jarunee Wonglimpiyarat, describes a country in the early stages of adopting a government policy toward university technology commercialization. The government realizes the importance of research as a basis for national innovative capability and thus launched urgent policies to support universities by endorsing national research universities in 2009. However, as indicated by the author, very few patents have been issued to the universities and even a smaller number have been commercialized by industry. The status of university technology transfer in Russia is the subject of Chapter 13, by Tatiana Pospelova. In Russia historically, applied research was conducted not at universities but mostly in government research labs. Only since 2009 has there been a government push toward an innovative economy that relies on academic research. The most obvious manifestation of this is the latest Russian legislation, which has given Russian universities the rights to all inventions funded by the state. However, in reality, the law is not enforced and when faculty believe that they have a worthy invention, they often form their own company outside the university. The author shows that the historical legacy at universities with regard to conducting basic research creates barriers for technology transfer and university–industry relationships. Chapter 14 on Italy, by Federica Rossi, Claudio Fassio, and Aldo Geuna, is very similar to Chapter 10 on Spain. Italian universities have a long tradition of interaction with industry, especially in applied fields such as engineering and chemistry. However, they began to formally acknowledge the importance of knowledge transfer activity and to establish dedicated infrastructures to support it only in the late 1990s. The case studies in this chapter provide a mixed picture, with a small group of institutions heavily engaged in institutional knowledge transfer and the vast majority barely involved. Chapter 15, by Ana Lúcia Vitale Torkomian, Marli Elizabeth Ritter dos Santos, and Thiago José Cysneiros Cavalcanti Soares, focuses on Brazil, which is also a latecomer to university technology commercialization. The Brazilian law on technological innovation came into effect only in 2004, mostly following passage of the U.S. Bayh-Dole Act. In accordance with the law, universities started to establish TTOs. However, the result was TTOs that mostly protect university intellectual property rights rather than focusing on commercializing technologies. The reasons mainly related to the distribution of R&D funding in Brazil, coupled with the fact that joint research between universities and companies there do not belong to universities. Chapter 16 is a timely piece on the state of university technology commercialization in China, by Chunyan Zhou. This chapter focuses on the commercialization of faculty consulting projects to firm-formation or developing "University-run Enterprises (UREs)." The chapter argues for government involvement in promoting university commercialization of technology. Concluding this section, Chapter 17, on Vietnam, by Tran Ngoc Ca, indicates that the country still has a long way to go with regard to university commercialization. The issues regarding university technology transfer have more to do with the basic role of universities in Vietnam, which were founded based on the Soviet model, separating teaching from scientific research and technology development. Universities thus make little contribution in terms of innovation from the universities to the local economy. Government policy to support commercialization is inconsistent and sometime contradictory. Overall management mechanisms for R&D and IPR provide little incentive for university staff to work more closely with firms. Even the establishment of a TTO is not a widely accepted practice and depends on the initiatives of individual universities.

Next, in Part V, we have five chapters by thought leaders in this field regarding the state of university technology commercialization. Chapter 18, by Martin Kenney and Donald Patton, explains how the technology transfer process at universities was influenced by the commercialization of biopharmaceutical inventions. However, this process does not fit other fields such as electronics and software. Unlike biopharmaceuticals, these fields require dialog between university and industry researchers. Moreover, according to the authors, involving the technology transfer administration in the commercialization will actually hinder the knowledge transfer. Chapter 19, by Frank J.M. Zwetsloot, Lodewijk L. Gelauff and Robert J.W. Tijssen, presents the difficulties in measuring university technology commercialization. Different institutions as well as reporting agencies use different measurements to represent their achievements. However, due to reporting differences, these measurements are incomparable. The authors encourage ranking experts to engage more directly with stakeholders to develop commonly acceptable definitions of key concepts. Chapter 20, by Guilherme Ary Plonski, strengthens the importance of evaluating universities' technology transfer within a specific context. Plonski shows that technology transfer in Brazil is a system in which universities are only one out of several players. Hence, by counting only universities' licenses we receive a very narrow picture on technology transfer in Brazil. Chapter 21, by Henry Etzkowtiz, discuss the impact of the Bayh-Dole Act in the U.S. on the role of universities in innovation. Lastly, Chapter 22, by Lita Nelsen, follows the development of university technology transfer in the U.S. and its contribution to the economy. Importantly, the chapter discusses current threats such as the decline in federal funding of basic research, and changes in patent law that may weaken the protection that patents offer to the development of university research.

We offer our final thoughts in Chapter 23, the Conclusion. The idea of university technology commercialization is not a bad one, especially when considering the amount of public funding invested in university research. However, attention needs to be focused on the characteristics of the university, the region in which it is located, and the resources available for commercialization. Our hope in presenting this volume is thus to demonstrate the need for more regional and national input in models of university technology commercialization. In particular, it should provide warning signals for universities and countries attempting to adopt a technology transfer model that is considered successful in another university, region, or country. Even the best technology commercialization models are not perfect. In sum, all that is glitters is not gold.

References

Bayh-Dole Act (1981) The Bayh-Dole Act: Patent Rights in Inventions Made with Federal Assistance. 35 USC 200–212.

Bercovitz, J., Feldman, M., Feller, I. and Burton, R. (2001) "Organizational structure as a determinant of academic patent and licensing behavior: An exploratory study of Duke, Johns Hopkins, and Pennsylvania State Universities." *Journal of Technology Transfer*, 26: 21–35.

Bercovitz, J.E.L. and Feldman, M.P. (2007) "Fishing upstream: Firm innovation strategy and university research alliances." *Research Policy*, 36: 930–48.

Blumenthal, D., Causino, N., Campbell, E. and Louis, K.S. (1996) "Relationships between academic institutions and industry in the life sciences: An industry survey." *New England Journal of Medicine*, 334: 368–74.

Breznitz, S.M. (2011) "Improving or impairing? Following technology transfer changes at the University of Cambridge." *Regional Studies*, 45: 463–78.

———(2014) *The Fountain of Knowledge: The Role of Universities in Economic Development*, Palo Alto: Stanford University Press.

Clark, B.R. (1998) *Creating Entrepreneurial Universities: Organizational Pathways of Transformation*, Oxford: Pergamon Press.

Clarysse, B., Wright, M., Lockett, A., Van De Elde, E. and Vohora, A. (2005) "Spinning out new ventures: A typology of incubation strategies from European research institutions." *Journal of Business Venturing*, 20: 183–216.

Cornell University Law Department (2005) "The objectives of the Bayh-Dole Act." Available at www4.law.cornell.edu/uscode/.

Di Gregorio, D. and Shane, S. (2003) "Why do some universities generate more start-ups than others?" *Research Policy*. 32: 209–27.

Etzkowitz, H. (1995) "The Triple Helix—university-industry-government relations: A laboratory for knowledge based economic development." *EASST Review*, 14: 9–14.

Etzkowitz, H. and Leydesdorff, L. (2000) "The dynamics of innovation: From national systems and 'Mode 2' to a Triple Helix of university-industry-government relations." *Research Policy*, 29: 109–23.

Feldman, M.P. and Breznitz, S.M. (2009) "The American experience in university technology transfer," in M. Mckelvey and M. Holmén (eds), *European Universities Learning to Compete: From Social Institutions to Knowledge Business*, Cheltenham, UK; Northampton, MA: Edward Elgar.

Freeman, C. (1995) "The national innovation systems is historical perspective." *Cambridge Journal of Economics*, 19: 5–24.

James, A. (2005) "Demystifying the role of culture in innovative regional economies." *Regional Studies*, 39: 1197–216.

Kenney, M. and Goe, R.W. (2004) "The role of social embeddedness in professional entrepreneurship: A comparison of electrical engineering and computer science at UC Berkeley and Stanford." *Research Policy*, 33: 691–707.

Kenney, M. and Patton, D. (2009) "Reconsidering the Bayh-Dole Act and the current university invention ownership model." *Research Policy*, 38: 1407–22.

Lawton Smith, H. (2006) *Universities, Innovation, and the Economy*, Abington: Routledge.

Lawton Smith, H. and Bagchi-Sen, S. (2012) "The research university, entrepreneurship and regional development: Research propositions and current evidence." *Entrepreneurship and Regional Development*, 24: 383–404.

Lawton Smith, H. and Ho, K. (2006) "Measuring the performance of Oxford University, Oxford Brookes University and the government laboratories' spin-off companies." *Research Policy*, 35: 1554–68.

Link, A. and Siegel, D. (2005) "Generating science-based growth: An econometric analysis of the impact of organizational incentives on university-industry technology transfer." *European Journal of Finance*, 11: 169–81.

Litan, R.E. and Mitchell, L. (2010) "A faster path from lab to market." *Harvard Business Review*, 88: 52–53.

Litan, R.E., Mitchell, L. and Reedy, E.J. (2007) "The university as innovator: Bumps in the road." *Issues in Science and Technology*, 23: 57–66.

Lockett, A. and Wright, M. (2005) "Resources, capabilities, risk capital and the creation of university spin-out companies." *Research Policy*, 34: 1043–57.

Lundvall, B.-A., Johnson, B., Andersen, E.S. and Dalum, B. (2002) "National systems of production, innovation and competence building." *Research Policy*, 31: 213–31.

Mazzucato, M. (2013) *The Entrepreneurial State: Debunking Public vs. Private Sector Myths*, New York: Anthem Press.

Mowery, D., Rosenberg, R.R., Sampat, B.N. and Ziedonis, A.A. (1999) "The Effects of the Bayh-Dole Act on U.S. university research and technology transfer," in L.M. Branscomb, , F. Kodama and R.L. Florida (eds), *Industrializing Knowledge: University-Industry Linkages in Japan and the United States,* Cambridge, MA: MIT Press.

Mowery, D.C., Nelson, Richard R., Sampat, Bhaven N., and Ziedonis, Arvids A. (2004) *Ivory Tower and Industrial Innovation University–Industry Technology Transfer Before and After the Bayh-Dole Act*, Stanford: Stanford University Press.

Mowery, D.C. and Sampat, B.N. 2001. "University patents and patent policy debates in the USA, 1925–1980." *Industrial and Corporate Change*, 10: 781–814.

Nelson, R.R. (1993) *National Innovation Systems: A Comparative Analysis*, New York: Oxford University Press.

——(2001) "Observations on the post-Bayh-Dole rise of patenting at American universities." *Journal of Technology Transfer*, 26: 13–19.

O'Shea, R.P., Allen, T.J., Chevalier, A. and Roche, F. (2004) "Knowledge networks as channels and conduits: The effects of spillovers in the Boston biotechnology community." *Organization Science*, 15: 5–21.

——(2005) "Entrepreneurial orientation, technology transfer and spinoff performance of U.S. universities." *Research Policy*, 34: 994–1009.

Owen-Smith, J. and Powell, W. (2001) "To patent or not: Faculty decisions and institutional success in academic patenting." *Journal of Technology Transfer*, 26: 99–114.

Rahm, D., Kirkland, J. and Bozeman, B. (2000) *University–industry R & D Collaboration in the United States, the United Kingdom, and Japan*, Dordrecht, Netherlands: Kluwer Academic.

Roberts, E.B. (1991). *Entrepreneurs in High Technology: Lessons from MIT and Beyond*, New York: Oxford University Press.

Russell, C. (1993) *Academic Freedom*, London: Routledge.

Sampat, B.N. (2006) "Patenting and U.S. academic research in the 20th century: The world before and after Bayh-Dole." *Research Policy*, 35: 772–89.

Schoenberger, E. (1997) *The Cultural Crisis of the Firm*, Cambridge, MA: Blackwell.

Shane, S. (2002) "Selling university technology: Patterns from MIT." *Management Science*, 48: 122–37.

——(2004) *Academic Entrepreneurship: University Spinoffs and Wealth Creation*, Cheltenham: Edward Elgar.

Siegal, D.S. and Phan, H.P. (2005) "Analyzing the effectiveness of university technology transfer: Implications for entrepreneurship education," in D.G. Libecap (ed.), *University Entrepreneurship and Technology Transfer: Process, Design, and Intellectual Property*, Amsterdam: Elsevier.

Siegel, D.S., Waldman, D. and Link, A. (2003) "Assessing the impact of organizational practices on the relative productivity of university technology transfer offices: An exploratory study." *Research Policy*, 32: 27–48.

Siegel, D.S., Waldman, D.A., Atwater, L.E. and Link, A.N. (2004) "Toward a model of the effective transfer of scientific knowledge from academicians to practitioners: qualitative evidence from the commercialization of university technologies." *Journal of Engineering and Technology Management*, 21: 115–42.

Thursby, J. and Thursby, M. (2003) "Enhanced: University licensing and the Bayh-Dole Act." *Science*, 301: 1052.

——(2005) "Faculty patent activity and assignment patterns," Roundtable on Engineering Entrepreneurship Research (REER), Georgia Institute of Technology. Atlanta, GA.

Zucker, L.G., Darby, M.R. and Armstrong, J.S. (2002) "Commercializing knowledge: University science, knowledge capture, and firm performance in biotechnology." *Management Science*, 48: 138–53.

Zucker, L.G., Darby, M.R. and Peng, Y. (1998) *Fundamentals or Population Dynamics and the Geographic Distribution of U.S. Biotechnology Enterprises, 1976–1989*, Cambridge, MA: National Bureau of Economic Research.

Part II
USA

3 The American experience in university technology transfer

Maryann Feldman and Paige Clayton

December 1980 was a watermark for American university technology transfer. The events of that month changed expectations about the commercialization of academic discoveries and set in motion new institutional policies and cultural changes that are still ongoing and unresolved. On December 2, 1980, the United States Patent and Trademark Office (USPTO) issued a patent to Stanford University entitled *Process for Producing Biologically Functional Chimeras* (#4237224). The patent covered the recombinant DNA (rDNA) technique developed by Dr. Stanley Cohen of Stanford University, California and Dr. Herbert Boyer of the University of California, San Francisco. At the time it was unusual for patents to be issued to a university discovery under research funded by the federal government. Indeed, the practice was for any intellectual property right to revert back to the federal government with each university able to petition the federal funding agency for permission to patent – an inefficient and cumbersome policy. But all this changed with the passage of the Bayh-Dole Act on December 12, 1980 (P.L. 96-517),[1] which granted universities ownership of intellectual property from federally funded research and obligated them to engage in practices to promote commercialization. The congressional testimony in support of the change was motivated by the perceived lack of American competitiveness and a desire to produce greater return from the significant public funding that had contributed to the prominence of American research universities. At the same time, American universities were searching for new revenue streams and ways to demonstrate their relevance.

The Cohen-Boyer commercialization program proved to be the ideal example to motivate the new technology transfer regime made possible by the passage of Bayh-Dole. By the time the Cohen-Boyer patent(s)[2] expired in 1997, Stanford University had received over $255 million in licensing revenues based on over $35 billion in product sales. Precisely how the Stanford University Patenting and Licensing Office was able to achieve this high rate of return is an interesting story in itself (Feldman, Colianni and Liu, 2008). The granting of 469 non-exclusive licenses created a flurry of activity but moreover conferred an advantage on startup companies that suddenly had legitimacy and a tradable asset when they signed up for the license. Certainly the widely adopted licensing program and the buzz it created helped launch the U.S. biotech industry (Feldman and Yoon, 2011).

But one major implication for American universities was the idea that there was significant revenue to be made from technology transfer. The Society of University Patent Administrators, founded in 1974 to address the concern that inventions funded by the U.S. government were not being commercialized effectively had achieved its mission. The Society changed its name to the Association of University Technology Managers (AUTM) and broadened its mission to promote technology transfer by providing a professional association for the new function. From the initial founding membership of 11 institutions, AUTM has grown into an international organization.

Over the ensuing 35 years absolutely every American Research University and even many undergraduate institutions and community colleges have created offices of technology licensing and transfer. Academics have changed their behavior to accept technology licensing (Bercovitz and Feldman, 2008). Scholars debate the desirability of these changes. For some, this new environment is key to promoting innovation and technological change and the hallmark of greater partnerships with industry and government (Etzkowitz, Leydesdorff and Geuna, 1999). To others, the emphasis on commercialization, intellectual property protection and greater engagement with industry erodes academic values, threatens the intellectual commons, and dilutes the mission of universities away from their core activities (Slaughter and Leslie, 1997). However, putting these important debates aside, this chapter will review the American experience in technology transfer by examining court cases involving university intellectual property as an interpretative lens. This litigation highlights contentious issues around technology transfer. Our analysis reveals that universities that have been more successful at technology transfer, have been at it longer, and have experienced a big hit have greater involvement with litigation. These court cases are shaping the unfolding relationships between universities, faculty members and commercial interests.

American technology transfer through the lens of litigation

As technology transfer has grown and become more prevalent, court cases have begun to reflect relational tensions between universities and industry, government, and other universities. There is a clear and ongoing debate over whether universities should, or even will be able to continue to legally maintain their sole status as educational organizations given their engagement with profit making activities.

Court cases affecting technology transfer at universities were found through an online keyword search of The Chronicle of Higher Education in June 2014. Articles were found from The Chronicle's website as early as 1970. Cases were found that began as early as 1988, and some were still ongoing at the time of the search. Forty-nine court cases were discovered using keywords: lawsuit, technology transfer, university, spinout, start-up, court case, and patent. The most influential cases identified are summarized in Table 3.2. The discussion follows major themes identified in reviewing the court cases.

While there is great interest in realizing public benefit for university research the fact that universities receive licensing revenues, which they then distribute to faculty inventors fuels this debate. Lawsuits questioning the appropriateness of revenue generating activities for non-profit educational entities have become more common over time. Such cases target the tax-exempt status of universities and research exceptions provided because of their educational purpose. The tactics used by some universities in technology transfer have raised question as to whether the university is aggressive for the sake of protecting knowledge, or for the sake of protecting monetary interests.

Court cases affect technology transfer by underscoring the diligence needed by universities if they are to compete for rights with companies that often have much larger budgets to litigate sometimes decade-long lawsuits. Cases disputing the language of contracts underscore a need for universities to employ professional technology officers who have the knowledge to protect the rights of universities and their faculties. Recent cases also illustrate the impact of contractual relationships dictated by technology commercialization on university technology transfer. Broken or misunderstood contracts and stringent intellectual property policies can easily alienate universities from industry and government agencies. Court cases not specifically involving a university can even affect their ability to transfer technology. Friend-of-the-court briefs issued by universities show their awareness of such possible impacts.

March-in rights

A trend exists in technology transfer court cases involving issues of intent of the Bayh-Dole Act. Several cases have involved the petitioning of Bayh-Dole "march-in" rights by plaintiffs or defendants. If petitioned, the right allows the federal agency that funded research leading to an invention to require the invention owner grant a license to the petitioner, even if the owner has already issued an exclusive license to another entity. Four conditions involving a necessity for the public good must be met in order to invoke these rights, though (35 U.S.C. § 203).

CellPro, Inc. brought a petition for the National Institutes of Health (NIH) to invoke its march-in rights after Johns Hopkins University, Baxter Healthcare Corporation and Becton Dickinson and Company brought suit against the company in 1994 claiming patent infringement. The plaintiffs argued CellPro's device, Ceprate, infringed on patents owned by Johns Hopkins that were exclusively licensed to Becton Dickinson, who then sold the license to Baxter. The patents covered a technique that isolates stem cells CellPro was using to treat cancer patients whose bodies were harmed by extensive radiation treatments (Blumenstyk, 1997a). The case was the result of a failed license negotiation between the parties (Blumenstyk, 1997b). CellPro argued the patents were invalid and an initial jury agreed, but a judge for the U.S. District Court for the District of Delaware overturned the verdict. The case went through another jury trial, which found that CellPro had willfully infringed and ordered the defendant to pay treble damages (Dunbar, 2001).

In 1997, CellPro petitioned National Institutes of Health (NIH), the invention's funding agency, to require Johns Hopkins to sell CellPro a license to the patent after a judge ordered a future injunction of sales of Ceprate. NIH denied the petition a week after CellPro was ordered to pay treble damages (Blumenstyk ,1997b), stating that Baxter and Johns Hopkins were taking reasonable steps to apply the patents toward the same technique, so there was no public health need that would be cause for CellPro to have a license to them (NIH, Office of the Director 1997). The case concluded in 1998 when the U.S. Court of Appeals for the Federal Circuit upheld the jury's decision (Johns Hopkins University et al. v. CellPro, Inc., 1998). CellPro announced in 2008 it would file for bankruptcy as a result of losing the case (Blumenstyk, 1998).

A group of patients suffering from Fabry disease brought a class action lawsuit against Mount Sinai School of Medicine and Genzyme Corporation in March 2011, accusing the defendants of negligence and violating the Bayh-Dole Act when they refused to break an exclusive licensing agreement and allow other companies to produce a medication of which Genzyme had a shortage. The drug, Fabrazyme, eased and lengthened the lives of patients who suffer from Fabry disease and was being rationed at an ineffective level to the patients due to a shortage that began two years prior. The patients sought damages from the companies for withholding a federally funded invention from the public. The suit was brought after a petition to NIH requesting it use its march-in rights was denied in December 2010. The petitioners called for NIH, who funded the drug's research, to demand the license be extended to other companies for manufacturing. NIH denied the request stating extension of the license would not solve the shortage problem (NIH, Office of the Director, 2010). The group re-petitioned NIH to march-in in 2011 and included a request in the petition for NIH to more clearly delineate conditions under which it would invoke its march-in rights (Blumenstyk, 2011b). NIH closed the second Fabry march-in case in February 2013 without ruling on the petition after the Fabrazyme shortage ended (Carik, et al. v. U.S. DHHS, 2013). A related case began in 2012 when another group of patients sued the U.S. Department of Health and Human Services, Mount Sinai, and other federal agencies over the shortage (Carik, et al. v. U.S. DHHS, 2013). The lawsuit was dismissed in 2013 by the U.S. District Court for the District of Columbia then dismissed again on appeal in 2014 by the U.S. Court of Appeals for the Federal Circuit (Carik, et al. v. U.S. DHHS, et al. 2014).

Challenges to tax-exempt status

Court cases involving technology transfer are one by-product of the expansion of the role of universities to include technology transfer and commercialization. The reach, strength, and efficacy of this expanded role have been questioned in several court cases since the early 2000s. A group of property owners challenged the tax-exempt status of several Princeton University buildings in 2011, claiming the buildings made money for the university rather than serving an educational purpose. The same group also questioned Princeton's overall tax-exempt status because of the hundreds of millions of dollars the university receives in royalties from a patent on the anticancer drug Alimta. It then distributes these royalties to faculty members – an action the property owners also view as a business activity for the school (Blumenstyk, 2013c). A New Jersey Tax Court Judge denied Princeton's motion to dismiss the case in June of 2013 (Offredo, 2013). As of February 2014 a court date had not been set, and the case was being settled out of court (Rappa, 2014). The outcome of this case could signal other citizens to bring similar suits against other research universities if the plaintiffs succeed in their challenge of Princeton's tax-exempt status based on the university's royalty profits and their subsequent distribution.

Assignment of rights

The United States Supreme Court agreed to hear a major case, the *Board of Trustees of the Leland Stanford Junior University et al. v. Roche Molecular Systems Inc. et al.* after it went through several rounds of appeals. In 2011 the Supreme Court decided through the case how patent rights were to be assigned when contractual agreements overlapped or contradicted. Stanford brought suit against Roche Molecular Systems in 2005 accusing the company of patent infringement on a device used to test for HIV (Huq, Goldberg, and Meagher, 2009; Kelderman, 2011). Roche held that it owned the patent in question, as well. The dispute arose because the Stanford researcher who developed the technology, Mark Holodniy, signed an agreement to assign rights of any future inventions to Stanford, and then also signed a Visitor Confidentiality Agreement at a company later acquired by Roche that assigned discovery rights to the company. The Supreme Court ruled the rights belonged to Roche because the Visitor Confidentiality Agreement was an immediate agreement while the Stanford agreement was only a promise to assign rights in the future (Huq, Goldberg, and Meagher, 2009). The major implication of this case for universities, outlined by the majority opinion, was that the Bayh-Dole Act did not automatically give them rights to the patented discoveries of their scientists; therefore, the wording of assignment agreements should be carefully articulated (Kelderman, 2011). Many universities and research institutions reached out to the Supreme Court arguing for a ruling in favor of Stanford, aware of the impact a verdict for Roche might have on their ability to argue patent rights (Blumenstyk, 2011a).

11th Amendment immunity

Universities have sought to downplay their economic activity as defendants in several technology transfer cases of the last decade. Some public universities have attempted to avoid lawsuits by claiming immunity from lawsuits under the 11th Amendment of the U.S. Constitution because of their legal status as government organizations. The 11th Amendment grants States and their agencies immunity from federal lawsuits initiated by citizens of another state. The University of Missouri claimed immunity under the 11th Amendment in a 2003 patent dispute case brought by Vas-Cath, Inc. Vas-Cath and Missouri both argued their own scientists were the first to invent a catheter used for dialysis, but the USPTO gave the patent rights to the university. When Vas-Cath appealed this decision to the U.S. District Court for the Western District of Missouri, Western Division, the university claimed immunity. The district court granted immunity in 2005 and dismissed the case (Vas-Cath, Inc. v. Curators of the University of Missouri, et al., 2005). When Vas-Cath appealed this decision, the U.S. Court of Appeals for the Federal Circuit held that Missouri could not claim immunity and remanded the case (Vas-Cath, Inc. v. Curators of the University of Missouri, et al., 2007a). The appeals court held the university waived its constitutional immunity when it participated in a federal administrative forum by asking the USPTO to hold an interference proceeding over the disputed patent and dismissed the appeal on that basis (Blumenstyk, 2007c). The case was ultimately dismissed by the Court of Appeals of the Federal Circuit in 2008 (Vas-Cath, Inc. v. Curators of the University of Missouri, et al., 2008) after the district court, upon remand, found Vas-Cath failed to state a claim under the rules of civil procedure (Vas-Cath, Inc. v. Curators of the University of Missouri, et al., 2007b).

Eleventh Amendment immunity was also claimed in *The Regents of the University of New Mexico v. Galen D. Knight and Terence J. Scallen.* The University of New Mexico filed suit against two scientists, Knight and Scallen, who developed a cancer treatment while at the university. Though the scientists signed over rights to the treatment in 1991, they refused to update the university's patent record in 1996. The university subsequently brought suit against the scientists and won the case, but the defendants were allowed to make counterclaims when they alleged the university had stolen their rights (Engber, 2004). The university claimed 11th Amendment immunity when subjected to the counterclaims, and the U.S. District Court for the District of New Mexico granted the immunity. On appeal the U.S. Court of Appeals for the Federal Circuit remanded the case, stating the district court incorrectly granted immunity to the university because the university had waived 11th Amendment immunity when it filed a lawsuit in federal court. On remand the district court dismissed Knight and Scallen's counterclaims. The scientists once again appealed, but in 2004 the U.S. Court of Appeals for the Federal Circuit affirmed the lower courts decision (The Regents of the University of New Mexico v. Knight, et al., 2004). These two cases outline the confusion that can arise over patent filing issues when inventors file for similar patents at the same time. Such cases may have been influential in the creation and passage of the new first-to-file patent law.

Experimental use exception

Another trend in technology transfer litigation is university defenses based on special treatment rights because of their educational legal status. A case brought against Duke University depicts such a defense based on a legal exception. When former Duke professor John M.J. Madey brought suit against the university for patent infringement in 1997, Duke argued it had not infringed due to an experimental use exception. This exception states that scientists can use patented inventions without a license if their research does not involve a business purpose (Blumenstyk, 2003). A disagreement between Madey and Duke over the operation of a research lab resulted in Duke removing Madey from his position as Principal Investigator. Following his removal Madey resigned from Duke entirely. When Duke continued to use Madey's patented technologies in his former lab at the university, Madey sued for infringement. In 2001, the U.S. District Court for the Middle District of North Carolina granted Duke this exception and partial summary judgment. The district court held Duke had not infringed because the patented technologies were used "solely for research, academic, or experimental purposes" in line with Dukes technology transfer policies, and because Madey had not proven any commercial intent on the part of Duke (Madey v. Duke, 2001).

Madey appealed the decision to the U.S. Court of Appeals for the Federal Circuit who found the district court incorrectly applied the experimental use exception and remanded the case. The Court of Appeals stated the district court focused too heavily on Duke's status as a non-profit when evaluating the merit of the experimental use exception, "suppressing the fact that Duke's acts appear to be in accordance with any reasonable interpretation of Duke's legitimate business objectives," and ordered the District Court to apply a more narrow understanding of the exception on remand (Madey v. Duke, 2002). The U.S. Supreme Court declined to hear Duke's appeal to evaluate the Court of Appeals finding, which kept the Court of Appeals' narrower definition of experimental use intact. Like the Stanford case, many universities petitioned the Supreme Court on behalf of Duke, fearing the implication of such a finding for technology commercialization at private universities (Blumenstyk, 2003). As the case progressed Duke attempted a "government license" defense, stating it had a right to use the patented materials because it was using them for the government. Duke also argued that because the materials were from government-financed research the government had a license to them under Bayh-Dole. The district court denied this defense in a 2006 motion for summary judgment, stating a university could not raise such a defense on behalf of the government, unless it was "for the government with its authorization and consent," which Duke had not proven (Madey v. Duke, 2006). Duke settled with Madey in August 2006. Terms of the settlement included returning Madey's lab equipment (Gallagher, 2009).

Doctrine of equivalents

The Supreme Court ruling in *Festo Corporation v. Shoketsu Kinzoku Kabushiki Co., LTD. (a/k/a SMC Corporation) and SMC Pneumatics, Inc.* (2008), however, affirmed universities' ability to protect patents from copycat inventors through the doctrine of equivalents. The doctrine of equivalents maintains that a patent holder may sue a competitor over a rival invention even if the competitor's discovery is not an exact copy. Festo sued SMC Corporation in 1988 for damages and infringement on two patents for technologies used in rods used to move goods (Festo Corporation v. Shoketsu Kinzoku Kabushiki Co., LTD, et al., 1993).

Festo acknowledged the infringement was not literal, stating SMC Corporation's device infringed under the doctrine of equivalents. A jury trial found SMC guilty in 1994. The U.S. Court of Appeals for the Federal Circuit upheld the decision, but the U.S. Supreme Court later took the case and remanded it to the Court of Appeals (Festo Corporation v. Shoketsu Kinzoku Kabushiki Co., LTD, et al., 2007). Upon rehearing, the Court of Appeals for the Federal Circuit held because the patent had been amended and made narrower before it was issued, the doctrine of equivalents did not apply and therefore SMC Corporation had not infringed (Blumenstyk, 2002c). The Supreme Court again heard the case and remanded in 2002, maintaining three exceptions existed that would allow the doctrine of equivalents to apply to an amended patent: the "equivalent may have been unforeseeable at the time of the application; the rationale underlying the amendment may bear no more than a tangential relation to the equivalent in question; or there may be some other reason suggesting that the patentee could not reasonably be expected to have described the insubstantial substitute in question" (Festo Corporation v. Shoketsu Kinzoku Kabushiki Co., LTD, et al., 2002). The U.S. Court of Appeals for the Federal Circuit subsequently remanded the case to the district court in 2003 (Festo Corporation v. Shoketsu Kinzoku Kabushiki Co., LTD, et al., 2003), where a jury trial found SMC Corporation guilty of infringement based on the doctrine of equivalents. In 2005, however, a judge for the U.S. District Court of the District of Massachusetts vacated the jury's decision holding SMC Corporation's equivalent patent would have been foreseeable to Festo professionals, so the infringement claim was not valid (Festo Corporation v. Shoketsu Kinzoku Kabushiki Co., LTD, et al., 2005). The U.S. Court of Appeals for the Federal Circuit affirmed the district court's decision in 2007 (Festo Corporation v. Shoketsu Kinzoku Kabushiki Co., LTD, et al., 2007) and in 2008 the Supreme Court declined to review the Appeals Court's decision, ending the 20-year long dispute (Festo Corporation v. Shoketsu Kinzoku Kabushiki Co., LTD, et al., 2008).

Inventor rights

Dr. Renee L. Kaswan sued the University of Georgia (UGA) Research Foundation over the Foundation's handling of a patent and license to a discovery she made that is used for Restasis eye drops. Dr. Kaswan was in the process of obtaining the patents herself when Allergan, Inc., the company the patent was licensed to, received FDA approval for the drug. The university decided not to transfer the rights to Dr. Kaswan because of the FDA approval and to let Allergan take the drug to market. Dr. Kaswan subsequently sued the Foundation and tried to have the decision invalidated when she discovered it had been made without her input. A Georgia Superior Court judge held in 2007 that the university did not have to consult with Dr. Kaswan about decisions regarding the patent. This ruling meant control of inventions patented through universities would be given entirely to the universities technology transfer managers in the Court's jurisdiction, making the inventor's desires legally irrelevant (Blumenstyk, 2008b). The seven-year dispute ended in a

2010 settlement in which UGA paid Kaswan $20.2 million (Shearer, 2010). Though this case did not set precedent, it could be persuasive in other courts.

Related precedents

Cases that do not involve universities can still have an impact on their ability to transfer technology and capitalize on its commercialization. In *MedImmune Inc. v. Genentech Inc.* the U.S. Supreme Court decided a patent's validity could be challenged in court by an entity that had agreed to license it and was already paying royalties. After licensing a patent from Genentech and paying royalties on the patent, MedImmune tried to have Genentech's patent invalidated in court (Blumenstyk, 2007b). The U.S. District Court for the Central District of California dismissed the case stating MedImmune did not have standing to sue. The district court based its decision on a U.S. Court of Appeals for the Federal Circuit precedent that stated, "a patent licensee in good standing could not establish a case or controversy under the Federal Constitution's Article III with regard to the patent's validity, enforceability, or scope." In 2007, though, the Supreme Court overturned the precedent and remanded the case, ordering it be decided on its merits. The Supreme Court held that a licensee has standing to sue without first having to break their patent license (MedImmune, Inc. v. Genentech, Inc. et al., 2008a). Several universities issued friend-of-the-court briefs arguing against such a verdict, fearing that it would prompt more companies to challenge universities' patents, and ultimately weaken the Bayh-Dole Act (Blumenstyk, 2007b). The case settled in 2008 (MedImmune, Inc. v. Genentech, Inc. et al., 2008a).

Universities may be drawn into court cases because of their relationship to the companies that license their technology. An example of this was seen in *AsymmetRx, Inc. v. Biocare Medical, LLC*. AsymmetRx sued Biocare Medical for patent infringement in 2007. When the United States District Court for the District of Massachusetts ruled in favor of Biocare in 2008 AsymmetRx appealed to the U.S. Court of Appeals for the Federal Circuit. Without resolving the merits of the case, the Appeals Court vacated the decision of the lower court and remanded. It held that AsymmetRx did not have standing to sue Biocare Medical for infringement on a discovery it licensed from Harvard University without naming Harvard a party to the suit (AsymmetRx, Inc. v. Biocare Medical, LLC, 2009). The Appeals Court stated Harvard could, however, bring suit against Biocare Medical without naming AsymmetRx a party. The discrepancy was due to the language of the licensing agreement (Huq, Goldberg, and Meagher, 2009). The court held that Harvard had not granted AsymmetRx all substantial rights, which would have allowed the company to sue independently (AsymmetRx, Inc. v. Biocare Medical, LLC, 2009). Harvard later joined AsymmetRx in arbitration against Biocare Medical (AsymmetRx, Inc., et al. v. Biocare Medical, LLC, 2010).

Universities were indirectly involved in two other cases found through The Chronicle search. Research Corporation Technologies (RCT) sued several companies, including Microsoft in 2001, for patent infringement. The University of Rochester became involved in the case because it owned the invention RCT commercialized and licensed to other companies (Blumenstyk, 2006a). The University of Utah was indirectly involved in *Association for Molecular Pathology, et al. v. Myriad Genetics, Inc., et al.* (2013). The plaintiff claimed three gene patents used to detect certain cancers that were owned by the university and licensed to Myriad Genetics were invalid (Blumenstyk, 2013b). The U.S. Supreme Court ruled in favor of the plaintiffs in 2013, holding "A naturally occurring DNA segment is a product of nature and not patent eligible merely because it has been isolated" (Association for Molecular Pathology, et al. v. Myriad Genetics, Inc., et al., 2013).

Patent infringement and license disputes

Court cases involving allegations of patent infringement and/or fraud constitute the majority of cases affecting technology transfer and appear the earliest out of the cases found from The Chronicle search. Universities regularly make such claims in suits against companies and/or individuals. Companies and/or individuals also make such claims against universities, though this trend is to be less common. Most patent infringement cases are concluded without the broad implications on technology transfer of the cases outlined previously. Still, the large number of cases universities have been involved in, and the monetary and temporal costs of them, has implications for universities and their ability to effectively commercialize technology.

Major cases

The rulings of some patent infringement and patent validity cases carry broad implications and are outlined in Table 3.2. In 2002, Ariad Pharmaceuticals, Inc., the Massachusetts Institute of Technology, the Whitehead Institute for Biomedical Research and Harvard College sued Eli Lilly and Company for patent infringement. The biomedical patent under question was owned by Harvard and the Whitehead Institute and exclusively licensed to Ariad (Blumenstyk, 2010c). A jury found Eli Lilly guilty of infringement in 2006, but in 2010 the U.S. Court of Appeals of the Federal Circuit reversed the verdict and declared Ariad's patent invalid because it did not fulfill the written description requirement (Ariad Pharmaceuticals et al. v. Eli Lilly and Company, 2010) and therefore was too broad (Blumenstyk, 2010c). According to USPTO, "To satisfy the written description requirement, a patent specification must describe the claimed invention in sufficient detail that one skilled in the art can reasonably conclude that the inventor had possession of the claimed invention" (USPTO, 2014a). The written description requirement has been the subject of much recent debate. Both parties of the Ariad v. Lilly case proffered different interpretations of the requirement. Ariad claimed the district court erred when it interpreted the written requirement being separate from the enablement requirement, but the Court of Appeals affirmed the distinction in Lilly's favor (Ariad Pharmaceuticals et al. v. Eli Lilly and Company, 2010). The enablement requirement states a patent claim must describe how to make and use the technology to be patented (USPTO, 2014b). The overturned decision was a great upset to the plaintiffs and many others who believed the narrow understanding of the written description requirement used in the court's decision could make it more difficult for universities to patent basic research (Blumenstyk, 2010c).

Patent validity is often brought into question in patent infringement cases as part of a defense. WARF endured considerable criticism during the 2000s because of its strict policies regarding the use of its patents on stem cell lines. The criticism was due to the fact that five of the 21 stem cells lines scientists could conduct research on during the George W. Bush Administration were patented to WARF. WARF aggressively protected its right to the patents, causing many organizations to criticize the Foundation and claim they impeded research progression (Blumenstyk, 2006c). Consumer Watchdog (formerly the Foundation for Taxpayer and Consumer Rights) challenged the patents' validity in court in 2006 by requesting inter parties reexamination of the patent (Consumer Watchdog v. Wisconsin Alumni Research Foundation, 2014). The organization argued the patents should not have been granted because the discoveries were too broad to be patent eligible (Blumenstyk, 2006c). The Patent Trial and Appeal Board disagreed with Consumer Watchdog, though, and affirmed the validity of WARF's patents. In 2014 and after several prior rounds of appeals (Basken, 2013a), the U.S. Court of Appeals for the Federal Circuit dismissed Consumer Watchdog's appeal of the Board's decision. The Court of Appeals held Consumer Watchdog ineligible to sue because the organization could not establish an injury in fact since it was not involved in stem cell research or commerce and was not a competitor of either WARF or WARF's licensee (Consumer Watchdog v. Wisconsin Alumni Research Foundation, 2014). Whether the Court of Appeals would have upheld the patent is unknown, as the case was dismissed before trial.

The Regents of the University of California filed a lawsuit against Genentech Inc. in 1990 for patent infringement on a discovery used in the company's human-growth hormone drug Protropin (Van Der Werf and Blumenstyk, 1999). Genentech countered arguing the patent was invalid. Though the jury trial held the patent was valid, it deadlocked over the case in June of 1999. A new trial was scheduled to begin in 2000 (Blumenstyk, 1999a), but the two parties reached a $200 million settlement in 1999 before the new trial began. The university had spent approximately $20 to $25 million on the case (Van Der Werf and Blumenstyk, 1999). Besides the enormous litigation costs, the case is illustrative of the longevity of some technology transfer disputes. The dispute began in 1978 when a Genentech scientist stole DNA from the university. Genentech acknowledged the theft and paid $2 million to the university in compensation in 1979, but many believe the DNA was used to invent Protropin. Genentech and the University of California stated the settlement was not an admission of guilt of patent infringement or guilt of the use of the stolen DNA for Protropin by Genentech (Van Der Werf and Blumenstyk, 1999).

Other litigation against universities

Onconome Inc. filed a lawsuit in 2009 against a researcher, Robert H. Getzenberg and the university that employed him during the time Onconome funded over $13 million of Getzenberg's research. The company accused the defendants of fraud and breach of contract and sought damages including money the company spent on licenses to commercialize Getzenberg's technology (Onconome, Inc. v. University of Pittsburgh et al., 2009; Blumenstyk, 2009b). Eli Lilly and the University of California have traded roles in several legal disputes. In 1993, Eli Lilly filed suit claiming the university breached an exclusive license contract when it invited other companies to seek licenses for the same patent (Blumenstyk, 1993). In 2003 several companies, including Biogen Idec, Genentech, and Genzyme, sued Columbia University accusing the university of seeking a patent for a technique the university already had an expired patent for, in an attempt to continue receiving royalties. The case resulted in several settlements. Though Columbia was able to keep its patent, it agreed not to enforce it against the companies (Blumenstyk, 2004c; Blumenstyk, 2005b).

Other litigation brought by universities

Most litigation is seen in cases where the university accuses a company, organization, or other university of patent infringement. These cases can take years to conclude, some lasting well over a decade. The longevity brings enormous litigation costs. *University of Colorado Health Sciences Center v. Wyeth Pharmaceuticals* (2004) lasted over 11 years. It began in 1993 when the Center brought suit against American Cyanamid (later acquired by Wyeth) for patent infringement. The university eventually won the case and $58 million in damages (Blumenstyk, 2004b).

Universities sometimes sue individuals directly over technology transfer disputes. In *West Virginia University v. Kurt L. VanVoorhies*, the university won rights to an invention VanVoorhies started working on when he was a graduate student at the university. VanVoorhies argued the university should not have rights to the invention because it was not complete until after he left the university. In a similar case, the University of New Mexico eventually dropped a lawsuit against former researcher Jonathan S. Nimitz for rights to discoveries Nimitz made after he left the university. The discoveries were variations on a compound he invented at the university (Blumenstyk, 2002b).

The University of Alabama at Huntsville sued Milton Harris for patent infringement after he made money from an invention he patented and spun-out while at the university. The university won the case. Harris paid damages and the university agreed not to continue with the patent claim (Burd, 2006). St. Johns University began a lawsuit against a former professor and graduate student, claiming they formed a company that profited from research they conducted while at the university without granting the university the monetary compensation it was owed (Blumenstyk, 2010d). WARF has also been involved in several lawsuits against companies: a 2001 license dispute lawsuit against Geron Corporation (Blumenstyk, 2006c); a 2003 patent infringement lawsuit against Sony and Toshiba (Blumenstyk, 2004a); and a 2006 patent infringement case against Arkopharma, LLC (Blumenstyk, 2006b). These types of court cases are not only an occurrence of the past decade. The University of Pennsylvania and University of Houston System filed lawsuits against an emeritus faculty member over patent infringement and former faculty member over failure to alert of an invention, respectively, almost 25 years ago (Grassmuck, 1990).

Other patent validity cases

Microsoft used a patent validity defense in 2003 when the University of California accused it of infringing on a web-browser technology patent. The USPTO affirmed the validity of the patents after Microsoft appealed the district court's decision awarding the university $521 million. The USPTO later reopened the investigation and the case was eventually settled in 2007 (Foster, 2007; Read, 2007). Pfizer Inc. raised the same defense when it was sued by the University of Rochester for patent infringement, but won the case. The U.S. Court of Appeals for the Federal Circuit affirmed the decision, and the U.S. Supreme Court declined to hear another appeal from Rochester (Blumenstyk, 2004d). In another case, the University of Minnesota and two of its researchers brought suit against Glaxo Wellcome claiming patent infringement. A patent validity defense was used and the case settled out of court (Blumenstyk, 1999b).

Litigation settlements

Most patent infringement cases brought by universities against companies ended in out-of-court settlements or orders to pay damages and/or future royalties. The University of Texas sued Research in Motion and settled for $1.8 million in 2005. Georgetown University sued Digene Corporation for patent-infringement and settled for $7.5 million with continued royalty payments in 2005 (Mangan, 2005). Emory University settled a six-year long dispute with GlaxoSmithKline and Shire Pharmaceuticals Group in 2002 over the rights to three anti-AIDS drugs. Emory received a monetary settlement and each party obtained licenses to the others' patents. The settlement also finalized the ending of a dispute over another patent that began in a lawsuit against GlaxoSmithKline's predecessor Glaxo Wellcome, even though the suit settled in 1999 (Borrego, 2002). Marvell Technology Group was found guilty of willful infringement on a patent owned by Carnegie Mellon University and ordered to pay $1.54 billion in damages to the university (DeSantis, 2014). Approximately seven other similar patent infringement or licensing dispute cases were found through the Chronicle search. These include: suits initiated by Cornell University and the Massachusetts Institute of Technology against separate defendants in 2002 (Blumenstyk, 2002a); a suit filed by the Washington Research Foundation against three cellphone manufacturers for patent infringement on Bluetooth technology in 2006 (Blumenstyk, 2007a); a suit Northeastern University and Jarg Corporation filed against Google in 2007 (Huckabee, 2007); a suit filed by Iowa State University against several companies in the early 1990s concerning technology used in facsimile machines (J.L.N., 1992); and a suit the University of Michigan brought against Learjet Corporation (Grassmuck, 1990).

Unintended consequences of litigation

Lawsuits involving technology transfer disputes can have surprising consequences. Micron Technology imposed a hiring ban on the University of Illinois-Champaign's students and suspended other activities with the university after the university brought suit against Micron for patent infringement. The university responded by asking the judge in the case for an injunction based on coercion, but the judge denied the request (Blumenstyk, 2013a). The University of Kansas sued NIH and Millennium Pharmaceuticals to add two inventors from the university to a patent. The patent only had a scientist from Millennium listed as inventor at the time. The university won the case in 2012 and added its scientists to the patent (Biemiller, 2012), thereby likely gaining more control over the patent, its licensing, and revenues. It is possible though, that filing suit against NIH may have harmed its important relationship with the funding organization (Blumenstyk, 2008c).

Other court cases

Some legal disputes over inventions arise when researchers change jobs and move to a new company or university. Florida State University accused American BioScience of stealing the inventions of a university researcher by hiring one of the researcher's postdoctoral students. Though a lower court ruled in favor of Florida State, the U.S. Court of Appeals for the Federal Circuit overturned the ruling and ordered the patents on inventions of the postdoctoral student be assigned to American BioScience. The company did, however, pay to settle claims that it stole trade secrets ("Despite Ruling", 2003).

Court cases show universities strongly assert their rights to inventions. One case resulted in a three and a half year prison sentence for the defendant, Petr Taborsky, in 1993 after he refused to turn over a patent to the University of South Florida on a discovery he made there as a student (Nicklin, 1993). Also in the early 1990s, the University of Minnesota sued a current professor, a former professor and three companies owned by the defendants and their families in an effort to recover alleged lost royalties and "diverted research-contract income" (Blumenstyk, 1992). A 2003 suit the Purdue Research Foundation and Cook Biotech brought against Stephen Badylak and ACell Inc. raised concerns about Purdue's actions. The plaintiffs accused former Purdue scientist Stephen F. Badylak of stealing research data from the university and helping a collaborator invent and patent a technology that became the basis for the ACell Inc. ACell is a competitor of a company, Cook Biotech, which Purdue had an ownership stake in. The case against Badylak was dismissed before it reached trial. ACell claimed the accusations were false, and the U.S. Court of

Appeals for the Federal Circuit sided with the defendant in 2006, holding ACell not guilty (Blumenstyk, 2007e).

University technology transfer litigation best practices

Universities are interested in safeguarding their economic interests. The commonly seen seven figure royalties licenses brought to universities have certainly increased their interest in economic self-preservation and prosperity. The court cases found through a search of The Chronicle of Higher Education illustrate a dilemma universities face. Universities must delicately balance the public interest with their own interest in insured longevity. The array of court cases impacting technology transfer and the recurring themes of the disputes highlight a lack of solidarity among universities with regard to how to best approach technology transfer litigation.

More proactively, university technology transfer offices (TTOs) have tried self-governance. Eleven universities collaborated in 2006 to produce a set of suggested guidelines, or best practices, for universities facing or considering technology transfer litigation. The guidelines are outlined in the white paper "In the Public Interest: Nine Points to Consider in Licensing University Technology" (Blumenstyk, 2007d) and were endorsed by the Association of University Technology Managers (AUTM) (AUTM, 2014). They include suggestions for limiting lawsuits to those only absolutely necessary, avoiding licensing to patent trolls (companies which aggregate patents for the purpose of future litigation), offering fewer exclusive licenses, and taking special concern over the language of contracts (Blumenstyk, 2007d). As of July 2014 over 100 universities and

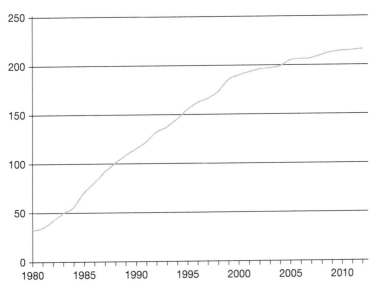

Figure 3.1 Cumulative number of technology transfer programs founded by year

institutions had endorsed the principles (AUTM, 2014). In 2013, however, AUTM began to reexamine its stance against patent aggregators as some argue aspects of aggregation may actually bring commercialization to more technologies (Basken, 2013b).

Relationship of litigation to university operations

Certainly litigation appears to have some relationship to university operations. The Wisconsin Alumni Research Foundation (WARF), founded in 1925 is the oldest university TTO in the United States and in 1968 was the first university to own the rights to patents of federally financed inventions. WARF frequently litigates and has a large enough endowment to bring lawsuits against any organization it feels may be infringing on its rights (Blumenstyk, 2006c). Of the 49 cases that were the subject of articles in *The Chronicle of Higher Education*, WARF was involved in four.

Several important trends in technology transfer licensing revenue, program age, and legal dispute involvement at American universities can be observed through data from AUTM's annual voluntary licensing survey. The majority of TTOs at universities were established after the Bayh-Dole Act. Figure 3.1 outlines the trend in program start dates. The year 1985 witnessed the most activity with the initiation of 15 programs. Office establishment tapered off by the early 2000s.

University license revenue has generally trended upwards, as shown in Figure 3.2. A sharp decline in total revenue occurred from 2008 to 2009, which may be attributed to the global recession. Total annual revenue and maximum annual revenue tend to follow the same trajectory, meaning the years with the highest

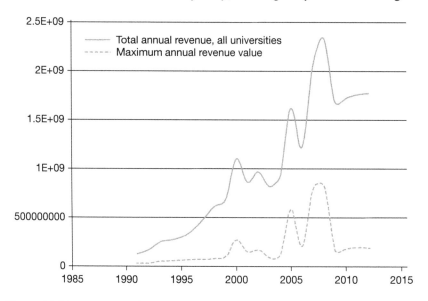

Figure 3.2 License revenue by year

maximum annual revenues tend to have proportionally high total annual revenues. The highest total revenue occurred in 2008, the same year the highest maximum revenue was attained. Northwestern University achieved the highest revenue in 2008, likely due to the December 2007 sale of a portion of its rights to the drug Lyrica (Blumenstyk, 2010a). Similarly, another unusually high total revenue occurred in 2005, due to the license revenue Emory University received for its sale of its future rights to two anti-AIDs drugs (Blumenstyk, 2005a).

A comparison of technology transfer program start dates, court cases, license revenue, and technology blockbusters provides a perspective on technology transfer trends in the U.S. University technology blockbusters, or "big hits," are defined as those technologies that bring in licensing or other revenues much higher than the average license revenues attained by the particular university. Such blockbusters have the potential to inflate universities' total revenue. Big hits were identified through a search of articles in the Chronicle of Higher Education. Because AUTM includes revenues from lawsuit settlements and equity sales in its overall license revenue category, such "blockbuster" settlements were included in the results. For example, Northwestern University's sale of equity in a startup company is an example of such a big hit that is a one time event.

Table 3.1 Revenue, blockbuster, legal dispute and program age correlations

Of the 23 universities with cumulative license revenue greater than $200 million:
52.17% (12) had at least one blockbuster
60.87% (14) were involved in at least one legal dispute
60.87% (14) had technology transfer offices/programs created before 1980

Of the 26 universities with at least one blockbuster:
46.15% (12) were involved in at least one legal dispute
46.15% (12) had cumulative license revenue greater than $200 million
38.46% (10) had technology transfer offices/programs created before 1980

Of the 35 universities involved in at least one legal dispute:
34.29% (12) had at least one blockbuster
40.00% (14) had cumulative license revenue greater than $200 million
45.71% (16) had technology transfer offices/programs created before 1980

Of the 30 universities with technology transfer offices/programs created before 1980:
33.33% (10) had at least one blockbuster
53.33% (16) were involved in at least one legal dispute
46.67% had cumulative license revenue greater than $200 million

Source: AUTM Licensing Survey, Fiscal Years 1991–2012.

Our findings indicated that of the 23 AUTM member universities with cumulative license revenue greater than $200 million, 52.17% of the universities had at least one blockbuster, 60.87% were involved in at least one court case, and 60.87% established TTOs or programs before 1980. These results depict a correlation between higher technology transfer licensing revenue, office or program age, blockbuster revenue earnings, and court case involvement. They suggest that the older and more successful a TTO is (when judged by cumulative revenue), the more likely that office will be to engage in a technology transfer legal dispute, and the more likely that office is to have attained its higher cumulative revenue due to one blockbuster license or settlement. Table 3.1 outlines the relationship between these variables.

These general trends can mask the fact that most universities net a loss in their technology transfer activities. A simple calculation of net revenue that subtracts total FTEs costs and total new patent filing costs found that of the 228 universities in the AUTM database for the years 1991 to 2012, where data was available, only 24.94 percent of the universities saw a net profit in any given year, with 76.02 percent incurring a loss in any given year. The universities that received the highest net profits out of the data for any given year were those described previously as the more litigious with the most blockbusters. The University of California System was found to have had some of the largest profits, as well as some of the largest losses in various years. Other than the California System, though, no university with one the highest net profits also had one of the largest net losses.

Table 3.2 Court cases

Case	Issue	Date Initiated	Date of Final Adjudication or Appeal (Jurisdiction)	Reference
The Johns Hopkins University, Baxter Healthcare Corporation and Becton Dickinson and Company v. CellPro, Inc.	March-in rights	March 8, 1994	August 11, 1998 (U.S. Court of Appeals, Federal Circuit)	Blumenstyk, 1997a; Blumenstyk, 1997b; Dunbar, 2001; Johns Hopkins University et al. v. CellPro, Inc., 1998

Case	Issue	Date Initiated	Date of Final Adjudication or Appeal (Jurisdiction)	Reference
Plaintiffs Anita Hochendoner, Earl Hochendoner, Anita Bova, Joseph M. Carik, Barbara J. Carik, Amber Britton, Shawn Britton, Cheryl Britton, Thomas Olszewski, Darlene Cookingham, and David Roberts, individually and on behalf of others similarly situated v. Genzyme Corporation and Mount Sinai School of Medicine of the City University of New York	March-in rights	March 9, 2011	Case dissolved by 2013 (U.S. District of Western District of Pennsylvania)	Blumenstyk, 2011b; Hochendoner, et al. v. Genzyme Corporation et al., 2011; NIH, Office of the Director, 2010
Consumer Watchdog, (formerly known as The Foundation for Taxpayer and Consumer Rights) v. Wisconsin Alumni Research Foundation	Patent validity	July 17, 2006	June 4, 2014 (U.S. Court of Appeals, Federal Circuit)	Blumenstyk, 2006c; Basken, 2013a; Consumer Watchdog v. Wisconsin Alumni Research Foundation, 2014; USPTO, 2007
Estate of Lewis, et. al. v. Princeton University and Borough of Princeton	Tax-exempt status	April 2011	Ongoing (Tax Court of New Jersey)	Blumenstyk, 2013c; Mulvaney, 2014; Rappa, 2014
Board of Trustees of the Leland Stanford Junior University v. Roche Molecular Systems, Inc.	Assignment agreements	October 14, 2005	June 6, 2011 (Supreme Court of the United States)	Blumenstyk, 2011a Huq, Goldberg, and Meagher, 2009; Kelderman, 2011; Board of Trustees of the Leland Stanford Junior University v. Roche Molecular Systems, Inc., 2006; Board of Trustees of the Leland Stanford Junior University v. Roche Molecular Systems, Inc., 2011

Table 3.2 continued

Table 3.2 continued

Case	Issue	Date Initiated	Date of Final Adjudication or Appeal (Jurisdiction)	Reference
Vas-Cath, Inc. v. Curators of the University of Missouri, Don Walsworth, Cheryl D.S. Walker, Anne C. Ream, M. Sean McGinnis, Marion H. Cairns, Angela M. Bennett, Thomas E. Atkins, Vicki M. Eller, Mary L. James and Connie Hager Silverstein	11th Amendment immunity	September 22, 2003	March 17, 2008 (U.S. Court of Appeals, Federal Circuit)	Blumenstyk, 2007c; Vas-Cath, Inc. v. Curators of the University of Missouri, et al., 2005; Vas-Cath, Inc. v. Curators of the University of Missouri, et al., 2008
John M.J. Madey v. Duke University	Experimental use exception	November 5, 1997	January 31, 2006 (U.S. District Court for the Middle District of North Carolina)	Blumenstyk, 2003; Blumenstyk, 2002d; Madey v. Duke, 2004; Madey v. Duke, 2006
MedImmune, Inc. v. Genentech, Inc. et al.	University indirectly involved	April 11, 2003	March 6, 2008 (U.S. District Court for the Central District of California) Settlement 2008	Blumenstyk, 2007b; MedImmune, Inc. v. Genentech, Inc. et al., 2008a; MedImmune, Inc. v. Genentech, Inc. et al., 2008b; MedImmune, Inc. v. Genentech, Inc. et al., 2013
Festo Corporation v. Shoketsu Kinzoku Kabushiki Co., LTD. (a/k/a SMC Corporation) and SMC Pneumatics, Inc.	Doctrine of equivalents	August 1988	June 9, 2008 (Supreme Court of the United States)	Blumenstyk, 2002c; Festo Corporation v. Shoketsu Kinzoku Kabushiki Co., LTD, et al., 1993; Festo Corporation v. Shoketsu Kinzoku Kabushiki Co., LTD, et al., 2007; Festo Corporation v. Shoketsu Kinzoku Kabushiki Co., LTD, et al., 2008

Case	Issue	Date Initiated	Date of Final Adjudication or Appeal (Jurisdiction)	Reference
AsymmetRx, Inc. v. Biocare Medical, LLC	University indirectly involved; substantial rights of licenses	June 27, 2007	September 18, 2009 (U.S. Court of Appeals, Federal Circuit)	Huq, Goldberg, and Meagher, 2009; AsymmetRx, Inc. v. Biocare Medical, LLC, 2009
Renee L. Kaswan v. University of Georgia Research Foundation and Allergan, Inc.	Patent ownership; University v. inventor control of patents	2004	Settlement 2010	Blumenstyk, 2008b; IP Advocate, 2014; Shearer, 2010
The Regents of the University of New Mexico v. Galen D. Knight and Terence J. Scallen	11th Amendment immunity	May 21, 1999	November 4, 2004 (U.S. Court of Appeals, Federal Circuit)	Engber, 2004; The Regents of the University of New Mexico v. Knight, et al., 2003; The Regents of the University of New Mexico v. Knight, et al., 2004
Regents of the University of California v. Genentech, Inc.	Patent infringement	August 6, 1990	January 7, 2000 (U.S. Court of Appeals, Federal Circuit) Settlement 1999	Blumenstyk, 1999a; Fran Finnegan & Company, 2014; Regents of the University of California v. Genentech, Inc., 2000; Rimmer, 2002/2003; Van Der Werf and Blumenstyk, 1999
Ariad Pharmaceuticals, Inc., Massachusetts Institute of Technology, The Whitehead Institute for Biomedical Research, and The President and Fellows of Harvard College v. Eli Lilly and Company	Patent infringement	June 25, 2002	March 22, 2010 (U.S. Court of Appeals, Federal Circuit)	Ariad Pharmaceuticals et al. v. Eli Lilly and Company, 2010; Blumenstyk, 2010c

Source: Compiled by the authors from sources in the *Reference* column of Table 3.2.

Conclusion

Data findings question the effectiveness of the United States model of university technology transfer and the way success in such a model is measured. Though many universities have been able to capitalize on the available monetary gains of active participation in technology commercialization, success has more often than not brought with it financial losses in terms of legal fees and licensing costs. Furthermore, blockbuster inventions are not the norm. As our findings and previous articles (Breznitz and Feldman, 2012; Feldman et al., 2002) indicate, most university technology transfer programs net a loss.

An overview of U.S. university technology transfer from a legal perspective, in conjunction with available data, outlines the ongoing debate over the merit of federal legislation like Bayh-Dole and other initiatives meant to promote university technology transfer. Several authors view Bayh-Dole critically, arguing the Act has had a detrimental effect (Sampat 2006; So et. al. 2008). Others continue to espouse its economic and innovation benefits. The overwhelming majority of universities incurring a loss from technology transfer activities lend credence to the idea that the current U.S. system needs revision. The costs of litigation concurrent with earning large profits bolster the argument that universities should carefully consider their strengths and weaknesses before devoted large numbers of resources to technology transfer. Still, the publicized profits gained by universities from blockbuster inventions or settlements may make pursuing commercialization at least monetarily worth its risk. But monetary risk does not address the issue of whether universities have stepped beyond their bounds of education and public service to behaving more like profit centered corporations. The arguments in favor and against this expanded role are unlikely to be resolved easily.

Technology licensing in the U.S. despite its problems most certainly will continue and evolve. Litigation is useful as a lens for understanding how the system is evolving, as future court cases are likely to determine the organizational configuration. The early gold rush that prevailed after the passage of Bayh-Dole is being tempered and technology transfer is beginning to look more like a routine function and an outlet for the greater public good.

Notes

1 For a summary of the Bayh-Dole Act, see www.autm.net/Bayh_Dole_Act1.htm.
2 The original patent application was split into three patents.

References

Ariad Pharmaceuticals et al. v. Eli Lilly and Company (2010). 598 F.3d 1336; 2010 U.S. App. LEXIS 5966; 94 U.S.P.Q.2D (BNA) 1161. Retrieved from www.lexisnexis.com/hottopics/lnacademic

Association for Molecular Pathology, et al. v. Myriad Genetics, Inc., et al. (2013). 133 S. Ct. 2107; 186 L. Ed. 2d 124; 2013 U.S. LEXIS 4540; 106 U.S.P.Q.2D (BNA) 1972; 24 Fla. L. Weekly Fed. S 276. Retrieved from www.lexisnexis.com/hottopics/lnacademic

AsymmetRx, Inc. v. Biocare Medical, LLC (2009). 582 F.3d 1314; 2009 U.S. App. LEXIS 20756; 92 U.S.P.Q.2D (BNA) 1113. Retrieved from www.lexisnexis.com/hottopics/lnacademic

AsymmetRx, Inc., et al. v. Biocare Medical, LLC (2010). 2010 U.S. Dist. LEXIS 128258. Retrieved from www.lexisnexis.com/hottopics/lnacademic

AUTM. (2014). Endorse the Nine Points to Consider. Retrieved from www.autm.net/source/NinePoints/ninepoints_endorsement.cfm

Basken, P. (2013a, July 3). After Utah's Loss on Genes, Wisconsin is Challenged Over Patent on Stem Cells. *The Chronicle of Higher Education*. Retrieved from http://chronicle.com.libproxy.lib.unc.edu/article/Groups-Ask-Court-to-Invalidate/140109/

Basken, P. (2013b, October 25). Under Financial Pressure, Universities Give Patent Buyers a Closer Look. *The Chronicle of Higher Education*. Retrieved from http://chronicle.com/article/Under-Financial-Pressure/142613/

Bercovitz, J. and M.P. Feldman. (2008). Academic Entrepreneurs: Organizational Change at the Individual Level. *Organization Science*, 19(1): 69–89.

Biemiller, L. (2012, April 6). U. of Kansas Researchers Win Credit for 2 Cancer-Drug Patents. *The Chronicle of Higher Education*. Retrieved from http://chronicle.com.libproxy.lib.unc.edu/blogs/ticker/u-of-kansas-researchers-win-credit-for-2-cancer-drug-patents/42156

Blumenstyk, G. (1992, December 9). University of Minnesota Sues 2 Professors Over Patents. *The Chronicle of Higher Education*. Retrieved from http://chronicle.com.libproxy.lib.unc.edu/article/University-of-Minnesota-Sues-2/70483/

Blumenstyk, G. (1993, March 31). Drug Company Sues U. of California on Marketing Rights. *The Chronicle of Higher Education*. Retrieved from http://chronicle.com.libproxy.lib.unc.edu/article/Drug-Company-Sues-U-of/73342/

Blumenstyk, G. (1997a, June 27). High-Stakes Patent Fight Features Research, Politics, Money. *The Chronicle of Higher Education*. Retrieved from http://chronicle.com.libproxy.lib.unc.edu/article/High-Stakes-Patent-Fight/74689/

Blumenstyk, G. (1997b, August 15). NIH Rejects Bid for License to Technology Patented by Hopkins. *The Chronicle of Higher Education*. Retrieved from http://chronicle.com.libproxy.lib.unc.edu/article/NIH-Rejects-Bid-for-License-to/75200/

Blumenstyk, G. (1998, October 9). Loser of Patent Fight with Johns Hopkins to File for Bankruptcy. *The Chronicle of Higher Education*. pp. A49. Retrieved from http://chronicle.com.libproxy.lib.unc.edu/article/Loser-of-Patent-Fight-With/30711/

Blumenstyk, G. (1999a, August 6). U. of California Patent Suit Puts Biotech Powerhouse Under Microscope A Billion-Dollar Patent Battle. *The Chronicle of Higher Education*. pp. A45. Retrieved from http://chronicle.com.libproxy.lib.unc.edu/article/U-of-California-Patent-Suit/20545/

Blumenstyk, G. (1999b, October 29). U. of Minnesota and Researchers May Receive Up to $300-Million in Patent Settlement. *The Chronicle of Higher Education*. pp. A54. Retrieved from http://chronicle.com.libproxy.lib.unc.edu/article/U-of-Minnesota-and/12609/

Blumenstyk, G. (2002a, January 25). Cornell and MIT Sue Companies Over Rights to Patents. The *Chronicle of Higher Education*. pp. A27. Retrieved from http://chronicle.com.libproxy.lib.unc.edu/article/CornellMIT-Sue-Companies/11082/

Blumenstyk, G. (2002b, May 17). Universities Try to Keep Inventions From Going "Out the Back Door". *The Chronicle of Higher Education*. pp. A33. Retrieved from http://chronicle.com.libproxy.lib.unc.edu/article/Universities-Try-to-Keep/5005/

Blumenstyk, G. (2002c, May 30). Supreme Court Ruling in Patent Case Expected to Benefit Universities. *The Chronicle of Higher Education*. pp. A28. Retrieved from http://chronicle.com.libproxy.lib.unc.edu/article/Supreme-Court-Ruling-in-Patent/115635/

Blumenstyk, G. (2002d, October 25). Court Ruling Revives Patent Lawsuit Against Duke U. The *Chronicle of Higher Education*. pp. A33. Retrieved from http://chronicle.com.libproxy.lib.unc.edu/article/Court-Ruling-Revives-Patent/19789/

Blumenstyk, G. (2003, July 11). Supreme Court Won't Hear Duke's Appeal in Key Patent Case. *The Chronicle of Higher Education*. pp. A25. Retrieved from http://chronicle.com.libproxy.lib.unc.edu/article/Supreme-Court-Wont-Hear/30065/

Blumenstyk, G. (2004a, March 19). Wisconsin Settles Playstation2 Lawsuit. *The Chronicle of Higher Education*. pp. A28. Retrieved from http://chronicle.com.libproxy.lib.unc.edu/article/U-of-Colorado-to-Collect/5700/http://chronicle.com.libproxy.lib.unc.edu/article/Wisconsin-Settles-Playstation2/16433

Blumenstyk, G. (2004b, April 30). U. of Colorado to Collect, Finally, $58-Million Drug-Patent Judgment. *The Chronicle of Higher Education*. Retrieved from http://chronicle.com.libproxy.lib.unc.edu/article/U-of-Colorado-to-Collect/5700/

Blumenstyk, G. (2004c, November 19). Judge Dismisses Challenge to Columbia Patent on a Biotechnology Technique. *The Chronicle of Higher Education*. pp. A27. Retrieved from http://chronicle.com.libproxy.lib.unc.edu/article/Judge-Dismisses-Challenge-to/9400/

Blumenstyk, G. (2004d, December 10). Supreme Court Declines to Hear Rochester's Appeal in High-Stakes Patent Case. *The Chronicle of Higher Education*. pp. A24. Retrieved from http://chronicle.com.libproxy.lib.unc.edu/article/Supreme-Court-Declines-to-Hear/31726/

Blumenstyk, G. (2005a, August 12). Emory U. Sells Rights to AIDS Drug, Betting on an Immediate Payoff. *The Chronicle of Higher Education*, pp. A26. Retrieved from http://chronicle.com/article/Emory-U-Sells-Rights-to-AIDS/27263/

Blumenstyk, G. (2005b, September 16). Columbia Patent Battle Winds Down. *The Chronicle of Higher Education*. pp. A37. Retrieved from http://chronicle.com.libproxy.lib.unc.edu/article/Columbia-Patent-Battle-Winds/27787/

Blumenstyk, G. (2006a, June 8). Lucrative Patents for U. of Rochester Are Unenforceable, Federal Judge Rules. *The Chronicle of Higher Education*. Retrieved from http://chronicle.com.libproxy.lib.unc.edu/article/Lucrative-Patents-for-U-of/119043/

Blumenstyk, G. (2006b, June 15). U. of Wisconsin Foundation Says Company's Dietary Supplements Infringe University Patents. *The Chronicle of Higher Education*. Retrieved from http://chronicle.com.libproxy.lib.unc.edu/article/U-of-Wisconsin-Foundation/ 119083/

Blumenstyk, G. (2006c, September 15). A Tight Grip on Tech Transfer. *The Chronicle of Higher Education*. pp. A28. Retrieved from http://chronicle.com.libproxy.lib.unc.edu/article/A-Tight-Grip-on-Tech-Transfer/3490/

Blumenstyk, G. (2007a, January 19). University Foundation Files Patent Suit. *The Chronicle of Higher Education*. pp. A28. Retrieved from http://chronicle.com.libproxy.lib.unc.edu/article/University-Foundation-Files/14501/

Blumenstyk, G. (2007b, January 26). Supreme Court Ruling May Disrupt Licensing. *The Chronicle of Higher Education*. pp. A31. Retrieved from http://chronicle.com.libproxy.lib.unc.edu/article/Supreme-Court-Ruling-May/1795/

Blumenstyk, G. (2007c, February 9). U. of Missouri Loses in Patent Appeal. *The Chronicle of Higher Education*. pp. A26. Retrieved from http://chronicle.com.libproxy.lib.unc.edu/article/U-of-Missouri-Loses-in-Patent/3141/

Blumenstyk, G. (2007d, March 16). New Guidelines Suggested for Licensing of Academic Inventions. *The Chronicle of Higher Education.* pp. A35. Retrieved from http://chronicle.com.libproxy.lib.unc.edu/article/New-Guidelines-Suggested-for/29927/

Blumenstyk, G. (2007e, April 6). Intellectual Property's Land Mines. *The Chronicle of Higher Education.* pp. A17. Retrieved from http://chronicle.com.libproxy.lib.unc.edu/article/Intellectual-Propertys-Land/5020/

Blumenstyk, G. (2008a, August 5). Microsoft Is Again in the Crosshairs of a University-Based Patent Suit. *The Chronicle of Higher Education.* Retrieved from http://chronicle.com.libproxy.lib.unc.edu/blogs/wiredcampus/microsoft-is-again-in-the-crosshairs-of-a-university-based-patent-suit/4146

Blumenstyk, G. (2008b, August 8). A Raw Deal, in a Researcher's Eyes. *The Chronicle of Higher Education.* pp. A1. Retrieved from http://chronicle.com.libproxy.lib.unc.edu/article/A-Raw-Deal-in-a-Researchers/5448/

Blumenstyk, G. (2008c, November 21). U. of Kansas Sues NIH to Gain Credit for Patents Used in Anticancer Drug. *The Chronicle of Higher Education.* Retrieved from http://chronicle.com.libproxy.lib.unc.edu/article/U-of-Kansas-Sues-NIH-to-Gain/1360/

Blumenstyk, G. (2009a, January 13). Inventor Behind Lucrative Eye-Drop Product Now Champions Faculty Patent Rights Online. *The Chronicle of Higher Education.* Retrieved from http://chronicle.com.libproxy.lib.unc.edu/article/Inventor-Behind-Lucrative/42230/

Blumenstyk, G. (2009b, September 4). Company Says Research It Sponsored at Pitt and Hopkins was Fraudulent. *The Chronicle of Higher Education.* Retrieved from http://chronicle.com.libproxy.lib.unc.edu/article/Company-Says-Research-It/48319/

Blumenstyk, G. (2010a, March 19). University Inventions Sparked Record Number of Companies in 2008. *The Chronicle of Higher Education.* Retrieved from http://chronicle.com/article/University-Inventions-Sparked/64204/

Blumenstyk, G. (2010b, March 19). Advocate for Faculty Inventors Makes Her Case to University Technology Managers. *The Chronicle of Higher Education.* Retrieved from http://chronicle.com.libproxy.lib.unc.edu/article/Advocate-for-Faculty-Inventors/ 64776/

Blumenstyk, G. (2010c, March 23). Federal Appeals Court Deals a Blow to Patenting Basic Research. *The Chronicle of Higher Education.* Retrieved from http://chronicle.com.libproxy.lib.unc.edu/article/Federal-Appeals-Court-Deals-a/64807/

Blumenstyk, G. (2010d, December 17). St. John's U. in $30-Million Patent Lawsuit Against Ex-Professor and Grad Student. *The Chronicle of Higher Education.* Retrieved from http://chronicle.com.libproxy.lib.unc.edu/blogs/ticker/st-johns-u-in-30-million-lawsuit-against-ex-professor-and-grad-student/29212

Blumenstyk, G. (2011a, February 22). In Case Before Supreme Court, a Battle Over Universities' Rights to Faculty Inventions. *The Chronicle of Higher Education.* Retrieved from http://chronicle.com.libproxy.lib.unc.edu/article/In-Case-Before-Supreme-Court/126479/

Blumenstyk, G. (2011b, April 17). Patients Take Aim at Medical School's Patent Deal on Life-Saving Drug. *The Chronicle of Higher Education.* Retrieved from http://chronicle.com.libproxy.lib.unc.edu/article/Patients-Take-Aim-at-Medical/127161/

Blumenstyk, G. (2013a, April 12). Tech Company Sued by U. of Illinois Takes It Out on Its Students. *The Chronicle of Higher Education.* Retrieved from http://chronicle.com.libproxy.lib.unc.edu/blogs/bottomline/tech-company-sued-by-u-of-illinois-takes-it-out-on-its-students/

Blumenstyk, G. (2013b, June 13). Academic Scientists Hail Supreme Court's Rejection of Gene Patents. *The Chronicle of Higher Education.* Retrieved from http://chronicle.com.libproxy.lib.unc.edu/article/Academic-Scientists-Hail/139813/

Blumenstyk, G. (2013c, July 8). Princeton's Royalty Windfall Leads to Challenge of Its Tax-Exempt Status. *The Chronicle of Higher Education.* Retrieved from http://chronicle.com/blogs/bottomline/princetons-royalty-windfall-leads-to-challenge-of-its-tax-exempt-status/?cid=wb&utm_source=wb&utm_medium=en

Board of Trustees of the Leland Stanford Junior University v. Roche Molecular Systems, Inc., (2006). 237 F.R.D. 618; 2006 U.S. Dist. LEXIS 53187. Retrieved from www.lexisnexis.com/hottopics/lnacademic

Board of Trustees of the Leland Stanford Junior University v. Roche Molecular Systems, Inc., (2011). 131 S. Ct. 2188; 180 L. Ed. 2d 1; 2011 U.S. LEXIS 4183; 79 U.S.L.W. 4407; 98 U.S.P.Q.2D (BNA) 1761; 68 A.L.R. Fed. 2d 617; 22 Fla. L. Weekly Fed. S 1069. Retrieved from www.lexisnexis.com/hottopics/lnacademic

Borrego, A.M. (2002, July 5). Emory Settles Patent Dispute Over AIDS Drugs. *The Chronicle of Higher Education.* pp. A26. Retrieved from http://chronicle.com.libproxy.lib.unc.edu/article/Emory-Settles-Patent-Dispute/8508/

Breznitz, S. and M. Feldman. (2012). The engaged university. *Journal of Technology Transfer,* 37: 139–157.

Burd, S. (2006, July 10). U. of Alabama at Huntsville Settles Patent Suit Against Professor and Company for $25-Million. *The Chronicle of Higher Education.* Retrieved from http://chronicle.com.libproxy.lib.unc.edu/article/U-of-Alabama-at-Huntsville/119387/

Carik, et al. v. U.S. DHHS (2013). 2013 U.S. Dist. LEXIS 168714. Retrieved from www.lexisnexis.com/hottopics/lnacademic

Carik, et al. v. U.S. DHHS, et al. (2014). 2014 U.S. App. LEXIS 8490. Retrieved from www.lexisnexis.com/hottopics/lnacademic

Consumer Watchdog v. Wisconsin Alumni Research Foundation (2014). U.S. App. LEXIS 10739. Retrieved from www.lexisnexis.com/hottopics/lnacademic

DeSantis, N. (2012, November 30). Supreme Court Will Take Up Case on U. of Utah's Controversial Gene Patents. *The Chronicle of Higher Education.* Retrieved from http://chronicle.com.libproxy.lib.unc.edu/blogs/ticker/jp/supreme-court-will-take-up-case-on-u-of-utahs-controversial-gene-patents

DeSantis, N. (2014, April 1). Judge Adds $366-Million to Patent-Lawsuit Award for Carnegie Mellon U. *The Chronicle of Higher Education.* Retrieved from http://chronicle.com.libproxy.lib.unc.edu/blogs/ticker/jp/judge-adds-366-million-to-patent-lawsuit-award-for-carnegie-mellon-u

Despite Ruling, Florida State U. Continues Battle Over Patents. (2003, July 25). *The Chronicle of Higher Education.* pp. A22. Retrieved from http://chronicle.com.libproxy.lib.unc.edu/article/Despite-Ruling-Florida-State/21898/

Dunbar, G. (2001). Real as Pro Wrestling: Johns Hopkins University v. CellPro and the Federal Court's Power of Review in Patent Infringement Actions. *Santa Clara High Technology Law Journal,* 18(2): 275–298.

Engber, D. (2004, November 26). U. of New Mexico Wins a Patent Ruling. *The Chronicle of Higher Education.* pp. A26. Retrieved from http://chronicle.com.libproxy.lib.unc.edu/article/U-of-New-Mexico-Wins-a-Patent/13826/

Etzkowitz, H., Leydesdorff, L., & Geuna, A. (1999). Book Reviews – Universities and the Global Knowledge Economy: A Triple Helix of University-Industry-Government Relations. *Economic Journal, 109*(456), F464.

Feldman, M.P., A. Colaianni, and C.K. Liu. (2008). Chapter17.22: Lessons from the Commercialization of the Cohen-Boyer Patents: The Stanford University Licensing Program. In A. Krattiger, R.T. Mahoney, U. Nelsen. J.A. Thompson, A.B. Bennett, K. Satyanarayana, G.D. Graff, C. Fernandez, and S.P. Kowalski, *Intellectual Property*

Management in Health and Agricultural Innovation: A handbook of best practices, Oxford; Davis CA. Volume 1: 1797–1808.

Feldman, M., I. Feller, J. Bercovitz, and R. Burton. (2002). Equity and the technology transfer strategies of American research universities. *Management Science*, 48(1): 105–121.

Feldman, M.P. and J.W. Yoon (2011). An Empirical Test for General Purpose Technology: An Examination of the Cohen–Boyer rDNA Technology. *Industrial and Corporate Change.* 21(2): 249–275.

Festo Corporation v. Shoketsu Kinzoku Kabushiki Co., LTD, et al. (1993). 1993 U.S. Dist. LEXIS 21434. Retrieved from www.lexisnexis.com/hottopics/lnacademic

Festo Corporation v. Shoketsu Kinzoku Kabushiki Co., LTD, et al. (2002). 535 U.S. 722; 122 S. Ct. 1831; 152 L. Ed. 2d 944; 2002 U.S. LEXIS 3818; 70 U.S.L.W. 4458; 62 U.S.P.Q.2D (BNA) 1705; 2002 Cal. Daily Op. Service 4539; 2002 Daily Journal DAR 5803; 15 Fla. L. Weekly Fed. S 320. Retrieved from www.lexisnexis.com/hottopics/lnacademic

Festo Corporation v. Shoketsu Kinzoku Kabushiki Co., LTD, et al. (2003). 344 F.3d 1359; 2003 U.S. App. LEXIS 19867; 68 U.S.P.Q.2D (BNA) 1321. Retrieved from www. lexisnexis.com/hottopics/lnacademic

Festo Corporation v. Shoketsu Kinzoku Kabushiki Co., LTD, et al. (2005). 2005 U.S. Dist. LEXIS 11621; 75 U.S.P.Q.2D (BNA) 1830. Retrieved from www.lexisnexis.com/hottopics/lnacademic

Festo Corporation v. Shoketsu Kinzoku Kabushiki Co., LTD, et al. (2007). 493 F.3d 1368; 2007 U.S. App. LEXIS 15942; 83 U.S.P.Q.2D (BNA) 1385. Retrieved from www. lexisnexis.com/hottopics/lnacademic

Festo Corporation v. Shoketsu Kinzoku Kabushiki Co., LTD, et al. (2008). 553 U.S. 1093; 128 S. Ct. 2903; 171 L. Ed. 2d 841; 2008 U.S. LEXIS 4800; 76 U.S.L.W. 3644. Retrieved from www.lexisnexis.com/hottopics/lnacademic

Foster, A.L. (2007, September 14). U. of California Settles Patent War with Microsoft. *The Chronicle of Higher Education.* pp. A23. Retrieved from http://chronicle.com.libproxy. lib.unc.edu/article/U-of-California-Settles/7063/

Fran Finnegan & Company. (2014). SEC Info: Genentech Inc. Retrieved from www. secinfo.com/d9N9s.5d.8.htm

Gallagher, J. (2009, May 5). Duke sues insurer to cover costs of Madey-laser suit. *Triangle Business Journal.* Retrieved from www.bizjournals.com/triangle/stories/2009/ 05/04/ story10.html?page=all

Grassmuck, K. (1990, July 25). Efforts to Protect Patents Bring Rewards and Lawsuits. *The Chronicle of Higher Education.* Retrieved from http://chronicle.com.libproxy.lib.unc. edu/article/Efforts-to-Protect-Patents/66547/

Hochendoner, et al. v. Genzyme Corporation, et al. (2011). Complaint in Civil Action. Retrieved from www.genomicslawreport.com/wp-content/uploads/2011/03/Hochendoner-v-Genzyme.pdf

Huckabee, C. (2007, November 23). Northeastern U., Tech Firm Sue Google Over Patent. *The Chronicle of Higher Education.* pp. A21. Retrieved from http://chronicle.com. libproxy.lib.unc.edu/article/Northeastern-U-Tech-Firm-Sue/31271/

Huq, A.A., D.S. Goldberg, and T.F. Meagher. (2009, November 1). Intellectual-Property Agreements: Are You Managing Your Rights? *The Chronicle of Higher Education.* Retrieved from http://chronicle.com.libproxy.lib.unc.edu/article/Cases-in-Point-/48971/

IP Advocate. (2014). Kaswan Case Study. Retrieved from www.ipadvocate.org/studies/ kaswan/10.cfm#Legal

J.L.N. (1992, November 18). Iowa State Continues Battle for Royalties on Fax Patent. *The Chronicle of Higher Education.* Retrieved from http://chronicle.com.libproxy.lib.unc. edu/article/Iowa-State-Continues-Battle/71623/

Johns Hopkins University et al. v. CellPro, Inc. (1998). 152 F.3d 1342; 1998 U.S. App. LEXIS 18626; 47 U.S.P.Q.2D (BNA) 1705. Retrieved from www.lexisnexis.com/ hottopics/lnacademic

Kelderman, E. (2011, June 6). Supreme Court Rebuffs Stanford's Bid to Assert Control of Invention. *The Chronicle of Higher Education.* Retrieved from http://chronicle.com. libproxy.lib.unc.edu/article/Supreme-Court-Rebuffs/127776/

Kelley, S. (2010, June 9). Hewlett-Packard, Cornell Reach Settlement in Patent Case. *Cornell Chronicle.* Retrieved from www.news.cornell.edu/stories/2010/06/hewlett-packard-cornell-reach-settlement-patent-case

Madey v. Duke (2001). 266 F. Supp. 2d 420; 2001 U.S. Dist. LEXIS 25242. Retrieved from www.lexisnexis.com/hottopics/lnacademic

Madey v. Duke (2002). 307 F.3d 1351; 2002 U.S. App. LEXIS 20823; 64 U.S.P.Q.2D (BNA) 1737. Retrieved from www.lexisnexis.com/hottopics/lnacademic).

Madey v. Duke (2004). 336 F. Supp. 2d 583; 2004 U.S. Dist. LEXIS 19182. Retrieved from www.lexisnexis.com/hottopics/lnacademic

Madey v. Duke (2006). 413 F. Supp. 2d 601; 2006 U.S. Dist. LEXIS 4356; 79 U.S.P.Q.2D (BNA) 1877. Retrieved from www.lexisnexis.com/hottopics/lnacademic

Mangan, K.S. (2005, August 3). U. of Texas Settles Patent-Infringement Case Against Blackberry Maker for $1.8-Million. *The Chronicle of Higher Education.* Retrieved from http://chronicle.com.libproxy.lib.unc.edu/article/U-of-Texas-Settles/120884/

MedImmune, Inc. v. Genentech, Inc. et al. (2008a). 535 F. Supp. 2d 1000; 2008 U.S. Dist. LEXIS 12198. Retrieved from www.lexisnexis.com/hottopics/lnacademic

MedImmune, Inc. v. Genentech, Inc. et al. (2008b). 2008 U.S. Dist. LEXIS 120336. Retrieved from www.lexisnexis.com/hottopics/lnacademic\

MedImmune, Inc. v. Genentech, Inc. et al. (2013). 2013 U.S. Dist. LEXIS 103836. Retrieved from www.lexisnexis.com/hottopics/lnacademic

Moser, K. (2008, July 8). Jury Orders Hewlett-Packard to Pay $184-Million in Patent Case Involving Cornell U. *The Chronicle of Higher Education.* Retrieved from http:// chronicle.com.libproxy.lib.unc.edu/article/Jury-Orders-Hewlett-Packard-to/41078/

Mulvaney, N. (2014, April 24). Princeton University to Pay Town $21.7 Million over 7 Years in New Deal for Tax-exempt School. *New Jersey On-Line.* Retrieved from www. nj.com/mercer/index.ssf/2014/04/princeton_university_to_pay_town_217_million_ over_7_years_in_new_deal_for_tax-exempt_school.html

Nicklin, J.L. (1993, August 4). Prison Term in a Patent Case. *The Chronicle of Higher Education.* Retrieved from http://chronicle.com.libproxy.lib.unc.edu/article/Prison-Term-in-a-Patent-Case/73426/

NIH, Office of the Director. (1997). Determination in the Case of CellPro, Inc. Retrieved from www.nih.gov/news/pr/aug97/nihb-01.htm

NIH, Office of the Director. (2010). Determination in the Case of Fabrazyme® Manufactured by Genzyme. Retrieved from www.ott.nih.gov/sites/default/files/ documents/policy/March-In-Fabrazyme.pdf

Offredo, J. (2013, June 29). Lawsuit Challenging Princeton University's Tax-exempt Status Won't be dismissed. *New Jersey On-Line.* Retrieved from www.nj.com/mercer/ index.ssf/2013/06/lawsuit_challenging_princeton_universitys_tax-exempt_status_ wont_be_dismissed.html

Onconome, Inc. v. University of Pittsburgh et al. (2009). 2009 U.S. Dist. LEXIS 117451. Retrieved from www.lexisnexis.com/hottopics/lnacademic

Rappa, J. (2014, February 19). Research Report: Summary of Arguments in Estate of Lewis et al. v. Princeton University and Borough of Princeton. Connecticut General Assembly: Office of Legislative Research. Retrieved from http://cslib.cdmhost.com/cdm/ref/collection/p128501coll2/id/274494

Read, B. (2007, August 1). Microsoft Seeks to Settle Long-Running Patent Dispute. *The Chronicle of Higher Education*. Retrieved from http://chronicle.com.libproxy.lib.unc.edu/blogs/wiredcampus/microsoft-seeks-to-settle-long-running-patent-dispute/3227

Regents of the University of California v. Genentech, Inc. (2000). 230 F.3d 1377; 2000 U.S. App. LEXIS 2333. Retrieved from www.lexisnexis.com/hottopics/lnacademic

Rimmer, M. (2002/2003). Genentech and the Stolen Gene: Patent Law and Pioneer Inventions. *Bio-Science Law Review*, 5(6): 198–211. Retrieved from http://ssrn.com/abstract=603221

Sampat, B. (2006). Patenting and US Academic Research in the 20th Century: The World Before and After Bayh-Dole. *Research Policy*, 35: 772–789.

Shearer, L. (2010, April 3). Drug's Inventor, UGA Foundation Settle. *Athens Banner-Herald.* Retrieved from http://onlineathens.com/stories/040310/uga_600934241.shtml

Slaughter, S., & Leslie, L. L. (1997). *Academic Capitalism: Politics, Policies, and the Entrepreneurial University*. The Johns Hopkins University Press, 2715 North Charles Street, Baltimore, MD 21218–4319.

So, A.D. et al. (2008). Is Bayh-Dole Good for Developing Countries? Lessons from the US Experience. PLoS Biology, 6(10): 2078–2084.

The Regents of the University of New Mexico v. Knight, et al. (2003). 321 F.3d 1111; 2003 U.S. App. LEXIS 3647; 66 U.S.P.Q.2D (BNA) 1001; 55 Fed. R. Serv. 3d (Callaghan) 856. Retrieved from www.lexisnexis.com/hottopics/lnacademic

The Regents of the University of New Mexico v. Knight, et al. (2004). 116 Fed. Appx. 258; 2004 U.S. App. LEXIS 23453. Retrieved from www.lexisnexis.com/hottopics/lnacademic

USPTO. (2007). Inter Partes Reexamination Communication. Retrieved from www.pubpat.org/assets/files/warfstemcell/913rejected.pdf

USPTO. (2014a). Manual of Patenting Examining Procedure. Chapter 2100: Section 2163. Retrieved from www.uspto.gov/web/offices/pac/mpep/s2163.html

USPTO. (2014b). Manual of Patenting Examining Procedure. Chapter 2100: Section 2164. Retrieved from www.uspto.gov/web/offices/pac/mpep/s2164.html

Van Der Werf, M. and G. Blumenstyk. (1999, December 3). Genentech Will Pay U. of California $200-Million to Settle Patent Lawsuit. *The Chronicle of Higher Education*. pp. A42. Retrieved from http://chronicle.com.libproxy.lib.unc.edu/article/Genentech-Will-Pay-U-of/5602/

Vas-Cath, Inc. v. Curators of the University of Missouri, et al. (2005). 2005 U.S. Dist. LEXIS 44600. Retrieved from www.lexisnexis.com/hottopics/lnacademic

Vas-Cath, Inc. v. Curators of the University of Missouri, et al. (2007a). 473 F.3d 1376; 2007 U.S. App. LEXIS 1402; 81 U.S.P.Q.2D (BNA) 1524. Retrieved from www.lexisnexis.com/hottopics/lnacademic

Vas-Cath, Inc. v. Curators of the University of Missouri, et al. (2007b). 2007 U.S. Dist. LEXIS 89932. Retrieved from www.lexisnexis.com/hottopics/lnacademic

Vas-Cath, Inc. v. Curators of the University of Missouri, et al. (2008). 274 Fed. Appx. 865; 2008 U.S. App. LEXIS 8536. Retrieved from www.lexisnexis.com/hottopics/lnacademic

4 Technology transfer paradox of success at Stanford University

"Don't fix" vs. "make it better"

Henry Etzkowitz

Introduction

This chapter focuses upon technology transfer at Stanford University, a hybrid liberal arts/engineering school with a practical orientation set by its founders. Believing that academic distinction required an industrial interlocutor, the university would have to take steps to facilitate its creation. Thus, Stanford's first President, David Starr Jordan, invested personal funds, along with engineering faculty members, to encourage spin-off firms in the Bay areas emerging electrical industry. Student government was established as an entity independent of the university and encouraged to organize student run businesses. Given this entrepreneurial academic orientation early informal faculty efforts to encourage technology transfer were fit for purpose. For example, Frederick Terman ran an informal patent licensing operation, reaching as far as Denmark, from his faculty office.

Stanford University's contemporary technology transfer regime is acknowledged by its peers to be an outlier, a case of outstanding success in a sea of modest university technology transfer performers, at least so far as income generation from technology transfer is concerned. Only relatively few universities earn significant funds from technology transfer to date or produce a large number of successful start-ups. On the one hand, the university has produced some of the largest and most successful firms to spin out of US universities, (e.g. Google, HP, Cisco, etc.), and on the other, "leaving on the table" the unrealized potential in discoveries of less entrepreneurially oriented faculty who would benefit from a more developed support structure, characteristic of university transfer regimes in less research intensive universities or in universities located in less innovation intensive regions, or both (Etzkowitz and Göktepe-Hultén 2015, this volume). We call this phenomenon "the paradox of success."

The paradox of success denotes impedance to a high-level of achievement becoming even higher through blindness to flaws that are obscured from observers as well as insiders. An attitude of "if it's not broken don't fix it" takes hold rather than the converse "if it's working well, make it better." In the following we discuss the evolution of technology transfer at Stanford, from an informal to a formal regime, including the opening up and resolution of a technology transfer gap that emanated from the double-edged sword of location in a region with a strong entrepreneurial ecosystem. On the one hand, such a fortuitous location facilitated the efforts of experienced entrepreneurs, while on the other, the abundance of entrepreneurial resources blindsided Stanford technology transfer office (TTO) from providing a higher level of assistance to a less entrepreneurially experienced faculty.

Licensing Life

"Licensing Life" is the process by which the commercializable outputs of the laboratory become tangible or intangible products and contribute to economic development in parallel with the codification of knowledge. "Licensing Life" links "Laboratory Life" to economic life, closing the loop between the creation of knowledge and its translation into use. The laboratory may be viewed as a bounded entity, producing data and transmuting it into publications, through a micro social/ technical process (Latour and Woolgar 1979), regulated by the classical norms of science (Merton 1942). Inputs, financial and otherwise, and outputs beyond publications, such as technology, may be "black boxed." Nevertheless, "Laboratory Life" is embedded, on the one hand, in collegial peer review and, on the other, in "Funding Agency life," the working of governmental and other organizations to distribute resources that make laboratory life possible.

A laboratory, by itself, can only metaphorically "raise a world"; however, coupled with a TTO and an entrepreneurial environment, a new social world can be created in the form of a technology-based start-up. If laboratory life is the transmutation of data into the production of articles, Licensing Life is the transmogrification of the inventions based on that data into economic activity. Scientists and their inscription devices to collect and record data are the protagonists of laboratory life, with journals as the object of their efforts, and the government research funding and peer review, post office, or Internet as intermediary. Licensing Life embodies a more complex intermediation process including the patent system, venture capital and angel funding. Moreover, licensing and laboratory lives are increasingly inter-twined: the laboratory becomes part of a productive force rather than a relatively isolated entity that generates knowledge as sole objective.

The counter-intuitive/counter-factual hypothesis explored herewith is that Stanford's technology transfer accomplishments might have been greater if a mentoring strategy had been targeted at neophyte entrepreneurs who often lacked sufficient knowledge of how to take advantage of regional resources. Not surprisingly, this is a strategy typically utilized by less favored schools, lacking serial entrepreneurs, for whom the choice is to nurture incipient talent or become a failed office. The analysis is primarily based upon research carried out in 2005, including participant observation in the Office of Technology Licensing (OTL) at Stanford University, archival research on informal engineering school technology transfer experience prior to the founding of a an administrative unit. This was followed up with interviews of the Stanford Student Government StartX Accelerator project conducted in 2012.

Most studies of US university technology transfer utilize the data provided by the Association of University Technology Managers (AUTM) annual survey, analyzing financial returns from e.g. Thursby and Thursby (2002) that provide a narrow view of technology transfer activities (Bozeman 2000).[1] A parallel literature analyzes organizational and policy issues—for example, George (2005) examines the evolution and strategic direction of an early office, while Jain and George (2007: 557) show the broader role of a TTO in "building legitimacy for a novel technology." Nelson (2005) analyzes the interaction of OTL and Stanford's music department as it incorporated the logic of transfer in a subsidiary and complementary relation to musical composition while Colyvas and Powell (2006) discuss the stages of legitimacy and acceptance of technology transfer among Stanford's faculty members.

It is reported that firms emanating from Stanford would constitute the world's tenth largest national economy with MIT's standing even higher, if they were cores of national, rather than regional, innovation systems (Eesely and Miller 2012). These two universities currently have similar technology transfer regimes although they began form different starting points of emerging and highly successful industrial regions in the latter part of the 19th century. Both offices espouse a marketing model of licensing intellectual property in the context of increasingly entrepreneurial academic scenes characterized by an increasing focus on start-ups as the preferred technology transfer method. Licensing to existing firms and going with a start-up, whether a spin-off emanating from the university or external entrepreneurs, is a difficult choice point. Although OTL attempts to make this decision on economic grounds, it is also influenced by the academic entrepreneurs preference, especially if they have strong support from academic colleagues.

A highly successful trajectory at Stanford University primarily relies on highly entrepreneurially oriented faculty and a rich entrepreneurial ecosystem. Stanford's OTL has generated $594 million in revenues since its founding (Page 2009). Although its primary expressed goal is seeing that the practical results of academic research are put to use, OTL also expresses pride in its income generation accomplishments in public presentations, citing ten patents that have each generated more than $10 million in income for the university and a current income of $50 million per year. A visitor's tour of its offices highlights plaques showing the highest income patents.

OTL's hallmark has been a marketing model of technology transfer. Neils Reimers, founding director of OTL, held that tech transfer offices were too focused on patenting rather than getting inventions into use. He instituted procedures to identify a wide range of firms that might be interested in an invention, followed up by contacts, traditionally by telephone and more recently via email. The marketing model was transferred to MIT in the mid-1980s after that school experienced difficulties with a venture capital model in which the university was deciding among various candidates to invest its funds, angering faculty who did not receive an investment. It has since become the prevalent US model.

OTL sees its mission, from its foundation until the current day, as one of facilitating technology transfer as an ancillary activity within the context of traditional academic goals of education and dissemination of knowledge. OTL advises faculty with an explicit "No" not to delay publication but also recommends they disclose as early as possible, noting the grace period offered by the US patent system between publicly announcing a result and having to file for protection. On the one hand, members of the office see their success as derived in large measure from the "entrepreneurial spirit" and collaborative culture of the Stanford faculty in contrast to university systems that are excessively hierarchical, with everyone "always looking after themselves." A licensing officer explained that, "We're not doing the licensing solely for the money; we're a university." On the other hand, "We don't want a company just to take something." The result of such balancing is negotiation of a moderate rate on the principle that maintaining good will is more important than obtaining maximum value.

Stanford is a median rather than a mode case like MIT, whose original mission was more narrowly focused on local science and technology-based mechanical industry (Etzkowitz 2002). Lita Nelson and Katherine Ku, respectively directors of technology transfer at MIT and Stanford, view their schools as pursuing a common approach. MIT abandoned an overt entrepreneurial stance in order to avert conflict among its faculty over whose venture it should fund in favor of Stanford's more arms-length marketing model of selecting from among both internal and external licensing opportunities. Niels Reimers, founder of Stanford's OTL and the inventor of the marketing model realigned MIT's efforts along Stanford lines as Boston and Silicon Valley pursued common venture-capital based high tech strategies, superseding their earlier differences as regions characterized by declining and emerging industries, respectively (Etzkowitz and Dzisah 2008).

Informal technology transfer at Stanford

An entrepreneurial culture had taken root at Stanford, well before establishment of a TTO, in contrast to universities where foundation of an office is an initial step in developing such a culture. As Dean of Engineering and then Provost, Terman expanded the economic base of the university in order to develop and attract talent. He began this project as a professor, capitalizing his research results through agreements with firms, exchanging disclosures for funds to support graduate students and encourage them to stay in the region. One of these fellowships allowed the duo of Hewlett and Packard to be reunited at Stanford, after a stint in the east, complete their masters' degrees under Terman's supervision and then go on to start the firm bearing their name.[2] At Stanford basic research grew up in tandem with commercialization, with firms interactions with faculty at times supporting academic interests to a greater extent than their own (Lecuyer 2005).

Professor Terman ran the virtual equivalent of a TTO from his faculty office in the Electrical Engineering Department during the 1930s. Terman owned the rights that he generated according to university policy and practice.[3] His key interlocutor on the industry side was a Stanford graduate who was head of the International Telephone and Telegraph (ITT) research lab in New York City. He negotiated an arrangement to provide a certain number of disclosures per year in areas of interest to the firm in exchange for funds to support graduate research assistants at Stanford. It was up to ITT to decide whether to patent and incur the costs of patent protection. He was also contacted by firms in the UK and Scandinavia and made similar deals. Thus, Terman notified a firm in the radio industry in Sweden that, "I expect that during the next 6 months to a year I will have a considerable number of disclosures to submit for your consideration. I have recently worked out an agreement for handling my developments in the US and certain foreign countries so that there is now considerable incentive to take the time necessary to write out descriptions of new ideas as they occur."[4]

A colleague in the electrical engineering department expanded upon the advantages of a firm's outsourcing some of its research to a university as there were

> no overhead or indirect costs and this, of course, constitutes the most obvious financial advantage of having Stanford do part of your research work. I know that the other advantages, including an independent point of view on problems and broadening of the total background of experience and associations, are well known to you ... the availability of fairly skilled grad student assistants at low cost ...[5]

A modest income earned from research findings with intellectual property potential, marketed to interested firms, helped support graduate students in electrical engineering. The disclosures to ITT were not translated into patents but appeared to serve as a way for an industrial lab to keep tabs on academic research and provide it with a modest subsidy.

Terman developed a "steeple of excellence" university development strategy, creating research groups in emerging fields of conjoint theoretical and practical potential. The objective, the key to Stanford's advance, was to achieve academic and economic development simultaneously. Terman held that "great institutions are created by a great faculty, not by paneled walls, acres of floor space, a co-op program, or even fancy gadgets in lecture rooms. What counts is first outstanding leaders on the faculty, second, intelligently planned support to enable these outstanding individuals to achieve their full possibilities in the environment in which they are placed, and third an outstanding group of students to be educated at both undergraduate and graduate levels." This process could be jump-started by, "raiding other institutions for about six outstanding mature men whose reputations were already well established, and whose fields were representative of the major fields of engineering."[6]

Initially pursued in a few technical areas and then across the university, this strategy transformed Stanford into a leading university in an academic generation of two decades. Fields were selected that had both scientific and economic potential and made best use of scarce resources. Sometimes, the way forward was not clear. For example, according to the Dean of Medicine, "At the same time the situation in physiology is such that we cannot expect at this time to recruit a really top drawer man … In time, a major strengthening of the Physiology Department is needed to make it comparable with Biochemistry and other medical sciences. However, this is not in the cards at the moment."[7] At other times, as in steroid chemistry, the way was clear and several promising candidates could be recruited simultaneously, making Stanford an almost instantaneous leader in a highly promising field (Djerassi 1992). Carl Djerassi, recruited to the chemistry department from the Syntex pharmaceutical firm in Mexico, maintained his position as the firm's research director as part of his employment agreement when it moved much of its activities to the Stanford Research Park.

In the early post-war, the founders of Varian Associates created a firm that was a seamless web with an academic laboratory. Indeed, it has been suggested that the company had more academic autonomy than the university research group that was subordinate to the needs of high-energy physicists (Lenoir 1997). Faculty members consulted, served on the Board, set strategy and sent their graduates to work in the company. Some company researchers moved in the other direction and took up academic positions. Patents developed in the university were the basis of the firm, with Varian undertaking patenting on behalf of the academics in exchange for an exclusive license.

Stanford's "Science Park" emerged as an unintended consequence of the transformation of an agricultural region into a high-tech conurbation. A shopping center, designed for a growing suburban population in the early post-war, utilized university land to generate rental income and support academic development. As receipts increased, Terman calculated how many professors could be hired. An industrial park, conceived as a follow-on venture to capture industrial firms relocating from San Francisco, succeeded despite these firms' lack of interest. Science-based firms, like Varian Associates, having originated at Stanford, wished to locate close to the university to maintain a collaborative relationship. Provost Terman understood the significance of their decision and made a research profile requirement for entry. This organizational modification gave birth to a science park movement that has evolved from a property development to a firm incubation model.

Stanford's formal technology transfer experience

The OTL was established at Stanford, as an administrative unit within the university, spun off form the contracts and grants office, which had official responsibility for patenting but had generated little return. Niels Reimers, a contracts and grants officer and initial director of OTL believed that the university could achieve better financial results through a unit specialized in the task.[8] In the early years, Riemers was its sole employee, assisted by students from Stanford's Graduate School of Business. The business students made it possible to extend OTL's reach, expanding what had been a legal model of gaining intellectual property protection into a marketing model of actively seeking out licensees and additional uses for an invention than those foreseen by its inventor. Behind the façade of successful innovation and financial success is a more complex reality of widely different levels of interest and involvement in technology transfer among faculty.

Typology of faculty technology transfer perspectives

A supportive environment for faculty entrepreneurship has been a recruitment advantage for Stanford as entrepreneurially oriented faculty gravitated towards Stanford before culture changed at other universities. Indeed, well after other universities had extended their control over intellectual property rights from federally funded research, Stanford, "placed the rights, when possible, in the hands of faculty, staff, and students." The policy was changed in the mid-1990s, however, to mandatory ownership by Stanford University (Gilmor 2004: 154). Nevertheless, de facto policy to this day implicitly favors licensing to faculty start-ups.

Divergent faculty perspectives on technology transfer and commercialization of research may be identified at Stanford based on interest and experience. Serial entrepreneurs, those with the most interest and experience, have "been there; done that, again and again." These are the faculty members who have successfully invented and licensed technologies, created and sold firms based on their discoveries, or more t precisely the discoveries of the members of their research groups. They are equally committed to basic research advanced discovery, and education. Indeed much of the basis for their entrepreneurial success derives from their role as mentor of student inventors in their research groups. In this context, they may contribute their own ideas as well as nurture the ideas of their students (Etzkowitz 1992).

Some serial entrepreneurs have evolved into informal entrepreneurial collectivities, pooling intellectual property and other resources with colleagues rather than only relying solely on their own efforts. For these experienced faculties, a disclosure to the university's TTO is both a box to be ticked and a valued resource for brainstorming additional applications of a discovery and additional contacts. However, the TTO will likely be primarily relying on the serial entrepreneur for leads to support the commercialization of their research rather than the other way around.

Stanford's serial entrepreneurs explore the multiple aspects of knowledge simultaneously, investigating theoretical and practical aspects, publishing and patenting as they go along; taking leaves of absence to engage in firm formation and/or sending out graduates to perform these functions backed up by an informal mentoring relationship, a formal advisory role on the firm's board of directors or Scientific Advisory Board and, quite possibly, a personal investment from funds earned from previous successes. These serial entrepreneurs have long time contacts with venture capitalists, links to angel networks and legal and accounting advisors at the ready to assist with evaluation of firm formation possibilities, in addition to the input from the university's TTO.

Opponents of technology transfer

On the opposite pole, are the opponents of commodification of academic knowledge, who hold for a strict division of labor between university and industry? In their view, academics should confine themselves to advancing knowledge while industry's responsibility is to put knowledge to use. The university's preferred means of knowledge transfer is through publication, with free access to all readers. Efforts to bridge the gap between the two spheres are viewed with suspicion. In this view university technology transfer is best limited to the narrowest possible extension of publication by taking out patents that should be licensed to all comers. The spread of a start-up culture in recent decades from the engineering school to the medical school, computer science and even more broadly is worrisome to these scholars. Many are humanities and social scientists who view the entrepreneurial ethos of contemporary Stanford as a passing phase and look forward to the return of one of their own, a tweedy historian or linguist, to the Presidency. He or she will then tamp down entrepreneurial fires and reorient the university to its true course of disinterested knowledge.

This group also includes scientists who, while cognizant of their official obligation to report commercializable research to the OTL, are philosophically in agreement with their anti commodification colleagues elsewhere in the university but are also aware that there is no penalty for failing to disclose. Indeed, it is highly unlikely that anyone will contact them to inquire if they have potential IP. OTL is so busy with serial entrepreneurs, or those aspiring to that status, that it has little if any time to bother with inventors uninterested in pursuing the intellectual property implications of their work.

The inventor disinterested in technology transfer

Formally compliant inventors meet their obligations under university and government policy but are unwilling to make an active effort to move the technology transfer process forward. Technology transfer is based on the premise of a cooperative inventor, interested and willing to assist in the process. But what happens when this is not the case? Some inventors who disclose are unwilling to support the transfer process, thereby reducing transfer potential in the absence of substitute support measures.

The involvement of the inventor is required to move the translation process forward A senior licensing officer recounted a failure case due to dependence on this assumption and inability to get the transfer process to move forward by finding a substitute for an uncooperative inventor. The officer took it personally in recalling the incident saying that the "camera still hurts me when I think of it … it was a way to get the right color as the human eye sees it." However, the inventor was interested only in the research aspects of the problem and wanted to move on to other tasks. He was willing to take only the most minimal role in the transfer process as an adjunct actor rather than as a proponent.

The licensing officer undertook some of the champion role and managed to organize an ad-hoc demonstration of the invention but it was a one-off event. The Sony Lab in Palo Alto provided the necessary equipment and technicians for a demonstration event but took back the equipment after an initial test. The licensing officer suggested to the inventor, "'You can rig it up yourself,' but he said, 'I do research; I won't waste time to spend a week doing something for people who don't see the light.' I never asked him, 'Will you give me the software?' I didn't think of that, so damned pissed off he didn't want to spend a few days to whip up a demo." Without the active participation of the inventor the transfer process did not move forward, despite OTL spending a considerable amount to acquire patents.

A new technological vision, no matter how great the potential, may wither on the vine. The licensing officer recounted that almost every company contacted asked to see it but "I couldn't demonstrate it. If it had a demonstration, it would have been the biggest project I handled in 20 years here. I even tried more; I mentioned my idea to put it on a chip. I knew that engineering students in our school, at one time or another, have to design and manufacture a chip. I told him to get together with so and so in engineering, an inventor, and get a student to make his chip. They never got together." Unfortunately, the licensing officer did not see it as part of his remit to introduce the project to the engineering school himself. Lacking a start-up process or take-up by an existing firm, the patents languished and were eventually abandoned.

This instance suggests the utility of a university technology transfer process that can provide translational and entrepreneurial support in order to be able to utilize the inventions of inventors who are willing to only minimally participate in the transfer process. The "inactive disclosers" go one step beyond those "active opponents " who refuse in any way to participate in commercialization of research and neglect to disclose. Although in formal abrogation of their employment contract with the university; there is rarely if ever any identification let alone enforcement procedure to catch potentially commercializable research if the inventor chooses not to reveal their work. Proposals to insert observers into research groups to watch for useful results have been summarily rejected as an intrusion on academic freedom or a potential counterproductive steering of the research process (Etzkowitz 1994).

Interested but inexperienced potential entrepreneurs

OTL plays an informal role in firm formation, initially by assessing the potential of the new technology as part of its marketing activities of contacting firms to see if there is any interest in licensing the new technology. This "marketing activity" also provides a basis for assessment of the start-up potential of the technology. Long-term licensing associates have good contacts in the Silicon Valley venture capital and legal communities. When they see an invention with significant potential for firm formation; they put the inventor into contact with potential sources of assistance, even if that help has not been requested. At that point it is up to the inventor "to pick up the ball." OTL does not directly engage in business development, a task that university TTOs explicitly undertake in emerging high-tech regions. Contemporary Stanford tech transfer practice relies on an informal dynamic to pull technology out of the university, without the need to provide in-depth support.

Stanford administrators with responsibility for technology transfer believe that it's unique location and the opportunities it offers, makes it unnecessary for the university to take more explicit steps, commonplace at other universities, such as provision of an incubator facility.[9] This laissez-faire attitude is encouraged by a pervasive empirical reality of serial faculty entrepreneurship, supported by the university's vast experience in technology transfer, through its OTL. A contemporary hands-off approach is paradoxically encouraged by a previous celebrated history of hands-on involvement by faculty members, like Terman, in facilitating technology start-ups (Lecuyer 2005).

However, it is often the case that OTL's marketing identifies potential areas of use and even users but does not result in an actual license. Firms typically view university-originated technology as too early stage. They want to see it in use and better yet, already generating revenues. Thus, they would rather pay many times more to buy a start-up that has gone through the development and innovation process rather than undertake this task themselves, even though a license could have been obtained for a fraction of the cost. For example, an interdisciplinary collaboration in technology transfer that we examined was spurred by the need for engineering expertise to build a device for automating a biotechnology discovery process, with academic and industrial applications.

A start-up encourages a sharp focus on the new technology.[10] Even in a large firm oriented to technological advance, focus is inevitably close to the market innovations.[11] Firms find it difficult to maintain focus on internally generated inventions; there are always new ideas coming along and calls to shift focus due to changes in strategic direction or the appearance of unexpected opportunities. These forces operate even more strongly when an invention has been brought in from outside and lacks an internal base of support. Awareness of these difficulties has led many firms to either support a start-up process through corporate venturing, or wait until an externally generated technology is embodied in a start-up that can be purchased and made into an operating division.

University technology transfer implicitly relies on faculty to at least take their work partway through the translational process and may stall if they are unwilling. OTL is currently one player among several in the Stanford innovation system, facilitating technology transfer and spin-offs. Indeed, disclosing to OTL is sometimes a matter of checking a necessary box, rather than seeking assistance, as part of a transfer and firm formation strategy developed by inventors and their angel investors. OTL also leverages the ecosystem, introducing neophyte inventors to venture capitalists, attorneys and other persons who might assist firm-formation. It is up to the inventor to pursue the lead as OTL takes a relatively passive approach once the introductions have been made. If the inventor decides to "transfer" by taking a position in a firm and bring their technology with them, as in the movement of "Orkut" to Google, so be it.

A proactive office must provide the necessary resources to pick up upon these inventions. In Germany the Fraunhofer Institutes specialize in these intermediary tasks. Lacking a Fraunhofer, the university must provide translational services to take advantage of inventions of minimally transfer active faculty. Not surprisingly, the Fraunhofer has identified a gap in US university technology transfer practice and has established units to fill this gap. Whereas in Germany there is an integrated system of such intermediaries, there are only a few such programs in the US where it is largely up to the university to fill the gap. In the US transfer model, a start-up firm is the modal organizational format to move the transfer process forward but in many research areas support for a start-up is weak or lacking due to the early stage of technology development/and or its location in a field that has not yet been perceived to have commercial relevance. Thus, a significant proportion of patented inventions languish unlicensed on TTO websites.

Until quite recently OTL has insufficiently addressed the intermediate group of faculty who have made discoveries that they duly report, and may have a moderate to strong interest in playing a role in commercialization. Their work often sits on the shelf as unlicensed IP, too little developed to be of interest to a potential licensee. To address these untapped opportunities OTL has created a "farm team" program through which an entrepreneurial team is recruited to commercialize inventions that the office has failed to transfer through the licensing process.

An OTL program, the so-called birdseed fund, offers modest funds to graduate students to work on translational research in between medicine and engineering has been established, requires a minimum effort of an application on the part of an inventor to activate the program. Recognition of Stanford's translational research gap, especially in emerging interdisciplinary fields, has inspired creation of various initiatives, such as BioX to encourage cooperation between engineering and the sciences, the "X" suffix designating an interdisciplinary and experimental intent of the program. In an earlier era, new sub-disciplines and departments such as applied physics were put in place to fill the gap between physics and electrical engineering.

Current programs fill gaps in the medical devices and biotechnology invention and translational research spaces. Each year the Biodesign program recruits an interdisciplinary group from medical, engineering and business disciplines to shadow clinicians in a different medical specialty each year. Asking questions and observing, they look for gaps in medical practice that a new technology or clinical method could fill. By the second quarter, a parallel student group who help work on fleshing out the initial concept joins them. Together, they create a prototype for testing and further development. Working the other end of the innovation continuum, moving form research to practice, rather than problem to invention, the Spark program selects a class of faculty, post-doctoral and PhD researchers from Stanford Medical School and related organizations like the local Veterans Administration Hospital whose research has led them to identify potential solutions to medical problems. Spark provides financial resources to carry the translational research process forward in the context of a once a week meeting. In alternate sessions participants share their work in progress and get a taste of the

Silicon Valley entrepreneurial eco-system through lectures from venture capitalists, attorneys and entrepreneurs.

Some TTO's have entrepreneurs in residence who are available to step in and fill the shoes of an inventor unable or unwilling to move the process forward. However, there are rarely a significant number available to step into the breach. At Stanford, a consultant frustrated with the inability of OTL to move a significant technology forward offered to initiate a start-up. Upon agreement, he immediately severed all connection with the office. US spin-off practice mandating strict separation is in strong contrast to Chinese university-run enterprises that are not only incubated within the universities but grow into large firms within the structure of the university (Zhou 2015).

The closest analogues in US practice are large government laboratories managed by universities under contract to the federal government. However, these units, like Los Alamos and Livermore national laboratories, both under the aegis of the university of California, are formally distinct from the university and geographically more and less distant. That said, others are adjacent to the university, like Stanford's SLAC, for the Department of Energy, or close enough, like MIT's Lincoln Laboratory for faculty and laboratory members to participate in each others venues, with lab staff mentoring students and faculty having significant lab research and administrative roles.

Resolving Stanford's paradox of success

Our 2005 study of (OTL) identified an "excluded middle" of inventors with commercializable research that was not being moved forward (Etzkowitz 2013). OTL with 25 staff members was primarily focused on serial entrepreneurs, whom they had worked with on successive commercialization projects, and did not have sufficient resources to seek out inventors who did not come to them directly. Occasionally, such an inventor was incentivized to find their own way to OTL but this was the exception rather than the rule. For example, a biology professor who did not believe in commercialization of research but wanted to see his invention built found a PhD student in the engineering school who was interested in founding a firm. He made that the condition of realizing the biology professor's goal of building his device and together they went through the OTL marketing and licensing process.

Nevertheless, this idiosyncratic example illustrated the existence of a broader entrepreneurial support gap at Stanford even though a solution was found in this particular case. Such a support structure has been created during the past decade or so and it has transformed OTL's role from the one organization among several technology transfer modes. At other universities, TTOs expanded to meet the needs of the intermediate group. Indeed typically lacking a corps of serial entrepreneurs, the intermediate group of uninitiated potential entrepreneurs were their only available clientele and they therefore had to expand their purview in order to meet their needs and remain relevant.

As Stanford University became more successful at technology transfer an invisible gap opened up as the TTO presumed that regional resources were doing enough to pull inventions out of the university without a push in the form of incubator and mentoring support form the office. Such a hands off policy fitted the needs of the university's corps of serial entrepreneurs but disadvantaged faculty who were interested in pursuing entrepreneurial projects but lacked experience in negotiating with fund raising, finding experienced and trustworthy partners and the other entrepreneurial skills. This attitude tended to neglect the potential contributes of neophyte entrepreneurs, leaving their intellectual capital "on the table" as it were.

The underachieving yet highly successful TTO was a victim of the paradox of success—the tendency to blind oneself to flaws in its business model that reduced its potential contribution. But who would take such an analysis seriously in the face of success? The deleterious consequences of the paradox of success were not addressed until some of the university's entrepreneurially oriented students who were especially affected by it, conduced their own study of barriers to entrepreneurship at Stanford and laid out a course of action to create an entrepreneurship mentoring and support structure to meet the needs of neophyte entrepreneurs.

Stanford student government's StartX accelerator

The StartX model does not follow the traditional conception of university–industry relations as divergent entities, operating according to different principles. StartX, a student initiated accelerator project that has spun off of Student Government as a 501C3 not for profit entity, is an intermediary organization that provides an experiential education process, and is located at the interface between university and industry, assisting the transition of student and faculty entrepreneurial projects into the business world. Instead of being on either side of a boundary between university and industry, StartX is an interface between these institutional spheres, arranging interaction into a network of connections and interactions between them. On the one hand StartX draws groups from the university into its tutorial process, while on the other mentors largely drawn from Stanford alumni who are active in start-ups and venture capital largely provide that process. The functioning of StartX exemplifies the reconceptualization of university–industry boundaries from defensive mechanisms designed to keep the two sides separate into integrative mechanisms, designed to intercalate them in a seamless web.

With the US government ideologically constrained from direct intervention, state government lacking resources and regional government virtually non-existent in Silicon Valley, Stanford University's student government acted as "Innovation Organizer," providing a support structure to fill a hidden gap in the university's innovation system. The StartX model intersects the university–industry divide as StartX itself incorporates modified elements of both academic and business practice in its organizational design. Technology firms in Silicon Valley have previously been analyzed as constituting a network of relatively autonomous professionals, with links occurring through informal interactions among various firms' employees, creating a group of like-minded individuals, sharing a common technological vision irrespective of employer (Saxenian 1999). StartX blurs the boundary between university and industry by creating an experiential educational process that assists the metamorphosis of intended into actual firms, drawing business people into an educational process while exposing academic firm founders to business reality in a nurturing manner.

A "paradox of success," in which high achievement is a justification for unwillingness to innovate and take further action, was hypothesized by the author after a stint as participant–observer in OTL, but it is a phenomenon that is difficult to discern, let alone prove, since it posits the potential of a higher level of achievement in an already successful venue.[12] The general attitude in the administration was that technology transfer at Stanford was working well, "[I]t's not on our radar."[13] Given the difficulty of proving a hypothetical the question of whether Stanford's innovation system was sufficient or insufficient rested until 2010, when in the midst of the great recession, creating ones own job became an increasingly attractive employment strategy. While a direct relationship between economic conditions and "necessity entrepreneurship" is difficult to trace, it is perhaps not surprising that an increase in entrepreneurial activity occurs in academia during an era when degrees, especially the PhD, less often lead to academic employment.

It is potentially misleading to focus upon StartX, as an entity in itself, as a cure-all to facilitate greatly expanded university innovation results generally. StartX's significant relatively quick effect was possible at Stanford because a number of other elements of a university innovation system were already in place, form a broad variety of entrepreneurial education initiatives, a well funded and well organized academic research system, and a network of entrepreneurs and venture capital firms surrounding the university. Absent these elements, and a StartX could wither on the vine as an isolated entity. Together with these elements, a StartX project can greatly expand the utilization of these resources, making it possible for a broader range of less experienced entrepreneurial projects to achieve take-off.

Underperformance in technology transfer

A larger unrealized potential of US universities in contributing to economic development, going well beyond the Stanford case, may be extrapolated from the experience of the University of Utah. Operating from a much smaller funded research base than MIT and Stanford, Utah has one of the highest rates of firm-formation in American universities.[14] Utah views start-ups emanating from the university as part of its main mission, along with educating students and performing research, rather than as an accidental byproduct of these activities as is still commonplace at most universities.[15] Participation in commercialization of research is credited in tenure and promotion proceedings, along with teaching and research. In contrast to schools where commercialization is de-facto relegated to the post-tenure career stage, junior faculty are encouraged, rather than discouraged, to be entrepreneurial since it is part of the academic reward structure.

A recent analysis of technology transfer and firm formation, presented at a seminar by Professor Loet Leydesdorff of Amsterdam University, based on the AUTM database, showed that seven firms had emanated from Stanford in 2010.[16] Having recently attended Demo Day, I, mentioned that StartX had assisted the formation of 12 firms per academic quarter or 36 firms during the 2010–2011 academic year. Indeed, following the seminar, it was found that the number of firms at StartX during the recently completed summer quarter had jumped to 29. If the AUTM data suggesting that Stanford, the world's leading entrepreneurial university, could only form seven firms, what hope was there for a European university? Indeed, the implicit conclusion was that the emerging economic and social development mission of the university was a misguided effort. Instead, critics propose that the university should return to its traditional teaching and research remit, as it is an unproductive waste of resources to engage in a "mission impossible" of promoting academic entrepreneurship.

Conclusion

Integration of economic and social development with education and research in academic institutions is concomitant with transition from an industrial to a knowledge-based society. MIT's pre-war industrial relations office provided a model for relations between government and universities during the Second World War (Etzkowitz 2002). In the post-war, technology transfer across legal and ideological boundaries provided a weak version of the seamless web among university–industry and government, created during the Second World War to develop and implement novel technologies. Starting with the foundation of universities specialized in agriculture space a select group of universities chosen for wartime R&D, US universities have assumed an innovation mission. This remit is integrated into the classic academic missions of education and research as universities acquire entrepreneurial education and technology transfer capabilities.

Learning from success is at least as important as the recently popular advice to learn from failure. Stanford is a mixed case, encompassing both failure and success. In recent years, intellectual property generated in the world's leading entrepreneurial university located in Silicon Valley, the world's leading entrepreneurial region, was subject to strikingly different fates. Stanford faculty distribute on a scale of technology transfer interest and experience: ranging from in principle, opposed to proponent, and in experience, from serial to neophyte entrepreneur. These entrepreneurial neophytes represent considerable commercialization potential but only if there is a business development support structure that goes considerably beyond traditional OTL services.

A relatively laissez-faire university technology transfer regime held over-optimistic assumptions that an entrepreneurially rich environment can provide all the necessary and sufficient ingredients to nurture a start-up. In other words, pull from the Silicon Valley did not require push form a Stanford University "innovation system." Under these conditions, projects that were too early stage to be licensed and required a start-up to move them forward either to the market or to the stage where an established firm would find them of interest to purchase, could easily be undertaken by serial faculty entrepreneurs, well integrated into the regional eco-system. However, less experienced faculty were left to fend for themselves, with an introduction to a venture capitalist that they were ill equipped to follow up.

Stanford experienced arrested development in technology transfer and entrepreneurship due to an over-interpretation of the extent of informal relations between the university and Silicon Valley, a phenomenon that was narrower than the university's technology transfer professionals expected, due to their focus on the university's relatively small but highly productive corps of serial entrepreneurs. Due to Stanford's great success primarily based on its serial entrepreneurs, OTL was not under pressure from the university's leadership to revise its model until the student government's StartX project appeared bottom-up, to fill the gap that aspiring student entrepreneurs identified in the university's technology transfer practice. These developments suggest that "the paradox of success," neglecting potential entrepreneurial activity, is being resolved and that Stanford's innovation system is revving up to produce even greater results than in the past.

The recent development of a technology commercialization support structure at Stanford, outside of Stanford University technology transfer is a consequence of a "paradox of success." On the one hand, the university has produced some of the largest and most successful firms to spin out of US universities, (e.g. Google, HP, Cisco, etc.), and on the other, "leaving on the table" the unrealized potential in discoveries of less entrepreneurially oriented faculty who would benefit from a more developed support structure, characteristic of university transfer regimes in less research intensive universities or in universities located in less innovation intensive regions, or both.

These entrepreneurial neophytes represent considerable commercialization potential but only if there is a business development support structure that goes considerably beyond traditional OTL services. Such a structure has been created during the past decade or so and it has transformed OTL's role from the one organization among several technology transfer modes. At other universities, TTOs expanded to meet the needs of the intermediate category. Indeed typically lacking a corps of serial entrepreneurs, the intermediate group of uninitiated potential entrepreneurs was their only available clientele and they therefore had to expand their purview in order to meet these faculty members needs and remain relevant.

Due to Stanford's great success based on a relatively small group of serial entrepreneurs, OTL was not under pressure from the university's leadership to revise its model until Student Government's StartX project acted bottom-up to fill the gap that aspiring student entrepreneurs had identified in the university's technology transfer practice. Thus, Stanford University's Technology Transfer Paradox—"if it's not broken don't fix it" vs. "if it's working well, make it better"—has been resolved in favor of the latter adage, albeit outside of the province of the university's OTL.

Notes

1 See Bozeman (2000) for a comprehensive survey of the technology transfer literature.
2 While Terman is often credited with initiating firm formation from Stanford in the 1930s, this phenomenon had precedent in the founding of Federal Telegraph (a firm where Terman interned as a young man) and Magnavox. A key to HP's early success was the concomitant rise of the Hollywood film industry, which required audio-visual technological innovations that coincided with Stanford research and development. Thus, HP's first sale was to the Disney Company.
3 His situation was equivalent in practice to the legal status of the Swedish "professors privilege." Indeed, Swedish sources often cite the similar status of the Stanford professor, until fairly recently, as justification for their regime.
4 Terman Papers, Stanford Archives, Box 12, Folder 3, 140239, Terman to Holstensson.
5 Professor Skilling to Buttner, ITT, 7 September 1944, Folder 2 III, correspondence 1940–42.
6 Fred Terman to Paul Klopsteg, Northwestern University, 20 March 1953, Terman Papers Series 3, SC160, Box 61, Folder 24.
7 Dean Always, Medical School to President Sterling 29 July 1959, Terman Papers Series 3, SC160, Box 61, Folder 1.
8 Author, interview with Neils Riemers, Carmel, CA 2005.
9 Author, interview with Katherine Ku, Director of OTL, 2005.
10 According to the AUTM Survey, 29% of university inventions follow this route.
11 It is difficult to get serious attention paid to a nascent technology without the impetus of a significant crisis such as Japanese competition that drove US semi-conductor firms out of the commodity DRAM market towards the newly emerging microprocessor, with its higher value added potential (Berlin 2005).
12 Author, talk to Stanford OTL staff meeting, July 2005.
13 Author, interview with Professor Arthur Bienenstock, Dean of Research, Stanford University, 2005.
14 New Survey Shows the University of Utah among Nation's Best in Generating Companies from Research (2007). Available online: http://unews.utah.edu/news_releases/new-survey-shows-the-university-of-utah-among-nation039s-best-in-generating-companies-from-research/ (accessed 12 February 2015).
15 Jack Brittain, President, Technology Venture Development, University of Utah "Commercialization Turnaround at Utah" Presentation at "Building the Entrepreneurial University Workshop", Stanford University, 12 November 2012.
16 Seminar, School of Management, London University, Birkbeck Fall, 2011.

References

Berlin, L. (2007) *The Man Behind the Microchip: Robert Noyce and the Invention of Silicon Valley*. New York: Oxford University Press
Bozeman, B. (2000) Technology Transfer and Public Policy: A Review of Research and Theory, *Research Policy*, 29: 627–655
Colyvas, J. and Powell, W. (2006) Roads to Institutionalization: The Remaking of Boundaries Between Private and Public Science. In B. Straw (ed.), *Research in Organisational Behaviour*, vol. 27, Oxford: JAI Press
Djerassi, C. (1992) *The Pill, Pygmys, Chimps and Degas Horse*, New York: Basic Books
Eesely, C. and Miller, W. (2012) Stanford University's Economic Impact via Innovation and Entrepreneurship. Available online: https://engineering.stanford.edu/sites/default/files/Stanford_Innovation_Survey_Executive_Summary_Oct2012_3.pdf

Etzkowitz, H. (1994) Knowledge As Property: The Massachusetts Institute of Technology and the Debate Over Academic Patent Policy, *Minerva,* Winter, 1994

Etzkowitz, H. (2002) *MIT and the Rise of Entrepreneurial Science*, London: Routledge

Etzkowitz, H. (2013) Silicon Valley at Risk?: Sustainability of a Global Innovation Icon Social Science Information, 52 (4): 515–538

Etzkowitz, H. and Dzisah, J. (2008). Unity and Diversity in High-tech Growth and Renewal: Learning from Boston and Silicon Valley, *European Planning Studies* 16 (8): 1009–1024

Etzkowitz, H. and Göktepe-Hultén, D. (2015) De-Reifying Technology Transfer Metrics: To Address the Stages and Phases of TTO Development, this volume (Chapter 5)

George, G. (2005) Learning to be Capable: Patenting and Licensing at the Wisconsin Alumni Research Foundation 1925–2002, *Industry and Corporate Change,* 14 (1): 119–151

Gilmor, S. (2004) *Fred Terman at Stanford: Building a Discipline, a University and Silicon Valley*, Stanford: Stanford University Press

Jain, S. and George, G. (2007) Technology Transfer Offices as Institutional Entrepreneurs: The Case of Wisconsin Alumni Research Foundation and Human Embryonic Stem Cells, *Industrial and Corporate Change*, 16 (4): 535–568

Latour, B. and Woolgar, S. (1979) *Laboratory Life*, Beverly Hills: Sage

Lecuyer, C. (2005) *Making Silicon Valley: Innovation and the Growth of High Tech, 1930–1970*, Cambridge, MA: MIT Press

Lenoir, T. and Lecuyer, C. (1997) Instrument Makers and Discipline Builders: The Case of NMR, in T. Lenoir *Instituting Science: The Cultural Production of Scientific Disciplines*, pp. 239–294. Stanford: Stanford University Press

Merton, R.K. (1942) Science and Technology in a Democratic Order, *Journal of Legal and Political Sociology*, 1, 115–126

Nelson, A. (2005) Cacaphony or Harmony? Multivocal Logics and Technology Licensing by the Stanford University Department of Music, *Industrial and Corporate Change* 14 (1): 93–118

Page, N. (2009) The Making of a Licensing Legend: Stanford University's Office of Technology Transfer. Available online: www.iphandbook.org/handbook/ch17/p13/ (last accessed 28 June 2010)

Saxenian, A. (1999) *Regional Advantage*, Cambridge: Harvard University Press

Thursby, J. and Thursby, M. (2002) Who is Selling the Ivory Tower: Sources of Growth in University Licensing. *Management Science*, 48 (1): 90–104

Zhou, C. (2015) China's Technology Transfer System: Political Mobilization of Universities for Economic Growth, this volume (Chapter 16)

5 De-reifying technology transfer metrics

To address the stages and phases of TTO development

Henry Etzkowitz and
Devrim Göktepe-Hultén

Displacement of goals

University technology transfer offices (TTOs) are undergoing transition from a marketing model, focused on sale of intellectual property rights, to an innovation model, focused on enhancement of academic entrepreneurship capabilities. TTO metrics, however, lag practice, having been institutionalized in the early 1990s, before they spread to less research-intensive schools. Reflecting the experience of research-intensive universities, they do not include the often hidden pre-commercialization activities of less research-intensive schools.

University technology transfer and academic entrepreneurship have become widely accepted strategies for job creation and economic growth. Although this is still a controversial proposition to some analysts of university technology transfer (Mowery et al., 2001), universities and policy makers are increasing their efforts to realize these objectives (Etzkowitz, 2013). Formerly confined to a relatively few universities, typically with engineering, agricultural and medical research capacities; formal technology transfer has spread throughout the academic universe, including to universities with only marginal research capabilities. The widespread institution of a third academic mission for economic and social development has increased the need for relevant metrics and policy support to assist under-resourced academic institutions.

The third mission has devolved upon various innovation mechanisms including science parks, incubators and TTOs. TTOs merit special attention as they have front line responsibilities for interfacing with academic inventors and firms as well as intermediaries such as incubators and science parks to insure the compatibility of transfer with other academic goals. Other observers argue that TTOs are a bureaucratic obstacle and that academic entrepreneurs can succeed on their own.

Serial entrepreneurs or star scientists at elite universities may not need extensive support, can have their own network. Support is often most needed at non-elite universities among the nascent entrepreneurs and inexperienced scientists. What pathway should non-elite universities follow? Is it possible to learn from elite universities and model their experience? Alternatively, should the focus be on learning from peers who have undertaken interesting experiments? Or must an aspiring university find a way by itself, through careful analysis of local resources and coalition building to access them? How can aspiring universities enhance their technology transfer capacity?

In this study we conducted interviews with directors of TTOs in non-elite universities and draw upon case studies of contemporary Stony Brook and the early history of Stanford. We have undertaken comparative case studies of 20 TTOs in the Bos-Wash Corridor of the US East Coast during 2004.[1] It is a broad geographical region with a variety of public and private research universities at different stages of development. The case study is used neither to test the hypothesis nor to validate the model, but as a rich illustration of the model, depicting a pattern that seems emblematic of the changes occurring at many nascent-TTOs. Data were collected through an e-mail questionnaire and followed up through face-to-face or telephone interviews.

The range of TTOs studied represent different stages and phases of TTO development, allowing us to present an analysis of the evolution of this organizational form, including nascent developments that might blossom into future trends. For example, at some schools we found survivals of the pre-marketing stage, a committee process to evaluate inventions that at more mature TTOs has given way to judgments left in the hands of TTO professionals. The sample of TTOs are mainly department type entities under an administrator within the university who typically has other significant responsibilities, either for research (Vice President for Research) or Provost, in charge of academic entities such as departments and centers. In some cases, especially when the TTO has succeeded in attracting some attention as part of an entrepreneurial mission for the university, the TTO is grouped along with other third agents (venture fund, incubator, entrepreneurial training, and start-up assistance) as an "Innovation Group" reporting to its own vice president.

We first discuss the limits of current TTO indicators then present findings from an in-depth interview study of TTOs in non-elite US universities, and related investigations, revealing gaps in TTO practice and metrics. We propose new metrics that capture capacity building activities and the expanded roles of nascent-TTOs. We argue quantitative indicators often lead to superficial comparisons, it is there useful to carry deeper, exploratory be incorporated in the surveys organized by university technology transfer professional associations. Although we have started the process of finding alternative indicators early on, and gained a detailed understanding of a number of nascent-TTOs, it is relatively hard process to quantify what we have observed, and propose new metrics to capture the innovation capacity building role of TTOs. This initial work would nevertheless contribute to the efforts of the Association of University Technology Managers (AUTM), which has recently started in finding alternative technology transfer indicators.[2]

The tyranny of big data

The quantitative analysis of university industry technology transfer, in particular role of TTOs has been more or less built on the base of the AUTM Surveys. Its superstructure consists of measures and data drawn from these sets of big data collected annually or less than annually. In some studies quantitative data is strengthened by additional interviews or other empirical observations. Most measures of TTO activities are focused around commercial output, including university licensing (number of licenses, licensing revenue), number of start-ups, equity positions, coordination capacity (number of shared clients), information processing capacity (invention disclosures, sponsored research), royalties, and patents (number of patents, efficiency in generating new patents) (Rothaermel et al., 2007). Indeed these indicators have been used internationally and several countries have modeled their own TTO surveys based on AUTM indicators. Indicators collected in the forms of big data, eventually manipulate the perceptions on the objectives and impacts of university industry technology transfer. They have even narrowed theoretical discussions, policy and practice into the measurement of the number of patents and university start-ups. Policy makers and administrators often with limited time for decision-making neglect diversity of technology transfer. The overestimation of quantitative indicators has eventually pushed policy-making targeting to increase number of patents and venture creation. In parallel to these developments we see a decline in less formal or countable technology transfer activities both scientists and TTOs could be engaged in.

Technology transfer channels that can be turned into numerical indicators, like licensing income, disclosures or patents attained, tend to obliterate valuable activities that are not easily subject to quantification. Statistical analysis of TTOs emphasize income generation at the expense of mentoring services to faculty members in developing the commercial implications of their research. Judged according to quantitative criteria, TTOs at emerging research universities may appear as failures, due to relative lack of income even as they perform an important academic and business development function that will only pay off in the longer term (Etzkowitz, 2013). Their work may become visible evaluation, if they are allowed the necessary gestation period, rather than being prematurely aborted as failures. Qualitative criteria are required to distinguish these pro-active mentoring offices, with their outreach activities, from the failed TTO, disconnected from its clientele, waiting patiently in its offices for lightening to strike.

An important characteristic of the AUTM Surveys and indicators is its prominence as policy instruments and as tools to provide comparative studies between universities, TTOs, nations, regions. Proxies that may partially indicate outputs have been reified into TTO objectives, taken-for-granted criteria with an aura of facticity (Berger and Luckmann, 1966). These measures best fit the experience of highly successful marketing TTOs, but may have the unintended consequence of narrowing the focus of such TTOs to serial entrepreneurs. Their efforts best contribute to existing measures, as opposed to providing support for the efforts of less entrepreneurially experienced faculty and students that may not show up in counts. Quantitative indicators of technology transfer at elite universities proceeds vigorously as they have the higher expenditure on research, recruit world-leading researchers with best graduate students, secure largest research contracts and have lucrative relations with leading business partners. Such universities have well-established technology transfer systems and can further support and invest in effective technology transfer infrastructure. Elite-TTOs were typically established in the 1970s and have high staffing levels, on average reaching to thirteen full-time employees, and above.

Elite universities know how to leverage their resources for patenting, licensing and spin-off and there has been a surge in patent applications, licensing agreements and of start-ups from these campuses.[3] A snapshot of academic patenting since 1980s showed patents assigned to universities have increased by more than 85 percent. The ten most active US universities account for the lion's share of growth in patenting. Royalty income derived from revenues is similarly skewed, and mostly in biomedicine patents. While on average most TTOs have returns under $5 million, there are a few outliers (Kenney and Patton, 2009). NYU, for example, received $195 million in 2006. TTOs at non-elite universities also have contributions to make to local business, campus and regions (Bradshaw et al., 2005) but these activities may be discounted by conventional output metrics.

TTOs are relatively new phenomena in many smaller US universities. According to the AUTM Survey low-performing TTOs have been established more recently. On average they have started business in the mid-1990s and have a limited number of full-time employees. They reflect very much the early stages of today's elite-TTOs. US$100 million in research funds has been considered the generally accepted minimum for supporting a TTO. However, there is considerable variation with some TTOs performing above their level and others below. We propose TTOs should pursue a broader set of goals like development of links with regional firms to support academic research. Nevertheless, such a reverse linear model of TTO practice should complement, not substitute for, the classic forward linear model of transfer.

It is at this modest academic level that the developmental role of the TTOs comes to the forefront. TTOs in aspiring universities have to perform a "scout" function going laboratory to laboratory speaking to faculty and students alerting them to the potential commercial implications of their research and assisting them in identifying research funds to carry their work forward to the point of patentability. Nascent-TTOs operate in a manner reminiscent of the original venture capital firm American Research and Development (ARD) that sent MIT graduates as technology scouts out into the university to find investment opportunities in the early post war.[4]

De-reification of technology transfer metrics

University technology transfer is currently in transition from a marketing model, focused on outputs such as invention disclosures, patents, licensing deals and spin-off companies to an innovation model focused on developing the research, entrepreneurial and absorptive capacities of academic institutions and regions. TTO indicators were formulated at the height of the marketing era, implicitly assume a linear understanding of technology transfer, and capture the countable outcomes from TTOs boundary-spanning role between academia and industry. These indicators increasingly lag TTO practice, especially in non-elite universities where nascent-TTOs have an important role to play in capacity building. However, this role may not be well captured by existing metrics, based on the experience of elite-TTOs.

Three stages of TTO development may be identified from a legal office for applying for patents to a marketing agent to sell and license patents and finally to a more an innovation (entrepreneurship) model. TTOs are currently in transition from the marketing to an innovation model in which the TTO takes on broader responsibilities for academic development and regional interaction. These transitions take place at an uneven rate and various universities may be located in different phases of transition or stuck in a particular stage. In elite universities with highly successful TTOs the transition to an innovation model typically takes the form of establishment of a broader administrative unit to encompass business development, entrepreneurial education and firm formation. If an elite university chooses not to expand its entrepreneurial activities administratively, the gap may be filled by parallel organizational initiatives, within and without the university.

Today's MIT, Stanford and Imperial College of the UK are the exemplars of university technology transfer. Conditions in aspiring universities, however, are significantly different from those in the best practice cases on various dimensions, including internal research strength and regional innovation environment. Is there an alternative strategy for non-elite universities to be successful in technology transfer? In non-elite universities, the TTO itself may take the initiative to informally broaden its remit to encompass innovation, realizing that its university and region do not yet have the research and absorptive capabilities to pursue a marketing model of technology transfer. Its sponsors may not recognize this expanded mission and the TTO may not be credited for these activities Alternatively, even if the conditions are not ripe for a marketing model such a nascent-TTO often persists in this vein, which may eventually become a living dead TTO, going through the motions of transfer with little result.

Stanford has been the object of emulation by many universities as evidenced by the stream of visitors to its TTO and the hiring of its alumni as consultants. While contemporary Stanford bears little resemblance to the aspiring universities of today, Stanford used to be an aspiring university in the early 20th century. Frederick Terman, the architect of Stanford's transition to a major research university, ran the virtual equivalent of a TTO from his faculty office in the 1920s and 30s. He was negotiating with companies for payments that he turned into bursaries for his students in exchange for disclosures that they could patent. Terman believed that occasional university patents could be made into a steady flow with appropriate encouragement. The next advance was the founding of a TTO in 1969, based on the principle that an active effort should be made to seek out firms to license the patent. Thus, began the transformation from the (legal) patenting to the (marketing) licensing TTO model.

Most universities have modest research funds, with researchers often uninterested in technology transfer and are located in regions with significant gaps in their ability to utilize research. In effect, aspiring universities must recreate the pioneering roles of leading universities in an earlier era. Otherwise, aspiring schools are doomed to a TTO fantasy, replicating the science park fantasy of the 1970s. Several schools and regions constructed low lying building similar to the Stanford Science Park that they had visited, expecting high tech firms to appear, not realizing the decades of prior work that had gone into creating the conditions for high tech firm formation. Non-elite/aspiring university TTOs typically view institutions they wish to emulate after success has already been achieved. They view the current status, policies, arrangements and procedures in place and assume that their replication will produce a similar result. However, later phase arrangements may not fit an initiation stage. The director of technology transfer at MIT, Lita Nielsen states that there is a "Chinese Wall" between academia and industry at her university. Strict rules are in place forbidding faculty members from playing an active role in firm formation. Decades earlier, the original venture capital firm, ARD used underutilized space at MIT like an incubator for the firms that it was helping MIT faculty members establish. Currently, it is said that Nielson merely turns the next card on her Rolodex to notify an area venture capitalist of the latest campus invention with start-up potential.[5]

If an aspiring entrepreneurial university adopts Stanford and MIT's current practices, it may likely impede its chances of success. In the early stages of developing technology transfer, aggressive steps were taken. A Stanford administrator noted that it was "not uncommon for a researcher working in a Stanford laboratory to be spending a couple of days a week at a faculty start-up before it appeared that this was not consistent with the basic principles of the institution. What we are trying to avoid is the kinds of connections between a Stanford faculty member's academic program, resources, facilities, people and their outside entity. We are trying to keep a barrier between those."[6] Contemporary Stanford tech transfer practice relies on an informal dynamic to pull technology out of the university, without the need to provide in-depth support.

The TTO universe encompasses diverse species that mutate from one from to another as ambitions and conditions change. Elite research universities that have only recently shifted from an ivory tower to an entrepreneurial mode have founded TTOs that have become peers of old established offices. A relatively few non-elite universities that have made the third mission a leading priority have also rapidly attained significant gains. We suggest a model of TTO development along two dimensions:

1 focus—legal, marketing and innovation
2 stage of development—capacity building, high performance and "living dead."

Multiple measures, both quantitative and qualitative, input, output and throughput are required to track this diversity. However, technology transfer metrics have not kept pace with developments in the field, especially the spread of TTOs to less research-intensive universities. Moreover existing metrics favor marketing results rather than capacity building tasks, inadvertently labeling some nascent-TTOs as failures.

Figure 5.1 shows the various tasks performed by TTOs and how they connect to each other.

Contemporary TTO metrics are essentially the ones that were developed to match the experience of research-intensive universities. These measures were solidified in the US in the early 1990s and then imitated elsewhere. However, the quantitative metrics that have been developed to demonstrate success of the TTO enterprise may be counterproductive in assessing the activities of emerging TTOs whose appropriate task is the development of research and commercialization capacities that will only pay off at a later date. Etzkowitz participated in this "game of legitimation by quantification" as a member of the AUTM statistics committee in the mid-1990s where he argued for qualitative case studies as a complement to the development of quantitative indicators.[7]

Etzkowitz and Stevens (1995) provides a prehistory of university technology transfer metrics, prior to the launching of the American University Technology Manager Licensing Survey (AUTM). Idiosyncratic studies from various sources, including individual members of the university technology transfer profession, the National Science Foundation (NSF) Board, the General Accounting Office and a Congressional Committee, tracked royalty income earned by academic institutions. The NSF study queried the top 36 recipients of federal funding, with 25 responding and reporting royalty income as follows:

1981	$7.3 million
1982	$9.2 million

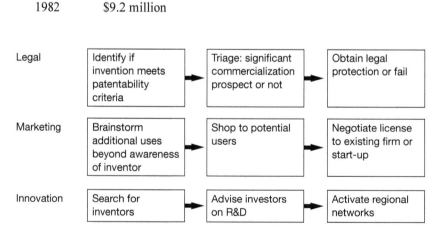

Source: Author's own work

Figure 5.1 Non-linear TTOs stages

A General Accounting Office (GAO) study found that 112 institutions reported royalty income for:

1986 $30.3 million

Four studies were conducted in 1988 by Marjorie Forster of the University of Maryland at Baltimore; John Preston, Director of Technology Transfer at MIT; Terri Wiley of the Indiana Corporation for Science and Technology; and the law firm Pravel, Gambrel, Hewitt and Kettleberger, producing a consensus figure for:

1988 $70.1 million

Two studies were available for 1989, 1990, the second AUTM Survey, carried out by Marjorie Forster and Steve Atkinson of Harvard Medical School. Another GAO study (University Research-Controlling Inappropriate Access to Federally Funded Research Results, GAO/RCED-92-104) carried out at the request of Representative Ted Weiss' Subcommittee on Human Resources and Intergovernmental Relations of the Committee on Government Operations. The study combined the figures for the two years into a single total, $113.1 million, with an estimated growth rate of 20–30% in royalties throughout the 1980s. For 1990, the data are rather better and cover 63 institutions:

1989 $89.2 million
1990 $125.4 million

For 1991, 1992 and 1993, comprehensive surveys are available from AUTM (Etzkowitz and Stevens, 1995). By the early 1990s data collection had been harmonized into production of a collective metric on the part of the technology transfer professional community, superseding individual members of the technology transfer community, government research funders, a government accounting agency and Congress.

Innovation capacity building remit

TTOs should be viewed in a new light as academic competence development units, helping faculty identify the commercial potential of their research, how to find funds to explore this potential and developing the regional infrastructure to facilitate technology transfer. Otherwise, TTOs are condemned to wait for the anomalous "big hit" to appear, an unlikely occurrence in an aspiring university. They need to create the infrastructure for increasing the university's research potential and translational research capacities. Simple "knowledge transfer" models that focus on performance indicators are unlikely to capture the capacity building roles of intermediary organizations and the full meaning of university–industry relations (cf. Hawkins, Langford and Sidhu, 2006). TTOs in peripheral regions and aspiring universities need to play a much more extensive role, creating the conditions making effective technology transfer possible. They are often not yet in a position to play an active role in patent licensing, venture creation and income generation.

Contribution to academic competence

At a TTO in a less research-intensive school, where disclosures are an occasional event, more time may be devoted to each case, even given a much smaller staff. The licensing office may make an effort to identify funds to move the research forward to commercialization, on the one hand, and identification of investors to help start a firm, on the other. As TTOs secure their financial base, they are more easily able to undertake capacity building activities but are less likely to do so. In the case of Binghamton University, the TTO director assisted faculty in identifying additional sources of funding to explore the commercial potential of their research. Consultancy and contract work as soft while patenting, licensing and spin-offs as hard activities. In Sweden, as elsewhere, soft activities are much more common among scientists, yet they are frequently neglected by the entrepreneurship support initiatives (e.g. TTOs) which tend to focus on the outcome oriented hard activities (Göktepe-Hultén, 2010). TTOs appear to take such activities for granted as an integral part of the academic tasks (Duberley et al., 2007) and have not yet included them in their tasks. TTOs may also look for industrial partners who have need of consultancy and cooperation with academics and facilitate contract research agreements. This is especially important for those inexperienced scientists and firms that do not have previous relations.

Contribution to the regional innovation infrastructure

A TTO in a region with a strong business development infrastructure can afford to play a narrower role than one in a developing region. An aspiring university TTO in a developing region faces contradictory pressures. On the one hand, the university will wish to see income return on the relatively few marketable inventions produced and so will encourage licensing to the highest bidder irrespective of location; on the other, local authorities wish to see commercialization and job creation in the region. To meet these dual objectives, such a TTO will have to play a leadership role, working with local government and industry to create an infrastructure to support development of a local high-tech cluster that can provide a context for technology transfer and retention.

The former director of the University of West Virginia TTO inspired regional authorities to form angel networks and the region's first venture capital firm. Some departments and centers recruited faculty who were, extremely interested in playing the game. It was noted that, a highly entrepreneurial faculty member, taking advantage of local resources and available state programs can lead a breakthrough of a university to becoming the site of a significant technological platform in a significant niche area, transforming a university's regional role. The need to fill gaps in the regional innovation environment brought the research institutions of Long Island together to engage in institution building. Out of these discussions, the Long Island Research Organization (LIRI) was formed to offer strategic management consulting to existing firms, especially in the declining defense industry. An affiliate was also established to provide seed venture capital. LIRI advised companies in the Long Island military industrial complex how to find new civilian outlets for their technologies. For example, a company working on detecting submarines was introduced to a medical instrument research group at North Shore Hospital. It was suggested to the company that its expertise in detecting valid signals from huge quantities of noise could also be applied to problems in medical diagnosis.

Emergence of internal competence

At Stony Brook the emergence of technology transfer as a university mission followed upon an earlier period that lasted until the early 1980s when there was no policy. The president of the university at the time recalled that: "The first person to do imaging was Lauterbur and when he sought to develop a patent for this concept the Research Foundation was not organized and they sat on it for a long time and by then it was too late and he was pressed from other quarters to publish it. [The university] could have made a bundle. I was determined that we wouldn't let that happen again."[8] This cautionary tale about the loss of intellectual property rights served as an impetus to change in university policy and the subsequent development of an organizational capacity for technology transfer.

Undertaking technology transfer involved an expansion of the university's mission. As one participant put it: "The very notion of technology transfer suggests some pragmatic and practical implication of ideas as opposed to conceptual transfer." When the question of marketing intellectual property rights from academic research first came up it was believed that the state constitution precluded a public university from engaging in business activities, even such ancillary conveniences as a bookstore or travel agency. It was initially thought that the state constitution would have to be changed to permit the university to engage in technology transfer. A further examination of the question found that reinterpretation would suffice. Thus, the university changed its rules to allow private business activities on campus and the university's Research Foundation, established to administer research funds, was given the additional task of marketing intellectual property.

The early to mid-1980s, marked the beginnings of an academic capacity to organize and manage technology transfer. A central university office had sole responsibility for dealing with the intellectual property rights generated by different campuses; harvesting whatever came in, identifying potential customers, arranging for protection. A faculty member recalled, "The first experience, which was really just my signing a piece of paper saying that I was going to get a little bit of money." Then, arising from this initial industrial involvement, "I had a company contact me asking if I knew of any laboratories that had developed a certain reagent for biodiagnostics and I said actually our lab has such a reagent and I would be really interested in testing the material. So I got in contact with [the] office up in which led to a licensing agreement which is in place now." The office with responsibility for patenting and licensing was located in the multi-campus university's central administration headquarters.

In a first step toward decentralization of technology transfer a division of labor was instituted between central administration and the local campus. A traditional business format of inside/outside partners was followed, with a centralized marketing capacity for all campuses maintained in the central administration, complemented at local campus by an individual with an industrial background interacting with faculty to identify marketable research. He "would literally walk down the halls of buildings, ask people what they were doing, and he would suggest that maybe they would want to write that down in their notebooks. He encouraged a highly selected set of disclosures. [The marketing person in central administration] took this technology and shopped it around using the contacts that he had been developing and he was very effective in that area."

Contribution to inter-firm collaboration

As firms want a broader technological framework than typically provided by a single invention, in addition to seeking out complementarities between technologies developed in their own university, TTOs are increasingly exploring collaboration with TTOs from other universities both to put together a package of technology for licensing (bundling) and as the basis for a start-up. Inter-university TTO cooperation is the basis for a new interface activities of the TTO. Hitherto the TTO was primarily focused on identifying industry partners or sources of government funding, especially at the state level, to move technology forward. Now the TTO is also focused in identifying relevant partners among its academic peers.

Some of the task of identifying partners has been handed over to an emerging group of firms that act as technology brokers. These companies seek out technologies from various universities and attempt to license them. To accomplish this goal, they also bundle different technologies from various sources. TTOs naturally try not to give away their most promising technologies to such firms. However, since the TTO is often resource strapped, passing on technologies to such firms may be an option to spread the workload. A few of these brokerage firms taken a further step and gone on to form firms based on such technological packages in addition to technology licensing, reprising the evolution of the TTO itself in including firm formation as well as licensing to existing firms among its tasks.

Creating the preconditions for innovation

The pool of research funds that a university is able to attract, based on the entrepreneurial academic capabilities of its faculty members, provides the necessary condition for technology transfer. Not surprisingly, nascent-TTOs receive fewer invention disclosures than elite-TTOs. On average elite-TTOs received 250 invention disclosures during 2006, while the latter group received 35 invention disclosures. As invention disclosures can be considered as the initial step behind commercialization, nascent-TTOs also lag behind in terms of patenting, licensing and spin-offs. On average, nascent-TTOs have applied for 24 patents and made less than 30 licensing deals. The director of an aspiring TTO described the faculty's low level of awareness of IPR issues and their efforts to raise the level: "Most scientists don't realize that publication of student's theses is disclosure. To promote outreach, we invite faculty to brown bag lunches, but maybe only three show-up."

Another outreach strategy was to attend orientation events for new faculty. To encourage participation the TTO targets a group of faculty members working in a common research field and try to get them involved in clusters. The best results came from a selective strategy, as explained by a TTO director: "If you target major thematic sponsored research faculty and use [them] as a primary conduit, collaborators they work with on and off campus and they will lead to other people. Nevertheless, whether at an aspiring or highly successful university, the common experience was that, disclosures are usually coming from repeat performers, who may or may not be building on things [done] there before."

For interested, newly involved faculty, another TTO officer found that it was best to "try to get to faculty when they first put their technology in as a proposal, sit down, and look at what they have." The objective of these sessions was to "sensitize faculty that there may be something coming out of the research they haven't thought about before [and] tell them what it might be." The surest route to enhanced awareness was a colleague's achievement. "Awareness depends on institutional success. When an academic department has had success with technology transfer, word will spread. A generational factor was also noted, with older faculty less inclined to technology transfer and some, dead set against it."

Since achieving a major success is an important signal to administrators, policy-makers and faculty about the importance of technology transfer many TTOs search for a "big fish." However, this may not be the most viable strategy, according to a TTO director who said that: "Everyone is still trying to go for a big hit, those are rare." It was pointed out that the "TTO might be hurt if expectations are raised and the blockbuster fails to materialize."[9] On the other hand, Northwestern University, which was not listed as one of the top performers, increased the licensing income from $4 million in 2005 to $30 million in 2006, largely due to one drug (Lyrica). Emory University, which took the top spot in 2005, had a major one-time boost (AIDS drug Emtriva that was sold for a one-time payment of $525 million.

An ideal objective is to build the reputation of the university in a research field with commercial potential either for an existing industry or with the potential of creating a new cluster. Building an advanced research capability in a field that generated basic research findings and pre-competitive research allowed a firm to re-invent its production capabilities and incentivized it to have a close collaboration with the university research center. The renewal of a large firm's technology and its retention in the region was a significant achievement.

Another TTO director used Hillary Clinton's book title "it takes a village to raise a child" to emphasize the need to "network resources" in a region in order to create a platform to support firm formation. The first step was awareness that entrepreneurship is a collective rather than an individual phenomenon. As the director put it, "Not just a couple of people, many are required in firm-formation and the support structure for firm-formation also requires a variety of types of persons to put together the elements to form a new venture including: Connectors (people who know everyone) and Mavens (people who love to teach money and technology people)." An organizational level may bring nascent entrepreneurs in contact with these resources. These groups include networking publications, industrial trade associations, state sponsored innovation support agencies such as high-tech venture councils, university-based programs, groups focused on capital raising, professional associations and accounting firms.

Some TTO directors adopt a "wait and see" strategy announcing the services of their office and counsel the university administration to be patient for results. Such directors are often replaced after becoming the object of dissatisfaction. In worst cases, a succession of wait-and-see directors manages a failed TTO with disheartened staff. A more useful response is the one adopted by a director who engaged with local business and political leadership and encouraged them to establish an angel network and the region's first venture capital firm in order to support start-ups from the university. This is similar to the response of Stanford's leadership in the early 20th century. Faced with the reality that graduates would leave the region for lack of appropriate employment, they helped establish technological firms so their engineering school could flourish.

The AUTM like indicators add additional bias to data collected on e.g. European universities and TTOs (see Audretsch and Göktepe-Hultén, 2015 for a discussion on European paradox and university patents). European experience also suggests that nascent-TTOs have a capacity development function. The ASTP survey showed that TTOs have been providing services beyond patenting, licensing, spin-off (ASTP, 2008). Beyond serving as a secondary support structure for industry and government, Japanese universities are encouraged to incubate thousands of firms and new knowledge-based clusters (Kneller, 2007). The obstacle appears to be the lack of complementary and intermediary institutions that can facilitate entrepreneurial activities despite the formation of a number of TTOs and business venturing agents and incubators. In Japan the establishment of intermediary institutions seems necessary before technology transfer can progress (Collins and Wakoh, 2000).

The largely failed Brazilian science parks of the 1970s and 80s, gave way to a smaller scale incubator model of firm formation, and then reappeared in the late 90s on a stronger footing after a sufficient base had been built (Etzkowitz et al., 2005). TTOs also appeared in Brazil as a follow on to incubators and entrepreneurial training initiatives that prepared the ground for technology transfer based upon intellectual property rights. TTOs at universities such as the Pontifical Catholic University of Porto Allegre in Brazil, a teaching university with aspirations to research and entrepreneurship, are quite well aware of the distance they have to travel. TTO and associated support structures such as incubator and science park facilities are geared to assist the transition of their universities to an entrepreneurial mode. Indeed, new approaches have been invented such as combined research groups and high tech firms to speed the transition process.

A first implication of this study is that capacity building activities should be seen as part of the organizational learning process on the way to a marketing mission. A second message is that currently premier TTOs may also learn from the experiences of aspiring TTOs and their own history. The contemporary Stanford office has more than 30 persons, including support personnel, most of whose time is occupied by dealing with serial entrepreneurs and inventors that show up at the office. The larger number of faculty, less entrepreneurially inclined, is relatively neglected.

Elite universities share some of the same conditions as non-elite universities, merely to a different degree. Thus, even at the most successful entrepreneurial universities, some faculty members require the same level of support as those at a non-elite university in order to pursue the commercial implications of their research. Conversely, at non-elite universities, there are typically some faculty members operating at the same high level of research and entrepreneurship as their peers at elite universities. Often they have trained at the same level of school and it is merely a matter of luck or contingency rather than achievement or skill that they are located at different levels on the academic ladder. There is continuity among schools rather than a dichotomy.

Move from big data towards new TTO metrics

Knowledge transfer between universities and industry may vary from simple collaboration in R&D, to mobility of people, lifelong learning and curriculum development relevant for industry. In addition to universities oldest missions of teaching and research the universities have become more and more entrepreneurial today. Universities are willing to see their knowledge set to practice and they are joining forces with industry to do so. The various pathways to an entrepreneurial university have been addressed elsewhere (Etzkowitz et al., 2005).

TTOs define their goals differently, and they act in different milieus. So while all TTOs would answer the same questions, the answers may not be unbiased to compare. However, an expectation for these measures should be to allow institutions identifying their own goals within a reporting of these metrics to provide community members better information and context through them, and whatever ancillary information an institution would provide. Our modest attempt is to show the diversity of technology transfer and the diverse roles that TTOs at less fortunate milieus undertake. However, this commitment should not be seen as an excuse or a justification for their existence. It is rather to show the potential risks in the case of their absence. We shifted the dominant focus from success cases to TTOs in aspiring research universities, often located in periphery regions. Our observations and interviews (over the years) emphasize comparison of key indicators (patents, licensing cost and /or revenues) across organizations or nations would lead to superficial differences or similarities. A focus on big data often misses the treatment of institutional, historical and legal and all other contextual factors.

Unlike studies based on the analysis of big data having top-down approach—or one fits all—our observations have matured over the years through a bottom-up process comprising discussions forth and back and re-observations. Our experiences add weight to the contention that "qualitative" and "quantitative" approaches result differently among universities within the same country despite the same legal framework. Likewise applying the same set of technology transfer indicators for cross-national analysis would not capture the diversity of technology transfer. The results often create an underperformance plot for some TTOs, even if big data could be normalized across different units.

We have questioned whether a marketing-focused TTO is the most effective strategy for such universities. This approach may work for a high-level research university, with cultural change a relatively simple matter due to peer examples from other entrepreneurial research universities and hiring of junior faculty from these schools. Under conditions of moderate or modest level of resources, what should non-elite universities do: take a long-range strategy and develop research strengths, adopt a short-term strategy with a focus on low-tech businesses development to aid local SMEs? How many policy and measures can they adopt simultaneously? There is no single answer or one-size-fits-all strategy, only some general guidelines for practice improvement and metrics development. In addition to the metrics for assessing value-creation, we propose a set of less conventional metrics by which we can understand and analyze what most TTOs in less fortunate environments are doing. We recognize this list as a work-in-progress and we aim to revise it in follow-up work. Nevertheless moving from marketing-focused TTO to a pre-commercial TTO will counterbalance the dominance of conventional indicators and provide a more holistic narrative on what TTOs are actually doing.

- Time and resources spent on faculty and student educational activities on technology transfer.
- Time and resources spent on identifying potential ideas that can be commercialized.
- Time and resources spent on generating funds/resources to support research.
- Time and resources spent on conflict of interest resolution among scientists.
- Time and resources spent on building a regional infrastructure.
- Time and resources spent on providing business support services and activities to the local companies.
- Time and resources spent on building collaboration between companies and university start-ups.
- Time and resources spent on cooperating with other university TTOs.
- Time and resources spent on building organizational competence/skills of TTOs.
- Time and resources spent on creating alternative strategies to reach scientists and commercialize research results.

The AUTM metrics were created to legitimate an emerging profession that had a precarious identity and give it easy-to-understand and visible, performance measures, accessible to policy makers, university administrators and the media. University technology transfer metrics have become an institutionalized routine practice to understand, justify and benchmark the marketing role of TTOs. Their widespread acceptance and imitation in Europe and Latin America, was an important step in the institutionalization of university technology transfer, making it an increasingly taken for granted part of the academic scene.

Importance of academic knowledge to economic and social development along teaching and research is accepted among policy-makers. With a few notable exceptions such as Beijing and Tsinghua universities in China, Oxford, Cambridge and Imperial College in the UK, and Karolinska in Sweden, world universities face circumstances similar to Binghamton, Porto Allegre and West Virginia. Most universities have relatively modest research funds, faculty at the early stages of awareness of the utility potential of their research and regions with significant gaps in their ability to commercialize research. Only a relatively few universities, such as Johns Hopkins, with extensive research capabilities and access to vast financial resources can quickly shift from an ivory tower to an entrepreneurial mode, joining the upper end of the success league, creating a biotechnology industry adjacent to the university in a relatively short time. Policies based upon the modus operandi of leading universities TTOs may misdirect followers as they assume the presence of a large pool of potentially commercializable research within the university, on the one hand, and the availability of means to translate this research into technology and firms locally, on the other. MIT, Stanford and Imperial College are the desired goal but their TTOs are not a relevant model for aspiring universities.

Developed in the era of transition from the patenting to the marketing model, TTO metrics need to be updated to reflect the current transition from the marketing to an innovation model. We recommend that AUTM, and its peers in Europe and Latin America collect data to encourage their TTOs to be active in the broad in a comprehensive way that captures the whole knowledge transfer and dissemination and allow researchers/faculty to be active in broad spectrum of knowledge transfer activities. Universities' role in technology transfer can therefore be fully assessed.

The indicators of university–industry cooperation are important in planning and evaluating the policies of R&D and higher education. Due to the diversity of knowledge transfer channels between universities and enterprises it is important to analyze the university–industry cooperation in a systematic way. To get an adequate understanding of the collaboration between universities and industry and its economic impact on society, appropriate indicators should be used.

De-reification of current metrics reveals unintended counterproductive consequences, especially for the broader universe of TTOs, created since the measures were established. Judged by the same criteria as TTOs that have already passed through the capacity development to the high performance stage, nascent-TTOs will almost inevitably fall short. Identifying less entrepreneurially experienced scientists or scientists without industrial contacts and female scientists, and helping them commercialize their research results should be credited. A focus on business development, attraction of resources for translational research and coaching and mentoring of nascent firms may boost a mid-level aspirant. The valuable role that TTOs play in capacity building in non-elite universities may not only become invisible but such TTOs may also be aborted, absent creation of relevant indicators.

The capacity building capabilities and metrics that we recommend for aspiring universities or nascent-TTOs are also relevant for elite universities and should be applied across the board rather than to a particular segment of the academic universe. The benefits of TTOs, beyond licensing fees and royalty revenues, can be, "significant but you have to measure them in the right way," said one TTO director. Just as AUTM created a survey in the early 1990s that legitimated the marketing model of TTOs, a new set of metrics is required to institutionalize a broader role as Innovation Organizer. The technology transfer profession has achieved a stable identity and is well positioned to take a leadership role, through its professional associations, in advancing the capacity building role of TTOs in aspiring universities.

The findings of this chapter indicate the importance of diverse performance indicators and their usage to measure the inputs, outputs and impact of university–industry collaboration. Thus, policies for university–industry collaboration should pay attention not only to the input and output measures as they mostly do today, but look also into the future and measure the possible effects of the created policies. Also, universities and enterprises should evaluate the cooperation and knowledge transfer between the parties.

Acknowledgements

Dr. Göktepe-Hultén gratefully acknowledges financial support from VINNOVA, the Swedish Governmental Agency for Innovation Systems.

Notes

1 The geographical region including the cities of New York Metropolitan Region, Boston, Long Island, Baltimore and Albany till Washington, DC area is commonly known as the Bos-Wash Corridor.
2 AUTM has initiated a New Metrics Subcommittee to investigate "Institutional Economic Engagement Index".
3 Although success in terms of numbers of patenting, licensing, spin-off may depend on experience, the effect of age may vanish with a major success or when controlled with other indicators.
4 ARD, in effect, combined the functions of a contemporary TTO, venture capital firm and incubator facility, with some firms in located in underutilized lab space and the university supplying some of the initial capital for the firm (Etzkowitz et al., 2005).
5 Personal communication with Ashley Stevens, Director of Technology Transfer, Boston University, August, 2007.
6 Etzkowitz's interview with Stanford administrator, June 2005.
7 Although this proposal for qualitative indicators was not taken up by AUTM at the time, the TTO of Stony Brook University commissioned a qualitative analysis of its incubator project (Etzkowitz and Stevens 1995).

8 Paul Christian Lauterbur (May 6, 1929–March 27, 2007) was an American chemist who shared the Nobel Prize in Physiology or Medicine in 2003 with Peter Mansfield for his work, which made the development of magnetic resonance imaging (MRI) possible.
9 Steve Brozak, WBB Securities Analyst, December 4, 2006.

References

Arundel, A., Kanerva, M., Bordoy, C. (2008) "Association of European Science and Technology Transfer Professionals,(ASTP), 2008 Summary Report for Respondents: The ASTP Survey for Fiscal Year 2007", Report produced by UNU-MERIT.

Association of University Technology Managers (2007) AUTM Licensing Survey: Fiscal Year 2006, AUTM.

Audretsch, D. and Göktepe-Hultén, D. (2015) "Does University Ownership Impede University Patenting in Europe", in Link, A. N., Siegel, D. S. and Wright, M. (eds) The Chicago Handbook of University Technology Transfer and Academic Entrepreneurship, Chicago: University of Chicago Press.

Berger, P. and Luckmann, T. (1966) The Social Construction of Reality: A Treatise in the Sociology of Knowledge, New York: Doubleday.

Bradshaw, T. K., Munroe, T., Westwind, M. (2005) "Economic Development via University-based Technology Transfer: Strategies for Non-elite Universities", International Journal of Technology Transfer & Commercialisation, 4 (3): 279–301.

Collins, S. and Wakoh, H. (2000) "Universities and Technology Transfer in Japan: Recent Reforms in Historical Perspective", The Journal of Technology Transfer, 25 (2): 213–222.

Duberley, J., Cohen, L. and Leeson, E. (2007) "Entrepreneurial Academics: Developing Scientific Careers in Changing University Settings", Higher Education Quarterly, 61 (4): 479–497.

Etzkowitz, H. (2002) MIT and the Rise of Entrepreneurial Science, London: Routledge.

Etzkowitz, H. (2013) "Mistaking Dawn for Dusk: Quantophrenia and the Cult of Numerology in Technology Transfer Analysis", Scientometrics, 97 (3): 913–925.

Etzkowitz, H., de Mello, J. M. C. and Almeida, M. (2005) "Towards Meta-innovation in Brazil: The Evolution of the Incubator and the Emergence of a Triple Helix", Research Policy, 34 (4): 411–424.

Etzkowitz, H. and Stevens, A. (1995) "Inching Toward Industrial Policy: The University's Role in Government Initiatives to Assist Small, Innovative Companies in the U.S.", Science Studies, 8 (2): 13–31.

Göktepe-Hultén, D. (2010) "University–Industry Technology Transfer: Who Needs TTOs?", International Journal of Technology Transfer and Commercialisation, 9 (1): 40–52.

Hawkins, R., Langford, C. and Sidhu, K. (2006) "University Research in an Innovation Society", presented at the Blue Sky II Conference, 26 September 2006, Ottawa, Canada.

Kenney, M. and Patton, D. (2009) "Reconsidering the Bayh-Dole Act and the Current University Invention Ownership Model", Research Policy 38 (9): 1407–1422.

Kneller, R. (2007) "Japan's New Technology Transfer System and the Preemption of University Discoveries by Sponsored Research and Co-inventorship", Industry and Higher Education, 21 (3): 211–220.

Mowery, D. C., Nelson, R. R., Sampat, B., Ziedonis, A. A. (2001) "The Effects of the Bayh-Dole Act on US University Research and Technology Transfer: An Analysis of Data from Columbia University, the University of California, and Stanford University", Research Policy, 30 (1): 99–119.

Rothaermel, F. T., Agung, S. D., Jiang, L. (2007) "University Entrepreneurship: A Taxonomy of the Literature", Industrial and Corporate Change, 16 (4): 691–691.

6 The commercialization of new drugs and vaccines discovered in public sector research

*Ashley J. Stevens,[1] Jonathan J. Jensen,[2]
Katrine Wyller,[3] Patrick C. Kilgore,[4]
Eric London,[5] Qingzhi Zhang,[6]
Sabarni K. Chatterjee,[7] and
Mark L. Rohrbaugh[8]*

Introduction

Historically, there was a clear distinction between the roles of public sector research and corporate research in the discovery of new drugs and vaccines to solve unmet medical needs: public sector researchers, primarily funded by Government sources, performed the basic research and elucidated the underlying mechanisms and pathways of disease and identified promising points of intervention, while corporate researchers performed the applied research that discovered the drugs that would actually treat the diseases and then carried out the development activities to bring the drugs to market.

However, the boundaries between the roles of the public sector and the private sector in the discovery of new drugs have shifted significantly since the dawn of the biotechnology era in the mid-1970s. The public sector now has a much more direct role in the applied research part of drug discovery than is generally realized. This shift in roles has been attributed to changes in biological research that made the results of academic research immediately applicable to drug discovery fortuitously coinciding with changes in the legal framework governing the ownership, management and transfer of the intellectual property resulting from public sector research.

This chapter documents this fundamental change and presents a detailed compilation of public sector inventions that have resulted in new drugs and vaccines.

In a previous article,[9] we showed that over the past 30 years, 153[10] new U.S. Food and Drug Administration (FDA) approved vaccines, drugs and/or new indications for existing drugs were created during the course of research carried out in public sector institutions. These drugs consisted of 93 small molecule drugs, 36 biologics, 15 vaccines, eight in vivo diagnostics and one over-the-counter (OTC) drug. We identified the disease indications where public sector research had the highest impact – cancer and infectious diseases. We identified the research institutions that have been most productive in discovering new drugs.

Finally, we showed that drugs discovered by public sector researchers have had a disproportionately high therapeutic impact.

In this article we further analyze our dataset to identify the timelines of the development programs, from the start of the scientific program that led to the discovery, to the actual discovery of the drug, to the initiation of development and finally to FDA approval. We analyze the complex, multi-step development pathways that brought these discoveries to a successful conclusion with market introduction. We quantify the economic impact of these drugs, which vastly exceeds the Federal Government's annual investment in biomedical research.

Our study is limited to the US. Public sector research institutions (PSRIs) in countries such as the United Kingdom (UK), Israel, Canada, Germany, France, the Czech Republic, Belgium, Australia and Japan have also made significant contributions to new drug discovery, and we present preliminary data on their contributions.

Background

The relationship between academia and the pharmaceutical industry has gone through a number of cycles. Following the Pure Food and Drug Act of 1906 and the Food Drug and Cosmetic Act of 1938, it was the transfer of drugs discovered at academic institutions, such as thyroxine (University of Minnesota), insulin (University of Toronto), vitamin D and coumadin (University of Wisconsin), penicillin (University of Oxford), neomycin and streptomycin (Rutgers), methotrexate (M.D. Anderson Cancer Center), and others, that transformed the pharmaceutical industry from peddlers of bogus "patent medicines" to an ethical, research-based industry.

However, in the early 1960s, the Kennedy Administration started claiming rights to patents discovered in federal laboratories and at universities funded by federal grants. A principle was established that federally funded inventions would only be non-exclusively licensed. This substantially reduced the incentive for any company to make the pioneering investment needed to develop an early stage academic invention to the stage of market readiness because others could then piggy-back on their investment when the technology's viability had been demonstrated.

In the mid-1960s, three cases made industry even more reluctant to develop university inventions that had received federal funding:[11]

- The lawsuit between the University of Florida and Robert Cade over rights to Gatorade, where title to the patents was disputed and the National Institutes of Health (NIH) prohibited Cade from seeking US patents on his invention;
- The controversy over the cost increases caused by the exclusive licensing of the phenylketonuria (PKU) test invented at the University of Buffalo, which reached the floor of the Senate; and
- The Government taking title to patents on the cancer drug 5-fluorouracil and non-exclusively licensing the patents when federal funds were used to support

the initial clinical testing. The drug's discovery and pre-clinical development had been funded and technically supported by Hoffman-La Roche.

A 1968 US Government Accountability Office (GAO) study[12] found that no drug the Government owned the rights to had ever been developed and reached the public, and another 1968 study[13] by the Harbridge House consulting firm described projects as being "contaminated" by federal funding because of the constraints that federal ownership of the intellectual property brought with it.

By the late 1970s, Congress was generally concerned about a perceived loss of US industrial competitiveness to Europe and Japan. It was discovered that the Government owned 28,000 patents and had managed to license fewer than 4% of them, including fully paid up licenses and licenses from the Government to the inventor of his/her own patent.[14]

One of the responses to the 1968 GAO and Harbridge House reports had been the establishment of the Institutional Patent Agreement (IPA) mechanism for universities and non-profits to own and manage their own patents by Norman Latker at the Department of Health Education and Welfare. However, the Carter Administration halted the IPA process[15] and a number of universities and small business groups therefore lobbied for the passage of the Bayh-Dole Act[16] to allow universities, non-profit research institutes, teaching hospitals and small businesses to own the intellectual property resulting from federally funded research and to license it on terms of their choosing. The bill was finally passed in a lame duck session of the 96th Congress.[17]

Bayh-Dole was a relatively straightforward piece of legislation, requiring institutions to:

- Notify the funding agency of invention disclosures within two months of receipt and whether they intend to take title within two years;
- File patents on inventions they elect to own and not abandon them without giving the funding agency notice;
- Not assign title to third parties other than to patent management organizations;
- Include notice of the Government's rights in patent applications;
- On request, report on the utilization of their inventions to the funding agency;
- Share any income they receive with the inventors and use the remaining income only for research and education;
- Collaborate with commercial concerns to promote the utilization of inventions arising from Federal funding;
- Give licensing preference to small businesses in the US; and
- Ensure that their exclusive licensees substantially manufacture products in the US for sale in the US market.

In addition, the US Government retained a non-exclusive license to practice the patent throughout the world and the right to "march-in" and grant additional licenses in the public interest if the invention was not being brought to practical application or meeting public health and safety needs.

Institutions were allowed to grant exclusive licenses for five years; the five-year limitation was removed four years later in an amendment to the Act.[18]

The Bayh-Dole Act provided no new funding and so did not require periodic reauthorization, which would have provided opportunities for Congress to amend the Act. The Act has therefore been in place for almost 30 years, with only one major amendment, in 1984.

The Stevenson-Wydler Technology Innovation Act of 1980[19] and the Federal Technology Transfer Act of 1986[20] established the foundation for technology transfer for Federal Government laboratories. Like their Bayh-Dole counterpart, these laws recognized the need for enhanced commercial dissemination of technologies from publicly funded research to private industry, establishing analogous mechanisms for laboratories of the US Government. For the first time, federal laboratories were required to grant licenses for commercial development of technologies invented in their laboratories and were incentivized to do so by being able to keep the proceeds within the laboratory. Inventors were given a share of the royalty income and laboratories were permitted to keep the remainder of the funds to support the cost of technology transfer and to further their research and training missions.

The Federal Technology Transfer Act also enabled federal laboratories to take a more active role in cooperating with companies developing technologies through Cooperative Research and Development Agreements (CRADAs). Some of the technologies licensed by the NIH were discovered as CRADA inventions, such as a method of administering Taxol, or were further developed under the CRADA mechanism with the licensee, such as Havrix, the first hepatitis A vaccine.

The historic roles of public sector and corporate research in drug discovery

Historically, there was believed to be a clear distinction between the roles of public sector and corporate research in the discovery of new drugs and vaccines to solve unmet medical needs. Although drug discovery occasionally is serendipitous, such as when the ability of sildenafil (Viagra) to treat male erectile dysfunction was observed as a side effect in an unsuccessful trial of sildenafil to treat angina, modern drug discovery is hypothesis driven and generally uses one of two scientific approaches:

- High throughput screening of large numbers of compounds against an assay to identify compounds that bind to a molecular target of interest; or
- Rational drug design based on detailed structural information about the molecular target of interest.

Traditionally, the role of public sector researchers, primarily funded by Government sources, was to perform basic research and elucidate the underlying mechanisms and pathways of disease and identify the molecular targets that would provide promising points of intervention in the etiology of the disease. Corporate researchers would then take the results of this basic research and carry out the applied research that discovered the actual drugs that would modulate the targets and treat the disease. The public sector basic research findings were transferred to industry at arm's length, via publications in the scientific literature and presentations at scientific conferences. They were available to all.

In the applied phase of the research, patents are applied for that will protect the investment the company will need to make in developing the product and bring it to market, and the knowledge can be localized to a single company.

An excellent example of this traditional, arms length paradigm was Julius Axelrod's Nobel Prize winning research at the NIH elucidating the basic mechanisms of neurotransmitters,[21] which provided the foundation for the pharmaceutical industry to discover an entirely new class of drugs, the selective serotonin reuptake inhibitors (SSRIs) such as Prozac, Paxil and Zoloft that have been immensely important in the treatment of depression and have also been extremely successful commercially.

There seems to be little dispute about the extent of the contribution of public sector basic research to drug discovery under this paradigm. Studies by Cockburn and Henderson[22] showed the complex inter-relationships between public and private research in the pharmaceutical industry. Zycher, DiMasi et al.[23] have shown that upwards of 80% of drugs are based on basic scientific discoveries made in the public sector, while Toole[24] has identified the complementary nature of public and private research in drug discovery. He summarized the research on the role of public sector basic research as follows:

> Most of this research highlights the role that basic research plays in opening new avenues to therapeutic outcomes. It is useful to think of the new therapies pursued by industry scientists as therapeutic jigsaw puzzles that must be completed before any new drug treatment can be brought to market. Public basic research provides either completely new puzzles or resurrects puzzles that were believed to be unsolvable. In either situation, almost all the case studies characterize the new puzzles emerging from public basic research as embryonic. *These puzzles are often in their earliest stages of scientific development and may embody only the faintest outline of a promising new therapy.* A key finding from these studies is that public basic research is characterized by a high degree of uncertainty in both its scientific maturity and its potential market applicability. Beyond supplying new ideas for therapies, public basic research can contribute to industry solutions by providing pieces of the puzzle or *by providing the clues required for discovering new pieces.* In the case studies, these pieces and clues take the form of methods for identification of target compounds, validation of these targets, methods for producing sufficient quantities of the compound for animal and human testing, and the design of laboratory models for animal studies. Because of the complexity and diversity of the puzzles confronting industry scientists, the pieces drawn from public basic research are rarely the "plug and play" variety. Information from this research must be shaped to fit the specific puzzle under investigation. Moreover, when public basic research only provides clues, new pieces must be invented to fit the puzzle (citations omitted; emphasis added).

Marcia Angell[25] quotes studies which showed that around 85% of the basic scientific research that led to the discovery of new drugs came from sources other than the drug industry. However, Angell is wrong when she states:

> And so on and so on. There is no question that publicly funded medical research – not the industry itself – is by far the major source of innovative drugs.

The studies she had just cited had shown that publicly funded medical research is the major source of the scientific leads that point to how innovative drugs could be discovered. These studies did <u>not</u> identify the actual drugs themselves.

Toole[26] discovered a quantifiable correlation between investment in publicly funded basic research and corporately funded applied research. He found that a 1% increase in the stock of public basic research led to a 1.8% increase in the number of successful NME applications after a lag of about 17 years. He further estimated that the total direct return to public basic research was 43% – i.e., a $1 increase in investment in public sector basic research yielded about $0.43 in annual benefits in NME innovation in perpetuity.

However, working in the technology transfer profession for many years, we observed that the boundaries between the roles of the public sector and the private sector in the discovery of new drugs had shifted significantly since the dawn of the biotechnology era. We saw that PSRIs were playing a much more important role in drug discovery than had previously been identified and documented and were having a significant role in the applied research phase of the drug discovery process, identifying the new drugs themselves and creating some, or all, of the intellectual protecting these new drugs. The primary objective of this study is therefore to document the extent of this new role for the public sector in the applied phase of the research and therefore in the creation of IP protecting the commercialized products.

The emergence of this new paradigm has been attributed to changes in biological research that made the results of academic research immediately applicable to drug discovery fortuitously coinciding with the establishment of the legal framework which governs public sector technology transfer described in the previous section.[27] Under this new paradigm, the results of public sector scientific research, in addition to being freely published in the scientific literature, can, to the extent they meet the criteria of novelty, utility and non-obviousness to constitute a patentable invention, be converted into intellectual property and then be transferred through commercial license agreements to a companies for further development.

Particularly in the life sciences, academic scientists have embraced this new paradigm. Murray[28] analyzed three years worth of articles in *Nature Biotechnology* from 1997 to 1999 and found that there was a corresponding issued US patent on just under 50% of the discoveries being reported, a phenomenon she termed the "patent-paper pair".[29] As Murray acknowledged, the discoveries submitted to *Nature Biotechnology* probably self select for those with commercial relevance, so the 50% figure she found may be higher than what would be found for the overall scientific literature. Lebovitz[30] examined the life science publications in *Science and Nature* in a six month period and found that 32.7% of the biomedical research articles surveyed in the study were associated with underlying patent applications, 17.9% directly covering the research disclosed in the scientific publication, and 11.7% related to an enabling technology that was utilized in the research.

Under the new paradigm that we are evaluating, we consider that a PSRI plays a role in the applied phase of drug discovery research if it, solely or jointly creates *product-specific* intellectual property pertaining to the drug that is transferred to a company through a commercial license. In most cases, the intellectual property is a patent or patent application. However, a few products have used proprietary biological materials developed and licensed by the institution. For example, MedImmune licensed proprietary strains of influenza virus developed by Dr. Hunein Maassab at the University of Michigan to develop FluMist, and FluMist is therefore included in our study.* Similarly the strain of *M. tuberculosis* used in the BCG vaccine and the trademark on the name "Tice" are owned by the University of Illinois and are licensed by them to the manufacturer, OrganonTeknica.

In this study we use the term "public sector research institute" in its broadest sense to include universities, research hospitals, not-for-profit research institutes and federal laboratories.

We use the term "drug" to refer to any product that received marketing approval from either the Center for Drug Evaluation and Research (CDER) or the Center for Biologics Evaluation and Research (CBER) of the FDA. We therefore include small molecule drugs, protein-based biologics, vaccines and *in vivo* diagnostics approved since 1970. Products that have received regulatory approval only outside the US are not included in this study.

There are multiple layers of patents protecting a particular drug. In this study, we classified patents into six categories.

We read all the independent claims of the 531 public sector, joint and company patents that we identified and classified the claims into the following categories:

Screening: Claims a way of detecting the existence of a condition or compound either in vitro or in vivo, and of identifying a molecule that is pharmacologically active against the condition.

Method of synthesis: Claims a specific way of making a compound or class of compounds, but does not cover the composition of matter of the pharmacologically active constituent of the marketed drug.

---

*   The University of Michigan has since received a U.S. patent on the strain used in FluMist.

Composition of matter: Claims the pharmacologically active molecule, or family of molecules, contained in the marketed drug, including peptides and proteins and the specific DNA sequences used to produce them.

Method of treating: Claims a way of treating a specific condition using the pharmacologically active molecule.

Formulation: Claims a way of delivering a compound, or a way or preparing a pharmacologically effective combination of compounds, but not the composition of matter of the pharmacologically active ingredient compounds which make up the combination.

Medical device: Claims an instrument or apparatus which does not achieve its primary intended purposes through chemical action and which is not dependent upon being metabolized for the achievement of its primary intended purposes.

We analyzed the patents as follows.

An individual patent frequently contained more than one type of claim, most often a composition of matter and a method of treating. Each patent was given a score of 1 in each category in which it had at least one independent claim. For example, if there were two PSRI patents protecting a drug, and one only had three independent composition of matter claims and the second had one composition of matter independent claim and two method of treating independent claims, it would have been given a score of two in the composition of matter category and one in the method of treating category

While the objective of our research was to comprehensively identify the public sector intellectual property underlying these drugs, including intellectual property jointly owned with a company, it was not one of our objectives to make a comprehensive identification of all the company owned intellectual property protecting the drugs. Our primary source for company owned intellectual property was the Orange Book, and so is most complete for small molecule drugs, including *in vivo* diagnostics, and is less complete for biologics and vaccines. The results are shown in Table 6.1.

For the PSRI solely owned patents, there were an average of 2.5 patents protecting each drug, and these patents had an average of 1.5 types of claim per drug. The most common types of claims were composition of matter which were found for 56% of the drugs, followed by methods of treating, found for 52%. Methods of screening patents were only found in 5% of the drugs and formulation patents in 10% of the cases.

We therefore use the term "discovered in whole or in part" through public sector research throughout the study.

Table 6.1 Types of patent claims protecting drugs

Patent ownership	PSRI		Joint PSRI & company		Company	
No. of drugs with patents	133		17		56	
No. of patents	329		45		157	
Average patents/drug	2.5		2.6		2.8	
No. of drugs with claims for:						
Screening	8	6.0%	2	11.8%	1	1.8%
Method of synthesis	38	28.6%	1	5.9%	10	17.9%
Composition of matter	85	63.9%	8	47.1%	43	76.8%
Method of treating	80	60.2%	13	76.5%	31	55.4%
Formulation	17	12.8%			9	16.1%
Medical device	2	1.5%				
Average types/drug	1.7		1.4		1.7	

Examples of the types of the different extents of the contributions of PSRIs to the discovery of specific drugs are as follows.

- In the case of Cialis, Cold Spring Harbor developed the screening technology and licensed it to ICOS Corporation, which used the tools to discover the actual active molecule, tadalafil, which it then took through clinical development. Cold Spring Harbor therefore does not receive royalties on sales of Cialis.
- In the case of Serafem, MIT showed that selective serotonin reuptake inhibitors such as fluoxetine hydrochloride, the active ingredient in Prozac, were effective in treating premenstrual dysphoric disorder and licensed it to Eli Lilly who had already carried out the safety and efficacy studies to secure FDA approval to market Prozac as an anti-depressant.
- In the case of ReoPro, SUNY isolated the 7E3 murine antibody that binds to fibrinogen to inhibit clotting and licensed it to Centocor. Centocor chimerized the antibody, creating abciximab. The clinical development was carried out by Lilly.
- In the case of Neupogen, Memorial Sloan Kettering cloned the gene for G-CSF and based on G-CSF's efficacy in regenerating neutrophils. Amgen's role was to develop the producing cell line and take the compound through clinical development.
- In the case of Taxol, Dr. Robert Horton, a chemist at Florida State University invented the semi-synthetic process for manufacturing Taxol from an extract of pine needles. This innovation freed Taxol from its dependency on the rare and slow growing Pacific yew tree as its sole raw material source and allowed Taxol to become a $1.6 billion dollar drug in its peak year of sales. Florida State licensed the process to Bristol-Myers, who had licensed the NIH's extensive clinical data on Taxol and method of administration to patients.

- In the case of Geodon, the University of Kansas discovered the use of cyclodextrins as a delivery agent for drugs and licensed them to CyDex, which partnered with Pfizer to formulate ziprasidone mesylate to treat schizophrenia. Pfizer carried out the clinical development.

In the case of biologics, there is frequently a layer of patents covering genetic engineering platform technologies that are needed to create and/or manufacture the drugs. Many of these platform technologies were created and are owned by PSRIs and are discussed in more detail below. If the only public sector contribution to a specific drug was through one of these platform technologies, we did not include that drug in our study, because the public sector did not contribute to the discovery of the specific, marketed product.

With the exception of the exclusion of such platform technologies, we deliberately use the term "discovery" very broadly, to refer to any intellectual property that protects the identification, composition of matter, method of treating, manufacture or formulation of a drug which was licensed by the PSRI to the corporate developer of the technology.

A broad range of contractual relationships between the public and private sectors is encompassed in our study. In some cases, such as Neupogen discussed above, the PSRI made the complete discovery itself and subsequently licensed the invention to the developing company. In other cases the relationship started with a collaboration between a public sector institution and a corporate collaborator, resulting in initial patents being jointly owned. In these circumstances, the corporate partner generally obtains a license to the PSRI's undivided interest in the patents. Other cases involved simultaneous inventions in the public and private sectors, resulting in interference proceedings, which were sometimes resolved through negotiation rather than through the patent office. Massachusetts General Hospital's interest in the arthritis drug Enbrel came through a license agreement structured to take into account a negative outcome should an interference be declared.[31] And finally, in a few cases, the developing company did not feel it needed a license to the public sector intellectual property, leading to litigation which resulted in a license being judicially imposed.

There are instances of academic research resulting in valuable drugs where the institution did not apply for a patent, to their considerable financial cost (although the public still benefitted from the product becoming available to them). These generally involved a new use for an existing drug, where there was adequate intellectual property protection available to protect the development of the drug for its original intended indication. For example:

- In the late 1950s, Dr. Gregory Pincus at the Worcester Foundation for Experimental Biology discovered that synthetic progesterones were effective female contraceptives. Pharmaceutical companies such as Syntex and G.D. Searle were only developing synthetic progesterones to treat menstrual irregularities, so Pincus' discovery would have been patentable as a new method of treating patent, but he failed to apply for a patent and therefore was unable to license his discovery; the contraceptive pill is therefore not included in our study. G.D. Searle, which marketed the drug, made some gifts to the Worcester Foundation, but the Foundation was ultimately absorbed into the University of Massachusetts in 1997.

- More recently, Dr. Lawrence Jacobs, Chair of the Neurology Department at the University of Buffalo Medical School, carried out the key clinical trial, funded by NIH, that showed the efficacy of intramuscular beta-interferon 1a in the treatment of multiple sclerosis. Biogen agreed to support the trial with their version of beta interferon 1a. Multiple sclerosis turned out to be the only major clinical use of beta-interferon 1a, which was the first product to which Biogen had retained development rights and which became its first clinical product under the trade name Avonex. Biogen subsequently gave the University of Buffalo $1.5 million to endow the Irvin and Rosemary Smith Chair in Neurology in the School of Medicine and Biomedical Sciences, which Jacob held until his death from cancer in 2002, considerably less than Buffalo would have received had they secured a patent on the new use of interferon 1a and licensed it to Biogen.

Avonex is in fact included in our study, not because of Jacobs' work, but because it was determined in litigation that Avonex infringed one of the Ringold patents jointly owned by Stanford University and Berlex,

As noted above, our study does not include the role of public sector research in developing the platform technologies discussed above that have contributed to the development of new classes of biological drugs. Such platforms include:

- The discovery of recombinant DNA technology at the University of California, San Francisco and Stanford University ("Cohen-Boyer");
- The discovery of bacterial production methods for recombinant DNA by the City of Hope Medical Center ("Riggs-Itakura");
- The discovery of production methodologies and chimerization techniques for antibodies at City of Hope Medical Center and Genentech ("Cabilly");
- The discovery of methods to produce glycosylated recombinant proteins in mammalian cells at Columbia University ("Axel");
- The discovery of methods to generate functional monoclonal antibodies at Columbia and Stanford ("Morrison-Herzenberg");
- The discovery of PEGylation techniques to extend the serum half-life of protein drugs at the University of Alabama Huntsville ("Harris"); and
- The discovery of siRNA methods of gene silencing at the University of Massachusetts and the Carnegie Institution, which was awarded the Nobel Prize in Physiology and Medicine in 2006 ("Mello-Fire").

These platform technologies have enabled very large numbers of products – essentially every genetically engineered product ever approved – and have been broadly licensed non-exclusively. Despite being licensed at relatively modest royalty rates, they have resulted in enormous royalty streams because of the multiple products covered and so have been among the most valuable academic patents ever issued:

- The Cohen-Boyer patents generated over $254 million in income before their December 1997 expiration.
- In 2002 a jury awarded City of Hope $300 million in damages in addition to the substantial royalties City of Hope had already received from Genentech for Riggs-Itakura.
- Cabilly generated $250 million in 2007 alone for Genentech, the exclusive licensee of City of Hope's interest (with City of Hope receiving approximately 38% according to Genentech's 2007 10K). City of Hope has reported over $2 billion in royalty income to the AUTM Survey since 1991.
- The Axel patents are estimated to have generated $790 million before their 2000 expiration.
- Stanford describes its interest in the Morrison-Herzenberg patents as currently being its biggest royalty generator.

Nonetheless, we did not include these products in our study because the platforms did not contribute to the discovery of specific individual drugs.

Finally, we did not include nutritional products which did not require FDA approval, though even here public sector research has sometimes played a role. For instance, Caltrate was discovered by the University of Texas Southwest Medical Center, while Caltrate Colon Plus was discovered at Dartmouth.

Disease pathway based intellectual property

There have been a few attempts to combine the old paradigm with the new when academic institutions which had identified new disease pathways attempted to obtain patents on any drug which modulates the newly discovered pathway.

The first and best-known example was when the University of Rochester received US Patent 6,048,850 titled "Method of inhibiting prostaglandin synthesis in a human host". The patent was issued on April 11, 2000 with claims to all methods of inhibiting prostaglandin H synthase-2 (PGHS-2, more commonly called COX-2), and the next day Rochester sued G.D. Searle, manufacturer of the first COX-2 inhibitor, Celebrex, claiming infringement. After a herculean fight on which the university reportedly spent tens of millions of dollars, culminating in an unsuccessful appeal to the Supreme Court, the patent was invalidated for lack of enablement.

The next case started when US Patent 6,410,516 "Nuclear factors associated with transcriptional regulation" was issued on June 25, 2002 to the President and Fellows of Harvard College, Massachusetts Institute of Technology and the Whitehead Institute for Biomedical Research, claiming all methods of inhibiting expression of a gene whose transcription is regulated by NF-κB by reducing NF-κB activity in that cell. The patent was exclusively licensed to ARIAD Pharmaceuticals, who sued Eli Lilly asserting that their osteoporosis drug Evista and sepsis drug Xigris infringed the patent. ARIAD won at the District Court level and was awarded \$65.3 mm in damages,[32] but the patent was invalidated for lack of written enablement by the Court of Appeals for the Federal Circuit (CAFC)[33,34] a decision which was reaffirmed at a rehearing *en banc*.[35] In the interim, Amgen filed suit against ARIAD to invalidate the patent and certify that its blockbuster arthritis drug Enbrel, and a second arthritis treatment, Kineret, did not infringe the patent. In September 2008, a federal judge in the US District Court of Delaware granted Amgen's motion for summary judgment of non-infringement of seven claims,[36] and in June 2009, the CAFC affirmed this decision.[37]

Lest it be thought that this degree of patent over-reaching is a purely academic phenomenon, in an interesting (and some might say hypocritical twist in view of the outrage they had expressed over the Rochester case) Pfizer (who had bought G.D. Searle), did precisely the same thing. Claim 24 of US Patent 6,469,012 "Pyrazolopyrimidinones for the treatment of impotence", issued on October 22, 2002 to Pfizer, Inc. was:

> 24. A method of treating erectile dysfunction in a male human, comprising orally administering to a male human in need of such treatment an effective amount of a selective cGMP PDE.sub.v inhibitor, or a pharmaceutically acceptable salt thereof, of a pharmaceutical composition containing either entity

and claimed all methods of treating male erectile dysfunction by administering a selective cGMP PDE-5 inhibitor. Immediately upon allowance of the patent, Pfizer sued Bayer and GlaxoSmithKline for their drug Levitra and Eli Lilly and their partner ICOS Corporation for their drug Cialis. Glaxo, Bayer and Pfizer entered into an agreement on a worldwide basis to settle the patent infringement and nullity proceedings.[38,39] The Lilly lawsuit was suspended while the US Patent and Trademark Office (USPTO) reexamined Pfizer's method-of-use claim and invalidated it on the basis that certain prior art rendered the claimed invention not new, and therefore unpatentable under 35 USC §102(b), and obvious and unpatentable under the doctrine of obviousness-type double patenting. The Board of Appeals and Interferences declared the patent invalid in February 2010.[40]

That said, it is possible to license drug discovery pathways on a collaborative basis, including know-how as well as patents. For example the erectile dysfunction drug Cialis discussed above was developed from a class of PDE molecules discovered using a yeast screen containing human genes invented and patented by Cold Spring Harbor Laboratory and licensed to ICOS at its formation in 1990. Cold Spring Harbor suggested the class of molecules to ICOS which then isolated the actual active compound, tadalafil, and confirmed its potential for treating erectile dysfunction. Cold Spring Harbor received 125,000 shares of ICOS stock, which was worth a considerable amount when ICOS' stock soared after its 1991 Initial Public Offering (IPO), but Cold Spring Harbor does not receive royalties on sales of Cialis since its patents do not cover the product tadalafil itself[41]. Cialis is therefore included in our study. Lilly bought ICOS for \$2.6 billion in 2006.

Methodology

This study uses the same dataset that was used in the NEJM article referenced in the Abstract. This section provides a fuller account of the methodology used to create the dataset than the word limits of the NEJM allowed.

There has been no systematic collection of outcomes of individual transfers of technologies invented by public sector researchers. Since 1991, the Association of University Technology Managers (AUTM) has conducted an Annual Licensing Survey[42] which provides aggregate statistics on the outcomes of academic institutions' technology transfer activities, but the specific technologies, their licensees and the success or failure of the licensees' development efforts are not identified.

Issued US patents have always been a matter of public record once they are issued and, since November 2001, US patent applications have been published 18 months after filing[29],[43] and are therefore also a matter of public record. Universities receive substantial numbers of patents, but again, patents contain no indication of whether a product covered by that patent ultimately reached the market.

Frequently, public sector technologies are licensed to small, privately owned companies that have no obligation of public disclosure of their financial status, business plans or partnerships. Nonetheless, such companies frequently make voluntary, though generally limited, disclosures about their activities. However, if the company files for an IPO, which is highly likely if the company is successful in developing a drug and partnering it with a large company, it will be required to make substantial disclosures to the Securities and Exchange Commission (SEC) about its business activities, including the technologies it has licensed and the financial terms of those licenses. These disclosures provide one area of systematic investigation.

Recombinant Capital,[44] a consulting company which was first bought by Deloitte and is now owned by Thomson Reuters, has systematically collected license agreements filed by biotechnology companies with the SEC since the earliest days of the biotechnology industry. Their databases, ReCap.com and rDNA.com, contain details of both the companies' in-licensing of technologies from universities, as well as their out-licensing of the same projects to larger companies after they have been advanced towards market entry. A search of this database with the keyword "university" yields over 1,000 hits. Again, however, this database contains no indication as to whether the technology was ultimately successful and resulted in a marketed product.

We therefore created a comprehensive database of successful drug discovery and development projects that owe their origin, at least in part, to inventions resulting from research carried out in the public sector.

Companies, whether large or small, are rarely motivated to publicly acknowledge that their key intellectual property was obtained from others. Rather, they prefer to promote their in-house technical capabilities and prowess to their investors. The first (and most difficult) step in our research was therefore to identify which drugs resulted from public sector research. We obtained this information from a diverse array of sources, as follows.

- The FDA's Orange Book contains details of certain of the patents protecting drugs that have received approval under New Drug Applications (NDAs) but not Biologics License Applications (BLAs). The Orange Book only lists patents still in effect, and only lists composition of matter, method of treating and formulation patents.
- A newer database created by Recombinant Capital, ReCap IP, contains the information from the Orange Book and links the patents listed in the Orange Book with information from the USPTO database, such as the assignee of the patents. One or more of the patents being assigned to a PSRI is *prima facie* evidence that there is a license to technology owned by that institution.[*]
- A number of AUTM sources were useful:

  - In 1994 and 1996, AUTM conducted Public Benefits Surveys[45] which identified a number of products that had reached the market based on licenses from universities, including a number of drugs.
  - Since 1997, the AUTM Annual Licensing Survey has included a series of Vignettes of individual transactions that have been self-reported by the institution. Some of these described successful drug discovery projects.
  - In 2005 AUTM started a systematic (but still voluntary) collection of success stories. These have been compiled in a database[46] currently containing 1,620 entries which are the bases for AUTM's "Better World Report" publications in 2006, 2007, 2008 and 2009. The biotechnology, health sciences and pharmaceuticals sections contain almost 140 stories and those that pertained to a marketed drug were added to our database.
  - As discussed earlier, the AUTM Annual Licensing Survey collects detailed statistics on various measures of technology transfer activity and performance at the level of individual institutions but does not identify specific transactions and outcomes. However, one of the metrics reported to the Survey is royalty income, and those institutions that have substantial royalty income frequently owe this to a marketed drug. We identified institutions with high royalty income and attempted to identify which owed their high income to marketed drugs, by browsing the institution's website, carrying out Google searches, etc.
  - The University of Virginia Patent Foundation has assembled a substantial number of success stories of academic licensing, and published them on its website.[47] Those that pertain to drug discovery were included in our study.
  - The NIH has identified and documented the drugs and vaccines that have resulted from licensing of inventions made in its intramural research program, that is, research conducted in Government laboratories at the NIH.[48]
  - The NIH's iEdison invention reporting system has a page listing a number of drugs discovered with funding from the NIH's extramural research program.[49]

---

*   ReCap IP is no longer available.

- A number of academic drug discoveries have led to litigation that revealed the role of the academic institution in the discovery of the drug. Publicly available information, such as the Complaints, Opinions, news stories and so forth, contain useful information.
- Academic institutions with substantial royalty incomes sometimes monetize the royalty stream by selling the right to receive the royalties to a third party. Sometimes the inventors sell their portion of the royalty stream independently of the academic institution. The specialized financial firms[50] that organize these transactions frequently make public announcements of the completion of these transactions and these revealed some public sector ownerships of which we were not previously aware.
- Finally, serendipity played a part – e.g., a front page story in the *Wall Street Journal*[51] about the roles of Duke and Genzyme in the development of Myozyme to treat Pombe disease resulted in Myozyme being added to the database; preparing a *Harvard Business School* case study on AngioMax and The Medicines Company[52] for a course on the management of innovation identified that AngioMax was the result of a collaboration between Biogen and the Wadsworth Center of the New York State Department of Health.

As a quality control measure, in the middle of May 2009, we emailed the list of products and discovering institutions that we had discovered as of that date to the list of technology transfer office (TTO) directors maintained by AUTM and asked for omissions and corrections. This step resulted in nine new products being brought to our attention.

The second step in our research was to determine the patents protecting each product. Our primary source of data here was the USPTO database.[53] Some of these patents were identified in the normal course of identifying that a particular drug should be included in our database. In order to gather as comprehensive a list of the underlying patents as possible, we searched FDA drug labels,[54] ReCapIP, and conducted internet searches, which would yield hits such as FDA patent term extension dockets or marketing websites dedicated to a particular drug. We further browsed the Federal Register for FDA patent term extension notices.[55] The browse products capability of ReCapIP was especially helpful because the primary view contains all underlying patents in the ReCapIP system, along with the corresponding assignee, without the user having to drill down further for that information. This allowed us to search through all of the products in the ReCapIP database methodically and efficiently to identify related public sector patents. Although the initial objective of this search was to identify patents protecting drugs already in our database, it yielded about 15 further drugs for inclusion in our study. The study by Sampat[56] using older versions of the Orange Book identified an additional nine drugs where the public sector patents had expired and these have been included.

The third step in our research was to determine as much as possible about how each drug was developed. The rDNA database allowed us to trace the various corporate transactions that drugs passed through on their way from discovery to market as they were licensed, acquired and divested from one company to another.

The fourth step in our research was to obtain information on the drug's approval process from the FDA's drug and biologic approval databases.

Using data from these primary sources, together with Internet searching, which frequently found articles that told the story of how the transition from bench-to-bedside had been brought about, we attempted to identify for each product:

- The Principal Investigator(s)/Lead Inventor(s) and his/her institution(s);
- The funding sources and dates of any federal grants;[57]
- The date of the earliest patent application cited in the issued patents;
- The date of issuance of the first patent covering the drug;
- The identity of the initial licensee and the date and terms of the license;
- The date, nature and value of any transactions by the initial licensee and subsequent sublicensees or assignees during the course of bringing the product to market, subdivided into those occurring before and those occurring after FDA approval;
- The dates of FDA approval of all the NDAs and BLAs incorporating that active ingredient;
- For drugs receiving NDA approval, the FDA chemical classification, whether the product received standard or priority review and whether it received orphan drug designation; and
- US sales of the product.

The cutoff date for our data collection was September 1, 2009 for drugs to have received FDA approval.

Results

Summary of the results in the prior article

The following are the findings that were published in the article in the *New England Journal of Medicine* referenced in the abstract earlier.

- 153[58] FDA approved drugs were discovered in whole or in part at US public sector institutions[59], including:
  - 102 NMEs (including eight *in vivo* diagnostics and one OTC product);
  - 36 biologic drugs; and
  - 15 vaccines.
- The NMEs approved from 1990–2007 represented:
  - 9.3% of all NDAs in this time period; and
  - 21.1% of NMEs receiving Priority Review.
- The 153 drugs fell in 16 therapeutic categories; Oncology and Infectious diseases were 50% of the total.

- The 153 drugs were discovered or co-discovered by 75 PSRIs including:
  - 22 by the NIH;
  - 11 by the University of California System;
  - 8 by Memorial Sloan-Kettering Cancer Center;
  - 7 by Emory University;
  - 6 by Yale University.

The identities of the 153 products are contained in Table 1 in the Supplementary Appendix to the NEJM article.

The translational process

In the balance of this chapter, we focus on the process by which the discovery made in the course of PSRI research was translated to the marketplace.

Initial developing company

We classified companies that were the initial licensee for the products into the three categories used by AUTM in its Annual Licensing Survey:

- Large company – a company with more than 500 employees
- Small company – a company with fewer than 500 employees
- Spin-out – a company formed specifically to develop the technology, a special case of a small company.

The distribution of licensees between these three categories is shown in Table 6.2. We classified the company according to its status *when the license was executed*. For instance, today Amgen is clearly a large company, with over 20,000 employees worldwide. However, when Amgen licensed Neupogen from Memorial-Sloan Kettering in 1986, it was a small company and is so classified in our study. Neupogen was one of the two products that propelled Amgen's growth.[60]

Some 92 different companies initially received licenses to the PSRI discoveries. Small companies (including the category of spin-out companies which were specifically founded to develop the drug) constituted 57.5% of the companies which initiated development of the drug.[61] The percentage of licenses with large companies we found, 42.5%, is a little higher than that typically reported in the

Table 6.2 Types of companies that initiated development of PSRI invented drugs

Type of entity	Number	%
Large entity	65	42.5%
Small entity	65	42.5%
Start-up	23	15.0%
Total	153	

AUTM Annual Survey, where the percentage of licenses with large companies was 35.1% in 2008. Since the AUTM Survey includes all types of technologies, it is possible that the difference is the result of life sciences inventions being more likely to be licensed by large companies due to the high costs and commercial demands to bring such products to market.

Marketing company

When the licensee is a large company, they generally have the resources to take the product to market. Our study confirmed that this is generally the case, though in a few instances an initial large company licensee gave the technology back to the university and it was relicensed to a spin-out which successfully developed it. For instance, the antibody that became Imclone's Erbitux was initially licensed by the University of California to Eli Lilly who subsequently terminated the license and returned it to the University of California, who relicensed it to Imclone. With mid-stage clinical data, Emory licensed emtricitabine to Gilead reportedly for a 14% royalty rate. Emory subsequently sold its royalty rights to Royalty Pharma and Gilead for $525 million. Glaxo initially licensed emtricitabine from Emory University, but terminated the license when the drug was in Phase 2 trials and returned it to Emory.

When the licensee is a small company or a spin-out company, the licensor generally expects that the small company will not have the resources to take the product to market and will need to find a partner at some point along the way.

Our study in general confirmed this model. Fifty-six different companies are currently marketing the 153 products, and their distribution is radically different from that of the initial licensees who commenced development of the drugs. Marketing rights to the majority of the drugs are now held by large pharmaceutical companies, as shown in Table 6.3. Glaxo sells the most drugs that originated in public sector research, 12, reflecting their strong presence in both vaccines and HIV, followed by Johnson & Johnson (J&J) with nine and Merck, Pfizer and Bristol-Myers Squibb with eight each. However, it is noteworthy that 32 of the products are marketed by 17 biotechnology companies founded relatively recently. These companies either developed the product themselves or acquired rights to them from a third party and have thereby evolved to become fully integrated biopharmaceutical companies (FIBCOs). Indeed, a higher number of the 153 products were being marketed by biotechnology companies until the most recent round of consolidation and acquisition of biotechnology companies by major pharmaceutical companies (e.g., AstraZeneca's acquisition of MedImmune, Lilly's acquisition of Imclone, Takeda's acquisition of Millennium, and so forth).

The transactions subsequent to the initial license by which these drugs migrated to the current marketers are discussed in more detail in the section on pages 000–000.

Table 6.3 Companies currently marketing PSRI invented drugs

Current marketer	Number	Current marketer	Number
GlaxoSmithKline	12	Lantheus Medical Imaging	2
J&J	9	Merck Serono	2
Bristol-Myers Squibb	8	Mission Pharmacal	2
Merck	8	Otsuka Pharmaceuticals	2
Pfizer	8	AGALinde	1
Eli Lilly	6	Alexion	1
Genzyme	6	Bausch and Lomb	1
Novartis	6	Bioniche Pharma	1
AstraZeneca	5	DuraMed	1
Wyeth	5	Enzon Pharmaceuticals	1
Amgen	4	Ferring A/S	1
Bayer Healthcare	4	Fontus Pharmaceuticals	1
Eisai	4	Forest Pharmaceutical	1
Roche	3	Genentech	1
Abbott	3	Genta	1
Baxter Healthcare	3	Ipsen	1
BiogenIdec	3	J&J Merck Consumer Pharm.	1
Gilead Pharmaceuticals	3	Mallinckrodt	1
Schering-Plough	3	Mylan Bertek Pharmaceuticals	1
Allergan	2	NitroMed	1
Astellas Pharma Inc.	2	Sanofi Aventis	1
BioVitrium	2	Santarus	1
Celgene	2	Shionogi	1
Cephalon	2	Shire	1
CSL Behring	2	Specialty European Pharma	1
Galderma SA	2	Takeda	1
General Electric	2	The Medicines Company	1
King Pharmaceuticals	2	Watson Laboratories	1

Development timeline

By making certain assumptions we were able to identify the timing and duration of the various phases of the development pathway of these drugs.

INITIATION OF THE DISCOVERY PROCESS

Patents that resulted from a federal grant are required to disclose the Government's rights in the patent application. We were able to identify 84 of the discovery projects in our study as having been federally funded. Of these, 19 arose from the

NIH intramural program alone (and thus did not involve grants) and 65 acknowledged funding by federal agencies, normally from the Department of Human and Health Services (DHHS) and most frequently from the NIH, the primary research funding agency of DHHS. Four of these involved joint funding with the Veterans Administration and one each was funded by the Department of Energy and the Office of Naval Research. Three were funded by both the intramural and extramural programs.

Of the extramurally funded products, 46 provided grant numbers in the patent. One patent only noted funding by the Veterans Administration. From the Computer Retrieval of Information on Scientific Projects (CRISP)[62] database, we were able to identify the date when the grant started for 23 of the products.[63] If the patent acknowledged multiple grants, we used the earliest start date of a grant naming one of the inventors of the patent as Principle Investigator (PI). When a grant number on the face of a patent did not correspond to any grant in the database, we attempted to reconstruct an actual grant number based on inventor/PI funding information. We were unable to obtain accurate grant information for 15 patents that noted NIH or HHS grant funding, possibly reflecting errors in the reported grant numbers.

We used the start date of the grant that led to the discovery of the drug as a proxy for the initiation of the discovery process.

PRODUCT DISCOVERY

Issued patents frequently claim priority to earlier patent applications, some of which may have matured into issued patents, while others may have been abandoned in favor of the later application as part of the prosecution strategy. In some cases, this results in a protracted prosecution history. The average prosecution time was 5.0 years, with a standard deviation of ±3.5 years. The longest prosecution history we found was 19.2 years and the shortest was 0.7 years.

We used the date of the earliest patent application from which the issued patent claims priority as a proxy for the date when the invention was made. We were able to identify a date of discovery for 148 of the products. As noted above, a few of the products are based on licensed biological materials for which we could not determine an invention date using our methodology.

In Figure 6.1[64] we plot the distribution of the discovery year of the products.[65] It is apparent that the number of products discovered each year appears to have taken a significant step up, from an average of roughly one every two years through the 1960s and 1970s to six in 1980. The rate continued to climb through the 1990s.

The decline since 1992–93 should not be interpreted as indicating a decline in public sector research productivity, but rather, as we show below, reflecting the long development timelines of public sector discovered drugs. Many of the drugs discovered since this peak are still making their way through the development pipeline.

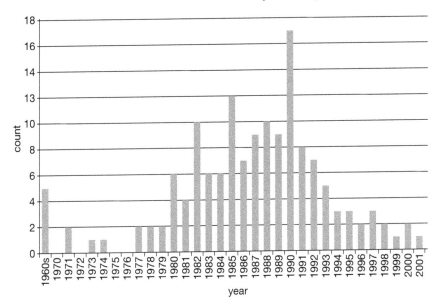

Figure 6.1 Number of PSRI discovered drugs by year

PRODUCT DEVELOPMENT

Academic institutions are rarely able to secure funding for drug development nor are they equipped with the infrastructure to take their drug discoveries very far down the development pathway. Thus, they must seek commercial licensees to develop their discoveries. We used the date of the initial license as a proxy for when preclinical and clinical development of the drug started.

When the initial licensee was a small entity the transaction was generally considered a material transaction and hence was required to be disclosed to the Securities and Exchange Commission (SEC) when the company filed to become publicly traded. In these cases we were therefore able to identify the date when the initial license was issued from Recombinant Capital's rDNA database. If the initial licensee was a large entity, the transaction was generally not considered to be a material transaction and hence was frequently not publicly disclosed or even announced. In these cases we asked the individual TTOs for the date of the transaction, and in many cases they were willing to supply this information.

If we were only able to determine the year of a transaction, we assigned it a date of July 1 of that year.

Some of the products were the result of research collaborations and we used the date of the initiation of the collaboration as the date of the license since companies are rarely if ever prepared to sponsor research at an academic institution without an agreement providing them an exclusive option to an exclusive license to any resulting intellectual property. However, the license terms are generally negotiated at the time of exercise of the option.

We were able to determine the date of the start of development for all 153 products.

ADDITIONAL TRANSACTIONS

Using the rDNA database, we were able to identify 191 additional transactions involving the technology. As shown in Table 6.4 and presented graphically in Figure 6.2, 44 of the 153 products in our database involved only one step in the development pathway while the remaining 109 products involved at least one additional transaction. Overall, around a third of the development pathways involved only one step, a third involved two steps and the remaining third involved more than two steps.

Table 6.4 Numbers of transactions in the development pathways of PSRI invented drugs

Steps in pathway	Number of products
1	44
2	53
3	37
4	14
5	3
6	2
	153

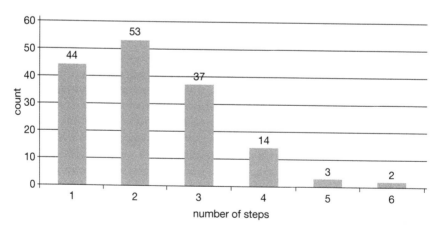

Figure 6.2 Numbers of transactions in the development pathways of PSRI invented drugs

We classified these additional transactions as to whether they occurred before or after FDA approval of the drug. The results are shown in Table 6.5. There are more additional transactions *after* FDA approval than before FDA approval.

Table 6.5 Number and timing of additional steps in the development pathways of PSRI invented drug pre- and post-FDA approval

Initial license	153	
Transactions pre-FDA approval	88	
Of which:		
Transaction 2		68
Transaction 3		14
Transaction 4		5
Transaction 5		1
Transactions post-FDA approval	103	
Of which:		
Transaction 1		75
Transaction 2		25
Transaction 3		3

PRODUCT APPROVAL

The date of product approval was obtained from the FDA CDER and CBER websites. We were able to identify the date of FDA approval for all 153 products in our database. Some drugs received multiple approvals (e.g., for additional indications, formulations or combinations). Two NMEs each received five NDAs.

We identified all the NDAs and BLAs approved for the molecular entities in our study. If a combination therapy contained two compounds which were both discovered in public sector institutions (e.g., Glaxo's Epzicom, a combination of Epivir, discovered by Emory University and Ziagen, discovered by the University of Minnesota) we only counted the NDA once.

Of the 108 compounds approved under NDAs in this time period, 32 had more than one NDA approved.

These 108 compounds had a total of 158 NDAs approved. The highest number of NDAs for a single active compound was five, for voriconazole, the active ingredient in Pfizer's Vfend.

Only one molecular entity had more than one approved BLA – filgrastatim, the active ingredient in Neupogen, where a PEGylated version with a substantially longer serum half life was approved as Neulasta.

The distribution of the number of NDAs and BLAs per molecular entity is shown in Figure 6.3. In Figure 6.4, we plot the number of drugs receiving their first NDA or BLA each year. In Figure 6.5 we plot the date of approvals of all NDAs and BLAs each year.

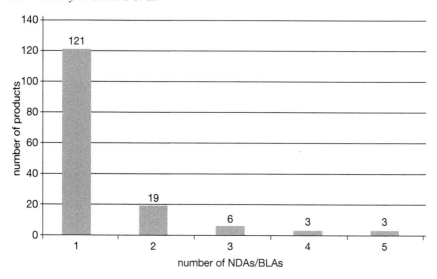

Figure 6.3 Number of BLAs/NDAs received per product for PSRI invented drugs

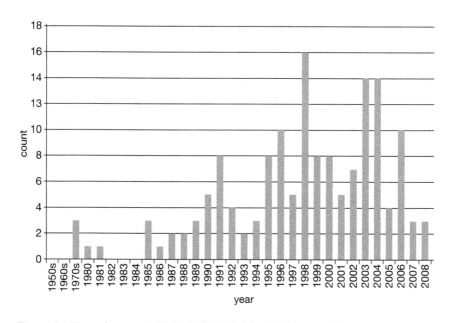

Figure 6.4 Year of approval of initial BLA/NDA for PSRI invented drugs

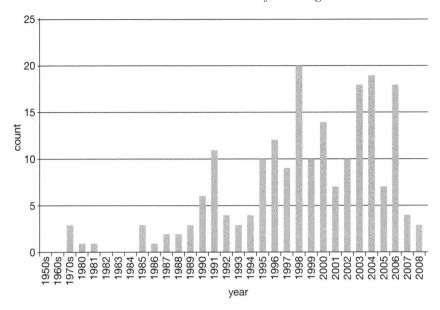

Figure 6.5 Year of approval of all BLAs/NDAs for PSRI invented drugs

RESULTS

The results of our investigations into the duration of the different phases are shown in Table 6.6 below.

The timelines are highly variable in length and reflect the highly diverse nature of the relationships we identified:

- Collaborative research projects that resulted in discovery of the product;
- Independent academic research that resulted in the discovery which was subsequently licensed to the corporate partner;
- Arrangements to avoid or preempt negative consequences of interference proceedings; and
- Situations where litigation resulted in an infringement judgment against the developing company and hence acceptance by the developing company of the validity of the PSRI's patent.

Table 6.6 Overall timelines of phases of product discovery and development of PSRI invented drugs

Phase	N	Mean	Median	Maximum	Minimum	Std. Dev
Start of research to discovery	22	5.57	4.22	16.70	0.75	3.75
Discovery to initial license	148	3.27	2.13	24.12	(9.09)	4.91
Initial license to FDA approval	153	8.10	8.24	23.00	(13.22)	5.39
Discovery to FDA approval	148	11.46	10.98	26.99	1.27	4.94

In the first of these situations, the date of the license will precede the date of discovery, while in the last, the date of the license will generally be subsequent to the date of FDA approval.

We show the distribution of the time from discovery through to FDA approval in Figure 6.6. The average time from discovery of the drug to FDA approval was 11.5±4.9 years of which the average time between the discovery and the initial license that initiated the development process was 3.3±4.9 years, while after the license was in place, the average time to FDA approval was 8.1±5.4 years. Based on a somewhat smaller number of data points, the discovery phase lasted an average of 5.6±3.8 years.

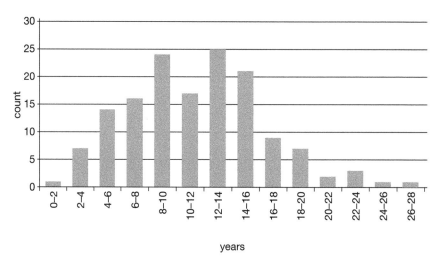

Figure 6.6 Distribution of timelines from invention to initial FDA approval for PSRI invented drugs

Development pathway

There have generally been thought to be two pathways for commercializing academic technologies:

- A one step pathway when the initial licensee is a large company which develops the technology and takes it to market itself:

  Academic Institution ➔ Large Co ➔ Market

- A two step process when the initial licensee is a spin-out or other small company, which carries out the early stage, high risk research to prove the viability of the technology and which subsequently partners with a large company for access to funding for the late stage, higher cost phases of development, manufacturing, global distribution and so forth, i.e.:

Academic Institution ➔ Small Co ➔ Large Co ➔ Market

However, one of the most surprising findings of our study was that both of these pathways are vast over-simplifications and Table 6.7 shows how the number of steps in the development pathway varies between the three categories of initial licensee.

As would be expected, where the initial licensee is a large company, a majority of the companies take the product to market themselves and there are no further transactions. However, in almost 40% of the cases, there are additional transactions. The additional transactions included:

- Termination of the initial large company partnership and replacement with a new partnership;
- Co-promotion agreements;
- Assignment of the license;
- Acquisition of the developing company;
- Acquisition of the product; and
- Monetizations of royalty streams.

In the cases where the initial licensee is a small company, the situation is reversed, with additional transactions in 94% of the cases. While 48% of the cases were the "classical" two step pathway, 44% had more than two steps. Notably, however, for five products (6% of the total), there were no further transactions and the small company is currently marketing the product itself. Our data clearly show therefore that the two step development pathway is a considerable over-simplification, with a consistent pattern of additional transactions, both before and after FDA approval of the product.

Products where the initial licensee was a spin-out company are skewed even more heavily towards a larger number of steps in the development pathway. In only one, or 3.5%, of the cases is the spin-out company marketing the product themselves while 35% of the cases involve a two step pathway and 60.5% of the cases involve three or more steps.

Table 6.7 Numbers of steps in development pathway of PSRI invented drugs by different types of initial licensee

Initial licensee	*Number of steps*						
	1	*2*	*3*	*4*	*5*	*6*	*Total*
Large entity	39	14	10	1	1	0	65
Small entity	4	31	18	10	1	1	65
Start-up	1	8	9	3	1	1	23
	44	53	37	14	3	2	153

One of the most complex pathways we identified is that for Macugen, a drug for the treatment of acute macular degeneration, which was discovered at the University of Colorado and involved seven transaction steps. The complete timeline of Macugen's development is as follows:

- The initial patent was filed by the University of Colorado in June 1990;
- The patent application was licensed by the University of Colorado to NeXstar in June 1991 for $1 million in stock and sponsored research funding;
- NeXstar was acquired by Gilead in 1999 for $550 million in stock;
- Gilead sublicensed rights to NX1838 to Eyetech, a new company, in 2000 for $7 million upfront and $25 million in milestone payments;
- Eyetech and Pfizer entered a Co-promotion agreement in 2002 for $75 million upfront, $25 million in equity purchase, $195 million in approval milestones and $450 million in post-approval milestones;
- The FDA approved Macugen in December 2004;
- The University of Colorado monetized part of its royalty interest in Macugen in January 2005 for an estimated $45 million;
- Eyetech was acquired by OSI Pharmaceuticals in June 2005 for $935 million in stock and cash;
- In August 2008, OSI divested its eye care business, primarily Macugen, to a new company, Eyetech, which primarily consisted of the Macugen salesforce, in exchange for potential future milestone and royalty payments.

There were six steps in the commercialization pathway of Rotarix, including three royalty monetizations, two by Children's Medical Center, Cincinnati, and one by Avant Therapeutics, the company formed by the merger of the initial licensee, Virus Research Institute, with T Cell Sciences.

Economic impact

Public sector discovered drugs have an economic impact at several levels:

- On the discovering institutions;
- On the developing companies; and
- On the marketing companies.

Economic impact on the discovering institutions

When a university licenses a drug to a company, the terms normally include a series of payments to the university. There will generally be an upfront fee, annual minimum royalty payments, milestone payments as the drug reaches key stages in its development and finally royalties on sales.

A recent study[66] collected and analyzed data on 155 transactions completed between 2005 and 2007 on drugs at all stages of development when the licenses were completed. 35% of the deals were from academic institutions. The study analyzed the deals by stage of development:

1 Preclinical;
2 IND filed through Phase II enrolled;
3 Phase II completed through Phase III enrolled;
4 Phase III completed through NDA submitted;
5 Marketed.

The study did not analyze the deals by type of licensor. Public sector discovered drugs will fall in group 1, but this group will also include deals by biotechnology companies who have advanced the drug further in development than a university typically will have been able to do, which will probably allow them to command a higher royalty rate.

For this group, the study found that, for deals with fixed royalty rates, the royalty rate averaged 4.2%, while those with tiered royalty rates had royalty rates that averaged from 4.5% on sales of less than $50 million to 7.5% on sales of $1 billion and more.

A 5% royalty on a drug with sales of $100 million would yield annual royalties of $5 million to the licensor, while a 7.5% royalty on sales of $1 billion would yield annual royalty payments of $75 million to the licensor.

The AUTM Annual Licensing Activity Survey (ALAS) shows that total royalty receipts by academic institutions have grown strongly since 1991, from $170 million to $3.4 billion in 2008. Royalties from marketed drugs have been substantial contributors to this increase in royalty income.

Most institutions have multiple licenses generating royalty income, so it is, in general, not possible to identify the income generated by each drug. However, over the past decade or so, institutions receiving royalties on drugs that have received FDA approval have started monetizing those royalty streams by selling the royalty obligations, sometimes back to the licensee or, more commonly, to partnerships which specialize in acquiring royalty streams and it is possible to identify the value of these monetizations. Table 6.8 identifies 35 royalty sales by academic institutions with a total value of $4.1 billion completed since 1990, with the pace appearing to have increased since 1999. We have included all monetizations that we have identified of drugs approved prior to our data collection cut-off of August 31, 2009, even if the monetization occurred subsequent to this date.[67]

Economic impact on the developing company

The multi-step development pathways identified in in the section on pages 000–000 were the result of a large number of transactions. We were able to track the reported value of many of these transactions in ReCap.[68] A certain amount of judgment was necessary in this exercise. For instance, in April 2007, AstraZeneca acquired MedImmune for $15.7 billion. The majority of MedImmune's drugs

Table 6.8 Sales of royalty streams from PSRI invented drugs by academic institutions and/
or the inventors

Date	Product	Licensor	Amount ($mm)	
6/1/90	Neupogen	Amgen	$75	
1/1/97	Synagis	Henry M. Jackson Foundation, Inventors	n/a	
1/1/98	TOBI	Seattle Children's Hospital	$12	
1/1/98	Thalomid	Children's Hospital	$5	
1/1/98	Taxol	Robert Holton (Florida State U.)	$32	*
1/1/98	Remicade	Jan Vilcek (NYU)	$66	
1/1/98	Enbrel (Foreign)	Hospital, Inventors	n/a	
12/1/99	Zerit	Yale University[1]	$125	
1/1/01	Clarinex	Inventor	n/a	
1/1/03	FluMist	University of Michigan	$10	**
1/1/03	AdVate	University of Connecticut	n/a	
9/1/03	Aldurazyme	LA Biomed[2]	$25	
1/22/04	Neupogen/Neulasta (US)	Memorial-Sloan Kettering[3]	$263	
1/1/05	Macugen	University of Colorado[4]	$45	
6/28/05	Tysabri	Fred Hutchinson Institute	n/a	
7/1/05	Emtriva	Emory University[7]	$525	
8/1/05	Remicade	NYU/Dr. Vilcek	$46	**
8/1/05	Neupogen/neulasta (Non-US)	Memorial-Sloan Kettering[8]	$142	
10/26/05	Humira	Scripps Research Institute[9]	$34	*
11/1/05	Rotarix	Children's Hospital Cincinnati Inventors	n/a	**
12/14/05	Rotateq	Wistar Institute[6]	$45	*
6/6/06	Embrel (US)	MGH[10]	$248	
4/1/07	Revlimid	Children's Hospital Boston	$131	
4/19/07	Enbrel (Foreign)	MGH[11]	$284	
5/1/07	Remicade	New York University[12]	$650	
7/1/07	FluMist	U. of Michigan[13]	$25	
12/1/07	Rotarix	Cincinnati Children's Hosp.[15]	$24	
12/18/07	Lyrica	Northwestern[14]	$700	
1/1/08	Relistor	U of Chicago Inventors	$8	
4/23/08	RotaTeq	Children's Hosp. of Phil.[16]	$182	
9/1/09	Myozyme/Lumizyme	YT Chen (Duke inventors)	$30	
2/1/11	Somavert	Ohio University	$52	
1/1/12	Myozyme/Lumizyme	Duke	$90	
3/12/12	Botox	U. of Colorado [18]	$30	
1/5/13	Lyrica	Northwestern Inventor	$148	**
	Total		$4,051	

*	Estimate
**	Sale by inventor

were discovered at PSRIs, so we attributed this transaction to the PSRI drugs and included the transaction in our analysis. By contrast, in March 2001, Johnson & Johnson acquired ALZA Corporation for $10.5 billion. Very little of ALZA's sales were from PSRI discovered drugs, so this transaction is not included in our study. We also did not include in the calculations the various major pharmaceutical company-pharmaceutical company mergers over the past decade – e.g., Pfizer's mergers with Pharmacia & Upjohn, Warner-Lambert, Wyeth-Ayerst, etc., though many of these companies were selling one or more PSRI discovered drugs.

We were able to identify the valuation of 23 of the 153 initial licenses and 144 of the 191 additional transactions. Over $143 billion was realized in the 144 transactions which followed the initial license transaction as shown in Table 6.9.

The average value per transaction is presented graphically in Figure 6.7.

In instances where there are a substantial number of transactions to provide meaningful data, the data show a steady increase in the value of technologies as they move from the initial license from academia into development and receive FDA approval.

The highest step up in valuation is with the first transaction after the initial academic license, where the mean value was 44 times higher than the initial academic license. Relatively few academic license valuations are in the database and they all have low valuations, reflecting the early stage nature of most academic technologies. It is extremely difficult to obtain federal funding for lead optimization, pre-clinical studies and toxicology, let alone clinical testing, so academic licenses are typically done at a very early stage. By contrast, the initial developer will generally develop the technologies to a significant value-added milestone before seeking a large company partner, so subsequent transactions are concluded at much higher valuations.

After the second transaction, valuations increase approximately two and a half-fold between each transaction for technologies with a substantial number of

Table 6.9 Number and value of transactions in development pathways of PSRI invented drugs

Transaction	Number	Value*	Avg. value / transaction*
Initial License	23	$99.0	$4
Transaction 2 Pre-FDA App.	51	$9,634.7	$189
Transaction 3 Pre-FDA App.	11	$5,522.0	$502
Transaction 4 Pre-FDA App.	5	$1,194.0	$239
Transaction 5 Pre-FDA App.	1	$24.0	$24
Transaction 1 Post FDA App.	54	$70,308.4	$1,302
Transaction 2 Post FDA App.	20	$56,002.2	$2,800
Transaction 3 Post FDA App.	2	$443.0	$222
Total	167	$143,227.3	

* Dollars are in millions

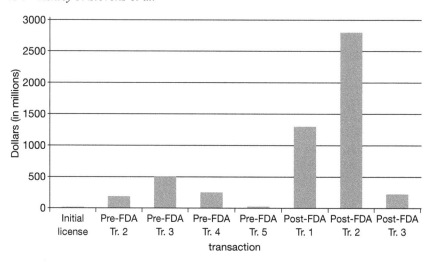

Figure 6.7 Average value of each transaction in development pathways of PSRI invented
drugs

transactions – the third transaction pre-FDA approval and the first and second
transaction post-FDA approval. There are relatively few technologies which had
four or five transactions before FDA approval or three transactions after FDA
approval, and in these cases, valuations stepped down. These transactions may be
indicative of the technology being "distressed" by the time of these late stage
transactions.

Probably the greatest economic impact of the commercialization of public
sector research is the market value of the successful companies that have resulted
from having commercialized a public sector discovered drug. For instance,
Amgen currently has a market capitalization of around $50 billion. Amgen is
currently selling 4 drugs that resulted from public sector research (Enbrel,
Neulasta, Neupogen and Sensipar), recently sold two others (Kepivance and
Kineret) to BioVitrum in a $130 million transaction and, as noted above, sells two
other major drugs, Epogen and Aranesp, which resulted from research carried out
but not patented at the University of Chicago. Virtually all of Amgen's market
capitalization can therefore be attributed to the results of public sector research.
However, creation of this market capitalization required an enormous private
sector investment to achieve. Analysis of the private sector investment needed to
translate these public sector investments into marketed products is beyond the
scope of this study.

Economic impact on the marketing company

The 2008 sales data for these drugs was kindly provided by IMS Health. The
search was carried out by generic name and then by brand name. Branded generic
sales were normally reported individually and all other generics as a single figure.

For Topamax, Gleevec and Botox, where only selected indications were invented in the course of public sector research, the sales for the relevant indications were obtained from IMS Health, Inc.'s National Sales Perspectives™ and National Disease Therapeutic Index™. For all other products, the data was obtained from IMS Health, Inc.'s National Sales Perspectives™.

Patent expiration had occurred for a number of the products and generic versions were available. Sales of generics were examined on a case-by-case basis to determine whether the generic formulations targeted the same indications as the brand version that originated in public sector research. For instance, Sarafem is a brand of fluoxetine hydrochloride approved for treatment of premenstrual dysphoric disorder (PMDD), a use discovered and patented by MIT. However, fluoxetine hydrochloride is better known as Prozac and we assumed that the majority of sales of generic fluoxetine hydrochloride are for treatment of depression, not PMDD, so only sales of Sarafem itself and of a branded generic called Selfemra specifically targeted to the PMDD market are included in the total.

The distribution outlets covered include Retail (Chains/Mass Merchandisers, Food Stores, Independents) Clinics, Mail Service, Non-Federal Hospitals, Long Term Care, Home Health Care, Federal Facilities, HMO, Misc-Prisons, Misc-Other, and Misc Universities but does not include sales from Long Term Facilities.

Eight products in this study were only identified after the data request was submitted to IMS Health. We were able to determine 2008 sales of all but one of these from company reports and we added these to the IMS data.

Certain drugs are sold to physicians who administer them in their office and are not captured by IMS's methodology. This is particularly true of Genzyme's enzyme replacement products Aldozyme and Myozyme. The sales reported in Genzyme's annual report were significantly higher than those reported by IMS and we included these figures in our analysis.

Total US sales of PSRI discovered drugs in 2008 were $39.9 billion. IMS reports on its website[69] that total US pharmaceutical sales were $291.5 billion in 2008, so PSRI discovered drugs accounted for 13.7% of the total.

IMS also reports that the global pharmaceutical market was $773.0 billion in 2008, so that the US market accounts for 37.7% of the global market. Assuming that US sales of PSRI discovered drugs are also 37.7% of the drugs' global sales, we estimate worldwide sales of the public sector discovered drugs to be $102.7 billion.

Twenty-one of the products had no sales in 2008 or had been withdrawn from the market.

The FDA conferred orphan drug status on 36 of the 102 NME products in our study, meaning that they treated a patient population of fewer than 200,000 patients. Three of the biologics also received orphan designation.

Twenty-eight of the products achieved blockbuster status with sales of over $1 billion worldwide while 12 of these had sales of over $1 billion in just the US. The three top selling drugs – Enbrel, Neulasta and Remicade – each had estimated worldwide sales of around $8 billion.

Comparison with other countries

We have initiated a comparable study of the contribution of PSRIs outside the US to the discovery of marketed drugs. We have so far identified 38 drugs discovered in nine countries. The drugs are shown in Table 6.10.

Table 6.10 Drugs discovered by non-US PSRIs

Drug	Discovering institution(s)	Country
Drugs not included in current study		
Ambisome	U. of British Columbia	Canada
Atracurium	U. of Strathclyde	UK
BioHep	Weizmann Institute of Science	Israel
Campath	Cambridge U.	UK
Copaxone	Weizmann Institute of Science	Israel
Daunoxome	U. of British Columbia	Canada
Exelon	Hebrew University of Jerusalem	Israel
Ferriprox	U. of Essex	UK
Frone	Weizmann Institute of Science	Israel
Hepsera	Academy of Sciences/ Katholic University in Leuven,	Czech Republic, Belgium
Interferon	MRC	UK
Ixempra	Helmholtz Centre for Infection Research	Germany
Levulan	Queen's University	Canada
Myocet	U. of British Columbia	Canada
Navelbine	CNRS	France
Periochip	Hebrew University of Jerusalem	Israel
Rebif	Weizmann Institute of Science	Israel
Relenza	CSIRO, Monash University	Australia
Removab	Helmholtz Zentrum München	Germany
Selectiose	CNRS	France
Taxotere	CNRS	France
Telbivudine	CNRS	France
Temodar/Temodal	Imperial College London/Aston University	UK
Tiorfan	Inserm	France
Tomudex	Institute of Cancer Research	UK
Varivax	Biken Institute at Osaka University	Japan
Viread	Academy of Sciences/ Katholic University in Leuven,	Czech Republic, Belgium
Vistide	Academy of Sciences/ Katholic University in Leuven,	Czech Republic, Belgium

Drug	Discovering institution(s)	Country
Drugs included in current study		
BeneFIX	University of Oxford	UK
Doxil	Hebrew University of Jerusalem	Israel
Epivir-HBV	University of Alberta	Canada
Erbitux	Yeda Research & Devel.	Israel
Gardasil	German Cancer Research Centre/ U. of Brisbane	Germany, Australia
Hepatitis B	Edinburgh	UK
Humira	MRC	UK
Sutent	Max Planck Society	Germany
Visudyne	University of British Columbia	Canada
Zinecard	CRC	UK

Of these drugs, 28 are not included in our US study, indicating that the discovery was made entirely by non-US institutions, while ten are also included in the current study, implying that both US and non-US public sector researchers made a contribution to the discovery of the drug. The discovering countries are shown in Table 6.11.

It is noticeable that these countries have contributed significantly fewer new drugs than their U.S. counterparts despite a comparable overall level of combined total spending on scientific research in these countries. One possible explanation for this difference is that for the majority of the study period, professors owned the rights to their inventions throughout most of Europe – the so called "Professors' Privilege" or "Teachers' Exemption". Only towards the end of the 1990s did most European countries adopt the US model, and today only in Sweden do the rights to academic inventions still reside with the professor. European institutions are now establishing offices of technology transfer at a rapid rate, though funding for these activities is an issue.

Table 6.11 Countries of domicile of non-US PSRIs that invented FDA approved drugs

Country	Number
UK	10
Israel	8
Canada	6
France	5
Germany	3
Belgium	3
Czech Republic	3
Australia	2
Japan	1

It is noteworthy that the UK, where a similar, institutional model of ownership to that established by the Bayh-Dole Act was introduced in 1988,[70] has the next most productive PSRIs. However, the number of drugs is substantially smaller than those discovered by US institutions. One of the reasons may be lower levels of funding for scientific research. In addition, substantial funding for technology transfer activities at the individual institutional level did not become available in the UK until around 1999, when "third stream" funding schemes were introduced. A recent article discussed in some length the much lower inclination of public sector research researchers in Europe to patent the results of their research.[71]

Discussion

There is little dispute that the pharmaceutical industry relies heavily on the results of basic scientific research carried out in the public sector to identify promising points of intervention at which to target drug discovery efforts.

However, there have been far fewer studies of the actual role of public sector research in the discovery of new drugs.

Our results are consistent with those of Kneller,[72] who looked at the discoverers of NME and new biologics approved between 1998 and 2007, updating an earlier study that had just looked at approvals from 1998 to 2003.[73] For this limited subset, Kneller found that 44.1% of all 252 NMEs and new biologics approved by the FDA during this time period originated from outside the large pharmaceutical companies; 2.5% originated in small pharmaceutical companies, 17.5% originated with biotech companies and 24.1% originated from PSRIs. Of the drugs that originated from public research, 35.2% were licensed to pharmaceutical companies and the balance was licensed to biotech companies. The PSRI contribution was 27.7% of NMEs given priority review, 17.6% of NMEs given standard review and 35.3% of new biologics.

Conclusions

We believe that two factors contributed to the increase in PSRI research productivity in drug discovery that started in 1980. On a technical level, the 1980s saw the automation and widespread diffusion of the fundamental techniques of biotechnology – recombinant DNA and monoclonal antibodies – beyond the academic institutions in the UK and on the east and west coasts of the US that had discovered them in the mid-1970s. While these techniques were available to the traditional pharmaceutical companies, they were clearly disruptive technologies and enabled the creation of numerous new drug discovery companies normally founded by the discovering professors and funded by venture capitalists. These companies licensed the drug discoveries those professors had made and started developing them.

However, one must look further to explain the increase in the public sector role in the drug discovery process. As we discussed above, in 1980 the Bayh-Dole Act allowed and incentivized academic institutions to protect and license their intellectual property, while the Stevenson-Wydler Act, along with the 1986 amendments under the Federal Technology Transfer Act provided similar incentives to federal laboratories. Our data appears to provide strong, albeit circumstantial, evidence that these Acts achieved their public policy objectives of facilitating the movement of publicly funded technologies to the marketplace for the benefit of the public.

We believe this study provides some of the most compelling data yet generated that these policy changes regarding the ownership and exploitation of the results of public sector research have had their desired effect, regardless of the source of funding. Our study shows that PSRIs:

- Increased the rate at which they identified and patented healthcare innovations as soon as the Acts were passed;
- Successfully licensed those innovations to companies that brought them to market;
- Displayed a preference for small businesses in their licensing, with 57.5% of the initial licensees being small entities;
- Discovered drugs that had a high medical impact, accounting for 21.1% of New Molecular Entities given priority review by the FDA over an 18-year period;
- Discovered drugs whose estimated worldwide sales in 2008 were over $100 billion, including twenty eight "blockbusters" with sales over $1 billion; and
- Contributed significantly to the treatment of rare diseases, with 36% of the NDAs approved receiving Orphan Drug designation.

Our study also showed that commercializing the results of private sector research:

- Created substantial wealth in the private sector, with $143 billion of capital value realized in transactions;
- Resulted in the creation of a number of sustainable, profitable fully integrated biopharmaceutical companies with substantial market capitalizations; and
- Resulted in substantial royalty streams to some of the institutions that have discovered these drugs, some of which have been monetized, resulting in substantial one time payments.

In short, one of the objectives of the Bayh-Dole Act was to integrate academic research into the commercial mainstream and our study shows that in the drug sector, at least, this objective seems to have been achieved.

Whenever the topic of drugs that were discovered in the public sector with public funding comes up in discussion, the next question is inevitably "Well, if the Government paid for this drug's discovery, why does it cost so much?" The large number of drugs we have identified in this study to have resulted from publicly funded research may elevate this discussion to a new level.

However, it is important to note that public sector research only pays for the *discovery* of these drugs. The cost to develop a drug is greater by at least two orders of magnitude and must be funded by the private sector. The only drug we have identified where substantial public funding was used in its development was

Taxol, where no patent protection on the composition of matter or use was available. The NCI invested $484 million to discover and develop Taxol from 1977 through 2002.[74] Bristol-Myers Squibb, who obtained exclusive rights to the Government's data through a Cooperative Research and Development Agreement (CRADA) with NCI which commenced in 1991, reported to the General Accounting Office that it spent an additional $1 billion on the development effort.

Our study was unable to discover either the expenditures by the public sector researchers to discover these drugs or the expenditures by the private sector to develop them.

- When we did the study, the dollar amount of grants was confidential and was not accessible via CRISP, so we cannot estimate the cost to discover these drugs. Anecdotally though, federal grants are typically in the $150,000–$500,000 per year range. Our data showed a time of 5–6 years from the start of a grant and the discovery of the drug, indicating that discovery costs are likely to be in the $1–5 million range. Subsequently, the amount of funding is available from the REPORTer system back to 1990.
- The pharmaceutical industry resolutely refuses to disclose the cost of developing individual drugs. There are the much-quoted figures of $800 million to $1.2 billion as the cost to develop a drug from the Tufts Center for the Study of Drug Development. However, these are the total economic cost of discovery and development and not the cost of developing an individual drug. The largest cost is the cost of failure while the second highest cost is the opportunity cost of capital. The out of pocket cost to conduct the pre-clinical and clinical development cost of an individual drug is a distant third, and is typically $200–500 million per drug.

Occasionally, it is possible to get hard data. Abbott laboratories received a $3.5 million grant from the NIH and used it to successfully discover Norvir, the first HIV protease inhibitor. In December 2003, Abbott raised the price of Norvir five-fold. This precipitated an outcry from the AIDS community and a march-in petition under Bayh-Dole was made. During an NIH committee hearing on the subject, Jeffrey M. Leiden, president of Abbott's pharmaceutical products group, said that the clinical development of Norvir had cost Abbott over $300 million.[75] The development cost was therefore 85 times higher than the discovery cost.

There is therefore a roughly 100- to 200-fold greater private sector investment needed to translate the public sector's investment in discovery into a marketed product. The imposition of price controls as a condition for rights to license a publicly discovered drug would certainly stop companies from making these substantial investments, thereby throwing out the baby with the bath water.[76]

The final issue that our study may raise is whether the Government should share in the substantial royalty income that some public sector institutions have received from successful federally funded drug discoveries. Such a provision was included in the initial draft of the Bayh-Dole Act but was taken out in the discussion on the Senate floor because it was decided that the Government's financial return should come from the taxation on the increased economic activity that would result from the commercialization of federally funded inventions. Studies have shown that the Government has received a far greater financial return through taxation by stimulating this economic activity then it would have received by collecting a fraction of the discovering institution's royalty income.[77]

Overall the public and private sector research programs in the US complement each other very effectively. While the traditional model which strictly divided basic and developmental biomedical research between the two sectors no longer applies, each sector plays an important role. The private sector is needed to conduct most of the developmental research as well as to manufacture and sell drugs. On the discovery side, the private sector discovers most of the new drugs, including many highly innovative ones. However, we have shown that between 10 and 20% of new drugs are discovered in the public sector, sometimes in collaboration with the private sector. Most interestingly, the public sector contribution is proportionally more than twice as innovative as the private sector.

Public sector researchers pursue new scientific fields of inquiry and are able to take more scientific risks than private sector researchers. They are also not limited in their research by business constraints to seek drugs for the most profitable markets. This may explain why the public sector has the greatest contribution to new vaccines, which have some of the lowest profit margins among biomedical products and a higher risk associated with safety because healthy people are vaccinated. Hopefully, this study will lead others to explore further how and why public sector researchers are more innovative.

This study raises tantalizing questions about how the retrenchment of the pharmaceutical industry from translational research might affect the contribution from publicly funded research to the discovery of new drugs and vaccines. The pharmaceutical industry's current narrow focus on target-based drug discovery leaves all sorts of cutting-edge knowledge, such as stem cells or nanotechnology, sitting "on the shelf", waiting to be translated into something useful. Traditionally, universities and public research institutions have stepped in and filled the void, but such cutting edge technologies are normally initially developed by venture capital backed companies, who make the necessary investment to prove the technology viable. Many technologies take 20 to 25 years from initial discovery to the regulatory approval of its first product. This is a long time period for venture capital and if the technology is sufficiently fraught with difficulty – such as gene therapy – venture capital eventually looses patience, investment reverts to what can be raised from basic science funding sources and progress slows to a crawl. The long history of gene therapy bears this out. The problem for the future is that venture capital is itself retrenching after 15 years of poor returns. Currently, the mantra among venture capitalists is that they are happy to start a company when the technology is a year away from entering Phase 1 testing. The challenge for academic institutions is to find the funding to bridge technologies through this "valley of death". Initiatives such as the NIH's Research Evaluation and Commercialization Hub (REACH) Awards, the NCI's Experimental Therapeutics Program (NExT) and NHLBI's Centers for Accelerated Innovations (CAI) could be crucial in this regard.

Acknowledgements and disclaimer

We wish to thank our many colleagues in TTOs throughout the US, too numerous to list, who have graciously responded to our many requests for information on specific drugs and who reviewed our initial list of products. We acknowledge helpful discussions with Fiona Murray and Bhaven Sampat.

We gratefully acknowledge the cooperation of IMH Health, Incorporated, who supplied us with data on the US sales in 2008 of the products identified in our study. The statements, findings, conclusions, views, and opinions contained and expressed in this article are based in part on data obtained under license from the following IMS Health Incorporated data information services: Sources: National Sales Perspectives™ January 2008 – December 2008, IMS Health Incorporated, All Rights Reserved™ and National Disease Therapeutic Index™, January 2008 to December 2008, IMS Health Incorporated. All Rights Reserved. The statements, findings, conclusions, views, and opinions contained and expressed herein are not necessarily those of IMS Health Incorporated or any of its affiliated or subsidiary entities.

Notes

1 Strategy and Innovation Department, School of Management, Boston University, Boston, MA.
2 Partners HealthCare Innovation, Boston, MA.
3 The Research Council of Norway, Oslo, Norway.
4 Rakoczy Molino Mazzochi Siwik LLP, Chicago, IL.
5 W.L. Ross & Co. LLC, New York, NY.
6 Qingzhi Zhang is an Assistant Professor at the University of the Chinese Academy of Sciences, Beijing.
7 Office of Technology Transfer, National Institutes of Health, Department of Health and Human Services, Rockville, MD.
8 Office of Science Policy, National Institutes of Health, Department of Health and Human Services, Bethesda, MD.
9 Stevens, A., Jensen, J., Wyller, K., Kilgore, P., Chatterjee, S. and Rohrbaugh, M. (2011). "The Contribution of Public Sector Research to the Discovery of New Drugs and Vaccines." *New England Journal of Medicine* 634 (6; February 10): 535–41 (www.nejm.org/doi/full/10.1056/NEJMsa1008268).
10 After data collection and analysis had been completed, the FDA approved Folotyn, which was discovered by SRI International, Southern Research Institute and Sloan-Kettering, and is licensed to Allos Therapeutics.
11 Stevens, A. "The Enactment of Bayh-Dole." *Journal of Technology Transfer* 29 (January 2004): 93–99,.
12 US General Accounting Office (1968). Problem Areas Affecting Usefulness of Results of Government-Sponsored Research in Medicinal Chemistry: A Report to the Congress, US Government Printing Office, Washington, DC.
13 Harbridge House, Inc. (1968). Government Patent Policy Study. Background Materials on Government Patent Policy, Vol. II (August 1976): 69–140, US House of Representatives Committee on Science and Technology.
14 Dr. Betsy Anker-Johnson, Assistant Secretary of Commerce for Science and Technology, testimony in hearings on Government Patent Policy before the Subcommittee on Domestic and International Scientific Planning and Analysis of the

Committee on Science and Technology, US House of Representatives, 94th Congress, 2nd Session, September 23, 27, 29; October 1, 1976, pp 896–97, quoted in Senate Judiciary Committee hearings on Bayh-Dole.

15 Bremer, H. Allen, J., Latker, N.J. (2009). "The Bayh-Dole Act and Revisionism Redux." Life Sciences Law & Industry Report, 3 (17; September 11): 1–13.

16 Public Law 96-517, codified at 35 USC §§ 200–212 with regulations at 27 CFR Part 401.

17 For a full account of the events leading up to and the passage of Bayh-Dole, see Stevens, A. (2004) "The Enactment of Bayh-Dole." *Journal of Technology Transfer* 29 (January): 93–99.

18 Found in Public Law 98-620, The Trademark Clarification Act of 1984.

19 Public Law 96-480, codified at 15 USC §§ 3701–3714 with regulations at 37 CFR Part 404.

20 Public Law 99-502, codified at 15 USC § 3710a.

21 "Julius Axelrod – Nobel Lecture." Nobelprize.org. October 8, 2010 (http://nobelprize. org/nobel_prizes/medicine/laureates/1970/axelrod-lecture.html).

22 Cockburn, I. and Henderson, R. Public-Private Interaction and the Productivity of Pharmaceutical Research. Cambridge, MA, National Bureau of Economic Research (NBER) Working Paper 6018, April 1997.

23 Zycher, B., DiMasi, J.A. et al. "The Truth About Drug Innovation: Thirty-Five Summary Case Histories on Private Sector Contributions to Pharmaceutical Science." Medical Progress Report No. 6 June 2008.

24 Toole, A.A. (1905). "Does Public Scientific Research Complement Private Research and Development Investment in the Pharmaceutical Industry?" *Journal of Law and Economics* 50 (1): February 2007.

25 Angell, M. 2004. The Truth About Drug Companies. Random House, New York.

26 Toole, A.A. (2010) "The Impact of Public Basic Research on Industrial Innovation: Evidence from the Pharmaceutical Industry." US Department of Agriculture, Economic Research Service, mimeo.

27 The 1982 Supreme Court *Chakrabarty* decision, which established the patentability of microorganisms, is considered to have been another critical factor in the rise of the biotechnology industry generally. Most biotechnology companies spun out of universities (see for example "BIO 2009 Member Survey Technology Transfer and the Biotechnology Industry" (available at http://bio.org/ip/techtransfer/documents/ Session2-Esham.pdf).

28 Murray, F. and Stern, S. (2007). "Do Formal Intellectual Property Rights Hinder the Free Flow of Scientific Knowledge? An Empirical Test of the anti-Commons Hypothesis." *Journal of Economic Behavior and Organization* 63 (4): 648–87.

29 During the time period covered by Murray's work, US patent applications were confidential and only issued US patents came into the public domain. In November 1999, Congress passed the American Inventors Protection Act (Public Law 106-113). Under this Act, US applications filed after November 29, 2000 have been published 18 months after priority date, together with the status of their prosecution.

30 Lebovitz, R.M. (2007). "The Duty to Disclose Patent Rights." *Northwestern Journal of Technology and Intellectual Property* 6 (Fall 2007): 36–45.

31 An interference is an administrative proceeding within the PTO between an issued patent and one or more patent applications, or between two or more patent applications, claiming the same invention to determine which group of inventors was the first to invent the invention.

32 www.sciencemag.org/cgi/reprint/312/5775/829c.pdf?ck=nck

33 www.cafc.uscourts.gov/opinions/08-1248.pdf

34 www.cafc.uscourts.gov/opinions/08-1248.pdf

35 www.cafc.uscourts.gov/opinions/08-1248.pdf

36 www.boston.com/business/ticker/2008/09/ariad_is_disapp.html

37 www.cafc.uscourts.gov/opinions/09-1023.pdf
38 Glaxo Annual Report 2004.
39 www.investor.bayer.com/user_upload/34/
40 http://jolt.law.harvard.edu/digest/patent/ex-parte-pfizer-inc
41 John Maroney, Personal communication.
42 www.autm.net/about/dsp.licensing_surveys.cfm
43 It is permissible to withhold a US patent application from publication if, at the time of filing, the applicant has decided not to file international applications claiming priority to the US application. This is unlikely to be the case for patent applications for pharmaceutical products because of the need to recover development costs from a worldwide market.
44 www.rdna.com/
45 Public Benefits Survey, Association of University Technology Managers, Deerfield IL, 1994. The 1996 study was not published, for reasons that are not clear, but AUTM made it available to us.
46 www.betterworldproject.net/products/index.cfm (accessed August 3, 2008).
47 www.uvapf.org/index.cfm/fuseaction/viewpage/page_id/115?CFID=1450853 &CFTOKEN=54000268& (accessed August 3, 2008).
48 www.ott.nih.gov/about_nih/fda_approved_products.html (accessed August 3, 2008).
49 http://s-edison.info.nih.gov/iEdison/commercial_report.jsp. The requirement for grantees to report FDA approved products that include technologies invented with NIH funded began for FDA approvals after January 2003.
50 www.dricapital.com/;   www.paulcap.com/InvestmentPlatforms/Healthcare/Portfolio InvestmentsList.aspx; www.royaltypharma.com/casestudies/cs-main.html
51 Anand, Geeta (2006). "Mothers' Tale, As Their Babies Tested New Drug, A Friendship Grew." Geeta *WSJ* December 12: p A1.
52 Harvard Business School Case 9-502-006, Professor John T. Gourville.
53 http://patft.uspto.gov/
54 www.accessdata.fda.gov/scripts/cder/drugsatfda/index.cfm?fuseaction=Search.Search _Drug_Name
55 www.accessdata.fda.gov/scripts/oc/ohrms/frsearch.cfm
56 "Ensuring Policy and Laws Are Both Effective and Just: Academic Patents and Access to Medicines in Developing Countries," *American Journal of Public Health* 99: January 2009.
57 Based on the statement of government interests in issued patents. Note that NIH intramural inventions do not identify a grant number because intramural investigators do not receive grants.
58 After data collection and analysis was completed, the FDA approved Allos Therapeutics' NDA for Folotyn (pralatrexate) for the treatment of patients with relapsed or refractory peripheral T-cell lymphoma on September 24, 2009. Pralatrexate was first synthesized by SRI International as a potential improved analog of edatrexate, an earlier anti-folate developed by SRI International and MSKCC. Preclinical development was performed by MSKCC and Southern Research Institute. SRI, MSKCC and Southern Research Institute licensed the technology to Allos in January 2003 when the drug was in Phase II trials (www.southernresearch.org/press/pr20090925.html).
59 We excluded drugs such as thyroxine, coumadin, nystatin, penicillin, streptomycin, neomycin, 5-fluorouracil, and the contraceptive pill that were discovered in the course of public sector research and introduced before the Kefauver Harris Amendment (Drug Efficacy Amendment) of 1962 ushered in the modern era of FDA regulation of drug approvals.
60 The other driver of Amgen's growth was Epogen, which was based on research carried out by Eugene Goldwasser at the University of Chicago, but not patented nor therefore licensed by the university. In accordance with our criteria, therefore, Epogen is not included in our study. The story of Amgen and Epogen is discussed in some detail in

Merrill Goozner's 2004 book *The $800 Million Pill: The Truth behind the Cost of New Drugs*. Berkeley and Los Angeles, CA: University of California Press.

61 The Bayh-Dole Act and the Stevenson-Wydler Act require recipients of federal funding to give small businesses in the US preference in granting licensees to their inventions. 35 USC §202(c)(7)(D) and 35 USC §209(c).

62 http://crisp.cit.nih.gov

63 Since a grant retains the same number through any number of competitive renewals, sometimes lasting decades, the grant start date is the original starting date of the grant. Since it is not possible from this database to identify the competitive cycle in which the invention was made, this number, the time in years for grant "start of research to discovery" in Table 6.6, will by definition be longer for inventions made in later years of a entire grant period.

64 This figure initially appeared in the NEJM article.

65 Note that the first column is for all drugs discovered prior to 1970.

66 BioPharmaceutical Royalty Rates and Deal Terms Report (2008). In J. Schaible, and J. McCarthy (eds), Licensing Executives Society (USA and Canada), Inc.

67 One monetization (Duke's January 2012 monetization for $90 million) was Duke's royalty streams from both Myozyme and Lumizyme. Lumizyme was approved on May 24, 2010, and so is outside the data cut-off window. It was not possible to determine how much of the monetization was for Lumizyme.

68 We follow the convention of the biotechnology industry and use as the "value" of a transaction the total of all the upfront and other pre-commercialization payments. This figure does not include future royalty payments because the magnitude of these is contingent on the sales that the drug achieves.

69 www.imshealth.com/portal/site/imshealth/menuitem.a953aef4d73d1ecd88 f611019418c22a/?vgnextoid=bb967900b55a5110VgnVCM10000071812ca2RCRD& vgnextfmt=default (accessed 27 December, 2009).

70 Richards, W.G. (2009). *Spin-Outs: Creating Business from University Intellectual Property*. Hampshire, UK: Harriman House.

71 Thangaraj, Harry, et al. (2009). "Dynamics of Global Disclosure through Patent and Journal Publications for Biopharmaceutical Products." *Nature Biotechnology* 27 (7): 614–18.

72 Kneller, R. (2010). "The Importance of New Companies for Drug Discovery: Origins of a Decade of New Drugs." *Nature Reviews of Drug Discovery* 9: 867–82

73 Kneller, R. (2005). "The Origins of New Drugs." *Nat Biotech* 23 (5): 529–30.

74 www.gao.gov/new.items/d03829.pdf (accessed 28 December, 2009).

75 http://pubs.acs.org/cen/news/8222/8222notw2.html (accessed 13 February, 2010).

76 See "A Plan to Ensure Taxpayers' Interests are Protected," July 2001 (www.ott.nih. gov/policy/policy_protect_text.html).

77 See, for example, William F. Swiggart, "The Bayh-Dole Act & the State of University Technology Transfer in 2003," a Panel Presentation at the 4th Annual Conference, Princeton Entrepreneurs' Network, Campus of Princeton University (May 29, 2003; available at www.swiggartagin.com/articles/Bayh_Dole_act.doc; last accessed 21 February, 2015), showing $5 billion in tax impact at the federal, state and local levels when total university royalty income was $850 million.

Part III

Developed countries

7 Island of bliss?

University technology commercialization practices in the Swiss innovation system

Christiane Gebhardt

Introduction: Island of bliss? How can a successful innovation system be made resilient?

Switzerland, a small state in the world market that lacks natural resources, has implemented a successful strategy of building up knowledge production as a globally competitive industry.[1] The transition of Switzerland into one of the leading nations in innovation and the capitalization of investments in innovation is confirmed by the OECD key performance indicators (OECD, 2011) – see, for instance, Figure 7.1. Not only is the current performance of the technology transfer model excellent, but also the long term indirect impact of innovation on the Swiss economy and labour market scores equally highly.[2] Currently, Switzerland is one of the most attractive destinations in Europe in terms of highly skilled workforces in both academia and the R&D intensive industries, has one of the highest immigration rates and one of the lowest unemployment rates in Europe.[3]

How can that successful Swiss innovation system be made resilient and Switzerland be prepared for further success in a changing world? Policies that address this issue must be assessed in the specific socio-economic context of Switzerland.

Outperforming all other EU member states in innovation rankings, Switzerland operates according to a different governance of innovation than surrounding EU countries[4] which takes the form of a historically developed federal system with strong cantons at sub-national level, a direct democracy and a policy of non-intervention at federal level. As a result, three types of higher education institutions constitute the basis of knowledge: federal universities, financed by the federal government; cantonal universities, financed (principally) by the cantonal governments; and regional universities of applied sciences, financed partly by the federal government and partly by the cantons of the respective region. With regard to knowledge and technology transfer, institutions in the ETH-domain (federal institutes of technology and federal research institutions) and universities of applied science research play an active role. As a result, 'doctoral projects in collaboration with firms' are highly relevant for the ETH-domain (41.8%) and 'thesis projects in collaboration with firms' (77.2%) for the universities of applied sciences (Arvanitis et al, 2008). The ETH domain was chosen for the early

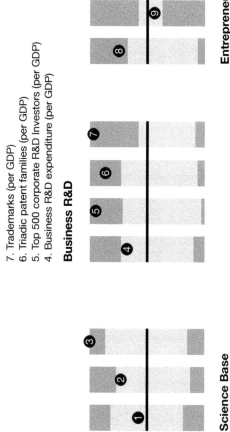

Middle range of
OECD values

Top/bottom 5
OECD values

Top half of OECD

OECD median

Bottom half of OECD

Science Base

1. Public R&D expenditure (per GDP)
2. Top 500 universities (per GDP)
3. Publication in the top-quartile journals (per GDP)

Business R&D

4. Business R&D expenditure (per GDP)
5. Top 500 corporate R&D Investors (per GDP)
6. Triadic patent families (per GDP)
7. Trademarks (per GDP)

Entrepreneurship

8. Venture capital (per GDP)
9. Patenting firms less than 5 years old (per GDP)
X. Ease of entrepreneurship index

Figure 7.1 Science and innovation indicators for Switzerland

institutionalization of a formalized technology transfer that became a role model for other Swiss universities.

The federal Swiss government has refrained from making direct investments in regional innovation and cluster programmes. However, the federal budget for university-based education, research and innovation (ERI) was a remarkable SF7.4 billion for the period 2013–2016. Federal expenditure of SF10.8 million was allocated to the *Eidgenössische Hochschulen*, ETH and EPFL, for the same period. Swiss cantons also fund universities and universities of applied sciences (80%); while the two technical research universities, ETH and EPFL, are funded 100% by the federal government (FDEA/OPET, 2012).[5]

Well-known success stories of family entrepreneurs – for example upgrading the mature textile sector for the production of smart fibres, or the transformation of family owned watchmaker firms into global brands by entrepreneurs such as Nicholas Hayek – define our image of the Swiss industrial landscape. In fact, Swiss global players control the innovation agenda: SF11 billion of the SF13 billion total of Science & Technology expenditure came from industry.[6] Currently, only a few large and globally integrated firms in the pharmaceutical and chemical industries are well connected with the top-tier ETH universities and fund joint applied science projects. Basic science initiatives of the Swiss National Fund and its six thematic initiatives relate to STEM disciplines, with an overall budget of SF122.9 million for the period 2014–2017.[7] Entrepreneurial spirit and the management skills of global players and, to a lesser extent, of medium sized enterprises appear to be strong stabilizing factors for Swiss innovation as well as for the Swiss economy.

The major players also shape the technology transfer model discussed here according to their needs. Adopting a socio-economic perspective, how different variables integrate into an innovation system, in which technology transfer is a wider concept of diffusiveness and permeability of knowledge, is analysed.

To date, therefore, the particular Swiss system of governance of the innovation system appears to be a model of success; that is, industry and strategy driving research and shaping the technology transfer model, with federal government policy driving education, providing the academic institutional base and defining the legal framework for relevant actors.

However, despite all the shiny new patents and the impressive numbers of licensing and spin-off developments, the streamlined technology model is tightly woven into an innovation system that might contain systemic risks in the form of industrial co-optation and emerging structural disparities between SME and global players.[8] Policy makers express some concern that the robustness of this self-perpetuating model might not be sustainable and feel ill-prepared to deal with systemic shocks. Lock-in, lack of variety and the gradual disintegration of SMEs could threaten future innovativeness. In striving for resilience in the Swiss innovation system there is a quest for strategic options, with regard to developing anticipatory policies, in order to prevent adverse developments before they appear on the scoreboards.

Notable programmes such as the German Leading Edge Cluster competition, or the German (university) excellence initiative, have to date been considered unthinkable in Switzerland. Equally, European Horizon 2020 programmes, such as World Clusters or regional innovation strategies/smart specialization (RIS), are not open to Switzerland. The Swiss federal government was forced to intervene financially, in order to safeguard joint science projects between Swiss universities and European partners, after a national referendum in Spring 2014 which voted against mass immigration was followed by a freeze on Swiss S&T funds imposed by the European Union.

Must Switzerland now open up to new policies and adopt a different approach to technology transfer to maintain its pole position in innovation and prevent structural disparities? Will government at federal level take on a new and more active role in the diffusion of knowledge and the Swiss governance of innovation?

The present study addresses the core issues of clarification of the operational mode and identification of the engines of innovation that drive the Swiss technology transfer model within the Swiss innovation system. In this context, technology transfer offices (TTOs) are embedded in the specific innovation system and are a system product rather that a stand-alone feature. In her study of Cambridge University in the UK, Breznitz shows that the success of technology transfer models relies on an amalgamation of external and intra-university factors, internal mechanisms and resources rather than on formulaic technology models per se (see Breznitz, 2011: 465). Other authors show that *diffusiveness* and *permeability* are to be found in the specific innovation system or ecosystem (Adner, 2006; Carayannis and Campbell, 2012; Mercan and Göktas, 2011) and constitute the condition for technology transfer.

The holistic approach taken here is an alternative method chosen by government officials of Swiss national agencies to validate and assess current Swiss innovation. The study employs a scenario technique, targeting the Swiss innovation system as a system constructed by relevant stakeholders, introducing a sensitivity analysis (Vester, 2001) and relying on complexity theory (Forrester, 1961; Schwanninger, 2006). It provides a system dynamics perspective as a heuristic for political decision-making.

The structure of the paper is as follows. It starts with a discussion of key concepts in innovation related to the Swiss innovation system and Swiss innovation policy, taking note of the diffusiveness and permeability of the innovation system; that is, an extended perspective on technology transfer. The central element in the Swiss innovation system – the role of academia and the mode of operation of technology transfer – is then considered in detail. The focus here is on the tier-one universities and their TTO offices, the role models for the diffusion of knowledge into industrial value in Switzerland. Following the introduction into the research method there is a discussion of key variables that comprise the 'genetic code' of the Swiss innovation system. A strategic analysis of the current state presents the engines of innovation as an underlying mechanism, revealing the systemic risks and trigger points or levers. The paper concludes with strategic scenarios for political decision making, focusing on the diffusiveness and permeability of the innovation system as a precondition for technology transfer and a key to resilience.

The Swiss innovation system

Innovation systems were introduced as an approach by Lundvall in 1992 and Nelson in 1993, focusing strongly on the components of the system – that is, organizations and institutions, the latter constituting the rules of the game (Lundvall, 1992; Nelson, 1993). According to this concept, an appropriate set of factors leads to innovation in products and services, following investments in Research and Development (R&D) by either public or industrial players – see Edquist (2011) for an overview. Cooke and Morgan (1998) and Cooke and Leydesdorff (2006) take this concept further and discuss *regionally* based innovative networks that involve universities and research institutions in regional innovation systems. Equally, *innovation clusters* assign a strong role to linkages between universities and industry (Ketels and Protsiv, 2013). In their effort to combine concepts, Swiss officials claim that innovation clusters such as the BioAlps[9] or the CleanTech Cluster[10] follow the underlying Triple Helix principles of a university, industry and government interaction.[11] They are in fact spatial conglomerations of similar and proximate industries, only partly located around universities and lacking a common mission of the networking members. Until recently the third Triple Helix strand, that of government, was effectively absent because there were no regional policies or national programmes to encourage networking and interaction. Swiss technology transfer was started as a bilateral rather than a cluster concept and has formed clusters ex post.

In Switzerland it is not necessary to use innovation policies as developmental measures. Innovation and Technology Indicators (ITI) forecast a trend towards future innovative growth. Equally, Marxt and Brunner, who discuss the European Innovation Scoreboard/Summary Innovation Index for 2009, identify an innovation leader position for Switzerland (Marxt and Brunner, 2009). Empirical analysis of knowledge clusters (Leydesdorff and Ahrweiler, 2014) and analysis of the R&D investment behaviour of clusters of Swiss pharmaceutical companies show that clusters that are already successful have a self-organized capacity to attract further investment and high level competences in order to generate wide variety and modularity for science-based developments and highly skilled employment (see Tinguely, 2013 for the general trend; Deakin and Leydesdorff, 2014).[12] In addition, knowledge clusters exhibit a tendency either to be more resilient to financial crisis developments or to recover more quickly after shocks (Delgado and Ketels, 2012).

In contrast, over-specialization carries the danger of lock-ins and regional risks when industries lose their competitiveness. Co-option of the innovation system by industry can lead to a closed system and reduced innovativeness (Leydesdorff and Ahrweiler, 2014). Due to favourable financial policies and attractive tax regimes, cantons in Switzerland have attracted the headquarters and research operations of global players. R&D related advanced manufacturing of high tech prototypes is a growing sector in advanced economies (Lester and Piore, 2004) – and also for Switzerland. However, regional problems can occur when high tech, highly mobile global firms move on to new markets or tax havens, or transfer production sites to regions with low labour costs (Vernon, 1979).

There is a downside to this self-organizing system. In an innovation system that is already successful, low tech SMEs might not be able to keep up with high tech sectors and compete with global players regarding the intake of new knowledge. Equally, medium sized firms tend to be more regionally embedded and provide stable employment opportunities, and are therefore considered an asset in regional innovation systems (Cohen and Levinthal, 1990). Unfortunately, SMEs are also notorious for lacking the absorptive capacity for knowledge and technology transfer (KTT) (Lewinthal and Levinthal, 1990). In their study on forms of Swiss KTT, Arvanatis et al showed that Swiss firms expect the availability of well-educated graduates and access to first class research results from the universities. These are the two most important groups of motives for KTT activities. According to their research, obstacles to KTT relate to 'deficiencies of science institutions' and 'cost, risk, uncertainty' (Arvanatis et al, 2007). In particular, small and medium sized enterprises tend to lack knowledge of university research programmes, especially if the research and KTT activities of the SMEs are narrow. It follows that although technology transfer is well organized between global players and tier-one universities, the diffusiveness and permeability of the innovation system systematically excludes weaker players such as SMEs.

Many regional innovation studies regard the university as a core player in an innovation system; that is, a provider and active promoter of regional innovation in concert with other players (Cooke and Morgan, 1998). Driven by large industries, this is particularly true for the Swiss clusters around the tier-one federal research universities: ETH and EFPL in the Greater Zurich and Lac Léman regions respectively, and Basel University in the Basel region. The Swiss map illustrates how the North–West distribution of biotechnology coincides with the locations of universities and firms in the pharmaceutical and chemical sectors. The success of the Swiss innovation system is due largely to the strong commitment of industry, led by the long-established direct engagement of chemical and pharmaceutical industries (followed by insurance, manufacturing and ICT). For example, ETH Zurich and EPFL Lausanne profit from a research cooperation programme with Microsoft Research in the ICT sector: Microsoft Research directly supports IT projects with funding of SF5 million.

Apart from creation and dissemination of knowledge by means of teaching and research activities, entrepreneurial universities engage in a so-called 'third role' in economic development through spin-offs, patents, licensing technology and applied research with industry (Etzkowitz and Leydesdorff, 2000; Urbano and Guerro, 2012; Atkinson and Pelfrey, 2010). In local networking models, universities play a critical role as a source of fundamental knowledge. They are therefore seen as key actors for the formation of new collaborative environments, increasing their innovation capabilities and engaging in continuous improvement (Etzkowitz et al, 2000; Kaufmann and Toedtling, 2001). Other authors claim that universities must be considered as a focal point for the development and dissemination of new knowledge and technologies for the design, development and commercialization of new products and processes (Flores et al, 2009).

Since the 1990s the Swiss federal technical universities ETH and EPFL have become crucial players and role models with regard to technology transfer policies and TTOs. They also provide services for Swiss Universities of Applied Sciences as well as other universities. All TTOs are organized by the Swiss Technology Transfer Association, founded in 2003, which is dedicated to the further improvement of technology transfer. ETH and EPFL have both contributed to the establishment of a highly developed and detailed system of rules and regulations relating to IPR, patents, the revenue split of royalties and support of inventors, as well as the involvement of TTOs. Other intermediaries, such as incubator facilities or training organizations, are mostly controlled by private investors (see Lawton-Smith, 2006 and Breznitz, 2011 for a general discussion of these features).

In both universities the incentives for engaging in technology transfer activities are based on monetary benefits – a positive correlation, according to Link and Siegel (2008). Successful technology transfer models also depend on the entrepreneurial culture at the respective university (Bercovitz and Feldmann, 2008). In this context, Thursby et al (2005) discuss the implications of licensing on research in the framework of a life cycle model of an academic scientist's career. The previous resistance of professors, more inclined to propagate independent ('free') research without immediate 'market value', has in many instances been overcome. Switzerland now has an academic system that seeks managerial competence alongside academic excellence in its scientific personnel and offers both high salaries and bonus payments linked to performance indicators and the outcome of appraisals.

In this context, many studies discuss the importance of managerial capabilities and the organizational location of intermediaries, with a special focus on TTOs (Clarysse et al, 2005: Lockett and Wright, 2005; Breznitz, 2011), with regard to successful spinning-off and commercialization. The role of management competences in building and maintaining adequate organizational structures and reaching consensus becomes more relevant in Triple Helix relationships in which technology transfer is of vital importance (Gebhardt and Pohlmann, 2013).

Successful transfer relies on a positive correlation between excellent management, good scientific content and a perfect match of supply and demand. It is important to emphasize that, above all, TTOs rely for their work on the attractiveness of the knowledge production, the compliance of professors and, last but not least, on the image and general performance of the university.

Swiss innovation policy

Regional innovation cluster programmes supported by central government and innovation programmes supported by regional governments are able to flourish and grow under European innovation policy. However, such programmes are not common under Swiss policy and to date have not been regarded as a political instrument for promoting economic development (EFI, 2011). Swiss clusters are spontaneous rather than policy-designed.

In contrast to neighbouring European countries, the Swiss government refrains from involvement in major innovation programmes, massive funding of technology transfer, translational themes and the financial promotion of regional networking; and innovation policies at cantonal level address instead the educational and vocational sector. The National Science Fund, NSF, is the federal agency that supports basic research in universities. Swiss based technology and incubator centres are not conceived as a policy instrument. Thierstein and Wilhelm (2001) address this issue and illustrate how technology parks were never set up with a view to establishing regional innovation. Claiming that Swiss technology and innovation policy is non-existent, Thierstein and Egger state that 'technology policy in Switzerland had been merely a special part of economic policy limited to design the regulations and to foster vocational education' (Thierstein and Egger, 1998).[13]

Griessen and Braun perceive lack of coordinated government intervention in innovation as a policy gap, which can be risky. They discuss a separation or institutional impermeability between basic research and higher education on the one hand, and technological research, applied science and professional education on the other, and call it the 'utilitarian divide'. A second gap concerns the division of responsibilities and competences between the federal government and the cantons. (Griessen and Braun, 2008): KTI, (the Commission for Technology and Innovation), a federal agency, was set up in 2005 to address this gap.

Technology transfer policies and the role of the Commission for Technology and Innovation (KTI)

Swiss innovation policy has long been to refrain from direct interference in the institutional landscape and in the industry-driven technology transfer model. Pioneers such as Henry Nestlé, Alexander Clavel (Ciba), John Rudolf Geigy, Fritz Hoffmann-La Roche and Alfred Escher (SKA) founded strong firms that survived the World Wars in a better state than competitors in neighbouring European countries. However, Switzerland lacked innovative start-ups, and the transfer of the Novartis research facilities to the Boston area in the USA was an alarming sign, even for the non-interventionist Swiss federal government. Following this, technology transfer became an issue propagated by the former SBF-State secretary Charles Kleiber.[14] One of the institutional results of the SNI was SwiTT (Swiss Technology Transfer Association) also promoted by Charles Kleiber.

Federal policies in the field of technology transfer struggled in the quest for the best funding model. A legal prototype for Swiss technology transfer was the Bayh–Dole Act of 1980, which allowed US universities the use of intellectual property created in their research departments. TTOs, which evolved alongside these debates, became an important and successful cornerstone in this technology transfer landscape.[15]

In 2002 a Swiss expert group visited the US to analyse US start-ups, including the North Carolina Research Triangle, Stanford University and MIT Mass.. Their report became very influential in creating a start-up culture in Switzerland. The vision of a 'Boston Area of Continental Europe' took shape, although a major and active role for the federal government was not possible in the Swiss political system. Technology transfer relied on entrepreneurial freedom and an active role of the university as a knowledge producer. Most importantly, universities were not to rely on a short-term financial income from licensing; professors would also receive a fair financial share from their inventions, and basic sciences would remain the fundamental aspect of university activities.[16]

To date Switzerland has focused on flanking action to improve, rather than to change, this model. In 2012, the federal government spent SF154.7 million on technology transfer and adjacent projects in research and development. In addition, the Federal Council of Switzerland and the Parliament authorized a SF40 million budget for projects related to promoting start-ups and for support for science and technology transfer (KTI, 2013).

Better integration of SMEs into the Swiss innovation system and the creation of new enterprises became a matter of concern in 2014. Consequently, the Swiss National Council (Bundesrat) in Bern assigned new political responsibilities in education, research and innovation policy to the State Secretariat of Education, Research and Innovation (SBFI). With the enactment and enforcement of Swiss national legislation regarding the promotion of research and the funding of entrepreneurs, high-tech start-ups, innovation networks, knowledge and technology transfer have gained greater importance in the political agenda. Funding for these activities is channelled through the national agency – the Commission for Technology and Innovation, KTI.[17] As a result of these organizational and legal changes, Swiss policy enables KTI to fund new forms of collaboration between (foreign) SMEs and universities.

There is some evidence of a trend towards policy driven changes and direct programmes: for instance, the agenda for energy policy 2020, which anticipates additional funding for energy research (SF142 million for the period 2013–2016).[18] A further policy change is the concept of federally commissioned implementation of national innovation parks, adopted by the Swiss Conference of Cantonal Ministers of Economic Affairs in June 2014.[19] These technology parks will support existing clusters (two will be set up in close proximity to ETH and EPFL) and promote industry activities – already strong and well-established – in the Basel region and the canton of Aargau.

While research of global players is self-financed and self-organized, Swiss small and medium sized enterprises very often lack the means to undertake research and development. The KTI therefore supports a technology platform and the setting up of instruments for science and technology transfer, to promote integration of SMEs into both the Swiss innovation system and international research activities. KTI also funds innovative start-up companies and maintains a consultancy service for SME innovation linked to European Programmes.[20] In the KTI report, the role of the state is specifically restricted to providing crucial framework conditions such as moderate taxes, a qualified workforce, infrastructures and logistics, political stability, legal security and enforceable rights. In addition, the assessment of innovation proposals is carried out with a clear focus on applicability and potential market success.

KTI received a budget of SF546.4 million for the period 2013–2016. In the legislation budget for 2011–2015 the guidelines for technology, research and innovation were stated for the very first time:

> Investments proposed for education, research and innovation have high priority and will be managed in close cooperation with the cantons and the industry. The instruments proposed contribute to three development goals:
>
> • Education: coverage of the demand of generally qualified and skilled personnel;
> • Research and Innovation: consolidating funding at the high level that has been achieved; and
> • Comprehensive Aspects of the Innovation System: designing Switzerland as a knowledge and skills location, which is also in agreement with the principles of equal opportunity, sustainability and competitiveness.
>
> (Bundesrat, 2012: S3123)

Significantly, entrepreneurial expertise is expected to drive development:

> Swiss firms have high quality awareness, a high orientation towards customer value and a global market perspective. All of these characteristics secure research and development and will result in successful market innovations.
>
> (Bundesrat, 2012: S3123)

The role of Swiss federal technical universities and TTOs in the commercialization of technology

In order to enable technology transfer, the Swiss federal government has focused on two technically oriented research universities, both to concentrate forces and resources and establish them as a prototype.[21] As a result of this approach Swiss universities have become attractive partners in basic research and for clinical studies.

A key role in this development is played in particular by the federal government agency 'Swiss National Fund' (SNF) which funds basic science and intramural research activities on a project and programme basis, including in addition Universities of Applied Sciences (*Fachhochschulen*). In 2012, SNF's funding totalled SF755 million, which represents an increase of 5.9% compared to 2011.[22] Most of the funding went to mathematics, engineering, natural sciences and technology ('MINT/STEM') related disciplines. University-based research amounted to SF487.8 million: ETH and federal laboratories attracted SF196.9 million; and Fachhochschulen SF17.5 million (SNF, 2012). Many projects were carried out in a globally integrated mode with international partners; that is, tier-one universities.[23] In Switzerland these research activities cluster regionally around ETH (Zürich) and EPFL (Lausanne), as well as the Universities of Fribourg, Basel, Lucerne, Bern (excluding CERN) and Lake Geneva. However, many of these relationships rely on bilateral agreements.

Swiss universities are spinning-off dozens of science-based start-ups every year. The TTO at ETH in Zurich has produced success stories such as GlycArt, a spin-off that Roche acquired for US$225 million in an all-cash transaction in 2005.[24] There is additional empirical evidence that ETH runs a successful technology transfer model: during the last five years ETH students and faculty launched approximately 20 start-ups per year in sectors such as information and communications technologies (ICT), medical engineering and biotechnology.[25] Similarly, in 2010 Logitech opened the doors of the Daniel Borel Innovation Center in the Quartier de l'Innovation at Ecole Polytechnique Fédérale de Lausanne (EPFL) in the Geneva region, maintaining the legacy of innovation and strong university support that originated with professors at EPFL in 1981.[26]

ETH is currently filing 80 new patent applications each year and has a record of accomplishment of some 260 spin-off companies that emerged from the institute between 1996 and 2012 (see Figures 7.2–7.5 for ETH and EPFL technology transfer indicators and data).

The focal points of ETH research include energy supply, risk management, developing cities of the future, global food security and human health. At EPFL the Laboratory for Production Management and Processes, created in 1995, carries out medium and long-term research for the manufacturing industry. The development of collaborative networks has been one of the main objectives in the research agenda of both organizations (Flores et al, 2009).

The Swiss technology transfer model was developed in these two federal institutes of technology, which both have a long-established tradition of

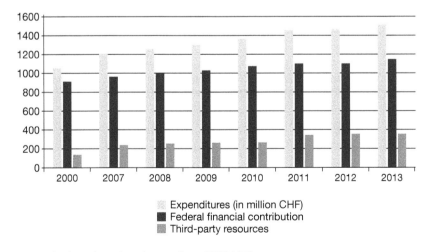

Figure 7.2 Financing of total expenditure ETH 2013

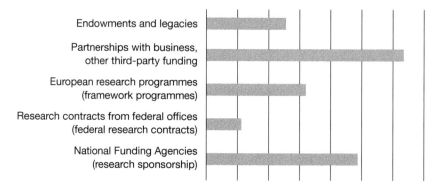

Figure 7.3 Origin of expenditures funded by third parties (ETH 2013)

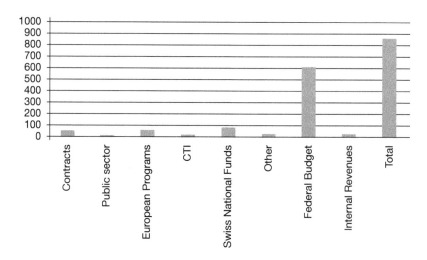

Figure 7.4 Expenditures by funding source: third party funding EPFL 2013 (in million CHF)

relationships with industry.[27] ETH and EPFL have mission statements that anticipate the transfer of knowledge to the private sector and to society at large. The number of spin-offs from Swiss universities and income from licensing are now criteria according to which they are ranked.

ETH itself has several additional support mechanisms for start-ups, including providing incubator space for the first two years. This includes access to ETH's scientific equipment, an especially valuable facility for life science companies, because investors are often reluctant to finance the instruments they need.

Ten cantonal universities and seven inter-cantonal universities of applied sciences have also adopted the model of licensing activities and TTOs developed in the late 1980s by EPFL and ETH. The driving force behind the development was the opportunity to generate income.[28] There are three strongly interrelated key components of knowledge and technology transfer: (1) *Patenting* a precondition

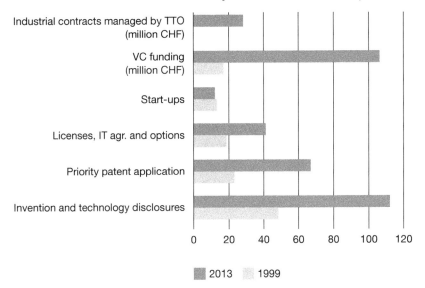

Figure 7.5 Growth in technology transfer (EPFL 2013)

for (2) *Licensing* and patenting and/or licensing as a main motivation for (3) *Starting a new firm* to exploit these assets. TTOs play a central role and provide detailed support for technology transfer at the federal technical universities. Swiss TTOs are active business developers, matchmakers, mediators and brokers.

It is apparent that a clearly stated mission, transparent rules for technology transfer and case-to-case evaluation[29] as well as assignment of the technology transfer task to the central TTOs have contributed to the success of Swiss technology transfer. Researchers, as well as venture capitalists and sponsoring firms, declare that 'you cannot escape the TTO' (from unpublished interviews with researchers at ETH and industry).

In line with this, Arvanatis et al (2008) state that intermediaries such as the TTO can successfully manage the obstacles to knowledge and technology transfer in Switzerland:

> Differing interests and attitudes and fear of losing scientific independence or neglect of basic research and scientific publication activities seem to be the most relevant impediments for scientific institutes to engage in KTT activities. These are primarily 'culture differences' between university and business that can be partly traced back [not only] to the different goals pursued by the university and the corporation but also to a lack of knowledge of the problems and interests of each other.
>
> (Arvanati et al, 2008)

Thus the professionalization of technology transfer has created a very structured environment for all players involved. Nevertheless, TTOs manage the commercialization with an awareness of academic careers:

Regulations anticipate that the right of ETH Zurich researchers to publish the project results must be secured in the agreement. However, publications can be delayed for a restricted time if necessary to allow for patent protection.

In principle the Swiss academic institutions own the intellectual property rights (IPR) to inventions and software generated by their professors and other employees. Software is generally protected by copyright but can also be protected by patents. There are variations from these principles, however, due to different laws at federal and cantonal levels. The professors own the copyright of authored work, including software. Most PhD students are employed by their university and fall under this rule.

Both TTOs claim that inventions are mostly disclosed to the TTO by the researcher without prompting, by means of disclosure forms. However, coaching sessions and seminar activities run by the TTOs have increased the visibility of the TTO services, reduced uncertainties and increased the number of disclosures. Generally, TTOs negotiate research agreements with industrial partners and contracts for the laboratories. Furthermore, TTOs evaluate the commercial potential, the legal aspects and the inventor's inclination to play an active role in marketing the technology, drafting the patent application, and in further development of the technology. This is seen as a benefit by many venture capital companies; but, sometimes, as an obstacle for academics regarding engagement in technology transfer activities because they – the academics – wish to dedicate more time to scientific work (Chardonnes, 2006). However, the new generation of academic personnel regards this system as a matter of fact and not as an obstacle (from unpublished interviews).

The TTOs act as a 'one-stop-shop' for the academic institutions and federal agencies, as well as for not-for-profit organizations and local authorities. TTOs also facilitate access to incubators; and EPFL offers financial support to innovative projects with high potential in which its collaborators are involved. Nine projects were funded by EPFL in 2012 by Innogrants, for average amounts of around SF100,000 per project. For ETH the Venture Incubator, started by McKinsey in 2010, fulfils this function: ETH supports potential start-ups with Pioneer Fellowships that allow for development of the technology in Innovation and Entrepreneurship Laboratories.

In addition, ETH and EPFL run activities to promote and fund technology transfer through loans and other forms of funding. For instance, a Swiss nationwide business plan competition 'Venturekick'[30] involves TTOs, the federal innovation promotion agency (KTI)[31] and consulting firms. Venturekick awarded about SF1 million in grants to 38 projects in Western Switzerland.[32] The Foundation for Technological Innovation (FTI) granted 13 loans of SF100,000 each in 2012 to EPFL Science Park PSE and regional high-tech entrepreneurs. PSE, as a contributing member, is associated with the operation of the FIT in sponsoring nominations and supporting entrepreneurs to develop their business.

In addition to the support and cultural stimulus, a so-called '3-Thirds Remuneration Scheme' is used by Swiss universities and institutes of technology.

The income is divided in equal parts between the institution, the laboratory and the researcher: the TTO receives a fee of 10–15%. Thus an inventor employed by EPFL or ETH is entitled to a share of the income received by the EPFL or ETH as a result of the commercial exploitation of an invention by a company having signed an agreement with the university.

The filing of patent applications follows a model of consensus building. Inventors, the head of the laboratory and the TTO evaluate the invention and decide whether or not to file a patent application. In case of disagreement the TTO makes the final decision. More importantly, the TTO covers the costs. The laboratory may sometimes file a patent, and meet the cost of doing so, in the institution's name, if the TTO declines: external patent attorneys support the application process. TTO officers very often follow a '30-months' policy: if the license agreement has not been executed within this period, the patent application is dropped or restricted to only a few countries. The strategy options are (1) non-exclusive licensing; (2) sole exclusive licensing to a start-up company; or (3) licensing to an existing company, all three of which are dependent upon the scope of technology, the market addressed and the time to market, and the further commitment of the inventor, because early stage technologies need the involvement of inventors. If the inventor is willing to start a firm the TTO will generally license first to the start-up. The academic institutions grant their start-ups a license while remaining the owner of the IPR: this policy is adopted because of the higher risk of bankruptcy involved with new start-up businesses (Chardonnens, 2006).

TTOs are also in charge of enforcing license agreements, in particular with regard to the payment of royalties and other remunerations due under the terms of the license. Licensees' agreements include clauses about bookkeeping and reporting obligations as well as audits of accounts. The constant interaction between the TTO and researchers and the training and consulting activities have contributed to the development of a positive culture concerning patenting and commercializing scientific knowledge. Swiss universities derive increasing levels of income from transfer activities, and high patent rankings prove the current success of the TTO role model and the policies that contributed to it.

Identifying risks and drivers: engines of innovation and the genetic code of the innovation system

Will an innovation policy which focuses on the enforcement of knowledge institutions and integration of SMEs be sufficient to make the innovation system resilient to future shocks? The evidence and performance indicators are a result of past policies and developments and, despite positive scoreboard indicators, there is a debate on the viability of the Swiss model. The following analysis sheds light on the future diffusiveness within the Swiss innovation model.

In the words of Forrester (1961) systems can be seen as 'wholes of elements, which cooperate towards a common goal'. In his 'Viable System Model', Stafford Beer specifies a set of management functions and their interrelationships as the conditions sufficient for the viability of any social system (Beer, 1981). According to Schwanninger (2006), 'understanding systemic behavior and the structure that generates it' becomes relevant. He sees system analysis as a means for 'exploring paths into the future and the concrete implications of decisions and assessing strategies as to their robustness and vulnerabilities' (Schwanninger, 2006).

The applied sensitivity model is a heuristic that underlines the interaction of different variables of different policy fields which constitute an assumed system constructed by the patterns stakeholders recognize.[33] The model does not rely on an institutional analysis but asks for variables that define the mechanism.

The sensitivity analysis takes into account different impact times of actions and the limited use of performance indicator sets for long-term decision-making in social and therefore complex systems. It sheds light on how the system reacts to intervention.

The ratio of output effects versus input effects assigns roles, to a greater or lesser extent, for every variable in the systemic model (see Figure 7.6).[34]

The analysis in Figure 7.6 illustrates that there are only a few active levers and a large number of critical, highly interconnected variables. Technology transfer and KTI policies for knowledge and technology transfer are addressed in (17) *Diffusion* and also comprise the invisible connection between educational and research sectors and the socio-economic impact of university–industry relations.

The systemic role and specific interdependencies of variables characterize the Swiss innovation system as being robust but also inert. There are many neutral and attenuating variables that contribute to resilience but hamper policy changes and new strategies. Accordingly, many self-organizing variables stabilize the system, among which are: (2) *Quality of Education*, (6) *Public Investments*, (14) *Degree of Employment*, (15) *Variety of the Technology Portfolio,* (16) *Inclusion,* (18) *Skilled Labour Supply* and (25) *Citizenship.*[35]

In this framework, (22) *Governance of Innovation* is a long-term product, as are (23) *Image of the Swiss Innovation System*, (21) *Robustness*, (1) *Quality of Living* and (3) *Quality of Research*. Policies directly addressing these variables would need to ignore the fact that the variables must be seen as indicators and outcomes rather than as active levers. Active levers, such as (13) *'Swissness'* and (9) *Infrastructure* are culturally specific: they address behavioural patterns and ways of doing things, such as the professional attitude of TTOs and self-conception as a service provider as well as consensus building on a case-by-case basis, which appears to be necessary for research and technology transfer. In addition, the high status of professional education in Switzerland, or the quiet pride in achievements and quality of work results, fall into this category (from unpublished interviews with experts).

The fragility of the innovation system is addressed by a large number of critical and highly interconnected variables: (7) *Private Investments*, (10) *Competitiveness*, (19) *Economic Strength*, (29) *International Connectivity*, (26) *International Positioning*, (27) *Legal Stability* and (24) *Policy*. In the Swiss innovation system *Public Investments* (6) made in a supply side fashion stabilize the system rather than these investments being used to drive policies. The model underlines the fact

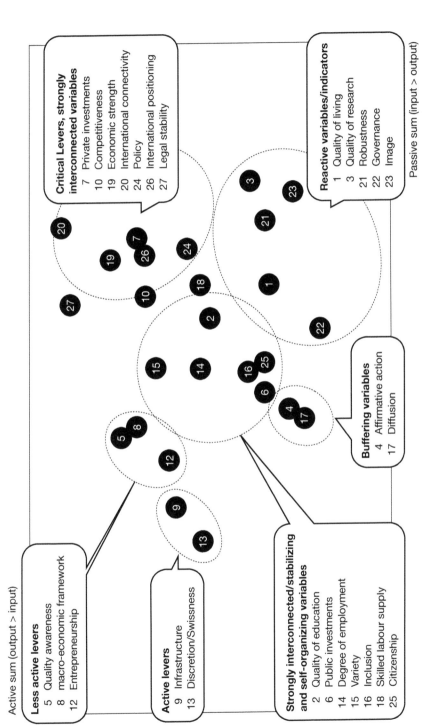

Active sum (output > input)

Less active levers
5   Quality awareness
8   macro-economic framework
12 Entrepreneurship

Active levers
9   Infrastructure
13 Discretion/Swissness

Strongly interconnected/stabilizing and self-organizing variables
2   Quality of education
6   Public investments
14 Degree of employment
15 Variety
16 Inclusion
18 Skilled labour supply
25 Citizenship

Critical Levers, strongly interconnected variables
7   Private investments
10 Competitiveness
19 Economic strength
20 International connectivity
24 Policy
26 International positioning
27 Legal stability

Reactive variables/indicators
1   Quality of living
3   Quality of research
21 Robustness
22 Governance
23 Image

Buffering variables
4   Affirmative action
17 Diffusion

Passive sum (input > output)

Figure 7.6 Systemic roles of variables in the Swiss Innovation System (identified by focus group for the system in focus)

that Swiss innovation policy addresses early system indicators and societal issues rather than research and technology. Only variables such as (9) *Infrastructure*, (27) *Legal stability*, (2) *Quality of Education*, (15) *Creation of Variety* and (20) *International Connectivity* are currently assigned to political action involving risk to a greater or lesser extent and addressed by programmes.

Engines of innovation

Three engines of innovation become prominent in the interdependency chart of the system model, when only strong relationships between variables are considered (see Figure 7.7).

Two key elements play a central role in linking the three subsystems (Figure 7.7): (3) *Quality of Research* and (5) *Quality Awareness*. Both are highly integrated into the system and involved in two mutually reinforcing feedback loops that play a crucial role with regard to the functioning of the system and the current economic strength of the country: they are called 'engines' of the system. The engines indicate that (3) *Quality of Research* as well (5) *Quality Awareness* ensure the adequacy of technology transfer. They also constitute the invisible link between the educational sector and the Swiss Research Excellence by means of cultural values such as (11) *Achievement Orientation*.

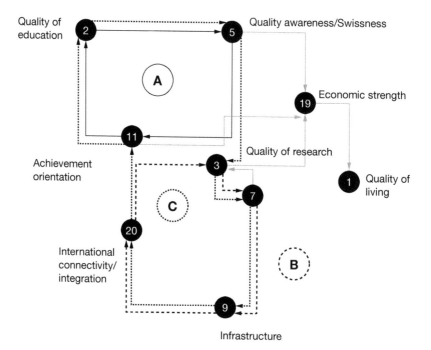

Figure 7.7 Engines of innovation within the model of the Swiss Innovation System

Engine One is driven by the cultural variable (11) *Achievement Orientation,* and has an effect on (5) *Quality Awareness* and (2) *Quality of Education.* Engine Two culminates in (3) *Quality of Research* which is fuelled by the investments, especially those of industry – (7) *Private Investments.* The financing of research by market players and the quality concern of citizens seem to be relevant for the adequate (9) *Research Infrastructure*[36] which has a positive effect on (20) *International Connectivity of the Swiss Innovation System.* Integration into global research is supported by market pull for international personnel in this sector and international investments. *International positioning* (26) leads to an enhanced global visibility, which in turn augments (3) *Quality of Research.*

Thus the system component (20) *International Connectivity* of the Swiss innovation system ensures the integration of the two central feedback loops (see Engine Three). Connection between economic and research sectors, as well as the integration and cooperation with international players, contributes to a self-organizing feedback loop that drives the entire system and at the same time functions with regard to the inclusion of Swiss society and opportunities for new players to participate.

In the model, stabilizing feedback loops dominate amplifying loops and indicate that the system is somewhat resilient not only to shocks but also to intervention.[37] The interrelationship shows that all stabilizing feedback loops integrate the following variables: (22) *Governance,* (24) *Policy,* and (6) *Public Expenditure.* The variables most embedded are (6) *Public Investments,* followed by (22) *Governance,* (24) *Policy* and (27) *Legal Certainty.* At the same time it is an inert system with many long cause-and-effect chains involving five or more variables, which implies that changes to the systems are difficult to accomplish.

The variable (7) *Private Investments* is not only a critical but also a strongly embedded variable. However, in contrast to (6) *Public Investments,* it is involved in amplifying feedback loops. If private investments slow down, changes to restore competitiveness will be difficult politically to make quickly.

Conclusion: systemic risks and some clouds on the horizon

The analysis proves that (5) *Quality Awareness* and (7) *Private Investments* are crucial variables that affect the robustness of the Swiss innovation system in terms of competitiveness and innovativeness culminating in (19) *Economic Strength.* They are influenced by the strong dependence on highly skilled labour and skilled immigrants in the research sector (see (18) *Skilled Labour Supply).* Apart from that, cultural variables such as (13) *Discretion* and (5) *Quality Awareness* contribute to a specific 'Swissness' that plays a distinctive role with regard to the excellence of research provided that the research is linked to the Swiss population and labour market. However, global investors and MNEs have different investment strategies to those of Swiss-based medium sized and medium technology firms – which can be described as being embedded better in the local ecosystem. MNEs prefer a stable and successful economy and a skilled workforce, with a focus on natural sciences, as well as highly specialized research activities and well-managed technology transfer (by the TTOs). The reservoir of skilled labour is a strong attraction for industry and for qualified individuals.

In that sense there is much of Bathelt et al's 'local buzz' in the pharmaceutical-driven North West regional innovation clusters (Bathelt et al, 2004). The situation is best characterized by a performance readiness of a population highly integrated into the innovation system. This integration results from the high level of employment and the institutional provision for lifelong learning activities in the educational system (so-called *Passarellen*). 'Global Pipelines' (Bathelt et al, 2004) are ubiquitous in the Swiss innovation system and show the same regional pattern. Following this, cluster policies for these sectors might instead enhance structural disparities. Equally, open programmes and new technology parks not having a quota for SMEs and variety will do the same.

Interestingly, although the education system and the research system are uncoupled – (considered critically by Griessen and Braun, 2008) – there are no gaps. The model illustrates how the latter picks up on the former. However, there is a danger that the self-organizing pattern of the major players is leading to a closing of the system or is distorted by (7) *Private Investment*, with a different cultural character that no longer relies on Swiss professions financed by public expenditure. In fact, private investment behaviour has already changed: there is a transfer of research activities to the USA and to China and a decline in industrial long-term funding of basic research in favour of product development. Swiss exports are under pressure due to a strong Swiss Franc which constitutes are severe financial problem for SME and impedes high R&D investments. At the same time, the trend anticipates larger, international research projects and a shift towards service sector activities such as ICT, innovative business models and social entrepreneurship as well as university spin-offs (KTI, 2013) that are related to the established industries.[38] Technology transfer generates good outcomes, but it is driven by accelerated innovation cycles: TTOs can play a crucial role in this process because management and good procedures accelerate the capitalization of knowledge.

The model shows that the current success of the Swiss innovation system relies heavily on legal and political stability in Switzerland and the inclusiveness and social living conditions that enable entrepreneurship and risk-taking in high-level technologies. The ability of the Swiss population, including young students and migrants, to integrate culturally in many fields, supported by the secondary level of education provision – (*Sekundarstufe 2*) – and the flexible employment sector represent an explanatory red tape. Switzerland has a strong model of *Flexicurity*, a liberal labour market with high levels of social protection.[39] The interplay of four variables contributes to the self-reinforcement of innovativeness: *Inclusiveness* (involvement of all players in the system); *Equal opportunities; Attractiveness for skilled labour;* and *High level of social recognition of crafts and professions outside the academic sector.*

The variable *Diffusion* represents the short- and long-term dialogue between science, education, industry and society. *Diffusiveness* is a precondition for the qualities and quantities the system needs and can supply: it stabilizes the system.

In this context, well-managed technology transfer and the KTI-initiatives will keep the communication channels open for feedback and minor corrective measures. There must be stronger incentives for TTOs and other technology transfer intermediaries to service an SME clientele. In a best-case scenario, KTI and government provide the means for generation of variety (of industries) and for innovative start-ups supported by private wealth and business angels, rather than focusing on the provision of start-ups for innovation shopping in the pharmaceutical sector. The latter is an existing self-organizing loop of private investment with a distinct regional pattern that contains the danger of increasing structural disparities.

Important parameters affecting culture are migration, the degree of inclusion within a society and the degree to which the Swiss economy can integrate into the global and European research landscapes without losing its identity ('Swissness'). Integration policy will therefore become a key component with regard to the sustainability of the Swiss innovation system. Balancing the integration of new cultures, in relation to human resources, investments and the enabling of new innovation-based economic sectors in concert with other countries and beyond the successful subsystem of pharmaceutical and chemical industries, will also become a key task for the Swiss government. The importance of embedded variables such as (7) *Private Investments* with strong linkages to (10) *Competitiveness*, (20) *International Inter-connectivity of the Innovation System* define where forecasts must lie.

Outlook and policy recommendations

Swiss technology transfer and the operating model used by TTOs draw on the diffusiveness and permeability of the Swiss innovation system. To date there are no gaps in the ecosystems and excellent brokers, such as university-based TTOs and KTI, the federal agency, integrate SMEs into that system at national level. Public investment in education as well as research universities will be the future basis for the quality of the research apparatus and for TTO operations, as well as for high tech manufacturing in ETH laboratories and the research departments of global players. The legal framework and the high quality of management in the universities provide a strong incentive for further investment. Copying best practice in technology transfer, the set-up of TTOs, federal research universities and STEM-related disciplines has so far proved a good way to transform Switzerland into one of the global players in science and research activities. It is possible that the scarcity of money at national level has prevented both the adoption of an approach that was too bureaucratic, and R&D overcapacities.

As an unintended consequence, federal and cantonal policies as well as industrial strategies have integrated ex post into a specific innovation system shaped by a specific governance of innovation. Vocational education and applied science ensure the inclusion and integration of new players into the innovation system. This provides a stable context for the TTO model so that rules and regulations in academia, industry and government relations are commonly understood and accepted by both Swiss society and the respective institutions. This framework enhances international attractiveness for future investment in R&D.

The analysis also makes it clear that government money invested in education is 'slow money' with an impact time of at least one generation. This time lag exemplifies the fact that Switzerland profits from small steps in past policies. However, the referendum of 2014 against immigration should be seen as a social indicator that the educational system and the existing governance of innovation is at its capacity limit and the perceived transformative capacity of Swiss society is being exhausted.

Although the system appears to be robust, there are risks. International investments and industrial R&D expenses of global players carry the danger of off-shoring. Fiscal policies and a weak European currency fuel this trend. There are signs of co-optation of the ETH–TTO technology model by the few Swiss global players that fund the system. This represents a new quality regarding the socio-economic development of the country. The disintegration of family owned SMEs and the collapse of southern regions should be seen as a dangerous trend, which cannot be compensated with large numbers of patents and publications in addition to high scoreboard rankings of top-tier universities. The shortcomings of dominant corporate strategies include destruction of variety, increasing disparities, dependency on highly mobile industries and a dysfunctional integration of Switzerland into the European innovation system.

The role of government in this is to provide diffusiveness and to allow for permeability in Swiss socio-economic development, rather than to promote large cluster programmes or to set up detailed transfer activities itself. To date, Swiss policy has sought to provide open channels and follow the principle of subsidiarity. There is a trend towards a new role for the federal government which involves the facilitation of European integration and resisting disparities that are arising. The governance of innovation that has shaped innovation thus far might take a new form.

Despite these challenges, there are no immediate policies at hand. The present analysis demonstrates that Swiss innovation policy lacks active levers for intervention and has no tradition, political culture or polity for direct federal political intervention. Internal dependencies in the Swiss innovation system demonstrate that the system is inert and has a tendency to stabilize itself, so that major policies might not succeed. The impending assignment to create new national technology parks close to existing clusters will therefore have counter-productive effects. It will fuel existing engines and accelerate further the disintegration process, unless countermeasures of the KTI agency in technology transfer and integration of mature industries and SMEs gather momentum.

The federal agency (KTI) will contribute to further success provided that it can generate variety and take into account the specificity and 'Swissness' of the Swiss innovation system. Accordingly, knowledge and technology transfer policies (TT) run by KTI will contribute to the resilience of the system if new players are included. Following this, the promotion of new science-based industries through interdisciplinary technology transfer and the integration of social sciences and humanities into knowledge and technology transfer becomes an important challenge for KTI. Related to this, the integration of SMEs in the Eastern and Southern regions of Switzerland operating outside the pharmaceutical sector, as well as of existing innovation clusters, is an important political challenge that is beginning to be addressed by KTI programmes.

The sensitivity model illustrates that current success and attractiveness relies on a stable legal framework and on a continuing integration of the Swiss innovation system into the international and European landscapes, especially in terms of vocational professions and integration of SMEs. This framework appears to be a key success factor and should not be disregarded in future innovation policies.

In terms of viability, a political concentration on the successful pharmaceutical and chemical clusters in Switzerland and a focus on a 'strengthening strength' paradigm of German innovation policy or a 'smart specialization strategy' as followed by the European Commission would be a risky strategy for picking winners in this advanced innovation system. Equally, more elaborate technology transfer initiatives to link federal laboratories and universities to existing industries, or even Regional Innovation Strategies anticipated in the European Horizon 2020 programme, would be the wrong approach for Switzerland and would only serve existing industries. This political focus would lead instead to a further closure of the successful subsystem, to overspecialization and increased regional disparity.

Innovation policy in Switzerland must be understood as a latecomer strategy of a less industrialized and small state. The country lacked both the cultural heredity of a dense industrial and research infrastructure (such as Fraunhofer, Max Planck or Helmholtz) of neighbouring countries such as Germany and a history of collaboration in the transfer of technology via these intermediaries.

Switzerland took a short cut in copying best practices and role models (such as MIT in the US and Cambridge in the UK, and other US research universities) and managed the TTOs effectively and with industry taking the lead role. It must not be forgotten that the Swiss innovation system is defined and supported by a direct democracy and by politicians who refrain of state interventionism. Minimal public investment is matched with industrial budgets: firms must pay if they need technology transfer. Globally competing MNEs will strive for the best option and force the research universities to live up to it. On the supply side, the Swiss government provides a well-educated and skilled workforce and students trained in STEM-related faculties.

It becomes apparent that the political system is a crucial factor in innovation studies and the specific governance of innovation provides the reasons for this. Direct democracy, Swiss federalism with powerful cantons and an absence of purposeful intergovernmental integration has defined and supports the Swiss innovation system. To date concerted actions and complex cluster programmes have been prevented (in contrast to, for example, German S&T and R&D system integration promoted and funded by Lander and Bund). The Swiss 'latecomer' strategy, low levels of federal investment, industrial R&D budgets, a legal framework and values supplemented the technology transfer model, whereby

TTOs are a product rather than a single success factor. Although these products are similar to other successful TTOs in different national contexts, the phenotype should not be mistaken for the genotype. The sensitivity analysis is therefore a powerful heuristic to unveil the genotype and identify the long-term risks of co-optation, structural disparities and European disintegration.

Acknowledgements

I would like to thank the experts of *Swiss Bundesamt für Bildung und Technologie/ Staatssekretariat für Bildung, Forschung und Innovation* for their input. I also acknowledge the work of Peter Pattis, lic. OEC HSG and René Klar, MA Universität Heidelberg, both researchers at Malik Management St. Gallen AG, Switzerland

Notes

1 In 2012 Switzerland had a population of 7.9 million and a GDP of US$ 632.2 bn. Research & Development activities account for 3 % of Swiss GDP. In 2009, the High Tech sector is the country's largest industrial employer and accounts for exports worth of a total of SF 63 bn. which is equivalent to 35 % of all goods exported from Switzerland.
   In: State Secretariat for Education and Research/ SER (2011) Report on Higher Education and Research in Switzerland, SER Bern, page 7.
2 According to the Economist Intelligence Unit, in 2013 GDP per head for OECD countries was about US$37,000 (PPP) while GDP per head in Switzerland was US$52,000US$ (PPP). Unemployment in OECD countries was 8%, while 3% of the Swiss population was unemployed in 2013.
3 European Commission Extra-EU mobility survey, June 2013: 66% of academic personnel at Swiss universities have a migration background and job satisfaction is high. See also: http://ec.europa.eu/euraxess/pdf/research_policies/more2/Report%20 on%20survey%20of%20researchers%20outside%20EU.pdf (accessed 4 September 2014).
4 'Switzerland's strong performance is linked to being the best performer in nine indicators, in particular in open, excellent and attractive research systems where it has the best performance in all three indicators and in economic effects where it has best performance in two indicators (Employment in knowledge-intensive activities and Licence and patent revenues from abroad). Switzerland is performing well above the EU average for most indicators, above all for international scientific publications, non-R&D innovation expenditures, community trademarks and new doctorate graduates' (EU, 2014: 72).
5 ERI (Education, Research and Innovation) period 2013–2016, cantonal expenditure increases by an average of 3.3% per year (from SF5.3 billion in 2004 to SF7.9 billion in 2016) and federal expenditure by an average of 4.7% per year (from SF4.3 billion to SF7.4 billion). In 2010, 55% of applied sciences at universities is covered by the cantons (25 by the confederation and 20% by other parties including student fees). See: FDEA/ OPET Bern (2012).
6 About SF9.1 billion come from industry out of a total of SF13.1 billion R&D spending; that is, 69% of the R&D funding comes from private business! Private research expenditures came mainly from globally integrated firms or multinationals in all sectors; that is, IT, food, pharmaceutical and chemical sectors. Research and Development expenditures of ten companies in the pharmaceutical and chemical

industry accounted for SF7.0 billion in 2011. Public funding: SF2.1 billion federal spending and SF890 million from cantons. SF685 million came from foreign sources (and SF305 million from others sources) (data based on Marxt and Brunner, 2013: data for 2004 and 2008).

7 www.sbfi.admin.ch/themen/01367/01677/index.html?lang=de#sprungmarke0_1 (accessed 20 August 2014).
8 World Economic Forum (2009).
9 www.bioalps.org (accessed 7 September 2014).
10 www.cleantech-switzerland.com (accessed 7 September 2014).
11 Beat Vonlanden, President of the West Schweizer Regierungskonferenz, Staatspräsident und Vorlkswirtschaftsdirektor des Kantons Freiburg, Schweiz at the go-cluster conference Berlin 6 March 2014.
12 The majority of all the patent cooperation treaties originated from three Swiss regions clustering around universities and the research-intensive industries: the Lake Geneva region with EPFL, and the Universities of Lausanne, Geneva and Fribourg, North West Switzerland (with Basel University and the University of North West Switzerland) and the Zurich region (ETH with Winterthur Campus and Zurich University).
13 Thierstein and Egger (1998).
14 Charles Kleiber was appointed State Secretary for Education and Research (SBF) in October 1997. He held this post for more than ten years. During his tenure, scientific research and higher education were significantly strengthened; new centres of excellence were established, international cooperation was intensified, resources for science were greatly increased, and a constitutional amendment was adopted, paving the way for a national area for science and research. See http://irgc.org/wp-content/uploads/2012/ 04/2008_KLEIBER__CV_ENG.pdf (accessed 27 February 2014).

   Kleiber's intention was to install Swiss Patent Offices because they were flourishing in Germany. As a pilot he chose Lausanne. Immediate protests came from Zürich – and, as a reaction, two agencies were planned. Ultimately, SNI/RSI (the Swiss Network for Innovation/Réseau Suisse d'Innovation led by former EPFL president Jean-Claude Badoux) used the model of Xavier Comtesse who was the first Swiss scientific consul in the United states and initiator of the Swiss House in Boston in 2000 (now Swissnex Boston). SNI faced massive criticism from the Swiss parliament and never took off as planned (source: unpublished interviews).
15 Interviews with SBFI officials ([unpublished] 2014).
16 Expertengruppe 'Start-up-Kultur USA–CH c/o Stiftung Technopark® Report on Enabling our Future. Stärkung der Start-up Kultur in der Schweiz aufgrund der Erkenntnisse aus einer Vergleichsstudie in den USA, May 2002.
17 Based on empirical research Thierstein and Wilhelms state that 43% of Swiss Incubator, Technology and Innovation centres, ITIs, are commonly set up by public business promoters, private companies or other private institutions such as foundations or business associations. Public institutions are engaged in 75% of all ITI centres, private companies engaged in 67% of all ITI centres. The study illustrates that one-quarter of all ITI centres were established exclusively by private companies providing simply space and out of rent seeking motives. www.kti.admin.ch/projektfoerderung/index.html?lang=de (accessed 24 March 2014).
18 FDEA/OPET (2012: 13).
19 SBFI Information from the State Secretariat for Education, Research and Innovation, SERI, July/August 2014. In addition to the two hubs surrounding Switzerland's two federal institutes of technology (ETH in Zurich and EPF in Lausanne), two projects for a network location have been put forward. In addition to issues surrounding location, the concept also includes participation criteria as well as aspects relating to scientific competence, the industrial surroundings and availability of land. In addition, the cantonal concept presents a general outline for a future national umbrella organization that will combine local initiatives to ensure both international marketing and quality assurance.

Both hub locations should be in the respective vicinity of the ETHZ and EPFL. While the Zurich site is expected to be developed on a portion of the former military airport, the Lausanne site will serve as the main hub for FIT-affiliated research institutes in the French-speaking cantons of Switzerland. In addition, two network sites will be established: one in the Canton of Aargau (InnovAARE Park near the Paul Scherrer Institute, Villigen) and the other in the north-western part of Switzerland (joint project 'BEST' conducted by Basel-Stadt, Basel-Landschaft and the Canton of Jura, Allschwil).

20 Since 1992 Switzerland has participated in programmes of the European Union. The main Swiss players are Staatssekretariat für Wirtschaft (SECO), Staatssekretaritat für Bildung, Forschung und Innovation (SBFI), Kommission für Technologie und Innovation (KTI) and Swiss National Fonds (SNF).

21 In terms of government budget appropriation or outlays for R&D (GBAGRD) Switzerland spent 2.37% of total government expenditures and internationally ranks behind only South Korea (2.99%) and the US (2.6%) (OEDC, 2011).

22 Funding is proposal driven, and NSF supported 3500 research proposals in 2012. Direct project funding was SF391.4 million for 2012, of which SF135.7 million was approved for basic research in mathematics, natural sciences and engineering, and SF155.5 million for biology and medicine. (Social sciences and arts, including economics and law, received SF84.8 million, interdisciplinary research SF15.5 million.) In 2012 mathematics (a platform science for many disciplines) enjoyed a 38% increase in funding. In medicine and biology the amounts for 2012 are stable and show an equal split between basic research in medicine and biology (biochemical, genetics, molecular research).

23 Out of 4057 international cooperations, 718 are with Germany and 625 with the United States (cf France: 443; UK: 390) (SNF, 2012).

24 www.swisslifesciences.com/swisslifesciences/db/detail.php?c=6296251k$Sn35KCa Mqk4s6 (accessed 24 March 2014).

25 www.handelszeitung.ch/unternehmen/eth-zuerich-22-spin-firmen-gegruendet

26 The creation of Logitech is due mainly to the invention of the mouse, which came out of the research performed by Jean-Daniel Nicoud, a professor at EPFL. He developed the first prototype, equipped with a ball and sensors, in the 1970s, and Logitech created a production model for Hewlett-Packard in the 1980s. http://actu.epfl.ch/news/a-logitech-research-center-opens-at-epfl (accessed 20 March 2014).

27 Statements in this section are based on work by Chardonnes (2006), a licensing officer at the Industrial Relations Office of EPFL. Her information paper on 'University technology transfer practices in Switzerland' is complemented with information on rules, regulations and templates on the ETH website: www.ethz.ch/en/the-eth-zurich/organisation/staff-units/eth-transfer.html (accessed 22 March 2014). For EPFL contracts http://tto.epfl.ch/ and the guide to TTOs http://tto.epfl.ch/Guide_SRI_1 were analysed (accessed 22 March 2014).

28 In 2007, incubator activities of ETH (130 spin-offs) yielded SF43 million profit and the turnover from Swiss university licensing totalled SF7.5 million in 2011 (NZZ, 10 October 2013): www.nzz.ch/aktuell/wirtschaft/nzz_equity/robsute-und-wachsende-spin-off-szene-schweiz-1.18164981 (accessed 2 September 2014).

29 Research Collaboration Agreements with partners from industry at ETH Zurich rely on this case-to-case evaluation. ETH emphasizes that it is important to define such projects clearly, so that they can easily be distinguished from other research projects carried out at ETH Zurich (especially within the same group).

30 www.venturekick.ch/index.cfm?CFID=386239662&CFTOKEN=65748440&page=129769 (accessed 7 September 2014).

31 The Swiss Commission for Technology and Innovation (KTI) brings together business angels, venture capital and universities, and has a strong focus on entrepreneurship training and start-up coaching. In 2004, the KTI set up Venturelab to provide free training for those who launch start-ups. Its goal is to help increase student awareness of entrepreneurship and 'trigger a new wave of Swiss entrepreneurs'.

32 More than SF11 million invested, over 298 start-up projects financed, more than 464 million in financing volume and 2433 jobs created: this is Venture Kick's track record since the private initiative was launched in autumn 2007 by a private consortium. See: www.venturekick.ch/index.cfm?page=129769 (accessed 24 March 2014) and Venture Kick (2013).

33 Vester states that 'the sensitivity model captures the perception of relevant stakeholders of the examined system and its socio-economic-ecological environment as a bio-cybernetic entity without getting lost in a countless number of factors and variables' (Vester, 2001). Following Vester's approach the Sensitivity Analysis focuses on the following key questions:
- Does the system have a tendency to stabilize itself?
- Is the system susceptible to disturbances?
- What are the internal dependencies within the system?
- What are the inter-linkages of the system's feedback cycles and its degree of variety?
- How a system will behave and react to one or other change inside or outside the system. Where in the system are interventions possible to keep the system viable?
See also: Vester (2001).

34 The focus group of innovation policy experts identified 26 variables that were sufficient to describe the model of the Swiss innovation system as the system in focus.

35 In 2011 approximately 20,000 were employed in the Swiss Research and Development Sector: 39% had no Swiss passport. Of academic personnel at Swiss universities 66% had a migration background (Swiss Bundesamt für Statistik, 2011): Eidgenössische Betriebszählung. 25% of the working population are migrants with a preference for full-time employment. The migrant population provides 22% of the total volume of work. See: Büro für Arbeits- und Sozialpolitische Studien (2011): Arbeitskräftemangel 2010–2030. Studie im Auftrag von Travail Suisse. Bundesamt für Statistik (2011): AVOL. Tatsächliches jährliches Arbeitsvolumen nach Geschlecht, Nationalität, Beschäftigungsgrad. Eidgenössische Kommission http://fimm.ch/fileadmin/Projekte/2011/2011_Sensibilisierung/Infodossier_Leistungen_Migranten_LANG_DE.pdf (accessed 22 March 2014).

36 Reasoning and definition of the focus group: Infrastructure has a positive impact on the system and on the image of the Swiss innovation system as well as on the attractiveness for local and foreign skilled labor; infrastructure is an important carrier of culture; an excellent research infrastructure is attractive for researchers.

37 Thirty-eight feedback loops are reinforcing, amplifying and short, and can lead to a fast dynamic overload of the system. There are also 185 stabilizing (long) feedback loops that show retarding impacts and stabilize the system on a whole.

38 www.kti.admin.ch/aktuell/00021/00139/00207/index.html?lang=de (accessed 7 September 2014).

39 Böhringer and Marti (2008).

References

Adner R (2006) Match your innovation strategy to your innovation ecosystem. *Harvard Business Review* 84: 98, 110.

Arvanitis S, Kubli U, Sydow N and Woerter M (2007) Knowledge and technology transfer (KTT) activities between universities and firms in Switzerland – the main facts: An empirical analysis based on firm-level data. *ICFAI Journal of Knowledge Management* 5(6): 17–75.

Arvanitis S, Kubli U and Woerter M (2008) University–industry knowledge and technology transfer in Switzerland: What university scientists think about co-operation with private enterprises. *Research Policy* 37(10): 1865–1883 (DOI: 10.1016/j.respol.2008.07.005).

Atkinson R and Pelfrey P (2010) Science and the entrepreneurial university. *Issues in Science and Technology* 26(4): 39–48.

Bathelt H, Malmberg A and Maskell P (2004) Clusters and knowledge: Local buzz, global pipelines and the process of knowledge creation. *Progress in Human Geography* 28: 31 (DOI: 10.1191/0309132504ph469oa).

Bercovitz J and Feldman MP (2008) Academic entrepreneurs: Organizational change at the individual level. *Organization Science*, 19(1): 69–89.

Böhringer P and Marti M (2008) Flexicurity, Bedeutung für die Schweiz. *Soziale Sicherheit CHSS* 1/2008, Bundesamt für Sozialversicherungen, S. 41–43.

Breznitz SM (2011) Improving or impairing? Following technology transfer changes at the University of Cambridge. *Regional Studies* 45(4): 463–478.

Bundesrat (2012) Botschaft über die Förderung von Bildung, Forschung und Innovation in den Jahren 2013–2016 (22 February 2012).

Chardonnes F (2006) University technology transfer practices in Switzerland. Online publication, available at: www.lesi.org/les-nouvelles/les-nouvelles-online/2006/june-2006/2011/08/08/university-technology-transfer-practices-in-switzerland (accessed 15 December 2014).

Carayannis EG and Campbell DFJ (2012) 'Mode 3' and 'QuadrupleHelix': Toward a 21st century fractal innovation ecosystem. *International Journal of Technology Management* 46(3/4): 201–234.

Clarrysse B, Wright M, Lockett A and Binks M (2005) Spinning out new ventures: A typology of incubation strategies from European research institutions. *Journal of Business Venturing* 20: 183–216.

Cohen WM and Levinthal DA (1990) Absorptive capacity: A new perspective on learning and innovation. *Administrative Science Quarterly*, 35(1): 128–152 [Special Issue: Technology, Organizations and Innovation]

Cooke P and Leydesdorff L (2006) Regional Development in the knowledge-based economy: The construction of advantage. *Journal of Technology Transfer* 31(1): 5–15.

Cooke P and Morgan K (1998) *The Associational Economy: Firms, Regions, and Innovation*. Oxford, UK: Oxford University Press.

Deakin M and Leydesdorff L (2014) The Triple Helix model of smart cities: A neo-evolutionary perspective. In: Deakin M (ed.) *Smart Cities: Governing, Modelling and Analysing the Transition*. London, UK and New York, NY: Routledge, pp 134–149.

Delgado M and Ketels C (2012) Assessing country competitiveness: The case of Spain – a neo-evolutionary perspective. In: Cooke P, Parrili MD and Curbelo JL (2012) *Innovation, Global Change and Territorial Resilience*. Cheltenham, UK: Edward Elgar, pp. 134–149.

Edquist C (2011) Design of innovation policy through diagnostic analysis: Identification of systemic problems (or failures). *Industrial and Corporate Change* 20(6): 1725–1753 (doi:10.1093/icc/dtr060).

EFI (Expertenkommission Forschung und Innovation) (Hrsg.) (2012) *Gutachten zu Forschung, Innovation und technologischer Leistungsfähigkeit Deutschlands 2012*. Berlin, Germany: EFI.

EPFL (2013) Lausanne Annual Report 2013. Available online at: https://documents.epfl.ch/groups/e/ep/epfl-unit/www/rapport/EPFL-annual-report-2013.pdf (accessed 15 December 2014).

ETH (2013) Zuerich Annual Report 2013. Available online at: www.ethz.ch/content/dam/ethz/common/docs/publications/annual-reports/2012/ETH_Annual_report_2012.pdf (accessed 15 December 2014).

Etzkowitz H and Leydesdorff L (2000) The dynamics of innovation: From national systems and 'Mode 2' to a Triple Helix of university–industry–government relations. *Research Policy* 29(2): 109–123.

Etzkowitz H, Webster A, Gebhardt C and Terra BRT (2000) The future of the university and the university of the future: Evolution of ivory tower to entrepreneurial paradigm. *Research Policy* 29(2): 313–330.

EU (2014) Innovation Union Scoreboard 2014. Brussels, Belgium: European Commission.

FDEA (Federal Department of Economic Affairs) and OPET (Federal Office for Professional Education and Technology) (2012) *Federal and Cantonal Funding in the Education Research and Innovation Sector 2004–2016*. Bern, Switzerland: FDEA and OPET.

Flores M, Boër C, Huber C, Pluss A, Schoch R and Pouly M (2009) Universities as key enablers to develop new collaborative environments for innovation: Successful experiences from Switzerland and India. *International Journal of Production Research* 47(17): 4935–4953.

Forrester JW (1961) *Industrial Dynamics*. Cambridge, MA: MIT Press.

Gebhardt C and Pohlmann MC (2013) Managing the organisation 2.0: Entrepreneurial spirit and general management competences as early indicators for cluster success and sustainable regional development – findings from the German Entrepreneurial Regions Programme. *Journal of High Technology Management Research* 24(2): 153–160.

Griessen T and Braun D (2008) The political coordination of knowledge and innovation policies in Switzerland. *Science and Public Policy* 35(4): 277–288. (DOI: 10.3152/030234208X310338)

Kaufmann A and Toedtling F (2001) Science–industry interaction in the process of innovation: The importance of boundary-crossing between systems. *Research Policy* 30(5): 791–804.

Ketels CHM and Protsiv S (2013) Clusters and the new growth path for Europe. *WWW for Europe Working Paper* No 14 Vienna, Austria: WIFO. Available at: www.hbs.edu/faculty/Pages/item.aspx?num=45185 (accessed 15 December 2014).

KTI (Kommission für Technologie und Innovation) (2013) KTI Tätigkeitsbericht 2013. Available at: www.kti.admin.ch/aktuell/00021/00139/00207/index.html?lang=de (accessed 15 December 2015).

Lawton-Smith H (2006) *Universities, Innovation and the Economy*. Abingdon, UK: Routledge.

Lester RK and Piore MJ (2004) *Innovation – The Missing Dimension*. Boston, MA: Harvard University Press.

Lewinthal CWM and Levinthal DA (1990) Absorptive capacity: a new perspective on learning and innovation. *Administrative Science Quarterly*, 35(1): 128–153.

Leydesdorff L and Ahrweiler P (2014) In search of a network theory of innovations: Relations, positions, and perspectives. *Journal of the American Society for Information Science and Technology* 65(11): 2359–2374.

Link A and Siegel D (2005) Generating science-based growth: An econometric analysis of the impact of organizational incentives on university–industry technology transfer. *European Journal of Finance* 11: 169–181.

Lockett A and Wright M (2005) Resources, capabilities, risk capital and the creation of university spin-out companies. *Research Policy* 34: 1043–1057.

Lundvall B-Å (ed.) (1992) *National Systems of Innovation: Towards a Theory of Innovation and Interactive Learning*. London, UK: Pinter.

Marxt C and Brunner C (2012) Analyzing and improving the national innovation system of highly developed countries: The case of Switzerland. *Technological Forecasting and Social Change*. Available online (doi:10.1016/j.techfore.2012.07.008 Elsevier).

Mercan B and Göktaş D (2011) Components of innovation ecosystems: A cross-country study. *International Research Journal of Finance and Economics* 76: 102–112.

Nelson RR (ed.) (1993) *National Innovation Systems: A Comparative Analysis*. New York, NY: Oxford University Press.

OECD (2010) *Science, Technology and Industry Outlook 2010* Paris, France: OECD.

OECD (2011) *Science and Innovation Indicators Scoreboard 2011: Highlights*. Paris, France: OECD.

Schwanninger M (2006) System dynamics and the evolution of the systems movement. *Systems Research and Behavioral Science* 23: 583–594.

SNF (2012) Swiss National Science Foundation, see: www.snf.ch/en/Pages/default.aspx (accessed 15 December 2014).

Thierstein A and Wilhelm B (2001) Incubator, technology and innovation centres in Switzerland: Features and policy implications. *Entrepreneurship and Regional Development* 13: 315–331.

Thierstein A and Egger UK (1998) Integrated regional policy: Lessons from Switzerland. *Environment and Planning C: Government and Policy* 16(2): 155–172.

Thursby MC, Thursby JG and Mukherjee S (2005) Are there effects of licensing on academic research? A life cycle view. *NBER Working Paper* No 11497. Cambridge, MA: National Bureau of Economic Research.

Tinguely X (2013) *The New Geography of Innovation: Clusters, Competitiveness and Theory*. Basingstoke, UK: Palgrave-Macmillan.

Urbano D and Guerrero M (2012) The development of an entrepreneurial university. *Journal of Technology Transfer* 37: 43–74.

Venture Kick (2013) Annual Report 2013. Zürich, Switzerland: Venture Kick.

Vernon R (1979) The product cycle hypothesis in a new international environment. *Oxford Bulletin of Economics and Statistics* 41(4): 255–267.

Vester F (2001) Simulating complex systems as sustainable organization by transparent sensitivity models. Lecture presented at Eurosim 2001 Congress, TU Delft, The Netherlands, 26–29 June 2001, Federation of European Simulation Societies, www.eurosim.info.

Vester F (2002) *Die Kunst vernetzt zu denken: Ideen und Werkzeuge für enien neuen Umgang mit Komplexität* (*The art of interconnected thinking: Ideas and tools for a new way of dealing with complexity*), Report to the Club of Rome. Munich, Germany: dtv (www.dtv.de).

World Economic Forum (2009) Global Competitive Report 2009–2010. Geneva, Switzerland: WEF. Available at: www.weforum.org/reports/global-competitiveness-report-2009-2010 (accessed 15 December 2014).

8 UK university models of technology transfer in a global economy

Helen Lawton Smith and John Glasson

The UK context since the late – 1990s

High profile success studies from the United States of America have long shaped the perceptions of the contribution that universities can make to innovation-led economic advance. Since the 1980s, the US has provided exemplars of national and local impacts of particular 'entrepreneurial universities'. They include Stanford and Silicon Valley (Etzkowitz 1983; Saxenian 1983) and MIT and Route 128 in Boston (Saxenian 1994; Etzkowitz 1993, 2002).

This chapter reviews the expectations on UK universities to contribute to economic and societal benefits to the country and to their localities. It does this by placing those expectations within a conceptual framework based on the triple helix model and the regional variant, regional triple helix spaces. This allows for an analysis of national and local specifics, role of government and kinds of impact which UK universities in particular might be expected to make and how they might do it. It focuses in particular on the local case of the county of Oxfordshire and of Oxford City – with its two universities and their innovative roles and interactions within the buoyant Oxfordshire high-technology economy. It also considers the cases of Cambridge University and Imperial College in London.

While universities in UK economic policy date back decades, it is only recently that it has become explicit as a local agenda. We here distinguish between the regional and local levels of policy making and delivery. This distinction in the UK represents a change in the political system. The regional scale in many countries represents a clearly defined area with administrative responsibilities encompassing many nodes of population and economic activity (see Howells 1999). Local here is characterised as a much smaller geographical unit with much more limited administrative powers and fewer nodes, such as a city, or in the UK, counties, which have a small number of towns and cities.

Since the Coalition government was elected in 2010, a series of reports have recommended local engagement as exemplified by the 2013 Witty Review of 'Universities and Growth'.[1] This represents a shift in policy from the previous Labour governments (1997–2010) where the focus was on the region, with much policy delivery to these administratively composite entities. 'In this chapter we examine the rationale for this change in policy and practice and position it within the context of other reports and policies which have an impact on UK universities' technology transfer activity in the global economy. The starting point in time is the 1990s.

It is then that major reports such as Dearing (1997) began to appear, which emphasised the central role of universities in the economy. Funding for the engagement of universities in economic development increased from that time. In part these changes were made possible by earlier changes in the UK system of higher education. Most notable in this expansion of higher education were the establishment of a set of research universities in the 1960s, the later creation (1992) of the 'new' universities (mainly former polytechnics, which were removed from funding by local education authorities), and the subsequent massification of universities as numbers of students have steadily risen (see the later section entitled 'A brief introduction to the UK university system').

In the first instance, policy was non-spatial (although with spatial outcomes). Later it included sub-national elements with the focus first on regions, later on cities and now on localities. In the UK, central government holds the purse strings not only for entrepreneurship and innovation-led economic growth but, perhaps more important, for science policy which has pronounced spatial outcomes. The continuing dominance of research funding in the 'Golden Triangle' of Oxford, Cambridge and London universities is the most obvious manifestation of this. European funding for scientific research and European regional policy (most recently that directed towards achieving 'smart growth based on innovation') has similar effects (Foray and Goenega 2013).

That being said, the link of universities to local development as a consequence of policies with a spatial basis is problematic. What is important is to understand the nature of regional/local economic specificity in the impact of universities (Storper 1997) as well as national and international impact of research and teaching. Goldstein (2009) raised a number of key policy relevant questions, two of which are taken as the basis for the discussion of UK policy. The first is: what kinds of changes in regional economic activity, or outcomes, is it reasonable to expect universities to make? This is both a political as well as an academic question. Goldstein lists a number of possible kinds of economic impacts: increased in aggregate regional income and employment; productivity gains, increases in innovative activity; new business start-ups; and increased regional capacity for sustained economic growth. He suggests that while the first is unproblematic as universities contribute more broadly to their local economies through their sheer scale of activity, there is less agreement about whether the other types of potential impacts can be attributable to universities.

The second is: how do universities stimulate economic development? Goldstein provides seven different types of possible activities: development of human capital (teaching), creation of knowledge (research); transfer of existing knowledge (technical assistance); technological innovation; capital investment, regional leadership and governance; and co-production of knowledge infrastructure and creative milieu. Goldstein also points out that estimating magnitude of impact is fraught with conceptual and measurement problems.

In policy, the focus is often on technology transfer as a means of stimulating innovation-led economic development, with the contribution of universities to technological advance identified as being embodied in the skills as well as in the wide spectrum of research from pure to applied. Goddard and Vallance (2013) identify universities as being essential urban 'anchor institutions'. They argue that universities, despite not having a democratic mandate to intervene, have a key role to play in local development because of their scale, local rootedness and community links. As such they represent a form of 'sticky capital' around which can be built local growth strategies.

This focus on universities as anchor institutions and as deliverers of local economic development may even bring universities into being further judged not only for their teaching and their research but also their local impact, as in the USA. This role of universities was underlined by the 2002 Great Cities Universities Consortium (GCUC) Report[2] which commented:

> urban universities have come to be judged, not only on their academic performance, but also on their ability to help communities identify, analyse and solve their most urgent problems created by a rapidly changing, culturally diverse environment dominated by computerized technologies.

Context – entrepreneurial universities in policy

UK higher education policy approach on the supply side draws on the notion of the 'entrepreneurial university' (Etkzowitz 1983; Clarke 1998) by which the university is the source of commercially available knowledge. The triple helix model of university–industry–government interactions (Etzkowitz and Leydesdorff 1995) and of 'open innovation' (Chesbrough 2003) both emphasise the increasingly diffuse and interactive nature of the innovation process. The concepts also include demand from industry for such information and intellectual property generated by universities (see Rossi and Rosli 2013). These reflect a preoccupation with the types of economic activity or outcomes that Goldstein (2009) suggested that universities might be reasonably expected to stimulate.

More recently, as we will show, focus of policy on the ways in which universities do make a difference at the regional level has broadened to include more systemic involvement as 'anchor institutions'. The regional triple helix spaces (Etzkowitz 2008: 75) encapsulates the idea that interaction between the three spheres would 'generate new initiatives for regional innovation' particularly with government as a driver of both demand and supply sides designed to stimulate interaction.

Supply and demand are necessarily context dependent. For example, affecting the supply side of what might be offered, universities are autonomous charitable bodies, and as such are constrained in their activities by the Charities Act. They are able to choose (subject to funding of research and outreach activities and academics' inclinations) whether and how much to engage in economic activities involving commercialisation of knowledge at geographical levels from the local to global. In France also, universities are autonomous institutions (Crespy et al 2007) whereas in Germany each federal state has its own higher education laws and funding (Koschatsky and Kroll 2007).

We focus here on what UK government documents identify as the main foci of policies from the supply side and stimulating demand from industry through collaboration; in other words, where each identify that universities should contribute to economic development per se and at the regional/local level. We show that it is only since the change of government in 2010 that universities are 'encouraged' to be engaged as local rather than regional actors. In England, as a separate system to Wales, Scotland and Northern Ireland, from the late 1990s, the engagement was through the nine regional development agencies (RDAs), which were multi-county organisations with wide powers to stimulate economic development in their regions. They were abolished in 2010–2011 and replaced by Local Enterprise Partnerships (LEPs). LEPs are joint local authority and business bodies designed to reflect genuine economic areas to promote local economic development. They can be seen as being mini-triple helix bodies as their boards include representatives from universities, business people as well as local government. By 2013, 35 of the 39 LEPs had a university representative on their board (Lawton Smith and Waters 2015). The government has introduced a series of programmes to support local economic activity including City Deals,[3] Enterprize Zones and the Growing Places Fund. Next we introduce the UK university system. This is followed by an outline of the major policy documents and funding initiatives.

A brief introduction to the UK university system

UK higher education has been on a rapid growth trajectory, particularly since the 1990s. In 1970, there were about 400,000 first degree students; by 2000 this had increased to 1,400,000 and by 2013 it was over 2,000,000. In addition, there has been a very large increase in postgraduate numbers, with currently around 600,000 students. As noted, crucial in this university growth was the addition of about 40 new universities, created in 1992 from the former polytechnics. More new universities have been created since and there are currently about 130 university institutions (number increases to over 160, when various other higher education institutions are included). Most have grown rapidly in numbers, especially following the lifting of a Government cap on numbers. The institutions range in size considerably from some with a few thousand students to many with over 30,000 students. There is also the Open University (distance learning) with over 200,000 students (2013). The previous Labour Government aimed to increase the participation of under-30s in UK higher education to 50% by 2010; the figure reached 49% in 2011–2012 – the final year before tuition fees trebled to £9,000 a year (DBIS 2013).

The overwhelming majority of UK universities can be classified as public sector universities. Until recently, the University of Buckingham was the only truly private sector university, although there are likely to be more private universities in the next few years (such as BPP University). The universities can also be classified by various quality rankings, and the rise up such rankings is a major driver of university activity. The annual ranking exercises, such as the Times Higher Education (THE) *World University Rankings*, include various mixes of factors including some of the following: entry standards, student satisfaction, research achievements, citations, peer reviews, industry income, international outlook, facilities spend and graduate prospects. The rankings are contentious, but are influential and important (especially for vice-chancellors!).[4]

UK universities are also organised into various self-interest/lobbying groups, including the Russell Group of research intensive universities (with over 20 members, such as Oxford, Cambridge, Imperial and London School of Economics and Political Science, LSE) and the University Alliance, largely made up of the more successful of the post-1992 new universities (again with over 20 members, such as Oxford Brookes, Plymouth and Portsmouth). Another significant group is Million+, so called because its constituent universities have more than a million students between them, mainly in the big-city post-1992 universities.

UK universities have multiple aims in their various mission statements, but all have a commitment to teaching quality, to research quality and, increasingly, to the growing third strand of entrepreneurial activities, often linked with their local and previously their regional economies. Such activities can include consultancy, industry spin-outs, support for inward investment and a variety of partnership arrangements (Glasson 2003). These relate to building increased capacity for sustained economic growth (Goldstein 2009) through institutional arrangements, building the industrial base through entrepreneurship and large company activity, physical infrastructure and through innovation. The mix of such activities varies between universities, and it is difficult to compare performance in the round, although it is possible to provide some crude and limited indicators.

Three UK examples of the kinds of changes which universities can be expected to and actually do make to stimulating economic development (Goldstein 2009) are given here. These are aggregate activity, new firms and research. For example, with regard to university spin-out companies a large number is a key indicator of an entrepreneurial university.

Aggregate income

UK higher education is a very significant component of the UK economy. A recent report (UUK 2014) has attempted to quantify this significance in terms of national output and employment. The analysis, for the academic year 2011–2012, includes those aspects of the UK economy which can be regularly measured. Unfortunately for this chapter that 'does not include any assessment of the value of the sector's collaboration with business or the impact of new ideas generated by universities or their graduates'. However, it does show that UK higher education is a major industrial sector contributing directly almost £40 billion – equivalent to 2.8% of UK GDP in 2011. When secondary or multiplier effects are added in, the contribution of the sector rises to over £73 billion of output and over

750,000 full-time equivalent jobs throughout the economy (equivalent to about 2.7% of all UK employment in 2011). The amounts of course will be distributed regionally, benefiting those areas which have several universities such as big cities like London and Manchester in England and Glasgow and Edinburgh in Scotland.

New firms

Table 8.1 shows one estimate of the top ten UK universities for the number of spin-outs, based on university intellectual property, for the period from 2000–2012. As the new firms tend to stay local, the outcomes are new job and wealth creation in areas close to the university (Zhang 2009). Not surprisingly the list is dominated by the Russell Group research intensive universities which have more 'raw material' to commercialise. On this indicator the post-1992 new universities fare less well, with none in the top ten and only one, Edinburgh Napier University, having more than ten spin-outs over the study period. However, the new universities are often strong on consultancy, partnerships with business and training for business, which are also important elements in the triple helix model per se and, where local/regional, within the second and third phases of the regional triple helix spaces model.

Research income

Nationally, it is the more research intensive universities that generate regional research incomes. However, as with aggregate income, the distribution is geographically uneven, with implications for local and regional multiplier effects to the extent that firms and other organisations have the capacity 'to use that knowledge to increase their productive or innovativeness' (Goldstein 2009: 19). Research intensive universities are defined as attracting an average annual research funding during 2007–2012 of at least £15 million. The 59 such UK

Table 8.1 Top ten UK universities for commercial spin-outs (2000–2012)

University	Number of spin-outs (2000–2012)
Oxford	92
Imperial College, London	88
Cambridge	82
Edinburgh	71
Strathclyde	60
Manchester	51
University College, London	48
Queens, Belfast	45
Bristol	40
Newcastle	39

Source: Created by authors based on data from Young Company Finance (2013) University Spin-outs Analysis.

institutions (from a total of 161) attracted almost £19 billion of the £20.4 billion of national HEI research spending, and employed 60% of their academic staff. These institutions' annual research income thus averaged £44,700 per full time equivalent (FTE) staff. It was highest, at over £50,000, in London, Eastern England and the South East, and lowest in Wales (£26,600) and Northern Ireland (£31,199) (Wood and Lawton Smith forthcoming).

UK universities in a policy context

In 1997, the incoming Labour Government inherited a situation where spending on universities and public sector research institutions – research, infrastructure and salaries – had been dramatically reduced under the previous Conservative Government (1979–1997). It attempted to address three problems: (i) under-funding for the science base; (ii) related to this, the associated lower levels of student numbers than competitor countries; and (iii) a lack of engagement with broader communities (economic and social). The Coalition government (Conservative–Liberal Democrat) elected in 2010 has maintained many of the same objectives, but as was suggested earlier, changed the geographical focus of delivery for some.

National policy

In Table 8.2 the agencies and specific targets arising from national policies are illustrated, and the Higher Education Innovation Fund (HEIF) discussed in detail later.

In particular in addition to the types of impacts discussed above, aggregate impacts, new business formation and research, policies generally fall into five more of Goldstein's seven categories which illuminate how universities stimulate economic development. These are the development of human capital (teaching and skills development); a combination of innovation related activities (including creation of new commercially relevant knowledge and transfer of existing knowledge patent and licensing, collaborative arrangements between industry and universities, raising finance for knowledge exploitation); regional leadership and governance; and co-production of knowledge infrastructure (laboratories, incubators and science parks). It also included civic activities (Goddard and Vallance 2013) and especially under the Coalition government, engaging in regional (here local) leadership and governance (see also Etzkowitz 2008). These also highlight how universities are complex institutions operating within policy frameworks at many geographical scales – global, national and local (Marginson 2004), and with interactions throughout those geographical ranges.

The tone was set by Dearing 1997 which argued for greater investment in higher education. This was followed in 2003 by two documents: a comprehensive overview of the benefits of higher education to individuals and the country in *The Future of Higher Education* and specifically on the role of universities as drivers of innovation, in the *Lambert Review of Business University Collaboration.*

Table 8.2 Examples of HEI programmes designed to foster innovation

Department	Initiative
OST/HEFCE	Joint Infrastructure Fund (JIF) (1998)
	Science Research Investment Fund (SRIF) (2001)
DfEE, DTI, HEfCE	1999 Higher Education Reach-Out to Business and the Community (HEROBC)
	• special funding for activities to increase universities' capability to respond to the needs of business and the wider community, where this will lead to wealth creation.
	• includes the promotion of spin-out companies
DTI/OST/ Engineering and the Engineering Physical Sciences Council (EPSRC)	1999 Science Enterprise Challenge (SEC) Fund
	• financed Enterprise Centres and the Foresight Directorate
	• encourages regional-level activity;
	• Faraday Partnerships
	• joint university–industry initiatives
	• Biotechnology Challenge Fund
OST/Treasury/Wellcome Trust and Gatsby Foundation	1999 University Challenge Fund (UCF)
	• seed funding to help selected universities make the most of research funding through support for early stages of commercial exploitation of new products and processes
HEFCE	• 2001–2004 Higher Education Innovation Fund (HEIF): £140m to knowledge transfer
	• 2004–6 HEIF 2: £187m
	• 2006–2008 HEIF 3: £238m
	• 2009–2011 HEIF4: £150m
	• 2011–15 HEIF 5: £150m
TSB (now Innovate UK)	2007
	• Knowledge Transfer Networks
	• Collaborative research and development
	• Knowledge Transfer Partnerships
	• Micro and Nanotechnology Centres
	• SBRI
	• International programmes
	• Catapult centres
CASE	Collaborative PhD level studentships designed to encourage research collaboration between industry and other non-academic organisations, funded by the research councils.

Source: Created by authors based on data in Lawton Smith 2012

In 2004 the Government published a ten-year investment framework for science and innovation (2004–2014), which very much was set within a triple helix framework as it emphasised the importance of the responsiveness of the UK science base to the needs of the economy.[5] The framework set out the Government's ambitions for science and innovation led economic growth. The Framework included details of the attributes and funding arrangements of a research system capable of delivering these ambitions. A target of raising total UK R&D from 1.9% of GDP to 2.5% of GDP by 2014 was set. Increasing funding, through the DTI and DfES, was at an average annual rate of 5.8 per cent in real terms over the Spending Review 2004 period (2004–2005 to 2007–2008). The target of raising total UK R&D to 2.5% has not been achieved, and in 2011 had in fact fallen to 1.8% of GDP, despite a diversity of programme initiatives, compared to 2.77% in the United States.[6]

Table 8.2 includes examples of each of the four main policy areas directed towards universities' capacity for stimulating economic development. The availability of funding under these programmes has influenced policy practice at the university level. It has provided the incentive and the means for universities to respond to the major government policies. For example, the Joint Infrastructure Fund and the Science Enterprise Fund (SEC) were directed towards co-production of knowledge infrastructure and associated creative milieu. SEC also targeted university–industry collaboration, as more recently does the Technology Strategy Board's (TSB) Catapult Centres.[7] The TSB's Knowledge Transfer Partnerships (KTP) is a skills and innovation based programme. A KTP[8] is: 'A relationship formed between a company and an academic institution ("Knowledge Base" partner), which facilitates the transfer of knowledge, technology and skills to which the company partner currently has no access. Each partnership employs one or more recently qualified people (known as an Associate) to work in a company on a project of strategic importance to the business, whilst also being supervised by the Knowledge Base Partner.' It is one of the UK's most successful technology transfer partnerships.[9] CASE studentships serve similar functions but at the PhD level.

Most policies under successive governments focus on the environment for universities to make changes in regional economic activity rather than on building innovation-based interactions between universities and industry. Even where environments are rich it is very difficult for a regional triple helix to be built. This is even though, since 2010, the environment created by public policy at the local level has changed to in principle being more locally driven, accountable and involving regional leadership and governance (Lawton Smith and Waters 2015).

The HEIF programme was set up in 2001 to support and develop a broad range of knowledge-based interactions between universities and colleges and the wider world, which result in economic and social benefit to the UK'.[10] It particularly focused on innovation activities such as technology transfer and knowledge exploitation. It provided funding for universities to support them in developing key activities such as: knowledge transfer, interactions with businesses and interactions with the wider community. SEC and UCF were set up as separate funds under HEIF 1. As the programme has expanded, it has become more commercially orientated and has sought to be more inclusive. Under HEIF3 it was intended that rather than the largest grants being awarded to the elite, research-led Russell Group of universities, support should be given for less research-intensive university departments. Similarly, in line with the Sainsbury Review recommendations that more funding be directed towards business-facing institutions, HEIF 4 declined to £150 million in 2010–2011 and is intended to redistribute funding from the richer to poorer universities. For the first time money was allocated by formula rather than by competitive bidding. An annual limit of £1.9 million per university was placed thus capping the amount that the Russell Group would receive (Lawton Smith 2012). In the funding round 2011–2015, allocations pegged at the same level as the previous round were performance-based.

An evaluation of HEIF in 2014[11] found that for every £1 of HEFCE knowledge exchange funding over the period from 2003 to 2012, £6.30 has been earned in gross additional income. The report acknowledges that the total benefits to the economy and society are likely to be greater. HEFCE noted that the analysis supports the conclusion of the Witty Review regarding the vital importance of HEFCE's funding for knowledge exchange.

More important than the level of funding for third mission activities, which varies between countries, is the effectiveness of that funding as measured against key objectives of the fund. By 2012, Public and Corporate Economic Consultants (PACEC) found that knowledge exchange fostered by HEIF had become a strategic activity for universities working to support and enhance research and teaching. In the European Union more broadly, evaluation procedures are being developed in the form of a three-year project designed to produce indicators for assessing universities' third mission impact.[12]

Oxfordshire and case studies of technology transfer from Oxford University and Oxford Brookes University, with Cambridge University and Imperial London comparators

It is no coincidence that Oxfordshire has a successful high-tech economy and that the county is also home to two major universities as well as a concentration of public and private sector laboratories. The collective impact as well as through considerable aggregate regional income is most significant for research, innovative activity, new business start-ups, skills, and co-production of knowledge infrastructure and creative milieu (Goldstein 2009).

Examples of research at the public and private laboratories include nuclear energy and space research at the former and electronics (Sharp) and materials (Infineum) at the latter. Within the county, Oxford itself has the good fortune, for a small city (2014 population of c150,000), of hosting two major universities which are widely regarded as the best in their groups. In a world of league tables there is much data to support this view. Using the criteria on teaching quality, research excellence etc. noted in the section 'A brief introduction to the UK university system', Oxford University is invariably right at the top of all UK universities, in a small cluster with Cambridge, and Imperial and UCL (both London); and Oxford Brookes University is regularly ranked as the UK's top modern/new university.

The impact of innovation related activities of the universities and other research centres, the government laboratories and research hospitals, is reflected in the dramatic shift in the nature of the Oxfordshire economy over the last 50 years. Reflecting those strengths, the Oxfordshire economy is strong in both high-tech and medium-tech manufacturing and services. Key high-tech manufacturing sectors in the county include: bioscience, medical-tech, and pharmaceuticals; physics related-cryogenics, instruments and magnets; engineering and electronics, including motorsports; and computer hardware and software. Oxfordshire is also particularly strong in high-tech services, including scientific R&D, telecoms, computer software consultancy, architecture and engineering consultancy, and technical testing and analysis. The wider high-plus-medium tech definition includes some other knowledge intensive activities which are important in the county – such as academic and scientific publishing, and motor vehicles. Overall the technology sectors contribute from 6.2% to 13.4% of Oxfordshire employment, according to which definition is used. The comparable figures for England as a whole are 5.1% and 9.8%. Estimates of the number of high-tech firms also varies, from about 1,500 (Oxford University and Science Oxford 2013) to about 2,000 (Waters and Lawton Smith 2012).

Every university has a distinctive history in transferring technology through formal means such as technology transfer companies and wholly owned companies, as in the case of Oxford, and through other civic forms of engagement. Next the two case studies illustrate ways in which co-located activities complement each other and so supply a range of expertise, skills and knowledge demanded by firms in the Oxfordshire high-tech economy. The one (Oxford) is focussed on science and technology research-based activities, the other (Oxford Brookes) on skills and applied research for both manufacturing and service sectors. Both universities are represented on the board of the Oxfordshire LEP at Pro-Vice-Chancellor (PVC) level. Therefore they are symbolically part of the local 'innovation space' even if budgets are small and they hold positions of influence because of the organisations they represent (Lawton Smith and Waters 2015). The degree of engagement in local governance reflects the independence of universities in the UK higher education system. Hence level of engagement depends on decisions made by individual vice-chancellors.

Oxfordshire has long had a history of coordinated activity that has sat alongside the universities and the local policy-making system. However, individuals and representatives from both have participated in its events. Historically the Oxford Trust was the main focus of coordinated activity. This is a charitable foundation, set up by Audrey and Martin Wood in 1985 'to encourage the study and application of science and technology' (the original founding ambition). They pioneered one of the original and most successful of Oxford spin-offs, Oxford Instruments, a world leading business especially in the area of cryogenics (Wood 2001). Another supportive facility is Oxford Venturefest. Launched in 1999 it is Oxfordshire's annual premier high-technology networking event. It brings together entrepreneurs, scientists, researchers, inventors, financiers, business angels and supporters to promote their ideas, and to introduce them to potential funding and the opening up of new markets.

Oxford University

Oxford University is one of the world's leading universities and was ranked second, after Caltech/US, in the World University Rankings 2013–2014 (THE 2013/14). The university's position in these rankings is due to several features: the university has a very high concentration of 'star scientists'; it specialises in genomics (THE 2013/14 ranked Oxford University first in the world for medical research); and it has been very active in the development of interdisciplinary research centres and groups cutting across traditional boundaries, many of which collaborate with international academic and industrial partners.

There are also strong links between university research and the major national hospitals based in Oxford, such as the John Radcliffe and Nuffield, ensuring easy access for the clinical studies that are necessary for putting research into action (Lawton Smith and Glasson 2005). The university employs over 4,000 staff in the STEM and medical fields alone, and over the period 2007/08 to 2011/12 has secured more external grant income in these fields than any other UK university, rising by an average of 9% pa to over £400 million in 2011/12 (Oxford of University/Science Oxford 2013). The university has some 20,000 students including 11,772 undergraduates and 9,850 graduate students, thus providing an impact through teaching and recruitment of graduates into the local economy.

Oxford University also has an elite commercialisation and technology transfer system, which enables it to act as a well-functioning 'entrepreneurial university' (Clarke 1998). Many, and a diverse range, of these have been supported by HEIF. This diversity relates back to the late 1980s with internal pressures on the university to capitalise on the growing number of spin-offs, rather than just the entrepreneurs becoming rich, and external pressures from the evolving national political agenda, as discussed in the section 'UK universities in a policy context'. At the heart of the commercialisation system is Isis Innovation, a wholly owned university technology transfer company. Although formed in 1988, it was not until 1997 that the spin-offs process really took off, with the appointment of Dr Tim Cook as MD, and the establishment of new commercialisation policies and procedures in 1995. Academics who have created intellectual property were obliged by their contracts of employment to form their spin-offs through Isis Innovation.[13]

> Isis now employs more than 60 people in three main divisions: Isis Innovation, the main organisation; Oxford University Consulting (OUC); and Isis Enterprise, a consultancy company which focuses on technology transfer. In 2008, Isis Innovation established Oxford Spinout Equity Management to manage the university's interests in its spin-off companies. Isis Innovation has been responsible for creating over 70 spin-off companies based on academic research generated within and owned by Oxford University, and has spun off a company every two months on average, with five formed in 2012. Since 2000, over £266 million in external investment has been raised

by Isis spin-off companies, and in 2013 five were currently listed on London's AIM market.

(Lawton Smith et al 2013)

Oxford University recognises that, 'transforming good research into good business is central to the UK's economic wellbeing'.[14] And, HEIF-supported activities 'have allowed the University of Oxford to stimulate and support the development of innovative ideas as they grow into young businesses'.[15] The 2011 award comprises £11.4 million over four years to July 2015. HEIF supported activities include helping Isis Innovation to set up the Isis Software Incubator (ISI) to encourage software businesses creation by university staff and students. Under HEIF funding, the Mathematical, Physical and Life Sciences Division established a Business Development team which has been active in liaising with key academics and supporting discussions with a range of small and large companies that wish to engage with the university. Other initiatives have taken place outside of government funding.

For example, many of Oxfordshire's largest high-tech firms originated in Oxford University, formed by staff or former students, mainly from departments of engineering science and metallurgy and more recently from medical research and life sciences. The oldest and many of the largest spin-offs, however, predated any efforts by the university to foster new business start-ups as they were established in the 1940s and early 1950s. In the 1970s and 1980s, the number of university start-ups increased. By the mid-1980s, some 40 firms had been established broadly defined as spin-offs (see Lawton Smith and Ho 2006). They include Oxford Instruments (scientific, industrial and medical devices), which employs nearly 2,000 people worldwide; Research Machines, the UK's leading educational computer manufacturer (1973); and Sophos (1981) (antivirus software), which by 2012 employed 1682 (Lawton Smith et al 2013).

However, Oxfordshire strengths in biomedical science are not reflected in the number of Oxford university spin-offs. In a four country study of healthcare research and commercialisation, it was found that Oxfordshire was diverging from comparator regions (Zurich (Switzerland), Medical Delta (Netherlands) and Biocat (Spain)) in translational activity in the form of the number of university spin-offs, where it has significantly fewer firms per se and also that its' firms were smaller on average (Lawton Smith, Bagchi-Sen et al forthcoming).

Over time, Oxfordshire with the help of Oxford University, has also developed a stronger knowledge infrastructure, although it has lagged behind Cambridgeshire in a number of respects (see Lawton Smith et al 2013). New spin-offs need appropriate physical infrastructure, such as science parks and business innovation incubators. Given its research excellence, the absence of an Oxford University-linked science park until the 1990s was unusual. The need for an Oxford Science Park was clearly recognised in many quarters, as noted in the summary to a 1988 report:

The rapid growth of science park developments in Britain since 1982 has now left the university and other academic institutions in Oxford in the unflattering position of not having access to this form of development. The science park concept offers a major opportunity to bring industry and education closer together in a dynamic exchange of problems and ideas.

(Glasson et al, 1988)

The breakthrough came with changes in Oxfordshire County Council planning policies in 1987, which allowed provision to be made for science based industries concerned primarily with R&D which can show a special need to be located close to Oxford University or to other research facilities in Central Oxfordshire. This allowed the Oxford Science Park to go ahead on land to the south of the city. It is a joint venture between Magdalen College, Oxford University and the Prudential Assurance Company Limited. It has been a success, with currently (2014) 60 companies on site: 43% bioscience; 31% computer hardware/software; and 26% others.

This development was followed in 2002 with the establishment by Oxford University of the Begbroke Science Park to the north of the city. Begbroke is closely integrated with the university's science and technology departments and acts as a catalyst for knowledge and technology transfer between researchers, industry and entrepreneurs. Begbroke currently hosts 30 high technology companies and 20 university research groups, and has about 450 staff on site. All the companies and groups focus on R&D, and their activities are spread roughly equally between materials, engineering, energy, medicine and pharma. The link of this science park to industry as well as its close ties with Isis Innovation, and the university's Department of Continuing Professional Development creates a strong university sphere or innovation space with potential for developing strong reciprocal relationships with industry (Oxford University/Science Oxford 2013), with two of the three spheres of the triple helix model becoming more interactive.

Oxfordshire's new firms, including university spin-offs, also benefit from a network of ten innovation centres in the County, offering business incubator facilities which are particularly important for the early start-up phase of new companies. Oxfordshire's universities have benefitted from government funding allocated at the local level through the City Deals initiative. The Oxford and Oxfordshire City Deal is based on the network of innovation and incubation centres which will drive business growth and an innovation support programme which will strengthen innovation networks.[14] Under the Deal four innovation hubs will be established along Oxfordshire's 'knowledge spine' at the site of government laboratories, Harwell and Culham in the south (the Harwell Innovation Hub and the UKAEA Culham Advanced Manufacturing Hub), to the life science BioEscalator for the life sciences sector in Oxford (Oxford University) and the advanced engineering hub at Begbroke (Begbroke Innovation Accelerator, Oxford University) in the north (Lawton Smith and Waters forthcoming).

Oxford University began to engage formally with the region in 1999 when it appointed a Regional Liaison Director. He was initially on secondment from Barclays Bank but was later funded under HEIF. The Regional Liaison Office was established under his leadership. At the time, the appointment of the Director, 'underline[d] the University's commitment to play a more prominent part in local economic development'. The office was absorbed into Isis Innovation in 2008. The post-holder, who retired in 2011 and who was not replaced, was the local point of contact with the university (Lawton Smith et al 2013) and served on local committees such as the Venturefest Board. In 2014 Oxford University was represented on the board by the Associate Director, Research Services and Head of Knowledge Exchange, the Executive Director, Entrepreneurship Centre at Saïd Business School. Oxford Brookes University was represented by a PVC.[16]

Oxford Brookes University

Oxford Brookes University is of a similar size to Oxford University, with about 19,000 students, of whom about 20% are postgraduate, including a strong PhD student base. In many ways it is complementary to Oxford University, with a greater emphasis on high level training and applied research. Research and knowledge transfer is a key part of the Oxford Brookes strategy, with a particular focus on providing a resource for the Oxford region. At the university level, support for research and developing more effective relationships with business is facilitated by the Research and Business Development Office (RBDO). Among its aims are the further development of research excellence in the university, and the increase in the range and volume of contract research and consultancy and the level and effectiveness of knowledge transfer. RBDO builds on the science and applied research strengths in many areas of the university, but particularly in the Faculties of Technology, Design and Environment (TDE), and Health and Life Sciences (HLS).

During the 2000s greater interaction with business across Oxford Brookes has been supported in part by resources gained in various rounds of HEIF. For example, under HEIF3 (2006/08), Oxford Brookes was the lead partner in CommercialiseSE – an integrated framework for accelerating the commercialisation of ideas in the South East region. The £5 million initiative was one of only eleven proposals nationally awarded funding from the competitive element of HEIF3. Amongst others, the partnership included eleven SE HEIs and six SE business sector consortia, involving world leading businesses based in the region. This initiative is an example of a regional triple helix space with multiple relationships within each of the triple helix spheres.

KTPs are another important knowledge transfer mechanism for Oxford Brookes. KTPs range from projects with small (often local) firms to major multi-nationals. For example, two KTPs with the Inter-Continental Hotel Group will help the Group to develop its enterprise risk management methodology, and to harmonise its business continuity and disaster recovery plans at thirty crucial sites around the world. The KTPs will 'enhance the Groups' risk intelligence and resilience to business disruptions'.

In terms of complementary relationships, Oxford Brookes is active in disciplines not offered by Oxford University, such as architecture, planning, real estate and construction. Moreover, the contribution to skills complements that of

Oxford University. Oxford Brookes also educates and researches in areas allied to, but connected to Oxford University's strengths, such as in health care. For example, although Brookes does not have a medical school, it does have over 3,000 students in nursing and subjects allied to medicine, and they represent a skilled labour force on which the local and regional bio-medical sector can draw.

In similar vein, the Department of Mechanical Engineering and Mathematical Sciences in TDE has over 700 students with many on undergraduate and postgraduate programmes in Automotive Engineering, Motorsport Engineering, and Racing Engine Design, which are closely linked with the motor industry in Oxfordshire. This includes BMW Mini and the various FI teams and suppliers with established homes in and adjacent to the county (e.g. Williams, Red Bull, Lotus, Caterham, Mercedes, Pro-Drive, Marussia and Force India). BMW Mini provides placements for around 40 engineering students each year.

In relation to technology transfer including technical assistance, the Advanced Engines, Propulsion and Vehicles Research Centre brings together scientific and industrial expertise to provide solutions for fuel efficient, low emission engines and vehicles; the Joining Technology Research Centre is a long established centre for research on the use of adhesives and sealants for the aerospace, automotive and construction sectors; and the Sustainable Vehicle Engineering Research Centre investigates the materials, design issues and drivetrain concepts that will allow the development of low mass, low emission, economical and safe vehicles. Thus we see that the innovation space in Oxfordshire is populated by complementary activities. However, these very often exist in parallel rather than form a coherent system of interactions. It is only recently with the formation of the Oxfordshire LEP and such initiatives as the City Deals that the intention of developing fully articulated policies designed at realising locally agreed goals (see Lawton Smith et al 2013).

Other major centres of technology transfer in Oxfordshire

Significant though the universities are in technology transfer in Oxfordshire, there are several other major public and private players, with varying links to higher education.

Thus a particular asset to the county is the longstanding presence of government laboratories. For example, there are around 150 organisations on the Harwell Campus and total employment of approximately 4,500. Harwell is home to some major science facilities, including the long established ISIS neutron source, and the more recent Diamond synchrotron. Nearby in the south of the county is Milton Park, where many of Oxfordshire's large and small high-tech enterprises are located. The site is now one of Europe's largest mixed-use business communities, with more science and bio-tech companies than anywhere else in Oxfordshire. It is currently (2014) home to some 200 organisations which, combined, employ around 6,500 people. Major companies include Research Machines (largest UK manufacturer of IT equipment for the schools sector), Taylor & Francis (one of the UK's largest publishers), Psion, Oxford Semiconductors, Bookham

Technology and many others. Milton Park also accommodates much of the Oxfordshire bio-science cluster. In Oxford, there are also some of the UK's major hospitals with strong research links to Oxford University.

Brief Cambridge University and Imperial London comparators

As noted in Table 8.1, Cambridge University and Imperial London provide close competition to Oxford University in the success of commercial spin-out activity in recent years. Indeed in several respects both have led Oxford University in some technology transfer initiatives. Like Oxford, Cambridge was a winner in the 2001 allocation of HEIF funding both for individual and collaborative grants.[17] Unlike Oxford the university continued with the HEIF funded collaborations through the Centre for Knowledge Exchange.[18] It has also been the recipient of the major awards in Table 8.2 such as the University Challenge Fund.[19] Where it differs from Oxford is in its earlier development of a knowledge infrastructure and in regional leadership and governance. However, its technology transfer system has been found to be less effective than that of Oxford and Imperial College in London.

In Cambridge, for example, the Cambridge Science Park was developed 20 years earlier than the first Oxford Science Park and many other universities had their science parks by the mid-1980s. The publication of the *Cambridge Phenomenon: The Growth of High Technology Industry in a University Town* (Segal Quince & Partners 1985) in part led to Cambridgeshire's profile as a leading cluster of high-tech firms or 'knowledge space'. The self-promotion of Cambridge as a premier UK high-tech location has been a constant and very effective feature of the Cambridge model, continuing through to the present day via internet initiatives such as the Cambridge2U website (www.cambridge 2you. com). Unlike in Oxford, academics inside Cambridge University have made a commitment to regional leadership and governance. Leading figures within the university and its colleges have pulled together key stakeholders to consider the prospects for growth in the sub-region. Two main initiatives are Cambridge Futures and Horizons. Cambridge Futures, a private-sector-led organisation, was set up in 1996 to stimulate thinking about the future development of Cambridge and to influence policy decisions. It was led by the Department of Architecture in the University of Cambridge, but involved a wide range of senior people in private, public and third sectors. In 2004, Horizons, a company limited by guarantee, was created to manage delivery of the growth strategy for Cambridgeshire (Lawton Smith et al 2013).

However, Cambridge University itself has been found to have considerable weaknesses in its technology transfer system, and it performs less well than Oxford, and even less well than Imperial (see later). The Cambridge commercialisation process started in 1983 when the Wolfson Industrial Liaison Unit (WILO), established by the Department of Engineering in 1970 as its own technology-transfer unit, became responsible for the commercialisation of university research as a whole. During the 1990s, Cambridge University also took steps to simplify the technology-transfer system 'to ensure greater efficiency and professionalism' (Breznitz 2011).

However, the outcome was far from effective, resulting in negative attitudes towards the technology-transfer office (TTO) and a reduced number of spin-offs. The creation of the Cambridge-MIT institute in 1999 was followed by the restructuring of technology-transfer units. In 2000 the WILO merged with the Research Grants and Contracts Office to form the Research Services Division (RSD), which operated several divisions dealing with sponsored research from research councils, charities and industry, including the WILO, which became the TTO. In 2002 with the help of the Higher Education Innovation Fund (HEIF), a new unit called Cambridge Enterprise, the Isis Innovation equivalent, was founded as an independent unit but it went into the RSD in 2003, and following changes to the university's IPR policy in 2005, the merged body became a single organisation.

In effect Cambridge adopted a very similar set of rules to those which had worked so well at Oxford: it would receive all control over inventions regardless of the source of funding. In principle this would encourage entrepreneurship, licensing and other forms of commercialisation because of the greater academic freedom to place inventions in the public domain. However, while Oxford's track record in terms of process has been in some respects better than Cambridge (Lawton Smith et al 2013; Breznitz 2011), neither have adopted the successful model developed by Imperial College. Indeed companies from both universities have benefited from that model.

Imperial's own-spin-off company, *Imperial Innovations*, was launched on the Alternative Investment Market on the London Stock Exchange in 2006. Until 2011, *Imperial Innovations* invested only in companies based on intellectual property developed at Imperial College. In January of that year, the company raised £140 million to invest in businesses built on intellectual property developed at or associated with the Universities of Cambridge and Oxford and at University College London, in addition to Imperial College London.[20] Indeed one of Oxford University biomedical spin-off companies, Oxford Immunotec, was listed on NASDAQ in 2013 having received support from Imperial Innovations. Imperial, like other major universities has benefitted from HEIF[21] and other government funding for innovation focused activities.

Conclusions

In this chapter, expectations on universities on the part of national government to contribute to economic and societal benefits to the country and to their localities are discussed. Those expectations are articulated in central government white papers and reports and set out an answer to the first question raised by Goldstein (2009): what kinds of changes in regional economic activity or outcomes can universities be reasonably expected to stimulate as 'anchor institutions' (Goddard and Vallance 2013)? The UK and the county of Oxfordshire, plus Cambridge University and Imperial are used as examples to answer Goldstein's second question on how universities stimulate economic development.

We show that universities are expected make multiple contributions to economic development. Here we focus on five groups of policies: development of human capital (teaching and skills development); a combination of innovation related activities (including creation of new commercially relevant knowledge and transfer of existing knowledge patent and licensing, collaborative arrangements between industry and universities, raising finance for knowledge exploitation); regional leadership and governance; and co-production of knowledge infrastructure (laboratories, incubators and science parks). The timeframe used in this chapter began with the 1990s when major reports such as Dearing (1997) began to appear which highlighted the necessity of properly funded universities so that they could play central roles in economic development. This was a response to the cutbacks in funding to the science base under successive Conservative governments (1979–1997). Since 1997, funding has been allocated, notably under the HEIF programme to facilitate all of these activities (see Table 8.2).

Under the following Labour Governments (1997–2010) the focus was on the region with multi-node regional development agencies having the remit and funding to initiate university involvement in economic growth strategies. Since the election of the Coalition government, the focus has been firmly on the local with government reports and funding directed towards creating local rather than regional triple helix spaces with the sight firmly set on the creation of the third phase of development, 'innovation spaces' (see Witty 2013).

University engagement in local economic policy strategies depends very much on the individual university. Some universities work individually to foster local development. Some like the 12 Higher Education Colleges in Yorkshire present a collective vision and strategy for contributing to economic development and growth.[22] Other models operate around the country.

In Oxfordshire, there is no similar co-ordinated collective activity 'to foster collaboration and partnership working in order to maximise the value and impact of higher education' to that in Yorkshire. The two universities are, however, through joining the LEP, becoming part of the system of local governance. Irrespective of whether being part of a system of governance will result in improvements in the county's economic performance, the chapter has shown that the two universities have complementary but different (positive) impacts on their local economy.

Oxford University (Russell Group) uses its resources to stimulate a wide range of commercial activities, many of which are underpinned by HEIF funding. In particular Isis Innovation has supported numerous university spin-offs, which have largely remained local (Lawton Smith and Glasson 2005) while Oxford University's Said Business School has used its HEIF funding to support programmes such as the Science Enterprise Centre (entrepreneurship education). Oxford University has also built its own science park (Begbroke), which has an incubator.

Oxford Brookes University offers different and complementary activities to the locality to Oxford University, reflecting its strengths in disciplines which are not present in Oxford University. HEIF funding has supported university–industry interaction. However, this has had a regional rather than a local focus, for example as lead partner in the CommercialiseSE programme. The KTP programme's geographical reach is local through to national.

However, despite the growth and success of the Oxfordshire high-tech economy, and the significant contributions of the universities in technology transfer, there is still concern that Oxfordshire is not realising its full high-tech growth potential, in comparison with other areas of the UK such as the Cambridge sub-region and the Thames Valley, and some high-tech cluster regions in Europe and beyond. There is particular concern about the physical constraints imposed on Oxford development by the Oxford Green Belt, by the congestion along the A34 trunk road through the county, by the lack of affordable housing for key workers, and by the political divisions between various local authorities and agencies which limits a consistent vision for the future economy.

The *Oxfordshire Innovation Engine* report (Oxford of University/Science Oxford, 2013) identified a number of recommendations relating to various infrastructures: research, soft, physical, and importantly to strategic direction and leadership. While the high-tech economy is booming – with both universities playing a key role in that success, the message from central government, as exemplified by the 2013 Witty Review of 'Universities and Growth', is that universities should be doing much more to play a full role in driving growth. The case made by Oxfordshire for national funding articulates that there are such problems at the local level, identified as a lack of leadership from within the universities. Hence issues relate not only to fragmentation – a lack of cohesion in vision and action – but also to structural problems that interaction between local triple helix actors themselves cannot solve.

More generally, the UK case, the Oxfordshire, Cambridge and Imperial examples in particular, illustrate that universities' local impact is never negligible (UK Universities 2014). However, that the success of incentives for interaction depends as much on the nature of the demand side (for example for skills, intellectual property and physical infrastructure) as well as what universities can supply. Clearly in Oxfordshire, there is work to do on both.

Notes

1   Witty, A (2013) *Final Report and Recommendations Encouraging a British Invention Revolution: Sir Andrew Witty's Review of Universities and Growth*, www.gov.uk/government/uploads/system/uploads/attachment_data/file/249720/bis-13-1241-encouraging-a-british-invention-revolution-andrew-witty-review-R1.pdf (accessed 27 October 2013).
2   *www.gcu-uec.org/GCUhistory.pdf.*
3   www.gov.uk/government/policies/giving-more-power-back-to-cities-through-city-deals (accessed 20 January 2015).
4   This ranking bears many similarities to the QS world ranking of universities, www.topuniversities.com/university-rankings/world-university-rankings/2013#sorting=rank+region=+country=+faculty=+stars=false+search= (accessed 21 April 2014).
5   www.berr.gov.uk/files/file28546.pdf (accessed 21 April 2014).

6 http://data.worldbank.org/indicator/GB.XPD.RSDV.GD.ZS (accessed 21 April 2014).
7 www.catapult.org.uk/ (accessed 1 September 2014).
8 www.ktponline.org.uk/ (accessed 20 August 2104).
9 http://ktp.innovateuk.org/faqs/ (accessed May 1 2015).
10 www.hefce.ac.uk/kess/heif/previous/ (accessed 1 May 2015).
11 www.hefce.ac.uk/news/newsarchive/2014/news86932.html (accessed 31 August 2014).
12 www.evollution.com/program_planning/defining-and-delivering-the-universitys-third-mission/ (accessed 21 April 2014).
13 www.admin.ox.ac.uk/rso/ip/ (accessed 21 April 2013).
14 www.isis-innovation.com/documents/HEIF_Brochure_2012.pdf (accessed 31 August 2014)
15 www.admin.ox.ac.uk/media/global/wwwadminoxacuk/localsites/researchsupport/documents/impactandke/Innovating_with_HEIF_at_Oxford__-_Brochure,_2012.pdf (accessed 1 May 2015).
16 www.gov.uk/government/uploads/system/uploads/attachment_data/file/276205/Oxford-Oxfordshire-City-Deal.pdf (accessed 18 February 2013).
17 www.venturefestoxford.com/about-venturefest/board-members/ (accessed January 20 2015)
18 www.theguardian.com/education/2001/oct/18/research.highereducation2 (accessed 1 September 2014).
19 www.hefce.ac.uk/media/hefce/content/about/staffandstructure/board/2007/117/B82a. PDF (accessed 1 September 2014).
20 www.enterprise.cam.ac.uk/news/2010/11/cambridge-challenge-fund-marks-ten-years/ (accessed September 1 2014)
21 http://w1ww.imperialinnovations.co.uk/about/ (accessed April 21 2014)
22 www.imperial.ac.uk/college.asp?P=5312 (accessed 1 September 2014).
23 www.yorkshireuniversities.ac.uk/(accessed 20 January 2015).

References

Breznitz, S (2011) 'Improving or impairing? Following technology transfer changes at the University of Cambridge', *Regional Studies* 45 (4): 463–478.

Chesbrough, Henry (2003) 'Open innovation: How companies actually do it', *Harvard Business Review* 81 (7): 12–14.

Clarke, B (1998) *Creating Entrepreneurial Universities: Organisational, Pathways of Transformation*, Pergamon Press: Oxford.

Crespy, C, Heraud, J-A and Perry, B (2007) 'Multi-level governance, regions and science in France: Between competition and equality', *Regional Studies* 41 (8): 1069–1084.

Dearing Report (1997) National Committee of Enquiry into Higher Education, https://bei. leeds.ac.uk/Partners/NCIHE/ (accessed 21 January 2015).

Department for Business, Innovation and Skills (DBIS) (2013), *Participation Rates in Higher Education 2006–07 to 2011–12*, DBIS: London.

Etzkowitz, H (1983) 'Entrepreneurial scientists and entrepreneurial universities in American academic science', *Minerva* 21 (2–3): 198–233.

Etzkowitz, H (1993) 'Enterprises from science: The origins of science-based regional economic cevelopment', *Minerva* 31 (3): 326–360.

Etzkowitz, H (2002) 'Incubation of incubators: Innovation as a Triple Helix of university–industry–government networks', *Science and Public Policy* 29 (2): 115–128..

Etzkowitz, H (2008) *The Triple Helix: University-Industry-Government in Action*, Routledge: London.

Etzkowitz, H, and Leydesdorff, L (1995) 'The Triple Helix—university-industry-government relations: A laboratory for knowledge-based economic development', *EASST Review* 14, 14–19.

Foray, D and Goenega, X (2013) The Goals of Smart Specialisation S3 Policy Brief Series No 01/2013, http://ftp.jrc.es/EURdoc/JRC82213.pdf (accessed August 28 2013).

Glasson, J (2003) 'The widening local and regional development impacts of modern universities—a tale of two cities (and north–south perspectives)', *Local Economy* 18 (1): 21–37.

Glasson, J, Thomas, K and Leary, M (1988) *The Need for an Oxford Science Park: Working Paper 107*, School of Planning, Oxford Brookes University: Oxford.

Goddard, J (2013) 'Keep universities anchored', www.researchresearch.com/index.php?option=com_news&template=rr_2col&view=article&articleId=1339223 (accessed 24 February 2014).

Goddard, J and Chatterton, P (1999) Regional development agencies and the knowledge economy: harnessing the potential of universities, *Environment and Planning* C 17: 685–699.

Goddard, J and Vallance, P (2013) *The University and the City*, Routledge: London.

Goldstein, HA (2009) 'What we know and what we don't know about the regional economic impacts of universities' in A Varga (ed.) *Universities, Knowledge Transfer and Regional Development*, Edward Elgar: Cheltenham, pp 11–35.

Howells, J (1999) 'Regional systems of innovation' in D Archibugi, J Howells and J Michie (eds), *Innovation Policy in a Global Economy*, Cambridge University Press: Cambridge, pp 67–93.

Koschatzky, K and Kroll, H (2007) 'Which side of the coin? The regional governance of science and innovation', *Regional Studies* 41 (8): 115–128.

Lambert (2003) *Lambert Review of Higher Education*, www.eua.be/eua/jsp/en/upload/lambert_review_final_450.1151581102387.pdf (accessed 21 January 2015).

Lawton Smith, H (2012) 'UK science and innovation policy' in S Mian (ed.) *Science and Technology Based Regional Entrepreneurship: Global Experience in Policy and Program Development*, Edward Elgar: Cheltenham, pp 74–95.

Lawton Smith, H, Bagchi-Sen, S, Edmunds, L Hassan, Hafen, B and Hogendoorn, P (forthcoming) 'Science, innovation and technology transfer paths: A study of divergent trajectories in the healthcare sector in the UK and Europe', *Journal of Technology Transfer*.

Lawton Smith, H and Glasson, J (2005) *High-Tech Spin-offs: Measuring Performance and Growth in Oxfordshire*, Oxfordshire Economic Observatory: Oxford.

Lawton Smith, H, Glasson, J, Romeo, S, Waters, R and Chadwick, A (2013) 'Entrepreneurial regions: Evidence from Oxfordshire and Cambridgeshire', *Social Science Information* 52 (4): 653–673.

Lawton Smith, H and Ho, K (2006) 'Measuring the performance of Oxford University, Oxford Brookes University and the government laboratories' spin-off companies.' *Research Policy*, 35: 1554–1568.

Lawton Smith, H and Waters, R (2015) 'Regional synergies in Triple Helix regions: The case of local economic development policies Oxfordshire', *Industry and Higher Education* (29) 1: 25–35.

Marginson, S (2004) 'Competition and markets in higher education: A "glonacal" analysis', *Policy Futures in Education* **2 (2): 175–244.**

Oxfordshire County Council (1998) *Economic Development Strategy for Oxfordshire, 1998/99*, Oxfordshire County Council: Oxford.

Oxford University/Science Oxford (2013) *The Oxfordshire Innovation Engine: Realising the Growth Potential*, SQW: Cambridge.

Rossi, F and Rosli, A (2013) Indicators of university–industry knowledge transfer performance and their implications for universities: evidence from the UK's HE-BCI survey CIMR Working Paper Number 13, www.bbk.ac.uk/innovation/publications/working-papers-1 (accessed 21 January 2015).

Saxenian, A (1983) 'The genesis of Silicon Valley', *Built Environment* 9 (1): 7–17.

Saxenian, A-L (1994) *Regional Advantage Culture and Competition in Silicon Valley and Route 128*, Harvard University Press: Cambridge, Mass.

SegalQuinceWicksteed Consulting (SQW) (2007) *Evaluation of the economic and employment growth of the southern central Oxfordshire Quadrant*, SQW: Cambridge.

Storper, M (1997) *The Regional World: Territorial Development in a Global Economy*, Guilford Press: London and New York.

Times Higher Education (THE) (2013/14) *World University Rankings 2013–2014*, THE: London.

Universities UK (UUK, 2014) *The Impact of Universities on the UK Economy*, UUK: London (see also www.universitiesuk.ac.uk/highereducation/Documents/2014/TheImpactOfUniversitiesOnTheUkEconomy.pdf)

Waters, R and Lawton Smith, H (2012) 'High technology local economies: geographical mobility of the highly skilled' in U Hilpert and H Lawton Smith (eds), *Networking Regionalised Innovative Labour Markets*, Routledge: Abingdon, pp 96–116.

Wood, A (2001) *Magnetic Venture: the Story of Oxford Instruments*, Oxford University Press: Oxford.

Wood, P and Lawton Smith, H (forthcoming) 'Universities in a metropolitan environment: The case of London' in D Audretch, E Lehmann, S Visama and M Meoli (eds) *University Evolution, Entrepreneurial Activity and Regional Competitiveness*, Springer: Berlin.

Young Company Finance (2013) University Spin-outs Analysis, www.spinoutsuk.co.uk/about-us/ (accessed 21 January 2015).

Zhang, J, (2009) 'The performance of university spin-offs: An exploratory analysis using venture capital data', *Journal of Technology Transfer* 34 (3): 255–285.

9 An analysis of the development of the Irish technology transfer system

Ciara Fitzgerald and Rory P. O'Shea

Introduction

This chapter outlines how the Irish government has set about transforming the nation's university R&D system to accelerate university–industry partnerships and encourage academic entrepreneurship. More specifically, the paper addresses the development of the Irish technology transfer system, the challenges that arose, the strategy objectives, the role of the state, and the core elements of the start-up ecosystem.

The chapter also presents examples of technology transfer in practice from universities in Ireland, incorporating specific examples of licensing, spinouts and IP management. It also reviews recent initiatives undertaken by some Irish universities to transition away from a 'bureaucratic control' model to a more 'entrepreneur-centred' system.

The analysis is sourced from policy reports and university data. It also draws on interviews with the leading university and government administrators responsible for implementing and monitoring the initiatives that have sought to strengthen and support Irish Technology Transfer Offices (TTOs). By presenting the contextual background of TTOs, the chapter reveals insights into the 'black box' of the TTO (Sanders and Miller, 2010; O'Shea & Allen, 2014) and gives a better understanding of how key actors have influenced their development in Ireland.

The case of the Irish technology system

To explore the development of the Irish technology transfer system we need to understand the academic entrepreneurship ethos in Irish universities. In researching TTOs in Ireland, it is interesting to note that the TTO institutional system evolved from a legacy structure of the Industrial Liaison Office, which appeared in Irish universities from the 1980s. Industrial Liaison Offices were tasked with engaging with industry yet their role did not embrace a culture of commercialisation. They focused more on building relationships with industry for student placement and guest lectures. Previous empirical studies of Ireland examined the role of the Industry Liaison Office in 1998 and found "little evidence of a proactive effort to work more closely with industry to widen the scope of the university's research results and to create new business employment" (Jones-Evans et al, 1999). The interest in commercialisation grew once the size of research income into the university increased over the past 15 years. This occurred in 2000, when Science Foundation Ireland (SFI) was established and delivered the first significant injection of research money to Irish universities, triggering the commercialisation agenda. The remit of SFI is to invest in academic researchers and research teams in Ireland's third level institutions. SFI grants are awarded to top-class scientists who are deemed most likely to generate new knowledge, leading edge technologies and competitive enterprises in the fields of science and engineering. The organisation was established to play a pivotal role in the implementation of Ireland's research and development strategy and ongoing economic development (Strategy for Science Technology and Innovation, 2006–2013).

Ideas about commercialisation were further enhanced with the Technology Transfer Strengthening Initiative (TTSI) in 2007. The initiative aims to build a coordinated national approach to technology transfer by Enterprise Ireland in partnership with Higher Education Institutes (HEIs). In 2007, a new department called the Technology Transfer Exploitation Network was established to manage the €230 million Technology Transfer Strengthening Initiative (TTSI) and to build up the technology transfer system in the country. In addition to managing the direct support to TTOs in Ireland and HEIs, the Technology Transfer Exploitation Network team also provided customised training events. According to a 2012 Higher Education Authority report, up to €30M had been invested into the programme between 2007 and 2012.

Historically, Irish universities were teaching-led yet some organic commercialisation did occur. There were examples of pioneering success at creating university spinoffs but they were sporadic. Iona Technologies was one of the first university start-ups to emerge from Trinity College Dublin, and is still an important firm in the evolution of technology entrepreneurship in Ireland. The founders left Trinity College to create the company and it was the first university affiliated start-up company to float on the NASDAQ stock exchange in the US. While the start-up was not officially deemed a university spinoff, because the academics had left Trinity and did not have to forfeit equity to the university, Iona remains Ireland's most recognised example of a company that emerged from a university and paved the way for other academics to consider starting a company. However, until the early 2000s, such success stories were the exception rather than the norm. Table 9.1 presents other spinoff stories that ended in acquisition: Changing Worlds from University College Dublin and acquired by Amdocs in 2008 for $60 million; Havok Technologies from Trinity College Dublin and acquired by Intel for $100 million in 2007.

Table 9.1 Sample of acquired university spinoffs

Company	University	Acquired by	Deal worth	Year	PI	Industry
Changing Worlds	University College Dublin	Amdocs	US$60m	2008	Prof Barry Smith and Prof Paul Cotter	ICT
Havok Technologies	Trinity College Dublin	Intel	US$100m	2007	Prof Hugh Reynolds and Prof Stevin Collins	ICT
BiancaMed	University College Dublin	Resmed	Undisclosed	2011	Dr Philip de Chazal, Dr Conor Hanley and Professor Conor Heneghan,	Medical Device
Stokes Bio	University of Limerick	Life Technologies	Eur 33m	2010	Professor Mark Davies and Dr Tara Dalton	Medical Device

Source: Created by authors based on data from Enterprise Ireland.

Political Agenda

Stemming from the Whitaker report in 1972, Ireland attracted a high number of manufacturing multinational companies because of low taxes and low labour rates. We advance the argument that foreign firms came here for these incentives rather than academic or scientific excellence. It was the Irish government that encouraged the university–industry linkages that triggered the TTO system rather than multinationals. R&D funding is an interesting metric to determine the commercial capability of the technology transfer system in Ireland, and the main source of research funding in the higher education sector comes directly from government. Direct government funding increased from €66 million in 2000 to €440 million in 2010, representing an almost seven-fold increase over the period. Overall, Ireland's performance in terms of higher education researchers (headcount) per 1,000 of the labour force, ranks 15th position out of 35 countries in the OECD at 5.3 per 1,000 (Forfás, 2013). The findings show that up to 2008 Ireland was making progress to increase the amount of higher education R&D (HERD). Specifically, in the period 2002–2008, HERD expenditure had more than tripled in nominal terms, peaking at almost €750m in 2008. However, due to an economic downturn in Ireland, there was a significant cut in government funding awarded to Irish universities from 2010–2014. The year 2010 saw a 5.5 per cent decline; total HERD stands at €708 million in 2010 (Forfás, 2013). The findings are shown in Figure 9.2.

Table 9.2 Summary of key results, 2000–2010, current prices

	2000	2002	2004	2006	2008	2010
Higher Education expenditure on R&D (HERD) – Euros	238m	322m	492m	600m	750m	708m
HERD as a % of GNP	.26	.30	.39	.39	.49	.54
Ireland\s Rank out of 35 countries	26	23	19	19	15	14
Researchers per 100 labour force	17	13	14	15	15	15

Source: Created by authors based on data from Forfás.

Another key metric in influencing underlying commercialisation activity of a country is patent counts. Applications for patents from Irish resident companies (whether foreign-owned or indigenous), institutions (such as universities) and resident individuals, fell in 2012 and were at the lowest level since 1982 (Irish Patent Office, 2012). One explanation is that with a few exceptions Ireland's dual industry structure and foreign-owned sector "does not carry out high value-added activities in Ireland" (Forfás, 2004: 21). The growth rate in patent filing at the European Patent Office between 1995 and 2000 was 26 per cent per annum. However, the number of Patent Cooperation Treaty (PCT) filings declined from 2008–2012 as illustrated in Table 9.3. An explanation for this may be due to the economic downturn in Ireland, which led to a significant cut in government funding awarded to Irish universities.

Table 9.3 Number of Patent Cooperation Treaty (PCT) filings by country of origin

	2008	2009	2010	2011	2012
Ireland	481	482	443	415	390

Source: Created by authors based on data from the World Intellectual Property Organization.

The European Innovation Union Scorecard (2013) captures the key strengths and weaknesses for Ireland in relation to the EU-25 member states. Accordingly, Ireland is classified as an innovation follower, with an innovation performance below those of leaders such as Sweden, Finland, Germany and Denmark, but still above the EU average. Ireland's relative strengths are in human capital and economic effects. Relative weaknesses are in finance and firm investments – the Irish venture capital (VC) industry is deemed to be particularly weak. Although the provision of venture capital for Irish companies has improved over the years, with Irish VCs investing €1.2 billion in Irish small and medium-sized enterprises (SMEs) since 2000, there is still much to be done in this area.

It is a subject of ongoing consideration for government and agencies like Enterprise Ireland.

Venture capital investment measured in terms of its percentage of GDP shows that in 2004 the US percentage was 0.2 per cent, the European average was 0.1 per cent and in Ireland the percentage was 0.042 per cent. However, recent budgetary changes in taxation have made Ireland a prime location for the establishment of global venture capital and R&D operations, according to a 2009 report by PricewaterhouseCoopers. This should, over time, assist not only in the expansion of activities on the part of multinational companies in Ireland, but also help to spur the creation and growth of indigenous Irish companies. Indeed, the Irish government has set up a framework for VCs to get money into the system and engage with universities. In 2013 the government launched a €175 million Seed and Venture Capital Scheme, 2013–2018. Through Enterprise Ireland, it makes funding available for investment in private seed and venture capital funds. In line with past practice, Enterprise Ireland will:

- make investment commitments to venture capital funds on pari passu commercial terms with the private sector
- not exceed more than 50 per cent of the total capital committed to any fund, and
- always ensure that any fund in receipt of an investment commitment under the scheme legally commits to investing, at a minimum, double Enterprise Ireland's commitment in Irish manufacturing or international trading SMEs.

The aim is to leverage domestic and international private sector/institutional capital into venture capital investment in Ireland. Therefore, there is no apparent preference between foreign VC and national VC.

Challenges of the Irish technology transfer system

With just seven teaching and research universities, Ireland is a small country and could be considered a latecomer to technology transfer activity. In recent decades it changed from being a low skilled country to becoming an advanced knowledge-based country with a significant number of high technology production sites. For all the focus, funds, and activity on technology transfer since the implementation of the Technology Transfer Strengthening Initiative, government and university leaders face tough challenges. First, any start-up needs to be competitive internationally because Ireland is too small a market to sustain them (Blumenstyk, 2010). They are encouraged to be export-orientated from the outset and become "Born Globals".

Furthermore, even though Ireland's commercialisation push is still in its infancy some hurdles are not significantly different from challenges faced by established TTOs in the United States, Britain and Canada. Finding venture capitalists to back early stage ideas is a global challenge and the "valley of death" funding trap is a real risk as start-ups look to finance long-term strategies. This is evident in the lacuna of successful IPO companies created since Iona Technologies out of Trinity College Dublin. This is not to say there have not been any spinoffs. Table 9.4 showcases the

Table 9.4 List of spinouts by university 2007/2011 cumulative

Categories
1 = Incorporated entity, built from IP from a HEI
2 = License concluded, working with EI and/or business partner to expand; typically employing 2–3 people
3 = Has won investment/sales and is an EI High Potential start up client; typically employing 5–10 people

University	Spinout	Year	Category
University of Limerick	Poly Pico Technologies Ltd	2011	1
Univeristy of Limerick	ALR Innovations	2011	2
University College Dublin	Applied Process Consulting	2011	2
University College Dublin	Wattics Ltd	2011	2
University College Dublin	Scream Technologies Ltd	2011	1
University College Dublin	Belfield Technologies Ltd	2011	1
University College Dublin	NewLambda Technologies Ltd	2011	2
Dublin City University	EcoVolve Limited	2011	1
Trinity College Dublin	Glanta	2011	3
Trinity College Dublin	Trimod Therapeutics Ltd	2011	3
Trinity College Dublin	Ussher Executive Education Ltd	2011	1
Trinity College Dublin	PBOC Ltd	2011	1
Trinity College Dublin	Aeriaq Filtration Ltd	2011	2
Trinity College Dublin	PixelPuffin Ltd	2011	1
Trinity College Dublin	Neuropath Ltd	2011	2
University College Cork	InfiniLED Limited	2011	3
University College Cork	Mitamed Ltd	2011	2
National Univeristy of Ireland, Maynooth	ISAAT	2011	1
National University of Ireland, Maynooth	Relational Frame Training	2011	1
National University of Ireland, Maynooth	ProFector Life Sciences	2011	3
Dublin City University	Pilot Photonics Limited	2011	3
Dublin City University	Scientia Sports Limited	2011	1
Dublin City University	Xcelerator Maching Translation Ltd	2011	1
Dublin City University	Sonex Metrology Limited	2011	3
Dublin Insitutue of Technology	Radical Coatings Ltd	2011	1
Dublin Institute of Technology	Sonic Ladder Ltd	2011	1
National University of Ireland, Galway	SEEVl Ltd	2011	1
National University of Ireland, Galway	Sindice Ltd	2011	1
National University of Ireland, Galway	Vornia	2011	1
University of Limerick	Learnopt Ltd	2010	2

Table 9.4 continued

Table 9.4 continued

University	Spinout	Year	Category
University of Limerick	Azotos Analytics	2010	1
University College Dublin	Bofinn Diagnostics Ltd	2010	1
University College Dublin	Careergro Ltd	2010	3
University College Dublin	Crop Research Ltd	2010	1
University College Dublin	Jlizard Ltd	2010	1
Trinity College Dublin	City Analytics Ltd	2010	1
Trinity College Dublin	Codex Oncology	2010	3
Trinity College Dublin	Synergy Flow	2010	1
Trinity College Dublin	Tolerant Networks Ltd	2010	1
Trinity College Dublin	Trinity Clinical Apps Ltd	2010	1
Trinity College Dublin	xcelerit Computing Ltd	2010	1
University College Cork	3PRO Energy Watch Limited	2010	1
University College Cork	Clinical Support Information Systems Ltd	2010	3
University College Cork	Thinksmart Technologies	2010	1
National University of Ireland, Maynooth	AniScan	2010	1
National University of Ireland, Maynooth	CereBeo	2010	2
National University of Ireland, Maynooth	Mutebutton	2010	3
Dublin City University	Astryne Ltd	2010	3
Dublin City University	GreenEgg	2010	1
Dublin City University	Jalico Ltd	2010	2
Dublin Insitutue of Technology	Moletest Ltd.	2010	1
Dublin Insitutue of Technology	Currency Traders Ltd	2010	1
National University of Ireland, Galway	Tethra Geo Ltd	2010	1
National University of Ireland, Galway	Peracton ltd	2010	1
National University of Ireland, Galway	DRIvEINTELL Ltd	2010	1
National University of Ireland, Galway	Cutting Edge Medical Devices Ltd	2010	2
National University of Ireland, Galway	Alternative Sustainable Energy Resources Ltd	2010	3
National University of Ireland, Galway	ALSE Waste Ltd	2010	1
Waterford Institute of Technology	FeedHenry	2010	3
Waterford Institute of Technology	Zolk C	2010	3
Royal College of Surgeons, Ireland	Surgacoll technologies Ltd	2010	3
Institute of Technology, Tralee	Niche Protein Limited	2010	1

University	Spinout	Year	Category
National University of Ireland, Galway	Analyze IQ Ltd	2009	1
Trinity College Dublin	Anemates Ldt	2009	1
University College Dublin	Aermon ltd	2009	1
University of Limerick	Bearna Medical	2009	2
National University of Ireland, Galway	Beckman Coulter Biomedical Ltd	2009	1
National University of Ireland, Maynooth	Beemune Limited	2009	3
Trinity College Dublin	BioCrio Ltd	2009	3
University College Dublin	Bioplastech ltd	2009	3
National University of Ireland, Maynooth	Blue Box Sensors	2009	3
Dublin Insitutue of Technology	Brim Brothers	2009	2
University College Dublin	Capstan Healthcare Ltd	2009	1
University of Limerick	Cauwill Technologies	2009	2
University College Dublin	Darius Medical Ltd	2009	2
National University of Ireland, Galway	Eagleedge Ltd	2009	1
University College Dublin	Equinome	2009	3
Dublin City University	Fairview Analytics	2009	1
University College Dublin	Future Buildings Consulting Ltd	2009	1
Trinity College Dublin	GoFer ICT Ltd	2009	1
University College Cork	Gourmet Marine	2009	3
University College Cork	HMEMZ Ltd	2009	1
National University of Ireland, Maynooth	iGeoTech Technologies Limited	2009	1
University College Cork	Keelvar Systems Ltd	2009	2
Trinity College Dublin	Kinometrics Ltd – Surewash Ltd	2009	1
National University of Ireland, Galway	KnowledgeHives	2009	1
University College Cork	Lee Oncology	2009	1
Dublin City University	Lexas Research	2009	3
Trinity College Dublin	Miravex Ltd	2009	3
Waterford Institute of Technology	Nubiq Technology Ltd	2009	2
National University of Ireland, Galway	Pro-cure Ltd	2009	2
National University of Ireland, Galway	Qpercom Ltd	2009	1
Trinity College Dublin	Recitell	2009	1
Trinity College Dublin	Share Navigator	2009	1
Trinity College Dublin	Sovotrin Therapeutics	2009	3

Table 9.4 continued

Table 9.4 continued

University	Spinout	Year	Category
National University of Ireland, Galway	TagCrumbs Ltd	2009	1
Dublin Insitutue of Technology	Trezur	2009	3
Dublin Insitutue of Technology	Breakout Gaming Concepts	2008	1
Trinity College Dublin	EmpowerTheUser Ltd	2008	1
Waterford Institute of Technology	Headway	2008	1
University College Dublin	Heystackes Technologies	2008	2
Trinity College Dublin	New Game	2008	1
National University of Ireland, Maynooth	Socowave	2008	3
Trinity College Dublin	Treocht Ltd	2008	3
University College Dublin	Advanced Diagnostics Laboratory	2007	1
University College Dublin	Ap Enveon	2007	1
University College Dublin	Biontrack	2007	1
National University of Ireland, Galway	Eirzyme Ltd	2007	3
Waterford Institute of Technology	Hash 6	2007	3
Royal College of Surgeons, Ireland	Neuro Research Services Ltd	2007	1
University College Dublin	Oncomark	2007	2
Dublin City University	Phive	2007	1
Dublin City University	Sera Scientific	2007	1
Trinity College Dublin	Sonitus Systems Ltd	2007	3
University of Limerick	Stokes Bio	2007	3
National University of Ireland, Galway	Theta Chemicals	2007	3
National University of Ireland, Galway	Triskel	2007	1

Sources: Created by authors based on data from Enterprise Ireland (www.enterprise-ireland.com/ EI_Corporate/en/Publications/Reports-Published-Strategies/Inventions-and-Innovations.pdf and www.hea.ie/sites/default/files/evaluation_framework_short_1.pdf).

volume of spinoffs while Table 9.1 (see earlier) shows the companies that sold out in their early stages of development.

Policy Initiatives

In the early 2000s a National Development Plan was devised to "upgrade" Ireland to a knowledge economy. The universities became key players in this strategy and had to step up their technology transfer capabilities to stimulate new firm formation. Numerous policy reports promoted closer links between industry and the universities, including "Ahead of the curve: Ireland's place in the global economy" (ESG, 2004); "Building Ireland's knowledge economy – the Irish action plan for promoting investment in R&D in 2010" (Forfás, 2004) and "Promoting enterprise – higher education relationships" (Forfás, 2007). Table 9.5 outlines other policy initiatives. These reports all contributed to influencing the policy agenda, supporting the role of the university in Irish economic development.

Table 9.5 Summary of policy initiatives

Title of Report	Recommendations of Report
White Paper on Industrial Policy, 1984	• Highlighted need to increase technology transfer from Irish HEIs to industry
Programme for Action in Education, 1984–1987	• Highlighted need to increase technology transfer from Irish HEIs to industry
Tierney Report, 1995	• Curriculum development and research endeavour be linked to the needs of business in Ireland
Barriers to Research and Consultancy in the Higher Education Sector, 1996	• Need to strengthen the interface between HEIs and industry based on application and exploitation of scientifically derived knowledge • Creation of a climate in which academics will be able and willing to interact with industry • Establishment of new institutional mechanisms and structures at college and national level to facilitate the development of links with industry
Building Ireland's Smart Economy, 2004	• Significant emphasis on the economic return for the major taxpayer funding of research
Strategy for Science, Innovation and Technology, 2006–2013	• Strategic priority to building research excellence and developing the third mission of universities and the strengthening of TTOs
Intellectual Property Protocol: Putting public research to work for Ireland	• Standardising national procedures and model contracts

Source: Created by authors.

While these reports played a role in creating an ethos for closer industry-academic linkages and building a foundation for university–industry technology transfer, the government's comprehensive plan to guide Ireland towards becoming a knowledge-driven economy was the Strategy for Science, Technology and Innovation 2006–2013. Its overarching vision was to ensure that: "Ireland by 2013 will be internationally renowned for the excellence of its research and will be to the forefront in generating and using new knowledge for economic and social progress within an innovation driven culture."

As a result of this strategy, research commercialisation and technology transfer emerged as new missions for Irish universities. Following on from this policy, the government published its "framework for sustainable economic renewal", entitled "Building Ireland's smart economy" (SSTI, 2006). The introduction explains that the framework "sets out the Government's vision for the next phase of Ireland's economic development". A significant part of the focus is the encouragement of research, innovation and entrepreneurship. The Innovation Taskforce was appointed to advise the government on how to turn Ireland into an international innovation hub and to support the development of a smart economy. The Taskforce examined options to increase levels of innovation and the rates of commercialisation of R&D on a national basis at university and non-university level. The aim was to accelerate the growth of indigenous enterprise and to attract new knowledge-intensive direct investment, building on the SSTI. Membership of the Taskforce included representatives from the private sector, third level education and relevant government departments and agencies.

In 2010, the Taskforce report recommended "making it easier for the entrepreneur" by "standardising national procedures and model contracts". The Taskforce also suggested developing a national IP Protocol with "ground rules" around ownership and setting up a national office that would be a single point of contact on all issues around IP for entrepreneurs in higher education. The outcome was the Irish central Technology Transfer Office, (cTTO) as outlined in the policy report "Intellectual Property Protocol: Putting public research to work for Ireland" (2012). Named Knowledge Transfer Ireland, its objective is to work closely with the university TTOs, sharing good practice and ensuring consistency in adoption and interpretation of policy by all stakeholders. TTOs are encouraged to operate to certain standards and processes, particularly around IP management.

The central recommendations of the report were as follows:
- the entrepreneur and enterprise must be at the centre of Ireland's Innovation efforts
- the goal is to strengthen entrepreneurial culture in Higher Education Institutes
- HR policies should be implemented that incentivise and reward innovation and commercialisation
- fair and supportive leave of absence policies should be introduced
- career advancement is based on valuing commercialisation as well as research and teaching
- develop and publish a national IP protocol which establishes "ground rules" around ownership and access to State supported IP
- adopt more meaningful metrics by which HEIs and TTOs are measured to reflect the IP Protocol
- link a proportion of state funding for HEIs to national metrics of innovation and commercialisation.

In 2014 there was a review of initiatives aimed at cultivating an entrepreneurial ecosystem in Ireland. Specifically the report, "Entrepreneurship in Ireland: Strengthening the startup community", outlines an initiative to create a national education strategy for entrepreneurship at all levels of the education system, supporting the potential of entrepreneurship education to encourage students to develop an entrepreneurial mindset. It encouraged HEIs to engage directly with graduate students without making any intellectual property claim, and with a policy towards easy access to IP for the public benefit. Furthermore, the report stipulated more must be done in Ireland to optimise relationships between academia and industry around the cross-fertilisation of research and commercialisation.

An independent review of the Irish Technology Transfer system was conducted and the following recommendations were made.

1   The State needs to continue to commit funding to the knowledge transfer initiative, accepting it as a cost/service base and not simply a mechanism to generate profit.
2   Emulate the UK model where they have a committed Higher Education Innovation Fund (HEIF).
3   Broaden the metrics beyond capturing volume to capturing count outcomes.
4   Embed knowledge transfer in the mission of universities along with teaching and research.
5   Reduce bureaucracy within the system.

It can be surmised that the Irish policy is positioning universities as critical ingredients in the nation's ability to remain competitive. The next section outlines the specific core support elements of the process.

Core Supports in the evolution of Irish TTOs

Enterprise Ireland (EI) is the government agency responsible for the development and promotion of the technology transfer system in Ireland through the Technology Transfer Strengthening Initiative. As part of its commitment to facilitating the commercialisation of research, it financially supports academic researchers to commercialise their work and to link with Irish companies through a number of funding schemes, including a Commercialisation Fund. Table 9.6 outlines the initiatives introduced by Enterprise Ireland to support researcher engagement with industry. This funding is critical to enabling TTOs to conduct their business and is the reason they exist in Ireland. Enterprise Ireland supports the salaries of many of the commercialisation specialists who work in the TTOs. In addition, Enterprise Ireland provides intense supports for Irish-owned businesses (employing between 10 and 250) involved in manufacturing and internationally traded services. It also supports start-ups and micro businesses (fewer than 10 employees) in the same sector, provided they have the potential to achieve rapid growth and international expansion. These are referred to as High Potential Start-Ups (HPSUs), of which about 70 receive Enterprise Ireland support each year. A university example is Metabolomic Diagnostics, a company spun out of University College Cork from infant research conducted by Professor Louise Kenny. It explores clinical exploitation of metabolomic technology for patient benefit, specifically the detection of pre-eclampsia based on a blood sample taken at 15 weeks.

Table 9.6 Enterprise Ireland initiatives supporting university–industry engagement

Proof of concept	• €50,000–€100,000 per project • 12 months duration • Staff on contract welcome to apply • 3 Calls for Proposals per year
Technology development	• €100,000–€400,000 per project • 18–36 months duration • Staff on contract welcome to apply • 3 Calls for Proposals per year
Innovation partnerships	• This programme supports collaborative research projects between Irish HEIs and companies. The financial support in this case is provided to the college. The proposal process and administration of the project is managed by the participating institute
Innovation vouchers	• SMEs spend their €5,000 vouchers in HEIs in exchange for innovative solutions to small business challenges. There is also the option for groups of 10 companies to apply for a "pooled innovation voucher" up to the value of €50,000 to spend with one research team
Commercial case feasibility support	• Funding support of up to €15,000 can be obtained by researchers in partnership with their Technology Transfer Office or equivalent office for a short Feasibility Project to scope and develop their commercial case for their technology in advance of submitting a Commercialisation Fund Support application to the programme
Commercialisation fund support	• Funding support is available for projects that address a "gap or need in the market" by developing innovative technologies that will ideally be ready for licensing to Irish industry or may form the basis of a new start up in 2–5 years. It is recognised however that some technologies may need a longer time to get to market than others. Proposals from all disciplines in the fields of Science and Engineering with costs ranging from €80,000 to €350,000 will be accepted

Source: Created by authors based on data from Enterprise Ireland.

The Enterprise Ireland 2013 annual report outlined its role in technology transfer in Ireland:

- €92 million invested in commercialising research and collaborative R&D for industry
- €65 million equity and venture capital investment in Irish enterprise in 2013 with TTSI support
- 34 companies were spun out from Ireland's colleges and 119 commercially viable packages of technologies and IP were transferred to companies
- a cTTO was established within Enterprise Ireland, providing companies for the first time with a comprehensive overview of research capabilities of all Irish universities, Institutes of Technology and specialist research centres
- supporting the VC environment, EI committed €175 million to a new Seed and Venture Capital Scheme (2013–2018) with funds of €700 million over to its lifetime available for investment in high-growth, early stage companies.

Currently, the TTOs are measured on the number of licenses, spinouts, and number of invention disclosures as part of the Technology Transfer Strengthening Initiative. By the end of 2012, participating institutions had more than doubled the number of inventions identified per year, more than tripled the number of licenses and options executed, and more than quadrupled the number of start-ups companies formed on the basis of university intellectual property (Enterprise Ireland, 2012). Relative to their levels of research support, Irish universities are comparable to their counterparts in the United States and the rest of Europe according to Enterprise Ireland. However, Enterprise Ireland does not trace the impact from technology transfer deals in terms of sales or growth levels. We believe this is a flaw in the system. If these performance metrics were captured, we could better evaluate the decision-making behind the investments and see if the chosen companies had the right strategies to compete in world markets. We could begin to see if the TTO programme was successful in developing growth-orientated Irish companies rather than lifestyle companies, as shown in Figure 9.1 (see also Enterprise Ireland 2012). The challenge might not be in creating spinoffs, but in scaling them from Ireland and keeping them here once they have attracted the attention of global VCs.

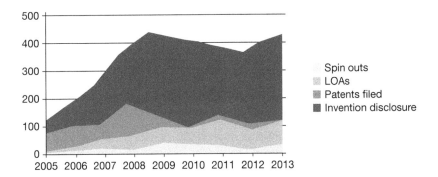

Figure 9.1 TTO Output 2005–2013

To set TTO targets, performance data is regularly collected and compared with international trends. In the recent EU Knowledge Transfer Report 2010–2012, Ireland was ranked first in Europe using a composite indicator of the knowledge transfer activities of public research organisations (start-ups, number of licenses, license income, research agreements, invention disclosures, patent applications and patent grants). According to Enterprise Ireland, the Technology Transfer Strengthening Initiative has been very successful, leading to a three-fold increase in the average number of spinout companies created in the five-year period since it was introduced. It rose from an average of seven per annum in the period 2002–2006 to an average of 24 per annum between 2007 and 2011. Furthermore, there has been a 400 per cent increase in the amount of technologies licensed to companies by Higher Education Institutes (Enterprise Ireland, 2012). From 2005 to 2010, invention disclosures increased from 135 to 431, patent applications increased from 83 to 101 licenses, options and assignments increased from 12 to 93, and the number of spinouts increased from 5 to 31. As regards the destination of licenses, in 2007–2010, 32 per cent of licenses from universities went to spinouts; a further 29 per cent went to Irish SMEs with 35 per cent going to multinational companies. The resource profiles and cumulative commercialisation outcomes are highlighted in Table 9.7.

In response to an increased focus on creating more spinouts, Enterprise Ireland launched a search for Business Partners in December 2008 – matching successful entrepreneurs with prospective spinout companies emerging from publicly funded research in HEIs. Once formed, new companies can also apply for support from Enterprise Ireland's High-potential Start-Up (HSPU) fund. These are companies that, in the view of Enterprise Ireland, can develop innovative technologies, products and services for sale on world markets.

In 2012, the government of Ireland announced they were extending the scheme and introducing a second round of support for the technology transfer system in Ireland. Quoting Feargal O'Morain (Head of Technology Transfer in Enterprise Ireland) from an interview conducted in 2012, "The extension of funding for a second phase of the Technology Transfer Strengthening Initiative will enable us to increase the flexibility and responsiveness of the system to make it a key resource for industry in Ireland." The objectives of the second phase include the development of an efficient and flexible response to industry's requests for access to intellectual property.

Enhancing commercialisation policies within Irish universities – examples

This section outlines three mini-case studies reflecting the transfer of Irish national strategy to the subnational level. The cases demonstrate how universities are reacting in various ways to Irish Government policy with regards to developing a more 'entrepreneurship centric' culture on campus.

Trinity College Dublin

Trinity College Dublin was founded in 1592. Today it boasts a 17,000-student population in the city centre campus occupying some 51 acres, including the Trinity Technology and Enterprise Campus. Trinity research has been the starting point for many pioneering Irish companies. From 2008–2013 the TTO has managed the protection of over 290 inventions and has successfully completed over 450 contracts with industry and produced 38 spinoffs. In the past two years, eight Trinity spinoff companies have attracted 60 million in venture investment. This venture capital investment performance outpaces any other Irish higher education institution.

Trinity recently launched an innovation and entrepreneurship strategy which identifies innovation and entrepreneurship as central feature of Trinity's future

Table 9.7 Cumulative output of technology transfer outputs 2010/2011

University	Type	Med school	Research income	Patent applications: IRE only	Patent applications: other than IRE	Patents granted: IRE	Patent granted: Outside IRE	License agreements	Spinout created
						2010/2011 cumulative			
University College Cork	Public	Y	EUR 70,333,000	7	39	4	11	34	5
University College Dublin	Public	Y	EUR 84,816,000	20	61	0	11	35	9
Trinity College, University of Ireland	Public	Y	EUR 81,977,000	9	48	1	8	21	13
National University of Ireland, Galway	Public	N	EUR 53,313,000	7	26	0	17	21	9
National University of Ireland, Maynooth	Public	Y	EUR 23,533,000	5	3	2	0	15	6
Dublin City University	Public	N	EUR 45,851,000	2	21	2	10	47	8
University of Limerick	Public	Y	EUR 42,533,000	7	24	4	10	62	4

Source: Created by authors based on data from Enterprise Ireland.

activity. A key component of this strategy is to develop the Office of Corporate Partnership and Knowledge Exchange (OCPKE) to promote Trinity as a partner of choice for industry and business, to support access to intellectual property, and to provide knowledge-based services to companies.

The OCPKE supports Trinity researchers with the identification, protection and commercialisation of Trinity's innovative research. It also facilitates and approves the formation of campus companies. The work of the OCPKE is underpinned by Trinity's "Principles for open innovation", which outlines an approach for effective engagement with public, private and social enterprises in order to stimulate knowledge transfer for social and economic development.

Trinity's approach to the transfer of knowledge and technology for commercial use is based on defining, and appropriately protecting, commercially useful intellectual property, so that it can accrue value and realise delivery of IP. Trinity will ensure that efficient and effective mechanisms for the deployment of IP are in place, consistent with its open innovation objectives.

The new policy on technology transfer is based on four principles:
1   optimising the rate at which campus companies are formed,
2   reducing real or perceived delays to forming a campus company,
3   maximising the level of knowledge transfer, and
4   ensuring a fair and reasonable return to college.

Trinity is open to a range of models for ownership of IP, licensing of IP and future assignment of ownership of IP to best exploit its commercial potential and ensure a future return. Trinity recognises and accepts that industry collaborators will be better placed to commercialise output than an academic institution, and, accordingly, Trinity will ensure that industry shall have the first right of refusal on all IP from collaborative projects on terms commensurate with the level of support from the industry partner. Provision will be made to enable other uses of IP, including licensing to newly created Irish-based ventures such as Trinity campus companies.

The mission of the office is based on the following principles:

- open innovation – the priority is to develop IP that is put to use in society
- not profit motivated – knowledge transfer for socio-economic return
- flexibility – Trinity is open to a range of models for ownership of IP
- user-friendliness – systems are in place to support and encourage industry engagement
- practical – they want to do fair deals quickly.

Uniquely among Irish universities, the OCPKE is part of a unit – Trinity Research & Innovation – which provides integrated support all along the research continuum, from funding applications, to contract negotiation, to technology transfer and entrepreneurship training. Its "gateway" policy, provides a one-stop shop "front door" that aims to proactively connect industry and academics, and minimise all barriers to commercialisation. Trinity wants to be recognised as a partner of choice for industry in collaborative and funded research. Interactions with industry partners, from spinouts to multinational corporations, will be governed by a user-friendly system to support and encourage engagement using a range of models including:

- collaborative research
- technology evaluation
- technology licensing
- internships
- researchers-in-residence
- entrepreneurs-in-residence
- fully funded research services.

According to Professor Vinnie Cahill, Dean of Research, "The purpose of the gateway approach is not to centralise all industry contact, but to offer visibility for new relationships. It also enables Trinity to be proactive in reaching out to industry and encourages the forming of new relationships."

The "front door" approach aims to:

- link enterprise and academia without barriers
- help companies to become more research-active
- enable quick decision-making and a streamlined approach to enterprise engagement.

The OCPKE will be responsible for managing all aspects of interactions with industry. It will support industry in getting involved in Horizon 2020, the EU Framework Programme for Research and Innovation. It will help businesses to access cutting-edge infrastructure and researchers, supporting all research projects from first steps to large-scale collaborations. It will develop business innovation, linked to more exports and jobs. Business leaders serving on a knowledge transfer and innovation committee will support the office. This committee will reinforce the enterprise-facing mission, and advocate for Trinity in the enterprise community.

In this model, the TTO encourages deal flow rather than short-term revenue maximisation objectives. According to Professor Cahill, "We see Dublin as the hub of a regional economic cluster marked by innovative companies, with Trinity acting as the city centre 'connector' for enterprise and academia. At the heart of our strategy is a drive to reach out and help enterprise to scale in a mutually enabling partnership for society and the economy."

Another important change in the development of Trinity as an innovation university was the revised equity investment procedure for the approval of campus company formation. This 2009 revision was at the instigation of the Associate Director of TR&I, Dr James Callaghan, with approval from the Finance Committee for the derogation of the College's IP Policy. The simplified process led to an immediate, significant increase in numbers of new companies. The reasons for this were identified as their equity policy of 15 per cent and an attitude of IP capture and protection rather than open innovation. The policy was changed to encourage deal-flow rather than IP-capture, with Trinity taking a 5 per cent equity stake in spinoff companies instead of 15 per cent, which was deemed to be a significant impediment for campus companies when they looked to attract further investment.

A wider Trinity strategy is to focus on encouraging student entrepreneurs. The university introduced the Launchbox to support potential entrepreneurs and "make it easier for them to set up companies". Furthermore, there is no expectation of financial return to the university from this activity.

Dublin City University (DCU)

DCU was established as a university in 1989, nine years after its original founding as the National Institute for Higher Education (NIHE). It has 11,760 students and 500 academic researchers and won approximately €35 million in research funding in 2013. The *Times Higher Education*'s "The 100 Under 50" has ranked it in the top 100 of the world's young universities (less than 50 years old) for three consecutive years. The DCU TTO, Invent, was launched in 2001. The purpose built incubation centre has 2,800 square metres of space for technology based start-up companies. Its mission is to support and encourage the translation of innovative research, inspired where possible by industrial partners, into new or enhanced products and services. The rationale is in line with the university's strategic objective to contribute to the development of the regional economy.

DCU's goal is to become "Ireland's University of Enterprise" and achieve this by working with researchers to identify innovations with commercial potential by engaging early on with industrial companies. Identifying and protecting intellectual property created at DCU, or in partnership with client companies, is seen as an important part of its role. The creation of new intellectual property, whether through patents, copyright or industrial designs, enables business partners to improve profitability, to enter new markets and to gain competitive advantage. The university uses extensive links with industry to help forge business and research partnerships and to market DCU's commercialisation opportunities and research capabilities both nationally and internationally.

DCU is beginning to experiment with innovative approaches to the management of technology transfer. In response to the challenge set by government in its Innovation Taskforce Report, which recommended that universities need to find ways to make it easier and faster for entrepreneurs to unlock innovation, DCU introduced a fast-track Licence Express scheme to make selected patent innovations available to industry and entrepreneurs in a fast and efficient manner. The scheme provides exclusive and non-exclusive template licences online to companies or entrepreneurs who must propose credible business plans. Proposals will be selected by DCU on the basis of potential impact to the Irish economy in terms of jobs or exports. Royalties will not be due for a period of four years and there will be no up-front payments due to the university. Ongoing royalties after the initial four years will be at a rate of only 1 per cent of net sales.

The motivation behind License Express was "to encourage a better relationship between university and potential industry partners", according to Richard Stokes, Director of Technology Transfer. It was recognised that "collaborative research is needed for innovative IP", thus the case was made for the fast track license. The objective is to get the technology out in the world for the benefit of society. Academics were not resistant to the introduction of the license because it was deemed preferable to the traditional approach where agreements are hastily secured in one to three months, followed by several months of change requests.

The introduction of the DCU Licence Express is part of a wider strategy to make DCU easy for industry and entrepreneurs to work with. However, it was decided not to go down the Easy Access IP model. Richard Stokes explained: "There will ultimately be a transaction cost involved in the management of all IP and so this cost must be covered somehow." The decision was made to introduce Licence Express as a "halfway house solution" between the traditional model and revolutionary models such as Easy Access IP.

The scheme is designed to make available to industry certain early stage technologies, which have been developed as a result of research carried out at DCU. Patents will have been granted or are pending, but the route to market or time to market may be unclear or dependent on other enabling technological or regulatory developments. As part of DCU's collaborative approach to working with industry and in the spirit of open innovation, DCU is offering licences to potential licensees on conditions set out below.

- No upfront licence fees will be due at the time the licence is signed, nor are there any milestone payments or royalty payments due during the initial development and sales period of four years.
- A flat royalty rate of 1 per cent of net sales will apply after the four-year royalty free period.
- DCU will not licence any patents under this scheme to patent aggregators or patent assertion companies. It intends that the licences will be granted to companies whose main business is the exploitation and development of technology through the manufacturing and sale of related products.
- Technology will not be assigned to licensees under this fast-track scheme.
- It will offer Exclusive and Non-Exclusive licences.

Dublin Institute of Technology (DIT)

Though it was established in its present form in 1992, DIT can trace an unbroken history back to the establishment in 1887 of the first technical education institution in Ireland. Currently there are approximately 22,000 undergraduate and postgraduate students. In 2014 it came 94th in the *Times Higher Education*'s "The 100 Under 50" ranking.

DIT Hothouse, the TTO at DIT, helps inventors and authors protect and commercialise their own IP. The centre has been jointly nominated for three awards at the Intellectual Property (IP) Awards 2014. The Hothouse has performed well in technology transfer metrics by completing between 10 and 20 per cent of the annual technology transfer licenses in Ireland, on just 3 per cent of the research expenditure since its formation in 2008. Hothouse has previously negotiated licences for DIT technologies with Sony, Sherman Williams, General Paints and ABB. Many more are in the pipeline.

DIT's Industrial Engineering Optics Centre (IEO) developed a groundbreaking individualised hologram to address a gap in the market for providing companies with a cost-effective means of combating the production of counterfeit products. The process involves digitally printing ink onto a light-sensitive polymer. The printed polymer is then exposed to a controlled pattern of laser light to convert the design into a unique hologram that can incorporate a serial number, barcode, company logo and other features. Having identified that the technology formed the basis for a business, DIT Hothouse worked with the research team to form Optrace, a DIT spinout company specialising in novel holographic security technology. Having formed in May 2013, Optrace is at an early stage in its lifecycle but is already achieving impressive results.

Another example is OptiWifi Ltd., a graduate of the 2012 Hothouse incubation programme and one of three finalists in the Docklands Innovation Park Awards 2013. The company's core technology was developed in DIT in the Communications Network Research Institute (CNRI). The company has seen strong growth and recently received investment backing from Telefonica, a world leader in the telecommunications industry. In February 2014, OptiWi-fi announced an agreement with O2 Wifi to deploy industry-first wireless network bandwidth optimisation across its UK and Irish networks.

DIT will only embark on a course of patenting and commercialisation if the technology warrants it and if the applicable researcher(s) support the process. It introduced an inventor ownership model when it founded the TTO in 2007, recognising that the creator has the moral and legal rights to the IP created, except where there are contracts with sponsors that require IP assignment, where DIT resources were used in the creation of the IP, or where administrative materials were developed for DIT.

DIT is also focused on:
- encouraging the protection of IP before publishing so that the IP retains commercial value
- enabling creators to choose to commercialise IP themselves or use DIT Hothouse, the TTO, or other means
- sharing up to 75 per cent of net revenues received from commercialisation with the creators, and
- assigning IP to colleagues and students in return for a negotiable equity stake for DIT, typically 15 per cent.

The IP policy is intended to create a more entrepreneurial environment in DIT to attract and retain world-class researchers, enhance collaboration with industry and raise the profile of DIT as a centre for excellence, commercially focused research and consultancy. The old IP policy allowed DIT to claim the IP generated by its employees and its students. The rationale is that the change encourages staff and students to be more innovative.

Everything created by students or staff at DIT belongs to them if three conditions are met.

1   Not required by a sponsor to assign the IP.
2   substantial DIT were not used resources while creating it the IP.
3   It wasn't something requested by senior managers while carrying out duties on behalf at DIT.

DIT is still the only university in Ireland to offer such an innovative model that avoids the TTO taking on the role of "IP police". According to Tom Flanagan, Director of Technology Transfer at DIT, the rationale is to instil trust in the TTO among academics "as they would be more inclined to assign their IP to the TTO if they felt a sense of ownership of the IP". They were enthusiastic when the model was introduced as it "endorsed a cooperative model". Academics are less willing to reveal new projects or IP to TTOs in universities with more traditional university ownership models, according to Flanagan. He said: "When they feel like they own it and see the effort the TTO puts in to protect and license IP, many are of the opinion that they will assign their IP to the TTO and take the royalty pay cheque and let the TTO do the hard work."

Conclusion

Systematic efforts have being made in Ireland to build up research and technology transfer infrastructure capability in order to manage the transition to an innovation-based economy. Whilst the government has implemented a vast range of technology transfer strengthening programmes and resources to stimulate R&D and knowledge transfer over the past decade, it was recognised by senior policy makers and a number of senior university administrators that there were still a number of "bureaucratic" roadblocks that needed to be overcome in order to effectively transfer knowledge from university labs to industry.

In this context, this chapter reviewed the role national policy makers played in developing a technology transfer system with a coherent institutional framework that facilitated the processes of knowledge transfer between industry and academia. The chapter also uncovered a number of 'top down' policy interventions that have been undertaken by three major universities in Ireland to restructure their technology transfer governance, incentive structures and policies in order to adopt a more 'entrepreneur-centric' approach to technology transfer.

The chapter also presented an analysis of the development of the technology transfer system in Ireland by analysing the external environment, the strategic capability and the culture and purpose of TTOs at a collective level. The objective was to present the complex, challenging environment in which the Irish TTOs operate as a boundary spanner and to explore the strategic environment in which they exist.

References

Blumenstyk, G. (2010) Ireland looks to academe to re-ignite its economy. The Chronicle of Higher Education. Available online: http://chronicle.com/article/Ireland-Looks-to-Academe-to/125447.

Enterprise Ireland (2012) Inventions and innovations, the positive impact of ideas from research on Irish industry and society. Available online: www.enterprise-ireland.com/ EI_Corporate/en/Publications/Reports-Published-Strategies/Inventions-and-Innovations.pdf.

Enterprise Strategy Group (ESG) (2004) Ahead of the curve: Ireland's place in the global economy. Dublin: Enterprise Strategy Group. Available online: www.forfas.ie/media/ esg040707_enterprise_strategy_group.pdf.

European Commission, 2013. Innovation Union Scorecard 2013. Available online: http:// ec.europa.eu/enterprise/policies/innovation/files/ius-2013_en.pdf.

Forfás (2004) From research to the marketplace: Patent registration and technology transfer in Ireland. Dublin: Forfás.

Forfás (2004) Building Ireland's knowledge economy – the Irish action plan for promoting investment in R&D to 2010. Dublin: Forfás.

Forfás (2007) Promoting enterprise – higher education relationships. Dublin: Forfás and The Advisory Council for Science, technology and Innovation.

Forfás (2013) Survey of research and development in the Higher Education sector 2010/2011. Dublin: Forfás.

Higher Education Authority (2013) Towards a performance evaluation framework: Profiling Irish Higher education – a report by the Higher Education Authority, December 2013.

Innovation Taskforce (2012) Intellectual property protocol: Putting public research to work for Ireland. Available online: www.enterprise-ireland.com/EI_Corporate/en/ Research-Innovation/Companies/IPP-Putting-public-research-to-work-for-Ireland.pdf.

Irish Patent Office (2012) Eighty Fifth Annual Report of the Controller of Patents, Designs and Trade Marks. Dublin: The Stationery Office.

Jones-Evans, D., Klofsten, M., Andersson, E. and Pandya, D. (1999) Creating a bridge between university and industry in small European countries: The role of Industrial Liaison Office. *R&D Management*, 29 (1): 47–56.

OECD (2006) Assessing and expanding the science and technology base. Paris: OECD.

O'Shea, R.P, Allen T.J. (2014) Strategies for Enhancement of University-based Entrepreneurship. Chapter 15, In Building Technology Transfer within Research Universities: An Entrepreneurial Approach. UK: Cambridge University Press, 2014.

Pricewaterhouse Cooper (2009) Ireland the investment opportunity. Irish Venture Capital Association.

Rothaermel, Frank, Agung, Shanti D. and Jiang, Lin (2007) University entrepreneurship: A taxonomy of the literature. *Industrial and Corporate Change*. 16 (4): 691–791.

Sanders, C. B. and Miller, F. A. (2010) Reframing norms: Boundary maintenance and partial accommodations in the work of academic technology transfer. *Science and Public Policy*, 37 (9): 689–701.

Strategy for Science, Technology and Innovation (2006–2013). Available online: www2. ul.ie/pdf/35659989.pdf

Trinity Strategic Plan (2014–2019) The Strategic Plan of Trinity College, Dublin.

10 Commercialization and technology transfer policies and intellectual property regimes in Canada[1]

Nicola Hepburn and David A. Wolfe

Introduction

Universities occupy a central place in the process of knowledge creation and dissemination in the contemporary economy. While the main research role of universities has traditionally been seen as the performance of basic research, they have come under increasing pressure in recent decades to expand this role into additional areas, particularly for the commercialization of research. The changes that have pushed the university system in this direction are part of a broader economic trend that has shifted the site for the performance of basic and applied research away from government and corporate research laboratories towards the university. At issue is the changing nature of the relationship between the universities and the broader innovation system in which they are embedded, as well as the changing nature of the research and development process within large corporations (Geiger and Sá 2008: 34).

The chapter examines the nature of Canadian policies for the commercialization of university-based research, as well as the tech transfer practices at a number of leading Canadian universities. Canada has one of the oldest federal systems in existence after the U.S., with the country organized into ten provinces and three northern territories. Unlike other federal systems, however, the jurisdictional responsibility for policy areas is not divided into watertight compartments with the result that both the federal and provincial governments share responsibility for key areas of post-secondary education (PSE), as well as responsibility for the university-based research system. Education policy (including the post-secondary system) was originally the exclusive preserve of the provinces from the time of Confederation in 1867, but with the creation of the National Research Council (NRC) during World War I, the federal government began to assume a more active role in supporting research and development activities across the country, including the PSE sector. In the decades since the end of World War II, the federal government has underwritten a greater portion of the cost of PSE and its funding of post-secondary research has expanded considerably. From the 1980s onwards the provinces also increased their spending on research in the post-secondary sector. At the same time, efforts to formulate a national approach to the commercialization of research results, comparable to the Bayh-Dole Act in the

U.S., came to naught with the result that the overall framework for technology transfer and the management of intellectual property has remained highly decentralized at the level of the individual universities. Partly as a consequence, both the federal and provincial governments have became increasingly concerned with the adoption and use of research results from Canada's post-secondary sector, with a significant increase in the number of programs targeting commercialization and technology transfer (Wolfe 2005).

This chapter begins with a survey of the range of federal and provincial policies that have been introduced in Canada to support university–industry partnerships and promote knowledge transfer between the two sectors. It reviews the nature of the IP policy regime in Canada and underlines the extent to which Canada has a highly decentralized IP regime in which virtually every university is free to determine its own IP policies. Finally, we provide a more detailed review of university tech transfer practices in Canada through a closer examination of five case studies of the role of the university technology transfer office (TTO) and the broader IP policies at some of Canada's most research intensive universities. We conclude with a discussion of some of the unique institutions that have been created to promote commercialization and tech transfer in Canada.

National innovation policy and programs in Canada

Canada is distinct from many of the OECD countries in the extent to which gross expenditures on research and development (GERD) are channeled through the higher education or PSE sector. Since the 1970s, responsibility for funding basic and applied research in the post-secondary sector was devolved from the NRC to three new federal granting councils. Federal contributions to post-secondary research expenditures increased significantly with the expansion of the role of the Medical Research Council, later transformed into the Canadian Institutes of Health Research (CIHR) along the U.S. model, the transfer of responsibility for research funding in the natural sciences and engineering from the NRC to a new Natural Sciences and Engineering Research Council (NSERC) and for the social sciences and humanities to the Social Sciences and Humanities Research Council (SSHRC) in 1976. Over the course of the subsequent decades, the federal government expanded its role of primary responsibility for funding most of the direct costs of sponsored research in the PSE sector. The extent of overlap of jurisdiction increased dramatically during the 1980s when many of the provinces responded to the shifting bases of global competitiveness by expanding their own programs to support targeted research through measures such as the Centres of Excellence program in Ontario, the Action Structurante program in Québec, the Alberta Heritage Fund and a number of others. In the late 1990s, federal spending on post-secondary research expanded further with the introduction of a major new suite of programs to support research at universities and community colleges, partly in response to increased spending in the U.S. (Doern and Stoney 2009). The result has been that PSE sector enjoys a high level of support for the conduct of its basic and applied research activities as can be seen in Table 10.1.

Table 10.1 Spending on research and development in the higher education sector, by source of funds, in millions of dollars

	2011/2012ʳ	2012/2013	2012/2013	2011/2012 to 2012/2013	
	millions of dollars	*% of total*	*millions of dollars*	*% of total*	*% change*
Total, spending	11,831.6	100.0	12,099.4	100.0	2.3
Higher education	5,192.7	43.9	5,416.5	44.8	4.3
Federal government	3,165.2	26.8	3,085.6	25.5	–2.5
Provincial government	1,255.0	10.6	1,340.5	11.1	6.8
Private non-profit	1,126.7	9.5	1,149.2	9.5	2.0
Business enterprise	966.2	8.2	980.1	8.1	1.4
Foreign	125.9	1.1	127.5	1.1	1.3

Source: Created by authors based on data from Statistics Canada, *The Daily*, July 25, 2014.
Available online: www.statcan.gc.ca/daily-quotidien/140725/dq140725b-eng.pdf.

Canada currently has several federally funded programs aimed at developing partnerships between academia and industry, strengthening university–industry linkages, and intensifying knowledge flows and technology transfer. The three granting councils, NSERC, SHHRC, and CIHR, along with the Canada Foundation for Innovation (CFI), each have programs to promote these goals. NSERC's *Strategy for Partnerships and Innovation (SPI)* outlines a four-point strategy that includes initiatives to build sustainable relationships, streamline industry access to NSERC sponsored research, facilitate human capital development, and address national innovation challenges. Moreover, the strategy is intended to double the number of firms participating in NSERC innovation-focused programs over five years. It also includes a suite of targeted partnership programs designed to help companies find highly qualified people, advance R&D, and build relationships with scientists and engineers in universities and colleges across the country. The objective of another program, the *Industrial Research Chairs*, is to intensify academic excellence, bolster university–industry collaboration and increase knowledge transfer between academia and the private sector, and to build critical mass in research fields that have not yet developed in Canadian universities but for which there is an industrial need. CIHR's *Research Commercialization Programs* fund initiatives that support the creation of new knowledge, practices, products and services in the health sciences and facilitate the commercialization of this knowledge through mechanisms such as proof of principle projects, which encourage collaboration between academia and industry in the promotion and support of the commercial transfer of knowledge and technology resulting from health research.

The federal *Network of Centres of Excellence (NCE)* program has attracted international attention as a precedent-setting model for connecting research and development to national economic and social well-being. The NCE program invests in networks and centres that stimulate leading-edge research in areas of importance to Canada, build on national and international partnerships, develop and retain world-class research capabilities and create innovative knowledge and technology transfer opportunities and mechanisms. *The Centres of Excellence for Commercialization and Research (CECR)* program is one of several NCE initiatives aimed at strengthening university–industry linkages in areas of national strategic importance by helping bridge the gap between innovation and commercialization. CECR supports the operating expenses and the commercialization activities of research centres in the key areas of the environment; natural resources and energy; health and life sciences; information and communications technologies; and management, business and finance. For example, the Centre for the Commercialization of Regenerative Medicine (CCRM) is a CECR Centre hosted by the University of Toronto, supporting the development of foundational technologies that accelerate the commercialization of stem cell- and biomaterials-based products and therapies. The focus of the CCRM is on addressing the barriers faced by the Canadian regenerative medicine industry, such as the licensing of early stage technologies to companies outside of Canada before their market value is realized.

There are also several examples of cross-agency collaboration to facilitate research-driven innovation. NSERC, SSHRC, CFI, the NRC and the Canada Excellence Research Chairs program created Automotive Partnership Canada (APC) in 2009, an initiative to fund $145 million in research over five years to support collaborative and transformative R&D activities to help the Canadian automotive sector achieve a higher level of innovation. Projects are industry-driven and aligned with strategic research themes. Broad competencies and state-of-the-art facilities across its 20 institutes enable the NRC to conduct research in a wide variety of fields that impact automotive technologies, such as advanced materials, manufacturing, information and communication, alternative fuels and aerodynamics. Through NRC Automotive, the agency invested $30 million over five years in Automotive Partnerships Canada. NRC Automotive emphasizes research that brings proof-of-concept technologies closer to commercialization and provides validation and demonstration of the applicability for actual use in vehicles.

Provincial and regional innovation policies in Canada

Canadian provinces have also introduced programs and policies to support university–industry linkages. Ontario has an elaborate system of programs that support university–industry knowledge flows and the technology transfer and commercialization process. The majority of these programs operate under the purview of the combined Ministries of Economic Development, Employment and Infrastructure (MEDEI), and Research and Innovation (MRI). MRI's Life Sciences Commercialization Strategy, launched in 2010, consists of life sciences initiatives to facilitate the commercialization of bio-medical research and technologies by attracting and supporting top scientific talent, facilitating greater university–industry collaboration, and improving international marketing and promotion activities. Three key initiatives of the strategy include: support to commercialize genomics research ($114.6 million GL^2 fund); support for the medical and assistive devices sector ($21.4 million HTX-administered fund); and support for early stage Ontario biotechnology companies ($7 million MaRS-administered fund).

The *Ontario Brain Institute* is a provincially funded research centre seeking to maximize the impact of collaborative neuroscience research and establish Ontario as world-class brain science hub. The OBI brings together researchers, clinicians, industry, patients and their advocates to foster discovery and develop innovative products and services to improve the lives of those living with brain diseases and disorders, including Parkinson's, Alzheimer's, epilepsy and autism.[2] To this end, the OBI plays a critical role in enabling the cross-fertilization of ideas and knowledge translation as well as improving the entrepreneurial and management capacity of Ontario's neuro-cluster in order to realize breakthroughs in the areas of pharmaceuticals, medical devices, diagnostic and non-pharmacological interventions.

The *Ontario Centres of Excellence (OCE)* delivers programs aimed at strengthening partnerships between academic researchers, entrepreneurs and industry to facilitate technology transfer to local firms. Some of these initiatives include:

- *The Industry Academic Collaboration Program (IACP)* is funded by the Ontario government and designed to leverage the capacity of the province's research institutions in order to help technology-based companies create jobs and economic growth by commercializing Ontario-based research discoveries. Under IACP, OCE offers a suite of programs that serve researchers, entrepreneurs and companies with the potential for commercial success. Through IACP, OCE seeks to leverage more value from provincial investments in research and innovation through effective technology transfer networks, and utilize the capacity of public research institutions to support industry-driven commercialization activities. IACP programs are divided into three main components: Collaborative Commercialization Programs which support industry–academic collaborations[3], Entrepreneurial Talent Programs which help college and university students and recent graduates develop entrepreneurial and business skills[4], and Technology Transfer Partnerships that facilitate technology and knowledge transfer as well as proof-of-principle demonstrations.
- The *Collaboration Voucher Programs* supports businesses working in partnership with research institutions to improve productivity and competitiveness. The voucher program consists of four different types: Voucher for Innovation and Productivity (VIP), Voucher for Commercialization, Voucher for E-Business and the Voucher for Industry Association R&D Challenge (VIA).

Quebec's *Politique nationale de la recherche et de l'innovation (PNRI)* was released in 2013, committing $3.7 million over five years to advance research and innovation activities in seven areas: aerospace, biofood, biotechnology, renewable energy and transportation electrification, creative industries, personalized health care and information and communication technologies. As part of this initiative, the Quebec government is to invest $130.2 million over three years to develop the Réseau recherche innovation Québec (RRIQ)[5] network. It is anticipated that the network will strengthen partnerships between researchers, businesses and innovation actors across the province, bringing together 120 Quebec organizations dedicated to knowledge transfer. The new network has been described as a vehicle for providing "a single entry point to those seeking to collaborate with universities and colleges" (Henderson 2013).

In Alberta, the Alberta Innovates-Technology Futures organization administers and supports a number of programs that promote public and private sector collaboration and advance knowledge and technology transfer across several industries. Initiatives include the *Alberta Biomaterials Development Centre* (ABDC), which facilitates the creation and commercialization of new products from forestry and agriculture fibre; *Centres for Research & Commercialization* which provide collaborative university–industry research hubs in four areas, glycomics, machine learning, geomatics technology, and biomedical technology; *nanoAlberta* devoted to R&D in nanotechnology; and the *Alberta Regional Innovation Network*, an integrated province-wide system that coordinates Regional Innovation Networks that provide entrepreneurial SMEs access to services and supports on a geographical basis.[6]

Intellectual property regimes in Canada

In Canada, there is no national obligation for universities to set policies for mandatory disclosure or a requirement for researchers to work with the university TTO. Many universities do require their inventors to disclose commercialization activities, but they do not universally require inventors to work with the university to commercialize research. Unlike in the United States, Canada has not tried to mandate ownership for the intellectual property generated from publicly funded research. In Canada, the ownership policies for intellectual property are determined by the universities themselves and are often included as part of faculty employment and collective agreements. Ownership of technology and discoveries created as the product of cooperative research with an industry or government research partner typically is determined *a priori* by some form of intellectual property agreement in place as part of the research agreement that covers the outputs of that research. Universities often require some retention of the rights to any discoveries for research or teaching purposes, but, generally, the research partner, particularly when it is private industry funding the project, retains some significant ownership of any intellectual property generated and/or an exclusive license to the intellectual property. Much of the research conducted on university campuses, however, is not covered by pre-existing research agreements and is funded by public research grants.

There is considerable debate as to which ownership regime is better at encouraging the commercialization of university-driven innovations (Kenney and

Patton 2009). University ownership of intellectual property offers some benefits. First, it is easier for university TTOs with experience at negotiating deals to ensure that the intellectual property is properly valued and that the developers are adequately compensated, as well as to ensure that the rights and interests of the university and the scientists and students involved in the development of the intellectual property are protected. Second, it reduces the time required to strike a deal with industry and investors. Those who favour inventor-owned intellectual property argue that it encourages more entrepreneurial thinking by faculty and students, encourages the creation of start-up companies, allows research staff who have existing relationships with appropriate receptors to negotiate their own deals as part of a broader commercialization plan, and increases the likelihood that the discoverer will remain involved and dedicated to a new commercialization opportunity (Kenney and Patton 2011). As we demonstrate below, current Canadian university practice consists of a mix of these various IP regimes, with some universities allowing for both. The resulting mix means that Canada lacks a uniform IP regime and that firms which are negotiating licenses for IP that originated at more than one institution may have to deal with the very different IP regimes in place at each.

University TTOs in Canada

Leading Canadian universities have experimented with various forms of their TTOs in an attempt to maximize the intellectual property captured and commercialized from the research activities of the institution. Despite this, there remains a considerable degree of diversity between the practices of different Canadian TTOs. As discussed earlier, this experimentation is driven, in part, by renewed emphasis on the role universities can play in stimulating economic growth. Different local factors, such as the availability of industrial receptors, the areas of science in which the research is being conducted, the availability of venture capital, technology transfer experience of faculty and TTO personnel, etc., have led universities to adopt different structural forums to make their technology transfer and commercialization procedures more effective.

In most Canadian universities the Vice-President of Research (or equivalent) is responsible for the development and implementation of intellectual property policies. Typically, their task is to coordinate university–industry relations and intellectual property management. There is a wider variation in organizational structures to coordinate these operations. Most commonly, the TTOs are located in the university and report directly to the Vice-President of Research or equivalent. TTOs established internally tend to be closely involved with faculty and students and coordinate all of the interactions between the university and firms, including the negotiation of joint research collaborations, sponsored chairs, and endowments, in addition to their role in handling technology licensing and commercialization agreements.

Alternatively, some universities have chosen to develop a not-for-profit corporation that serves as an arms-length TTO. These organizations typically exist outside the university's organizational structures, although often with university-appointed leadership, either through a board of directors or with top management selected by the university. These organizations are intended to minimize the potential for conflict-of-interest and to let the office operate slightly removed from the university culture. These (usually) not-for-profit corporations tend to focus more on the intellectual property consultancy and commercialization roles of the technology transfer processes, leaving the negotiations of joint-research agreements and sponsored research to the offices that are organized directly under the university's operating structure.

One of the challenges facing university technology transfer managers in Canada is the lack of receptors that are in a position to acquire university-generated technology. Several reports from the Council of Canadian Academies and the federal Science, Technology and Innovation Council have documented the low levels of business expenditure on research and development (BERD) in Canada as a major shortcoming in the operation of the Canadian innovation system and a critical contributor to Canada's low level of productivity performance (Council of Canadian Academies 2009, 2013; Science Technology and Innovation Council 2013). The lack of firm-based R&D significantly reduces the receptor capacity of the private sector, in other words, the potential for firms to adopt and use the intellectual property resulting from university-based research. This has created the dilemma of too many federal and provincial programs designed to promote the commercialization of university research without the necessary demand from the private sector to adopt and utilize that research.

Start-ups can become a viable option for transferring technology from the university to industry in circumstances where there is industrial activity in a related sector but where the firms are resistant to license technology. Many firms have found that it is either too costly or too disruptive to establish new business units to try to develop university generated intellectual property and prefer to allow others to assume the risk of starting up the firm, and pay to acquire an established firm. This has become a common tactic for pharmaceutical and biotechnology firms. This, however, is something that typically only larger firms have the resources to do. Small and medium-sized enterprises are not large enough or diverse enough in their operations to take on these sorts of acquisitions. There are certainly examples of small and medium-sized enterprises that have made these sorts of acquisitions, but they commonly occur early in the development of new platform technologies and new radical technologies before the industry has had a chance to coalesce and the commercial potential of the new technology is fully realized.

The predominance of small and medium-sized enterprises in the Canadian economy constitutes a further challenge for the dissemination and commercialization of university-based research results. The surveys of innovation conducted by Statistics Canada indicate that larger companies have more linkages to universities than small and medium-sized enterprises. This difference in the industrial structure of the Canadian economy is seen as a key factor in explaining the lower levels of productivity increase in Canada over the past two decades given that small and medium-sized enterprises are also slower to adopt new technologies as well as invest in research and development (Niosi 2008; Council of Canadian Academies 2009). The overall predominance of small and medium-sized enterprises in the Canadian economy clearly represents a significant challenge for the dissemination of research from universities to private firms.

Some industries require substantial upfront capital costs that can constitute a barrier to university-based start-ups. The software side of the information and communications technology sector has had low capital barriers to entry, with software development requiring a typical personal computer. Biotechnology has seen considerable start-up creation over the last few decades primarily because of the similarities between the necessary facilities and processes between the academic and industrial laboratory. This has allowed for commercial activities to take place at the academic laboratory until the level of commercial activity necessitated (and justified) acquiring separate commercial laboratory space. Especially in the case of medically related technologies, the availability of venture capital, thanks to the market potential of some of these technologies, has also facilitated the shift to a start-up or spin-off firm. Spin-off company creation in Canada is often seen as a vehicle for commercializing Canadian technology due to the lack of available receptor firms. The three main fields where start-ups occur in Canada are health science (including pharmaceutical and medical devices), information communications technology, and engineering and material sciences (Gertler and Levitte 2005; Barker and Cooper 2008; Gertler and Vinodrai 2009).

The next section surveys the technology transfer practices of five of Canada's leading research-intensive universities: the University of British Columbia, the University of Alberta, Queen's University, the University of Waterloo and the University of Toronto. The survey is not intended to be definitive, but rather to provide an overview of the diverse range of approaches to promoting the commercialization of university research in Canada. To provide a better context for the ensuing discussion, Table 10.2 sets out some key indicators with data on the performance of the respective university TTOs.

University of British Columbia

The University of British Columbia's University–Industry Liaison Office (UILO) was founded in 1984, making it the first office of its kind at a Canadian university. The UILO is an example of an internal TTO, functioning as a unit of the Office of the Vice-President of Research and serves both of UBC's campuses, as well as its five affiliated hospitals. The office has 36 staff, making it one of the largest TTOs in Canada. Eleven staff members facilitate the knowledge mobilization of university developed research. Within the Knowledge Mobilization Group, there are a number of practice areas including life sciences, information technology, physical sciences, education, arts, and forestry. UBC operates with an institution-owned intellectual property policy, taking ownership and rights to all inventions and discoveries made by faculty, staff, and students through the course of conducting research using university facilities. Inventors receive 50 per cent of

Table 10.2 Indicators of technology transfer and commercialization at selected Canadian universities

Indicators of technology transfer and commercialization at selected Canadian universities

Year	Institution	Full-time employees	Total Research expenses	Licensing income	US Patents issued	Formed
2012	Queen's Univ.	16	$177,871,009	$2,294,145	10	1
2013	St.Michael's Hospital	1.5	$60,293,198	$181,089	2	0
2013	Sunnybrook Health Sciences Cen	1	$80,535,843	$531,684	3	2
2013	Univ. Health Network	11.5	$302,808,069	$2,350,913	22	2
2013	Univ. of Alberta	16.3	$423,148,252	$833,029	16	5
2013	Univ. of British Columbia	19.5	$520,278,306	$5,359,876	21	5
2013	Univ. of Toronto (excluding affilia	25.36	$418,351,678	$3,004,965	10	12
2013	Univ. of Waterloo	7.5	$194,494,158	$559,124	4	11

Note: St. Michael's Hospital, Sunnybrook Health Sciences and University Health Network are affiliated research hospitals of the University of Toronto.

Source: Created by authors based on data from AUTM, STATT Database 2014.

net value generated though equity income and royalties from intellectual property. If the university does not decide to protect with a patent or license the discovery, its rights can be assigned back to the inventor. Researchers who do not wish to commercialize the discovery, but choose instead to publish the results in the public domain, are not required to assign the rights to the discovery to the university. The UILO employs an entrepreneur-in-residence who heads up the New Ventures Initiative at UBC.

The UILO is somewhat unique in that despite being an internal office of the university, it has an advisory board consisting of key stake holders that meets twice a year, including the university, government, industry, capital funds, and technology transfer organizations. The board has two main responsibilities, to oversee and review the operations, policies, procedures, and governance of the UILO, as well as to facilitate relationships between the UILO and the public sector and act as an external advocate for the UILO. The UILO uses a wide range of new mechanisms to supplement the traditional licensing practices employed by TTOs. It is participating in Flintbox, a global intellectual property exchange designed to provide easy and open access to university-based innovation. Flintbox was founded in 2003 by UBC Research Enterprises (UBC-RE), a subsidiary of the University and was recently acquired by Wellspring Worldwide. Flintbox establishes a site for research and industry to build relationships by combining direct access to innovation with a network of users in more than one hundred countries worldwide. In addition, the UILO is participating in the West Coast Licensing Partnership to achieve increased value by aggregating its licensing efforts (Livingstone 2009).

University of Alberta and TEC Edmonton

The University of Alberta's TTO is an external not-for-profit joint venture between the university and the Edmonton Economic Development Corporation (EEDC), named TEC Edmonton. The TEC acronym stands for Technology, Entrepreneur, and Company Development. TEC Edmonton was formed in 2006 by the amalgamation of two university units (the Technology Transfer Program and the Spinoff Company Development Program) and two EEDC initiatives (Deal Generator and the VenturePrize Business Plan Competition). The organization services both the University of Alberta, as well as offering services to firms and independent inventors in the Edmonton city-region as a whole.

The underlying premise of the TEC Edmonton model is that it is community owned, and focused on community outcomes. Authority over the organization is granted by the two parties to an appointed Board of Directors consisting of eight members, half of whom are nominated by the university and half by the City. There is a nominating committee which selects potential members with a strong technology background and makes recommendations to the Board and the joint venture partners. One key benefit of the joint venture model and the representative basis of the Board of Directors is that it fosters increased collaboration between the university and the broader tech community in Edmonton.

TEC Edmonton offers four main services: *technology transfer, business development, entrepreneur development*, and *funding and finance*. To facilitate technology transfer, the University of Alberta has an inventor-owned intellectual property policy stipulated in the University of Alberta Faculty Agreement. The university requires inventors to disclose discoveries to TEC Edmonton, but inventors can chose to commercialize independently or through TEC Edmonton's technology transfer team. The heritage of TEC Edmonton's Technology Transfer unit is the Industry Liaison Office of the University of Alberta which was formed in 1994 in the office of the Vice-President (Research). Today, the 12-person technology transfer team is the largest group of Intellectual Property professionals in Alberta with the expertise to manage commercialization ventures.[7] Core responsibilities of the technology transfer team include the following.

- Managing intellectual property (IP): assessing, advising and developing IP protection strategies.
- Negotiating, drafting and managing the legal agreements required to establish a successful commercial relationship, and/or transfer technology to a licensee company or new venture.
- Working with inventors to assemble the elements needed to test the commercial feasibility of new technologies, such as assisting them in seeking relevant research and development funding.

TEC Edmonton's business development team consists of 20 Executive-in-Residence (EIRs) and Business Development Associates who provide customized advice to select early stage companies where they can directly contribute to their success. This can include assisting businesses with the development of strategic and operational implementation plans, including technical and market opportunity assessments; business, marketing, financial plans; investor presentations; and corporate finance materials. It also provides one on one coaching and mentoring to help entrepreneurs grow viable high-technology businesses. It coordinates a network of Angel investors through Alberta Deal Generator who provides funding for early stage companies and it provides management and board expertise to start-up or early stage companies.

The Entrepreneur Development team at TEC Edmonton also offers a range of business training and entrepreneur education to help businesses grow that includes providing technology based inventors access to *TEC Source*, a user-friendly on-line form designed to connect them with TEC Edmonton in order to provide customized resources for their needs. They offer a *Business Basics for Innovators* program to help inventors, entrepreneurs and students understand the fundamentals of growing a business and learn to overcome barriers to success. It develops entrepreneurial skills and talent through outreach programs such the *Go-To-Market* and *International Go-To-Market programs*, which combine a comprehensive go-to-market curriculum through applied learning, access to industry and personalized mentoring. Finally, it collaborates with professional service providers in the community to provide free business advisory and development services through the *TEC Source Advisory Panel*. The panel members consist of volunteers with expertise in financing, taxation, intellectual property, corporate law, management, marketing and product development.

In addition to the four core services mentioned above, entrepreneurs may also benefit from the TEC Edmonton business incubator, the TEC Centre. The TEC Centre is located on the fourth floor of Enterprise Square in downtown Edmonton and provides lab and office space to 22 companies with over 80 staff between them.[8] Most of the tenants are early stage high tech businesses in life sciences, ICT, nanotechnology and agriculture, who benefit from a number of resources offered by the TEC Centre including, meeting rooms with internet access, delivery management services, central reception and mail services, access to IP protection services, business plan development, mentoring, seed funds, a business centre, and presentation tools. The TEC Centre was created with the support of $15 million from Western Economic Diversification Canada (Federal Government program), $15 million from Alberta Advanced Education and Technology (Provincial Government program), and $7.5 million from the City of Edmonton.

Overall, TEC Edmonton enjoys a strong track record in achieving its goals. In 2013, it was named the 17th best university business incubator in the world by the University Business Incubator Index. TEC Edmonton credits this high placement to the strong collaborative relationship it has maintained between the city and the university which has enabled it to bring business advisory, technology management and entrepreneurial training services to both university researchers and local firms. Notably, due to the quality of resources TEC Edmonton provides, about 90 per cent of University of Alberta inventors choose to use its services. Indeed, in 2012–13, of the 119 start-up clients TEC Edmonton supported, 34 per cent were University of Alberta spin-offs and projects.[9] Moreover, through tech transfer activity enabled by TEC Edmonton, University of Alberta's total licensing revenue for that period was $831,958.[10]

Queen's University

Queens University formed PARTEQ (Partners in Technology at Queen's) in 1987 to provide an arms-length, not-for-profit corporation which serves as the technology transfer and commercialization organization for the university, and is an early example of such an external TTO. Despite its arms-length status, PARTEQ operates as a traditional TTO. The Executive Director of the company reports to the Vice-President (Research) and conflict resolution with the company is mediated through the university. PARTEQ employs eight people, including three staff responsible for patent development, and four commercial and business development staff.

Queen's has an inventor-owned intellectual property policy. This policy for faculty is enshrined in the Faculty Collective Agreement and in university senate policies covering students and staff members. Inventors are not required to commercialize, but if they chose to they are required to disclose their inventions to the university. PARTEQ, however, is granted the first right to evaluate the discovery and make an offer to the inventor for intellectual property development. If PARTEQ makes an offer, the inventor is not required to accept it and may seek alternative commercialization options. The university receives 25 per cent of all net proceeds exceeding $500,000 gained from the intellectual property. This policy also extends to hospital appointees (Kingston General Hospital), but does not extend to staff of the hospital. In the case of a staff invention, the hospital retains ownership of the intellectual property.

PARTEQ has several funding sources that it leverages to help move technologies forward to commercial viability. The PARTEQ Proof of Principle (POP) Fund (sponsored by the Ontario Ministry of Research and Innovation) provides funding for each stage of commercialization activities such as intellectual property protection, prototype development, market assessment, business plan development, and new company start-up costs. PARTEQ also manages the TriColour Venture Fund as a joint venture with the Queen's School of Business. This fund provides equity investments up to $150,000 to firms, selected by business students who are responsible for evaluating the investment opportunities available and monitor those investments. This program combines a business-talent development program with the provision of seed finance to firms in the Queen's community. Additionally, PARTEQ delivers the Atherton Entrepreneurship Awards, which provides seed funding of up to $34,000 annually to encourage and assist a Queen's University undergraduate or graduate student, post-doctoral fellow, professor or research associate in developing promising new entrepreneurial ventures in science or engineering.

In 2008 Queen's University also launched the Innovation Park. The Innovation Park was funded primarily through a $21 million grant from the provincial Ministry of Research and Innovation to build an incubator centre with the obligation to help build public–private partnerships within the Kingston Region. The Park brings together a community of academic researchers, industry, government and not-for-profits to generate cutting-edge ideas, drive technology transfer and push new products, processes and services into the marketplace. Innovation Park offers leased space to secure and fully equipped facilities as well as access to the specialized R&D machinery early stage businesses need to succeed. Moreover, tenants benefit from a range of innovative services offered, including innovation acceleration, technical, research and commercialization services.

Another initiative jointly funded by the governments of Ontario and Canada and established by PARTEQ Innovations in 2009 is the *GreenCentre Canada*, which brings together academic researchers and industry partners to develop clean, less energy-intensive alternatives to traditional chemical products and manufacturing processes, providing a range of commercialization services to develop early stage technologies to meet specific industry needs. Consisting of industry members who assess and validate technology opportunities, commercialization managers with experience in chemistry and materials innovation, and scientific teams in catalysis, fine chemicals/pharmaceuticals, polymers and materials and petrochemicals, the Green Centre offers "a holistic commercialization program" that includes a range of technical, commercial and business development components.[11]

University of Waterloo

The University of Waterloo is an exemplary entrepreneurial university in Canada, highly committed to advancing its region's innovation agenda and contributing to local economic development. This institution has been described as "a critical catalyst" in advancing the region's innovation efforts "through its ability to generate and attract the talent that underpins academic and applied excellence in science, math and engineering, support for local firm-based R&D, and its explicit institutional support for entrepreneurial activity at the local level" (Bramwell and Wolfe 2008: 1176). The university's success in the production of new ideas, the flow of knowledge and technology transfer is attributed to the robust linkages it has established with local and non-local firms in areas of exceptional growth potential like ICT, environment and energy, health informatics, and software engineering. Its capacity for generating and attracting talent to the region is leveraged by a strong Cooperative Education Program that provides students and firms with an ideal interface for developing new ideas, sharing knowledge, skills development and training, facilitating entrepreneurial activities and engaging in social learning. In addition, the university's innovative Intellectual Property policy, which grants full ownership of IP to the creator, encourages faculty researchers and/or students to commercialize their ideas (Kenney and Patton 2011). According to Bramwell and Wolfe (2008), this IP policy initiative and the university's Co-op program have driven the establishment of a large number of high profile start-ups and spin-offs in the region – developments that contribute directly to growth and innovation in the local and regional economy.

A number of offices that report through the Vice-President of Research assist Waterloo members in accessing national (e.g., NSERC, SSHRC, CIHR, CRC, etc.) and international grant programs, as well as negotiating government research contracts where applicable. Some of these offices include Research Finance, Research Partnerships, Office of Research Ethics, and Institutional Research. In particular, the Waterloo Commercialization Office (WatCo) provides intellectual property development and commercialization services to the University of Waterloo community to advance research innovations into the marketplace.

Members of the university who develop intellectual property and intend to pursue commercialization of the IP are required to inform the Vice-President of Research and WatCo of the nature of the intellectual property and the intentions of the creators for the intellectual property. Inventors have the choice to commercialize their discovery on their own, or they can choose to use the services of WatCo. If the researcher chooses to collaborate with WatCo, they continue to own the IP, but assign the right to WatCo to commercialize on their behalf.[12] WatCo's team manages the entire commercialization process for Waterloo researchers by following through with a number of activities, including:[13]

- Confirming technology pedigree – resolve legal issues relevant to licensees and investors
- Assessing opportunity – define and position the opportunity in commercial terms
- Protecting IP – create an "asset" and preserve commercial opportunity
- Developing prototype – validate performance and advance commercial readiness
- Accessing WatCo's network of business and investor contacts
- Providing intellectual property protection (e.g. patents).

Researchers that partner with WatCo in the commercialization of technology receive 75 per cent of profits and WatCo receives 25 per cent of profits; half of WatCo's share will be allocated to the researcher's faculty.[14] If the inventor decides to commercialize their own technology, they are not required to provide any funds back to the university. It is this aspect of the University of Waterloo intellectual property ownership policy that has made it the most liberal example of the inventor-owned policy regime in Canada. The university counts on receiving charitable donations, industry-funded research projects, and other ancillary benefits as a result of this policy. It also believes that it can attract higher quality and more entrepreneurial-minded faculty to the university by using this approach.

University of Toronto

In 2009, the Office of the Vice-President Research at the University of Toronto underwent an extensive reorganization which saw the previous Innovations Group transformed into the new Innovations and Partnerships Office (IPO), which included the industrial contracts function, as well as the disclosure, intellectual property and commercialization groups that report to the VP Research. The IPO is an internal TTO and serves the typical function of assisting in the assessment of discoveries, the application of possible intellectual property protections, and the commercialization of the intellectual property. The office also negotiates government and industry joint-research contracts. It is supported by 25 individuals who provide services to researchers from a range of practice areas including physical sciences and engineering, biomedical and life sciences, social sciences and humanities and information communications technology. This number of staff, however, does not include employees at the University of Toronto affiliated hospitals.

The University of Toronto has a hybrid intellectual property ownership policy. The inventor and the university have joint ownership at the time of invention. The researcher, however, has the right to commercialize independently from the university. Inventors who commercialize the invention independently will assume responsibility for their own commercialization activities such as patenting, legal, investment, marketing and investment negotiation. Moreover, net revenues generated are split 75 per cent to the inventor and 25 per cent to the university; revenues received by U of T are distributed to the inventor's department, faculty and the Connaught fund to help support future research at U of T.[15] On the other hand, inventors also have the option of letting MaRS Innovation (MI), discussed in more detail in the next section, or the IPO provide commercialization services.[16] These services include:

- Securing intellectual property rights to protect the invention from copying and unauthorized replication
- Securing financial support for further research and development or proof of concept work
- Managing and executing legal contracts related to confidentiality, material transfer, collaboration, sponsored research, commercial options and licenses, etc.
- Marketing and promoting the innovation to the broader marketplace while assuring the researcher's rights and interests are best represented
- Incorporating a company and participating as a shareholder.

If the university accepts the offer, the inventor is required to assign full ownership of the intellectual property to the university. If the technology generates revenue, 20 per cent of that revenue is collected by the university as a management fee, and the remaining 80 per cent is split between the inventor (75 per cent) and the university (25 per cent). As is the case at other universities, if the university is unsuccessful at commercializing the technology, ownership reverts back to the inventor.

The formation of the IPO and the establishment of new mechanisms to allow IPO to interact more effectively with MI have helped reshape the institutional culture at the university and realigned support services for innovation and commercialization more effectively. This reorganization has also enabled the office to work closely with faculty on industry sponsored research at the university and to further develop services to support entrepreneurship and knowledge translation activities.

Commercialization centres, business incubators and accelerators

There are numerous examples of commercialization centres and business incubators and accelerators operating in Canada. Two accelerators in the Waterloo region stimulate collaboration between local firms, universities, colleges and government agencies in order to drive innovation and commercialization across the high-tech sector: *the Accelerator Centre* and the *Communitech Hub: Digital Media and Mobile Accelerator*. The Accelerator Centre along with the Ontario Centres of Excellence and the University of Waterloo technology transfer commercialization office (WatCo), are partners in the Accelerator for Commercialization Excellence (ACE) which works closely with other commercialization entities such as Communitech to provide seamless access to commercialization resources for start-ups, entrepreneurs, and investors in the Waterloo Region.[17]

The *Communitech Hub: Digital Media and Mobile Accelerator* was established in October 2010 with the support of major investments from the Province of Ontario, the Government of Canada and other key partners. Today, the Hub provides an attractive location in the heart of the region for entrepreneurs, government agencies, companies, technology incubators, and academic institutions to interact in a 44,000 square foot state-of-the-art roof. Among the many features of the Hub are the immersive 3D H.I.V.E (Hub Interactive Virtual Reality Environment) provided by Christie Digital, one of the key private sector partners, 3D-capable event space, and virtual conferencing facilities. In addition to Christie Digital, the Hub also has representatives from some of the larger firms in the region, including Blackberry, Open Text and Google. Through a wide range of programs administered by Communitech, the Hub's mission is to build global digital media by mentoring tenant start-ups, creating linkages with more established companies in the region, and helping secure financing for digital media ideas. Since 2010, the Hub has played a key role in technology company deals totaling more than $500 million and has supported the creation of over 800 new companies.

Many Canadian universities have also established business incubators and accelerators focused on students. For example, in 2013, the Ontario government announced the introduction of Campus-Linked Accelerator (CLA) funding which would provide $20 million over two years to allow post-secondary institutions to create and improve entrepreneurial activities that would benefit students and youth within their regions, and to integrate existing entrepreneurial activities with investors, industry and other stakeholders in their region.[18] Ryerson University's Digital Media Zone (DMZ), located in downtown Toronto and discussed in more detail below, is one of Canada's largest incubators and collaborative workspaces for entrepreneurs and an ideal candidate for CLA funding. Between April 2010 and January 2014, 123 start-ups have joined the DMZ, and 70 per cent of those companies still exist or have been successfully acquired (Clegg 2013). The DMZ provides numerous resources, such as mentorship and business development counseling, networking opportunities, company promotion opportunities, and funding. In particular, two initiatives are offered to facilitate the growth of member start-ups: the DMZ Incubation Program and the DMZ Accelerator Program. The Incubation Program is a semi-structured four-month initiative that provides start-ups with support for validating their business model, R&D, iterating on their prototype, identifying pilot customers and isolating the market for their product. The Accelerator Program is a three-phased structured program, ranging from six to 18 months, intended to assist start-ups in designing and executing on their business plans.

The Ontario College of Art and Design's *Imagination Catalyst*, was launched in 2011 to promote creative knowledge transfer and launch commercializable ideas. Faculty, graduate students, post-graduate students and alumni join Imagination Catalyst to create a for-profit company, a social enterprise or a not-for-profit, or license their designs to a manufacturer or publisher. Imagination Catalyst provides these individuals with mentorship, workshop and networking opportunities, a workspace, as well as facilities to support testing and prototyping. More recently, Imagination Catalyst launched the Take-It-to-Market incubator, an experiential entrepreneurship program and incubator aimed at helping start-up teams launch their enterprise or commercialize their research within a year.[19]

On March 19, 2014, the Nova Scotia government announced funding to support the creation of four "sandboxes" where university and college students, innovators and industry can work together to develop new businesses.[20] The sandboxes will be established and operated under the following partnerships: The Island Sandbox (Cape Breton University and NSCC Marconi Campus); the Community Sandbox (Saint Mary's University, NSCAD University and Mount Saint Vincent University); the Nova Scotia Agriculture Sandbox (Dalhousie University and Acadia University); and the ICT Sandbox (Dalhousie University, St. Mary's University, NSCAD University and Volta Labs). These new initiatives are based on approaches used at the Massachusetts Institute of Technology and the University of Waterloo, and will provide a combination of academic programs and entrepreneurial, professional and management services and resources. The Nova Scotia government has committed to provide each centre with $150,000 per year for up to three years.

Case study of a key intermediary: the MaRS Discovery District

The MaRS Discovery District, located adjacent to the University of Toronto and major downtown teaching and research hospitals, is driven by the demand-pull model of tech transfer, conducting market research for young companies, providing incubation and business advisory services, linking to the relevant industry leaders, and connecting emerging companies (many of which are affiliated with publicly sponsored research hospitals and universities) to the local and international angel and venture capital communities (Evans 2005; Treurnicht 2008: 28). The MaRS Discovery District houses several technology transfer programs, most of which are funded by the federal government and the Government of Ontario.

As a Centre of Excellence for Commercialization and Research (CECR) funded by the federal government, MI is the chief commercialization organization for the intellectual property generated in the areas of therapeutics, medical devices and diagnostic imaging, information and communications technologies, and advanced manufacturing and clean technologies by its 16 members. Located within the MaRS Discovery District, MI taps into the $1 billion of annual research and development in Toronto's growing research hub, though it remains a separate, not-for-profit organization with an independent mandate, board of directors and staff. MI is designed to build linkages between Toronto's academic, health care and research communities to support the development of a health sciences cluster, enabling MI to bundle research assets together, from both a scientific and business perspective, while keeping the individual integrity of the IP intact.

The commercialization process involves several steps. As noted above, the University of Toronto and its affiliated research hospitals send their research disclosures to MaRS and after MI has chosen the most commercially promising discoveries from the hundreds of submitted prospects, it attracts investors interested in these technologies. MI then establishes an agency agreement between itself and the member organization for the commercialization of a specific discovery, ensuring that institutional intellectual property policies are compatible. A "deal team" is formed, comprised of the inventor, MI project manager, representatives from the member's TTO, and experts in product development or regulatory matters.[21] MI also manages and funds the process of patent filing and issuance, develops a business case for the intellectual property, and undertakes project planning on its commercialization. The organization also finds funding to bridge the technology gaps to strengthen the discovery's business case.

As of January 2014, MI has helped launch 26 start-up companies,[22] including VitalHub, a spin-off of Mount Sinai Hospital that uses an iPhone-based system to give health professionals remote access to patient records and test results from a hospital's internal data network. A number of these start-ups supported by MI are graduates of the University of Toronto Early Stage Technology (UTEST) program. UTEST provides young software companies with start-up funding, office space in the MaRS Discovery District, mentoring and business strategy support.[23] Promising companies that are not yet ready for traditional incubators may receive up to $30,000 in start-up funds. The program is jointly administered by the Innovations and Partnerships Office at University of Toronto and MI.

Beyond MI, MaRS provides several other services, funded by the provincial government and in partnership with key industry, government and academic stakeholders in order to support knowledge flows and technology transfer across a broad range of sectors:

- *MaRS Incubator:* Emerging science and technology firms eager to be part of the MaRS community can apply to be part of the MaRS Incubator which provides space for academics, researchers, entrepreneurs, mentors, investors across the innovation spectrum with the opportunity to meet, share ideas and collaborate.[24]
- *Excellence in Clinical Innovation and Technology Evaluation (EXCITE)* partnership was created to establish effective pre-market evidence development and evaluation of medical technologies. EXCITE will harmonize health technology evaluation into a single, premarket evidence-based evaluation process for technologies with disruptive potential and specific relevance to health system priorities.[25] MaRS EXCITE represents a partnership between the health system (Ontario Health Technology Advisory Committee), the government (Ministry of Health and Long term Care and the Ministry of Research and Innovation), Academia (i.e. Council of Academic Hospitals of Ontario and academic centres specializing in clinical trials methodology and execution, classified as "Methodological Centres" and other specialized areas of health technology evaluation), MaRS, health innovators, and industry (MEDEC and HTX).[26]

- *MaRS Commons* is a physical space and a community that supports the most promising web and mobile start-ups, helping these emerging companies grow successful global businesses through a combination of education, networking and mentorship.[27] The MaRS Commons community consists of three pillars: mentors and staff; start-ups, and partners from industry and academia.
- *JOLT* is an early stage start-up accelerator for high-growth web and mobile companies.[28] Located in the MaRS Commons, JOLT provides entrepreneurs with the space, capital, design expertise and mentorship they need to accelerate market validation. JOLT clients benefit from increased founder education by participating in exclusive workshops, fireside chats, power lunches, etc. They are provided with market intelligence, legal and finance services as well as technology advice and networking opportunities.[29]
- Funded by the Province of Ontario under the purview of the Ministry of Research and Innovation, the *Investment Accelerator Fund (IAF)* is a seed fund that assists emerging Ontario technology companies to bring their products and services to market. The fund provides entrepreneurs and innovators with the connections and resources they need to launch new ventures. The IAF program is managed by MaRS and delivered through the Ontario Network of Entrepreneurs (ONE), a collaborative network of organizations across Ontario, designed to help commercialize ideas. The IAF invests in early stage, privately held companies with no significant revenue or institutional investment. These companies must demonstrate their potential to achieve high growth and be enabled by truly innovative technologies that can provide the new venture with sustainable competitive advantage.[30] In 2013, the *Youth Investment Accelerator Fund (Youth IAF)* was launched to invest in technology-based start-ups founded by young entrepreneurs under the age of 30.

Conclusion

This chapter provides a comprehensive review of the array of policies implemented by the federal and provincial governments in Canada to promote more effective industry–university linkages and facilitate the commercialization of research from universities and affiliated research hospitals. It highlights both the highly regionalized nature of the Canadian innovation system and policies for technology transfer and the decentralized nature of the IP policy regime in which Canadian universities enjoy tremendous latitude to determine their own practices. It provides insights into some of the best practices pursued by the TTOs at leading Canadian universities and policy lessons that can be drawn from these cases for other jurisdictions.

From the brief overviews of the university TTOs above, we see that regardless of whether the offices are internal or external to the university, for the most part they are similarly staffed and have a similar mission. UBC has developed a set of Global Access Principles to help distribute their innovations world-wide. UBC believes that this more international focus will be a future trend in commercialization, but this approach raises questions about the fairness to domestic tax payers who are funding much of the research, yet potentially not seeing the full economic growth benefits that come from domestic commercialization of the technologies developed at the university. This global approach relies less on the receptor capacity of regional firms. The University of Alberta's TEC Edmonton structure, in contrast, is far more locally focused. One of its key mandates is to provide commercialization services, not just to the University of Alberta community but to companies within the City of Edmonton as a whole. Queen's, similarly, uses PARTEQ and the Innovation Park to help stimulate local innovation and regional growth. Universities with closely associated incubator facilities, not surprisingly, have a local focus to their commercialization and firm development strategies. Given the political and economic capital dedicated to these facilities, it ought not to be surprising that the TTOs might align their activities and resources to assist the incubator. These more locally focused approaches rely on there being an abundance of local receptors to support commercialization.

Distinct from the practice in the U.S., Canadian universities each establish their own intellectual property regimes. None of the universities covered in this survey have precisely the same intellectual property and commercialization policy. Their policies range from UBC's institution-owned regime through to Waterloo's inventor-owned policy. Yet, as one unravels the specifics of these policies, it becomes clear that in both of these extremes when the universities' TTOs act as the commercialization manager they assume ownership of the intellectual property. There is a practical advantage in this approach as it allows for potential licensees to negotiate with a single owner. The difference, therefore, between institutions, aside from the specific compensation percentages to inventors, is the options presented to the research from the point of disclosure to the time TTO takes over as the commercialization agent. In all of the cases presented above, should the university not be able to find a suitable receptor for the license, ownership of the intellectual property reverts back to the inventor. It is only the University of Waterloo that allows the inventor to retain ownership of the intellectual property, yet does not require the inventor to pay a percentage of revenue back to the university if the intellectual property is successfully commercialized. The University of Toronto has a hybrid-ownership policy whereby the university and the inventor have initial ownership of the discovery, but, as discussed, if the TTOs commercialize the intellectual property they require the inventor to assign ownership to their respective universities.

Many of the TTOs covered in this survey draw upon and benefit from significant commitments and assistance from local, provincial and federal governments in helping them to establish broader regional innovation support structures. Where these government and non-government organizations are in place, universities can focus on their key role of creating and commercializing their own technologies, allowing technology transfer staff to focus on core activities. Similarly, the research direction that university researchers have taken might either lag behind or outpace the knowledge pool that receptors might be working with. These factors will have an impact on the amount of commercialization activity that is taking place between universities and receptor firms. The variety that we see in the form and function in the various TTOs in the above case examples likely relate to universities trying to negotiate the particular series of opportunities and challenges presented by their unique combination of receptor development, governmental and non-government innovation and commercialization support infrastructure, and the particular knowledge areas that the university faculty are working in.

Notes

1 Research assistance on the role of the TTOs was provided by Andrew Munro, which the authors gratefully acknowledge.
2 www.braininstitute.ca/about-us; www.braininstitute.ca/research (accessed on February 17, 2014).
3 These programs include Market Readiness, Collaborate-to-Commercialize, SmartStart, High Performance Computing, Colleges Ontario Network for Industry Innovation (CONII), and Medical Sciences Proof-of-Principle. www.oce-ontario.org/programs/collaborative-commercialization (accessed February 17, 2014).
4 These programs include the On-Campus Entrepreneurship Activities, Experiential Learning Program, Entrepreneurship Fellowships and Connections. www.oce-ontario.org/programs/talent-programs (accessed February 17, 2014).
5 Quebec Research and Innovation Network (QRIN).
6 www.albertatechfutures.ca/Home.aspx (accessed on February 17, 2014).
7 www.tecedmonton.com/AboutTEC/tabid/56/language/en-US/Default.aspx (accessed February 18, 2014).
8 www.tecedmonton.com/BUSINESSSERVICES/TECCentre/tabid/77/Default.aspx (accessed February 18, 2014).
9 http://news.ualberta.ca/newsarticles/2013/july/tec-edmonton-named-17th-best-university-business-incubator-in-the-world (accessed February 18, 2014). The UBI Index team assessed 150 leading university-associated incubators in 22 countries.
10 www.research.ualberta.ca/MobilizingKnowledge/Commercialization.aspx (accessed February 18, 2014).
11 www.greencentrecanada.com/about-us/ (accessed on February 17, 2014).
12 http://uwaterloo.ca/research/waterloo-commercialization-office-watco/intellectual-property/protecting-your-intellectual-property (accessed February 18, 2014).
13 http://uwaterloo.ca/research/waterloo-commercialization-office-watco/commercialization-services (accessed February 18, 2014).
14 http://uwaterloo.ca/research/waterloo-commercialization-office-watco/partnership (accessed February 18, 2014).
15 www.research.utoronto.ca/wp-content/uploads/documents/2013/07/RevenueReport Form2013_2013-06-26.pdf
16 www.research.utoronto.ca/wp-content/uploads/documents/2013/09/Invention CommercializationFAQs1.pdf (accessed February 18, 2014). MaRS Innovation is a Centre of Excellence Commercialization and Research and is U of T's partner in innovation and commercialization. Under an agreement between the university, its affiliated research hospitals and MI, MI has the first opportunity to select the most promising research results from University of Toronto's top faculties and affiliated research institutes. Its portfolio, built through intellectual property disclosures from member institutions, turns research into businesses through industry partnerships, licensing arrangements and start-up companies.
17 www.acexcellence.ca/about (accessed February 17, 2014).

18 www.fin.gov.on.ca/en/budget/ontariobudgets/2013/bk5.html (accessed April 14, 2014).

19 www.ocadu.ca/research/imaginationcatalyst/Take_It_To_Market_Incubator_Program.htm (accessed on February 17, 2014).

20 http://novascotia.ca/news/release/?id=20140319003 (accessed on April 14, 2014).

21 http://marsinnovation.com/how-we-work/for-inventors/ (accessed on February 18, 2014).

22 http://marsinnovation.com/category/portfolio/start-up-companies-portfolio/ (accessed on February 18, 2014).

23 http://marsinnovation.com/company/university-of-toronto-early-stage-technology-utest/ (accessed on February 18, 2014).

24 www.marsdd.com/facilities/office-facilities/incubator/ (accessed on February 18, 2014).

25 www.marsdd.com/aboutmars/partners/excite/ (accessed on February 18, 2014).

26 http://excite.marsdd.com/who-is-involved/ (accessed on February 18, 2014).

27 www.marsdd.com/aboutmars/initiatives/ (accessed on February 18, 2014).

28 www.marsdd.com/aboutmars/initiatives/ (accessed on February 18, 2014).

29 http://jolt.marsdd.com/jolt-network/benefits/ (accessed on February 18, 2014).

30 www.marsdd.com/aboutmars/partners/iaf/ (accessed on February 18, 2014).

References

Barker, M. and D. Cooper. 2008. "Research Infrastructure and the Economy: An exploration study on the link between CFI investments and Canadian university spin-off company growth." Ottawa: Canadian Foundation for Innovation.

Bramwell, A. and D.A. Wolfe. 2008. "Universities and Regional Economic Development: The Entrepreneurial University of Waterloo." *Research Policy* 37 (September): 1175–87.

Clegg, L. 2013. "Digital Media Zone at Ryerson University Celebrates 2013 As Its Most Successful Year." Press Release (January 13) Ryerson University, Toronto, Ontario.

Council of Canadian Academies. 2009. *Innovation and Business Strategy: Why Canada Falls Short*. Report of the Expert Panel on Business Innovation in Canada. Ottawa: Council of Canadian Academies.

Council of Canadian Academies. 2013. *The State of Industrial R&D in Canada*. Report of the Expert Panel on the State of Industrial R&D in Canada. Ottawa: Council of Canadian Academies.

Doern, G. Bruce and Christopher Stoney, eds. 2009. *Research and Innovation Policy: Changing Federal Government–University Relations*. Toronto: University of Toronto Press.

Evans, J.R. 2005. "The Academic-Commercial Interface in a Knowledge-Driven Economy: A view from MaRS," in *Creating Knowledge, Strengthening Nations: The Changing Role of Higher Education*, eds G.A. Jones, P.L. McCarney and M.L. Skolnik. Toronto: University of Toronto Press, pp. 273–82.

Geiger, R. and C. Sá. 2008. *Tapping the Riches of Science: Universities and the Promise of Economic Growth*. Cambridge: Harvard University Press.

Gertler, M.S. and Y.M. Levitte. 2005. "Local Nodes in Global Networks: The geography of knowledge flows in biotechnology innovation." *Innovation and Industry* 12 (4): 487–507.

Gertler, M.S. and T. Vinodrai. 2009. "Life Sciences and Regional Innovation: One path or many?" *European Planning Studies* 17 (2: February): 235–61.

Henderson, M. 2013. "Quebec's New Research and Innovation Policy Aims to Boost R&D to 3% of GDP." *Re$earch Money* 27 (16): 1.

Kenney, M. and D. Patton. 2009. "Reconsidering the Bayh-Dole Act and the Current University Invention Ownership Model." *Research Policy* 38: 1407–22.

Kenney, M. and D. Patton. 2011. "Does Inventor Ownership Encourage University Research derived Entrepreneurship? A six university comparison." *Research Policy* 40 (8): 1100–112.

Livingstone, Angus. 2009. "Technology Transfer: Structures, strategies & functions for the future." Presentation to the ACCT Conference. Victoria, B.C., November 9.

Niosi, J. 2008. *Connecting the Dots Between University Research and Industrial Innovation. IRPP Choices* 14 (14). Montreal: Institute for Research on Public Policy.

Science, Technology and Innovation Council. 2013. *State of the Nation 2012. Canada's Science Technology and Innovation System: Aspiring to Global Leadership.* Ottawa: Science, Technology and Innovation Council Secretariat.

Treurnicht, I. 2008. "University Research and Industrial Innovation: How can Canada compete and win?" *IRPP Choices* 14 (14). Montreal: Institute for Research on Public Policy.

Wolfe, D.A. 2005. "Innovation and Research Funding: The role of government support," in *Taking Public Universities Seriously*, eds F. Iacobucci and C. Tuohy. Toronto: University of Toronto Press, pp. 316–40.

Part IV
Developing countries

11 University technology transfer

The case of Spain

Adela García-Aracil,
Elena Castro-Martínez,
Joaquín M. Azagra-Caro, Pablo D'Este and
Ignacio Fernández de Lucio

Introduction

The Spanish Higher Education (HE) System and university technology transfer strategies have changed profoundly in the last few decades. Since the 1980s, Spanish universities have become more research oriented, and the importance of knowledge and technology transfer has increased and had an impact on the performance of universities. Starting in the early 1990s, several interface infrastructures have been developed to foster university–business interactions. This chapter provides an in-depth discussion of the transformations to the university technology transfer system in Spain. The full potential of the benefits from university–industry relationships has not been realized and differs among universities. Our investigation implies that the role of Spanish universities as key agents in the processes of technology transfer and innovation needs to be developed further.

The chapter is structured as follows. The sections will provide an overview of the national context of HE in Spain; a review of current science policy, and the relationships among the various actors involved in innovation activity; a description of the main support mechanisms and the agents involved in promoting university technology transfer; an example of two Spanish public universities' technology transfer activities; and a discussion and some conclusions.

National industry and R&D context

Since the 1950s, the service sector in Spain has grown and currently represents 66% of the economy. This expansion has been at the expense mainly of the primary sector, although, over the last few years, the industry sector, which presently accounts for 17% of GDP, has also begun to decline (OECD, 2013). Retail, tourism, banking and telecommunications constitute a large part of service sector activity. Up to the onset of the financial crisis in 2008, the construction industry was growing, and represented a larger proportion of the economy than in most European countries. The Spanish economy's sectorial characteristics – notably the construction sector's boom and bust cycle, the relatively large weight of low-knowledge intensive services and low level participation in education due, in part, to the increased wages for unskilled jobs during the long expansion prior to the crisis – are one of the main explanations for the high incidence of temporary employment and sharp increase in unemployment since 2008. Official data shows that unemployment levels are high (26%), especially among young people between 16–24 year of age (45%) and women (55%). Individual level data suggest that participation in dual work-training programmes, which is low in Spain, would markedly improve the transition to work among Spanish youth (INE, 2013b).

Spending on research and development (R&D) has increased several times, but the 2012 figure of 1.3% of GDP, or €13,392 million, was considerably below both the European (EU-28 2.06%) and OECD country (2.4%) averages (see Table 11.1). Since the onset of the 2008 crisis, business sector expenditure on R&D has decreased and in 2012 was €7,094 million compared to €7,454 million in 2007.

Table 11.1 shows a divergence in the structure of R&D expenditures, with 53% accounted for by firms (see column 2 relative value of 0.69/1.30) and 47% by universities and government. In addition, the resources devoted to R&D in Spain are unevenly distributed among the 17 regions (or autonomous communities – CCAA): over 69% of the economic effort and 65% of human R&D expenditure is concentrated in four regions (Madrid, Catalonia, Andalusia and the Basque Country). Of these, only the Basque Country performs higher than the European average due to its productive structure and high presence of industry (2.19% of GDP). Ten of the 17 regions spend less than 1.0% of GDP on R&D activity and in eight (Andalusia, Cantabria, Galicia, Murcia, Extremadura, Canary and Balearic Islands and Valencian Community) the business sector was responsible for less than half of total R&D expenditure. Graph 11.1 depicts R&D activity in the Spanish regions.

Table 11.1 R&D resources in 2012

Indicator	Spain	UE-28
R&D expenditure (% GDP)	1.30	2.06
R&D expenditure (% of GDP) by:		
Firms	0.69	1.30
Government	0.25	0.26
Universities	0.36	0.49
Nº FTE R&D personnel (% of active population)	0.91	1.09
Firms	0.39	0.57
Government	0.18	0.15
Universities	0.34	0.36
Nº FTE Researchers (% of active population)	0.55	0.68
Firms	0.19	0.31
Government	0.09	0.08
Universities	0.26	0.27

Source: INE, 2013c. FTE: Full time equivalent.

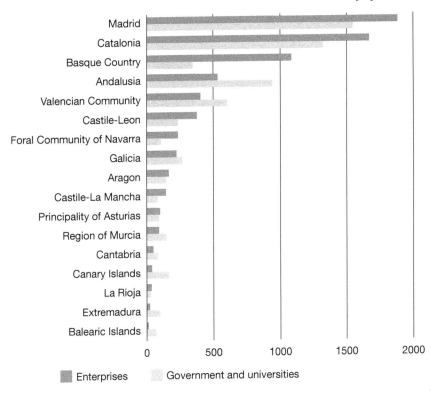

Source: INE, 2013c

Graph 11.1 Domestic expenditures on R&D in 2012: distribution by region and by sector of performance (million €)

Science policy and the scientific environment

Regulatory framework

Spain has a good supply of institutions and well-established programmes to promote links between the public research system and industry. However, in December 2011, responsibility for the governance of science and innovation activities was split between the Ministry of the Economy and Competitiveness (MINECO) and the Ministry of Industry, Tourism and Commerce (MINETUR) (Azagra-Caro, 2009). In 2012, MINECO distributed 68.9% of the Spanish State Budget and MINETUR 25.7% (Fernández-Zubieta, 2013).

MINECO is responsible for designing and implementing the four-year National Plans, national government's main tool for programming long-term financing for research. In 2012, MINECO also drafted the Spanish Strategy for Science, Technology and Innovation (2013–2020) setting out the rationale, objectives and indicators of Spanish R&D and innovation policy and the National Plans. The Seventh Plan (2013–2016), which was approved on 1 February 2013, sets the national strategy, its priorities, programmes, coordination mechanisms, costs and sources of funding and shows a further decline in the resources devoted to science and innovation (€2,012 million compared to €8,123.9 million in 2007).

The regional governments of the Spanish CCAA have shared with the national government responsibilities in promoting R&D, being responsible for their public research organizations (PROs) and funding policies to promote R&D, although sometimes large delays occurred regarding the lack of coordination between national and regional departments supporting public R&D due to insufficient expertise for funding management.

Spain also receives European funding and benefits from shared infrastructure and facilities. According to European Commission data (EC, 2013), the number of Spanish participants in Framework Programme 7 was 9,836 representing €2,848.59 million. Spain benefits also from the EU Cohesion Funds, which have expanded the R&D budgets of eligible Spanish regions quite substantially. Also, between 2000 and 2006, the contribution to Spanish R&D and innovation, and the information society, from EU Structural Funds amounted to some €4 billion (Tortosa, 2006; EC, 2009). Investments in R&D, innovation, entrepreneurship, transport and environmental projects accounted for €12 billion of structural funding (35% of the total allocation for Spain) (EC, 2009). However, from 2013, Spain was no longer eligible for Cohesion Funding. This implies successful convergence with the other member states, but reduced public support for R&D.

The innovation system actors

Business firms

Firms in Spain are mostly small and medium-sized enterprises (SMEs); however, there are many more micro firms (<10 employee) and many fewer large firms (>250 employees) enterprises than in other European countries. For example, the number of Germany's large firms is five times than Spain's and they account for 55% more jobs in relative terms.

The Spanish manufacturing sector is concentrated mainly in low, medium-low and medium-high technologies such as food products, textiles, chemicals, metal products, machinery and equipment and transport equipment. In Spain there is a relatively smaller number of high-tech enterprises, and their contribution to GDP is lower than the European average. Private spending on R&D remains relatively low compared with other OECD countries. In 2010 to 2012, only 25.9% of Spanish companies were involved in activities that could be described as innovative (INE, 2013d), and the number of innovative enterprises fell from 36,183 in 2008 to 18,077 in 2012.

There is also a shortage of qualified human resources. Many Spanish companies that engage in innovation activity lack suitably qualified personnel and, despite of efforts to increase firms' absorptive capacity, it remains low or non-existent

(Fernández-Zubieta, 2013). The problems identified are: (i) insufficient R&D personnel, especially in firms; and (ii) a mismatch between the supply and demand of doctoral graduates, especially those specializing in science and technology (Cañibano and Castro, 2011; POCARIM, 2013).

Universities

Spanish universities are among the oldest in the world. The University of Salamanca was founded 1215 and the University of Valladolid in 1292. These early universities were small institutions focused on law, philosophy and theology. In the 19th century, when Spain adopted the Napoleonic HE system, Spanish universities became subject to state laws and standards (García-Aracil, 2007). In the 1970s, a new model emerged, with a shift from an elite to a mass HE system. An important legal reform was enacted in 1983 in the form of the University Reform Act (*Ley de Reforma Universitaria* – LRU), which democratized the internal structure of universities and involved a change from direct state intervention to institutional autonomy.

In 2001, the legislative reform *Ley de Ordenación Universitaria* (LOU) dictated a transition to a model that included knowledge transfer among universities' core objectives, and promoted a large-scale structural reorganization of the sector (adaptation to the Bologna Declaration, the European Higher Education Area and the European Research Area) of the Spanish HE system. Further reforms include the enactment in 2009 of the Spanish Strategy University Framework (Estrategia Universitaria 2015) (Ministerio de Educación, 2010) to encourage the exploitation of university knowledge by industry and universities' commitment to supporting their regions.

Universities provide most of the tertiary education in Spain, and are responsible for a large proportion of its research activity. In 2013, there were 50 public and 29 private universities. Private universities account for only 10% of university spending on R&D, with most research activity taking place in public universities (INE, 2013c).

University R&D activities are funded by the National R&D Plans, the Spanish CCAA R&D policies and European funds (see Graph 11.2). Universities receive additional funding from providing services to firms, under the LRU 1983 and the LOU. Universities have more freedom to allocate the finance from research contracts with industry than public funding, and some goes to increasing the remuneration paid to academics. Most university researcher salaries are paid out of "general university funds", which in 2012 represented 70% of total intramural R&D university expenditure. The resources available to the universities also include loans to invest in R&D infrastructures, and the sale of other services than R&D.

Universities are responsible for a large proportion of the scientific publications in Spain: they produced around 60% of the publications listed in the Web of Science Database (e.g. Science Citation Index Expanded, Social Sciences Citation Index, Arts and Humanities Citation Index, Index Chemicus and Curren Chemical Reaction). Universities produce the most publications in all scientific areas except

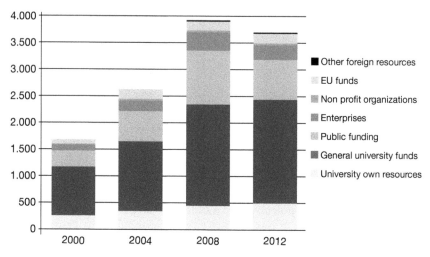

Source: INE, 2013c and previous years.

Graph 11.2 Evolution of the source of funds for R&D in universities in Spain (millions of euros)

medicine, where hospitals (linked in most cases to universities) generate more scientific literature than universities (CRUE, 2012).

Public research organizations (PROs)

PROs conduct a large proportion of the R&D activities supported by public funds, and accounted for 18% of national R&D expenditure in 2012. There are eight main PROs attached to the State Secretariat of Research, Development and Innovation, which account for 43% of government R&D expenditure: Spanish Council for Scientific Research (CSIC), National Institute for Aerospace Technology (INTA), Institute of Health Carlos III (ISCIII), Geological and Mining Institute of Spain (IGME), Spanish Institute of Oceanography (IEO), Centre for Energy, Environmental and Technological Research (CIEMAT), National Institute for Agricultural Research and Technology and Food (INIA), and Canary Institute of Astrophysics (IAC). Other PROs and research units engaged in scientific, technological and/or industrial innovation research are attached to other ministries. These organizations account for 34% of government R&D expenditure (INE, 2013c).

Private non-for-profit foundations

Private non-for-profit organizations (PNFPO) in Spain are less important than similar organizations in other European countries, and their expenditure on R&D accounted for 0.01% of GDP in 2012 (EU-28 value is 0.03%) (EUROSTAT, 2013).

Business sector–university relations

An overview of the organizations that collaborate for innovation provides a picture of the relationships among business sector and university actors. Table 11.2 shows that small enterprises that have introduced a new product or process have low levels of cooperation for innovation although collaboration with universities is higher than with most other types of organizations except supplier firms. In the case of large enterprises, levels of cooperation with universities increase substantially.

In general, Spanish firms cooperate with universities less than firms in the more advanced EU countries. The percentage of German and French firms that cooperate with universities was 14% and 13% respectively in 2010, compared to 9% for Spain, just ahead of Italy, Bulgaria and Romania (EUROSTAT, 2013). Relationships between Spanish universities and companies do not significantly affect firms' innovation performance; the most influential variable is internal R&D (Vega-Jurado et al., 2008).

Table 11.2 Innovative enterprises (IE) which have cooperated with other actors to conduct their innovative activities in 2009–2011

	Less than 250 employees	*250 and more employees*	*Total*
Total IE companies	22,681	1,783	24,464
% of IE companies respect to total companies	14.7	52.3	15.5
% of IE companies that have cooperated in innovation in 2009–2011	24.6	48.4	26.3
% of IE companies that have cooperated respect to total companies	3.6	25.3	4.1
Companies that have cooperated with (%):			
other companies in the same group	5.7	26.5	7.2
Suppliers of equipment, materials, components or software	11.1	28.3	12.3
Private sector clients	6.7	15.4	7.4
Public sector clients	2.4	7.4	2.7
Competitors or other enterprises inside their same branch of activity	5.4	14.8	6.0
Consultants or commercial laboratories	5.9	18.7	6.8
Universities or other higher education units	7.5	23.8	8.7
Public research organizations	3.8	13.6	4.4
Technological centres	6.4	17.5	7.1

Note: IE = Firms involved in innovation activities during the period 2009–2011.

Source: INE, 2012.

There are certain barriers to communication between universities and companies, which reduces the transfer of knowledge. There is no tradition of cooperation between universities and companies, which makes communication difficult, and the culture of these organizations is very different. This hinders the free flow of technology and knowledge from universities to industry. Spanish companies are less innovative than the EU average, and tend to innovate on their own rather than through collaborations (FCYD, 2011).

Commercialization of university technology

Government bodies linking universities and companies

Spanish R&D policy has always prioritized the promotion of knowledge transfer and exchange between universities, PROs and society. The National R&D Plans include several instruments to achieve this; from 1988 to 2011, the Interface Structures (IFS) have been in place. The IFS are designed to promote and catalyse interactions among relevant actors in order to facilitate innovation and technology transfer activity and to increase the competitiveness of firms (Fernández de Lucio et al., 1996). The Spanish innovation system includes several IFS (see Table 11.3).

Table 11.3 shows the significant increase in IFS as a result of the introduction of knowledge transfer offices (OTRI) and science parks (PC). Up to 1986, the legal framework did not allow extra budgetary revenues to public universities and in order to provide research services to firms, some universities created University–Enterprise Foundations (FUE), which had private participation and managed the resources provided by companies. After the enactment of a new law, which resulted in publication of the National R&D Plan, OTRI took over the FUE to promote contracts between universities and firms. University managers were keen to control this new and increasing source of funds.

The development of science parks was encouraged by the ministry responsible for science and innovation policy since 2000, to promote university–industry relationships through the exploitation of EU regional funds (BOE December 8, 2000). Although IFS generally promote links between universities and companies, their influence varies. We discuss this in more detail below.

Table 11.3 Evolution of interface structures in Spain

	1988	*1995*	*2005*	*2010*
University–Enterprise Foundations (FUE)	15	15	19	19
Knowledge Transfer Offices (OTRI)	0	55	86	101
Scientific Parks (PC)	0	n.a.	15	48
Other Specialized IFS	0	7	10	22
Total	15	77	130	190

Source: 1988 and 1995 data: Fernández de Lucio et al. 1996; 2005 and 2010 data: Ministry of Education and Science, Ministry of Economy and Competitiveness (www.apte.org)

Knowledge Transfer Offices (OTRI)

The OTRI were created at the end of 1988 within the National R&D and Innovation Plan framework and were aimed at fostering and facilitating cooperation between researchers in public institutions and private companies, at both the national and European levels. The OTRI try to identify societal and economic demand and promote the transfer of technology between the public and private sectors by facilitating interactions between academia and society in order to transfer the results of university research. All Spanish universities and PROs have an OTRI (Castro-Martínez et al., 1991; Fernández de Lucio et al., 1996; Represa et al., 2005), and most are part of a network established in 1997 as a permanent working group under the auspices of the General Assembly of the Spanish University Chancellors' Conference (CRUE). Currently, 69 universities (all the public universities and some private ones) belong to the OTRI network and 24 Spanish research centres are associated with it. One of the objectives of the university OTRI network is to encourage the development of university structures to promote and manage the supply of technology and knowledge, and relations between universities and business. A geographically distributed network of small units has been established to forge links with and provide detailed knowledge on the respective local environment (Castro-Martínez et al., 2008).

Table 11.4 presents some knowledge transfer indicators for Spanish universities. The main activity of the OTRI between 1989 and 1995 was related to R&D contracts between public institutions and private companies. Since then, they have become involved in support for university patenting, licensing and spin-off activities. The growth in R&D capabilities in firms and universities seems to be correlated to the development of technical and scientific infrastructures. University OTRI have increased the number and quality of their

Table 11.4 Evolution of main knowledge transfer indicators of the Spanish universities

	1989	1995	2003	2007	2011
Number of universities asking the questionnaire	32	48	58	62	65
Number of OTRI staff (FTE)	64	154	294	499	621
Number of R&D contracts	695	3.270	7.958	10.113	6.631
Revenues from R&D contracts (M€)	8	120	258	408	258
Invention disclosures submitted				692	1282
National patent applications	24	140	317	434	612
PCT patent extensions			107	192	351
Number of license contracts and option agreements			78	190	212
Revenues for licenses (M€)			1,69	1,94	2,44
Number of spin off created			87	120	111

Source: CICYT until 1995; from 2003 Red OTRI (www.redotriuniversidades.net).

technical staff helped by the working groups, training programmes and other activities offered by the network to improve their management skills. Most OTRI are now supported by their respective universities following initial government support for their establishment.

Science and technology parks

The first science and technology parks (STPs) in Spain appeared in the mid-1980s and were established by the governments of the newly created autonomous communities (CCAA). The more industrialized regions saw STPs as tools to promote industry diversification. Initially, eight STPs were established in the CCAA of the Basque Country, Madrid, Catalonia, Valencia, Andalusia, Castilla y León, Galicia and Asturias, between 1985 and 1993. By 2000, there were 14 STPs supported by regional governments, universities and the municipalities. This great expansion of the STPs took place when the Ministry responsible for Science Policy, since then, decided to give support to these structures using funding from the EU to foster innovation. Today, there are 68 STPs in Spain (APTE, 2013), although there are no precise data on how many are in operation. These parks are spread across all the CCAA, with a high presence in Catalonia and the Basque Country.

In December 2012, the 46 STPs linked to the Association of Science and Technology Parks of Spain (APTE) hosted 6,206 companies and institutions (500 in 1997), focused on information technology (27%), followed by engineering, consultancy (12%), industry (10%) and R&D (10%). In 2012, the companies and institutions located in these parks accounted for 146,669 employees, 20% of whom worked in R&D, and had a turnover of €21.587 million (192% increase on 1997) (APTE, 2013).

It could be said that STPs generally have not achieved the expected results or justified the amount invested. For example, the parks set up by universities have not increased the interaction between research groups and local companies. However, since many of these parks are quite new, it is difficult to find concrete evidence of their performance and results.

Technology transfer activities carried out by the Spanish universities

Since 1989, Spanish universities and PROs have implemented various mechanisms for cooperation with companies, starting with consulting and R&D services. The portfolio of the services offered has developed and includes student placements, joint supervision of students, training programmes, consultancy, technical services, R&D contracts, joint research projects, scientific personnel exchange programmes, patents, licenses, spin-off activity and R&D institutes shared with enterprises. However, the most common activities are internships, consulting and technical services, and R&D contracts.

A survey of the relationships between universities and companies, conducted by the "Fundación Ciencia y Desarrollo" (FCyD) in 2010 (FCYD, 2011), shows that for those companies that collaborated with universities (54%) the main mechanism was training students (77%), followed by consultancy agreements (17%) and collaborative research projects (14%). The new mechanisms for university–industry collaborations, such as patents, licences, spin-off companies and joint R&D centres are being promoted by the universities although the establishment of joint R&D facilities has been hampered by the economic crisis and the general lack of resources.

Table 11.4 shows that patenting and licensing activity accounts for less than 1% of net contract R&D despite the sharp increase in the number of patents filed by universities and PROs. In this framework, increased intellectual property rights protection mechanisms in universities and PROs has been prompted by a combination of factors. First, government is keen to improve Spain's innovation performance; second, the universities are keen to optimize the scientific knowledge they produce and to improve their position in the HEI rankings; third, academics are keen to incorporate aspects of knowledge transfer into their curricula.

The interest of OTRIs in applying for protection and marketing intellectual property is relatively recent. The 2011 Science Act Article 15 specifies that teachers and researchers have a duty to reveal to their institutions any research findings that might need protection, and to participate in the transfer of these results. Table 11.4 shows that Spanish patent applications from universities have increased from 140 in 1995 to 612 in 2011. This increased patenting activity is reflected in the number of licenses, which nearly tripled between 2003 and 2011, but is not reflected in increased income. This situation is due to the weakness in the Spanish productive system, which makes it difficult to license patents to companies and mostly leads to the creation of spin-offs to allow academics to commercialize their research results. In this case, the university has a share in the company as payment for the assignment of patent rights.

Entrepreneurial activity in the form of spin-off[1] establishment has also favoured the creation of STPs in universities. The set-up of the spin-offs was enhanced considerable in the early years of this century, although this instrument is not formally collected in the Universities reform till 2007. Universities have responded to the change in the law by creating specific regulations to govern the establishment of these companies, although not all universities have reacted in the same way.

The number of university spin-off companies established (see Table 11.4) is around 120 per year in the period 2007–2011. This activity has been driven partly by the desire of universities to perform well in the ranking for knowledge transfer performance, and this spin-off activity includes any university initiatives, including those undertaken by students. Some academics set up firms to give them more freedom for research not governed by the university administration and bureaucracy (Morales-Gualdron et al., 2009). Thus, the numbers in Table 11.4 may not reflect genuine spin-off companies.

Therefore, there are many national-level public support programmes for the creation of innovative technology companies on STPs, as well as other initiatives of the different autonomous governments which have had a positive impact on the creation of technology-based companies. All these initiatives try to encourage university entrepreneurial activities. However, for a high increase of entrepreneurial activities, OTRIs should integrate all activities involved in the third mission in their own strategy with a clear decision about the quality of the companies created, beyond the achievement of reaching good university indicators or rankings.

Knowledge and technology transfer in context: discussion of two Spanish universities

We compare two Spanish public universities, established more than 500 years ago, which are comparable in size. They are considered traditional universities which added technical disciplines in the 1980s, but which differ in their strategic approaches, and management and organization of their knowledge and technology transfer activities. The selected universities are Universidad de Valladolid (UVA) and Universidad de Santiago de Compostela (USC) (see Table 11.5).

The USC's OTRI was set up in 1989 within the framework of the National R&D Plan and responsible to the Pro Vice-Chancellor for Research and Innovation. Its mandate is to manage knowledge transfer mechanisms (consultancy and R&D contracts, patents, licence and spin off) and competitive public research funds. In 1989, USC's OTRI had 3 staff, which in 2011 had increased to 22 personnel with an annual budget of €152 million. The USC's OTRI remains under the direct control of the university.

Table 11.5 Overview of the main data of UVA and USC

	UVA	*USC*
Main data		
Foundation year	1295	1495
Location – region	Castilla y León	Galicia
Total annual expenses (million €)	195.7	228.8
Size (number of undergraduate students)	24,298	24,998
Staff (full time academic staff)	2,801	2,294
R&D inputs		
Total annual R&D expenses (million €)	60.5	106.1
R&D public funds (competitive calls, million €)	15.4	37.0
of which coming from regional funds (%)	*31.5*	*42,4*
of which coming from national funds (%)	*60.6*	*43,0*
of which coming from UE funds (%)	*7.9*	*14,6*
R&D personnel (FTE)	3,830	2,677
Researchers (FTE)	3,022	1,608

Source: INE, 2013e; CRUE, 2012

In 1989 the USC announced a policy to promote protection of intellectual property at the university. The scheme consists of a set of actions for providing information, specialized training and advice services to professors and researchers, and establishing an efficient IPR decision and management system. This has increased patenting activity. The high quality research and the greater professionalization of the OTRI's management have contributed to this increase. In 2011, USC was ranked among the top ten patenting organizations in the Spanish Patent Office: it was responsible for 49 invention disclosures, 27 national priority patent applications and 30 priority patent extensions. In 2007, USC was ranked first for licensing revenues (€293,000), and at the end of 2011 was maintaining 250 patent families and 6 licences and was receiving €70,000 from licensing revenue.

At the end of the 1990s, USC began to actively promote spin-off creation and set up an incubator, UNINOVA, which was one of the first university incubators in Spain. In 2000, the OTRI published a set of procedures for spin-off creation and created a risk capital society (UNIRISCO) with two other public Galician universities and several financial and private investors. In 2005, USC and 15 other Spanish universities and 9 investment companies, created a risk capital management society (UNINVEST), which manages I+D UNIFONDO, a capital fund of €18.5 million to provide seed capital for university spin-offs.

Since 2008, USC's OTRI has developed its IPR management processes, hired experts in the technologies in which the university is most active (e.g., biopharma) and focused on the coordination of licences and spin-offs, working with other university organizations located in the same EMPRENDIA building (UNIRISCO and UNINOVA). It supports entrepreneurship activity by faculty and students through a new proof-of-concept programme (funded by regional government), which benefits from the expertise of external experts, and accounts for €200,000 per year.

In 2011, the UVA published 811 ISI-indexed articles, 45% of them in the natural sciences, 30% in technology fields, 17% in medicine and 8% in humanities and social sciences, and produced 149 doctoral graduates, while USC published 1,529 ISI-indexed articles, 52% of them in the natural sciences, 33% in medicine, 11% in technology areas and 4% in humanities and social sciences and produced 238 doctoral graduates (CRUE, 2012). Although UVA has more full-time academic staff than USC (see Table 11.5), USC is more productive in terms of scientific production and obtaining research funding from competitive calls.

The UVA's OTRI was set up in 1989, within the framework of the National R&D Plan, as a unit responsible to the Pro Vice-Chancellor for Research. In 1997, this unit was transferred to the UVA's General Foundation (Fundación General de la Universidad de Valladolid), a non-profit organization set up to improve R&D management. In 2011, the OTRI employed 17 staff, with an annual budget of €814 million, 12% from public subsidies, 8% from contract overheads, 1% from licensing revenues and 79% from the university's General Foundation budget. From its creation, OTRI's activity has consisted mainly of supporting research and consultancy contracts, which represent an important percentage of university R&D funding. However, since the establishment of the university's Science Park and Incubator in 2007, there has been a stronger focus on spin-off promotion.

UVA has an active IPR policy designed to increase patenting activity through the establishment of an integrated IP management system, an IPR fund, and a programme to help students learn about how protect their inventions. In 2011, the UVA was maintaining a total of 116 patent families, received €66,000 in licensing revenue, and applied for three more licences.

Table 11.6 compares UVA and USC's technology transfer policies and strategies.

Table 11.6 Overview of UVA and USC dealing with technology transfer (2011)

	UVA	USC
OTRI resources		
Staff (including director)	17	22
Budget (million €)	814	152
IP management		
IP framework	1 OTRI set up in 1989, but management was transferred to the UVA General Foundation. 2 Patents Act allocates patents property to university. 3 UVA policy and regulations (1997) establish the procedure and benefits distribution. 4 OTRI promotes and manages IPR.	1 OTRI set up in 1989, but remain under direct control of university. 2 Patents Act allocates patents property to university. 3 USC policy and regulations (1989) establish the procedure and benefits distribution. 4 OTRI promotes and manages IPR.
Approach to generating invention disclosures from academics	1 The academic identifies a result with potential industrial use and communicates it to Pro Vice-Chancellor for Research. 2 OTRI manages the intellectual protection process, with academic collaboration. 3 OTRI manages the patent valorisation process and negotiates conditions with potential clients. 4 OTRI develops an integral system to manage IPR in 2010. 5 If UVA decides not to protect a research result, the academic can do it on its own. In this case, UVA has a right to 25% of the revenues obtained.	1 The academic identifies a result with potential industrial use and communicates it to the OTRI. OTRI elaborates, with the help of the academic, a report on the suitability of intellectual protection. 2 OTRI manages the intellectual protection process, with academic collaboration. 3 OTRI manages the patent valorisation process and negotiates conditions with potential clients. 4 OTRI coordinates IPR valorisation with spin off creation. 5 If USC decides not to protect a research result, the academic can do it on its own. In this case, USC has right to 10% of the revenues obtained. 6 USC offers seed capital.

	UVA	USC
IP management *continued*		
Distribution of revenues arising from IPR licensing	1 Inventors: 60% 2 Their department: 10–17% 3 University: 30–33%	1 Inventors: 60% 2 Their department: 20% 3 University: 20%
Output and Impact Indicators		
Incomes from technical an R&D contracts (period 2006 to 2011)	55,453 million €	97,569 million €
Level of university patenting (period 2006–2011)	• 56 national priority patent applications • 14 PCT patent applications • 116 patent families	• 127 national priority patent applications • 76 PCT patent applications • 250 patent families
Number of license generating income (period 2006–2011)	23	25
Income from licenses (period 2006–2011)	261,800€	660,000€
Number of university spin-offs	None (OTRI does not manage spin offs)	2002–2011: 42 (from research results or capacities, excluding student start-ups)
Science parks/ incubators	Yes, from 2007	Yes, the first incubator was created in 1999 (UNINOVA). In 2008 a scientific park was opened with its own incubator. In 2009 started Campusvida. Since 2012 the USC have its own proof concept programme which had invest 275,000 € in 9 projects.
Employment impact/ growth	No data available	1999–2011: USC has created 272 enterprises (spin off & start up), with 800 employees.

Source: Economic, R&D statistics and general data: www.ine.es; Universities data: www.educacion. gob.es; Spanish legislation: www.boe.es; Universities organizational and legal information: www.usc.es and www.uva.es; Knowledge transfer data, information and valuations: OTRI network annual survey; UVA and USC OTRI person in charge.

Conclusions

Since the mid-1980s, public support for R&D in Spanish universities has been associated with increasing levels of knowledge and technology transfer to businesses and other non-academic sectors. However, partly as a result of the low absorptive capacity of the Spanish production system (i.e. SMEs in low and medium-tech sectors), the knowledge transfer mechanisms that have experienced stronger growth are largely connected to relatively unsophisticated channels that generally involve contracting of R&D services such as consultancy agreements, provision of technical services and R&D contracts. Income from R&D contracts increased steadily to a peak of €408 million in 2007, before experiencing a sharp decline as a result of the economic crisis, reaching €258 million in 2011 (equivalent to 2003 levels). Conversely, other channels such as licensing of intellectual property have exhibited more moderate growth. Licensing revenues from patents have remained below 1% of the revenues generated from R&D contracts, despite the fact that the total number of national and international patents has exhibited a continuous growth over the period analysed in this study.

Public policies to support R&D activities in universities have mainly focused on setting well-defined incentives to foster research. This focus contrasts with the comparatively weaker efforts to incentivize knowledge and technology transfer activities from universities. As a result, Spanish universities have not developed a clearly defined strategy to support technology transfer activities, feeding into a university system that is characterized by the existence of markedly heterogeneous structures for transferring knowledge and fostering interactions with diverse social and economic agents.

This heterogeneity characterizing university knowledge and technology transfer support structures is epitomized by the contrasting cases of Universidad de Santiago de Compostela (USC) and Universidad de Valladolid (UVA). Comparative analysis shows that two universities of similar age, size (number of academic staff and undergraduate students), coverage of scientific areas and located in similar socio-economic environments, exhibit markedly different research performance and degree of involvement in technology transfer activities. Data shows that USC produces twice as many ISI journal publications and graduate students, spends 50% more on R&D, and has a higher number of patents and spin-offs, as compared to UVA. We argue that the better performance of USC is largely due to highly coordinated research and technology transfer policies that have triggered a cultural change within the university. A key role in making this change possible has been played by OTRI at USC, which succeeded in managing a high-level integration between itself and other key actors within the university. By contrast, UVA's management of R&D and transfer activities have been far less integrated, with the management of technology transfer activities being outsourced to an organization outside the university.

Acknowledgments

The authors would like to thank the OTRI network for data from the Annual Knowledge Transfer Survey; and Yolanda Calvo (UVA's OTRI director) and José Luis Villaverde (USC's Valorization, Transfer and Entrepreneurship Unit director) for their help in understanding the context of their universities and activities.

Note

1 We adopt the definition of spin-off or spin-out used in the OTRI network survey, i.e. a new company whose business is based mainly on knowledge created in a university/ PRO, generally (but not necessarily) with university research staff involvement.

References

APTE, Asociación de Parques Científicos y Tecnológicos de España (2013). *Directorio de Parques Científicos y Tecnológicos 2013*, APTE, Málaga.

Azagra-Caro, J. M. (2009). ERAWATCH Country Report 2008. *An assessment of research system and policies: Spain.* http://cordis.europa.eu/erawatch/index.cfm

BOE, Boletín Oficial del Estado (2000). ORDEN de 5 diciembre de 2000 por la que se establecen las bases reguladoras para la concesión de ayudas a Parques

Científicos y Tecnológicos, y la convocatoria para las solicitudes de ayudas correspondientes al año 2000. 8 December 2000, pp. 42921–42927.

Cañibano Sánchez, C., Castro Martínez, E. (2011). El sistema español de innovación. In: Berumen, S.A. (coord.) *Los sistemas de innovación en Europa*, pp. 23–65. Madrid: ESIC.

Castro Martínez, E., Fernández de Lucio I. (1991). Hacia un Sistema integrado Ciencia-Tecnología-Industria, *Actas del Simposium International New Tecnologies and Socieconomic Challenge*, pp. 315–324, Institut Catalá d'Estudis Mediterranis, Barcelona.

Castro Martínez, E., Fernández de Lucio, I., Molas Gallart, J. (2008). Theory and Practice in Knowledge Transfer: The Emergence of "Interface Structures". In B. Laperche, D. Uzunidis and N. von Tunzelmann (eds) *The Genesis of Innovation. Systemic Linkages between Knowledge and Market*, pp. 146–161. Edward Elgar: Cheltenham UK.

CICYT (1995). *Plan Nacional de I+D 1996–1999*, Madrid.

CRUE, Red OTRI Universidades (2006, 2007, 2008, 2009, 2010, 2011, 2012). *Encuesta de Investigación y Transferencia de Conocimiento de las Universidades Españolas*, Madrid.

EC, European Commission (2013). Country participation. Success stories. http://ec.europa. eu/research/fp7/index_en.cfm?pg=country-profiles

EC, European Commission (2009). European Cohesion Policy in Spain. http://ec.europa. eu/regional_policy/sources/docgener/informat/country2009/e_en

EUROSTAT (2013). Science, technology and innovation statistics. http://epp.eurostat.ec. europa.eu/portal/page/portal/science_technology_innovaon/introduction (accessed 20 December 2013).

FCYD (2011). Informe CYD 2011. Barcelona: FCYD.

Fernández de Lucio, I., Conesa, F., Garea, M., Castro, E., Gutiérrez, A. and Bodegas, M. A. (1996). *Las Estructuras de Interfaz en el Sistema Español de Innovación. Su papel en la difusión de la tecnología*, 2 vols., Universidad Politécnica de Valencia, Valencia.

Fernández-Zubieta, A. (2013). *ERAWATCH Country Reports 2012: Spain*. European Commission, ERAWATCH.

García-Aracil, A. (2007). Expansion and Reorganization in the Spanish Higher Education System. In A. Bonaccorsi and C. Daraio (eds) *Universities Strategic Knowledge Creation*, pp. 376–340. Edward Elgar: Cheltenham UK.

INE, Instituto Nacional de Estadística (2011). Encuesta sobre Innovación en las Empresas. www.ine.es

INE, Instituto Nacional de Estadística (2012). Encuesta sobre Innovación en las Empresas. www.ine.es

INE, Instituto Nacional de Estadística (2013a). Cifras de Población y Censos Demográficos. INE: Madrid.

INE, Instituto Nacional de Estadística (2013b). Encuesta de Población Activa. www.ine.es

INE, Instituto Nacional de Estadística (2013c). Estadística de las actividades de I+D. www.ine.es

INE, Instituto Nacional de Estadística (2013d). Encuesta sobre Innovación en las Empresas. www.ine.es

INE, Instituto Nacional de Estadística (2013e). Estadística de la Enseñanza Universitaria en España. www.ine.es

MECD, Ministerio de Educación, Cultura y Deporte (several years: 2004–2013). *Datos y Cifras del Sistema Universitario Español*, Secretaría General Técnica Subdirección General de Documentación y Publicaciones, Madrid.

Ministerio de Educación (2010). Estrategia Universidad 2015. The contribution of universities to Spanish socio economic progress. Available online: www.educacion.es/dctm/eu2015/2011-estrategia-2015-ingles.pdf?documentId=0901e72b8091009a (accessed 3 March 2015).

Morales-Gualdron, S., Gutiérrez-Gracia, A. and Roig-Dobón, S. (2009). The Entrepreneurial Motivation in Academia: A Multidimensional Construct. *International Entrepreneurship and Management Journal*, 5 (3): 301–317.

OECD (2013). *OECD Economic Outlook: Statistics and Projections*, No. 94. Paris.

POCARIM (2013). *Mapping the Population, Careers, Mobilities and Impacts of Advanced Research Degree Graduates in the Social Sciences and Humanities*. European Commission, 7FP.

Represa, D., Castro-Martínez E. and Fernández de Lucio, I. (2005). Encouraging Protection of Public Research Results in Spain. *Journal of Intellectual Property Rights*, 10 (September) 382–388.

Tortosa, E. (2006). La I+D en el marco autonómico. In J. Sebastian and E. Muñoz (eds) *Radiografía de la investigación pública en España*. pp. 70–95.

Vega-Jurado, J., Gutiérrez-Gracia, A., Fernández-de-Lucio, I., Manjarrés-Henríquez, L. (2008). The Effect of External and Internal Factors on Firms' Product Innovation. *Research Policy*, 37: 616–632.

12 University technology commercialization

The case of Thailand

Jarunee Wonglimpiyarat

Introduction

Thailand is one of the emerging tigers in Asia attempting to become a knowledge-based economy through deepening national technological capabilities. This chapter discusses the case of university technology commercialization with a focus on Mahidol University, one of the national research universities in Thailand and the leading universities in Asia. The case of Mahidol University provides an interesting example of the Thai university playing an active role in promoting academic entrepreneurship through the technology transfer process. The case of Mahidol University has set an example of successful university in terms of technology commercialization for other universities in Thailand to follow.

This chapter is concerned with the university technology commercialization in Thailand. The study includes the discussions of the government policies to support entrepreneurial innovations and uses Mahidol University, one of the national research universities, as a case study to explore the process of university technology commercialization. The structure of this chapter is as follows. Following this introductory section, the section 'Background of Thailand's economy and the government policies to support university technology commercialization' provides a background of Thailand's economy. It also discusses the government policies to support university technology commercialization. The section 'University technology commercialization in Thailand' discusses the process of university technology commercialization in Thailand. The section that follows this ('Case study of Mahidol University') provides an analysis of the case study of Mahidol University, the oldest institution of higher learning in Thailand with outstanding research in medical sciences, to understand its system and mechanisms to manage the university research and promote innovation commercialization. The conclusion to this chapter offers policy recommendations to enhance the capacity of university technology transfer and commercialization.

Background of Thailand's economy and the government policies to support university technology commercialization

Background of Thailand's economy

In recent years, Southeast Asian countries have shown their commitments towards creating a knowledge-based economy through innovation development. Their innovation performance can be seen from the World Bank's Knowledge Economy Index shown in Table 12.1. Currently, there is a trend of Southeast Asian governments' attempts to promote knowledge transfer from the universities to industry and technology commercialization. For example, the Malaysian government has introduced incentives for university researchers and inventors to publish, patent and commercialize their research results including cash rewards on disclosure of an invention and funding for initial development when a patent is granted. Similarly, the government of Indonesia has tried to motivate and facilitate research commercialization by providing resources, funding and incentives under the National System of Research Development and Application of Sciences and Technologies (R&D Act) and the Government Regulation No. 20 of 2005 on Technology Transfer of Intellectual Property (IP) and Research Findings (TT Regulation) (OECD, 2013). The government of Singapore, an innovation driven economy, has launched various entrepreneurial financing programs to support technology commercialization. Major universities having extensive networks with the industry are the National University of Singapore (NUS), Nanyang Technological University (NTU) and Singapore Management University (SMU) (Wong et al., 2007; OECD, 2013)

Thailand is located in the Southeastern part of Asia with a total area of 513,120 square km. It is the second largest economy in Southeast Asia (after Indonesia) having a population of 69.5 million. In 2011, the World Bank has upgraded Thailand's income categorization from a lower middle income to an upper middle income economy. Thailand can be seen as a late adopter of small- and medium-sized enterprise (SME) policy to support entrepreneurial development (Thailand

Table 12.1 Knowledge economy index of Southeast Asian countries – Year 2012

	Rank	Knowledge economy index (KEI)	Economic incentive regime	Innovation	Education	Information and communications technology (ICT)
Indonesia	107	3.11	3.47	3.24	3.20	2.52
Malaysia	48	6.10	5.67	6.91	5.22	6.61
Philippines	92	3.94	4.32	3.77	4.64	3.03
Singapore	23	8.26	9.66	9.49	5.09	8.78
Thailand	66	5.21	5.12	5.95	4.23	5.55
Vietnam	103	3.40	2.80	2.75	2.99	5.05

Source: The author's design, based on the World Bank Group (2014).

adopted policies later than other Asian countries like Taiwan and Singapore whose SME innovation policies were adopted since the 1980s). The overview of economic and innovation performance of Thailand is shown in Table 12.2. The economic growth of Thailand is one of the world's fastest growing with an average growth rate of 5% per year. In 2013, Thailand was ranked 27th (out of 60 countries) according to the International Institute for Management Development (IMD)

Table 12.2 Overview of economic and innovation performance of Thailand

Indicator	Year	Thailand
Population (million)	2013	69.5
GDP	2012	USD 366 billion
GDP growth (%)	2011	0.1
	2012	6.4
	2013	3.7
IMD world competitiveness ranking	2010	26
	2011	27
	2012	30
	2013	27
IMD world competitiveness ranking	2013	27
Ranking in economic performance	2013	9
Ranking in government efficiency	2013	22
Ranking in business efficiency	2013	18
Ranking in infrastructure	2013	48
– Ranking in scientific infrastructure	2013	40
– Ranking in technological infrastructure	2013	47
WEF competitiveness ranking	2010	38
	2011	39
	2012	38
	2013	37
WEF competitiveness ranking	2013	37
Ranking in basic requirements	2013	49
Ranking in efficiency enhancers	2013	40
– Ranking in technological readiness	2013	78
Ranking in innovation and sophistication factors	2013	52
– Ranking in innovation	2013	66
Knowledge Economy Index (KEI) Ranking	2012	66
KEI Index	2012	5.21
Research and development (R&D) expenditure	2012	USD 740 million
% of R&D expenditure to GDP (approximate)	2012	0.22
R&D personnel (FTE per 10,000 people)	2012	9.1

Source: The author's design, based on the Institute for Management Development (IMD) (2010, 2011, 2012, 2013), World Economic Forum (WEF) (2010, 2011, 2012, 2013) and World Bank (2013).

world competitiveness ranking and 37th (out of 148 countries) according to the World Economic Forum (WEF) Global Competitiveness Report. The research and development (R&D) spending is 0.22% of gross domestic product (GDP) whereby the public and private sector account for 60% and 40% of total R&D investments respectively.

Innovation system and the role of universities, incubators in the commercialization of technologies

Based on the national innovation system (NIS) framework, Figure 12.1 presents an overview of the national innovation system and role of universities, incubators in the commercialization of technologies of Thailand. The national innovation system (NIS) is the interactive system of existing institutions, private and public firms (either large or small), universities and government agencies, aiming at the production, diffusion and exploitation of knowledge within national borders (Lundvall 1992, 1998, 1999, 2003). In other words, interorganizational interactions among various actors and institutions give rise to the development of innovation system. The major industrial clusters in Thailand are formed near the Science Park in the Northern Bangkok and Technolopolis or Innovation Park in Bangkok metropolitan area. These technology clusters were established to emulate the successful high-tech clusters of US Silicon Valley. From seeing a thriving innovative cluster of the US, the Thai government has tried to create the clusters to support technology commercialization. The Northern Bangkok Industrial Cluster was established with the working environments to promote academic research and technology transfer (Wonglimpiyarat, 2010). The Northern Bangkok Industrial Cluster is situated in the area surrounded by the Science Park, universities and industries. The major universities providing a source of knowledge to support the growth of the cluster are the Asian Institute of Technology (AIT), Sirindhorn International Institute of Technology (SIIT), Thammasat University, Rangsit University and Bangkok University. These universities are located near Navanakorn, Rojana, Bangkradi industrial estates to enhance R&D collaboration and university technology commercialization.

The Technolopolis or Innovation Park of the National Innovation Agency is located at the nexus of universities in central business district of Bangkok. The cluster comprises the universities of Mahidol University, King Mongkut's University of Technology North Bangkok, King Mongkut's Institute of Technology Ladkrabang, King Mongkut's University of Technology Thonburi, Kasetsart University and Chulalongkorn University. These universities are located in the Bangkok metropolitan area and in close proximity to industrial estates and export zones. NSTDA Science Park and NIA Technolopolis/Innovation Park provide necessary infrastructure and facilities to support R&D activities of start-ups as well as university spin-offs. In reducing the risks of failure in new venture formation, the parks also offer innovation financing programs to support innovative and commercialization projects. The financing programs of NSTDA Science Park are, for example, the Industrial Technology Assistance Program

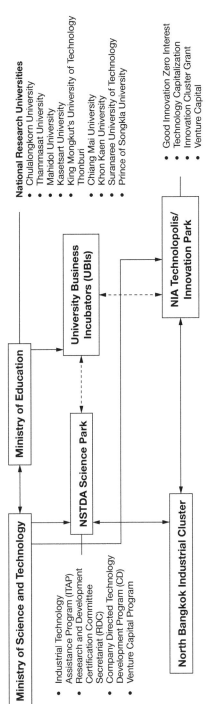

Figure 12.1 Overview of the national innovation system and role of universities, incubators in the commercialization of technologies

(ITAP), the Company Directed Technology Development Program (CD), the Venture Capital Program and R&D tax incentives. The financing programs of NIA Technolopolis/Innovation Park are, for example, the Good Innovation Zero Interest Technology Capitalization, the Innovation Cluster Grant and venture capital. The Thai government has encouraged the universities to use these programs to support start-up companies and foster university spin-offs.

Government policies to support university technology commercialization

The Thai government plays an important role in strengthening the innovation system through the national policies. The SMEs in Thailand account for 99.5% of total businesses, employing over 60% of the total workforce.[1] Realizing the importance of SMEs on job creation and economic growth, the government has paid special attention to supporting new start-ups and entrepreneurial ventures. The evolution of government policies to support SME development is shown in Figure 12.2. Interestingly, it can be seen that from 1990s onwards, the Thaksinomics policy is a major policy framework to support entrepreneurship. The policy initiatives since 2000s are aimed at enabling Thailand to transition from middle income trapped economy to higher income economy. Interestingly, the Bank of Thailand has also introduced the Financial Sector Master Plan II (Years 2010–2014) as a national entrepreneurship policy to revive economic growth (supporting and developing entrepreneurs through policy-based institutions including commercial banks and financial institutions). Given the importance of innovation in creating jobs and building economic development, the Thai government has linked science and technology (S&T) with the 11th National Economic and Social Development policies (Years 2012–2016) to support the university research activities and increase utilization of research results.[2] The Thai government has introduced various policies and programs to encourage the creation of new entrepreneurs as well as support the development of technological and innovative capabilities of firms.

The Thai government plays an important role in driving the national innovation system. To strengthen the national competitiveness, the government recently (Year 2009) launched the policy initiatives to enhance its R&D capability and promote technology commercialization through the establishment of national research universities. The government has put prime importance on promoting the university research capability by providing the budget amounting THB 9,450 million (or approximately USD 295 million) for the period of three years to support nine universities being selected as national research universities. In particular, the government through the Ministry of Education has encouraged the creation of the university business incubators (UBIs) and technology licensing office (TLO) to foster the research and innovation for technology transfer and commercialization. Table 12.3 discusses the external and internal factors influencing the ability of universities to transfer technologies from the public to the private market.

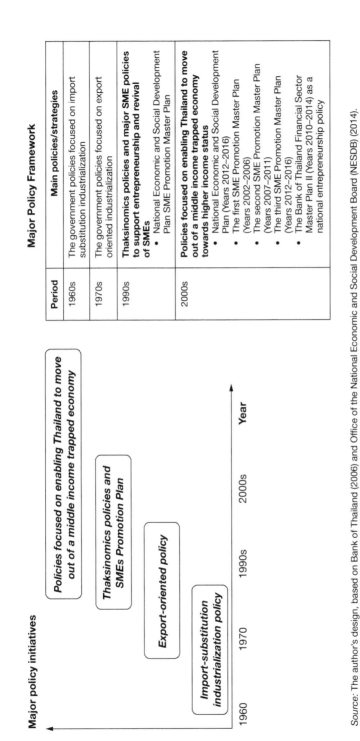

Major policy initiatives

Major Policy Framework

Period	Main policies/strategies
1960s	The government policies focused on import substitution industrialization
1970s	The government policies focused on export oriented industrialization
1990s	**Thaksinomics policies and major SME policies to support entrepreneurship and revival of SMEs** • National Economic and Social Development Plan SME Promotion Master Plan
2000s	**Policies focused on enabling Thailand to move out of a middle income trapped economy towards higher income status** • National Economic and Social Development Plan (Years 2012–2016) • The first SME Promotion Master Plan (Years 2002–2006) • The second SME Promotion Master Plan (Years 2007–2011) • The third SME Promotion Master Plan (Years 2012–2016) • The Bank of Thailand Financial Sector Master Plan II (Years 2010–2014) as a national entrepreneurship policy

Policies focused on enabling Thailand to move out of a middle income trapped economy

Thaksinomics policies and SMEs Promotion Plan

Export-oriented policy

Import-substitution industrialization policy

1960   1970   1990s   2000s   **Year**

Source: The author's design, based on Bank of Thailand (2006) and Office of the National Economic and Social Development Board (NESDB) (2014).

Figure 12.2 Major government policies to support SME development in Thailand

Table 12.3 Factors influencing the ability of universities to transfer technologies from the public to the private market

External factors	Internal factors
• Government policies via the Office of the Higher Education Commission to support the establishment of the university technology licensing office (TLO) in encouraging the transfer of knowledge from the university to industry.	• The university policy on building knowledge and competencies including the intellectual property (IP) policies. The IP policies provide guidelines on the ownership and proceed sharing to encourage protection and utilization of university IPs.
• The national policies to support the establishment of university business incubators (UBIs) via the Office of the Higher Education Commission under the Ministry of Education. The aim of establishing UBIs is to encourage wide use of university research as well as of intellectual properties (IPs).	• The ability to establish university-industry linkages and coordination with the industrial sector (professional networking services provided by TLO and UBIs) to bring academic research towards the commercialization stage.
• The Ministry of Commerce via the Department of Intellectual Property (DIP) introduced policies to support SME intellectual property and innovation.	• The university's ability to provide financial supports in facilitating the TLO and UBI to develop and transfer potential technology for commercialization.
• The Ministry of Industry via the Office of the Small and Medium Enterprises Promotion (OSMEP) enacted SME promotion policies through various programs of grants, venture capital, business matching services.	• Availability of resources and managerial capabilities as well as skills to manage the university TLO, particularly the specialist skills in business negotiation.
• The Office of the Small and Medium Enterprises Promotion (OSMEP) under the SME Promotion Act B.E. 2543 introduced the SME promotion plans as the national policy framework to support SMEs. The SME promotion plans were formulated in accordance with the National Economic and Social Development Plan.	• The ability to decrease inefficient procedures and bureaucratic red tape process of the university TLO and UBI operation in order to enhance the process of technology transfer and commercialize university research.
• The IP system in Thailand is still weak due to lack of clear policy to improve the utilization and commercialization of IPs in the right direction.	• The provision of VC funding support covering various stages of business development particularly the pre-seed stage and the availability of funding support to help successful spin-offs expand their operations or market their innovations.

Source: The author's design.

In 2004, the government, through the Office of Commission on Higher Education (CHE), Ministry of Education, launched the innovation policy of setting up UBIs in attempts to promote academic entrepreneurship. The UBIs are instrumental to support new ventures with entrepreneurial mentoring and advisory services. In addition, the government has enacted the policy initiative of establishing a TLO as a channel for university research commercialization in 2006. The university professors and researchers of the government research institutes provide such mentoring and advisory services. By helping establish the system for transferring knowledge to industry, this would not only generate revenues for the university but also enhance linkages between universities and industries to promote university research commercialization.

University technology commercialization in Thailand

In Thailand, the universities are recognized as the main source of scientific knowledge and research. According to the Scopus database, more than 90% of the research output in Thailand is generated by universities. The government realizes the importance of research as a basis towards national innovative capability and thus launches urgent policies to support universities by endorsing the national research universities in 2009. Particularly, the Office of CHE, Ministry of Education selected nine universities as flagship national research universities to encourage knowledge dissemination and research commercialization (Table 12.4).

Table 12.5 presents a list of universities with intellectual property (IP) management units and TLOs supported by the Office of CHE, Ministry of Education. There are currently 35 UBIs established with 327 cases incubated and 60 new enterprises created.[3] The performance of the national research universities is shown in Table 12.6. The nine national research universities are major universities with strong research capacity in Thailand where the government aims to upgrade them into world-class universities (Figure 12.3). Up to now, there are 10 universities in Thailand with the IP Management Unit and TLO set up in

Table 12.4 National research universities in Thailand

Name of national research universities
1. Chulalongkorn University
2. Thammasat University
3. Mahidol University
4. Kasetsart University
5. King Mongkut's University of Technology Thonburi
6. Chiang Mai University
7. Khon Kaen University
8. Suranaree University of Technology
9. Prince of Songkla University

Source: The author's design, based on University Business Incubators Thailand (2014).

coordination with CHE to promote IP commercialization. The main goal of the national policies to support the establishment of UBIs and TLOs is to open up commercial opportunities for university research which would thereby help strengthen the country's economic competitiveness in the long run.

Table 12.5 List of universities with IP management unit and TLO in Thailand

Name of universities with IP management unit and TLO
1. Mahidol University
2. Chulalongkorn University
3. Silpakorn University
4. Kasetsart University
5. Chiangmai University
6. Khon Kaen University
7. Burapha University
8. Prince of Songkla University
9. Suan Dusit Rajabhat University
10. Rajamangala University of Technology Thanyaburi

Source: The author's design, based on University Business Incubators Thailand (2014).

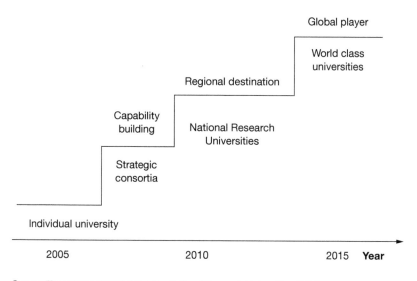

Source: The author's design, based on National Research Universities (2014).

Figure 12.3 Goal of the national research universities in Thailand

Table 12.6 The performance of the national research universities in Thailand

Activities	2011		2012	
	Target	*Output*	*Target*	*Output*
Academic performance				
– Publication	2,008	2,078	1,538	1,145
– Patent	86	124	93	98
Postgraduate education				
– Enrolment of graduates	1,654	2,321	1,061	1,384

Source: The author's design, based on the Office of Commission on Higher Education (2012).

Acknowledging that universities are a central source of knowledge, the Thai government attempts to follow the success of US research universities (the entrepreneurial university model) in driving innovation and economic growth (Etzkowitz, 1983; Clark, 1998; Wong and Singh, 2007). The government sees the establishment of national research universities as the key policy priority in building research capacity and enhancing national competitiveness. Realizing that universities are a major source of knowledge for innovation, the Thai government has tried to encourage faculty and researchers to bring their research results to the marketplace. The Office of CHE, Ministry of Education and Ministry of Science and Technology have encouraged these research universities to undertake research projects focused on solving the problems of the country as well as the problems affecting the industrial sector.

Taking into account the ability of university technology commercialization, the process of technology transfer from university to industry at present is not effective in terms of bringing academic research towards commercialization. During the years 1995–2004, there were 140 patents awarded to the universities but only six of them were transferred to industry, showing the low level of university research commercialization (Krisnachinda, 2009). Although the government has introduced various entrepreneurship policies/programs to support SMEs, the operation of university TLOs is seen as inefficient and bureaucratic, obstructing the process of commercializing university research. Nevertheless, among the universities in Thailand, Mahidol University is an interesting case with outstanding performance in terms of promoting academic entrepreneurship through the technology transfer process. It has set an example of a successful university for other universities in Thailand to follow. The following section will focus particularly on the case study of Mahidol University, one of the national research universities in Thailand and the leading universities in Asia, to understand the process of university technology commercialization.

Case study of Mahidol University

Background and policies governing the university research

Mahidol University is one of the nation's leading research universities with research strengths in medical sciences. The university is also at the forefront in introducing technologies and research results to benefit the Thai society. Mahidol University was top among Thai universities in the Times Higher Education World University Rankings Years 2010–2011 (ranked at 306) and was 61st in the Asian University Rankings Years 2012–2013 by Times Higher Education. Mahidol University originates from Thailand's first hospital, Siriraj Hospital, founded in 1888 and later renamed by H.M. King Bhumibol Adulyadej. The university was named after H.R.H. Prince Mahidol of Songkla, father of H.M. King Bhumibol Adulyadej who is widely regarded as 'Father of Modern Medicine and Public Health in Thailand'. The university currently has six campuses: Phayathai campus, Bangkok Noi campus, Salaya campus, Kanchanaburi campus, Nakhon Sawan campus and Amnaj Charoen campus.

Mahidol University has a vision of becoming a world-class university and the Wisdom of the Land. In achieving this vision, the university has committed in various activities to promote internationalization of education and research. The university is outstanding in scientific and medical research and has distinguished itself as a clinical trial center for examining the effectiveness of vaccines for cholera, rotavirus, poliomyelitis, malaria, varicella, human papilloma virus and human immunodeficiency virus (HIV). The rise of knowledge-based economy has led the role of Mahidol University to focus on dissemination of university knowledge to industry and commercial market. The university has placed a strong emphasis on research activities so as to generate new knowledge from the research base.[4]

The main support programs of Mahidol University providing assistance for the activities of technology transfer and commercialization are the Division of Research Management and Development and the Center for Intellectual Property Management. Mahidol University's Division of Research Management and Development is responsible for establishing the policies governing the conduct of research in the university, research funding and overseeing the management of the university's research programs. Figure 12.4 presents the sources of funding for R&D performed at Mahidol University.

By far, most research funding comes from domestic funding (66%), followed by international funding (17%), government (10%) and the university's own income (7%). The university has adopted a performance-based research funding principle from the Research Council of New Zealand in which each faculty research potential and accomplishments are taken into consideration in addition to merits of the project. Concerning the role of Mahidol University to encourage research undertakings, the university has allocated THB 16,910,000 (or approximately USD 528,438) of its revenue to set up a Central Instrumental Facility (CIF) providing scientific and research equipment to support innovative

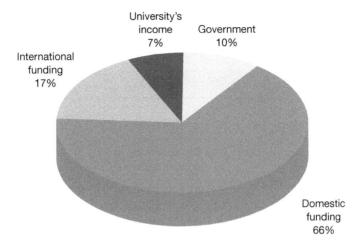

Source: The author's design, based on Mahidol University (2012).

Figure 12.4 Sources of Mahidol University research funding

research. The CIF is presently managed by the Division of Research Management and Development to allow students, researchers and instructors to make use of high-quality instruments for conducting research activities.

The role of Mahidol University in technology commercialization

The Center for Intellectual Property Management was set up by Professor Emeritus Dr. Pornchai Matangkasombut, a former Rector of Mahidol University, to promote commercialization of IP. The structure of Mahidol University Center for Intellectual Property Management (MUCIP) is shown in Figure 12.5. Currently, there are nine staff working for the center.

Table 12.7 shows the proceed sharing policies of the Mahidol University. According to Mahidol University's IP policy and regulations, the university retains ownership of IP rights. The distribution of licensing revenue generated from domestic IP is as follows: 50% of the net income goes to the creator(s), 30% to the university, and the last 20% is evenly split between faculty and the department. For international IP, the benefit to the creator(s) increases to 75% with the rest being divided as follows: 15% to the university, 5% to the faculty and 5% to the department. The policies of license revenue sharing take into account net income after deduction of all related expenses. The net income must be distributed within 60 days of the university's receipt of licensing revenue. Such license revenue sharing provisions aim to provide incentives for creators/researchers in promoting IP performance.

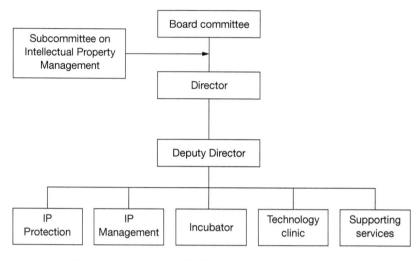

Source: The author's design, based on Mahidol University Center for Intellectual Property Management (2014).

Figure 12.5 Structure of Mahidol University Center for Intellectual Property Management

Table 12.7 Proceed sharing policies of Mahidol University

	Percentage of profit sharing (Domestic IP)	*Percentage of profit sharing (International IP)*
Creator(s)	50%	75%
University	30%	15%
Faculty	10%	5%
Department	10%	5%

Source: The author's design, based on World Intellectual Property Organization (WIPO) (2007).

Mahidol University support programs to enhance and promote technology transfer and commercialization also include Mahidol University Business Incubator (MUBI). The MUBI was created in 2004 and managed under the Center for Intellectual Property Management where the university receives some financial assistance from the Office of CHE, Ministry of Education. The MUBI has set policies focused on supporting start-up companies and projects with commercial potential. Specifically, the incubator provides incubation services to encourage research take-up in the areas of healthcare, medicine, life sciences, medical equipment, biological and biochemical materials. The incubator also provides technology commercialization programs and organizes inventor forums as well as training services to help entrepreneurial start-ups get ready for marketing their innovations.

The MUBI supports high potential projects which could be further developed to be university spin-off companies. The Center for Intellectual Property Management also helps the companies incubated in the MUBI find partners from the private sector who are interested in marketing and licensing to make co-investments. The MUBI supports university faculties, researchers and students to start new ventures from their research outputs/projects. Currently, it receives annual financial support amounting USD 3.09–15.43 from the Office of CHE, Ministry of Education to develop its R&D capacities.[5]

Given the research expertise in medicine, Mahidol University also established the biotechnology pilot plant to support biomedical research and Good Manufacturing Practice (GMP) plant for drug production. The establishment of these pilot plants aims to improve a solid application of potential research in industrial and commercial sectors. The MUBI has organized the Millionnaire Ladder program providing training courses in innovation management, business plan writing and marketing to help the students and graduates learn the knowledge and skills necessary to start their own businesses. The MUBI has also initiated the Open Lab program by facilitating investor access to high potential research projects for further development into commercial innovations. These are the university support programs attempting to bridge the gap between research and commercialization.

Realizing the importance of university technology transfer, Mahidol University has encouraged participation of faculty members in setting up research clusters to expedite research commercialization. Apart from the university research funding, the faculties also obtain external research grants from the government agencies such as the National Research Council of Thailand, Thailand Research Fund, National Science and Technology Development Agency, National Innovation Agency. In particular, the faculties are encouraged to undertake the translational research with the support from Stang Holding Company Limited, a company assuming the role of venture capitalist to provide venture capital (VC) investments to start-ups.

Mahidol University encourages the faculties to undertake collaborative research (integrated research projects) with other institutions. For example, the Mahidol University research staff from seven faculties worked with the staff of the Electricity Generating Authority of Thailand and Chulalongkorn University to develop a database system detailing integrated biodiversity at the Plant Genetic Conservation Area of Srinagarindra Dam. This is an example of collaborative research partnerships between universities and the government sector to produce research outcomes which are beneficial to the communities. Importantly, Mahidol University sees that the academia–government collaboration serves as a necessary mean to strengthen research capacity of each party personnel and support the establishment of research scientist networks. This type of networks not only helps reinforce the body of knowledge in academic research but also gives the faculties practical experiences in applying their academic work to benefit the society which would thereby improve the country's economic competitiveness.

The university policy to support technology transfer activities can be seen from the setup of MUCIP. Figure 12.6 depicts the process of IP management at Mahidol University.

The MUCIP has worked closely with the Division of Research Management and Development to protect the university's IPs and oversee the process of technology transfer. The setup of MUCIP has helped increase the number of university IPs as can be seen in Table 12.8. The Technology Clinic was also set up under MUCIP with the help of the Ministry of Science and Technology in promoting the process of technology transfer to benefit community and for industrial use.

Concerning the role of university in developing spin-offs, Mahidol University has established Stang Holding Company Limited, a venture capital (VC) company to provide VC financing for the start-ups. Stang Holding Company was established in 2005 with a registered share capital of THB 100 million (or approximately USD 3 million). It is a private VC firm set up in collaboration between Mahidol University (providing 60% funding), the Small and Medium Enterprise Development Bank of Thailand (providing 20% funding) and the National Innovation Agency (providing 20% funding) with the aim to increase the commercialization of potential research. The fund provides equity capital to finance projects with commercial potential up to 15% of total project investments (or up to 10% of registered capital and not exceeding THB 20 million (or approximately USD 0.6 million)). Figure 12.7 presents the overall operation of Mahidol University's research commercialization process.

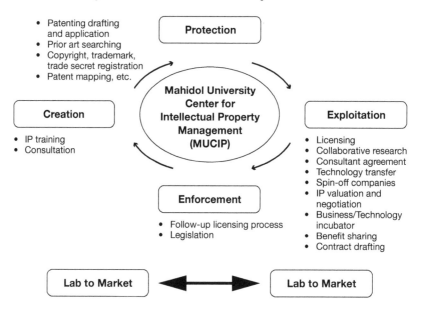

Source: The author's design, based on Mahidol University Center for Intellectual Property Management (2014).

Figure 12.6 Mahidol University's IP management

Table 12.8 IP performance of Mahidol University

	Applied				Approved			
	2009	*2010*	*2011*	*2012*	*2009*	*2010*	*2011*	*2012*
Patent: Thai	33	24	23	39	1	-	2	3
International	-	1	-	-	2	2	1	-
Petty patent	28	20	23	22	12	12	30	19
Copyright	23	29	20	52	17	28	27	49
Trademark	1	-	4	2	-	3	1	4
Trade secret	-	13	1	-	-	13	-	1
Total	85	87	71	115	32	58	61	76

Source: The author's design, based on Mahidol University (2012).

MUCIP and Stang Holding Co., Ltd. serve as mechanisms to facilitate the transfer and exploitation of knowledge. Their operation can be seen as an important link between academia and industry. The MUCIP and Stang Holding Co., Ltd. both support the progress of projects from the research to commercialization stage as indicated by the direction of arrows shown in the figure. Concerning the results of a research project, the research outputs can be divided broadly into two categories: intellectual properties (IPs) and publications. The generation of IPs can help solve production problems or lead to the development of new innovations. The MUCIP will provide assistance on licensing and transfer of technology to the industrial sectors, depending on the technological readiness for commercialization as well as the private sector readiness to purchase IP rights. If it is not in a mature stage for licensing out and needs further development, the Mahidol University Business Incubator (MUBI) would provide incubation services and a broad array of services to improve the commercial potential of technology and help entrepreneurs develop a new venture. The Stang Holding Company would further offer funding support to assist the creation of new business spin-offs.

The successful spin-off companies of Mahidol University are, for example, Go Green Co., Ltd., X-Zell Biotec Co., Ltd., Aclires International Ltd., Xcellerex, Inc. and MU Business Co., Ltd, etc. The university also works with Laddawan Fund Co., Ltd. to set up the Siam Bioscience Co., Ltd. to carry out biomedical R&D which would help Thailand locally manufacture its own drugs and reduce its dependence on importing prescription drugs from other countries. Table 12.9 provides examples of successful spin-off from Mahidol University. The case of Mahidol University has shown that the university plays an active role in promoting university technology commercialization. It also shows that the dynamic interactions and linkages between university and industry are important in supporting the successful process of technology transfer towards commercialization (Etzkowitz, 2002, 2011; Etzkowitz and Leydesdorff, 1998, 2000).

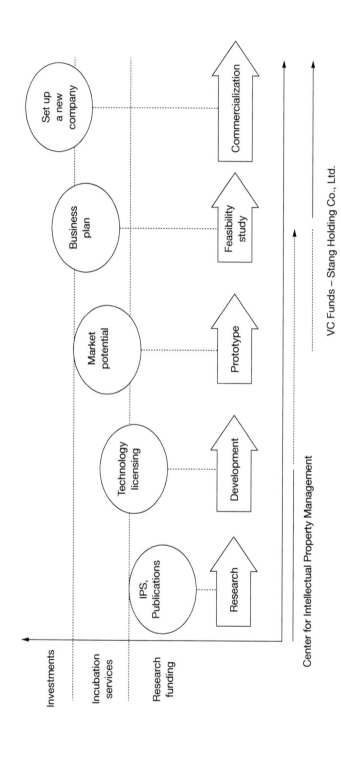

Source: The author's design, based on Mahidol University (2012).

Figure 12.7 The research commercialization process of Mahidol University

Table 12.9 Examples of successful spin-offs from Mahidol University

Name of company	Description
X-Zell Biotec Co., Ltd.	X-Zell Biotec is the first spin-off company from Mahidol University in 2009. The company is based on Thailand Science Park. It is a biotechnology company offering life science products and services including custom conjugation for antibodies, proteins and fluorescent dyes, enzymes and particles, cell culture media, reagents, monoclonal antibodies.
Go Green Co., Ltd.	The company was established in 2009 and based in Nakhon Pathom, Thailand. The company develops and distributes eco-health related products and services. Go Green has developed MosHouse, an innovation which lures and traps disease-carrying mosquitoes. The product is used to control the Aedes aegypti mosquito which causes dengue fever.
Xcellerex Inc.	The company provides proprietary technologies in producing biomolecules and innovative medicines. Xcellerex offers biomanufacturing capacity which helps improve speed and flexibility while also reducing costs in biopharmaceutical manufacturing compared to those of conventional practices.

Source: The author's design, based on X-Zell-Biotech (2014), Stang Holding (2014).

Conclusions

This chapter explores the university technology commercialization and government policies to support transfer and commercialization of R&D in Thailand with a particular focus on the case study of Mahidol University, the leading research university in medical sciences. The government, through the Office of CHE, Ministry of Education, plays an important role in supporting university technology transfer and commercialization. The Thai government recently launched policy initiatives to assist commercialization of university R&D by supporting the setup of incubators and technology licensing offices to foster efficient technology transfer and IP exploitation.

The case study of Mahidol University, a leading research university in Thailand, provides an example of the university playing an active role in promoting research activities and advancing technology-driven innovations towards commercialization. The university has implemented the government policy in building and strengthening research capacity and encouraging innovations through the establishment of Mahidol University Business Incubator (MUBI), MUCIP and Stang Holding Company Limited. The university has R&D excellence in medical science together with policies and procedures to support spin-offs and start-ups. The university has also organized various programs and forums to assist academic entrepreneurship and facilitate technology transfer from university labs to industry. The case of Mahidol University has set an example of being the entrepreneurial university for other universities to follow.

Currently, the Thai government is supportive of university–industry collaboration to encourage IP utilization. However, it is still an early stage of policy implementation. It is a challenging task of the Thai government to place emphasis on R&D investments and strengthen the university–industry relationships. Given the important role of universities in influencing knowledge creation and transfer, the government should allocate more R&D budget to support university research and encourage private sector involvement to bring research results for public use and commercialization (translational research). Further, the government should provide an enabling environment to foster the conduct of research activities such as ease of capital access, provision of financial and tax incentives to encourage VC investments and improve IP exploitation. It is necessary that the universities themselves also need to focus on improving their strengths and working in tandem with the industries based on the strengths of each university for the commercialization of university research results. These policy implications and recommendations would be useful for other economies to better exploit university technologies under the national innovation system approach. The improvement of university technology transfer and commercialization would thereby help drive future economic growth of Thailand.

Notes

1 The rest of the total workforce is mostly employed in the service sector where tourism is one of the most important service industries in Thailand (according to the source data of Office of the National Economic and Social Development Board).
2 Office of the National Economic and Social Development Board (NESDB).
3 Organization for Economic Co-operation and Development (OECD) (2011), OECD Studies on SMEs and Entrepreneurship Thailand: Key Issues and Policies, Paris.
4 The vision of Professor Emeritus Dr. Pornchai Matangkasombut, former rector of Mahidol University.
5 In 2013, the Office of Commission on Higher Education (CHE), Ministry of Education, set up a USD 172 million venture capital (VC) fund to support entrepreneurial start-ups with an aim to create between 5,000 and 10,000 new enterprises annually.

References

Bank of Thailand (2006), *Thailand's Financial Sector Master Plan Handbook*, Bank of Thailand, Bangkok.

Clark, B.R. (1998), *Creating Entrepreneurial Universities: Organisational Pathways to Transformation*, IAU Press/Pergamon, Oxford, New York, Tokyo.

Etzkowitz, H. (1983), 'Entrepreneurial Scientists and Entrepreneurial Universities in American Academic Science', *Minerva*, 21 (2–3): 1573–1871.

Etzkowitz, H. (2002), 'Incubation of Incubators: Innovation as a Triple Helix of University-Industry-Government Networks', *Science and Public Policy*, 29 (2): 115–128.

Etzkowitz, H. (2011), 'Creative Reconstruction: From Isolated Innovation Mechanisms to a Triple Helix Regime', *International Journal of Technoentrepreneurship*, 2 (3–4): 210–226.

Etzkowitz, H. and Leydesdorff, L. (1998), 'A Triple Helix of University-Industry-Government Relations', *Industry and Higher Education* 12 (4): 197–258.

Etzkowitz, H. and Leydesdorff, L. (2000), 'The Dynamics of Innovation: From National Systems and "Mode 2" to a Triple Helix of University-Industry-Government Relations', *Research Policy*, 29: 109–123.

Institute for Management Development (IMD) (2010), *The Institute for Management Development (IMD) World Competitiveness Yearbook*. Available at: www.imd.org (accessed: 31 March 2014).

Institute for Management Development (IMD) (2011), *The Institute for Management Development (IMD) World Competitiveness Yearbook*. Available at: www.imd.org (accessed: 31 March 2014).

Institute for Management Development (IMD) (2012), *The Institute for Management Development (IMD) World Competitiveness Yearbook*. Available at: www.imd.org (accessed: 31 March 2014).

Institute for Management Development (IMD) (2013), *The Institute for Management Development (IMD) World Competitiveness Yearbook*. Available at: www.imd.org (accessed: 31 March 2014).

Krisnachinda, N. (2009), 'Thailand's Experience in Fostering University–Industry partnership', *WIPO development of university–industry partnerships for the promotion of innovation and transfer of technology Thai Report*, World Intellectual Property Organization (WIPO).

Lundvall, B. (1992), *National Systems of Innovation: Towards a Theory of Innovation and Interactive Learning*, Pinter, London.

Lundvall, B. (1998), 'Why Study National Systems and National Styles of Innovation?', *Technology Analysis & Strategic Management*, 10 (4): 407–422.

Lundvall, B. (1999), 'National Business Systems and National Systems of Innovation', Special Issue on Business Systems, *International Studies of Management and Organisation*, summer volume.

Lundvall, B. (2003), *National Innovation System: History and Theory*, Aalborg University, Aalborg, Denmark.

Mahidol University (2012), *Mahidol University Annual Report 2012*, Committee Annual Report, Salaya, Nakhon Pathom.

Mahidol University Center for Intellectual Property Management (2014), *Structure of Mahidol University Center for Intellectual Property Management*, Mahidol University. Available at: www.mahidol.ac.th (accessed: 20 June 2014).

National Research Universities (2014), *Goal of the National Research Universities in Thailand*. National Research Universities, Office of the Higher Education Commission. Available at: www.nru.go.th. (accessed: 20 June 2014).

Office of the National Economic and Social Development Board (NESDB) (2014), *The National Economic and Social Development Plan*. Available at: www. nesdb.go.th (accessed: 20 June 2014).

Organisation for Economic Co-operation and Development (OECD) (2013), *OECD Reviews of Innovation Policy – Innovation in Southeast Asia*, OECD, Paris.

Stang Holding (2014), *Spin-off Portfolio Companies*. Stang Holding, Mahidol University Group. Available at: http://stangholding.mahidol.ac.th (accessed: 25 June 2014).

The Office of Commission on Higher Education (2012), *Statistics on the Performance of the National Research Universities*. Bureau of International Cooperation Strategy, Ministry of Education. Available at: www.inter.mua.go.th (accessed: 23 November 2014).

The World Bank Group (2014), *The World Bank's Knowledge Assessment Methodology*. Available at: www.worldbank.org/kam) (accessed: 25 June 2014).

University Business Incubators Thailand (2014), *Thailand National Research Universities and Business Incubators*. Available at: http:// www.ubi.mua.go.th) (accessed: 12 January 2014).

Wong, P.K., Ho, Y-P and Singh, A. (2007), 'Towards an "Entrepreneurial University" Model to Support Knowledge-Based Economic Development: The Case of the National University of Singapore', *World Development*, 35 (6): 941–958.

Wonglimpiyarat, J. (2010), 'Commercialisation Strategies of Technology: Lessons From Silicon Valley', *Journal of Technology Transfer*, 35 (2): 225–236.

World Bank (2013), *World Bank Data*. Available at: http://data.worldbank.org (accessed: 31 March 2014).

World Economic Forum (WEF) (2010), *The Global Competitiveness Report*. Available at: www.weforum.org (accessed: 31 March 2014).

World Economic Forum (WEF) (2011), *The Global Competitiveness Report*. Available at: www.weforum.org (accessed: 31 March 2014).

World Economic Forum (WEF) (2012), *The Global Competitiveness Report*. Available at: www.weforum.org (accessed: 31 March 2014).

World Economic Forum (WEF) (2013), *The Global Competitiveness Report*. Available at: www.weforum.org (accessed: 31 March 2014).

World Intellectual Property Organization (WIPO) (2007), *Technology Transfer, Intellectual Property and Effective University–Industry Partnerships: The Experience of China, India, Japan, Philippines, the Republic of Korea, Singapore and Thailand*. WIPO Publication No. 928E, Geneva.

X-Zell-Biotech (2014), *X-Zell-Biotech: Spin-off Venture of Mahidol University*. Available at: www.x-zell.com (accessed: 25 June 2014).

13 University technology transfer

The globalization of academic innovation in Russia

Tatiana Pospelova[1]

Introduction

Making the transition to a science-intensive economy is one of the main goals of the Russian government because the prospects for social and economic development in Russia, with its great intellectual and industrial potential, as well as for overcoming the country's reliance on the exportation of raw materials, developing high technology, and maintaining high economic growth rates, depend on it. The country's progress is linked not only to the availability of new ideas and breakthrough technologies but also to the speed with which those technologies are commercialized and turned into new products.

Much recent research is devoted to the problem of the *new role of universities*, which are regarded as being among the key conduits of support for and reinforcement of innovation (Etzkowitz et al., 2000). Along with *education and research*, which are the first two functions of universities, the university has gained a third function, an *entrepreneurial* function, related to the commercialization of the products of research (Slaughter and Leslie, 1997). The entrepreneurial university is the next step after the implementation of a research university model, which will enable a new balance among science, education, and innovation. Facilitating the commercialization and transfer of scientific activity—and thereby technology—is a critical aspect of the entrepreneurial university. Technology transfer in Russia cannot be studied without due consideration for the country's history, especially the regime changes in the twentieth century and the formation of a new country after the breakup of the Soviet Union. The process of establishing a system for transferring technology in modern Russia, however, is only just beginning. Russia has an opportunity to use the effective elements of the Soviet system of technology transfer to build its own up-to-date system. At present, technology transfer has been hampered by several problems, such as the absence of infrastructure and specialists in this area and a weak economy (which has not rebounded since the collapse of the Soviet Union).

This chapter discusses the current state of Russia's efforts to develop technology transfer. Since 2008, Russia has focused on knowledge-based economic development. Universities have been at the center of changes related to technology transfer, and the Russian experience may offer some lessons for other transitional economies (Feige, 1994).

The chapter proceeds as follows. The first section offers a historical perspective on technology transfer in Russia. The second section introduces a structure for our analysis in terms of external (public policy initiatives and infrastructure) and internal (intellectual property rights and human resources policy) factors. The third section discusses current developments regarding technology transfer in Russia at Lomonosov Moscow State University, the Tomsk State University of Management Systems and Radio Electronics, and the Skolkovo and Academpark science parks. The fourth section analyzes the current impediments to the commercialization of technology, both cultural and institutional. The fifth section concludes the paper and offers recommendations for future steps to improve technology transfer in Russia.

Historical perspective and legislation

Technology transfer in Russia can be divided into three stages. The first stage consists of the years after the conclusion of World War II (1945–1985), the second comprises the period of the collapse of the Soviet Union (1985–2008), and the third is the current period (2008–present).

The first stage: The postwar years in the Soviet Union (1945–1985)

The Soviet/Russian model of economic development has historically relied on a system of central planning and politically controlled research. During the Soviet period, all resources were publicly owned and centrally administered. Government authorities planned the volume of production for goods and services and regulated prices. Investment decisions were also made at a central level. One major drawback of a planned economy was its inability to respond quickly to scientific and technological developments, so it could not take advantage of changes that would increase economic efficiency in a timely way.

State control played a critical role in the commercialization of research in Russia. Although large-scale basic research was conducted mainly at institutions that were part of the Academy of Sciences, the practical application of their results was dictated by the state. Research and development (R & D) took place only if it was requested by the industrial and sectoral ministries. Moreover, the products that emerged from such research were created automatically, regardless of economic rationale, as they were under the patronage of government authorities.

One example is in wood products. After the beginning of the cold war, the government decreed the production of some items because of their military application: in particular, different types of cellulose were used in the manufacture of aircraft, ballistic missiles, and so forth. But after the cold war ended, the industry needed to refocus and modernize in order to find its place in both the domestic and international economy.

Several main research fields were established in which the Soviet Union became a leader: defense industry, space exploration, and medicine. The choice of these sectors was directly related to the Soviet Union's goal of becoming a superpower, and world leadership in these sectors was considered strategically important during the cold war. To attain that leadership under the economic conditions in which it started, the country used a five-year plan for national development, devised by the leadership of the Communist Party of the Soviet Union. New technologies in other fields that did not interest the government rarely reached the point of being ready for the commercial market, and efforts to bring the products of scientific research to market were notable for their indecision and an absence of enthusiasm. Although the Soviet Union developed to the point of taking the lead in basic science, it did not succeed in creating an effective mechanism for innovation that could be used for improving general economic conditions. Research teams as well as individual scientists had almost no economic incentives for commercializing their inventions. Thus it failed to close the economic gap that already existed with the developed countries of the West after World War II, and the gap only grew wider. Moreover, government funding began to decline, such that by 1985 the amount of basic research had fallen sharply, and new technologies had almost ceased to be developed.

The second stage: The collapse of the USSR and its aftermath (1985–2008)

The post-Soviet scientific complex inherited many features of the Soviet system, in which university research did not play the main role. The largest volume of applied research was carried out at research institutes and was aimed mainly at strengthening the country's defense capabilities. By the time the Soviet Union collapsed in 1991, 75% of the funds allocated for research had been used to fund projects with a military application. In the 1990s, the number of universities in Russia increased, but the number of scientists decreased significantly, in part because, after the collapse of the Soviet Union, it became legally possible to conduct private business. Because of the declining financing for scientific work, many scientists were forced to engage in work that was unrelated to research. In the 2000s, the financing for scientific research stabilized, and the number of researchers at universities began to grow again (Trofimec, 2013).

By this time, the first pieces of the innovation infrastructure had been established, mainly at leading universities, and they began to engage in transferring technology; in the early 1990s, science and technology parks and business incubators were created in Russia supported in part by universities and government agencies. Because these represented a new initiative in the country, it took time for specialists and society to adjust to the transition to a knowledge-based economy.

During this period, technology transfer between universities and industry took place largely as contract work, so the relationships between developer-professors and companies grew one by one. This model has the disadvantage of instability because it depends on individual personal relationships and it is difficult to scale.

At this stage, institutions of higher education in Moscow, Tomsk, and Zelenograd became examples of contract technology transfer systems, in which the universities became centers for both developing and implementing concepts and created special technical innovation zones for their specific technical specialties in the priority areas of science, engineering, and technology. This was possible because these universities already possessed a strong scientific base and were in the forefront.

Because under Soviet rule the state owned all intellectual property, in the late 1990s problems began to arise with the definition of intellectual property rights (IPR) in a nonstate context. This gap was filled by studying global experience and practice. Two Russian universities, St. Petersburg State University and Ural State Technical University, became members of international associations for university technology transfer (the Association of University Technology Managers [AUTM] in the United States[2] and the ASTP [Association of European Science and Technology Transfer Professionals]-Proton in Europe[3]) of their own volition, not on state instruction. Because they offered an opportunity to study international experience through cooperation with other universities that were members of the associations, these two Russian institutions became regional centers and leaders in the theory and practice of technology transfer.

Currently, these schools are affiliated with the Association of Entrepreneurial Universities of Russia (AEUR) and are among the top ten leading Russian universities with respect to "innovation and entrepreneurship," according to the National Rating of Classical and Research Universities of Russia. Their international experience relates to innovative infrastructure facilities and the construction of the interaction between the various departments of universities. Participation in such events later became a factor in the creation of such institutions as the Center for Technology Transfer and Entrepreneurship, the Center of Innovative Marketing Management, the HR Center, and the Center of Innovation Activity at Ural State Technical University. The university is involved in a close partnership with industry through the establishment of jointly equipped centers for the development of competence and specialized laboratories for training and production. One example of this cooperation is the educational, scientific, and innovative complex organized at the Institute of Radio Engineering and Information Technology, the largest electronics manufacturer and scientific development and automation production center in the Urals.

The third stage: Current period (2008–present)

Since 2008, the Russian government has been paying more attention to the development of innovative activities in the country, as illustrated by remarks by the then-president of the Russian Federation, Dmitriy Medvedyev, to the Federal Assembly:

> In the last century, through extreme efforts our agrarian country was transformed into one of the most influential industrialized nations of the time;

it led the creation of a number of advanced technologies of the time such as space, missile, and nuclear. But in a closed society with a totalitarian political regime, we could not maintain that position. In the twenty-first century, our country again requires comprehensive modernization. Instead of an economy based on basic raw materials, we will create a smart economy, producing unique knowledge and new things and technologies. New technologies are the key to Russia's transition to a new technological level and gaining a leading position in the world.

Specific actions designed to help the Russian economy develop and related to the growth of innovation are outlined in the "Conception of Long-Term Social and Economic Development of the Russian Federation Until 2020," approved by the government (Mau and Kuzminova, 2012). Thus, at that time, the foundations were laid at the government level for integration between scientists, the state, and the business community.

Since 2009, the Russian government has paid particular attention to the creation of technology transfer centers on university campuses. The main goal of a technology transfer center is to carefully protect an invention and bring it to market. The functionality of many technologies developed at universities is not clear. Taking all this into account, the specialized centers of technology transfer should work toward further technological improvement, the continuation of research and accumulation of new knowledge, collaboration with big companies, and conducting joint research (Engovatova, 2013).

Analytical structure

Technology transfer is a complex process that involves interaction between educational institutions and industry. Internal and external factors play a critical role in its implementation within the university.

Factors external to the university

Public policy and infrastructure

Public policy aimed at transformation of the university culture and the development of cooperation between universities and business mainly includes the following.

1   *Change in the types of institutions of higher education and the designation of universities as important to the government.* The most promising universities were selected to receive additional funding. Lomonosov Moscow State University and Saint Petersburg State University were both awarded special status as the oldest universities, with over 200 years of history, and were the only ones in Russia to be included in the Shanghai Academic Ranking of World Universities. The goal of the giving them additional funding is to create conditions that allow them to become involved in innovative activities

and therefore build regional centers of economic and social growth and focus on certain industrial sectors. The key goal is the development of interaction between institutions of higher education and industry by improving technology transfer and the work of scientific organizations and promoting the development of research, science, and infrastructure for institutions of higher education (Pospelova and Ivashchenko, 2013).

2   *Approval of federal law no. 217-F3 of August 2, 2009, "On the Application of Amendments to Certain Legislative Acts of the Russian Federation Concerning the Issues of the Establishment of Business Companies by Government-Financed Academic and Educational Institutions in Order to Practically Apply (to Introduce) the Products of Intellectual Activity."* The main purpose of this law is to provide actual adoption by industry of the results of research and technology activities, paid for with state funds and legally owned by government-financed institutes for science and education. These initiatives are quite significant for the commercialization of the products of research and technology activities at institutions of higher education. In the past, companies were not allowed to be founded on university campuses. Now, if any office at the university owns intellectual property, its staff is permitted to pursue commercialization of it, and these companies enjoy a number of advantages, such as tax breaks. The only condition is that the university is permitted to have no more than one-third ownership in the resulting new enterprise. One example is the company Lactocore, which was established at Moscow State University, where it continues to operate.

3   *Government support for development of the infrastructure for innovation at federal institutions of higher professional education (by decree of the government of the Russian Federation no. 219 of April 9, 2010).* The decree stipulates government support for the development of innovative infrastructure at educational institutions. These policies have the potential to build, equip, and modernize universities in Russia, and the resulting measures contribute to the development of collaboration between universities and the private sector and attract leading scientists to Russian universities.

One striking example of this support is the government's funding of the appointment in 2013 of Kendrick D. White as vice-rector for innovation at the largest university in Nizhny Novgorod, Nizhniy Novgorod State University. White, who has an MBA in finance and international business from Northwestern University, has more than twenty years' experience in innovative entrepreneurship and promotion of technological projects in Russia. At present, it is too early to talk about the results of White's work, as he was appointed to this position only in late 2013. He is engaged in to implementing the strategy of university development based on the concept of an entrepreneurial university.

Over the past five years, the Russian government has amended some laws related to information technology in the hope of improving efficiency in the commercial use of technology developed with state funding. At present, laws are being amended in the following areas of state policy with respect to technology transfer in Russia, which are critical to the further development of technology transfer:

- the formation and improvement of conditions for the most effective utilization of innovations developed using state funding
- the formation and development of technology transfer infrastructure,
- support for entrepreneurship.

Lack of funding and motivation at many universities has hindered the opening of technology transfer centers and the hiring of specialists in this field, so these amendments should prove helpful.

These changes should help initiate the development of technology transfer. Public funds are designed, first, to help motivate the development of universities and infrastructure. Then, universities should develop their own technology transfer. For its part, the government has taken a big step by passing changes in the legal rights of universities.

Development of innovative infrastructure

The presence of an effective innovative infrastructure that will allow universities to take on their new entrepreneurial role is an important factor at this stage. This infrastructure includes basic elements such as business incubators, science parks, centers for technology transfer and commercialization management, and technology parks (Ivashchenko and Engovatova, 2012). An analysis of innovative infrastructure at Russian universities indicates that the necessary elements of innovative infrastructure (at minimum: a business incubator, technology park, and a technology transfer center) are present at only five universities in Russia: the Moscow Institute of Physics and Technology (a state university), Samara State Aerospace University, National Research Tomsk State University, Bauman Moscow State Technical University, and Southern Federal University (Engovatova, 2013).

From the Russian university's perspective, two main activities are associated with the development of technology transfer: (1) establishing collaboration between businesses and universities; and (2) assistance with the creation of spin-offs (Kornyakov et al., 2012). Universities are starting to work with companies, in cooperation with the Russian Technology Transfer Network (RTTN). Established in 2002 as part of an initiative by two innovation centers in Obninsk and Koltsovo, this network now brings together more than fifty innovation centers from forty regions in Russia and member countries of the Commonwealth of Independent States specializing in technology transfer. The network supports national and regional innovation infrastructure, which allows them to effectively disseminate technological information and help find partners in the implementation of innovation. Members of the network provide services on technology transfer to clients in their region (innovative companies or scientific and educational organizations).

The innovation centers all use the following four-step business process.

Step 1: Identification of the client's potential for engaging in the transfer of technology. This consists of a detailed examination of the client organization to determine its technological competencies and needs. Typically, this occurs in the course of an audit, which should result in an action plan to achieve technological improvements, the purchase of the necessary technology, and the acquisition of experience or know-how in pursuance of those objectives.

Step 2: Compilation of technological profiles. Technological profiles (of the technology request or offer) are compiled for the purpose of exchanging information between the centers and members of the network. The profiles are intended to generate interest and introduce the available technology or explain the specific technological needs of a company to potential partners and others. RTTN uses an adapted form of the technological profiles compiled by of the European Enterprise Network, which is the largest information and consultancy *network* in *Europe and supports* small business, in particular with respect to innovation.

Step 3: Search for partners in technological cooperation. A search is conducted to identify partners in the creation and development of technology using a shared database of technological profiles. Additional opportunities for finding foreign partners arise from RTTN's participation in the European Enterprise Network (EEN), which allows members of the Russian network to share information with EEN's membership spanning fifty countries.

Step 4: Negotiation and agreement. The innovation centers provide support in negotiations between the client and potential partners up to the conclusion of a contract. They help them understand the obligations normally required of both sides, according to international norms. Moreover, they act as middlemen if the client and potential partners are having trouble agreeing to terms.

Factors internal to the universities

Internal factors include policies related to intellectual property rights (IPR) and human resources. Most of the scientific inventions created at traditional Russian universities came out of a rich cultural heritage. Lomonosov Moscow State University is more than 250 years old, and it is famous for its inventions; the Moscow Physical-Technical Institute is more than sixty years old. A shift from being a traditional educational institution to an entrepreneurial one takes time. Many universities are not ready for commercialization of scientific knowledge, since they are unfamiliar with the process. Furthermore, they do not have a clear understanding of all the benefits that accrue from the successful launching of technology outside the university.

   This situation is changing due to the fact that more institutions of higher education have become involved in technology transfer through holding specialized conferences, eminars, and webinars, and new associations are beginning to form. For example, building on the knowledge gained by membership in international organizations, Russian universities joined with the Skolkovo Fund to create the Association of Entrepreneurial Universities of Russia (AUER) in 2011.[4] AUER members have the opportunity to share experiences, including those relating to technology transfer, when they meet annually at a conference to discuss the results and strategic development plans. They also have access to online resources and a quarterly magazine and hold online meetings and webinars.

Intellectual property rights (IPR) policy

The Commentary on the Patent Law of the Russian Federation, promulgated on September 23, 1992, stated that all IPR belong to the university. However, the state has the right to set special conditions in contracts with the university, and, in turn, the university can set its terms in contracts with scientists there. If an invention is created under the contract, the inventor receives a reward. In addition, all rights to inventions created by academic staff at the university also belong to the university (Bichkova, 2011).

In reality, after many scientists working at the university realize that they have created worthwhile technology, they open their own companies outside the university and register the inventions in their own name. In Russia there is no law to prevent this, which is why many inventions created at the university are commercialized without university involvement.

Human Resources Policy

The process of transferring technology is rather complicated, requiring a team of specialists. Universities complain about the lack of infrastructure and people capable of clearly translating the language of researchers and developers to industry and vice versa. Now Russia is going through a process of learning and inviting foreign specialists, techno-brokers-entrepreneurs-scientists who are at the intersection between the academic world (developers, academics) and industry. The main task for the specialists is the promotion of successful practices in the commercialization of technology, the formation of strong connections among universities, research institutions, and industries, and organization of professional training in technology transfer.

Because Russia suffers a shortage of specialists in the field, universities there that focus on the entrepreneurial aspect of technology transfer have to confront problems such as a lack of practical skills among technology transfer department specialists and a lack of continuing education programs for academic staff, postgraduate, and undergraduate students in the creation of small innovative companies and cooperation with existing businesses. Today professors with practical experience in leading a business work for many technology transfer departments.

Current environment for technology transfer

First results: Two institutions of higher education and two science parks

A program for developing a knowledge-based economy, in which attention is focused on technology transfer, has been in place since 2008. The program includes a list of activities projected to take place until 2020; however, it has already yielded preliminary results with respect to contributing to effective technology transfer.

Lomonosov Moscow State University (MSU)

The MSU campus is home to fifteen schools and forty faculties.[5] The university is considered to be at the forefront in Russia regarding the humanities and the sciences. The university was designated as having national importance, which drives it to continuously engage in innovative activities as a principal institution of higher education in Russia.[6] The strategic importance of innovation is just beginning to be understood in the country, and the first important steps toward this understanding have already been taken.

In 1992, MSU and the Ministry of Industry created MSU Science Park, part of the organizational structure engaged in technology transfer today. Today there are more than fifty parks of this kind in Russia. The main tasks for the MSU Science Park,[7] one of the first technology parks in Russia, include the following.

1   The creation of positive conditions for MSU departments planning to spin-off companies as well as scientists, undergraduate and postgraduate students, and alumni, who are planning to open start-ups and become entrepreneurs in high technology.
2   The creation of a positive environment for the existing small and medium-size innovative companies that are interested in mutually profitable collaboration with universities and the use of their human resources and scientific potential.

Since 2004, MSU Science Park has offered annual educational programs to encourage students at various schools to create innovative projects, which thus far have been mainly in IT, bioengineering, pharmaceuticals, and medicine. Those who complete the program have an opportunity to take part in a two-week educational training program at MIT in the United States, organized by Global Innovation Labs,[8] in which the participants can present their projects to international experts. The Foundation for Assistance to Small Innovative Enterprises in Science and Technology plays an important role at MSU Science Park, by providing space for companies, attracting mentors, and offering consulting services. At present, MSU Science Park is home to more than fifty companies organized by university graduates and scientists from MSU and other universities.

Some of the entrepreneurs go to MSU Science Park from the MSU accelerator, which was established in 2010 as part of the university's program aimed at supporting innovative entrepreneurship by helping to speed up companies' entrance to the market. The accelerator provides its residents with initial investments, access to university infrastructure, such as office space and lab equipment, help in the design of a business model, and, most importantly, an opportunity to turn an idea into a working business in the course of four months.

Special attention is paid to interdisciplinary projects that require the involvement of students from different departments as well as project managers from both universities and companies. Such programs created at universities include the three-month program Formula for Success, IT Formula, at MSU Science Park. The teams consist of undergraduate and postgraduate students in the humanities and the sciences at MSU who work with faculty members in the Department of Economics and at MSU Science Park as well as guest lecturers. The program finale is a demo day, to which business angels are invited. The finalists have an opportunity to attract investment, and the winners receive a chance to become residents at the MSU business incubator, which also opened in 1992. In the past few years, participation in such programs has become obligatory for postgraduate students in the Department of Business. Their course of study includes a final project, and part of their final grade is a performance review. Continuing education courses are very popular, as undergraduate and postgraduate students can take them in different departments. In particular, the "Introduction to Business" course at MSU has high attendance mainly because of the lectures given by famous entrepreneurs.

MSU Science Park and the MSU business incubator have already shown good early results. Over $3 million in investment has been attracted. The market evaluation of resident companies at the MSU business incubator is over $11.5 million, which is a good sign for the future.[9]

MSU has been completing projects on the creation of subdivisions promoting the development of entrepreneurship and scientific and production integration since 1990. At present, MSU promotes the development of technology transfer in many ways.

- It funds a Chair of Innovation Economy (2007).
- It has a business club founded by the economics faculty (created in 2009).
- It created a laboratory for innovation business and entrepreneurship called the innovationStudio (created in 2010).
- It offers a program for schoolchildren called PRE.incubator, supported by the Chair of Innovation Economy (created in 2011).
- It opened a Center for Innovation Consulting (created in 2011).
- It hosts the Center for National Intellectual Reserve and the fund National Intellectual Development (TSNIR/FNIR) (created in 2012).

Tomsk State University of Management Systems and Radio Electronics (TUSUR): Regional experience

TUSUR is a leading regional institution of higher education, one of the first results of attempts to create entrepreneurial universities. The main task for the contemporary industrial university in Russia is actively participating in economic development not only nationally but regionally. The strategic purpose of TUSUR as an industrial university is to create a high-performance cultural, educational, scientific, and innovative environment to provide efficient training for specialists in science-intensive high-technology sectors of the economy.

The university is particularly interested in entrepreneurial activities to create innovative technologies at the university and in their commercialization. The university plans to develop the ability to reach world standards in the development of science, engineering, and technology. Thus it is making a real contribution to the creation of a center for education, studies, and designs in Tomsk and to the transition of the national economy to innovation-based development (Kobzyeva et al., 2012).

In addition, TUSUR takes part in international conferences (e.g., the annual Triple Helix International Conference) and has been a member of the Triple Helix Association in Russia since 2012. In October 2012, TUSUR hosted an AEUR conference in Tomsk on the "Development of Entrepreneurial Universities as Backbone Elements of Territorial Innovative Clusters."

TUSUR has had a business incubator since 2004, and its successful members include 3dbin, Sectar, Comprel, Medical Electronics, and Biotok. Among future entrepreneurial activities planned at TUSUR are the development of international cooperation and assistance in the promotion of start-ups in international markets. The International Center California-Tomsk promotes promising developments among Tomsk scientists in electronics and information technology in the U.S. market. The International Center Toronto-Tomsk cooperates with Canada and focuses on power electronics and software development. The Russo–Canadian company TechBridge intends to promote and sell products and services produced at TUSUR. The company's activities are connected with the provision of services such as offshore software development, web design and web development, and mobile development by specialists from Tomsk to the Canadian market. Engineers from Tomsk are considered strong professionals; their services are cheaper than those of their counterparts in Canada. Moreover, that work in the IT industry may be performed remotely.

TUSUR plans to develop cooperation with the cluster "Information Technology and Electronics of the Tomsk Region." This cluster is on the Russian government's list of fourteen Russian pilot clusters, which underlines the importance that it places on strengthening the ecosystem.

Experience in constructing innovation centers: project Skolkovo and Academpark

Project Skolkovo is another initiative of the Russian government. In February 2010, the then-President Dmitriy Medvedyev announced the creation of a modern scientific and technological innovation center and invited the leading scientists at Russian institutions of higher education to go there. The innovation center will be financed primarily from the national budget (Kommersant, 2010). Skolkovo concluded a cooperation contract with MIT, so there is an exchange of experience between the two universities through internships for students and researchers. This collaboration helps to attract foreign professors. Among the priority goals of the project are:

1   creating a core of major international innovation companies in Skolkovo;
2   making a powerful university the heart of Skolkovo: this would be a source of personnel and technology for creating start-ups.

Those engaged in research at Skolkovo are exempt from the value-added tax and taxes on land and property until their annual sales volume reaches $35 million and total profits $10 million. Research at Skolkovo concentrates on five priority areas: energy, information technology, communications, biomedicine, and nuclear technology.[10] In the future, it will significantly affect the propensity of academics to spin-off companies.

Skolkovo is still being constructed; indeed, more time is needed before such a tremendous project can be expected to produce results. For comparison, let us consider a smaller but similar project, the Novosibirsk technology park Academpark, which began to be built in 2008 and opened in 2010. The government allocated to it a total of about $166 million (of which $70 million was for modernization of infrastructure).

According to the Academpark website, the following are some of the first results of the project as of 2013.

• Number of registered resident companies: 240.
• Number of projects: 600.
• Number of jobs created: 7,300.
• Main businesses: Internet and software.
• Ten of the best resident companies over the period 2008–2014 showed an increase in turnover of 534%.
• Academpark reached the breakeven point by the beginning of 2014.

Recent progress in spin-off creation

According to statistics on spin-off activity from January 1, 2012, to January 1, 2013, the number of jobs created grew from 3,360 to 4,216, an increase of 25% year on year. In all, 1,000 spin-offs were created at universities during this period. These companies have been established in a number of regions in which the strongest universities of Russia are concentrated: Moscow, St. Petersburg, Republic of Tatarstan, Nizhny Novgorod, and Tomsk.

Eighty percent of these companies operate in three priority areas: information and telecommunication systems (29%); energy efficiency, energy conservation, nuclear power (28.3%); and environmental management (21.5%). Most of the staff are professors, followed by scientists, graduate students, and undergraduate students. According to a survey conducted by the Center of Research and Science Statistics of Moscow, the average age of employees over the period decreased from 38 to 37.35 years old as of January 1, 2012 (Abaev, 2012).

Spin-off companies experienced significant growth. Large Russian cities, especially Kazan, Moscow, and Saint Petersburg, showed active involvement by entrepreneurs, students, investors, and other concerned parties. Target conferences and meetings take place, with some international companies, such as Angel Hack and Start-up Point, pursuing active innovation development. In recent years, leading Russian companies such as Yandex (a leader in the Russian search engine market) and Kaspersky Lab successfully launched summer schools where students are able to demonstrate their projects and ideas. Universities produce more and more spin-off companies, mainly due to organized business incubators. The chief executive officer of the Zet Universe start-up, Danila Kornev, who is in charge of the development of an intuitive and attractive visual interface for information management and search with the help of an endless desktop for Windows-based laptops or tablet computers, stated [in an interview with this chapter author in September 2014]:

> Having had the experience of working for Microsoft and Google, I decided to start my own project. In 2010 my team got into one of the first incubators in Moscow at the National Economic Academy. Analyzing the experience of those years, I can say that the program didn't help us much except in providing us with office space. However, you cannot imagine how motivating it was for us to work with people who believed in us and pushed us forward. Only four years ago, there were not many young people setting up start-ups in Moscow. In this respect, the opportunity to use the university infrastructure helped us a great deal.

Current difficulties and low efficiency of technology transfer in Russia

The distinctive character of Russian universities is due to the historical peculiarities of the Russian Federation, where entrepreneurship emerged only about twenty years ago. This legacy has left them with some problems that need to be addressed in order for technology transfer to advance.

First of all, Russia needs to develop an entrepreneurial culture. The most important factor in creating an entrepreneurial university is the presence of an entrepreneurial culture, which encourages academic staff to evaluate research results from the perspective of their commercial and intellectual potential. Employees at technology transfer offices can change the attitude of the university researchers and professors with respect to the results of their research by encouraging their interest in the practical implementation of their product. This can happen only if those employees can find business partners and correctly explain to the professors all the advantages of commercializing their inventions and the research created at the university.

One successful example is the Innovation and Technology Center at Nizhny Novgorod State University. In addition to providing assistance to inventors and researchers in the development of business and patent strategies, the center works closely with business partners by offering consulting services to Russian and foreign entrepreneurs and industrial structures interested in using new technologies and product launches. The staff of this department consists of professors who are lawyers or have experience in venture capital-financed business.

Changing the culture is the responsibility of the university, where the next generation of specialists and entrepreneurs will be trained. This process is complicated by the presence of a number of university staff who are supporters of traditional methods and are opposed to innovation. It will take time to educate the population, so that it can learn about all the benefits of the knowledge-based economy. Their adaptation to a new entrepreneurial culture will lead to changes everywhere in the future.

In addition, it is critical for universities to take whatever steps are necessary to form an entrepreneurial culture. Both professors and students need to understand the benefits that can be reaped from the commercialization of intellectual property.

Second, one impediment that arises in developing that culture is that researchers and developers usually do not know the market and often have little idea about how their research results can be transformed into a marketable product. This is because, under central planning in the Soviet Union, developments in science contributed to new technologies in areas such as military and space, which were run by the state. Although the Soviet Union was first worldwide in basic science, it could not create an effective mechanism for implementing innovations in the private sector, where such developments could lead to an improvement of the economy and society in general. Because the country was closed to the outside world for a long time, scientific societies and individual scientists did not have economic incentives for commercializing their inventions, which created a development gap between Russia and Western countries that continues today.

Third, most Russian businesses are not interested in the implementation of new Russian technologies or financing scientific research. For the most part, they are oriented toward short-term results, and only a few take into consideration the long-term goals of the company—mainly due to their mistrust of the government, corruption, and bureaucracy (Pudkova, 2011). In addition, the country faces significant obstacles in introducing innovative products to local and foreign markets, developing a legal framework, and protecting IPR.

Business spokespeople claim that the problem is not only the lack of interest but the fact that Russian technologies are not ready for commercialization. One solution to this is the development of small innovative entrepreneurs who can prepare innovative products for sale—not merely written papers on the subject but actual business plans.

Fourth, the venture capital industry in Russia is quite weak. Because it is still immature, it has a low tolerance for risky projects, which innovations in Russia often are. The regulations to which many existing funds are subject aim to provide some protection and lower risk, with the success of the projects considered only secondarily. Moreover, Russian investors sometimes demand more than 40% ownership of a company in exchange for their participation, which puts a damper on business development. In recent years, this tendency has been changing, but rather slowly.

Fifth, some problems are also associated with underdevelopment of the legal framework for innovative activity, of the stock market, of the services market, and a lack of infrastructure. There are problems with corruption in the country, which has led to an outflow of international investment.

Conclusion

Over the past seventy years, university technology transfer in Russia has undergone several phases of transformation. Under central planning, all activities related to the commercialization of science and scientific knowledge were controlled by the state. Since 2008, a transformation associated with building a knowledge-based economy has been taking place, including the development of human capital, interaction between science and industry, promotion of the development of small innovative business, such as start-ups and spin-offs, as well as the development of the venture capital industry and improvement in the investment climate. Improving the efficiency of technology transfer is one of the priority tasks for both institutions of higher education and the government. In 2008, the development of technology transfer was included in the government's long-term strategy on economic development in Russia until 2020. This strategy is in the process of implementation. Today, it is possible to enumerate the first positive results in the development of technology transfer in Russia and a number of urgent issues for the country to confront.

Given the experience of the advanced industrialized countries, the development of innovation infrastructure has an important role in technology transfer, a long and costly process. Russia is paying attention to this issue, establishing infrastructure, such as science parks and business incubators. However, the interactions between these institutions have come in fits and starts. Improving efficiency and management is a key and urgent task for Russia, as is addressing the lack of an entrepreneurial culture, a negative attitude toward entrepreneurship among the scientific community at universities that is a legacy of the Soviet past, bureaucracy, and political instability. In early 2015, the Russian economy began to face a crisis, in no small part from rising interest rates and the imposition of trade sanctions by a number of countries, which have a negative impact on the development of innovation in general. In this regard, the universities' strategy with respect to technology has changed. That has caused universities to shift their focus from international to domestic economic activities in order to continue their technological development. From now on, universities, in collaboration with state agencies, are concentrating on modernizing and strengthening the domestic economy, going it alone if necessary.

Despite these problems, some positive changes have taken place, such as amendments in legislation, the establishment of innovative infrastructure, growth in start-up and spin-off activity, encouraging results at Moscow State University and TUSUR, and the initiation of the Skolkovo project. The Russian people have a clear understanding that economic development cannot continue to be based only on the extraction of natural resources. One alternative is the development of a "smart" economy, based instead on the commercialization and implementation of innovation in the production of goods and services. The imposition of sanctions has led a number of industries to raise the question of engaging in import substitution, in part to address the anticipated increase in requests from private companies that universities develop things that will be impossible to buy abroad due to those sanctions. This will contribute to local market development.

Technology transfer from universities to the private sector is beginning to receive more attention from corporations. Russian companies are beginning to work with universities and thus indirectly with Intel and Microsoft. In recent years, major Russian IT companies, such as IBS, Yandex, and Kaspersky Lab have entered into partnerships with universities to conduct joint projects. This offers Russian universities an opportunity to understand the needs of companies and present technology transfer in the proper perspective.

In conclusion, further change will be necessitated by the many problems Russia still faces. The economic crisis creates some complications but also a chance for Russia to develop an economy built on innovation. Building a knowledge-based economy takes many years, even under more favorable conditions. Among those that have been successful, Israel took twenty to twenty-five years to build its economy into its current high-tech powerhouse. In view of Russia's territorial dimensions and special circumstances, it has a long way to go before it can construct innovation ecosystems with effective technology transfer.

Notes

1 Tatiana Pospelova is a PhD student at the School of Economics, Lomonosov Moscow State University. Her main research activities concern the theory of the Triple Helix and the possibility of implementing this concept in Russia. E-mail: pospelova_t@mail.ru.
2 www.autm.net.
3 www.astp-proton.eu.
4 http://marchmontnews.com/Technology-Innovation/Central-regions/17860-Association-Entrepreneurial-Universities-Russia-created.html.
5 MSU's website, www.msu.ru/info/struct/#inst/.
6 Action plan to implement programs to improve competitiveness ('roadmap') of the Federal State Autonomous Educational Institutions, 2009, http://ria.ru/edu_crisis/20091021/189919384.html.
7 Scientific Park of MSU website, www.sciencepark.ru/ru/about/.
8 Global Innovation Labs website, www.innovationlabs.net.
9 MSU business incubator website, http://inmsu.ru/ru/ob-inkubatore/.
10 *Eureka Annual Review*, 2011.

References

Abaev, A.L. (2012) 'Centers of forecasting of scientific technological development as a modern element of innovational infrastructure of universities', *Bulletin of Moscow State Academy of Business Administration Series: Economy* 6: 15–23 [in Russian].

Bichkova, O.E. (2011) 'Sustainable development of entrepreneurship in the field of higher education', *Modern Scientific Research* 1: 17–20 [in Russian].

Clark, B. (2004) *Sustaining Change in Universities: Continuities in Case Studies and Concepts*, Berkshire, UK: Open University Press.

Engovatova, A. (2013) 'Organizational models of innovation infrastructure at Russian universities', PhD dissertation, Moscow State Lomonosov University [in Russian].

Etzkowitz, H., Webster, A., Gebhardt, C., and Cantisano Terra, B.R. (2000) 'The future of the university and the university of the future: Evolution of ivory tower to entrepreneurial paradigm', *Research Policy* 29 (2): 313–330.

Eureka Annual Review 2013. Available at: www.eurekanetwork.org/c/document_library/ get_file?uuid=5de379b9-1c28-49b0-bbef-f71a49f2de0d&groupId=10137/.

Feige, Edgar L. (1994) 'The transition to a market economy in Russia: Property rights, mass privatization and stabilization', in Gregory S. Alexander and Grażyna Skąpska (eds), *A Fourth Way? Privatization, Property, and the Emergence of New Market Economics*, New York: Routledge, pp. 57–78.

Ivashchenko, N.P., and Engovatova, W.W. (2012) 'Contemporary tools of the innovative policy of the state as concerns Russian higher education institutions', *MIR* (Modernization. Innovation. Growth.) 3: 46–54. Available at: http://istina.imec.msu.ru/ publications/article/3412738/ [in Russian].

Kobzyeva, L.V., Pudkova, V.V., and Uvarov, A.F. (2012) 'Experience of the interaction between TUSUR and institutions of development of Russia', *Innovative Russia* 3, 11 (169): 57–59 [in Russian].

Kommersant. 2010. 'The state will invest 54 billion rubles in the center "Skolkovo"'. Available at: www.kommersant.ru/doc/1482479/ [in Russian].

Kornyakov, M.B., Ruposov, V.L., and Zvezdin, A.V. (2012) 'Directions of development of innovation activity of R&D of RSTU', *Bulletin of Irkutsk State Technical University*, 68 (9): 266–270 [in Russian].

Mau, V.A., and Kuzminova, Y.E. (2012) *Strategy-2020: New Model of Growth—New Social Policy. Final Report on the Results of the Expert Work on the Actual Problems of Russia's Social Economic Strategy for the Period Until 2020. Book 1; Under Scientific Edit*, Moscow: 'Delo' Publishing House of Ranepa [in Russian].

Pospelova, T. and Ivashchenko, N. (2013) 'The process of the formation of entrepreneurial university in Russia', *Triple Helix Association Journal Helice* 2 (2): 14–18.

Pudkova, V.V. (2011) 'Development of cooperation between the university and government in generation of hi-tech business', *Innovations* 5 (4) 37–42 [in Russian].

Regnum. (2013) 'On MSU territory there will be a scientific technological cluster "Vorobjevi Gori"'. Available at: www.eurekanetwork.org/c/document_library/get_ file?uuid=a78cc883-c513-4601-bc00-fa047d68956e&groupId=10137/ [in Russian].

Slaughter, Sheila, and Leslie, Larry L. (1997) *Collective Bargaining in Higher Education*, Baltimore: Johns Hopkins University Press.

Trofimec, V.E. (2013). 'Conditions of professional work of young scientists in national science (according to the date of social research). Available at: http://charko.narod.ru/ tekst/cb7/tro.html [in Russian].

14 The role of institutional characteristics in knowledge transfer

A comparative analysis of two Italian universities

Federica Rossi, Claudio Fassio &
Aldo Geuna

Introduction

Although academics in Italian universities have a long tradition of interactions with industry, especially in applied fields such as engineering and chemistry, most university institutions have begun to formally acknowledge the importance of knowledge transfer, and to establish dedicated infrastructures to support it, only since the late 1990s. Italian policymakers' interest in promoting interventions to support university–industry knowledge transfer is also relatively recent. Empirical studies provide a mixed picture, with a small group of institutions heavily engaged in institutional knowledge transfer, but the majority barely involved. These studies also provide evidence of sustained interactions with businesses outside of the institutional university set up, which are not included in institutional statistics on university–industry knowledge transfer. Following a general overview of the university–industry knowledge transfer system in Italy, this chapter focuses on a comparative case study of the two universities (University of Torino and Politecnico of Torino) based in Torino, the capital city of the Piedmont region in North-West Italy, to explore contrasting models of knowledge transfer engagement.

The chapter is structured as follows. The next section provides a brief overview of the Italian university system and the recent literature on knowledge transfer by Italian universities, and the impact of institutional factors in particular. The following section introduces the comparative case study, describing the two universities and comparing their involvement in knowledge transfer. Italy is characterized by a relatively late institutionalization of knowledge transfer activity, and a very important role of formal and informal channels that bypass the university institutions (Bodas Freitas et al. 2013). In the fourth section we analyze the views of companies and industry investors on the transfer of knowledge from these two universities. Based on two original datasets, we highlight the factors that facilitate knowledge transfer from the perspectives of companies and industry inventors in the same region as the two universities. The final section concludes with a discussion of the differences between the approaches of the two universities to knowledge transfer.

Italian universities' knowledge transfer activities

In 2013, there were 96 university institutions in Italy. These included 76 traditional "bricks and mortar" universities, 11 virtual universities providing distance learning courses, six schools for advanced post-graduate studies, and three universities specialized in teaching the Italian language and culture to foreign students. Despite the system's formal homogeneity (universities are the only institutions authorized to award bachelor level and higher degrees but were granted some degree of autonomy from central government during the 1990s), there are remarkable differences among Italian universities. They have different histories,[1] traditions, and cultures, and different relationships with their local economies. The system includes both public and private institutions. The public university system expanded substantially between 1960 and 1990 but most of the universities established since the early 1990s are private institutions (Rossi 2009). Universities also differ greatly in terms of size (the system includes a small number of large universities and a larger number of small and medium-sized universities) and the mix of disciplines taught (on average, larger universities are more diversified and smaller ones are more specialized – Rossi 2009).

While several attempts have been made to introduce criteria for allocating funds to reward high quality research and knowledge transfer, the largest share of government funds continue to be distributed to universities on the basis of historical costs, with some small corrections to account for the number of enrolled students, exam completion, and past research performance. Historically public universities have had little incentive to diversify their income by commercializing their research and teaching activities. In 2009, only 1.1% of university research and development (R&D) was funded by business, compared with 6% in the US, 8% in Spain, and 14.3% in Germany (Geuna and Sylos Labini 2013).

The importance of private collaborations between academics and industry

The relatively small share of university R&D funded by business may not provide an accurate picture of the extent of university–industry knowledge transfer in Italy. The figure of 1.1% accounts only for business-funded R&D performed with the formal involvement of university institutions. Academics in Italy tend to interact with business without the involvement of the university, and recent evidence suggests that a relevant share of knowledge transfer activities is informal, or formal but not organized through the university (Bodas Freitas et al. 2012).

Muscio (2010) analyzes 197 Italian engineering and physics departments in 2007, and finds that most knowledge transfer activities involve collaborative and contract research, consulting, sale of patents and royalties, researcher mobility to and from departments, and "soft" forms of transfer such as participation in events organized by companies, conferences, joint supervision of graduate students, and personnel exchanges. Almost half of these collaborations are initiated directly between companies and individual professors, with no involvement of intermediate actors. If third parties are involved these are usually other universities and/or research centers, and other companies; only 20% of cases involved a university knowledge transfer office (KTO).

Evidence from industry confirms that a large share of the collaborations between academics and industry bypass the university institution. Based on a survey of a representative sample of industrial firms in the Italian region of Piedmont, Bodas Freitas, Geuna and Rossi (2013) find that direct, contract-based interactions between academics and industry researchers are as frequent as research contracts mediated by the university institution. While institutional interactions mostly involve large firms which vertically integrate R&D activities, small firms prefer direct personal interactions involving an open innovation strategy. This suggests that direct collaborations with university researchers allow firms that lack material and social/cognitive resources, to interact with a university in order to benefit from knowledge transfer.

The importance of interactions not mediated by the university institution is highlighted also by studies of academic patenting. The share of business-owned academic patents (i.e. patents with at least one academic in the list of inventors) is a rough indicator of the importance of collaborative activities that do not involve the university institution since businesses tend to claim ownership of patents generated in collaborative research and particularly if these activities are funded by industry with no direct institutional involvement of the university. Data for the period 1994–2001 collected by Geuna and Rossi (2011), suggest that in Europe, most academic patents (50%–80%) are business-owned (Figure 14.1). Della Malva et al. (2007) confirm that most (72%) Italian academic patent applications filed at the European Patent Office (EPO) between 1994 and 2001 were assigned to companies, while Lissoni and Montobbio (2012) show that the share of business-owned academic patents in Italy in the period 1995–2001 is comparatively higher than in France, the Netherlands, or Denmark. The situation has not changed substantially in recent years. As a result of legislation introduced in 2005, Italy is one of only two countries in Europe (the other being Sweden) where academics enjoy the so-called "professor's privilege" – that is, they own the intellectual property for any inventions emerging from their publicly funded research activities. However, because of the high costs of patent filing, most academics transfer these rights to the university institution,[2] or in the case of research carried out with industry, to the collaborating companies. If the research is industry-funded, the contracting company generally stipulates ownership of the rights to any resulting intellectual property. Therefore, although the share of university-owned patents has increased in all countries over time, in Italy this increase has been due mainly to a decrease in the share of patents owned by government research institutes, with business-owned academic patents remaining very important.

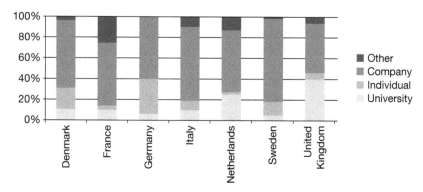

Figure 14.1 Shares of patents with at least one academic inventor, according to ownership (university ownership, individual ownership, company ownership, other ownership), 1994–2001

Public policies supporting university–industry knowledge transfer

Italy lacks coordinated and effective public policies to support universities' knowledge transfer. The responsibility for science, innovation, and technology policy is split between central and regional government. Central government supports and coordinates pre-competitive research, and provides generic incentives such as R&D tax credits (OECD 2011); regional governments implement policies designed to support local businesses through the provision of services and/or grants, and other funding. Interventions aimed at developing a knowledge transfer infrastructure have been fragmented. The first publicly funded science and technology parks date back to the early 1980s but it was mainly in the 1990s that a variety of other structures were created: EU-funded Business Innovation Centers, development agencies, special agencies of the chambers of commerce, technology centers, and others (Muscio and Orsenigo 2010). There are numerous centers that support technology transfer and innovation in different ways; however, most are small, not specialized, poorly integrated, and vary greatly in the services offered, their business models, and their involvement in technology transfer activity (IPI 2005). This contrasts with the situation in countries such as Germany and Sweden, where effective, publicly funded KTOs have been set up at regional level (Sellenthin 2006).

The development of an infrastructure for university–industry knowledge transfer in Italy

As Italian universities cannot rely on a solid external infrastructure to support their knowledge transfer activities, they have developed internal structures to manage their interactions with businesses, and to support research commercialization and the creation of spinoff companies. However, these efforts are recent: in most cases, the organizational structures to facilitate knowledge transfer were not set up until the 2000s. Most KTOs were established between 2001 and 2008,[3] with growth concentrated especially in 2004 to 2006. According to NetVal (Network per la Valorizzazione della Ricerca Universitaria, Italy's main association of university technology transfer offices), in 2011, 59 of the 61 Italian universities surveyed had a formal KTO (NetVal 2013). Figure 14.2 shows that Italian KTOs are much younger on average than those in the other European countries surveyed except Ireland (ProTon Europe 2012).

In the same period, most universities formulated internal policies to regulate interactions with business. Baldini, Fini, and Grimaldi (2015) study the 64 Italian universities with science, technology, engineering, and mathematics (STEM) departments. They report that in 2000 none had spinoff, patenting, or consultancy policies but by 2007, 60% had at least one of these initiatives in place. Most university knowledge transfer policies are fairly similar, with less prestigious universities emulating the policies of their more prestigious competitors (Baldini et al. 2010).

The KTO system in Italy is immature, and the variety of organizational forms is limited with most structures focusing on a narrow set of activities. The most common structures are patent filing and management offices, Industry Liaison Offices and incubators to support university spinoffs (Muscio 2010). Most of these structures serve a single university, are publicly owned, and are managed by a university professor (Muscio 2010). KTOs in Italy tend to be smaller (see Figure 14.3) than those in most other European countries, with the exception again of Ireland (ProTon Europe 2012), and this small size, according to international evidence,[4] is associated with lower efficiency.

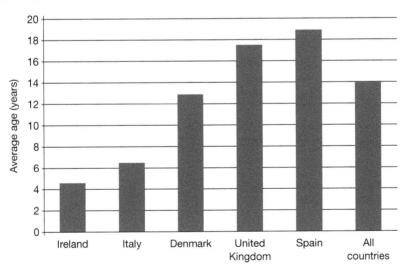

Figure 14.2 Average age of KTOs, 2011

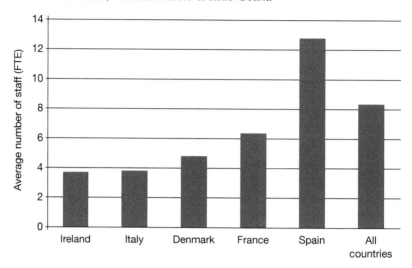

Figure 14.3 Average number of staff of KTOs (FTE), 2011

Almost half of the 61 Italian KTOs included in the NetVal (2013) survey are linked to, or hold equity in, a science park, and/or an incubator. Most KTOs see intellectual property management as their main function, followed by support for spinoff companies, and licensing. Management of collaborative research and contracts with industry are less important but still relevant, while provision of continuing professional development courses, management of research funds, management of seed capital funds, provision of technical services, and management of science parks or incubators are much less frequent (NetVal 2013).

Italian universities' abilities to engage in knowledge transfer appear very skewed, with the best knowledge transfer performers doing significantly better than the rest. The best five performers have almost twice the ratio of technology transfer staff to academic staff than the remaining universities, and their average patent stock, number of licensing contracts, and licensing revenues are much higher (NetVal 2013).

Several recent studies highlight some basic characteristics of Italian universities, KTOs, and university researchers which promote interactions with industry. The following are the most relevant.

1   *Scientific excellence.* Research quality is a very important determinant of the likelihood of interactions with industry. Sciacca (2012), using panel data for 69 Italian universities in 2006–2009, found that research-oriented universities – those that are ranked higher for scientific productivity, very large universities, and technical universities ("politecnici") – have a larger share of research funding from industry. Muscio and colleagues (2013) found that business funding to Italian departments is positively affected more by these departments' academic research performance, which provides a quality

signal to industry, than by the presence of a KTO (Hewitt-Dundas (2012) presents similar findings for the UK). Abramo et al. (2009 and 2011) found that the number of Italian universities' collaborations with industry is positively influenced by the size of the university, the scientific excellence of its academics, and the proximity of collaborators. However, there are differences across disciplines: a separate analysis on a specific field, pharmacology, suggests that scientific excellence does not play a significant role.

Matricano et al. (2013) found that the likelihood of creating a university spinoff in Italy increased with the quality and size of the university's academic staff (number of research projects, share of projects coordinated by the university, and number of tenured academics), and differed according to disciplines (biotechnology and engineering are particularly likely to generate spinoffs). Similar relationships are reported in several international studies such as O'Shea et al. (2005) for the US, and Caldera and Debande (2010) for Spain.

2   *Institutional size.* Bruno and Orsenigo (2003) suggest that a critical mass of researchers is needed to improve the ability of Italian institutions to interact with firms. Institutions with more research staff not only have more resources but also enjoy greater prestige and higher visibility, and have more efficient procedures for the establishment and management of collaborations (Muscio and Nardone 2012). Several international studies suggest that the size of the university is positively related to the level of technology transfer (Belenzon and Schankerman 2009), measured in terms of amount of private research funds (Von Tunzelmann and Kraemer Mbula 2003), number of interactions with companies (Bruno and Orsenigo 2003; Landry et al. 2007), and spinoff creation (O'Shea et al. 2005). However, Muscio (2010), investigating engineering and physics departments in Italy, found that the size of the university did not substantially affect the interaction of the department with business.

3   *Policies and incentives.* Muscio, Quaglione, and Vallanti (2013) provide evidence that limiting the amount of money that researchers can earn from consulting and contract research, and increasing the university's overhead fees have a negative effect on participation in these activities by Italian engineering and physical sciences departments. Baldini, Fini, and Grimaldi (2015) focus on a subset of 64 Italian universities with STEM departments and find that having policies in place to regulate consultancy, patenting, and spinoff creation increases academic entrepreneurship. This is in line with international evidence. For example, Caldera and Debande (2010) find that Spanish universities' adoption of clear rules for dealing with conflicts of interest increase the number of R&D contracts and the amount of R&D income, while university regulation of researchers' participation in contract research has the opposite effect. Technology commercialization activity is shown to benefit from well-defined licensing contracts (Jensen and Thursby 2001; Macho-Stadler et al. 2007), higher royalty shares for academic

inventors (Lach and Schankerman 2004), and the inclusion of patents and licenses in the criteria for promotions and tenure negotiations (Geuna and Muscio 2009), while optional disclosure and unclear intellectual property rights policies have been shown to lead to conflicts over ownership and poor KTO performance (Fisher and Atkinson-Grosjean 2002).

4   *Size and quality of KTO.* Baldini, Fini, and Grimaldi (2015) find that having a KTO, and in particular running more professional technology transfer operations (affiliation to a professional technology transfer association and staff trained in technology transfer), increases academic entrepreneurship in Italian universities. Muscio (2010), using original data from interviews with 197 university departments in Italy, finds that, while the establishment of a KTO per se does not increase the frequency of university–industry interactions, KTOs that are managed by knowledge transfer professionals rather than academics, are more involved in mediating university–business interactions (Siegel et al. (2003) report similar results for the US). Nosella and Grimaldi (2009) use data from a survey of 43 Italian universities in 2005 and find that the presence of a KTO, on its own, does not affect the rate of spinoff creation but that the number of technology transfer staff, the number of services provided by the KTO, and the KTO's relationships with external organizations make a positive difference. Algieri, Aquino and Succurro (2013), using data on 58 Italian universities in 2009, find a positive effect of KTO's resources (financial and human) on the rate of spinoff creation. Fini et al. (2011), study Italian academic spinoff companies and find that the existence of both institutional and regional infrastructures to support technology transfer facilitates the creation of spinoffs, however the marginal effect of institutional infrastructures on productivity decreases in contexts where regional support mechanisms make a positive marginal contribution to productivity. That is, in highly supportive regional innovation systems, the contribution of institutional infrastructure is less important.

Several international studies emphasize the importance of KTO staff competences and experience (e.g., Friedman and Silberman 2003; Markman et al. 2008; Lockett and Wright 2005; Siegel et al. 2003). However, studies of UK and European contexts find that KTOs generally lack both scientific expertise and business skills and capabilities (Geuna and Nesta 2006; Chapple et al. 2005), and are of variable quality (Lambert 2003), which is in line with recent evidence from the NetVal (2013) survey.

A comparative case study: The University of Torino and the Politecnico of Torino

In order to illustrate different models of university engagement in knowledge transfer activities, we present a comparative analysis of the two universities based in Torino, the capital of the Piedmont region in North-West Italy. These institutions share the same socioeconomic environment, and operate within the same legal and regulatory framework but differ in origin, history, size, specialization, and institutional mission. A comparison of these institutions allows us to explore the relationship between institutional characteristics and the nature of these universities' involvement in knowledge transfer.

A brief overview of the two universities

The University of Torino, which is medieval in origin (founded in 1404), has 27 departments covering a wide range of disciplines including humanities, social, natural, and medical sciences. Compared with the average Italian university, the University of Torino's undergraduate and post-graduate education provision is oriented more towards the social sciences and less towards science, humanities, and medicine (Geuna et al. 2009). Based on data from the Italian Ministry of Education (MIUR), at the end of 2012 the university had approximately 63,000 enrolled students and employed almost 2,000 tenured academics (more than 3,000 if temporary contracts are included), and just over 1,900 permanent and temporary administrative and technical staff. The University of Torino is one of ten Italian universities that enroll more than 50,000 students.[5] The Politecnico of Torino was founded in 1859 and includes 11 departments, focused on architecture and engineering. At the end of 2012, its student enrollment was almost 29,000 and it employed just over 800 tenured academics (more than 1,000 including temporary contracts), and almost 900 permanent and temporary administrative and technical staff. Despite being a specialized technical university, the Politecnico is larger than about 75% of Italian universities in terms of enrolled students. The large numbers of students per academic staff in these universities is in line with the Italian average, and is one of the highest in Europe (Geuna and Rossi 2015).

The incidence of PhD students in the student population at the Politecnico of Torino (2.8%) is higher than the national average (2.2%) and higher than the University of Torino (1.8%). A more obvious indicator of research intensity is the scientific productivity of the university's academics, measured for example, in terms of publications per researcher. However, data on academics' publications aggregated by university or by department are not collected systematically. Moreover, since there are significant differences in publication practices across fields, the two universities are not easily comparable. According to the ISI Science Citation Index (expanded) data for the period 1995–2001, the University of Torino was ranked 12th for scientific productivity among the 31 universities with a medical school, while the Politecnico of Torino had the second highest index of scientific productivity among the three Italian politecnici, after the Politecnico of Milano (Conferenza dei Rettori delle Università Italiane 2002). Data from the Aquameth database (Daraio et al. 2011) built on ISI data for the same period, suggest that the number of publications per tenured academic staff at the University of Torino compared to the average for other large universities, is higher for the technical and medical sciences, and lower for the natural sciences, the humanities and social sciences. In terms of research impact (citations per researcher or per publication), the University of Torino is ranked third among universities with a medical school, while the Politecnico of Torino is ranked second among the politecnici (Conferenza dei Rettori delle Universita Italiane 2002). Aquameth data indicate also that the University of Torino has a particularly high number of citations per publication compared to other large universities. Both universities are relatively better positioned in technical and scientific disciplines than in social sciences and the humanities.

Scellato, De Rosa, and Riva (2007), using ISI Science Citation Index (expanded) data for 2005, provide more detailed information on the scientific production of these two universities. In 2005, the Index included 600 articles published by Politecnico researchers and 1,453 articles published by university researchers.[6] Almost 50% of the Politecnico's publications were in technology, engineering, and computer science, while almost 50% of the university's publications were in medicine, biology, biotechnology, and pharmacy. Both institutions had a sizeable share of publications in the physical sciences. Researchers from the Politecnico participated on average, in smaller collaborations (in most subject areas the University of Torino has a higher average number of co-authors, and average number of different institutions per publication) but collaborated more often with foreign institutions and were more frequently first authors. In most subjects, the Politecnico's publications were more interdisciplinary (greater average number of different subject categories per article).

The ability to secure competitive public research funds is another indicator of university research strength. Data for the period 2000/01–2004/05 (Daraio et al. 2011) show that the Politecnico attracted a high level of competitive research funding per tenured academic staff, higher than the national average and the other politecnici. The figure for the University of Torino was lower than the national average and other large universities. This is confirmed by data from Consiglio Nazionale per la Valutazione del Sistema Universitario (2008), which show that in 2006 the amount of competitive research funds per tenured academic staff was over €90,000 at the Politecnico, and over €58,000 at the university. This difference can be explained by the university's above-average share of staff in social sciences (research fund allocations in this field are usually lower than in the natural, technical, and medical sciences) and by the particularly low level of research funds obtained by the university in these subjects (Comitato di Indirizzo per la Valutazione della Ricerca 2006).

The two institutions' knowledge transfer infrastructures and policies

The University of Torino has a small, relatively new infrastructure to support knowledge transfer, focused almost entirely on patenting and spinoff activities. The university's KTO (Settore Brevetti e Trasferimento di Conoscenze) was set up in 2001. In addition to providing training for academic staff related to intellectual property issues, the office is involved mainly in managing patent applications and licensing. The University of Torino introduced a formal intellectual property policy in 2003 (updated in 2009). If the academic inventor agrees to transfer the economic rights to exploitation of their invention to the university, the university pays all the costs of the patenting process, from a special central patenting fund and a matching contribution from the inventor's department. The academic is entitled to 50% of any profits from the commercialization of his or her invention, the remaining 50% being shared between the patenting fund and the department or research center to which the academic is affiliated. In 2003, the university also issued a formal policy on spinoff companies which entitles the university to a minority stake (between 5% and 49%) in any spinoff companies created to exploit intellectual property held by university staff. In 2006, it set up an incubator (a joint venture with three local government bodies), to host university spinoffs in the chemical, pharmaceutical and biotech fields. The incubator provides office and laboratory space at reduced rentals, and financial support for the purchase of equipment.

Company-sponsored research and consultancy contracts are another important channel for knowledge transfer. The University of Torino's Research Office deals with these contracts. Any intellectual property emerging from contracts funded, fully or partially, by private companies, is usually assigned to the business partner. The Research Office also manages research projects funded by national and international government bodies.

The knowledge transfer activities of the Politecnico are managed through several structures, the oldest of which is its "Ufficio contratti", which currently employs about ten staff. While the office deals with patent applications,[7] licensing, and spinoffs, its main activity historically has been management of company-funded research and consultancy contracts (Cuttica 2012). The Politecnico published its first intellectual property policy in 2001; the most recent one (2007) contains similar provisions to the university's, with academics having the right to assign the intellectual property of their inventions to the Politecnico in exchange for the latter covering all patenting expenses. Half of the profits from commercialized inventions are assigned to the inventor, with the remaining 50% going to the Politecnico (10% to the academic's department or research center, 40% to the KTO to support patenting expenses). The Politecnico has had a spinoff policy since 2003; the most recent one was published in 2012 and stipulates that the university should have an equity stake of between 5% and 40% in spinoff companies set up by its staff (a broad category that includes current students and recent alumni). Career-related incentives have been included to encourage staff to invest their time in the creation of spinoff companies (possibility to switch to a part time academic post or to take a sabbatical in order to work in the spinoff without this affecting career progression). Most spinoffs are hosted in the Politecnico's incubator, I3P, which was set up in 1999 and is currently the largest university incubator in Italy. Like the University of Torino's incubator, I3P is a joint venture with local government bodies and local organizations.

The Politecnico's knowledge transfer infrastructure also includes other components, such as two project management offices (one for projects funded by national structural funds, and the other for European Union funded projects), a contact point for businesses (Innovation front end), a venture capital hub launched in 2007, with an office at the Politecnico representing 27 Italian and international venture capital and business angel funds, and a Business Research Centre project, launched in 2008 which promotes the localization of company research centers on the Politecnico campus. This last initiative has resulted in several multinational companies (including General Motors, ST Microelectronics, Indesit, Avio, Pirelli, Prima Industrie) establishing research units in the Politecnico.

A study by Rolfo and Finardi (2014) compares the university and the Politecnico of Torino in terms of research personnel attitudes to knowledge transfer. The authors collected detailed data on the individual research laboratories' research projects, and studied how scientists transferred them to the commercial sector by publicizing them on two technology transfer portals. They infer that in the University of Torino, knowledge transfer activities are driven by the involvement of departments rather than individual scientists, while the reverse applies to the Politecnico. Moreover, in the university, knowledge transfer initiatives appear to be concentrated in the hands of laboratory directors, while at the Politecnico these activities are more diffused and laboratory directors are more often collaborators in projects than project leaders. This suggests that the knowledge transfer culture is different in these two institutions, and that knowledge transfer initiatives are more concentrated and hierarchical in the university and more diffused and egalitarian in the Politecnico.

Engagement in knowledge transfer by the two universities

We consider patent filing and revenue from patenting and licensing activities, creation of spinoff companies, contract research and consulting, to compare the knowledge transfer activities of the university and the Politecnico of Torino. Data on the output from these knowledge transfer channels is collected by the university institutions. This does not cover all the knowledge transfer activities of these institutions. For example, it does not include all the interactions with the public sector, the media, and the general public and specific communities or groups which are especially important for the social sciences, arts, and humanities. It also does not include education-related knowledge transfer activities (joint supervision of graduates, industry support for PhD students, or university–industry personnel exchanges). In addition, many interactions between academics and external stakeholders take place outside institutional channels (Bodas Freitas et al. 2012).

Filing of patents and revenue from patenting and licensing activities

Patenting activity at Italian universities has intensified in recent years (Baldini, Grimaldi and Sobrero, 2006). Italian academics can retain the intellectual property rights to their scientific discoveries but the costs of patenting are prohibitive for an individual and most academics transfer these rights to their institutions. In addition, since the early 2000s, universities have more actively pursued the commercialization of research results. In 2012, the Politecnico of Torino had a portfolio of 172 patents, 44 dating from the six years between 2001 and 2006 and the remaining 128 filed in the six years to 2012. Since then, patenting activity has slowed and several patents (19) have been abandoned. The University of Torino's patent portfolio has also increased significantly, and in 2011 included 95 patents, 40 filed since 2010 (in 2001 the university only held four patents). In 2011, the University of Torino filed 12 patents and the Politecnico filed 27; the Italian average was 6.2 (NetVal 2013) (see also Figure 14.4).

The revenues from licensing in Italy are very skewed, with the five best performing universities accounting for more than half of all licenses and 95% of all licensing income in 2011 (NetVal 2013). While Italian universities registered an average of 1.3 licenses and earned €8,100 from licensing activity, the top five universities had 6.6 licenses and earned €61,400 from licensing. Of the 95 patents held by the University of Torino, 22 have been licensed representing an average of 8.1 patent applications and two licenses per year, in the period 2001–2012 (Università degli Studi di Torino 2012). The average number of patents filed by the Politecnico in the period 2001–2008 was ten per year and the average number of licenses per year was 2.25 (Politecnico di Torino 2008).

Despite the recent increase in university patents, the share of academic patents granted to companies is likely to remain high. Torino hosts the research centers of several large companies which historically have engaged in collaborations with researchers at the Politecnico, as well as several private and public research institutions to which numerous academics from the Politecnico and the University of Torino are affiliated: academics are not required to notify their university employers about inventions realized in the course of their research activity carried out at these institutions or to share the proceeds from their sale.

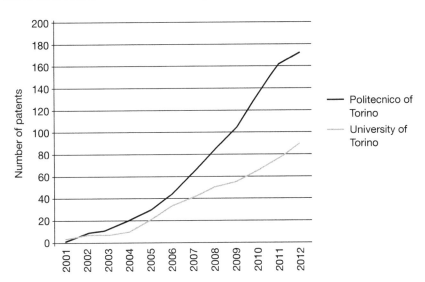

Figure 14.4 Cumulative number of patents filed by the Politecnico and University of Torino since 2001

Spinoff activity

The most recent NetVal (2013) survey identified 1,082 companies active in 2012, spun-off from public research conducted in universities and public research organizations. Of these, 87% were established in the period 2002–2012 (96 were established in 2011). The five most active universities and public research organizations in terms of spinoff creation are responsible for almost 30% of these spinoffs, with the Politecnico accounting for 5.7%. The Politecnico is the most active creator of spinoffs among Italian universities. In January 2014, the number of companies hosted by the I3P incubator since its establishment in 1999 was 156, of which 85 had already left the incubator, 30 had closed down, and six had been acquired. These companies, which specialize mainly in information and communication technology, engineering, and industrial technology, also include start-ups not spun off directly from research carried out at the Politecnico; the number of active Politecnico spinoffs is 62 (NetVal 2013). In 2011, the I3P incubator launched an incubation program for digital and new media companies which has attracted 59 such projects. The 2013 UBI Global Benchmark Report on 150 spinoffs in 22 countries ranks I3P as fourth in Europe and 11th in the world based on a set of performance indicators (I3P 2014).

The University of Torino has seen a substantial increase in the number of spinoffs: 25 of the 27 spinoffs established between 2001 and 2012 were established after 2007. Seven of the 27 spinoffs active in 2012, had received an equity stake from the university, and 13 were hosted in the university's incubator. The incubator includes a total of 19 companies employing 133 staff and accounting for 12 patents.

Contract research and consulting

The importance of private financing for university research has increased for all Italian universities. Between 2001 and 2009, the share of financing received from the Italian Ministry of Education (MIUR) dropped from 73% to around 63%, while there was an increase in income from tuition fees (from 10.7% to 12.7%) and in funding from other sources (which includes contracts with public bodies, businesses and charities) (from around 12% to almost 18%) (Geuna and Sylos Labini 2013).

At the University of Torino, third-party contracts[8] for research, consultancy, and services amounted to €14,577,472 in 2012 (down from €18,178,221 in 2010). Of this, approximately €12,055,000 was for research activities, and 24.6% of the university's overall research funding came from external (i.e. non-ministerial) sources (Università degli Studi di Torino 2012). In 2011, third-party contracts for research, consultancy and services provision by the Politecnico amounted to €20,886,325, almost half of the total research funds from external sources. Third-party contracts have increased in number, but increased only slightly in value since 2011 (Politecnico di Torino 2012). The amount of third-party funding per tenured academic is slightly more than €25,000 at the Politecnico, and slightly more than €7,000 at the university.

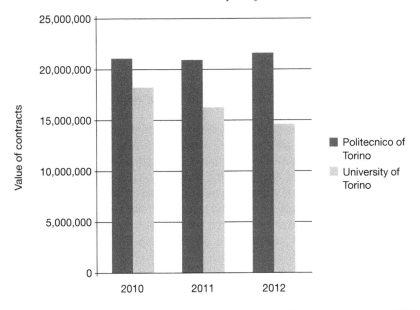

Figure 14.5 Value of Politecnico and University of Torino third-party contracts, 2010–2012

The perspective of companies and industry inventors on interactions with regional universities

To further explore differences in the knowledge transfer processes of the two universities, we investigate what drives companies' and industrial inventors' choices of collaborator. We rely on two original surveys conducted in 2008–2009, one addressed to companies and the other to inventors. All those surveyed were based in Piedmont, that is, in the same institutional, social and economic setting, which allows us to control for some of the determinants of different types of interactions.

The UIPIE questionnaire was administered in autumn 2008 to a sample of 1,058 representative firms in the Piedmont region; we obtained 1052 valid responses. The sample was developed and validated by the local chamber of commerce, which administered the questionnaire with its quarterly regional economic foresight survey (Bodas Freitas et al. 2013). Of the 1,052 companies that responded to the survey, 100 stated having collaborated with a university institution in the previous three years. Of these, 83 had collaborated with at least one of the two universities in Torino: 17 companies had collaborated with the University of Torino, 55 with the Politecnico of Torino, and 11 with both universities.

Compared with the 72 companies that collaborated with other universities, the 28 that collaborated with the University of Torino were significantly more likely to belong to the food industry, and significantly less likely to belong to textiles, transportation, or other manufacturing. They were also significantly less likely to have an R&D department. Compared with the 34 companies that collaborated with other universities, the 66 that collaborated with the Politecnico of Torino were significantly less likely to belong to the food or chemical industries, and significantly more likely to belong to the mechanical or other manufacturing sectors. They were also larger on average although this difference is only weakly significant.

Some differences emerge also with respect to the nature of the collaborations. Companies were asked whether their collaborations with university institutions were aimed at R&D, provision of services to support the firm's production activities (e.g. safety and quality testing and analysis), or support for the firm's business development via organizational, management, logistics, marketing, or legal consultancy. Compared with the companies that collaborated with other universities (72), those that collaborated with the University of Torino (28) were significantly more likely to pursue a greater number of different objectives. Compared with the companies that collaborated with other universities (34), those that collaborated with the Politecnico of Torino (66) were significantly less likely to engage in collaborations to provide organizational, management, logistics, marketing, or legal support.

Eighty-nine respondents stated that although they did not collaborate with a university institution (they had not signed a contract with either a KTO, a department, or the university), they had contracts with individual academics (private contractual relationships), that is, almost as many companies as those that collaborated with the university institutions. However, due to space limitations, we could not collect more detailed information about these interactions through the UIPIE survey. Private contractual relationships were investigated in more detail in the PIEMINV survey.

The PIEMINV questionnaire was administered in autumn 2009 and spring 2010 to the population of inventors with a Piedmont address, that had applied for an EPO patent in the period 1998–2005, which included some 4,000 patents and 3,000 inventors (Bodas Freitas et al. 2014). We were able to identify 2,583 valid addresses for company inventors and obtained 938 valid responses from questionnaires (response rate 36%). After eliminating responses from inventors employed at public research institutions at the time of the invention (for which previous information was not available), we were left with 915 observations.

The questionnaire was designed to investigate various aspects of university–industry interactions and to enable quantitative measurement of the local universities' contribution to the invention process. Additional information (number of employees, revenue, legal status, industry) on the firms employing the inventors was collected from the CERVED database of Italian company accounts. Further information on company size was collected for firms with non-Italian ownership and firms not present in the CERVED database. Finally, information was collected on inventors' patents.

Inventors were asked to indicate which universities they collaborated with, and how often. Of the 815 inventors who responded to this question, 570 stated that they had collaborated with at least one university (through any channel) in the previous two years; 36 inventors had collaborated with the University of Torino, 305 with Politecnico, and 146 with both.

Table 14.1 shows that the Politecnico of Torino is ranked first for interaction frequency, followed by other Italian universities. The other two Piedmontese universities (Torino and Piemonte Orientale) are less important, although there is a clear localization effect, with 58% of inventors declaring collaboration with one of the three. Forty-six percent of company inventors interacted at least every two years with a non-Piedmontese university, and 29% with a foreign university (13.4% with a US university), indicating a high level of internationalization in the university–industry interactions of innovative Piedmontese companies.

The prevalence of interactions with the Politecnico may be due to an alumni effect since the Politecnico is an elite technical university that specializes in disciplines that tend to dominate inventors' technology classes (especially mechanical and electrical engineering). Many (208) of the inventors in our sample were Politecnico graduates. Figure 14.6 shows the numbers of inventors that graduated from each of the universities who subsequently interacted with each university. Although some subsamples are relatively small, there is a strong correlation between the degree-awarding institution and the university with which the inventor interacts. This confirms the importance of networks of relationships, such as alumni networks, for driving university–industry relationships.

The PIEMINV survey allows us to explore in more detail the channels of interaction with academic research used by the inventors. Almost all the inventors who collaborate with the University of Torino also collaborate with the Politecnico

Table 14.1 Frequency of interactions with different universities

University	Frequency of interaction (%):			
	Very frequent	*Frequent*	*Not frequent*	*Rare*
Politecnico of Torino	5.40	9.00	15.60	25.40
Other Italian University	5.80	8.20	9.80	17.20
Other European University	2.80	4.50	6.30	10.90
University of Torino	1.60	3.20	5.00	12.50
US university	0.90	2.10	4.00	6.40
Other foreign university	1.00	0.70	2.80	5.30
University of Piemonte Orientale	0.60	1.20	2.30	4.90

Note: Rare is 1 interaction every 2 years; not frequent is once or twice a year; frequent is 3–6 times a year; very frequent is every 1–2 months. There was also an alternative (not reported here) of no interaction.

Source: Authors' own elaboration of PIEMINV data.

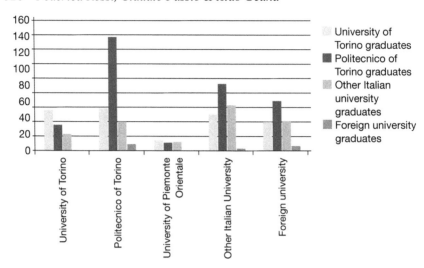

Figure 14.6 Graduates by institution and interactions with different universities

(146 out of 182), while there is a substantial group of inventors (305) who collaborate only with the Politecnico.

Compared with the 265 inventors who collaborate with other universities, the 305 inventors who collaborate only with the Politecnico of Torino are significantly more likely to patent in mechanical engineering, machinery, or transportation (and significantly less likely to patent in instruments, chemicals and materials, and pharmaceuticals, and biotechnology). They are significantly more likely to seek solutions to technical problems, and less likely to seek information about other relevant sources of knowledge or to seek legal, marketing, or organizational advice. Concerning their preferred interaction channel, they are less likely to attend academic conferences and read scientific literature, since these are not common ways of accessing academic knowledge in applied fields such as engineering. These inventors are significantly more likely to engage in direct contracts with individual academics – probably because collaboration is aimed mostly at finding solutions to specific problems. They are also significantly less likely to engage in institutional collaborations with a university institution (whether funded by the company or public funds), shared facilities with a university, recruitment of graduates, and staff exchanges with a university.

Compared with the 534 inventors who collaborate with other universities, the 36 inventors who collaborate only with the University of Torino are significantly more likely to patent in chemicals and materials, pharmaceuticals, and biotechnology (and significantly less likely to patent in mechanical engineering, and machinery, and transportation). They are significantly more likely to attend academic conferences and read scientific literature but significantly less likely to engage in staff exchanges with a university.

Finally, compared to the 424 inventors who collaborate with other universities, the 146 inventors who collaborate with both the university and the Politecnico of Torino are significantly more likely to patent in instruments, and less likely to patent in the process industries and in mechanical engineering, machinery, and transportation. They appear more likely to seek information about other relevant sources of knowledge, and to engage in all the forms of interaction considered.

Conclusions

This chapter provides an overview of the evidence on the knowledge transfer activities of Italian universities, and the evolution of the institutional setting in which these activities take place. Empirical studies using Italian data highlight the importance of private contractual collaborations between private companies and individual university researchers; they show the positive effects of academic excellence and university size on the success of research collaborations between universities and private firms. They show also that the overall success of knowledge transfer practices increases with the size and quality of the KTO and depends crucially on the specific incentives put in place by each institution.

The chapter provides a careful analysis of the knowledge transfer activities at the two largest universities (the University of Torino, and the Politecnico of Torino) based in Piedmont, in North-West Italy. While these and most other universities in Italy, have only recently developed institutional infrastructures to support knowledge transfer activity, their profiles of engagement are different, due to their different scientific specializations, different research quality (the University of Torino is more heterogeneous), different histories of collaboration with industry, and different cultures.

Politecnico academics historically have engaged in interactions with industry, based mostly on personal contracts and informal contacts, although the university institution has also benefited from a large number of research contracts with industry. The Politecnico's former knowledge transfer infrastructure was directed to research contracts. Over time, the Politecnico has strengthened its knowledge transfer activities, emphasizing those that involve direct interactions with industry for R&D activities including especially creation of spinoffs and hosting of laboratory facilities. Patenting activities have increased but are not the main focus and have been rationalized in recent years.

The model of knowledge transfer in the University of Torino is more diverse and includes several activities that have produced mixed results, and successful strategies that are concentrated in a few disciplines (most spinoff activity is related to chemistry, pharmacy, and biotechnology, most collaborative and contract research is in medicine and the natural sciences). It is likely that the University of Torino's knowledge transfer activities are underrepresented since it is specialized in academic fields (the social sciences and humanities) whose knowledge transfer activities are less well captured by the indicators used.

Company and inventor surveys suggest that interactions with the University and the Politecnico are fostered by the presence of social networks generated through alumni connections (particularly important for the Politecnico). Companies and inventors that interact with the two institutions have different sectoral and technological profiles, with the university attracting collaborations from the food industry and inventors patenting in chemicals and materials, pharmaceuticals and biotechnology, and the Politecnico attracting collaborations from the mechanical industry and inventors patenting in mechanical engineering, machinery, and transportation. Inventors seek the support of Politecnico to solve technical problems, and prefer direct contracts with individual academics. Companies that interact with the university do so for a variety of objectives. The few inventors that interact only with the university are more likely to access the scientific literature and to attend academic conferences. These findings confirm the more targeted approach to knowledge transfer typical of the Politecnico, focused on finding solutions to technical problems through direct, often personal interactions between academics and industry researchers, and the more heterogeneous model adopted by the university, characterized by multiple objectives – including business consulting activities – and a variety of channels of interaction due most likely to the more diverse set of academic subjects offered.

Since most Italian public universities are more similar to the University of Torino (a diverse range of departments and a traditional focus on teaching and research) than the Politecnico (focused on a few technical disciplines, and with a long tradition of interactions with industry), we would expect the model adopted by the university to be more prevalent in the country. The evidence at national level suggests that most Italian universities have only recently set up dedicated knowledge transfer infrastructures and policies, and that the system is immature, with few established organizational models, small dedicated structures still mostly managed by academics rather than by knowledge transfer professionals, and a dearth of knowledge transfer competences. This situation is compounded by the absence of coordinated policies at the regional and national levels; initiatives to support university–industry knowledge transfer are fragmented and poorly funded. However, in the last decade, progress has been made towards the establishment and consolidation of a university knowledge transfer infrastructure – including physical offices and facilities as well as soft skills and supportive regulations – largely due to the universities' own efforts.

Acknowledgements

The authors are grateful to Francesco Lissoni for access to the EP-INV database produced by CRIOS-Bocconi. We thank Guido Romano and Andrea Gavosto for access to CERVED data, and Paolo Checchelli for his help in building the PIEDINV database. We are grateful for financial support from the IAMAT Project coordinated by Fondazione Rosselli, the European Union (FP7) Project "An Observatorium for Science in Society based in Social Models – SISOB" Contract no.: FP7 266588, and the European Union (FP7) Project "PICKME" Contract no.: FP7 266959.

Notes

1 A fairly large share (23%) was founded before the French Revolution, especially in the Middle Ages, and another 17% were established in the 19th and early 20th centuries. The largest group (60%) includes universities founded after World War II. See also Antonelli et al. (2013) for a historical analysis of the evolution of Italian universities in the first half of the 20th century.
2 The university acquires the right to commercially exploit any invention that has not been commercialized in the five years since the patent was granted.
3 In 2000, a Ministerial Decree allowed universities to set up Industry Liaison Offices and to organize and invest equity in spinoff companies (Muscio and Orsenigo 2010).
4 See among others, Rogers et al. (2000), Thursby and Kemp (2002), Nosella and Grimaldi (2009), Caldera and Debande (2010), Curi et al. (2012), and Algieri et al. (2013).
5 The other nine are Bari, Bologna, Catania, Florence, Milan, Rome La Sapienza, Naples Federico II, Padua and Palermo.
6 Note that the ISI Science Citation Index (expanded) does not include humanities and arts journals, and includes a limited number of social sciences journals, thus, it excludes a significant part of universities' scientific publications, especially from those that are particularly specialized in these disciplines. In 2008, the University of Torino's catalogue of research products (a very broad aggregate including books, book chapters, articles, and other publications, as well as software, databases, materials, etc.) included over 5,000 items, of which 2,347 were articles. Similarly, in 2007, the Politecnico's catalogue of research products included approximately 1,100 articles. For both universities, the actual number of articles produced was much higher than the yearly numbers reported in the ISI Science Citation Index (expanded) two years earlier: 67% higher in the case of University of Torino, 37.5% higher in the case of the Politecnico.
7 Both the university and the Politecnico outsource the filing of the patent applications to external organizations.
8 The definition of "third party" adopted here includes private companies and also public administrations and charitable trusts (two of which play very important roles in funding research activities in Torino's universities).

References

Abramo, G., D'Angelo, C.A., Di Costa, F., and Solazzi, M. (2009) 'University–industry collaboration in Italy: A bibliometric examination', *Technovation* 29 (6): 498–507.
Abramo, G., D'Angelo, C.A., and Di Costa, F. (2011) 'University–industry research collaboration: A model to assess university capability', *Higher Education* 62 (2): 163–181.
Algieri, B., Aquino, A., and Succurro, M. (2013) 'Technology transfer offices and academic spin-off creation: The case of Italy', *Journal of Technology Transfer* 38 (4): 382–400.
Antonelli, C., Crepax, N., and Fassio, C. (2013) 'The cliometrics of academic chairs. Scientific knowledge and economic growth: the evidence across the Italian Regions 1900–1959', *Journal of Technology Transfer* 38 (5): 537–564.
Baldini, N., Fini, R., and Grimaldi, R. (2015) 'The transition towards entrepreneurial universities: An assessment of academic entrepreneurship in Italy'. In A. Link, D.S. Siegel and M. Wright (eds) *The Chicago Handbook of University Technology Transfer and Academic Entrepreneurship*, Chicago, IL and London: University of Chicago Press.
Baldini, N., Fini, R., Grimaldi, R., and Sobrero, M. (2010) 'The institutionalisation of university patenting activity in Italy: Diffusion and evolution of organisational practices'. Working Paper SSRN–id1632430. Available online: http://ssrn.com/abstract=1632430 (accessed September 2014).

Baldini, N., Grimaldi, R. and Sobrero, M. (2006) 'Institutional changes and the commercialization of academic knowledge: A study of Italian universities' patenting activities between 1965 and 2002', *Research Policy* 35 (4): 518–532.

Belenzon, S. and Schankerman, M. (2009) 'University knowledge transfer: Private ownership, incentives, and local development objectives', *Journal of Law and Economics* 52 (1): 111–144.

Bodas Freitas, I.M., Geuna, A., Lawson, C., and Rossi, F. (2014) 'How do industry inventors collaborate with academic researchers? The choice between shared and unilateral governance forms'. In P.P. Patrucco (ed.) *The Economics of Knowledge Generation and Distribution: The Role of Interactions in the System Dynamic of Innovation and Growth*, London: Routledge.

Bodas Freitas, I.M., Geuna, A., and Rossi, F. (2012) 'The governance of formal university–industry interactions: Understanding the rationales for alternative models', *Prometheus* 30 (1): 29–45.

Bodas Freitas, I.M., Geuna, A., and Rossi, F. (2013) 'Finding the right partners: institutional and personal modes of governance of university–industry interaction', *Research Policy* 42 (1): 50–62.

Bruno, G.S.F. and Orsenigo, L. (2003) 'Variables influencing industrial funding of academic research in Italy: An empirical analysis', *International Journal of Technology Management* 26 (2/3/4), 277–302.

Caldera, A. and Debande, O. (2010) 'Performance of Spanish universities in technology transfer: An empirical analysis', *Research Policy* 39 (9): 1160–1173.

Chapple, W., Lockett, A., Siegel, D.S., and Wright, M. (2005) 'Assessing the relative performance of university technology transfer office in UK: Parametric and non-parametric evidence', *Research Policy* 34 (3): 369–384.

Comitato di Indirizzo per la Valutazione della Ricerca (2006) 'Relazione finale'. Available online: http://vtr2006.cineca.it/php4/vtr_rel_civr_index.php (accessed April 2014).

Conferenza dei Rettori delle Università Italiane (2002) 'La ricerca scientifica nelle università italiane. Una prima analisi delle citazioni della banca dati ISI'. Available online: www.crui.it/HomePage.aspx?ref=1051# (accessed April 2014).

Consiglio Nazionale per la Valutazione del Sistema Universitario (2008) *Nono rapporto sullo stato del sistema universitario*, Rome, Italy: Ministero dell' Istruzione Università e Ricerca.

Curi, C., Daraio, C., and Llerena, P. (2012) 'University technology transfer: How, inefficient are French universities?', *Cambridge Journal of Economics* 36: 629–654.

Cuttica, A. (2012) 'Il trasferimento tecnologico al Politecnico di Torino. Industrial Liaison Office, Cittadella Politecnica, Innovation Front End: Il sostegno all'innovazione come servizio al territorio'. In M. Bianchi and A. Piccaluga (eds) *La sfida del trasferimento tecnologico: Le Università italiane si raccontano*, Milan, Italy: Springer, pp. 63–70.

Daraio, C., Bonaccorsi, A., Geuna, A. et al. (2011) 'The European university landscape: A micro characterization based on evidence from the Aquameth project', *Research Policy* 40 (1): 148–164.

Della Malva, A., Breschi, S., Lissoni, F., and Montobbio, F. (2007) 'L'attività brevettuale dei docenti universitari: L'Italia in un confronto internazionale', *Economia e Politica Industriale* 34 (2): 43–70.

Fini, R., Grimaldi, R., Santoni, S., and Sobrero, M. (2011) 'Complements or substitutes? The role of universities and local context in supporting the creation of academic spin-offs', *Research Policy* 40: 1113–1127.

Fisher, D. and Atkinson-Grosjean, J. (2002) 'Brokers on the boundary: Academy-industry liaison in Canadian universities', *Higher Education* 44 (3–4): 449–467.

Friedman, J. and Silberman, J. (2003) 'University technology transfer: Do incentives, management and location matter?' *Journal of Technology Transfer* 28 (1): 17–30.

Geuna, A. and Muscio, A. (2009) 'The governance of university knowledge transfer: A critical review of the literature', *Minerva* 47 (1): 93–114.

Geuna, A. and Nesta, L. (2006) 'University patenting and its effects on academic research: the emerging European evidence', *Research Policy* 35 (6): 790–807.

Geuna, A., Riva, M., and Rossi, F. (2009) 'Posizionamento degli Atenei Torinesi nel panorama nazionale', Rapporto sull' Impatto degli Atenei sull' Area Metropolitana, Fondazione Rosselli.

Geuna, A. and Rossi, F. (2011) 'Changes to university IPR regulations in Europe and the impact on academic patenting', *Research Policy* 40 (8): 1068–1076.

Geuna, A. and Rossi, F. (2015) *The University and the Economy. Pathways to Growth and Economic Development*, Cheltenham: Edward Elgar.

Geuna, A. and Sylos Labini, M. (2013) 'Il finanziamento pubblico delle università italiane: venti anni di riforme incompiute', Department of Economics and Statistics Cognetti de Martiis. Working Papers 201319, University of Torino.

Hewitt-Dundas, N. (2012) 'Research intensity and knowledge transfer activity in UK universities', *Research Policy* 41 (2): 262–275.

I3P (2014) I3P Innovative Enterprise Incubator, presentation. Available online: www.i3p. it/files/I3P_Pieghevole_dic2012.pdf (accessed April 2014).

IPI – Istituto per la Promozione Industriale. (2005). 'Indagine sui centri per l'innovazione e il trasferimento tecnologico in Italia', Dipartimento Centri e Reti Italia, Direzione Trasferimento di Conoscenza e Innovazione, Roma.

Jensen, R. and Thursby, M. (2001) 'Proofs and prototypes for sale: The licensing of university inventions', *American Economic Review* 91 (1): 240–259.

Lach, S. and Schankerman, M. (2004) 'Royalty sharing and technology licensing in universities', *Journal of the European Economic Association* 2 (2–3): 252–264.

Lambert, R. (2003) *Lambert Review of Business–University Collaboration*, London: HM Treasury.

Landry, R., Amara, N., and Ouimet, M. (2007) 'Determinants of knowledge transfer: evidence from Canadian university researchers in natural sciences and engineering', *Journal of Technology Transfer* 32 (6): 561–592.

Lissoni, F. and Montobbio, F. (2012) 'The ownership of academic patents and their impact. Evidence from five European countries', *Cahiers du GREThA*, n. 24, Oct.

Lockett, A. and Wright, M. (2005) 'Resources, capabilities, risk capital and the creation of university spin-out companies', *Research Policy* 34 (7): 1043–1057.

Macho-Stadler, I., Perez-Castrillo, D., and Veugelers, R. (2007) 'Licensing of university inventions: The role of a technology transfer office', *International Journal of Industrial Organization* 25 (3): 483–510.

Markman, G.D., Siegel, D.S., and Wright, M. (2008) 'Research and technology commercialization', *Journal of Management Studies* 45 (8): 1401–1423.

Matricano, D., Guadalupi, L., Tutore, V.A., Andreottola, F., and Sorrentino, M. (2013) *The Creation of Academic Spin-offs: Evidences from Italy* (Essays in Management, Economics and Ethics), Italy: McGraw-Hill.

Muscio, A. (2010) 'What drives the university use of technology transfer offices? Evidence from Italy', *Journal of Technology Transfer* 35 (2): 181–202.

Muscio, A. and Nardone, G. (2012) 'The determinants of university–industry collaboration in food science in Italy', *Food Policy* 37 (6): 710–718.

Muscio, A. and Orsenigo, L. (2010) 'Politiche nazionali e regionali di diffusione della conoscenza', in P. Bianchi and C. Pozzi (eds), *Le politiche industriali alla prova del futuro – analisi per una strategia nazionale*, Bologna: Il Mulino.

Muscio, A., Quaglione, D. and Vallanti, V. (2013) 'Does government funding complement or substitute private research funding to universities?' *Research Policy* 42 (1): 63–75.

NetVal (Network per la Valorizzazione della Ricerca Universitaria) (2013) 'Seminiamo ricerca per raccogliere innovazione'. X Rapporto Netval sulla Valorizzazione della Ricerca Pubblica Italiana.

Nosella, A. and Grimaldi, R. (2009) 'University-level mechanisms supporting the creation of new companies: An analysis of Italian academic spin-offs', *Technology Analysis & Strategic Management* 21 (6): 679–698.

OECD (Organisation for Economic Cooperation and Development) (2011) *Economic Survey of Italy*, Paris: OECD.

O'Shea, R.P., Allen, T.J., Chevalier, A. and Roche, F. (2005) Entrepreneurial orientation, technology transfer and spinoff performance of US universities', *Research Policy* 34 (7): 994–1009.

Politecnico di Torino (2008) Relazione Nucleo di Valutazione Anno 2008. Available online: http://areeweb.polito.it/strutture/svi/relazioni/relazione_2008.pdf (accessed April 2014).

Politecnico di Torino (2012) 'Il Politecnico in numeri'. Available online: www.polito.it/ateneo/documenti/numeri/numeri2013.pdf (accessed April 2014).

Politecnico di Torino (2013) 'Il Politecnico in numeri'. Available online: www.polito.it/ateneo/documenti/numeri/numeri2012.pdf (accessed April 2014).

ProTon Europe (2012) *The ProTon Europe Ninth Annual Survey Report* (Fiscal Year 2011). Report produced by Istituto di Management, Scuola Superiore Sant'Anna, for ProTon Europe. Available online: www.pg.infn.it/cntt7/sites/.../Proton%202011%20report%5B1%5D.pdf (Last accessed: September 2014).

Rogers, E., Yin, J., and Hoffmann, J. (2000) 'Assessing the effectiveness of technology transfer offices at U.S. research universities', *The Journal of the Association of University Technology Managers* 12: 47–80.

Rolfo, S. and Finardi, U. (2014) 'University third mission in Italy: Organization, faculty attitude and academic specialization, *Journal of Technology Transfer* 39 (3): 472–486.

Rossi, F. (2009) 'Increased competition and diversity in higher education: An empirical analysis of the Italian university system', *Higher Education Policy* 22 (4): 1–25.

Scellato, G., De Rosa, G., and Riva, M. (2007) *Scoreboard per la valutazione e comparazione del sistema regionale di innovazione del Piemonte*. Torino: Fondazione Rosselli.

Sciacca, M. (2012) 'Industrial funding path analysis in the Italian university system', in R.J. Howlett, B. Gabrys and Musial-Gabrys, K. (eds) *Innovation through Knowledge Transfer*, Berlin: Springer.

Sellenthin, M.O. (2006) 'Beyond the ivory tower. A comparison of patent rights regimes in Sweden and Germany', Linkoping Studies in Arts and Science, No. 355, Linkoping University (Sweden).

Siegel, D.S., Waldman, D. and Link, A.N. (2003) 'Assessing the impact of organizational practices on the relative productivity of university technology transfer offices: An exploratory study', *Research Policy* 32 (1): 27–48.

Thursby, J.G. and Kemp, S. (2002) 'Growth and productive efficiency of university intellectual property licensing', *Research Policy* 31 (1): 109–124.

Università degli Studi di Torino (2012) 'Relazione sulle attività di formazione, di ricerca e di trasferimento tecnologico – anno 2012'. Available online: www.unito.it/unitoWAR/ShowBinary/FSRepo/Area_Portale_Pubblico/Documenti/R/relazione_ricerca_2012.pdf (accessed: September 2014).

Von Tunzelmann, N. and Kraemer Mbula, E. (2003) 'Changes in research assessment practices in other countries since 1999', HEFCE commissioned report, SPRU, University of Sussex.

15 The Innovation Law, the creation of technology transfer offices and their impact on the Brazilian innovation landscape

Ana L. V. Torkomian,
M. Elizabeth R. dos Santos and
Thiago J. C. C. Soares

Introduction

During the past decades entrepreneurial dynamism has increased both in universities and scientists, reshaping the academic landscape by transforming knowledge into intellectual property (Etzkowitz, 2001). In response to the pressures of a rapidly changing society (Rodrigues, 2011), universities are increasingly engaged in technology transfer processes, which can be characterized as a second academic revolution[1] (Etzkowitz, 2003).

According to Torkomian (2011), despite the Brazilian government's efforts to promote technological innovation in the country, there is still quite a long way to go. One of the main challenges faced in transforming the knowledge generated through research and development into innovation regards the low investments in R&D, especially by companies.

In 2012 Brazilian expenditures in Research and Development (R&D) represented 1.24 percent (U$ 35.6 billion) of its Gross Domestic Expenditure (GDP). When compared to developed nations, this number appears to be quite modest. In the same year Germany invested 2.98 percent of its GDP in R&D (U$ 102.2 billion), while the United States invested 2.79 percent (U$ 453.5 billion), and China 1.98 percent (U$ 293.5 billion) (Ministério da Ciência, Tecnologia e Inovação [MCTI], 2014a). The share of the Brazilian companies in R&D investments represented, in 2012, only 45.1 percent of the total expenditures (MCTI, 2014a), whereas in advanced countries over 70 percent of these costs are covered by private companies (Santos & Torkomian, 2013).

In 2013 the Brazilian National Institute of Industrial Property – INPI (acronym for Instituto Nacional de Propriedade Intelectual) occupied 10th place among the offices with the most patent applications (World Intellectual Property Organization [WIPO], 2014). However, most of the applications in Brazil are filed by non-residents. In 2012, for example, of the 33,395 applications filed, 76.6 percent were by non-residents. From 2000 to 2012 the number of applications filed by residents increased by 21.1 percent, from 6,448 to 7,810. On the other hand, the applications filed by non-residents increased by 80.3 percent, from 14,191 in 2000 to 25,585 in 2012 (MCTI, 2014a). This clearly indicates that the increase and number of patent applications received at INPI does not directly reflect the results of the national effort to promote and spread technological innovation within the country.

Until the 1990s, the role of universities in the innovation process was not clearly perceived. Consequently, the interaction between universities and companies was not included in the university's research agenda and was considered a marginal activity, not embedded in the institutional policies (Santos, 2010). In this perspective, there was no concern with the protection of intellectual property rights, as the universities lacked the adequate tools and procedures to put this into practice and also the governmental entities responsible for evaluating the academic production did not consider intellectual property rights a valuable asset for the academic career.

However, since the Innovation Law entered into force, this scenario has changed, hence the role of universities in the Brazilian Innovation System has been realigned. Enacted on December 2, 2004, the Innovation Law created incentives for scientific and technological innovation in a productive environment, striving for technological autonomy and industrial development in Brazil. Among others, the Law stipulates that public scientific and technological institutions (STIs)[2] must establish a Technology Transfer Office (TTO) to manage their innovation policies.

This chapter analyzes the role this Innovation Law plays in the intellectual property (IP) protection and technology transfer (TT) in Brazilian STIs, both public and private, through the creation of TTOs and definition of innovation polices. It also outlines the evolution and activities performed by seven TTOs in Brazil's southeastern and south regions, 10 years after the enactment of the Innovation Law. These cases were analyzed using the results of interviews carried out with the directors of these offices.

The remainder of this chapter is organized as follows. The next section describes Brazil's innovation scenario before the Innovation Law and the background for its creation. The third section provides a general overview of TTOs activities in Brazil after the Innovation Law was enacted. It also summarizes some of the main achievements of TTOs in Brazil between 2006 and 2013. The fourth section presents the cases of seven TTOs, located in the south and southeast regions. Finally, the fifth section concludes the study.

The political and economical background for the creation of the Innovation Law

Historically, the lack of coordination between government, companies and universities has been one of the main characteristics of the Brazilian Innovation System. Since the 1980s, many governmental programs aiming to approximate these three components of the system have been put into practice, hence much progress has been reached thanks to these initiatives.

Regarding the STIs, the first attempt to establish an institutional mechanism to manage innovation was the creation of Technological Innovation Nucleus – NIT (acronym for Núcleo de Inovação Tecnológica), designed in 1981 and implemented by the National Council of Scientific and Technological Development – CNPq (acronym for Conselho Nacional de Desenvolvimento Científico e Tecnológico), in order to improve the links between academy and industry:

> The NIT were small teams (two to five people), located in universities or research institutes and specifically designed to promote the link between market demand and the real and potential R&D supply, acting as inducers of technological innovation. The NIT team belonged to the institution, and should act permanently as promoters of technological innovation.
>
> (Stal, 1997, p. 34)

Probably inspired and influenced by the Bayh-Dole Act, signed in United States in 1980, this program was a very innovative proposal, even when compared with similar initiatives from developed countries. Considering the period when it was conceived and put into practice, the program was very well developed in terms of the planned activities. Despite government efforts, the project had a very short life and was stopped in the late 1980s. Just a few NIT were incorporated into their host institutions. There was not an appropriate national environment or even enough maturity in academia, industry, or the government to put into practice these innovative ideas and carry them out successfully. On the other hand, it should be emphasized that there was a positive result in that the NIT spread the idea of technological innovation in their host institutions, causing links with industry to prosper in several cases (Stal, 1997).

Another example of a short-lived project was the FINEP-TEC, led by the Financier of Studies and Projects – FINEP (acronym for Financiadora de Estudos e Projetos), a government development agency. This project was created to encourage cooperation between universities and companies through joint R&D projects. The excessive number of guarantees required by FINEP for companies to have access to funding was one of the reasons for the low demand, which contributed to the discontinuation of the program (Stal, 1997). The positive result of the FINEP-TEC project was the creation of TTOs at universities that were enrolled. In some universities, these offices have remained active and have been reinforced by new government policies.

Only at the end of the 1990s new laws changing the previous regulation of international trade and IP led universities to new ways to innovate, promote TT and manage innovation through structures such as TTOs, incubators and technological parks, requiring "substantial transformation in university ethos and additional non-academic competencies" (Maculan & Mello, 2009, p. 109). One of the new competencies was IP management, which has been increasingly stimulated in academia.

It was in this context that the discussion and proposal of a Brazilian Technological Innovation Law emerged. In 1996, Roberto Freire, a Federal Deputy, inspired by the French Innovation Law, proposed the first draft of this

Law in Brazil. His motivation was based on the need for an economy founded on scientific and technological innovation, "the economy of the future". Thus, the state had a major role to play in enforcing these policies to promote the integration of scientific and technological knowledge into the Brazilian market (Rede de Propriedade Intelectual, Cooperação, Negociação e Comercialização de Tecnologia [REPICT], 2004). The proposal coincided with the demands of the technology managers in the community, who then met at the Annual Meeting of the Intellectual Property, Commercialization, Negotiation and Technology Commercialization Network of Rio de Janeiro – REPICT (acronym for Rede de Propriedade Intelectual, Cooperação, Negociação e Comercialização de Tecnologia). This network played an important role in promoting and creating an environment conducive to effective discussions about the Law.

This started a long period of discussions and debates in many workshops and seminars that were held across the country before the enactment of the Innovation Law. Other legal landmarks were achieved at this time. Among them, the Law 9.279, from 1996, which regulates rights and obligations related to industrial property and replaces the Law 5.772, which enacted the first industrial property code in Brazil, in 1971[3]; the Decree 2.553, from 1998, which regulates rights and obligations related to federal public employees' industrial property; and the ordinance 322 of the ministry of education and sports, also from 1998, which regulates rights and obligations related to industrial property of the agencies or entities of the ministry of education.

The Innovation Law was finally signed in December 2004. The main reason behind this was to overcome the inconsistencies between public and private relationships, and also to provide the legal mechanisms to improve university–company interaction. This Law is regarded as the most important milestone to promote technological innovation in Brazil and to realign universities with the knowledge economy. Its main objective is training and achieving national technological autonomy and industrial development, placing emphasis on innovation and IP protection.

The Law was designed to provide research and innovation incentives, covering important support mechanisms for the construction of alliances between STIs and the industry, such as cooperation agreements. Moreover, the Law also establishes that laboratories, infrastructure and human resources be shared with companies and non-profit organizations; incubation of small firms in public STIs; provision of R&D services for industrial firms; and the creation of TTOs (Maculan & Mello, 2009; Brasil, 2004). Among others, the Law also foresees the possibility of STIs signing TT and licensing agreements, as well as the inventors' shares of royalty revenues resulting from technology transfer agreements. This share is of at least 5 percent and at most 33.3 percent, at the institution's discretion. The legal obligation regarding a TTO carrying out the innovation management at public universities and research institutes as required by this law was the basis of the changes made within these institutions.

However, the implementation of TTOs was only the first step in the innovation process. Protecting an academic research result and transferring it to the market involves a complex set of actions and institutional decisions. It is faced with a bumpy road, since the introduction of new dynamics in the managing of research results culminates in cultural conflicts and legal barriers, passing through the lack of specialized human resources which makes IP management in the university environment a constant challenge.

While adequate laws alone are not enough to ensure results, the creation of specialized offices to manage IP may prove to be ineffective if not followed by appropriate TT mechanisms. Thus, legislation has a crucial role to play in guiding procedures and solutions to a more effective outcome.

Nevertheless, the experience with IP and TT management precedes the signing of the Law. According to Santos (2005), the first record of a patent application filed by a university in Brazil dates back to 1979, when the Federal University of Rio de Janeiro applied for a patent, which was granted in 1985. In the 1980s there was a reduced number of patent applications filed by universities, with two peaks recorded: one in 1987, with 32 filings, and another in 1989 with 37. Both were caused by the entry of the State University of Campinas (Unicamp) and the University of São Paulo (USP) into the IP system as universities with systematic patenting activities (Póvoa, 2008). In the 1980s, USP and Unicamp created structures dedicated to managing IP. In 1984, Unicamp first established IP policies through the Permanent Board of Industrial Property – CPPI (acronym for Comissão Permanente de Propriedade Industrial), with actions centered on helping scientists in the process of filing patent applications to the National Institute of Industrial Property – INPI. A similar mechanism was implemented at USP in 1987, with the creation of the Advisory Group for Development of Inventions – GADI (acronym for Grupo de Assessoramento ao Desenvolvimento de Inventos). These actions were put into practice by the universities themselves rather than being organized by state or federal entities, and they focused more on the protection of IP than on the commercialization of technology (Santos & Mello, 2009).

It was only at the end of the 1990s that IP acquired importance in the national scenario, especially because of the Trade Related Intellectual Property Rights (TRIPS)[4] agreement and the commitment derived from its implementation through Brazilian laws. This fact, together with the implementation of new governmental programs encouraging university–industry partnerships, marked a fresh stage in the national context of promoting technological innovation. From 1996 to 1997, the number of university patent applications filed at INPI doubled from 24 filings in 1996 to 50 filings in 1997. Since then, increasingly significant numbers have been achieved. Figure 15.1 shows the development of IP protection applications by STIs in Brazil between 2010 and 2013 (including patents, computer programs, trademarks, industrial designs, cultivars, among others).

In this new scenario of increased IP protection, the improvement of IP management has become essential for academic institutions, particularly as they seek to intensify their relationships with industry and the relevance of their work for society's needs. In this context, the TTOs now play a mandatory role, mainly in public institutions, and their main function regards the management of IP issues. But considering the great diversity, in terms of research volume and

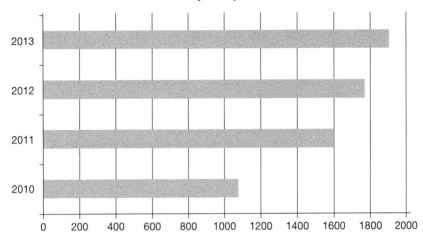

Figure 15.1 IP applications filed by Brazilian scientific and technological institutions (2010–2013)

Sources: MCTI (2014b), adapted by the authors.

regional commitment, among other aspects that characterize Brazilian research institutions, some of these TTOs have added this function to the previous one of managing the university–industry linked activities.

Technology transfer offices in Brazil: a general overview

As established by the Innovation Law (Brasil, 2004), every public scientific and technological institution (STI) must have a TTO to manage its innovation policy. The minimum competencies of these offices are: to oversee the enforcement of the institutional policy to foster the protection of creations and technology transfer; to assess the results from research activities and projects to meet the requirements of the Innovation Law; to assess requests from independent inventors to "adopt" and nourish an invention; to promote the protection of creations developed at the institution; and follow up on the processing of requests and maintain the institution's IP titles (Santos & Torkomian, 2013).

Each year, the STIs provide information to the Ministry of Science, Technology and Innovation – MCTI (acronym for Ministério da Ciência, Tecnologia e Inovação) about the results of their efforts to protect IP and transfer technology. As regards the Innovation Law, STIs are considered public administration agencies which include research in their institutional missions, either pure or applied. The Law does not oblige private institutions to provide information, but volunteered registration of such institutions is part of the database of MCTI. In 2013, the form, known as Formict, was filed by 261 institutions, of which 74.3 percent were public institutions (MCTI, 2014b).

Considering all the institutions, 69.4 percent informed that they have innovation policies, that is, formal documents with general guidelines to direct innovation related actions, for the protection of IP and TT. From the institutions which have implemented innovation policies, "non-disclosure or confidentiality", "development of cooperation projects with third parties" and "partnership agreements" were the most frequently supported activities by their policies, whereas the least frequent were "permission to researchers to temporarily leave without pay to form an enterprise", "permission to researchers to temporarily leave to collaborate with another STI", and "assignment of creation rights to the creator in order to carry the invention in his or her own name".

Of the group of institutions which provided information, 166 (63.6 percent) reported that their TTOs are implemented. In 66 institutions (25.3 percent), the TTOs were under implementation, and in 29 (11.1 percent), they had not been implemented at that time. The TTO activities with the highest implementation rates were: to follow the filing process and keeping the institution's IP titles (70.7 percent); to assess the convenience and promote the protection of the creation developed in the institution (68.5 percent); and to ensure supporting the institutional policy to encourage the protection of IP (66.4 percent).

The offset to the TTOs' focus on the matter of IP protection is that many institutions already had effective actions in this field: 56.7 percent (148 institutions) informed they had IP filed or granted in 2013. However, 43.3 percent (113 institutions) informed they had no patent filed.

In 2013, 271 IP applications were granted, and 1,901 were filed. These numbers show a 7.5 percent increase when compared with the previous year. According to the institutions, 91.7 percent of the applications were filed in Brazil, 8.0 percent were filed abroad, and 0.3 percent both in Brazil and abroad. Usually, applications filed abroad only occur if there is a partnership with foreign institutions (companies or scientific and technological institutions) in the research development. Regarding the applications granted, 90.8 percent were filed in Brazil, and 8.9 percent abroad, and 0.4 percent both in Brazil and abroad.

Regarding the types of IP application, 1,198 are for invention patents, 259 are for computer software, and 247 for trademarks. There were also other protection requests: 101 for design, 42 for cultivars, 39 for utility models, and 15 for other types of protection. Patents of invention represent about two thirds of the total of applications. The sectors that had the most applications for this type of protection were: manufacturing (29 percent, 553 applications), professional, scientific and technical activities (7 percent, 115 applications), human health and social services (6.6 percent, 126 applications), and agriculture, livestock, forest production, fishing and aquaculture (6.4 percent, 122 applications). From the protection applications for manufacturing industries, patents of invention stand out in the pharmaceutical industry (10.2 percent, 193 applications), chemical industry (5.4 percent, 103 applications), diverse products (2.3 percent, 43 applications), machines and equipment (2.2 percent, 42 applications), food (1.7 percent, 33 applications), electrical materials (1.7 percent, 32 applications), plastic and rubber (1.1 percent, 21 applications), metallurgy (0.8 percent, 16 applications), and oil refining and biofuels (0.7 percent, 13 applications).

The information provided also shows that only 45 STIs signed contracts in 2013. Altogether, there were 1,943 technology contracts, of which 64.1 percent were IP licensing; 9 percent were know-how transfer; 7.5 percent were research, development and innovation partnership agreements; 4.2 percent regarded co-ownership; 3.6 percent were nondisclosure agreements; 0.3 percent were biological material transfer; 0.3 percent were cooperation agreements for sharing laboratories, equipment, tools, materials and other facilities with micro and small technology innovation-related companies, for the advancement of incubation activities; 0.1 percent regarded the assignment of intellectual property rights; 0.1 percent were related to permission to use laboratories, equipment, tools, materials and facilities by national companies and private non-profit organizations for research activities; and 11 percent for other purposes. These technology contracts amount to US$ 122 million.

A significant impact of the Innovation Law on STIs' activities has been evident in both public and private institutions, as observed in the recent data collected by the Ministry of Science, Technology and Innovation, presented above (MCTI, 2014b). The following deserve comment:

- A substantial increase in the number of respondent institutions, from 43 in 2006 to 261 in 2013. This shows that the STIs are gradually adhering to the Law, creating and consolidating their TTOs, either with their own resources or using government incentives through public calls for the creation and consolidation of TTOs. It also reflects the result of the effort made by MCTI to extract information from a greater number of universities and research institutes and thereby have a general overview of the country.
- The number of private scientific and technological institutions (67 – 25.7 percent of the total respondents) that reported IP and TT activities. These institutions are not compelled to submit a report, as the Technological Innovation Law only obliges public institutions to do so. Nevertheless, the number and percentage of private institutions participating in Formict increases every year, which indicates that the Innovation Law exerts an impact on these institutions, even if not directly. These institutions are increasingly more aware of the benefits that IP commercialization can bring to them and to society as a whole.
- The remarkable increase in the number of already-implemented TTOs, 166, which represents 147 more than in 2006 when the first survey was conducted. This is a result of the time elapsed since the first initiatives and the government's financial support for implementing TTOs through a public call.
- The increase in the number of patents filed by universities and research institutes. Between 2010 and 2013 this increase was of 54.6 percent, from 775 to nearly 1200 applications, which represented ca. 15 percent of all patent applications filled by residents in Brazil this last year.
- The important revenue increase derived from technology contracts, which include IP licensing, know how transfer, research cooperation agreements,

coownership agreements, among others. In 2006 the total income was of less than US$500,000, whereas in 2013 it was of over US$74 million.

Analyzing the performance of the TTOs gives rise to some deliberations. While the data shows that an increasing volume of research results reaches the market, there is still no consensus among the Brazilian research community about the importance of academic TT (Martins, Andrade & Torkomian, 2011). It remains a resistance which stems from the impression that economic interest in academic research may undermine the social perspective of science development and the public nature of knowledge dissemination. Even though the number of patent filings has increased significantly in the context of STIs and that patents are considered a measure of the researcher's academic merit, the dilemma of publishing versus protecting has not been fully resolved. There are researchers who still resist protecting their research results, opting for publication as the only acceptable way to disseminate knowledge (Santos, 2010).

In Brazil, the largest source of revenue within TT has been the completion of joint research between universities and companies, results that quite often are not protected and do not always constitute innovations in the market. Nevertheless, there are several programs from both the federal government and state development agencies that fund part or even the full development of cooperative research projects between STIs and companies.

Finally, it is important to emphasize that despite the still existing resistance, in general terms TT has produced a positive impact on how the social relevance of academia is perceived. In order to broaden this impact, with society remaining as the main beneficiary, it is essential to continue pursuing the balance between the different roles played by STIs, emphasizing and prioritizing the social aspect of TT.

Innovation in Brazilian scientific and technological institutions: the case of seven universities

Although the Formict report provides a general overview of the activities of the Brazilian TTOs, we deemed it important to study in depth these structures, choosing some cases for further investigation. These cases were chosen from the TTOs of universities and represent links to federal public institutions (two TTOs, one from the state of São Paulo and the other from Rio de Janeiro), state institutions (three TTOs from the state of São Paulo) and private institutions (two TTOs, one from the state Rio Grande do Sul and the other from Rio de Janeiro).

Despite the other cases of well-succeeded TTOs in other regions of Brazil, six of the chosen cases are concentrated in the southeast region (four of them in Sao Paulo and two in Rio de Janeiro) and one in the south (in Rio Grande do Sul). These offices were chosen due to their prominent positions in Brazil on issues such as: number of patent applications, percentage of licensed patents, revenues earned from royalties, number of spin-offs generated, relationships with business incubators or technology parks, among others.

Thus, the following topics are based on the interviews with TTO directors of the following institutions, in alphabetical order: Federal University of Rio de Janeiro – UFRJ (acronym for Universidade Federal do Rio de Janeiro); Federal University of São Carlos – UFSCar (acronym for Universidade Federal de São Carlos); Pontifical Catholic University of Rio de Janeiro (or PUC-Rio, acronym for Pontifícia Universidade Católica do Rio de Janeiro); Pontifical Catholic University of Rio Grande do Sul – PUCRS (acronym for Pontifícia Universidade Católica do Rio Grande do Sul); State University of São Paulo – Unesp (acronym for Universidade Estadual Paulista); State University of Campinas – Unicamp (acronym for Universidade Estadual de Campinas); and, finally, University of São Paulo – USP (acronym for Universidade de São Paulo).

The interviews covered the following topics: how the Innovation Law impacted TTOs in Brazil; practices and policies to promote innovation; IP protection; TT practices; startup incubators and technology parks; TTO networks; and the main challenges faced in creating and establishing an entrepreneurial culture in Brazilian research institutes and universities. The next sub-section brings a brief description of the universities studied.

The interviewed institutions

The Federal University of Rio de Janeiro – UFRJ was founded in 1920, under the name University of Rio de Janeiro. Reorganized in 1937, when it was renamed University of Brazil, UFRJ has held its current name since 1965. UFRJ has three campuses and over 55,000 undergraduate students, 11,000 graduate students, and 4,000 faculty members. It offers 182 undergraduate courses, 152 certificate courses, 92 Academic Masters, 15 Professional Masters and 86 Doctorate (PhD programs) (Universidade Federal do Rio de Janeiro [UFRJ], 2015). The UFRJ Innovation Agency, the TTO of UFRJ, was created in 2007. The University has also created startup incubators and technology parks.

The Federal University of São Carlos – UFSCar, created in 1968, initiated its academic activities in 1970. The university has four campuses and is the only higher education federal institution in the interior of the state of São Paulo. The university community includes 1,179 faculty members, 922 technical and administrative staff, 1,498 undergraduate students, 1,939 enrolled in distance learning undergraduate majors, and 6,048 graduate students. UFSCar offers 61 undergraduate courses and 47 graduate programs, with 41 Academic Masters, 8 Professional Masters and 26 Doctorates (Universidade Federal de São Carlos [UFSCar], 2015). The TTO of UFSCar, the Innovation Agency of UFSCar, was created in January 2008 and absorbed previous intellectual property divisions of the University.

The Pontifical Catholic University of Rio de Janeiro – PUC-Rio, a non-profit philanthropic institution, was the first private higher education institution in Brazil. Founded in 1940, PUC-Rio offers 42 undergraduate and 100 graduate courses. It includes over 1,250 faculty members, 13,000 undergraduate students, 1,350 Master students and 970 Doctorate students (Pontifícia Universidade

Católica do Rio de Janeiro [PUC-Rio], 2015). The Puc-Rio Innovation Agency was created in 2009, from the Intellectual Property Business Office – ENPI (acronym for Escritório de Negócios em Propriedade Intelectual), which was the previous TTO of PUC-Rio, founded in 2003.

The Pontifical Catholic University of Rio Grande do Sul – PUCRS, founded in 1948, is a private institution located in Porto Alegre, the southernmost capital city in Brazil. With more than 30,000 students, 1,500 faculty members and 5,000 administrative and technical staff, PUCRS offers 67 undergraduate programs, over 100 options for certificate courses, 24 Master's and 21 Doctorate courses (Pontifícia Universidade Católica do Rio Grande do Sul [PUCRS], 2015). The Technology Transfer Office of the University was created in 2005 and currently integrates the INOVAPUCRS, a network of innovation and entrepreneurship that includes, among others, a science and technological park and a startup incubator.

The State University of São Paulo – Unesp, established in 1976, resulted from the incorporation of separate higher education institutes of São Paulo. Unesp is a successful model of a multi-campus university in Brazil, it has 24 campuses distributed throughout the state of São Paulo. It counts with over 3,700 faculty members, 36,250 undergraduate students, and 12,800 graduate students, offering 179 undergraduate courses and 129 graduate programs, with 119 Academic Masters, 13 Professional Masters and 101 Doctorates (Universidade Estadual Paulista [Unesp], 2015). Founded in 2007, the Unesp Innovation Agency incorporated a previous division of intellectual property of the university, created back in the early 2000s.

The State University of Campinas – Unicamp was founded in October 1966. Unlike most Brazilian higher education institutes, which were mostly created with the unification of pre-existing schools, Unicamp was created from an idea that encompassed all of its current setup. Even before it was installed, it had already attracted over 200 foreign professors from different fields and about 180 others coming from the best Brazilian universities. Currently, the research produced at Unicamp represents roughly 15 percent of all Brazilian university research. The university counts with over 1,750 faculty members, 18,300 undergraduate students and 16,200 graduate students, offering 70 undergraduate programs and 156 graduate programs, with 14 certificate courses, 74 Masters and 68 Doctorates (Universidade Estadual de Campinas [Unicamp], 2015). The TTO of Unicamp, Inova Unicamp, was created in July 2003 and is one of the most actives TTOs in Brazil.

One of the most prestigious institutions of higher education and research in Brazil and Latin America, the University of São Paulo – USP was founded in 1934, with the unification of several pre-existing schools. With campuses distributed over seven cities, USP has over 92,000 students and 6,000 faculty members, offering 289 undergraduate courses and 222 graduate programs (Universidade de São Paulo – [USP], 2014). The TTO of the university, the USP Innovation Agency, was founded in February 2005 and can be defined as a "cooperation network" composed of several offices. In each USP campus there is an office composed of employees of the USP Innovation Agency and in some cases staff and faculty of the respective campus.

A general overview of the universities presented above can be found in Table 15.1, represented below.

Table 15.1 General overview of the studied cases until 2014

Institution	Name of TTO	Foundation of the university	Number of faculty members	Foundation of TTO	Number of TTO staff*
UFRJ	UFRJ Innovation Agency	1920	4,000	2007	18
UFSCar	Innovation Agency of UFSCar	1970	1,200	2008	13
PUC-Rio	PUC-Rio Innovation Agency	1940	1,250	2003	4
PUCRS	PUCRS Technology Transfer Office	1948	1,500	2005	8
Unesp	Unesp Innovation Agency	1976	3,730	2007	11
Unicamp	Innovation Agency Inova Unicamp	1966	1,750	2003	45
USP	USP Innovation Agency	1934	6,000	2005	68

*Including interns.

Sources: Elaborated by the authors.

The impact of the Innovation Law in Brazilian universities and research institutes

Before the Innovation Law, only a few Brazilian universities and research institutes had organizations responsible for their IP and TT. Even when this was the case, they were often a department of a larger university support organization, and not a separate and independent structure, lacking the resources and support to fulfill its mission. In this sense, the enactment of this Law was fundamental to sensitize both the administration and faculty of the universities regarding the importance of establishing and institutionalizing a division responsible for their IP, one that could facilitate the TT process to the industry.

The Innovation Law played a major role in defining the type of cooperation agreements that could be crafted between universities and industry. In addition, the Law provided a clearer aspect regarding IP ownership; promoting entrepreneurship; creating technology-based companies; and the sharing of laboratories, equipment, tools, materials and other facilities with micro and small companies related to technological innovation activities.

Even the TTOs that existed before the Law, such as the Innovation Agency Inova Unicamp, had to adapt their internal procedures regarding relationships with industry, IP protection and TT. Yet, there were some unforeseen special cases, meaning that there is still room for improvement.

The Law did not homogeneously impact all university departments and institutes. The IP concept permeated some sectors more than others. There is now a higher acceptance by researchers with regards to the formalities needed in relationship agreements with other social agents. It can be said, overall, that thus far and despite the absence of instruments that can make the Innovation Law more effective, it has brought very positive results to the innovation landscape in Brazil.

Furthermore, it exerted a significant impact on private institutions, notwithstanding the fact it had no legal influence over them. In these cases the Law serves mainly as a guiding document, especially for the creation of TTOs and definition of IP and TT institutional policies.

It can then be stated that the Innovation Law, through the creation of TTOs and definition of innovation policies, provided a higher visibility of IP and TT activities in the internal and external academic community, both in private and public institutions.

TTOs practices and policies to foster innovation

The TT process in most Brazilian universities is still at its early phase. In order to foster innovation in the academic environment, many of the TTOs have begun offering entrepreneurship courses and seminars to undergraduate and graduate students, faculty members, and even to the community outside academia. The USP Innovation Agency, for example, offers two entrepreneurship courses to the academic community. The first one, "Entrepreneurship and Innovation", is intended to undergraduate students, while the second one, "Technological Innovation Projects Management", is offered in partnership with FIESP (Federation of Industries of the State of São Paulo) and CIESP (Center of Industries of the State of São Paulo) and intended to graduate students, focused on teaching and applying innovation measures to entrepreneurs in the state of São Paulo.

Nevertheless, it is not uncommon that divisions in the university other than TTOs perform those activities. At PUC-Rio and PUCRS, for example, entrepreneurship courses are not ministered directly by the TTOs, but by other university institutes. At PUCRS, the Entrepreneur Center is responsible for these courses, while at PUC-Rio, the university's Business Administration Department performs the activities related to entrepreneurial education.

In addition, all TTOs interviewed stated they promote activities such as contests of ideas and products. The TTO of the Federal University of Rio de Janeiro – UFRJ Innovation Agency, for example, in partnership with the startup incubator of COPPE (a UFRJ Institute of Graduate Studies and Research in Engineering), promotes yearly the idea contest "Empurra que Vai" – or in English

"Push it, it will work". The ten best-placed competitors have a week of mentoring with well-known entrepreneurs, in order to optimize their projects for the final presentation to the jury. The competition offers a two thousand dollars prize to the best innovative business idea.

In some cases, there are additional mechanisms used to stimulate entrepreneurial activities within Brazilian universities. Unesp, for example, enacted a policy in 2011 that provides scores for faculty members who seek protection for their research output. These scores are taken into consideration in the university's career progression program. Another example is the Inventors Award, an initiative of the TTO Inova Unicamp in partnership with the rectory of the university. This initiative aims to foster innovation in the academic community by rewarding researchers involved in IP protection and TT activities.

All the TTOs studied stated they have a well-defined IP and TT policy, some of them even dating back to before the Innovation Law was enacted. These policies usually define, among others, the researchers' obligation to disclose their inventions; IP rights; general rights and duties of the inventors and university; terms for cooperation agreements between the university and companies; and the sharing of royalties among the inventors, university and other support entities or departments in the case of licensing.

Due to an exclusivity clause in their contracts, Brazilian public researchers are not usually allowed to actively work on spin-off companies while performing their regular academic activities. However, they can own shares of these companies and assume roles such as consultants or as members of the supervisory board. The Innovation Law foresees that public researchers, provided they are not on the probationary phase, may be granted unpaid leave for up to three consecutive years to constitute a company, provided it is an entrepreneurial activity related to innovation. Thus, if the enterprise fails, the researcher has his/her position at the university secured. This is one of the points that deserves more attention in the Law, since it has not been effective. This may happen due to several reasons, namely the researchers' lack of confidence that it will not harm their academic career, lack of entrepreneurial culture, or even the absence of stimulus within academia.

In order to promote the services they offer, some offices organize meetings with the various research groups of their institutions. This is especially important when considering that many academics – both students and faculties – are not aware that their research results may have market potential or that they could earn royalties from technology licensing. Many of them simply have little knowledge about the activities performed and services offered by their TTO, as suggested by a study conducted by Martins, Andrade and Torkomian (2011), which analyzed how researchers of UFSCar perceived the TTO.

According to the interviewees, the continuous training process of the TTO staff includes their participation in events and specific training programs, both in Brazil and abroad. There are also training programs offered in partnership with entities such as the National Institute of Industrial Property – INPI, the World Intellectual Property Organization – WIPO, and the Innovation and Technology Transfer

Managers National Forum – FORTEC (acronym for Fórum Nacional de Gestores de Inovação e Transferência de Tecnologia).

Some other TTO training and capacitation programs in Brazil are funded by government and state development agencies, such as FINEP, CNPq, CAPES (acronym for Coordenação de Aperfeiçoamento de Pessoal de Nível Superior, in English Higher Education Personnel Training Coordination) and FAPESP (acronym for Fundação de Amparo à Pesquisa do Estado de São Paulo, in English Research Support Foundation of the State of São Paulo). The staff of UFSCar's Innovation Agency, for example, participated in a training project funded by FAPESP focused on implementing and adapting the best practices of well-succeeded offices from the United States, Spain, Portugal, Scotland and England. The project Inova TT, funded with resources from the FINEP Technology Innovation Award – category scientific and technological institutions – paved the way for an entirely new level of TT activities at Unicamp. It sought to map and redraw the IP and TT processes of Inova, in order to improve the capacity of both supplying and negotiating technologies of the university.

The capacitating and training programs have been significant to the Brazilian TTOs, given that there are often no specific skill-sets and market experience determined for TTO staff in the STIs. These qualified skill-sets are only achieved through trainings or work experience. The survey conducted by Formict for 2013, as mentioned earlier, found that 26.6 percent of the TTOs' active staff has a background in Engineering, Chemistry or Physics; 17.5 percent in Administration or Economics; 12.9 percent in Law; 8.5 percent in Biological Sciences; 3.2 percent in Social Communication; and 31.4 percent in other areas (MCTI, 2014b).

Intellectual property practices

The TTOs from Brazilian institutions to a large extent play a rather reactive role in finding patenting technology inside the university. The usual process flow requires the researcher to disclose an invention to the office, which will then analyze its market potential and protection feasibility.

From the seven TTOs studied, only the USP Innovation Agency and the Inova Unicamp are positioned as more proactive than reactive in activities related to technology prospecting for patents. These offices put effort to identify technologies with protection and licensing potential while still in their development phase, to not miss TT opportunities.

All the interviewees agree that the main challenge to establishing proactive activities lie within the reduced number of TTO staff when compared to the number of researchers, departments and laboratories of the studied universities.

The offices strive to increase the number of invention disclosures by organizing meetings, seminars and workshops aiming to promote IP protection to faculties and students. However, a large portion of the academic community is still unaware of the possibility or benefits of patenting activities.

The criteria used to decide whether an invention disclosure will be protected or not are not standard within the studied universities. USP and Unesp strictly analyze whether the legal requirements for the patent application are fulfilled or not. The process at PUCRS consists in a prior art search by the TTO followed by an analysis of external consultants, also involving market representatives whenever possible. At PUC-Rio, an invention is only protected if it meets the legal requirements and presents either market potential or benefits to society. The analysis at UFRJ consists of the inventor completing a questionnaire, followed by at least one interview. The aspects evaluated are the target group, market potential (albeit approximate), main competitors, and the existence (or not) of an undertaking or participant company in the invention, among others. At UFSCar there is an internal committee responsible for evaluating the patenting feasibility of inventions. The criteria used by this committee are related to the technical and commercial feasibility of the invention. Finally, Unicamp considers the patentability requirements under the Industrial Property Law.

As mentioned earlier, not all TTOs perform a market potential assessment of inventions before filing the respective patent applications. Some offices use external help to either perform the market potential assessment for them or to train their staff to do so. As a matter of fact, most of Brazilian TTOs lack the capacity to properly perform such analysis, which can be noted when the quantity of patents managed by the offices is compared to the quantity of crafted licensing agreements. The disparity between patenting and licensing activities could also be understood as a consequence of a strategic decision from TTOs to protect as many inventions as possible (without worrying about their market potential), in order to increase the institution's reputation in the scientific community.

Nevertheless, it can be said the criteria used by TTOs for filing patent applications are gradually becoming more rigid in Brazil. Offices are rethinking their strategy, given the high number of patents without license agreements. In addition, universities are starting to drop patents that are not licensed within a period of time. In these cases the inventors usually have the right to keep the patent, provided they pay the maintenance fees.

Table 15.2 shows a general overview of the IP protection activities performed by the studied TTOs.

Table 15.2 Overview of IP protection activity of the studied cases until 2014

Institution	Patent applications in Brazil	Patent Cooperation treaty applications	Patent applications abroad	Prominent patenting fields	Protected computer programs	Protected cultivars	Protected trademarks	Further protected technologies*
UFRJ	319	42	60	n.a.	21	n.a.	n.a.	5
UFSCar	132	27	29	Engineering and Chemistry	15	21	4	0
PUC-Rio	63	21	32	Engineering and Earth Sciences	51	0	75	7
PUCRS	106	36	50	Engineering, Chemistry and Human Health	28	0	85	0
Unesp	205	33	54	Human Health and Instrumentation	74	0	144	8
Unicamp	830	115	116**	Chemistry	89***	n.a.	n.a.	n.a.
USP	1024	50	72	Health and Personal Care	n.a.	n.a.	n.a.	n.a.

* Including industrial design, geographical indications, integrated circuit topography, among others.
** From 2005 to 2014
*** From 2009 to 2014

Sources: Elaborated by the authors.

Technology transfer practices

The Innovation Law ensures inventors of STIs the share of at least 5 percent and at most 33.3 percent of the royalties resulting from technology transfer agreements, regardless of whether these are spin-offs or licensing contracts. In five of the seven cases studies, the share of royalties granted to inventors was of 33.3 percent. At USP, this share was 30 percent. At PUC-Rio, the inventor receives the first US$ 4,000 earned in royalties and then 30 percent of the royalties that exceeds this amount.

From the seven TTOs studied, three stated to be proactive in TT activities: those belonging to UFSCar, Unesp and Unicamp. These offices perform constant market assessments to find companies for cooperation agreements and technology licensing. There is a continuous commercial dissemination work of the protected technologies, aimed at finding partners interested in bringing these into the market. In 2014, for example, Inova Unicamp found directly 110 companies to craft partnerships with the university, through either TT or R&D cooperation agreements.

In Brazil TT is usually performed by offices with more experience. In order to craft license agreements, these offices frequently organize meetings to promote their technologies among target companies. It could be said that TT through licensing is much more frequent in Brazil than the creation of spin-offs, especially in research institutes.

From the seven studied universities, only Unicamp and UFRJ promote activities that explicitly target the creation of spin-offs. The Inova Unicamp annually organizes the so-called Challenge Unicamp, which is a competition of business models, focused on encouraging the creation of technology-based companies from Unicamp's protected technologies. The TTO staff pre-selects the technologies for the challenge based on their potential to create a spin-off company. The evaluation committee (first and second phase) and jury (final round) are made up of TTO staff, specialists on the respective technology, sponsors and other guests. At the 2015 edition, the winning team was rewarded with a pre-acceleration at the Baita startup accelerator; a Green Belt Six Sigma course; US$ 1,200 for each member; a trophy; and a certificate of participation as finalist. At UFRJ, there is the initiative COPPE-IDEA, organized by the UFRJ startup incubator of COPPE and intended to encourage the creation of spin-offs from UFRJ research outputs and the interaction with companies to generate new products, processes and services.

In Brazil, TT has not been an exclusive activity of TTOs. At PUC-Rio, PUCRS and UFRJ spin-off activities and research cooperation agreements with the industry are often assigned to startup incubators, tech parks or entrepreneurship related bodies. This usually takes place at institutions which had implemented and consolidated startup incubators or technology parks prior to the TTO. The TTOs of these institutions are mainly concerned with activities related to IP protection and licensing.

From the TTOs studied, only the Inova Unicamp actively works supporting spin-off activities. In addition to providing information, the TTO approaches the various stakeholders involved, though mentoring services, events and seminars. It also advises their spin-offs about possible opportunities that could result in obtaining financial resources. Unesp and UFSCar are also involved with spin-offs, but not as intensely as Unicamp. They support these companies by providing information to issues related to opening businesses, building business models, finding resources from venture capitalist or the government, among others.

Table 15.3 shows a general overview of the TT activities performed by the TTOs studied.

Startup incubators and technology parks

There is no standard model that portrays the relationship of the TTOs in Brazil with startup incubators or technology parks. In five of the seven studied cases (UFRJ, PUC-Rio, PUCRS, Unicamp and USP), the universities have incubators at one of their campuses. In general, these incubators were created prior to the creation of the TTOs (as mentioned earlier, many of the TTOs in Brazil are the outcome of the development of previously existing structures in universities). Currently, some TTOs even manage these startup incubators, as seen at Unicamp and USP.

At USP, since 2014 the TTO is also responsible for managing the technology parks linked to the university: the Technology Park of São Paulo/Jaguaré and the Technology Park of Ribeirão Preto. The Unicamp Science and Technology Park is also linked to its TTO, which maintains contact with other parks in the region of Campinas and in the interior of the state of São Paulo.

At PUC-Rio, the startup incubators are managed by the Genesis Institute, responsible for fostering innovation within the university. The TTO, in turn, provides the incubators with IP protection services, as also done at PUCRS. At PUCRS, both TTO and incubator are located within the technology park of the university, the TECNOPUC, which favors the interaction of the PUCRS Technology Transfer Office with companies from the incubator and the park.

The management of the UFRJ Innovation Agency is a member of the university's technology park Deliberative Board,[5] where the startup incubator of COPPE (a UFRJ Institute of Graduate Studies and Research in Engineering) is installed. The relationship between the UFRJ Innovation Agency and the Technology Park of UFRJ is incentivized by the physical proximity of these structures. Many of the TTO events take place at the facilities of the Technology Park of Rio. Concurrently, the TTO also actively participates in the events of the park.

The Innovation Agency of UFSCar represents the university at local initiatives of startup incubators and technology parks, which also includes an office at ECOTEC, one of the tech parks in São Carlos that UFSCar is affiliated to. São Carlos, home of the main university campus, also has the São Carlos Science Park and the ParqTec Foundation, which manage a network of startup incubators.

Similarly to the TTO of UFSCar, the Unesp Innovation Agency also has an office at a tech park, the Sorocaba Technology Park. This office is in charge of disseminating the activities and tasks performed by Unesp within the park. The

Table 15.3 Overview of TT activities of the studied cases until 2014

Institution	Licensing of patents in Brazil	Licensing of patent abroad	Licensing of computer programs	Licensing of cultivars	Licensing of further technologies*	Licensing total	Prominent licensing fields	Earned royalties in 2013 [1,000 UU$]
UFRJ	n.a.	n.a.	n.a.	n.a.	n.a.	n.a.	n.a.	n.a.
UFSCar	13	0	1	170	3	187	Agribusiness and Materials Engineering	265.00
PUC-Rio	2	0	4	0	0	6	Computer Science	n.a.
PUCRS	4	0	0	0	0	4	Engineering, Telecommunication, Medical Equipment	0.43
Unesp	6	1	4	0	1	12	Human and Animal Health, Agribusiness, Medical and Agro Equipment, New Materials	0
Unicamp	n.a.	n.a.	n.a.	n.a.	n.a.	91	n.a.	227.00
USP	37	1	2	0	5	45	Pharmacy, Machines and Equipment, Materials	640.00

* Including trademarks, industrial design, geographicalindications, integrated circuit topography, among others.

Sources: Elaborated by the authors.

Unesp Innovation Agency also interacts informally with several startup incubators throughout the state of São Paulo.

Networks

Given that TTOs act as an interface between the university and the industry, as they face similar challenges, their managers set up FORTEC in May 2006 (Torkomian, 2009), a non-profit private civil association. FORTEC is a representative body of the TTOs' technology managers in Brazil, which is similar to the Association of University Technology Managers – AUTM in the USA. In 2014 it had 215 associated TTOs, a 5.4 percent increase when compared to 2012. The goals of FORTEC are to:

- promote the culture of innovation, intellectual property and technology transfer;
- strengthen and disseminate the role of STIs;
- support the creation and institutionalization of TTOs;
- encourage professional training of all TTO staff;
- establish, promote and disseminate best practices for TTOs;
- support the representation of TTOs in the government and other civil society organizations;
- map and disclose the activities and indicators of TTOs;
- support the events of interest of its members;
- promote cooperation and networking activities among its members;
- contribute to the proposal of public policies related to technological innovation, intellectual property and technology transfer at the national, state and municipal levels;
- encourage research, scientific and technological development, innovation, intellectual property and technology transfer at the national, state and local levels;
- foster and cooperate with the training and development of professionals involved in the effort of innovation management, intellectual property and technology transfer for STIs operating in the country;
- promote cooperation and exchanges with associations and other bodies, both public and private, in Brazil and abroad; and
- develop, on their own or as required by its members or external bodies or partners, the studies, surveys, research, diagnostics, projects, tools, systems, programs, courses, seminars and publications related to its scope of operation and consistent with the principles of FORTEC.

The benefits perceived by TTOs from their participation in networks and in particular at FORTEC, are the result of the training provided at meetings and workshops, sharing of best practices, exchange of experiences with other TTOs, expansion of contacts and, finally, the result of having created a relationship network that favors the interaction and search for partners for joint activities.

All the studied TTOs also participate in state networks of Technology Transfer Offices. This is crucial to concentrate efforts in actions at the state level, such as public policy proposals to governments and funding agencies. Those located in Rio de Janeiro, the UFRJ Innovation Agency and PUC-Rio Innovation Agency, are members of the Technology and Innovation Network of Rio de Janeiro – REDETEC and of one of its thematic networks, the Intellectual Property and Technology Commercialization Network of Rio de Janeiro – REPICT, co-founded by PUC-Rio in 1998. REDETEC is a non-profit association that congregates the leading universities, research centers and development institutions of the state of Rio de Janeiro, bringing the companies closer to their associates, in order to promote the socio-economic and technological development of the state of Rio de Janeiro. REPICT played an important role not only in Rio de Janeiro, but also in the entire country. It was the cradle of discussions and reflections regarding STIs' IP and TT issues.

The TTOs of the state of São Paulo (Innovation Agency of UFSCar, Unesp Innovation Agency, Inova Unicamp and USP Innovation Agency) are regarded as the founders and participants of the São Paulo Inova Network, currently managed by Unicamp, whose goal is to congregate forces to strengthen the initiatives aimed at protecting intellectual property, the generation and transfer of technology and the promotion of innovation in the state of São Paulo. Finally, PUCRS Technology Transfer Office is affiliated with the Rio Grande do Sul Intellectual Property Network – RGPI (acronym for Rede Gaúcha de Propriedade Intelectual), which is responsible for strengthening the protection of scientific and technological knowledge and innovation developed in the state of Rio Grande do Sul.

Two additional networks were mentioned by USP and Unicamp: the National Association of Entities Promoting Innovative Enterprises – ANPROTEC (acronym for Associação Nacional de Entidades Promotoras de Empreendimentos Inovadores) and the RedEmprendia, a network of Ibero–American universities that promotes innovation and entrepreneurship.

Five of the seven studied TTOs (those of UFSCar, PUCRS, Unesp, Unicamp and USP) also stated they are affiliated with the National Association of Research and Development of Innovative Companies – ANPEI (acronym for Associação Nacional de Pesquisa e Desenvolvimento das Empresas Inovadoras), in order to communicate with and have access to innovative companies interested in innovation partnerships with universities.

Challenges

The creation of TTOs in Brazil was not a simple process. However, the most challenging task was not actually creating these offices, but rather establishing and structuring the process that came after. One of the main difficulties regards assembling the staff necessary to run the offices. The competences required to occupy the foreseen positions were often not available at the institutions. Much of the staff was transferred from other departments and bodies of the university to work at the TTOs, performing tasks that were not yet clearly defined. As a consequence, some of the staff did not adapt to their new posts and left the TTOs. Resources from government funding agency programs such as FINEP, CAPES and CNPq were essential to build the competences necessary to run the TTOs properly.

Despite all the dissemination work of the activities related to intellectual property, the practice of disclosing inventions, which is the first step for filing patent applications, has not yet been fully set up within the academic community in Brazil. One of the main issues regards how well the researchers understand the function and importance of invention disclosures and this misunderstanding often results in incomplete information in the application forms. As a matter of fact, IP related activities are frequently underestimated or even unknown by researchers.

Many of the disclosed inventions are rejected due to lack of novelty. It is also not unusual that prior publications hinder the protection of important discoveries. Due to their lack of knowledge about the IP laws, many researchers do not recognize the need to communicate an invention to the TTO before disclosing it somewhere else. Furthermore, as the focus on publishing originated from the official university performance assessment rules, it does not promote IP protection or other entrepreneurial activities by the academic community.

Other challenges regard the dissemination of patent based tools to support the initial drafting of projects and consequently the development of research in such a way that the results are aligned with the state of the art. Thus, a continuous reiteration about the importance of IP protection is imperative. Researchers, students and universities must learn to assess the intellectual and commercial potential of their research outputs and be more proactive in the commercialization of their technologies.

The main barriers to academic entrepreneurship in Brazil, according to the interviewees, regard the researchers' and students' lack of information and entrepreneurial culture. Nevertheless, the participation of students and faculty members in academic activities related to entrepreneurship has increased over the last few years in Brazil.

Final considerations

The data presented in the third section shows that the number of TTOs in Brazilian institutions is rapidly increasing. According to Torkomian (2009), the first TTOs in Brazil were founded 10 years before the Innovation Law. Now, 10 years after the Innovation Law, there are more than 200 TTOs in Brazil, which justifies the existence of different stages of internal structuring and maturity levels.

There are noticeable disparities among the Brazilian STIs, where some of them are not fully familiar with the steps needed to participate in the innovation process. However, there is a large number of Brazilian universities equipped for TT and they already carry out significant activities in this field, as shown in the case studies presented in this chapter.

Nevertheless, the focus of many Brazilian TTOs has been more on protecting technology than on transferring it to the industry. This latter activity is much more difficult and requires skills that academia is not accustomed to doing. In addition, TT activities in Brazil focus on providing licensing to companies already established in the market. Thus, the stimulus for creating spin-off companies is one of the points in the Innovation Law that still requires closer attention from the government.

The results of Brazilian STIs are still modest in terms of earned royalties. However, more important than increasing the revenues from royalties earned by universities is to transfer academic discoveries to the market, which refers to the role played by STIs in compliance with their mission to contribute to the economic and social development, thereby benefitting society at large.

Notes

1 The first academic revolution dates back to the nineteenth century, integrating research as a university function, in addition to the teaching task (Etzkowitz, 2003).
2 According to the Innovation Law, a STI is defined as a public administration body or entity whose institutional mission includes performing basic or applied scientific or technological research activities (Brasil, 2004).
3 Although the Law 5.772 was the first industrial property code in Brazil, IP issues had already been regarded – albeit secondarily – in other Brazilian laws from the 1940s.
4 TRIPS, or Trade Related Aspects on Intellectual Property Rights, is an agreement signed in 1994, during the negotiation of the General Agreements on Tariffs and Trade (GATT) (World Trade Organization [WTO], 2015). According to the World Trade Organization (2015) "it establishes minimum levels of protection that each government has to give to the intellectual property of fellow WTO members".
5 The Deliberative Council is the highest agency of the park, responsible for defining its long-term policies.

References

Brasil (2004). Lei da Inovação Tecnológica. Pub. L. No. 10.973 (2004). Retrieved from www.planalto.gov.br/ccivil_03/_ato2004-2006/2004/lei/l10.973.htm
Etzkowitz, H. (2001). The second academic revolution and the rise of entrepreneurial science. *IEEE Technology and Society Magazine, 20*(2), 18–29. doi:10.1109/44.948843
Etzkowitz, H. (2003). Research groups as "quasi-firms": the invention of the entrepreneurial university. *Research Policy, 32*(1), 109–121. doi:10.1016/S0048-7333(02)00009-4
Maculan, A. M., & Mello, J. M. C. (2009). University start-ups for breaking lock-ins of the Brazilian economy. *Science and Public Policy, 36*(2), 109–114.
Martins, P. V., De Andrade, R. S., & Torkomian, A. L. V. (2011). Percepção de Professores de uma Universidade Pública sobre seu Núcleo de Inovação Tecnológica. In *XIV Congresso Latino-Iberoamericano de Gestión Tecnológica - ALTEC 2011.*
Ministério da Ciência Tecnologia e Inovação. (2014a). Retrieved December 22, 2014, from www.mct.gov.br
Ministério da Ciência Tecnologia e Inovação. (2014b). *Relatório FORMICT, 2013. Política de Propriedade Intelectual das Instituições Científicas e Tecnológicas do Brasil* (p. 52). Brasília.

Pontifícia Universidade Católica do Rio de Janeiro. (2015). Retrieved January 7, 2015, from www.puc-rio.br

Pontifícia Universidade Católica do Rio Grande do Sul. (2014). Retrieved December 18, 2014, from www.pucrs.br

Póvoa, L. M. C. (2008). *Patentes de Universidades e Institutos Públicos de Pesquisa e a Transferência de Tecnologia para Empresas no Brasil* (Doctoral dissertation). Universidade Federal de Minas Gerais, UFMG, Brasil.

Rede de Propriedade Intelectual, Cooperação, Negociação e Comercialização de Tecnologia. (2004). O Projeto de Lei de Inovação: Qual é a Lei mais adequada para alavancar a Inovação Tecnológica no Brasil? In *VII Encontro de Propriedade Intelectual e Comercialização de Tecnologia e II Workshop de Propriedade Intelectual ANPROTEC.* (pp. 87–124). Rio de Janeiro: Rede de Tecnologia do Rio de Janeiro, INPI, Brasília, ANPROTEC.

Rodrigues, C. (2011). Universities, the Second Academic Revolution and Regional Development: A Tale (Solely) Made of "Techvalleys"? *European Planning Studies, 19*(2), 179–194. doi:10.1080/09654313.2011.532664

Santos, M. E. R. dos. (2005). *La Gestión de la Transferencia de Tecnología de la Universidad al Sector Productivo: Un Modelo para Brasil* (Doctoral dissertation). Autonomous National University of Mexico, UNAM, Mexico.

Santos, M. E. R. dos. (2010). The Formation of a National Technology Transfer Network: The Case Study of FORTEC (Brazil). Beyond the First World News – Innovation for International Development. Retrieved December 28, 2010, from www.beyondthefirstworld.com/?page_id=1086

Santos, M. E. R. dos, & Mello, J. M. C. (2009). IPR Policy and Management at University Technology Transfer Offices in Brazil. In *7th Biennial International Conference on University, Industry and Government Linkages.* Glasgow, Scotland.

Santos, M. E. R. dos, & Torkomian, A. L. V. (2013). Technology transfer and innovation: The role of the Brazilian TTOs. *International Journal of Technology Management & Sustainable Development, 12*(1), 89–111. doi:10.1386/tmsd.12.1.89

Stal, E. (1997). *Centros de Pesquisa Cooperativa: um Modelo Eficaz de Interação Universidade-Empresa* (Doctoral dissertation). Universidade de São Paulo, USP, Brasil.

Torkomian, A. L. V. (2009). Panorama dos núcleos de inovação tecnológica no Brasil. In M. E. Ritter dos Santos, P. T. M. de Toledo, & R. de A. Lotufo (Eds.), *Transferência de tecnologia: estratégias para a estruturação e gestão de núcleos de inovação tecnológica* (pp. 21–39). Campinas: Komedi.

Torkomian, A. L. V. (2011). Transferência de tecnologia, inovação tecnológica e desenvolvimento. In A. M. M. de Azevedo & M. A. Silveira (Eds.), *Gestão da Sustentabilidade Organizacional: Desenvolvimento de Ecossistemas Colaborativos* (pp. 101–114). Brasil: Gráfica Bandeirantes.

Universidade Estadual de Campinas. (2015). Retrieved January 7, 2015, from www.unicamp.br

Universidade de São Paulo. (2014). Retrieved December 20, 2014, from www.usp.br

Universidade Estadual Paulista. (2015). Retrieved January 7, 2015, from www.unesp.br

Universidade Federal de São Carlos. (2015). Retrieved January 7, 2015, from www.ufscar.br

Universidade Federal do Rio de Janeiro. (2015). Retrieved January 7, 2015, from www.ufrj.br

World Intellectual Property Organization. (2014). World Intellectual Property Indicators. Geneva.

World Trade Organization. (2015). Undestanding the WTO: the Agreements. Retrieved February 3, 2015, from www.wto.org/english/thewto_e/whatis_e/tif_e/agrm7_e.htm

16 China's university technology transfer system

Political mobilization and academy for economic growth

Chunyan Zhou

Introduction

The "Great Wall" between the university and the economy was torn down in the 1980s as part of a mobilization to achieve rapid economic growth in China. Solid concrete walls, replaced by porous picket fences, symbolized the social responsibility of the university. The third mission of the university germinated at the behest of government and the Party, making contribution to economic growth as well as social development an academic task. Acknowledging technology demands through consulting for industry, the university developed applied-orientation research, followed by creation of its own high-tech firms. As we shall see, the university technology transfer system is broader than the activities of a technology transfer office (TTO) focused on the commercializable results of academic research. Rather, it is concerned with promoting the utilization of technology at various levels, derived from sources within and without the university, nationally and internationally.

The Association of University Technology Managers (AUTM) defines university technology transfer (UTT) as "the process of transferring scientific findings from one organization to another for the purpose of further development and commercialization."[1] Knowledge spillover from campuses in a knowledge-based society promotes economic development in a given region, typically through UTT, including faculty's consulting for industry (technology service), commercialization of lab research (technology license) and firm-formation based on new inventions and new ideas (technology self-application). The Chinese university can itself own and run a group of companies, called university-run enterprises (UREs), to spillover knowledge/technology and help support the university.

This chapter analyzes the key characteristics of China's UTT and focuses on a triple helix path through the UTT system, referring to the activities from faculty consulting to firm-formation or developing UREs. It is argued that the driving role of the government under the Communist Party of China (CPC) – that is, political mobilization, is the most important engine propelling UTT to promote economic growth. The UTT system will evolve as a consequence of the evolution of the government-pulled and Party-led triple helix to a university–industry–government interactive one or "overlapping triple helix".

University technology transfer: problems and challenges

UTT has become part of the academic research ethos. The importation of a strong research ethic from Germany, combined with a lack of resources to support research, created an impetus to consult for industry in U.S. universities in the mid-nineteenth century (Jencks and Riesman 1968, Etzkowitz 2008). An analogous resource-lack driven academic transformation took place in China in the 1980s as student numbers increased without a concomitant increase in funding. China's universities didn't charge tuition until 1998. As the higher education developed fast, a funding gap appeared. In order to supplement the inadequate resource, the university started to provide technology/knowledge for the society, simultaneously developing its research and service mission.

Three factors play critical roles in UTT: the potential of research for use; the development needs of regional industries, including agriculture; and the interest of universities in regulating the commercialization process in order to protect their reputations, since many discoveries have health and medical implications (Apple 1989). On one hand, China UTT is primarily short of the first factor, the capacity in research and industrial application of the results with commercialization potential, even though it is gradually improving in the recent decade.

For example, He, Wu and Zhou (2007) analyzed the contribution of UTT to Beijing regional growth and found that patent licensing was minor compared to other UTT methodologies. China is a major manufacturing base and is becoming one of the largest consumption markets in the world. Nevertheless, most its production activities still hover in low end of the industry chain, finishing the final products in the production and processing stages or doing outsourcing, rather than in the early stages of new idea formation, R&D and product design, on the other. A "domestic innovation gap" has thus been identified as a national issue.

Technology transfer from university to industry takes place in multiple ways, including:

1   providing entrepreneurship education to train new entrepreneurs
2   consulting for existing firms
3   jointly developing projects by university and industry
4   sharing rare facilities for R&D
5   providing technology patent licensing
6   creating new firms to apply new technologies born on campus.

These ways embody the university's three missions as a primary social institution: teaching, research and service for the society. The university is good at 1–3 based on its teaching tradition and tight connections with industrial practice, but poor at 4–6, especially 5 and 6, caused by quantity, quality and the relatively low licensing rate of university technology patents.

The quantity of the granted patents has not been a main issue in the UTT. Traditionally, China suffered from a lack of products with intellectual property rights (IPRs), which has seriously decreased the sustainable innovation potential of technical enterprises. From the 1950s to 1970s, manufacturing industry fell into a declining technological spiral due to lack of technology imports on the one hand and the low level of indigenous technology, on the other. From the 1980s, as China opened to the world, imported technologies played a predominant role in industry. Concomitantly, the recent number of IPRs of China has risen significantly, as national investment to science and technology (S&T) enterprises is great and increasing rapidly; it reached ¥1,200 billion in 2013 (Ding 2014). The number of patents granted, both resident and non-resident, ranked second worldwide in 2012 (WIPO Statistical Country Profiles 2013). According to the State Intellectual Property Office of the PRC, the total number of the granted patents was 233,000 in 2014; among them 163,000 (70 per cent) are domestic (Li 2015).

Nevertheless, the commercialization rate of research results is only around 10% (Ding 2014). The quality of the granted patents is a key problem in the commercialization process. This is partially caused by the corrupted administration system in research support, which results in government funds used improperly. The failure of the research evaluation system, which favors publications over technology invention and application, makes the result even worse. It is a long-term and arduous effort for the UTT officers to increase the rate of utilization.

Government-pulled and Party-led triple helix

UTT in China is a key feature of a Party-led, government-pulled and university–industry joint combat strategy for economic growth. The UTT concept has been extended to include science parks, incubators, high-tech industrial development zones, expanding the third mission of the university, to grow the economy. These imported innovation mechanisms were utilized in a different way, and on a significantly larger scale, than in their country of origin with quantitative increase morphing into qualitative change as a comprehensive organizational network of interface is created.

Recent developments in China include establishment of technology transfer units in most universities, working among the university, local government and industries. For instance, Zhejiang University established a special department, the local liaison department, to enhance the university's linkage with local government agencies and industrial firms. Many other universities have established a Science and Technology Enterprises Department to enhance the linkage.

China's innovation mobilization strategy

The state ownership of university and industry insures that only government can be an organizer for innovation, with government driving the other two spheres to achieve regional innovation. The government thus mobilizes the university and industry for national strategy. In recent decades, the National Science and Technology Conference (Beijing, January 2006) has indicated that university and industry should further contribute to innovation. Through policies and measures, government encourages overlapping between state-owned universities and state-owned companies. For example, in 2009 the government issued five measures to push universities to jointly work with industrial firms and research institutes, including "Suggestions on Strengthening Universities to Economic and Social Development" to encourage university–industry–research institute collaborations to build industrial technology alliances, and jointly develop colleges with industrial features by the Ministry of Education and other agencies (up to 2009, 22 have been involved). Thus, innovation in university–industry collaboration modes to promote UTT and establish R&D and industrialization bases for research application has become a high priority in the mobilization for transition to a knowledge-based society.

Technological application activities in the universities are increasing as government takes a lead in providing resources. There have been special "joint fund" projects to support the China National Science Foundation's (CNSF's) collaborations with center government agencies, local government and corporations from the CNSF since 1999, which aim at funding fusion, greatly enhancing the application of the research results which generated in campuses and research institutes. The "joint fund" has supported 1,265 projects from 1999 to 2008, with a total of ¥680 million. CNSF also prescribes that projects with industrial potential can obtain priority during the application.[2]

Universities can obtain additional government funding through national research projects from the Ministry of Education and S&T Ministry, e.g., 863 Program (1986),[3] National Climbing Project (1991)[4] and 973 Program (1997)[5] "knowledge innovation program" of the Chinese Academy of Sciences implemented by China Academy of Science (1998), as well as various local projects/programs. The central government enhances its investment in university research in relative proportion to general university funding growth. This policy greatly improved university abilities in basic and applied research. In addition, Project 985[6] and Project 211[7] play important roles in developing research ability of the university as well.

A rapidly growing state-owned university system forms the basis of the government-pulled triple helix. A state-owned industry system is the other basis. Although China has tried to transform from plan into market economy since the end of 1970s, the government (central and local) still has tremendous administration rights. Indeed, administration plays a more important role in social economic operation than the market mechanism, through large-scale state-owned enterprises controlling most national resources. Before reform in 1978, private enterprises didn't exist in the economic system. Although private enterprises are increasingly significant as an economic factor, the state-owned system retains a dominant position. Government agents still control market dealings and executive intervention plays a very important role. Social and economic activity embodies the state's will, even only the top leader's idea.[8]

Through university–industry cooperation, local government tries to build a platform for enterprises, using its financial resources, including Ministry of Science and Technology, Ministry of Education, China Academy of Science and

CNSF. Some big projects are also organized for innovation. For example, Liaoning Provincial government set up a Platform for Information Service and a Network for Large Facility Use, which attracted over 100 research institutes, universities and enterprises to participate. Even a small alliance usually consists of units from government, university, research institutes and industrial firms. For instance, Shaoxing Textile Research Alliance was established by 3 local governments, 6 universities, 4 research institutes and 22 local textile firms in 2006, aiming to transferring applicable technology, promoting research cooperation, and improving research capacity of the local textile cluster. The alliance as a servicing platform helps its members to establish and develop technology transfer centers in Shaoxing City, assists them to obtain funding from government and industry sources and provides information for sharing among the members. Professors were organized to make contracts with the firms in Shaoxing and campus research results were displayed to the firms. Some large-scale consulting activities were designed to increase the number of consulting contracts signed and academia–industry collaborations. The consortia undertook 70 governmental R&D projects, and 10 cooperative R&D projects, all input R&D expenditure 40 million CNY, and obtain 400 patents in 2006–2007 (Qian 2007).

The Party's role in mobilization for economic growth

UTT is not only government-pulled, with university and industry in collaboration, but also Party-led. China's political, economic, education and cultural systems are interwoven. The political power system is so strong that other systems lose their own trajectories in response to the political one. Political authority of the state is dominant, distributing economic and social resources by fiat.

Indeed the CPC political system plays a more important role in social economic operation than the government administration and market mechanism, through large-scale state-owned enterprises controlling most national resources. The Party in power governs above all the triple helix spheres, including universities, industry and government. The Party's will decides the triple helix shape. In other words, the Party shapes the government-pulled triple helix and the path of UTT. In addition, the Party is always combined with the state, as well as all other social institutions, in playing a guiding role, whenever it deems necessary, throughout the entire society.

Given that the state is still predominant despite the existence of a significant private sector and an emerging Civil Society; as a result, the government administration must follow the Party's will that controls the vast majority of material and spiritual resources to lead the activities of university and industry, including technology transfer. The outlines of this hegemonic social structure, if not its ideology, are replicated in all social organizations and interactions among them, giving a different form and meaning to apparently similar phenomena such as the U.S. spin-off firm and the Chinese university-run enterprise (URE).

Government-pulled and Party-led triple helix

To develop research universities has been looked upon as a measure to fulfill the objective of effective indigenous technological innovation. As all Chinese research universities are public or state-owned, controlled or directly run by the government, they thus respond quickly to mandates and signals from their sponsors. In this context, academic entrepreneurship transcends simple knowledge capitalization as the university interacts with innovative actors from other institutional spheres in a variety of ways to promote regional growth through well-funded initiatives in recent years. These interactions form a government-pulled university–industry–government triple helix (Etzkowitz and Zhou 2008).

In this triple helix, research in universities is increasing rapidly as government takes the lead in providing resources. As a whole, the central government continues to enhance its investment in university research. Relatively, it is a stable increase as university funding increases. This policy greatly improved university ability in basic and applied research. In addition, Project 985 and Project 211 also play important roles in developing research ability of university. Special funding is available from the CNSF, Ministry of Education (MOE) and S&T Ministry (MOST) to support university–industry collaboration projects. Indeed, CNSF prescribes that projects with high industrial potential can obtain priority during the application process. The policy oriented the research in Pasteur's quadrant (Stokes 1997).

The state-owned system retains an overwhelming position, even though the private sector is increasingly significant as an economic factor. Social activity must embody the state's will, even only the top leading circle's idea. Government agencies still control market dealings and executive intervention plays a very important role. The university and industry as main innovation actors are thus mobilized by the government, which forms a government-pulled and Party-led triple helix and endows the UTT unique characteristics. Such a triple helix has following characteristics.

- Government designs, initiates, organizes and controls national, regional and local significant projects for innovations, economic growth and social development (strong administration).
- Virtually all research universities, key research institutes and large-scale enterprises are affiliated to central or local government (state ownership).
- The top leader's thought is paramount and orients the Party and government to make policies and formulate measures to implement them (political authoritativeness).
- Anything can be built through national or local government plans, programs or projects to fulfill state goals in innovation and development (mobilization thinking).
- The government establishes and manages primary innovation institutions in a region, such as high-tech developed areas, university science parks, incubators, technology market, intellectual right exchange platforms and information system in science and technology (top-down innovation).

We cannot say there is no government-pull in innovation in any country. In fact, in some circumstances, periods or emergencies, the American government took the lead in innovation, in direct or indirect ways (Etzkowitz, Gulbrandsen and Levitt 2001; Etzkowitz 2008; Mazzucatto 2013). However, it is a characteristic that should be specially highlighted for understanding China.

University entrepreneurship

Projects and programs such as "Project 211" and "Project 985" were invented to promote university research and technology transfer capacity. The government formally emphasized the significance of indigenous innovation at the National S&T Conference held in Beijing on 11 January 2006. It was simultaneously decided to enhance the role of universities and research institutes in technological innovation, beyond basic research tasks. As a result, some Chinese universities began a transition to the entrepreneurial mode, as entrepreneurs (Zhou and Peng 2008).

Although industry–university collaborations can be traced back to the 1950s and even earlier, S&T enterprises created with university resources (firms formation) only began to appear in the 1980s. Since the First National Science Conference held in 1978 concluded that science and technology is the leading source of productivity, the university was expected actively to play a role in regional innovation. The Chinese university started its entrepreneur career. It has developed its own firms, UREs, from early 1980s, but in the meantime keeps the tradition, providing consultant services for existing firms. UREs in China developed with surprising speed during the 1990s, encouraged by national policies. A few universities have created some of the largest and most successful high-tech enterprises in the country. Tsinghua Tongfang, Beida Fangzheng, Beijing Zhongnong Tiannuo Science Developing Co. Ltd. and Beijing Futong Environmental Engineering Co. Ltd. are among the UREs that have earned significant monies for their university's development.

Academic research results with commercialization potential were rarely transferred to industry. Thus the university has to fulfill technology transfer and knowledge capitalization through establishing UREs. Most of UREs started from low-tech and then grew up to higher-tech industry. Their path to growth is low-tech to capital and then to high-tech enterprises. They are neither spin-offs, nor start-ups: UREs are actually enterprises possessed and established by universities.

China's academic institutions (universities and research institutes) play a much more direct role in firm formation than is typical of U.S. universities. Some admittedly are on the way to becoming good research universities. They have developed the necessary research bases for commercialization of knowledge, but the research results did not spill over enough to develop high-tech entrepreneurship, impacting the regional economy. Some external factors to be propitious to the development include strong support to universities from the government, natural collaboration relationship between university and industry, and service consciousness to contribute to the economy as well as university growth in recent decades.

The government increasingly encourages university entrepreneurial activities. The National Conference of Science and Technology (in 2006) embodied the idea to construct a Chinese National Innovation System, with the university contributing to achieve indigenous innovation in regions. Industry was originally expected to be the prime mover in technology-based firm formation. In an important document, "Solution on Implementing Outline of the Science and Technology Plan for Enhancing Independent Innovation Capability" (issued by CPC Central Committee and State Council in January 2006), enterprises were encouraged to take the lead in technological innovation, with the expectation that the university will assist them. When this strategy did not produce results, government encouraged universities, through a combination of incentives and budget cuts, to substitute for industry in creating firms from a large repository of knowledge about advanced, if not leading-edge technology, that resided in the university. These policies are expected to continue to influence university–industry relationship in the next 30 to 50 years.

Local government plays a critical role in establishing various transfer channels, working with local universities. As university entrepreneurship ability increases, UREs with high technology support from high quality researchs on campus are expected to upgrade national and regional old industrial conurbations and promote newborn industries. Some UREs spin-off from their mother institutions to the market, becoming listed companies. Non-faculty professional managers are hired to operate the formerly academic administered UREs. The mother university acts as a stockholder through investing in technology. University and firms are more deeply involved, sharing R&D resources through cooperative research, joint venture or research projects, patent licensing, etc.

The university tradition: Faculty technical aid to industry

Most Chinese universities were built in the 1950s when the needs of industrial production were primary, since the newborn PRC faced the issue of recovering its economy. Thus teaching in the universities has been tightly combined with industrial and agricultural practices. The faculties were oriented to application purposes and providing technical aid for industry. However, such a university– industry linkage can be called "university's aid to industry" – that is, institutions in industry and university as state affiliated parts generally collaborate with each other for technique improvement. Usually, individual factories or entire industrial sectors asked for university help to resolve specific technical problems. Universities passively waited for the requests from industries. Since the 1980s when university research recovered, its regional role has become one of assisting import of technologies. At that stage, the state strategy was to access techniques from other countries; faculties were thus encouraged to be consultants for existing firms to help them understand the new technologies.

This is similar to industrial consultation, which is the starting point of U.S. UTT, having become an important practice of professors in some universities as well as bringing a financial return to their faculties. Professors such as V. Bush in MIT in the 1930s learned about firm technological needs through consultation and brought problems back to labs on campus to start further theoretical investigation while they dealt with the practical problems (Etzkowitz 2002).

As research resources are concentrated in a few highly reputed universities, they contributed the most to consulting activities. For example, under the leadership of faculty in Peking University a consultation firm was organized, with more than 200 business or technology experts living in different cities and divided into 5 groups depending on their expertise. A series of books on consultation (edited by authors at Peking University) was published by Zhongxin Press at the turn of the new century. International Technology Transfer Centers were established to find new technologies that the industries need.

Moreover, multidisciplinary researchers worked together to promote industrial development, e.g., through initiating consulting platforms. Typically, 36 universities headed by University of Science and Technology of China made contracts with hundreds of joint projects with Chaohu City Administration of Anhui Province for solving industrial problems in May 2007, with a total investment CNY 60 million. These projects aim at pushing university–industry interaction and further applying technologies generated from campuses through building new rural areas, joint labs and engineering technology centers.

UREs vs. spin-offs

UREs have three typical characteristics: (1) university takes up all or part equity; (2) those who operate UREs basically come from university staff or students, especially at the very beginning; and (3) R&D of UREs mainly relies on their mother universities. In fact, as potentially successful new tech firms, UREs expand campus knowledge application and contribute to developing the basic research strength of their mother sponsors. Since these companies typically operate as a university-owned entity or under the umbrella of the university, the distance between firm and academic lab is virtually non-existent, with the same people often occupying key roles in both venues.

Although universities in both U.S. and China are encouraged to create enterprises, UREs are quite different in their essential nature. A spin-off by definition is an economic entity of academic origin that becomes an independent entity, whereas a URE is a business enterprise that remains part of the administrative structure of the university. UREs evolve from owners to stockholders; however, before they grow up to list companies the university is their home and may include its annual budget with the UREs. This is a big difference from spin-offs which are not under an umbrella from the beginning. The latter doesn't have any ownership with the university, but has academic or personal connections. UREs can freely use the mother institution's resources, including labs facilities, and are controlled by the university/research institute.

There is an umbilical cord connecting baby to mother, even though they have been born and are growing.

The development of UREs has raised the issue of university's purity and missions. There have increasingly been complaints that the university is becoming "industry." For example, university is competing with enterprise actors in innovation through its advantage in high-tech research; the tension between university and industry is increasing; and since university has its own companies; excessively competitive university–industry relationships will eventually induce a difficult technology transfer from university to industry; and so on.

The role of university in a society is generally determined not only by the economic logic, but also by the social division of labor. The division prescribed that the university is an institution for education and production of knowledge. Historically, universities have been shaped by, drawn their agenda from, and been responsible to the communities that founded them. Each generation has established a social contract between the university and the society it serves. Today, an array of powerful social, economic, and technological forces is driving change in the needs of society and the institutions created to respond to those needs (Duderstadt 1999). Ownership of UREs that have intruded industrial elements into the university really becomes an improper focus of university–industry relationship. In addition, a university should be a social commonweal enterprise – that is, non-profit-making, by social contract; however, UREs made them rich. The poor professors nicknamed "Stinking Number Nine" before the end of 1980s now are becoming a rich class, changing their poor scholar image.

Spin-offs in Boston and Silicon Valley exemplify that universities have made tremendous contribution to local economic and social development. Many UREs from some universities such as Tsinghua University, Peking University, have also taken the leading role in China's high-tech industry. Tongfang, Wangxin, Dongruan Gufen and Founder respectively established and operated by Tsinghua University, Zhejiang University, and Northeastern University, have become the No. 3, 12, 15 and 25 Chinese Top-100 S&T Firms in early 2002 (Eun et al. 2005). They exemplify the advantages of UREs as high-growth enterprises. Based-on huge self-interest (Table 16.1) considerations, universities are reluctant to give up the ownership of UREs.

The hierarchy between UREs and the university is generated by the political and economic system. The birth of UREs is due to a state-owned system in which it was natural to ask: just as government has its enterprises at the national and local level why cannot a university have its own firms, especially since university, government and industry are all state creatures? This statist logic is at one and the same time the competitive advantage and the Achilles' heel of socialist market economy.

While it may be untenable in "neo-liberal" institutional logic theory[9] (Thornton and Ocasio 2008), it is commonplace in China's innovation practice that government, university and industry all create capital through their firms. Ideally, they should have shared (overlapping) functions (Zhou 2014a) as independent institutional spheres in an optimum triple helix, rather than one sphere dominating

Table 16.1 Total assets of group companies of UREs in China

Mother university with UREs group companies	2010		2013	
	Ranking	Total assets (billion CNY)	Ranking	Total assets (billion CNY)
Peking University (Beijing)	1	67.523	1	117.656
Tsinghua University (Beijing)	2	50.604	2	97.120
Northeastern University (Shenyang)	3	11.946	3	16.409
Tongji University (Shanghai)	4	7.115	4	12.699
China University Of Petroleum (Huadong)	7	3.984	5	9.502

Adapted by the author. Data source: Official website of Science and Technology Development Center, Ministry of Education. Available online: www.cutech.edu.cn/cn/kjcy/xbcytj/2012/05/1331845780456224.htm (accessed 28 February 2015).

the others, but that is not the contemporary model. It is hypothesized that a stronger role for the state will be legitimized in western innovation theory and practice while a more equal division of labor in setting innovation course and direction will emerge in China (Etzkowitz and Etzkowitz 2014).

While some convergence is expected; significant difference in the role of university, industry and government in various triple helix configurations may also be expected, creating a natural experimental design. May the most innovative and productive system that best serves the people emerge!

University patenting

Chinese university research is not characterized by a shortage in quantity, but of quality and technological usability. UTT is generally accomplished by means of IP licensing agreements (contracts) between universities and private companies or publicly owned commercialization agencies, rather than published papers' number, which is increasingly growing up. From 2003 to September 1 2013, there were 1,143,000 papers published by Chinese, ranking second worldwide. The papers are cited a total of 7,098,800 times, ranking no. 5 in the world. In 2012, the number of papers which are cited over the average times is 43,500, accounting for 26.4 per cent of the total number of papers in the year. Among them 81.8 per cent of the papers were contributed by the university and 16.9 per cent came from research institutes (ISTIC 2013). However, this seems not to improve the 10 per cent commercialization rate (Ding 2014). It is that the quantity of university patents of high quality is a key in UTT in reality.

The Silicon Valley economy has continued to flourish partly because the region is home to several world-class research universities. In addition to Stanford University, the University of California System also plays a vital role. The latter has been the leader among U.S. universities in creating patents (Munroe and

Westwind 2009). Universities have also been an important research force in China since 1980s, even though it has a tradition that state-owned research institutions take most national critical projects. University capacity in knowledge production, application and dissemination, together with technology demands from the industries and interest overlapping between university and industry, determine UTT's possibilities and necessity in China (Zhou and Peng 2008).

In recent years, the number of the Chinese invention patents has grown up dramatically (Table 16.2). A university's contribution to patents granted is also rapidly increasing. Tsinghua University, for example, ranks 15th in the IEEE Spectrum Patent List of 2012,[10] with 1,168 granted patents (ISTIC 2013). The capacity of university knowledge application and production is enhancive. This provides the possibility for UTT to industry, although applying the patents to industries is still a big issue.

URE capital generation

Since the 1970s, the office of technology transfer in U.S. universities has adopted multiple methods to transfer technology. Some of them operate incubators or science parks. Moreover, many university-originated start-ups, as they became successful, acted as angels to newly emerging firms, providing a source of venture capital (Etzkowitz, Solé and Piqué 2007). In pace with capitalization of knowledge, there is a move from Mode 1 where the university was an independent space for discovery, beyond control, with government as a key funder, the main guarantor, to Mode 2 typology – i.e. an organization engaged in high levels of interaction with a range of stakeholders where sustainability is a function of a broader legitimization as seen through the eyes of the state, private partners and, indeed, society as a whole (Gibbons et al. 1994; Dooley and Kirk 2007; Rinne and Koivula 2009, Gibb et al. 2013). The financial resources of the higher education institutions in China basically come from state appropriations, mainly used for daily operation – including staff salaries, infrastructure, disciplines development, teaching and research work; no special funds can be used for UREs. For most UREs, the first

Table 16.2 The numbers of granted patents: 2012 vs. 2002

Country	Patent grants. Resident (rank)		Patent grants. Non-resident (rank)		Patent grants. Abroad (rank)	
	in 2012	*in 2002*	*in 2012*	*in 2002*	*in 2012*	*in 2002*
Japan	224,917 (1)	108,515 (1)	49,874 (3)	10,677 (6)	118,567 (1)	67,136 (1)
China	*143,808 (2)*	*5,868 (8)*	*73,297(2)*	*15,389 (3)*	*8,294 (12)*	*480 (21)*
USA	121,026 (3)	86,976 (2)	132,129 (1)	76,542 (1)	107,892 (2)	56,873 (2)
Germany	21,485 (6)	23,096 (4)	3,168 (16)	3,019 (13)	55,640 (3)	36,378 (3)

Adapted by the author. Data source: IPs data draw from WIPO, 2013 Statistical Country Profiles. Available online: www.wipo.int/ipstats/en/statistics/country_profile/ (assessed 20 February 2015).

investment came from the mother university (with partners); and they usually have their own technological resources (IPRs or imported high-techs) and products. As capital increases, they invest in other industries or products.

For example, the Founder Group, one the best UREs of Peking University, established in 1986, has 70% of its total shares held by Peking University and 30% by the group's management. As the decision-maker and founder of Founder Group, Academician Wang Xuan invented the Chinese-character Laser Phototypesetting Technology and laid a solid foundation for the future development of the group. Nowadays, Founder is investing in its development in IT, real estate, medical/pharmaceutical, financial and commodity trading industry.[11] Beida Jade Bird Group was established in 1992, based on a national key research project – namely the Jade Bird Project – undertaken by Peking University together with 20 other research institutions. However, Peking University Biotech Co., Ltd. is a joint venture by Wearnes (WBL Corporation Limited) in Singapore, Peking University and Beijing Holdings Limited. Another URE of Peking University – PKU High-Tech – has become a listed company in Shanghai and Shenzhen Stock Exchange to raise private capital. This became an important financial channel for UREs. See Figure 16.1.

Some national university science parks exemplified government–university collaborations. For instance, the Science Park of Lanzhou was initially funded by

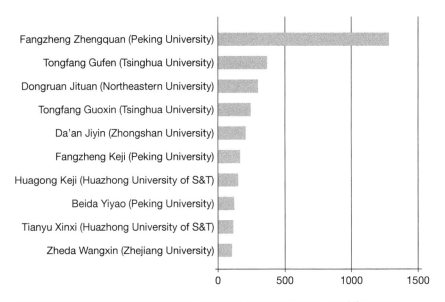

Adapted by the author. Data source: *Xueqiu*, online available at http://xueqiu.com/S/SH601901, accessed on 28 February 2015.

Figure 16.1 The stock value of top 10 UREs at stock exchanges (as at 27 February 2015; unit: 100 million)

Lanzhou University and Chengguan District Government of Lanzhou City, and then attracted private capital through the stock market. There is a movement away from a system which is almost completely supported by central or local public funding to a situation with multiple non-direct public financial resources such as fees, research grants, local development money, donations, contract research and philanthropy (Williams 2009). Financial channels for URE development are increasingly widened. Even if the university withdraws support for UREs, they will expand following business and market rules.

UTT in a government-pulled triple helix

The government policies and laws play a critical role in promoting the innovation system, the development of science and technology, knowledge industrialization and high-tech industry. UTT has attracted greater government attention in recent years. The university is working with government and industry in contributing to economic growth.

University–government interaction: Joint ventures

National centers of technology transfer were first established in six top-ranking universities: Tsinghua University; Shanghai Jiaotong University; Xi'an Jiaotong University; China East University of Science and Technology; China University of Science; and Technology and Sichuan University. Some universities have even set up international centers of technology transfer to introduce technology from other countries. To date, 276 national technology transfer demonstration agencies have been appointed by the Ministry of Science and Technology. The problem persists of how a university can generate technologies instead of importing them from abroad – that is, how to enhance research and its commercialization. Innovative tools such as the university science park, incubators, and new and high tech development zone are utilized to advance innovation.

a. Jointly developing national university science parks

The national university science park model is in the overlapping area of university and government, a "battlefield" for the interaction between them. It tightly connects government and university, becoming one of the most important facilities for commercializing research on campus. University science parks are developed to incubate high-tech firms based on technologies from campuses and imported from all over the world. The essential purpose of the incubator is to educate a group of people to act as an effective organization. Since the first university science park was established adjacent to Northeastern University in Shenyang City in 1989, the Ministry of Science and Technology and the Ministry of Education jointly initiated 93 national university science parks. Additionally, some small science parks also play active roles – for example, the Safety Technology Industrial Park in Hangzhou, established by Zhejiang Police

Vocational College and local government in 2007. Fourteen small firms in the safety technology field incubated in the park. The small park located on the campus plays an innovation role as an incubator.

The science park idea came from the co-evolution between Stanford University and Silicon Valley. However, this earliest ancestor was formed naturally, rather than created. "The evolution of the Valley as a global center for high-tech innovation was almost totally organic, rather than intentional. Certainly, the creation of the Stanford Industrial Park was an intentional effort to provide a center of high technology located near a university that shared its vision, but virtually every other aspect of the emergence of the Valley's prominence was unplanned, unexpected and unintended on the macro level" (Munroe and Westwind 2009: 51). Stanford is a natural incubator; providing a support structure for teachers and students to initiate new ventures: intellectual, commercial and conjoint. The university is also a seedbed for new interdisciplinary scientific fields and new industrial sectors, each cross-fertilizing the other. Thus, tying the generation of economic activity to the university can create a self-sustaining dynamic of economic and social development based upon its traditional features. Nevertheless, the rise of a science park movement is impossible without effective policies from the government.

b. Jointly constructing new and high-tech development zones.[12]

Constructing development zones appears to be a movement across the country. Each province has several high-tech development zones, assessed as national or local level. For example, by 2009 there were 5 national new and high-tech development zones and 25 at province level, located in 14 cities of Liaoning Province. They contribute to regional innovation and development with 36,914 enterprises registered in them up to 2009, including 3,406 industry, 1,574 foreign capital enterprises and 51 branch agents of the World Top 500 Enterprises. Province Government has recognized 831 of the total as high and new-tech enterprises. In 2009, their gross industry product was ¥ 170.41 billion, of which ¥ 34.71 billion was used for infrastructure.

University–industry interaction: the University–Enterprise Cooperation Committee

Much of Chinese industry in which manufacturing is dominant operates with low-tech and/or imported technology in a cheap labor and natural resources economy. Firms are very weak in absorptive capacity and innovation ability in traditional industries. The transition to understand and respect IPRs seems to require a longer period of time. The enterprises thus have to give much more effort to engage in their own R&D activities than those firms in technologically developed countries. In fact, industry is the main investor for R&D activities in the society. In 2012 the total national R&D expenditure of China was ¥ 1029.84 billion, including ¥ 784.22 billion (76.2 per cent) from the enterprises, ¥ 154.89 billion (15 per cent) from state-owned research institutes, and ¥ 78.06 billion (7.6 per cent) from universities.[13]

On the one hand, government calls on universities to serve industrial firms to improve their existing technologies and find new applied ones. As IP from some campuses increase, firms increasingly choose the university as a technology source. The university no longer confines itself to basic or applied research, but works with industry on R&D and commercial products. This involvement in industrial R&D also promotes the basic or applied research goals on campus by expanding the support for research. Not surprisingly, the university, as producer of knowledge and industry as the user, need each other, with a common goal. Typically, under government leadership, a University–Enterprise Cooperation Committee was established to enhance the linkage.

The case of Northeastern University can better explain the phenomenon. The Northeastern University (NEU) of China led by the former Ministry of Metallurgy and subsequently by the Ministry of Education before September of 1998, was initially jointly managed in 2001 by the Department of Education, Liaoning Province and Shenyang City. The decentralization further ignited the university's local economic service mission at the same time as government played a growing role in building university–industry links. The case of NEU and its largest URE, Neusoft, illustrates that the government plays a critical role between the university and the local industrial firms.

A typical example of government's role in university–industry links is the University-Enterprise Cooperation Committee of NEU, established 2 November 1991 (Zhou 2014b). Within the first year of the Committee's life, more than 500 university–industry contracts were signed, worth ¥ 270 million, creating an economic value of ¥ 2 billion. It consists of the Economic and Trade Committee of Liaoning Province Government, the Educational Department of Liaoning Province Government, NEU and 35 of the largest state enterprises in Liaoning Province. Regularly, representatives from the Economic and Trade Committee are responsible for organizing meetings and forums to report the demands from the industrial firms and the university. Government agency thus becomes a "regional innovation organizer," playing the role of a leading institution of university–industry cooperation and innovation to make a "consensus space" (Etzkowitz 2008). According to relevant rules, first NEU must announce its newest research achievement to the membership enterprises, and transfer technology to them as a priority. Second, in the selection of research problems and training talents, it should consider the needs of membership enterprises. Enterprises, in turn, should issue their technology needs and problems to NEU to address.

The University–Enterprise Cooperation Committee of NEU aims at strengthening university–industry linkages. The Committee commissioned relevant Liaoning departments to organize an annual conference to summarize existing linkages. Participants include relevant NEU leaders and experts, the principals of administration and technology in given enterprises, as well as the directors of science and technology in each city government of Liaoning Province.

Government supports university and industry through making financial resources available to them, including those from the Ministry of Science and Technology, the Ministry of Education, the China Academy of Science and the CNSF. The university is expected to contribute to local innovation in three ways: providing entrepreneurship education; helping industry to resolve problems; and establish joint R&D centers and support UREs, especially from the research in its labs. Industry is encouraged to rely on university research to renew existing or achieve new technological innovation and products.

Guanxi Network and Collective Cooperation

"Guanxi"[14] denotes interpersonal relationships in the specific and narrow meaning of informal social connection. Guanxi or social connection is very important in any culture; however, it has been one of the most important factors to be successful in the society. Typically children learn how to make Guanxi with their teachers from their parents; the young generation working for the government or the Party follows the old to make Guanxi, which may either cause corruption for the common interest or may result in productive results. Guanxi could develop jointly from official work opportunities, personal family contacts, business partnership or former colleagues, students, teachers, etc. The combination of official and personal Guanxi is usually used to fulfill great ambitions through collective cooperation.

Guanxi is also one of the most important elements in building networks for UTT in the society. Newcomers, through their Guanxi, join the networks and then make more Guanxi within them. At the same time, new joint venture ideas and new projects appear; new technologies are imported, developed and applied; knowledge/technologies generated on campus are transferred.

UTT beyond the TTO: the USST[15]

The university technology transfer center (UTTC), the counterpart of TTO, promotes UTT as an independent department of university. The TTC of University of Shanghai for Science and Technology (USST), among the earliest, was established in July 2007, and has been chosen to show its operation.

USST Technology Transfer Co., Ltd. was formed by USST Science Park Co., Ltd. and Shanghai SAST Investment Co., Ltd. with ¥ 5 million joint investment, charged with building a "Technology transfer platform of Advanced Manufacturing Industry." It implements mechanisms in which the Board decides major issues, and is guided by USST Department of Scientific Research in operation. The TTC works with the government and industrial firms to establish 6 branch TTCs in different cities and 14 technology transfer stations to commercialize its 539 granted patents in 2008–2010. This is fostered by the integration of technology transfer related resources and the use of internal and external resources to enhance technology transfer performance. It now has around 150 staff, working for administrative offices, technical marketing, project services, financial management department, international cooperation and expert advice department. Moreover, it has also set a TTC office in the university to find research results that can be commercialized or firms formed.

1   The TTC organized 4 consulting teams in new energy and energy-efficient technologies, optoelectronics and information technology, advanced manufacturing technology and equipment, as well as medical equipment. Newsletters with relative technology info can regularly be published.
2   The TTC signed comprehensive scientific and technological cooperation agreements, and creates several industry–university–research institute collaboration offices/virtual research institutes and branches of the TTC, together with a number of municipal government agents.
3   The TTC joins network of UTT and established "Shanghai TTC Coalition."
4   The TTC actively collaborates with government agencies; for instance, it hosts Shanghai University Technology Market with 4,000 square meters in its science park, which becomes a big platform for the university–industry–research institute, together with three important agencies: the Education Committee; the Science and Technology Committee; and the Yangfu District Government of Shanghai City.

6. Case study: Triple helix path of Tsinghua's technology transfer system

Munroe and Westwind (2009) summarized the seven key elements of Silicon Valley's innovation eco-system: research universities; entrepreneurs; investment capital; workforce; social professional networks; business environment; and quality of life. In fact, Stanford University as an entrepreneurial university, plays a pivotal role in the evolution and success of innovation economies. The entrepreneurial university mode has been experiencing tests theoretically and practically. The voice from opponents (e.g., Collini 2012) and proponents (e.g., Etzkowitz 1983, 2002; Etzkowitz and Viale 2010; Zhou 2008) has never stopped. There are also proponents with conditions. For example, Rosenberg and Nelson (1996) think that the entrepreneurial university mode should be highly praised and supported in land grant universities, rather than in all university systems. This can be clarified through distinguishing between university entrepreneurship activity and entrepreneurial university (Zhou and Peng 2008).

Oriented by the government, university entrepreneurship idea is practiced throughout the university system. A few top universities are evolving into an entrepreneurial mode. Tsinghua University exemplifies the process following a government-pulled triple helix model.

In summary, the entire Tsinghua Technology Transfer System, as a vast enterprise, goes well beyond a usual TTO. It exemplifies UTT in a government-pulled triple helix model. It focuses on making cooperation between the university and UICC member units, encouraging and organizing experts/scholars to visit local areas, providing services in project feasibility studies, engineering consulting, corporate diagnosis, hosting and participating in exchange activities in technology transfer, and establishing enterprises relying on research achievements of Tsinghua. It combines the functions of Stanford Office of Technology Licensing and StartX Accelerator, a support structure to fill a hidden gap in the university's innovation system, modifying elements of both academic and business practice, blurring the boundary between university and industry by creating an experiential educational process that assists the metamorphosis of intended into actual firms, drawing business people into an educational process (Etzkowitz 2013a, 2013b).

Tsinghua University, born in 1911, partly funded by the "Gengzi Indemnity," also known as Boxer Indemnity, first functioned as a preparatory school (called Tsinghua Xuetang – Tsinghua Imperial College) for those students who would be sent by the government to study in the United States. Tsinghua is one of the most important bases in training higher-level talents and scientific research. As a comprehensive, research-based and open university, it has trained two National Chairmen (Hu Jintao and Xi Jinping) and over 600 national academicians. Tsinghua is ranked No. 1 among China's universities of Science and Engineering, No. 1 in patent numbers, and No. 1 in national science and technology reward numbers in 2015 (CUAA-Team of China University Evaluation 2015).

As a dedicated research-intensive university, Tsinghua sets its three primary functions as creating knowledge, initiating technological innovation, and contributing to society (in addition to teaching). These functions underwent an evolution process following the national needs. Since the 1990s China has developed "research universities" through Project 211 and Project 985. Service for the society based on highlighting teaching's connection with practice in industrial and agriculture production in 1950s and 1960s is evolving from consulting for industry into a more direct formation, establishing firms from the laboratory research results.

Tsinghua highlights both basic and applied research. It undertook large numbers of projects from the 973 and 863 Programs, the National Key Technology R&D Program, along with other basic research programs from the CNSF and some national Ministries. Additionally, the university developed a large number of applied technologies meeting national goals and general industrial demands. The university continually strives to promote the commercialization of technology to participate actively in national and regional development, and contribute to society. In spite of some arguments supporting the purity of traditional university missions, the third mission became undisputed when the government supported it in the mid-1990s, to alleviate university financial shortage and to achieve technology transfer from the campus to industries. Tsinghua commits itself to domestic and international technology transfer as a bridge, through the Tsinghua technology transfer system (TTTS) and by actively developing science parks, including the world's largest, as well as UREs. TTTS consists of the Department of Science and Technology Development, the University–Industry Cooperation Committee, the Department of Overseas Projects, and the International Technology Transfer Center. It uses the domestic and overseas resources of Tsinghua to move technologies to industrial firms.

Working at U-I interface: Tsinghua University–industry cooperation committee (UICC)

After the state clearly confirmed academic entrepreneurship, the UICC was founded in July 1995 as a non-profit-making organization for enhancing university–industry collaboration and technologies' contribution to economy. It plays an active role in promoting exchange and cooperation among Tsinghua's academic departments, research centers and industries. The UICC is working as a bridge between domestic and overseas industries. It makes considerable effort in promoting economic, technical and cultural exchange and cooperation between Chinese enterprises/regions and overseas partners. Through seminars, exhibitions, conferences and training programs, the UICC promotes the interconnection and create opportunities for technical and industrial cooperation. Its missions include the following.

- To strengthen cooperation, especially with regard to the exchange of talent and information, between university and industry.
- To study the trends of technology development so as to accelerate research into and development in those areas of greatest value to the national economy.
- To help enterprises solve technical and managerial problems arising in production, thereby strengthening their competitiveness and overall capabilities.
- To serve as a bridge between domestic and overseas enterprises, facilitating the flow of talent and information in both directions.

Depending on members' needs, the UICC as an industrial liaison department provides them with: information related to research and development activity and progress in Tsinghua; workshops, seminars and symposia between enterprises and academia, creating the communication platform to explore potential cooperation; planning and coordinating for members on specific events, such as recruiting graduate students, setting up scholarship, high-level speeches, as well as public relation activities; customizing services provided by various centers under the UICC umbrella (for instance, the Business Intelligence Center provides intelligence consulting to enterprises and organizations at home and abroad); the latest information to support its clients in product development, technological innovation and market expansion. Meanwhile, the Development Strategy Research Center provides analysis and consultation to make strategic decision for enterprises and governments.

The UUIC staff composition is as shown on Figure 16.2.

The UICC domestic department is charged with Tsinghua collaborations with domestic enterprises. Its functions include: (1) assisting the enterprises to raise their technological innovation capacity through founding joint R&D institutions, making university–industry–research institute linkages, increasing S&T investment, developing independent IPRs and protecting technology interest; and (2) guiding the enterprises to strengthen technological innovation and

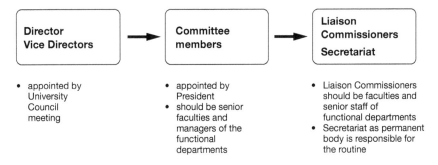

Figure 16.2 UICC's staff structure

Source: adapted by the author; data source: Official Website of Tsinghua University Technology Transfer System. Available online: www.kfb.tsinghua.edu.cn/qhw/index.htm (accessed 28 February 2015).

competitiveness in market, through providing help in technological development, improvement and import, collecting demand information for the enterprises, and finding the expertise to solve the problems – providing S&T information from Tsinghua University and other sources – along with organizing conferences and seminars.

Tsinghua collaborates closely with domestic industry, setting up engineering master training stations in about 20 domestic enterprises, thereby fostering high-level talent for industry; it has also established more than 100 stations in 30 provinces for distance education. These programs use the Internet, satellite and other measures to transmit information. In addition, the university has created joint laboratories and/or research centers – between Tsinghua academic departments and domestic industry. The UICC has had 144 Domestic members[16], (123 enterprises, 14 local S&T departments, 6 Management Committees for Development Zones and 1 Association).[17]

Founded in 1996, the UICC overseas department has a contract with 40 members abroad, including well-known international companies such as IBM, GM, P&G, Motorola, Toshiba, Hitachi, Samsung, EDF, France Telecom, etc.

Working in a triple helix: The Department of Science and Technology Development (DSTD)

Founded in 1983, the DSTD is a centralized management unit, authorized by the president in charge of scientific and technological cooperation between Tsinghua University and the provinces, municipalities and enterprises, and signs technology contracts based on research achievements of Tsinghua University.

The DSTD is dedicated to promoting a close and effective combination of technological and intellectual resources of Tsinghua University with the regional economy, in order to fully configure and use Tsinghua resources, services for Chinese social education, technology and economic development. It functions as follows.

- Contract management – audits, sign, and manage Tsinghua contracts in technology development, technology transfer, technical consulting, technical services and patent licensing.
- External cooperation – conducts technological cooperation between Tsinghua University with local governments and enterprises.
- Technical bids – organizing Tsinghua's relevant schools/departments to participate in the technical bids of provincial/ municipal projects.
- Jointly apply projects: organizes the university and enterprises jointly to apply key projects in national, province and city level and technology transfer projects such as university–industry–institute collaborations.
- Joint research – organizes joint research for cooperation projects with local governments and enterprises.
- Dissemination: participates in high-tech achievement exhibitions and conferences organized by local units on behalf of Tsinghua University.

The External Cooperation Office is responsible for the university's cooperation with local governments and enterprises. To date, Tsinghua University has signed "comprehensive cooperation agreements between the University and province" with 25 provinces, and "University–City cooperation agreements" with over 80 prefecture cities. It has over 20 "industry–university–research institute cooperation offices" and more than 100 domestic and oversea "joint R&D institutions." In addition, it collaborates with 170 universities in 32 countries, more than 200 enterprises, international organizations and governments in 27 countries. These greatly promote technology transfer and firm formation of Tsinghua (Table 16.3).

The Contract Management Office focuses on technology contract management, including:

1   signing technology contracts
2   identifying and registering technology contracts in management authority of Beijing's technology market and implementing tax incentives
3   submitting applications for research projects such as the Torch Program, the Spark Program and the Key Promotion Project.

Office of University–Industry–Research Institute Collaboration (OUIIC)

Resources from the university, local industry and government form an integrated legal entity, the OUIIC. The headquarters are located at the Department of Science and Technology Development (DSTD) of Tsinghua. It functions as shown in Figure 16.3.

Table 16.3 Technology transfer contracts of Tsinghua University in 2012

	No.	Accounting for the total number (%)	Contract amount (10K)	Of the total contract amount (%)
Tech development	602	31.05	60,905.45	48.93
Tech service	905	46.67	39,936.07	32.09
Tech consulting	385	19.86	15,369.47	12.35
Tech license	47	2.42	8,252.51	6.63
Total	1939	100	12,4463.50	100

Source: Adapted by the author. Data source: www.kfb.tsinghua.edu.cn.

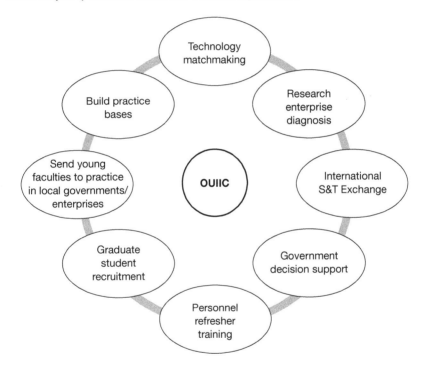

Figure 16.3 The functions of office of university–industry–institute collaboration

Source: adapted by the author; data source: official website of Tsinghua University Technology Transfer System. Available online: www.kfb.tsinghua.edu.cn/qhw/index.htm (accessed 28 February 2015).

University–region cooperation fund

A numbers of University–Region Cooperation Funds have been developed in the Tsinghua Technology Transfer System, together with local governments and enterprises, such as Guangdong Province–Tsinghua Academic Venture Fund

(1994), Hebei Province–Tsinghua Science and Technology Cooperation Development Fund (1996), Yancheng City–Tsinghua Science Venture Fund (1996), Liaoyang City–Tsinghua Science and Technology Development Fund (1998), Anshan City–Tsinghua research seed money (2002), Tsinghua–Huawei Technology Development Fund (1998), China Textile Import and Export Corporation–Tsinghua applied technology development fund (2000), Jinan Iron and Steel–Tsinghua Science and Technology Achievements Award Fund (2001), Ancaijituan Chair Professorship Fund (2001), as well as Wuxi Tsinghua Science and Technology Achievements Transformation Fund, Erdos Technology Cooperation Fund, Long Spoon Technology Cooperation Fund, Anshan Tsinghua Research Seed Fund, and Tongling Qinghua Cooperative Fund, etc. The investment came from multiple sources, including individuals, enterprises, government agencies and foundations. These funds incentivize university–industry and university–government interaction, greatly promoting UTT and regional economic growth.

Joint research and development institutes

The Joint research and development institutes have been working as a local innovation platform since 1999. According to *The Relevant Provisions (Trial) on Declaring and Approving that Tsinghua University Establishes Joint R&D Institutions with Enterprises, May 2000*, the applications should be approved by Tsinghua DSTD. Up to September 2013, there had been 116 joint R&D institutes operating, 107 among them with enterprises as partners.

UURR cooperation model

The UURR Model – named from cooperation between Tsinghua University (U) + a foreign university (U) + a region in China (R) + a region abroad (R) – effectively integrates resources in the universities and the regions to achieve development of both universities and regions. Tsinghua University + Iwate University (Japan) + Zhejiang Province + Iwate Prefecture (Japan) and Tsinghua University + Fraunhofer Institute for Production Technology (IPT) + Jiangsu Province + Nordrhein-Westfale (Germany) have been organized and conducted. This cooperation enables lifting the triple helix interaction to international level that a well-known foreign university/industrial corporation would join.

Global vision: Tsinghua international technology transfer center (ITTC)

Established in June 2001, the ITTC collaborates with Russia, America, France, Poland, Japan, etc. It focuses on both Tsinghua technology commercialization and importing foreign mature and advanced technologies; at the same time, it also helps domestic enterprises understand and absorb the technologies. The State Economic and Trade Commission and the Ministry of Education identified it as one of the "National Technology Transfer Centers" in September 2002.

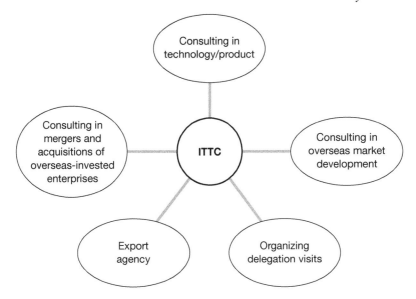

Figure 16.4 The ITTC's functions

In order to conduct international technology transfer, in June 2002 the ITTC established COWAY International Technology Transfer Co. Inc., an operating entity. The tasks involve: transfer and graft foreign advances technologies and projects, technology transfer and agents, research projects' market investigation, screening, analysis, evaluation and demonstration, technology integration as well as localization of products and technologies (see Figure 16.4). In addition, the center provides consulting and business services, projects, programs (plans) and design. Recently it highlights the polymer and biotech field.

The ITTC relies on Tsinghua's academic resources to assess and judge emerging technologies and developed comprehensive partnership with 22 provinces and more than 60 cities with Tsinghua's broad social resources. The ITTC has developed numbers of international partners – for example, Fraunhofer Institute for Production Technology (IPT), Verein Deutscher Ingenieure (VDI), Cornell University, State Research Center of Russia, Belarus National Technology Transfer Center, and so on. Moreover, it also co-founded the China–France Environment and Energy Center and Chine–America Energy Technology Center for further international technology transfer to domestic enterprises.

Conclusion: political mobilization, UTT regime and evolution of the triple helix

The new economics of science have revealed the commercialization potential of science and the triple helix theory has been used to analyze the success of knowledge-based regional innovation in a developed capitalist country, the USA. However, how can these concepts be applied to specific situations in developing socialist China where the future of the university is mostly dependent upon government's orientation? In the recent past, unstable policies have caused uncertainty in universities. This is partly due to the fact that universities are strongly controlled by government. There are at least three factors to take into account: new government policies, development of (venture) capital guarantees; and enhanced knowledge production abilities on campus. The solution of the ownership problem of URE's is the focus of current policy changes.

Although UTT has evolved from faculties consulting for industries to firm-formation the UREs in the Chinese HEI system and a government-pulled triple helix model are quite different from "spin-offs" in the USA. The government plays very active roles in technology transfer, through supporting platforms and bridges, organizing university–industry joint activities as well as policies to encourage university–industry collaboration. The scale and scope of UTT is noteworthy: TTOs of leading universities extend their activities across the country though subsidiary units. They establish joint ventures, further extending their reach. The human resources committed to UTT are of an order of magnitude greater than at leading U.S. universities. Nevertheless, China's UTT is still in the early stages of transition of from a technology transfer regime focused on existing technologies to one based on invention.

The triple helix of China is unbalanced due to the over strong power from the one-party political and state-owned economic system. The UTT path is evolving from a government-pulled triple helix, directed by the Communist Party through the government, into a university–government–industry interactive triple helix, with goals and objectives set collaboratively and new ideas arising bottom-up as well as top-down. When the private sector grows up and the government decentralizes, when the Party gives the government and university enough executive autonomy, a transition process from government-pulled to interactive triple helix will begin. This is a complex and arduous journey because it will refer to politics, economics, education, social improvement and so on, depending on evolution of the three spheres per se and change of their relationship. The world incubator award given several years ago to a Chinese university with several hundred firms in its facility in comparison to much smaller numbers in competing European projects exemplifies the scale and scope of the UTT regime. Through political and social mobilization, quantitative change may result in qualitative change as universities increase their prominence in the innovation system.

Notes

1 AUTM official website: About technology transfer. See www.autm.net/Tech_ Transfer/14733.htm (accessed on 20 February 2015).
2 See http://news.sciencenet.cn/htmlnews/2009/2/216363.html (accessed on 20 February 2015).
3 The National High Technology Research and Development Program of China – also known as the "863 Program" because it was issued in March 1986.

4 The "National Climbing Program" promotes basic research. It ensures that the research with significance can be organized and implemented by central government, according to the trends of scientific development and the need of China's economic growth.

5 The National Basic Research Program (known as the "973 Program" because it was issued in March 1997) is implemented by the Ministry of Science and Technology (MOST).

6 "Project 985" began in May 1998 (hence its title). It is a project to promote the development and reputation of the Chinese higher education system by founding world-class universities in the twenty-first century. The project involves both national and local governments allocating large amounts of funding to certain universities, to build new research centers, improve facilities, host international conferences, attract worldwide faculty and visiting scholars, and help Chinese researchers attend international conferences.

7 "Project 211" is a project of National Key Universities and colleges initiated in 1995 by the Ministry of Education of the People's Republic of China, with the intent of raising the research standards of high-level universities and cultivating strategies for socio-economic development. The name for the project comes from an abbreviation of the twenty-first century and 100 (approximate number of participating universities). China today has more than 118 institutions of higher education (about 6 per cent) designated as Project 211 institutions for having met certain scientific, technical, and human resources standards and offer advanced degree programs.

8 Indeed, even sophisticated Chinese observers are somewhat taken aback when various pronouncements of US President Obama on infrastructure and education policy appear to have little influence on policy, at least not immediately. Their paradigm is exemplified by Deng Xiao Ping's visit to an underdeveloped region, Shenzhen, and his drawing a figurative circle, mandating the rise of a new urban conurbation that in fact appeared in succeeding years. Although few pronouncements have such weight, a top-down cultural mind-set is well in place.

9 The German scholar Alexander Rüstow coined the term "neo-liberalism" in 1938 at the Colloque Walter Lippmann.

10 See http://news.tsinghua.edu.cn/publish/newsen/6055/2013/20130107145004087331257/20130107145004087331257_.html (accessed on 20 February 2015).

11 See www.founder.com/templates/T_Second_EN/index.aspx?nodeid=192

12 In China it is actually called "New and High Technology Development Area", not only "high-tech", since imported technologies are even used more.

13 National Bureau of Statistics, Ministry of Science and Technology, Ministry of Finance. (2013) *Statistical Bulletin of the National Science and Technology Funding*. 26 September 2013.
  【国家统计局、科技部和财政部,《2012年全国科技经费投入统计公报》, 2013年9月26日】

14 Guanxi – 关系 in Chinese – means various of "social connections" among acquaintances, friends, relatives, colleagues, classmates, roommates, etc.

15 The case in this section came from H. Fang (2013). Inquiring into and Analyzing about Technology Transfer Performance in Universities. *China Science & Technology Resources Review*, 45 (3): 36–40.
  方厚政, 大学技术转移绩效探析, 中国科技资源导刊, 2013年5月, 第45卷, 第3期, 36–40.

16 See www.kfb.tsinghua.edu.cn/kfb/page/zhishichanquan/lianheyanfajigou/shenpiguiding.htm

17 Data source: Official Website of Tsinghua University Technology Transfer System. Available online: www.kfb.tsinghua.edu.cn/qhw/index.htm (accessed on 28 February 2015).

References

Apple, R. (1989) Patenting university research: Harry Steenbock and the Wisconsin Alumni Research Foundation. *ISIS* 80 (303 – September), 375–394.

Collini, S. (2012) *What Are Universities For?* London: Penguin.

CUAA–Team of China University Evaluation, *Development Report on 2015 China's University*, January 2015.

Ding, J. et al. (2014) Weird phenomenon of research funding: ¥1, 200 billion investment but 10% commercialization rate of research results. *Xinhuanet*, 22 December.
【丁静 等, 科研经费怪象：年投入1.2万亿元 科技成果转化率仅10%,《新华网, 2014年12月22日】

Dooley, L. and Kirk, D. (2007) University–industry collaboration grafting the entrepreneurial paradigm onto academic structures. *European Journal of Innovation Management*, 10 (3): 316–332.

Duderstadt, J. J. (1999) The future of higher education: New roles for the 21st-century university. *Issues in Science and Technology*. Available online: http://deepblue.lib.umich.edu/bitstream/handle/2027.42/88249/1999_Future_Roles_for_Higher_Education.pdf?sequence=1

Etzkowitz, H. (1983) Entrepreneurial scientists and entrepreneurial universities in American academic science, *Minerva*, 21 (2–3): 1573–1871.

Etzkowitz, H. (2002) *MIT and the Rise of Entrepreneurial Science*. Routledge: London and New York.

Etzkowitz, H. (2008) *The Triple Helix: University–Industry–Government–Innovation in Action*. London: Routledge.

Etzkowitz, H. (2013a) Mistaking dawn for dusk: Quantophrenia and the cult of numerology in technology transfer analysis. *Scientometrics*, 97 (3): 913–925.

Etzkowitz, H. (2013b) StartX and the paradox of success: Filling the gap in Stanford's entrepreneurial culture. *Social Science Information*, 52 (4): 605–627.

Etzkowitz, H. and Etzkowitz, A. (2014) Europe of the future and the future of Europe: The innovation/austerity choice. *Hélice*, 3 (11). Available online: www.triplehelixassociation.org/helice/volume-3-2014/helice-issue-11/europe-future-future-europe-innovationausterity-choice

Etzkowit, H., Gulbrandsen, M. and Levitt, J. (2001) *Public Venture Capital*, New York: Harcourt Professional Publishing, 2nd edn.

Etzkowitz, H., Solé, F. and Piqué, J. M. (2007) The creation of born global companies within the science cities: An approach from triple helix. *ENGEVISTA*, 9 (2): 149–164.

Etzkowitz, H. and Viale, R. (2010) Polyvalent knowledge and the entrepreneurial university: A third academic revolution? *Critical Sociology*, 36 (4): 595–609.

Etzkowitz, H. and Zhou, C. (2008) Building the entrepreneurial university: A global perspective. *Science and Public Policy*, 35 (9): 627–635.

Eun, J-H., Lee, K. and Wu, G. (2006) Explaining the university-run Enterprises in China: A new theoretical framework and applications. *Research Policy*, 35 (9): 1329–1346. Available online: www.ciber.gatech.edu/workingpaper/2005/019-05-06.pdf

Gibb, A., Haskins, G. and Robertson, I. (2013) Leading the entrepreneurial university: Meeting the entrepreneurial development needs of higher education institutions. In: A. Altmann and B. Ebersberger (eds) *Universities in Change: Managing Higher Education Institutions in the Age of Globalization*. New York: Springer-Verlag.

Gibbons, M., Limoges, C, Nowotny, H., Schwartzman, S., Scott, P. and Trow, M. (1994) *The New Production of Knowledge: The Dynamics of Science and Research in Contemporary Societies*. London: Sage.

He, J., Wu Y. and Zhou, L. (2007) A positive study on contribution of university technology transfer to regional economic growth of the capital region. *Studies in Science of Science*, 25 (5): 871–876.

【何建坤，吴玉鸣和周立，大学技术转移对首都区域经济增长的贡献分析，《科学学研究，第25卷，第5期，2007年10月】

ISTIC (Institute of Scientific and Technical Information of China) (2013) *China International Science and Technology Statistics Results*. 27 September 2013.

【中国科学技术信息研究所，，《中国国际科技论文统计结果，2013年9月27日】

Jencks, C. and Riesman, D. (1968) *The Academic Revolution*, Garden City, NY: Doubleday.

Li, Q. (2015) The number of China granted patents in 2014 reached 233K. *China Intellectual Property News*, at the official website of the State Intellectual Property Office of the P.R.C. Available online: www.sipo.gov.cn/zscqgz/2015/201502/t20150212_1075284.html

李群，2014年我国发明专利授权量达23.3万件，《知识产权报》，中华人民共和国国家知识产权局官网

Mazzucatto, M. (2013) *The Entrepreneurial State: Debunking Public vs. Private Sector Myths*, London: Anthem Press.

Munroe, T. and Westwind, M. (2009) *What Makes Silicon Valley Tick?: The Ecology of Innovation at Work*, Herentals B-2200 Belgium: Nova Vista Publishing.

Qian, X. (2007) Textile: Using a variety of methods to promote innovation through university–industry–research institute alliances. *Today Science and Technology*, 3: 24–25.

【钱信军，纺织：产学研联盟六管其下促创新，《今日科技》，2007.03，24–25】

Rinne, R. and Koivula, J. (2009) The dilemmas of the changing university. Chapter 10. In: M. Shattock (ed) *Entrepreneurialism in Universities and the Knowledge Economy. Diversification and Organisational Change in European Higher Education* (*Society for Research in Higher Education*), Milton Keynes, UK: Open University Press.

Rosenberg, N. and Nelson, R. R. (1996) The roles of universities in the advance of industrial technology. In: R. S. Rosenbloom and W. J. Spencer, W. J. (eds) *Engines of Innovation*, Cambridge, MA: Harvard Business School Press.

Stokes, D. (1997) *Pasteur's Quadrant – Basic Science and Technological Innovation*, Washington DC: Brookings Institution Press.

Thornton, P. H. and Ocasio, W. (2008) Institutional logics. In: R. Greenwood, C. Oliver, K. Sahlin and R. Suddaby (eds) *The SAGE Handbook of Organizational Institutionalism*, Thousand Oaks, CA: Sage.

Williams, G. (2009) Finance and entrepreneurial activity in higher education in the knowledge society. Chapter 2. In: M. Shattock (ed) *Entrepreneurialism in Universities and the Knowledge Economy. Diversification and Organisational Change in European Higher Education*, Maidenhead: Open University Press and SRHE, UK.

WIPO (2013) WIPO Statistical Country Profiles. Available online: www.wipo.int/ipstats/en/statistics/country_profile/.

Zhou, C. (2008) Emergence of the entrepreneurial university in evolution of the triple helix: The case of Northeastern University in China. *Journal of Technology Management in China*, 3 (1): 109–126.

Zhou, C. (2014a) Four dimensions to observe a triple helix: Invention of 'cored model' and differentiation of institutional and functional spheres. *Triple Helix*, 1 (October): 11.

Zhou, C. (2014b) The path to the entrepreneurial university: A case study of Northeastern University in China. In: T. J. Allen and R .P. O'Shea (eds). *Building Technology*

Transfer within Research Universities: An Entrepreneurial Approach, Cambridge: Cambridge University Press.

Zhou, C. and Peng, X. (2008) The Entrepreneurial University in China: Nonlinear paths. *Science and Public Policy*, 35 (9): 637–646.

17 University system in Vietnam
Some technology transfer practice

Tran Ngoc Ca

Introduction of the university system

Over the last 20 years, Vietnam has experienced the new challenges of globalization and is undergoing a double transition, from a centrally planned economy to a market-oriented system and from inward orientation toward greater regional and international economic integration. While it is changing, Vietnam still remains an agricultural economy and society, with three-fourths of the population living in rural areas and two-thirds of the labor force still working in an agricultural sector characterized by low productivity. In this situation, there is a need for a broad spectrum of knowledge transfer, technologies and scientific research activities to upgrade existing production capabilities. At the same time, changes in the policy and market environment are influencing the behavior of science and technology organizations, including universities and the nature of their interactions with firms.

It is worth noting that until the mid-1980s, under the centrally planned economic system, both state enterprises and private firms were unable to fully appreciate the requirement for technology innovation because of the absence of competitive pressure in previous decades. As a result the R&D and learning capacity within firms has failed to develop. It has also been difficult for economic actors to link to knowledge institutions to develop joint research activities or product innovation. The exception is in the few industries, such as telecom and energy (oil and gas, power generation), where the rate of innovation is higher and relatively high levels of investment resources are available. Vietnamese exports began with basic primary products like rice, seafood and cashew nuts, and have moved gradually to manufactured goods such as textiles, garments, footwear and electronics. This shift requires manufacturing technology that can help firms in achieving the quality and other technical standards of international markets. The abolition of trade protection in the framework of regional agreements such as the Association of Southeast Asian Nations (ASEAN), the ASEAN Free Trade Agreement (AFTA), and the World Trade Organization (WTO) have eventually led to similar competitive conditions for the domestic market. In this context, the country needs to increase competitiveness of economy at an international level, and pursue industrialization and modernization while joining international economic institutions and regimes.

This chapter first provides an introduction to the university system in Vietnam and its development context. R&D activities in enterprises and the university sector are then identified. Technology transfer activities are analyzed and the subsequent section discusses the policy setting of technology transfer. The cases of five specific institutions are described to give a detailed picture of technology transfer in Vietnamese universities. The chapter concludes with analyses of some overall emerging issues in the technology transfer systems within the Vietnamese university system.

Structure of the overall research system

In the above-mentioned context, the whole science, technology and research system in general, and the university structure in particular, is being shaped by an evolving social–economic setting. These new structures and characteristics place new demands on the science, technology and higher education system in Vietnam, which can be divided into four groups. First, research has been undertaken mainly in three academies: Vietnam Academy of Science and Technology (VAST); Vietnam Academy of Social Sciences and Humanities (VASS); and Vietnam Academy of Agriculture Sciences (VAAS). These institutions have gradually shifted from more basic research to applied oriented research during last 15–20 years. The next group includes government research institutes (GRI) organized under different ministries such as industry and trade, construction, transport, etc. These institutes are oriented more toward applied research activities serving the need of their own respective agencies and companies. The corporate sector itself (except for few large state-owned companies which have their own R&D units) carries out little R&D, and mainly takes care of minor technical changes and improvement. Finally, there is the research undertaken in universities. In addition to two Vietnam National Universities (VNU), one in Hanoi and another in HoChiMinh City, there are universities under the management of the Ministry of Education and Training (MOET). In contrast to universities in most of East Asia, the university system in Vietnam originated in the context of a Soviet model that separated teaching from scientific research and technology development. This image of the universities has begun to change only in the last 15 years or so, during which attempts have been made by government to re-orient them toward research and innovation. An analysis of the university system in Vietnam should take this specific feature into account.

In general, both training and R&D provided by universities have to serve the production needs of firms or social needs of public at large. Local enterprises often complain about the difficulties in finding enough skilled labor for their production activities (Pham Minh Hac, 2000), and the traditional mandate of universities in Vietnam has been to produce human resources rather than to engage in research. The general context of Vietnamese production points to the need for an innovation system and universities capable of serving firms. However, universities still have to continue with their traditional mandate – that is, primarily the provision of a labor force for domestic enterprises and second for firms resulting from FDI. At the same time, many universities have begun to overcome their old mode of operation, in which teaching was divorced from research, by becoming involved in R&D projects and small-scale experimental production. However, the bulk of R&D activities are conducted not in universities but in research institutes under line ministries and in academies. There is very modest financing of R&D mainly from the state budget, which represents around 80% of total national expenditure on S&T. More than two-thirds goes to applied research and technological development and the rest to basic research (Tran Ngoc Ca, 2011).

To date, most publicly funded R&D is conducted in government research institutes and only a limited number of university faculties have adequate resources for significant R&D. The research infrastructure is below international standards, and such research that is being carried out tends to be theoretical and supply driven. The tertiary education system as a whole is under stress, as a massive expansion in student numbers since 1990 has been accompanied by only a modest growth in faculty numbers (Perkins and Anh, 2010). A research university is still quite a new concept in Viet Nam and research is not a prominent activity for the majority of faculty staff. Only about 20% of university professors are involved in research projects (Tagscherer, 2010).

R&D in universities

In 2005 there were 147 laboratories managed by higher education institutions, but very few were world-class and many did not perform high quality research. The most important and productive were and still are concentrated in a few places. Only a limited number of faculties and academic departments at Viet Nam's universities and colleges have sufficient personnel, equipment and other resources to perform serious R&D. Among them, the two VNU and the two largest polytechnics (Hanoi University of Science and Technology and Ho Chi Minh City University of Technology) are the most research-intensive bodies in the Vietnamese university system. They are currently intensifying efforts to become internationally recognized research universities.

Only about 4% of government expenditure for S&T is currently assigned to universities, which accounts for approximately 15.3% of universities' R&D expenditure. The remaining 84.7% funding for university R&D expenditure comes from contracts with other organizations, of which, 29.2% is from enterprises; 6.7% is from other organizations; and 48.8 % is from international sources (Tran Ngoc Ca, 2006). For a comparative perspective, in some OECD countries the figure is much higher. For example, the share of university R&D in total R&D expenditure spending is 20% in Sweden, 26% in Denmark and 17% in Germany. Other developing countries also have quite high ratios: for example 39% in Brazil, 35% in Cuba and 32% in Uruguay, while China has 9% and Russia 6% (Brundenius and Goransson, 2011). This might be explained by the fact that universities in Vietnam are doing much less R&D than comparative government R&D institutes under state agencies.

From 1996 to 2002, universities implemented some 3,800 R&D projects both of basic and applied oriented research in various areas such as agriculture, healthcare, industry, etc. Many universities have established their own R&D units (centers, divisions). By the end of 2002, within the university sector there were 167 research divisions and 147 centers dealing with technology development and offering consultancy activities. There has also been some movement toward more entrepreneurial activities within university circles, with teaching staff doing more consulting for firms or local governments on a contractual basis. Table 17.1 shows the number of higher education institutions in academic years from 1995 to 2013.

Almost all universities and colleges fall under the administration of the Ministry of Education and Training (MOET), which is also responsible for primary and secondary education. For the academic year 2007, there were 345 universities and colleges employing some 61,300 lecturers (MOET, 2008).

Research programs at universities have encountered several problems. Many universities are far from being considered as "centers of excellence for R&D" lacking autonomous status. Although their operations have become much more independent than before, they still have to follow many directives and comply with the regulations of either the MOET, or in some cases, their line ministries. In public universities, faculty and staff face constraints in terms of salary ceilings, rigid human resource management regulations and lack of financial incentives. In short, they are still deemed as government officials, rather than academics and have little ability to behave entrepreneurially. Despite the move to abolish the separation between teaching and research, there has still been a well-documented lack of research and weak linkages between research and teaching.

The present incentive scheme does not promote a proactive approach among teaching staff in universities. There are few mechanisms to encourage them to interact with other institutions and firms. Cooperation is usually short term, and relies mainly on personal and informal relationships. As such, other than grooming the new graduates, the contribution of university activities tends to be isolated in nature. In the existing system, universities have not seen technology transfer activities as crucial for their own continued survival. Consequently any such technology innovations are commonly not seen as particularly attractive by firms. In fact, the facilities and practical engineering knowledge of universities frequently lags behind those of the firms themselves.

Another issue faced by universities is that of human resources for teaching and undertaking research. The number of professors and lecturers is relatively small compared with the number of students: one professor has to teach about 30 students, while in other countries this ratio is about 1:15. Meanwhile, student enrolment is increasing. Between 1995 and 2005, for instance, the student numbers increased by 4.43 times (from 297,900 to 1,319,754 students), while the teaching staff increased by just 2.09 times (from 22,750 to 47,616 lecturers). Due to this overload of teaching, university staff members simply do not have sufficient time left for R&D and other learning activities. An ageing staff population is another problem, since the majority of professors and associate professors are over 55 years old, with few replacements in the pipeline. During the 1990s and 2000s,

Table 17.1 Universities and colleges in Vietnam

	1995	2000	2001	2002	2003	2004	2005	2006	2007	2010	2013
Universities and colleges		*178*	*191*	*202*	*214*	*230*	*277*	*322*	*345*	*414*	*420*
Public	109	148	168	179	187	201	243	275	288	334	337
Non-public		30	23	23	27	29	34	47	57	80	83
Teachers (thousands)		*32.4*	*35.9*	*38.7*	*40.0*	*47.6*	*48.6*	*53.4*	*61.3*	*n.a.*	*n.a.*
Public	22.8	27.9	31.4	33.4	34.9	40.0	42.0	45.7	54.4	n.a.	n.a.
Non-public		4.5	4.5	5.3	5.1	7.6	6.6	7.7	6.9	n.a.	n.a.
Students (thousands)		*899.5*	*974.1*	*1,020.7*	*1,131.0*	*1,319.8*	*1,387.1*	*1,666.2*	*1,928.4*	*n.a.*	*2,178.6 (for 2012)*
Public	297.9	795.6	873.0	908.8	993.9	1,182.0	1,226.7	1,456.7	1,662.5	n.a.	1,885.2
Non-public		103.9	101.1	111.9	137.1	137.8	160.4	209.5	265.9	n.a.	323.4
in which: full-time training	173.1	552.5	579.2	604.4	653.7	729.4	836.7	917.2	1,123.0	n.a.	n.a.
Public		452.4	480.8	493.8	529.6	601.8	698.4	754.9	918.2	n.a.	n.a.
Non-public		100.1	98.4	110.6	124.1	127.6	138.3	162.3	204.8	n.a.	n.a.
Graduates (thousands)		*162.5*	*168.9*	*166.8*	*165.7*	*195.6*	*210.9*	*232.5*	*n.a*	*n.a.*	*n.a.*
Public	58.5	149.8	157.5	152.6	152.6	180.8	195.0	216.5	n.a	n.a.	n.a.
Non-public		12.6	11.4	14.2	13.1	14.8	16.0	16.0	n.a	n.a.	n.a.

Source: Statistical Yearbooks (various issues). Elaborated by author.

many scientific and engineering disciplines failed to attract talented young students and consequently a shortage of human resources in the university system is predicted. Within the higher education system, entrepreneurship is not an embedded tradition. The most entrepreneurial characteristic apparent to date is reflected in the desire of teachers to do "outside the class" teaching in order to supplement their income. The low basic salary of academic staff is offered as an explanation for this.

In terms of infrastructure and other teaching and R&D facilities, although the system has seen some recent investment for upgrading, this resource has mainly gone to larger universities. Many universities still use equipment and facilities dating from the mid-1970s. Library systems in many universities are small and outdated in both their quality and the scope of coverage. The bulk of foreign language literature also dates back to the 1970s. There has been a lack of electronic links with the national library or investment in centralized information and librarian systems. Moreover, the rate of literature use is often low due to the poor English capability of the staff and/or their current teaching workload. As a result, teaching curricula are often outdated, repetitive and lack innovative approaches. In terms of international cooperation, rapid changes in the international landscape have caused difficulties in long term planning. This has sometimes led to the selection of unsuitable organizations for cooperative activities thus placing the academic system in a disadvantageous position.

Starting in the middle of the last decade, Vietnamese universities have witnessed several changes, some being more radical than others. First of all, the government prioritized the drive to create new type of universities, sometimes referred to as research universities, or universities of international level or standard. The government set up a range of partnerships with various foreign partners from Europe and Asia to form a number of such universities, for instance the Vietnam–Germany University, Vietnam–France University and Vietnam–UK University. These projects received a substantial amount of investment amounting to several hundred million USD from both Vietnamese government and international donor governments. In addition, a number of corporate or private universities arrived on the scene, some of these new universities being funded by large corporations. Examples of these institutions are the Petroleum University funded by state-owned PetroVietnam and FPT University funded by FPT IT Group. A second initiative is the more noticeable move to develop high-tech activities in the country as a result of the enactment of the High Tech Law in 2008. Universities as well as R&D institutes began to make increased efforts to develop high-tech research programs and training for high-tech human resources in areas like ICT, biotechnology or nanotechnology. These efforts have been noted by international donors like World Bank or ADB who are supporting government in forging closer links between research and higher education, and in creating centers of excellence in various forms (OECD-WB, 2014).

Technology transfer activities in universities

In general, the technology transfer activities of universities are supposed to serve the need of enterprises and communities, and farmers. However, according to some studies, among research institutes and universities, their share of cooperative activities with enterprises is still low (NISTPASS, 2000). As provided in Table 17.2, a survey of linkages between R&D institutes, universities and industries reveals that universities are delivering less cooperation with firms even than research institutes.

Overall, different types of firms exhibit different behavior and extent of engagement with regard to innovation. The SME sector in general is weak and generally tends to source its R&D externally, relying little on R&D institutions and universities (VCCI, 2012; Tran Ngoc Ca, 2011). Large corporations are even more likely to follow this pattern, while FDI firms tend to rely on their home country R&D organizations. Therefore, this suggests that there are few opportunities for Vietnamese R&D institutions and universities to play a significant role in helping firms, and even when they do, these activities are mainly concerned with incremental and minor technical change. In the context of weak linkages, universities' share of R&D funding is low. Data from recent empirical studies has also revealed weak linkages between R&D, postgraduate education and the needs of the economy and the production sector (NISTPASS, 2000; Tran Ngoc Ca and Nguyen Vo Hung, 2011).

A number of observations can be made. First, while universities contributed actively to the training needs of the society and economy, their direct technology service to enterprises has been insignificant. This is a quite understandable situation, given that for a long period of time, the cultural tradition within Vietnamese universities has been directed entirely toward an overriding mandate to provide teaching.

Table 17.2 Sources of innovation of Vietnamese firms

Sources of information	All activities (%)
Originated from the production processes	89.7
Follow other enterprises (domestic/foreign)	36.2
Suggestions/requirements of customers	48.3
Suggestions of suppliers/contractors	10.3
Information from professional associations	10.3
Cooperation with research institutes	6.9
Cooperation with technical colleges/universities	5.2
Investigated or survey in aboard	34.5
Provided by domestic consulting agencies	13.8
Provided by foreign consulting agencies	3.4
Participate in fairs/exhibitions	39.7

Source: NISTPASS (2000). Elaborated by author.

Second, overall links between industries and research institutes and universities are not close and there has been an absence of technology network organizations to connect universities and production activities. Coordination of research activities between R&D institutes and enterprises is very weak or almost absent. In many case, the research agendas of universities tend to rely on what the researchers know rather than on market needs. As a result there is a mismatch between industries and research performance. There have been attempts to create a technology market which brings together technology intermediary organizations such as consultancies, financial brokers, and IP lawyers, but these are currently too new to evaluate fully.

Third, the research capability of enterprises is also weak and negatively influences the development of university–industry linkages. Companies could not identify the technical issues that could address their business problems, who was capable of solving these issues, and how. As a result of this weak technology market structure, there is a communication gap between firms and universities in technical discussions.

As seen in this section, the weak linkage between universities, research institutes and enterprises in general, and between universities and firms in particular, are still undermining attempts by universities to transfer technologies to address the needs of the local economies where universities are located. There is a general view among firms that there is a demand for technology and training services provided by R&D institutes and universities. However, the demand has barely been met, and the strength of the relationship between firms and society with universities is less than satisfactory.

Policy instrument for technology transfer

Overall policy framework

The first ever Vietnamese legal document that regulated technology transfer activities was the Ordinance on Technology Transfer approved in 1988. However this Ordinance mainly created the legal framework for technology transfer contracts with foreign countries, in order to make the negotiation, conclusion and the contract performance compliant with international rules. Then, in 1995, the Civil Law created the legal framework for technology transfer contracts between the seller and buyer. Due to its general nature, these documents have not impacted much on technology transfer agreements from the domestic university system.

In 2005, in the process of modification of the Civil Law, the section on technology transfer was adopted separately into the new Law on Technology Transfer in 2006. The content of this law has clearer regulations, workable conditions and is compatible with international rules for technology transfer. For example, the government cannot now intervene in the process of technology transfer contracts. There are also new regulations concerning the IP rights of technology created by state funded projects. According to these the IP rights of technology created by this type of project is allocated to the organization conducting the S&T activities; and that organization can transfer, manufacture or use that result to contribute to business production. The related organization also can decide on the division of the benefit and the income between the author of the technology and the S&T organization at the point when the product or service is commercialized or manufactured. This change has encouraged R&D institutes and universities to conduct technology transfer by allowing them to receive direct benefit from their work. More specifically for universities, the Ministry of Education and Training (MOET) in 2008 has issued Decision No. 78/2008 to regulate IP activities in universities. However this Decision has not been implemented fully and consequently the IP management units in universities have not yet developed their full potential.

To spur demand from the corporate sector for university R&D and technology transfer, some policy measures have been introduced to allow the non-state enterprises and scientific and technological organizations (including universities) to create funds investing in R&D activities by themselves. The most notable policy is the Decree 119 of PM in 1999 on investment for R&D and innovation activities in firms. More recently, a new government initiative has created the National Program on Technology Innovation and the National Technology Innovation Fund (NATIF) which provides more funding for firms' innovation enabling companies to secure more resources for cooperation with universities in technology development, innovation and transfer. All the above measures and policies encourage the enterprises to invest more in R&D as well as technological innovation activities in cooperation with universities. Some universities have already begun to make use of these new policies and are working with firms in technology transfer agreements.

The system of programs and organizations for technology transfer

Since the 1980s, Vietnam has organized State-level S&T programs in key fields to advance socio-economic development. In recent years, around 15 to 20 programs were run each year in areas such as ICT, Biotech, Healthcare, Agriculture, Advanced material and others). Half of these programs relate directly to the creation of new technology for applications in relevant production sectors. The Ministries and Provinces also have their own science and technology (S&T) programs to create new technology applications. Aiming at creating closer links between universities and firms, since 1990s, the government has established four techno-economic programs for ICT and biotechnology technology applications to speed up the transfer process.

For agriculture and the development of rural and mountainous areas, the government has created an application program for new agricultural technology in order to transfer new technologies to farmers and rural areas. Within this program, the mobilization of financial support from local sources and from farmers has been successful in encouraging the transfer of new technology to farmers. In 2004, the Ministry of Science and Technology also began to implement the program for the application and transfer of technology for the socio-economic development of rural and mountainous areas during the period 2004–2010. This program conducted 288 projects in 60 provinces and cities with funding of USD35 million, of which around USD14 million was from the central government budget (39.7%) and more than USD21 million was contracted by companies, private sector and provincial government budgets (60.3%). These projects transferred many technologies to farmers and local communities in agriculture, aquaculture, healthcare and new infrastructure for rural development.

Since the 1990s, systems have been established for agriculture extension, fishery extension, industrial extension and the scientific and technological application centers in provinces. These organizations support technology transfer for farmers, medium sized and small enterprises in rural area. Many workshops, seminars, conferences and projects have been conducted to transfer technology to users. During the 2000s, SATI (State Agency for Technology Innovation) was created under Ministry of Science and Technology to promote a network of technology application and transfer centers around the country.

Besides the above organizations, networks of scientific and technological information centers of the government and provinces established during the 1970s and 1980s have disseminated the scientific and technological information for business production activities in agriculture, industry and the enterprises, cooperatives and locals.

In 2000, the government initiated a project for the development of technology market mechanisms by creating technology transaction centers in selected large cities like Hanoi and HoChiMinh City as well as providing more incentive policies. In 2005, a decision by Prime Minister was enacted on technology market development. In these cities, technology trading floors were established, which allowed technology sellers and buyers to communicate directly to trade technology and it also facilitated transfer activities.

The government also organized the technology trade exhibition (or TechMart) activities around the country to facilitate and bring together technology sellers and buyers, research institutions, universities, domestic and foreign enterprises and facilitate negotiations for transfer contracts. In addition, post-TechMart measures have been undertaken to follow up sales and transactions. In addition, the establishment of the online TechMart has created favorable conditions for communications and technology exchange.

Other policies relevant to technology transfer and application

According to the Law on Science and Technology (2000) and the Decree No. 81 (2002), profits gained from the assignment or transfer of R&D results shall be divided among the scientists who have created the technology, the technology owners, the scientific and technological organizations of the scientists and the intermediaries. Where the technologies are created with the use of State budget, the authors shall receive a maximum of 30% of the technology transfer price, while the authors and collectives organizing the successful application of science and technology (S&T) results shall be rewarded by the S&T result – using parties with a maximum value being equal to 30% of the after-tax additional incomes for a period of 3 years. The intermediaries may receive at most 10% of the technology transfer price. This is a significant and progressive change in the policy for technology transfer.

According to the later enacted Law on Technology Transfer of 2006, which was based on the practical learning experience of the Bayh-Dole Act of the US among others, government shall assign the ownership of technology from results of public funded R&D to the organizations which organized such activities such as universities or R&D institutes. Revenue from public funded technology transfer activities shall be distributed as follows: the author of an invention (such as university research staff) shall be entitled to 20–35% of the income from the technology transfer contract. Under this Technology Transfer Law, the National Program for Technology Innovation has been established to improve national technological capacity and increase the effectiveness of technology transfer activities; also to facilitate small and medium enterprises to replace outdated technology, to apply and master progressive technology transferred from overseas to Vietnam. Government science and technology organizations are also permitted to mortgage the state owned assets which have been assigned to them to set up loans for implementation of technology transfer activities.

Under the Law on Investment of 2006, the state is obliged to create favorable conditions for technology transfer and ensure the lawful rights and interest of parties, including any capital contribution in the form of technology, in order to encourage investment and help to transfer advanced technology in Vietnam.

As can be seen above, the legal and institutional framework for technology transfer activities, from foreign or domestic organizations, or internal transfer among domestic organizations, has now been created.

Experiences at specific universities

To understand better specific experiences of technology transfer in universities, this section provides analyses of five universities as examples of how technology transfer activities were organized, what were problems and issues emerged.

Hanoi University of Science and Technology (HUST)

Hanoi University of Science and Technology (HUST) was established by government decree on March 6, 1956. HUST consists of 14 faculties and 25 institutes and centers. Over the years, HUST has trained more than 80,000 engineers and 1,800 masters and doctors. In addition to five key laboratories working on engineering such as Automation, Electrical and Electronics Engineering, Mechanical Engineering, HUST hosts the following organizations:

- International Training Institute for Materials Science
- Automation Research Centre
- Bach Khoa Internetwork Security Centre

- Biomedical Electronics Centre
- Centre for Development and Application of Software
- Centre for Education and Development of Chromatography
- Centre for High Performance Computing
- Centre for Research and Development of High Technology
- Centre for Talents Training
- International Research Institute on Multimedia Information, Communication and Application
- BK Network Information Centre
- Materials Science Centre
- Polymer Centre
- Polytech Company
- Renewable Energy Research Centre.

HUST has 1,800 staff, including 1,500 lecturers and 240 professors and associate professors, 450 of whom possess doctorates. The university annually enrolls 35,000 undergraduate and 2,000 graduate and postgraduate students. With teaching as its key mandate, skills development constitutes the main type of cooperation between HUST and local enterprises. The HUST gives support to firms through training and re-training of staff and upgrading of technological expertise. Contracts for technical services and other R&D activities for firms represent another kind of university linkage with industry, and HUST also provides firms with consultancy services on technology innovation, transfer and equipment upgrading.

To develop linkages with local enterprises, the university has created several incubators for technology and business development. Funding for R&D comes from three main sources: (1) the state budget for programs and projects; (2) the business sector through contractual arrangements; and (3) international organizations via development assistance.

In some cases technology transfer from HUST to organizations such as Department of Science and Technology under Hanoi city or other provinces has been significant. In engineering subjects, such as new material technology, polymer and composite technology for electrical, electronics and bioengineering, HUST has carried out research to create technology applicable solutions for transfer to several economic sectors including transport, agriculture, aquaculture, environment protection, telecom, automation and power generation.

One of the noteworthy examples is *Polyco*, a company acting as the commercial arm of HUST to deal with technology transfer needs. The company has 850 staff and is self-financing, earning income from technology transfer contracts. Polyco (Polytechnical Mechanical, Thermal, Electrical and Refrigeration Engineering Company Limited.) was a spin-off from the R&D activities of HUST. Professor Dinh Van Nha, gained his PhD in Russia in automation technology in 1975. He worked at HUST in different capacities such as Director of Automation Center of HUST, focusing on areas of automation for brewery production, construction material, food processing, energy conservation and new energies. Over time,

Professor Nha and his colleagues have undertaken more than 500 research and technology application contracts, published more than 60 scientific articles and supervised hundreds of undergraduate and postgraduate students. He received many medals and awards for his achievements. In 1994, Professor Nha and the group of HUST scientists set up Polyco as a university spin-off specializing in the implementation of automation technology in several productive sectors. Over (almost) 20 years, Polyco has grown into a large industrial group consisting of 11 member companies, 4 research institutes and colleges and 20 design centers. Currently Polyco is one of the leading corporations in Vietnam for manufacturing research and technology transfer in the food industry and cold temperatures. The company is now among the strongest organizations in Vietnam specializing in design, manufacture, equipment installation and supply, technical consulting and technology transfer (turnkey method) in the following fields:

- Food processing equipment – food processing equipment for breweries, milk, alcohol, fruit and food processing plants in turnkey contract
- Pressure equipment – steam boilers, oil automatic heaters, coal heaters (low, medium and large capacity); refrigeration system with capacities up to millions of Kcal/h; CO_2 recovery system, bottling line system, compressed-air system
- Other fields – air conditioning and ventilation system for hotels, modern buildings, conventional halls and factories; electricity system, measurement, control and automation system; water treatment, waste – water treatment, industrial and civil constructions.

In recognition of its success, the company has received many awards and medals from both government and international organizations such as WIPO. The technology transferred was conducted at a large scale. Revenue growth was a factor of 1.5 to 2 times annually. Polyco has delivered many package contracts (EPC contractor) in design, construction, equipment supply and installation of production lines, for alcohol and brewery plants of capacity 50–120 million liters/ year in many provinces and cities. In addition, Polyco worked jointly with several large foreign corporations (Krones Group, KHS Group, Siemens) to deliver international projects. The founder of the company, Professor Nha, is currently Director of the Omega Research and Training Institute, and Vice CEO of the Polyco Group.

Polyco is one of few successful spin-off companies from HUST for the purpose of technology commercialization and transfer. Despite the fact that the main mandate of HUST is still to deliver training it is one of leading universities in providing technology transfer activities. There are a number of policy and legal provisions designed to promote creation of start-up companies from within HUST. In addition to Decision No. 78/2008 that applies to all universities, HUST has also introduced some of its own regulations. By Decision No. 150 on May 2008, the Rector of HUST issued new regulation governing the management of the IP activities of staff and students within the university. Several objects of IP are regulated, including patents, industrial designs, know-how and trademarks created by the projects funded via HUST or using HUST facilities. The regulations also cover copyrights in arts, science, broadcasting as well as new species of plants. These regulations apply to all projects and programs under HUST. The Science-Technology (S&T) division of HUST has overall responsibility for IP management, and within the S&T division, there is a sub-divison of IP. This sub-division takes care of advising staff and students in working with IP issues such as registration, protection of IP rights and their commercialization. Before the creation of the IP sub-division in 2006, the total number of granted patents or utility solution for HUST was around 20. Since its creation, this total has risen to 30 and 15 trademarks have been granted.

Nevertheless, these regulations are still somewhat unclear and detailed guidance is not always available, and the absence of communication mechanisms is an obstacle to strengthening linkages between university and companies. A system of match making or brokering is not considered adequate to bridge the gap between the technology that the university has to offer and the needs of firms that are potential users of that technology.

HoChiMinh City University of Technology (HCMUT) under Vietnam National University

HCMUT is located in HoChiMinh City, the economic hub of the country, and the university staff utilizes this advantage to develop technology transaction activities for economic purposes. The university maintains close relationships with local firms and other organizations like provincial authorities, departments, extension organizations, and as a result has contributed significantly to production and business activities in HoChiMinh City and other provinces in the Mekong river delta.

Established October 27, 1957 the university was known as the Phu Tho National Center of Technology. It included four partner colleges: College of Civil Engineering; College of Electrical Engineering; College of Industrial Arts Engineering; and Vietnam National Maritime Engineering. In 1972, the university was renamed the National Institute of Technology, and was the only center in South Vietnam to train technical engineers and experts. On January 11, 1974, the National Institute of Technology was merged into Thu Duc Institute of Polytechnic and renamed the University of Technology, running a postgraduate training program for the first time. After the national reunification in 1976, the university was renamed as HoChiMinh City Polytechnic. Being one of the three largest universities of technology in Vietnam, the mission of the HoChiMinh City Polytechnic is the training of engineers majoring in the fields of construction, industry, natural resources exploration and exploitation, and environment preservation. Since 1981, HCMUT has expanded its scope into postgraduate training.

The Vietnam National University, Ho Chi Minh City (VNU-HCM) was founded in 1995. Ho Chi Minh City Polytechnic joined the 9 members of VNU-

HCM and was renamed as University of Technology. It has two campuses: one is located in the inner of HoChiMinh City and the other in the outskirts of the city. The first campus has 117 classrooms, 96 laboratories, 3 workshops and 1 library.

The university provided academic programs for 34 undergraduate majors. They are classified in the following types of educational programs:

- Formal and informal undergraduate education
- Postgraduate education
- Cooperative and twinning program with national and international partners – two years of study at HCMUT and the remainder of the academic programs at the cooperative universities and institutions in others countries
- Education program for the gifted and talented
- PFIEV (Programme de Formation d'Ingénieurs d'Excellence au Vietnam) in cooperation with France
- Advanced Program –a national project that enables HCMUT to implement the training on the organization system of the Electrical and Electronics Sector, in cooperation with the Department of Electrical and Engineering, University of Illinois at Urbana-Champaign, USA.

HoChiMinh City University of Technology offers bachelor degrees, 31 master's degrees and 38 doctorates in 11 faculties, as follows:

- Faculty of Applied Science
- Faculty of Civil Engineering
- Faculty of Chemical Engineering
- Faculty of Computer Science and Engineering
- Faculty of Electrical and Electronics Engineering
- Faculty of Environment
- Faculty of Geology and Petroleum Engineering
- Faculty of Industrial Management
- Faculty of Materials Technology
- Faculty of Mechanical Engineering
- Faculty of Transport Engineering.

In terms of international cooperation, HCMUT has partnerships with many international universities including the University of Illinois at Urbana-Champaign; University of Heidelberg, Germany; Protestant University for Applied Sciences Freiburg, Switzerland; Johannes Kepler University of Linz, Austria; University of Leeds, UK; Waseda University, Japan; Advanced Institute of Science and Technology, Japan; National University of Singapore; and Nanyang Technological University, Singapore. It has cooperated with some companies like the Norwegian group Roxar AS assisting the university in building a high-tech laboratory.

In the field of technology transfer and commercialization activities, HCMUT is one of the most active in the country. To deliver both applied oriented research and technology application in contractual projects, the university has created multiple centers, including the: Applied Research Center for Construction Technology; Polymer Technology Research Center; Research Center for Mechanical Equipment and Technology; Research Center for Industrial Technology and Equipment; and Renewable Energy Research Center. In addition, the university has set up a number of organizations for the purpose of commercialization and technology transaction such as the Polytech Company (POTECO), the Center for Research and Training Support in Business Administration, and a Consulting Office for Enterprises. Under POTECO, for instance, there are a number of smaller member companies such as the Construction–Installation Enterprise, the Material Technology and the Environment Center. Among them, the most notable organization is **BKC** (Bach-Khoa Construction Consulting Company; Bach-Khoa means Polytech). BKC was set up in 2002, with 45 staff, of which 3 have PhDs, 8 with masters and 28 with bachelor degrees. Many lecturers and staff from the university are associates of the company. The company's main mission is conducting planning, design and implementation for construction projects. On the business side, the company has transferred some technologies, developed by HCMUT staff, to other companies in areas such as construction survey, planning, monitoring, quality control and assurance and project management. These technology solutions have been widely implemented in many projects including irrigation, construction and building of industrial, infrastructure and housing projects. In just 5 years, the company has conducted 250 consulting projects for 170 clients, worth of USD2 million.

Like HUST, HCMUT also has a Division for Science and Technology, including IP and technology transfer. This is common practice for many universities, but the extent of their involvement in technology transfer and IP management varies, depending on their mandate to conduct consultancy. More often than not, it is companies created by university staff (like BKC) that are the most active in pursuing technology transfer projects rather than the IP units.

The most important contribution of HCMUT to society remains the training of human resources. However, HCMUT also tries to address the needs of society and companies via the previously mentioned organizations which link the university to firms and other actors. These entities aim to improve the local economy through multiple channels, including solving specific technical problems in production and business operations in firms, technology transfer and services. Via this structure, HCMUT can supply various kinds of consultancy services in R&D, testing, standardization, metrology, quality control and other technical solutions. HCMUT conducts these activities via agreements with firms which implement cooperative programs and projects, or in partnership with business associations such as the Plastics Association, Automation S&T Society, Mechanics Society, and the Association for Leather and Shoe Industry. Many large-scale state-owned enterprises in industries like garments, plastics, mechanical engineering, construction, brewery, or seafood processing have become long-term partners of HCMUT and have benefited substantially from this partnership.

Can Tho University (CTU)

Can Tho University was established as Can Tho Academy on March 3, 1966 in Can Tho, a city hub for agriculture business in the Mekong river delta, several hundred kilometers south of HoChiMinh City. It has a mandate to work in such fields as agriculture, veterinary medicine, irrigation, agricultural mechanical engineering and agriculture economics. The main functions of the CTU are undergraduate, graduate and postgraduate training, as well as research and technology transfer for the Mekong river delta. The university has seven faculties (now called colleges), and many research institutes and centers with a total of 1,100 staff, of which 735 (or 68.7%) participate in teaching and R&D activities. These colleges work in areas such as Agriculture and Applied biology, Aquaculture and fisheries, Engineering Technology, Environment and natural resources, ICT, Rural development and Natural sciences. CTU has various research centers such as the: Research Institute for Climate Change, Software Center, Biotechnology Research and Development Institute, and Mekong Delta Development Research Institute.

Apart from its main and long-term mandate to provide training, CTU is involved in various fields of scientific research and technological development. These are primarily applied projects in agriculture, biotechnology and aquaculture. Among the notable results of the CTU in this area are projects on rice varieties research (with more than 30 new types of rice having been approved as national varieties), the project of farming systems, technology transfer for pig farming, agro-based food processing, biotech for agriculture and the production of various type of aquaculture products like shrimp artemia and new breeds of fish. Supply of services for agricultural needs is also a widespread activity in the university. To commercialize and pursue these activities, CTU has established units like the Company of Plant Protection and the Laboratory on Tissue Culture. The most active organization working on technology transfer is *Center for Services and Technology Transfer (CSTT)*, which was established in 2012. The center, employing around 20 staff, has been tasked with advising the CTU leadership on the management and implementation of technology development and transfer activities, organizing transfer process and incubation, and commercialization of research results of the university. Acting as a bridge between different colleges and the farmers, the center has focused on transferring technologies to a number of production activities, depending on the strengths of respective colleges. For example, the College of Agriculture has worked on: new crops and breeds of rice; fruits like mango, watermelon, plums; and developments such as a new crop of rice with anti-drought, pest-resistance features. The College of Aquaculture has worked on diseases and higher yields for different types of fish and shrimp, and better farming systems for aquaculture. These technologies were transferred to farmers and cooperatives in partnership with the center.

In addition to the above organizations supporting linkages with farmers in the delta, CTU benefits from extensive networks that facilitate cooperation with international associations, societies and firms around the world. This helps the university to upgrade its infrastructure, facilities, capabilities and knowledge base, and has given rise to various fellowship exchange programs. CTU has 27 cooperative projects with foreign and international organizations, the budget for which totals roughly USD10 million. Some of the most well-known projects have included cooperation with US universities on climate change impact in the Mekong river delta, and the training of agro-based technicians in cooperation with European partners.

There are not many large-scale industrial firms in the region and farmers, with their small-scale and family based production, are the main users of innovation and technology transfer from the CTU. These activities are often implemented via small-scale projects by provincial local authorities such as Department of Science and Technology or Department of Agriculture to support farmers groups at district or commune levels. The most significant impacts are job creation and formation of new business opportunities. Along the coast of three provinces – Soc Trang, Bac Lieu and Ca Mau (the furthest southeast provinces of the country, facing the South China sea) – technology transfers from CTU enable farmers to combine planting and raising shrimp artemia together with salt production, and to increase the productivity of catfish production.

CTU also cooperated with the provinces to implement technology transfer in 59 projects in agriculture and rural development. This has led to new job creation and the formation of new business opportunities for farmers. The university also assisted local provinces in Project Mekong 1000, which aims to train 1,000 provincial managers to degree level. Additionally, CTU has been involved in various development consultancy projects for the region. Interestingly, the university has also published a scientific journal describing its research and technology transfer activities for dissemination among farming and rural communities.

In the technology transfer process, CTU has faced a number of difficulties. Regulation on setting up spin-off companies is complicated and there is a lack of effective financial incentives (such as tax exemptions). The overload of teaching time by lecturers is one of the reasons discouraging their research. As a result, research commercialization tends to be one-off rather than a regular activity. Complex IP protection issues also cause difficulties within the university research environment.

To evaluate technology transfer activities in CTU, one can say that, traditionally, training still remains its main mandate and research activity has only come into focus in the last 15 years. This change has created many new challenges. Unlike other universities, CTU aims primarily to serve the need of farmers having very low purchasing power, and thus derives limited revenues from commercialization of research. This raises a need for strong government support for technology transfer. So far, most commercialization measures of CTU have to be done via central or local governments, which have budgets for various programs to support farmers. Nevertheless, it is widely believed that policy so far has not been supportive enough for the university to play an increased role in this agriculture-based region, whether in training or in technology innovation and dissemination. Despite the recent efforts of many institutions to align university activities with the needs of farmers,[1] long-term planning and strategic orientation including investment program that help farmers to have more affordable or even cost-free technology services are still not adequate. So far, technology transfers from CTU to the region tend to have immediate but only short-term effects. Products from these technologies mainly serve the domestic market and lack international competitiveness.

Hanoi University of Pharmacy (HUP)

Hanoi University of Pharmacy, formerly known as the Indochina Medicine School, was established by decree of the French government on January 8, 1902. The school was responsible for training medical doctors, pharmacists and doing some research in tropical diseases. The training of pharmacists started in 1926.

On September 29, 1961, the Ministry of Health decided to split Hanoi School of Medicine–Pharmacy into two schools: the Hanoi Medical University; and Hanoi University of Pharmacy. The university has 18 departments and centers in areas such as organic and inorganic physical chemistry, analytical chemistry, biochemistry, pharmaceutical chemistry, pharmacognosy, pharmaceutics, traditional pharmacies, industrial pharmacies, clinical pharmacies, pharmacology, microbiology and botany. The HUP also has number of laboratories, including working on Good Manufacturing Practice (GMP), pharmaco-kinetics, quality assurance and a botanical garden.

The university has different academic training programs, e.g.: PhD, master, first-level specialized pharmacist, second-level specialized pharmacist (graduate programs), five-year regular pharmacist, four-year irregular pharmacist, second-degree pharmacist and three-year junior pharmacist. It also provides collaborative training programs such as: the Mekong Transregional master program (Master of Pharmaceutical Science); the Pharmacovigilance and Epiedemilology DU program; and the Pharmaceutics DU program. During 1961–2013, more than 15,000 pharmacists were trained in HUP. Currently there are 5,066 students of all types studying at HUP: 4,261 undergraduate, 805 graduate (2013–2014). There are around 50 international students each year at HUP, coming from Laos, Cambodia, Mongolia, France, the United States, Japan, Thailand, Sweden, Belgium and Netherlands. The university cooperates in a network of more than 100 partners and exchange programs with more than 10 countries.

In research activities, HUP produced the *Journal of Pharmaceutical Research and Drug Information*, which is considered one of the most respected journals in the field of pharmaceutical sciences in Vietnam. The university conducts 30 university-level projects, 4 ministry-level projects, 3 projects for Hanoi Department of Science and Technology, and projects funded by National Foundation for S&T Development. Research focus areas of HUP include:

• Medicinal plants and traditional pharmacy – research on traditional remedies, medicinal plants conservation and how to prepare and process traditional medicines

- Phytochemistry – isolation of natural compounds, structure elucidation, semi-synthesis and studying on biological activity and pharmacology
- Drug quality control
- Pharmaceutical formulation – study on the stability and pharmacokinetics of products in order to improve bioavailability to ensure the therapeutic effects
- Pharmacology and pharmacokinetics
- Organic synthesis (immune-stimulants, anti-malarials, contraceptives)
- Mathematical design of experiments (optimization) applied in pharmaceutical sciences
- Community pharmacy
- Pharmaceutical administration and epidemiology.

The university does not commonly create companies or spin-off organizations for technology commercialization and transfer. Most issues related to IP or technology transfer are managed by a division of S&T management. Recently, however, the university set up its first commercial company called **Duoc Khoa (DK) Pharma Co. Ltd** to address the need for new drugs that can be used for treatment of patients at affordable costs, The company was spun-out from the university in 2001 with a mission to turn traditional knowledge in medicines into technology and commercial products to serve the need for healthcare. The company was created by Dr. Tran Van On, Dean of Department, for a traditional medicinal plant of HUP and a group of other scientists. Currently, the company has 123 staff, of which 10 have PhD and master's degrees in Pharmacy and 24 with bachelor degrees. In cooperation with network of researchers within and outside HUP, the company aims to provide affordable drug products based on traditional plants, using advanced extraction technologies. The company also has partnerships with international organizations such as Cosmetic Valley (Paris), Tesoro Spin-off (Prague) and Chiang Mai University in Thailand. The company has an R&D division, project management division, a factory for traditional pharmacy, and a production unit for eye care products. It has opened a drug store and a farm working on Good Agriculture Practice (GAP).

DK Pharma works in some areas such as R&D of herbal medicines, tea products, extracted by-products; plus provision of consulting services for communities and farmers in planting and harvesting traditional medicinal plants. Key products of DK Pharma include 40 various types of medicines, ranging from eye care, plant-based antibiotics to products that increase immunology capacity, treating rheumatism, liver infection, diabetes, vitamins and other functional foods. DK Pharma now supplies its semi-processed products to more than 20 other pharmaceutical companies, and many of these products were IP protected by patents and trademarks held by the Vietnam National Office of IP.

The case of DK Pharma shows that even non-engineering universities like HUP have begun to see positive results from their efforts to secure and deliver technology commercialization and technology transfer projects.

As we can see from the specific examples described, many universities have good interactions with local authorities, entrepreneurs, farmers, and other end-users by building a long-term plan and strategy with the local community. The technical outreach activities of universities have often been conducted very professionally; however, the existing divisions of science and technology management at these universities are still not sufficiently active. Instead, in some large universities, a number of companies have been spun-off from the R&D activities at the universities. These organizations (such as Polyco, DK Pharma, CSTT or BK Construction) eventually grew into larger companies and performed successfully, dealing with the commercialization of research results and transfer technologies to communities and firms.

However, these successful cases are not very numerous and the majority of other universities have limited direct collaboration activities and contracts with the private business sector. One reason for this is that the business sector often undervalues domestic expertise in comparison to a foreign offer. Because part of the research budget of most universities is government funded, both the business sector and the university complain about the excessive bureaucratic financial procedures. Finally, the success of a few selected universities also depends on the individual entrepreneurship and leadership of university managers which not everyone can always possess.

Technology transfer in Vietnamese universities: issues and problems

The main contribution of Vietnamese universities has been the training of human resources for economic development, satisfying the needs of firms and other organizations. Most universities perform this task rather well in terms of quantity but are often lacking in terms of quality. There is little contribution in terms of innovation in local firms, and the clustering effect of innovation from the universities for local economies is therefore limited.

Yet, there are some instances of innovation and learning in the university system. Most universities are involved in consultancy activities, supplying various kinds of services to local productive units, firms or farmer households. Universities offer minor technical improvements that serve demands for import substitution or that address specific needs in the areas of tropical climate production and socio-economic development. Nevertheless, there has been no major technological breakthrough by universities, and their role in upgrading the technological level of production in the country is still limited.

Concerning firms' perceptions of university–industry linkages, firms widely cite a desire for greater cooperation and assistance from universities and R&D organizations. However, local firms tend to accumulate technological learning from other sources, such as other domestic firms and foreign suppliers and buyers, rather than from local universities. Moreover, the reverse effect of local firms on activities in the universities is also limited. There are several reasons for this. Both firms and universities lack the expertise for negotiating with one another, for learning and for sharing information, and for absorbing new knowledge. Many transactions between firms and universities are based on informal and personal relationships, as the institutional mechanisms to facilitate this process such as technology intermediaries (consultancy, business agents, investment lawyers, angel investors) are rarely in place. A further problem is that the overall structure and dynamism of markets do not sufficiently encourage firms to innovate.

To date, the policy environment is not sufficiently developed to facilitate technology transfer and market transactions between universities and their clients. Inconsistent and sometimes contradictory policies together with unsuitable institutional frameworks still create obstacles for university and firms to work together. Overall management mechanisms for R&D and IPRs provide little incentive for university staff to work more closely with firms. The establishment and operation of a technology transfer office (TTO) or other forms of commercial units within the university system is not a widely accepted practice and progress relies on individual initiatives within particular universities. Lack of support in terms of funding, training and connection for this vital institution tends to slow down interactions between universities and others actors and the roles of individual scientists, inventors, managers and entrepreneurs have received inadequate attention. The lack of an entrepreneurial culture in the university system is also a key constraint limiting the contribution of university entrepreneurs to business operations. Despite existing legal and policy frameworks being in place, their enforcement and implementation are not always fully functional.

As our analysis shows, universities face many barriers in managing their technology transfer relationships. Due to the lack of essential resources such as finance, viable investment is a frequent problem. Concerning time resources, the preoccupation with teaching limits time available for research and other related activities. University staff members have little knowledge of IPR and commercialization skills and there is no effective mechanism to address this weakness. The recipients of university services (especially from agriculture-based institutions such as CTU or HUP), including farmers and other disadvantaged groups of population with low purchasing power, have created only a small payback for the commercialization of research and technology transfer. To date, most commercialization projects are carried out via central or local provincial governments, which have budgets for various programs to support farmers or small firms. There is a strong need for the provision of free public technical services involving government support in technology transfer.

Although universities play an important role in the technology transfer process and promote social and economic development both directly and indirectly, they are still unable to realize their full potential due to weak government policy implementation, lack of basic commercial knowledge and the passive attitude of their staff.

Among other indicators, the function and performance of universities are evaluated on the basis of their research activities together with the transfer of its output to production and users. Due to existing barriers to technology transfer, many university staff members tend to commercialize the research output directly out of the lab by their private efforts. Despite the fact that all universities have divisions for science, technology management and also deal with IP issues, their companies are more active in real technology transactions.

As this analysis of cases has shown, there is an imperative to improve the government policy environment. First, financial sources from the government for university activities are still much lower than adequate for serving the need of communities. In addition, the payment and accounting system for financial clearance is very cumbersome, thus preventing universities from using them more intensively for technology extension or transfer activities. Furthermore, the salary regime in Vietnam, despite various improvements, is still not adequate.

Second, proposals to increase time resources for lecturers and professors for the purpose of conducting research and the provision of technical transfer services, while much discussed, have not been implemented.

Third, the enhancement of management capability in IPR and commercialization is another vital policy issue. Intellectual property policies have still not been clearly communicated to university staff, scientists and other technical workers to encourage them to commercialize their research outcomes. In general, the current legal framework on IPR has been completed, in compliance with the Law of IPR enacted in 2006, but key problems remain with the dissemination, implementation and enforcement of the Law. Many scientists, researchers and teachers at universities have stated that they lack knowledge about IPR, that administrative procedures are too complex and IP applications take too long to complete.

As mentioned earlier, the transfer of research outcomes to society should be addressed by special policies which are geared to the provision of low-cost public services for the poor or disadvantaged such as farmers, women, children or ethnic minorities. This is especially true for universities such as CTU and HUP working in areas of social need such as agriculture, farming and healthcare. Without these policies, universities cannot be expected to provide services to these disadvantaged groups.

Several recommendations can be made to improve policy. First, research should be included as a key mission of universities, which should also receive additional investment in both basic research and applied research. Research programs in universities should be focused on social and economic effects and research activities should be oriented to the real needs of users. Finally, it is essential to promote technical outreach activities such as technology extension and transfer to enable universities to work closely and directly with relevant "external organizations" such as hospitals, pharmacy manufactures, agriculture manufactures, firms and associations.

Priority must be given to increasing the quality of training activities throughout the higher education system. Beyond this, a longer-term vision and a strategic approach should replace short-term planning aimed at earning fees and securing other benefits for the university system. To overcome the separation of research and teaching, universities should have more autonomy and stronger incentives to encourage innovation research. Investment should be more selective to avoid wasting resources and fragmentation. Modern university management methods such as peer review, international advisory committees and performance-based evaluation for both R&D and teaching quality should be thoroughly applied. The internationalization of the university system, hiring more international staff and achieving internationally competitive salary levels and management techniques, as well as rigorous evaluation criteria and a greater emphasis on teaching quality, could create a push for more competition and quality. The model of private universities built as centers of excellence might be a sensible option.

Balancing the need for commercialization of research, teaching and serving the public needs is not an easy task for universities. Establishment of companies to act as commercial arms or TTO, a TLO (technology licensing organization) would seem to be appropriate given Vietnam's circumstances. To develop technology markets is one of the central tasks of the increasing linkage with production. These and other new mechanisms should be based on the overall principle of moving in the direction of a market economy, with the state focusing on macro-level regulations. This should be seen as a long-term process, requiring determination and flexible solutions for each specific circumstance.

Policy makers should pay attention to both quantitative and qualitative aspects of university–industry linkages. Priority should be given to enhancing the capability of university staff through financial and other incentives, as well as to the organization of R&D system, IPR issues and evaluation of research results. At the same time, a key challenge is to increase the capability of universities to meet the technological innovation needs of enterprises. Although much remains to be done, progress is being made in turning university behavior into more business friendly and innovation-oriented directions. The result may be that Vietnamese universities will develop more productive patterns of interaction with firms and with local economies.

The cases studies also show that there has been a gap between established policies and their implementation in promoting technical extension and transfer mission. The existing policy framework, especially on financial incentives, management mechanisms, salaries and IPR, strongly influences the implementation of mission statements adopted by universities. Hence, the government should introduce an adequate and more specific mechanism to support these types of activities.

Note

1 One example of these supporting activities is mentioned – the Ministry of Science and Technology program to support farmers in rural and mountainous areas via science and technology innovation.

References

Brundenius, C. and Goransson, B. (2011) *Universities in Transition. The Changing Role and Challenges for Academic Institutions*. IDRC, Switzerland: Springer.
Ministry of Education and Training (MOET) (2008) *Data on Education and Training*. Available online: www.edu.vn/data/
NISTPASS (2000) *Research and Postgraduate Training*. Report of RAPOGE project Hanoi.

OECD-WB (2014) "Science, Technology and Innovation in Vietnam." In the series OECD Reviews of Innovation Policy, published jointly by OECD and WB. Available online: http://dx.doi.org/10.1787/9789264213500-en

Perkins, D.H. and V.T.T. Anh (2010) "Vietnam's Industrial Policy: Designing policies for sustainable development." Policy Dialogue Paper, No. 1, Ash Institute, Harvard University, Cambridge, MA.

Pham Minh Hac (2000) Education and Human Resources. Proceeding of the conference *Using Knowledge for Development*. Hanoi 1998. World Bank and NISTPASS.

Tagscherer, U. (2010) "Analysis and Assessment of Industry–Science Linkages in Viet Nam." Study for the OECD *Review on Innovation in South East Asia*. Germany: Fraunhofer ISI.

Tran Ngoc Ca (2006) "Universities as Drivers of the Urban Economies in Asia. The case of Vietnam." Policy Research Working Paper, No. 3949 (June). World Bank: Development Research Group.

Tran Ngoc Ca (2011) "Review of Viet Nam's Innovation Policy." Background Paper prepared for the Joint OECD-World Bank Review of Viet Nam's National Innovation System.

Tran Ngoc Ca and Nguyen Vo Hung. (2011) "Vietnam: Current debates on the transformation of academic institutions." In *Universities in Transition. The Changing Role and Challenges for Academic Institutions*, C. Brundenius and B. Goransson (eds). IDRC, Switzerland: Springer.

VCCI (2012) *Vietnamese Enterprises Sector*. Report of Vietnam Chamber of Commerce and Industry, Hanoi.

Part V

What about university technology transfer?

18 In university technology transfer one size does not fit them all

Comparing the biological sciences and information technology

Martin Kenney and Donald Patton

Over the last four decades, university research outputs have become increasingly important for leading edge technological developments and economic growth in a number of nations and, in particular, the U.S. Advances in science and engineering research and research techniques have become increasingly important for technological innovation (Hicks et al., 2001; Narin et al., 1997; Rosenberg and Nelson, 1994). In some fields, such as pharmaceuticals and information and communication technologies (ICT), university research has formed the basis of new firms and, in certain cases, new industries.[1] Universities, because of their role in training students and conducting scientific research, have received significant attention from policy-makers.

Given the multifaceted role of the university in knowledge-creation and dissemination, it is remarkable how the social scientific understanding of technology transfer has fixated upon patentable inventions and technology licensing. This chapter suggests that this fixation not only underestimates the technology transferred, but more importantly, mischaracterizes the transfer process itself, which as Perkmann et al. (2013) have observed is more often a process of engagement than of direct commercialization. We suggest that the current misunderstanding of technology transfer is caused by the belief that the field of pharmaceutical biotechnology is a valid characterization of reality for all other disciplines. The process of technology transfer in the field of pharmaceutical biotechnology is characterized by patents and a relatively unidirectional, linear process from university invention to final product, often intermediated by a venture capital-financed new firm. Hereafter, we will refer to this as the biotechnology model.

The commercialization of biotechnology was the catalyst for the most important U.S. government technology transfer policy, the Bayh-Dole Act of 1980, which was meant to encourage the patenting and licensing of university research advances based on federally funded research. Such a policy, it was believed, would accelerate commercialization and improve U.S. international competitiveness (Berman, 2008). While university patenting was increasing prior to the passage of Bayh-Dole, the post-1980 period witnessed further growth, though it is unlikely that Bayh-Dole "caused" this growth (Mowery et al., 2004). The success of the U.S. biotechnology and ICT industries prompted many OECD and other industrializing-economy governments to enact Bayh-Dole-like laws in the hopes of promoting university–industry technology transfer (Mowery, 2008).

The biotechnology model, perhaps because of its simplicity or possibly for the hopes of university administrators have of receiving significant income by licensing a research-derived invention, is widely touted by many. By examining technology commercialization in both biotechnology and ICT, we conclude that the biotechnology model will mislead policy-makers and researchers on how technology transfer in other fields of university research operates, and that applying the biotechnology model across campus is problematic.

The final problem with using biotechnology to think about technology transfer is that the industry it represents, pharmaceuticals, is in fact a small, though very profitable, industry with relatively low employment. For example, according to the World Health Organization (2014) the entire industry has sales of approximately US$300 billion a year. In 2014, the package software industry alone had $400 billion in sales (Statista, 2014), and this is only one portion of the ICT industries. While biotechnology has transformed the ways in which we think about life itself, it is the ICT industries that have transformed how we organize the society within which we live.

The biotechnology model

Biotechnology was born in the 1970s when the basic science of molecular biology developed "genetic engineering." Today, biotechnology comprises a variety of techniques that began with recombinant DNA and the development of monoclonal antibodies and grew into to a vast variety of techniques for manipulating and using living organisms and products (for a discussion of the industry's birth, see Kenney 1986). While biotechnology has also been influential in agriculture, its greatest impact has been in pharmaceuticals – an industry in which the products can be effectively protected by patents. Because many of the inventions that became products are the result of basic research many recent biotechnological inventions have their origins in university laboratories. The typical pattern is that the research funded by NIH and/or NSF results in a promising invention (usually a bioactive molecule) that is patented by the university and then licensed to a small firm funded by venture capital that further develops the molecule and begins clinical trials.

Only a few of these firms succeed, while many fail as their candidate drug fails trials. In contrast, those molecules, whose value is embodied in a small firm, showing promise are acquired by big pharmaceutical firms. This pattern has become so prominent that large pharmaceutical firms downsized and replaced their research operations with a strategy of acquiring smaller firms having a promising drug (see, for example, Higgins and Rodriguez, 2006). This development model fits a linear process in which the invention is developed in the university and then transferred to industry. While the transfer process does require interaction between the inventing laboratory and the commercial entity licensing the molecule (Siegel et al., 2004; Thursby and Thursby, 2003), as can be seen by the frequent inclusion of the university inventors in the management team and/or as members of scientific advisory boards (Powell and Padgett, 2012), the central role of basic science means that the knowledge is more likely to flow from academia to industry.

Given the costs and time necessary to develop and test a drug, patents are an important means of protecting these investments. It is this intellectual property that the university capitalizes upon in its negotiations with those interested in commercializing the invention. While research shows that even in biotechnology, a naïve "linear model" conceptualization of the links between university research and industrial innovation is not entirely justified, it is sufficiently congruent with reality to make for a workable model. Biotechnology was the ideal technology for the patent-based commercialization envisioned by Congress when passing Bayh-Dole.[2]

The information and communication technologies

If biotechnology can be understood as a basic science that resulted in the creation of a technology, and whose new innovations continue to be fed by basic research, ICT, which are for the most part located in engineering colleges, have a different pattern. The background of departments of electrical engineering can be traced to the rise of science-based industries in the late 19th century and the need for personnel with university degrees to staff new firms such as General Electric and Westinghouse (Noble, 1977). While the electrical industry was considered a science-based industry, much of the important early research was undertaken in large corporate laboratories with universities largely relegated to producing graduates. Though MIT was already introducing a more science-based curriculum, it was only after World War Two that electrical engineering was transformed into a research-based discipline, supported by research funding from the Department of Defense. DoD funding strategies affected the types of projects undertaken and indirectly influenced the economic effects of this research.

The Department of Defense had a liberal policy toward intellectual property in both industry and academia (National Research Council, 1999: 119–120) and supported research commercialization as long as DoD received a royalty-free license to any patents granted. Not only were many new firms in the early computer industry founded to commercialize DoD-funded research but, in many cases, DoD was an early and price-insensitive customer. This allowed firms high profit margins that supported further product development (National Research Council, 1999: 165) – a feature of particular importance to small research-based startups.

In ICT, the relationship between university and industry is complex, and industry has had an important role in conducting cutting-edge research. For example, semiconductors firms often conducted applied research in cutting edge fields such as surface science, and research at Bell and IBM Laboratories was of such a fundamental nature that their researchers won Nobel Prizes.

There have been few studies of the commercialization of university research results in ICT. Balconi and Laboranti (2006), in a study of microelectronics researchers at Italian universities, found that students were the most important form of knowledge transfer and that patents were comparatively unimportant. In a study of Dutch university faculty relationships, Bekkers and Bodas (2008: 1845) found that for computer science the most important method of engaging with industry was through "scientific output, students and informal contacts" and "collaborative and contract research." Moreover, they found that in electrical engineering the most common method was contacts via alumni or professional organizations.[3] Agrawal and Henderson (2002) found that for transferring knowledge from the MIT Departments of Mechanical and Electrical Engineering patenting was a minor activity and that they accounted for less than 10% of the knowledge transferred.

A recent study of electrical engineering and computer science at UC Berkeley found that patents were rarely used to protect technology that proved to be valuable to industry (Kenney et al., 2014). Examples of technology transferred from UC Berkeley research include software-based advances such as BSD UNIX (operating system software), GENIE (time-sharing system software), SPICE (semiconductor design software), and INGRES (relational database software). The research for each of these software programs was funded by the Department of Defense and/or NSF and freely released to the all interested parties. In each case, the software was fundamental for the establishment of new firms and the introduction of new products.

These software programs could have been patented and then marketed by the technology transfer office (TTO) in an attempt to commercialize the software, but none were. By adopting an open source strategy the technology was widely diffused and became the foundation for new industries. One example is the development and commercialization of the SPICE semiconductor design software, which is also an excellent example of the deep bi-directional relationships between firms and UC Berkeley researchers. As discussed by Lécuyer (2014), the SPICE (Simulation Program, Integrated Circuit Emphasis) project began in the late 1960s when Berkeley's integrated circuits group began developing software to simplify increasingly complex microchip design. In the late 1960s a junior faculty member and a group of graduate students designed a circuit simulation program while the faculty member was simultaneously on sabbatical at Fairchild Semiconductor. Using funding from the military, a state program to support semiconductor research, and the NSF, a group of faculty members recruited students and professors to improve the SPICE algorithms that were made universally available.

User feedback was essential for improving SPICE and extending its applicability. Because it was free and unpatented, the software was adopted by industrial users who identified problems with the software and sometimes shared their improvements with the UCB team. The end result was that SPICE became the best software design program available and became the basis of an electronic design automation software industry centered in Silicon Valley. In the case of SPICE, UCB did not benefit directly, but the open source nature of the project encouraged firms to contribute code and suggestions to the university researchers that were then able to improve the software.

While Kenney et al. (2014) and Lécuyer (2014) focus on the comparative lack of patenting of software developments at the University of California, there is evidence that MIT computer science operated in a similar manner as it openly released a number of software programs that have had significant economic importance.[4] It is quite possible that open release has created greater economic value than would have been the case if the technologies had been patented and then licensed. Recently, Greenstein and Nagle (2014) show that the value of the descendent of the HTTP server software, Apache, which was developed at the University of Illinois and publicly released, accounted for somewhere between $2 billion and $12 billion in value. This study suggests that there has been a "large potential undercounting of 'digital dark matter' and related IT spillovers from university and federal funding."

Conclusion

The intensive focus by researchers and policy-makers on patenting and licensing ignores the more prevalent model, which is one in which university–industry technology transfer is a process characterized by considerable feedback and iteration (Colyvas et al., 2002) that entails multiple channels of interaction and knowledge flow between academia and industry. Attention focused on formal tech transfer misses the far more economically valuable technology transfer taking place outside of the administrative channels of technology licensing. Most technology transfer is part of a movement of technology, people, resources, and knowledge between industry and the university. These bidirectional and informal human and information flows are normally not dependent upon TTOs. Technology licensing is only one of a multitude of channels through which technology and knowledge flow into and out of the university.

While "closer university–industry relationships" are hailed as vital to the U.S. economy and the subject of a large scholarly literature, we still know surprisingly little about the microdynamics of these relationships and the most effective metrics for measuring them. The emphasis in recent U.S. policy on patent-based channels of interaction and knowledge transfer is reflected in the similarly "patent-centric" focus of much of the academic literature on university–industry research interactions. With the exception of pharmaceuticals, in most industries, university patents and licenses were reported to be of less importance compared with publications, conferences, informal interaction with university researchers, and consulting (Agarwal and Henderson, 2002; Nelson, 2012).

As we have asserted, interaction between academic and industrial researchers is vitally important and TTOs rarely have any role to play in the preponderance of these interactions. In certain fields industrial research may uncover fundamental problems that can initiate or even "lead" the academic research agenda. This was clearly the case in light-emitting diodes and semiconductors.[5] Historically scientific instruments, a small but lucrative industry, have been intimately related to the university and technology transfer (Rosenberg, 1992). It is possible that the earliest university–industry interactions were in scientific instruments; as inventor/scientists such as Galileo began their scientific careers building instruments such as telescopes, a field where they had to interact with not only fellow scientists but also commercial lens-makers (see Biagioli, 2006). From renaissance telescopes to contemporary probe microscopy, in the field of scientific instruments university researchers and industry (initially these were craftspersons) scientists and engineers have had deep networks of interaction that were productive prior to the introduction of Bayh-Dole or the establishment of technology licensing organizations (in addition to Biagioli, see Lenoir and Lécuyer 1995 on nuclear magnetic resonance; Mody 2014 on probe microscopy; and Riggs and von Hippel 1994 on surface chemistry). Scientific instruments, while resembling the EE/CS story also has its peculiarities, but certainly does not fit the biology narrative.

The diversity of knowledge-based interactions between university and "industrial" (including agricultural) innovation is remarkable. There are vast differences by technology and academic field in how knowledge creation is created and diffuses. University–industry interactions are complex and heterogeneous. They occur through diverse channels and often are bi-directional. Finally, the character and content of transfer may shift over time. The varied nature of academic research calls into question the validity of a universal "biotechnology-based" model to describe or structure technology transfer (Kenney and Patton, 2009: 2011).

Our research results suggest that simple counts of academic patents, licensing revenues, or startups are poor measures of the "performance" of universities in developing or transferring technologies and knowledge. Such data overlook and even devalue other forms and channels of transfer and interaction. In the case of SPICE and BSD-Unix, the absence of patents certainly encouraged transfer and adoption. Further, the absence of patents did not preclude new firm formation. In other cases, such as the Cohen-Boyer and Axel patents there is no evidence that patenting was necessary for adoption.

These contrasts suggest that no single template for designing and managing university–industry relationships is likely to be effective without flexibility to accommodate differences among industries and research fields. Such flexibility should accommodate contrasting approaches to the management of intellectual property and its licensing. The need for flexibility in technology transfer strategy and policy is insufficiently recognized in U.S. universities' policies toward the management of university–industry relationships and patenting.

Universities, or, put more properly, university researchers contribute to industrial technological advancement in a wide variety of ways. Patents and licensing assuredly are important in some fields, and far less so in others. Remarkably despite the innumerable academic studies of TTOs, with the exception of patentable materials, these transfer offices are largely irrelevant to most technology transfer. Moreover, the current fixation on patenting may lead to policies inhibiting other societally more important channels of interaction.

Notes

1 In the case of pharmaceuticals and biotechnology, see Kenney (1986) for an early statement. In the ICT industries, the interaction between industry and university research is more complicated; see, for example, National Research Council (2012).
2 One important caveat is that many of the most valuable university inventions in biotechnology, such as the Stanford-University of California Cohen-Boyer recombinant DNA patents or the Columbia University Axel Transformation patents were on fundamental techniques necessary for creating new drugs and operated largely as taxes on users and could not be argued as "necessary" for adoption (see, Colaianni and Deegan-Cook 2009; Kenney and Patton 2009).
3 In contrast, they found that for biology the most important method of engagement was through patents, whereas for what they termed "medical science" the method of engagement was through "contract or collaborative research."
4 The role of universities, specifically UC Berkeley and MIT, in the formation of the open source software movement is not often recognized (for exceptions, see Bretthauer 2001).
5 For an industry insider's view on the relationship between industry and the university in semiconductors, see Moore and Davis (2004).

References

Agrawal, A. and Henderson, R. (2002). Putting patents in context: Exploring knowledge transfer from MIT. *Management Science*, 48 (1): 44–60.

Balconi, M. and Laboranti, A. (2006). University–industry interactions in applied research: The case of microelectronics. *Research Policy*, 35 (10): 1616–1630.

Bekkers, R. and Bodas Freitas, I. (2008). Analysing knowledge transfer channels between universities and industry: To what degree do sectors also matter? *Research Policy*, 37 (10): 1837–1853.

Biagioli, M. (2006). *Galileo's Instruments of Credit*. Chicago: University of Chicago Press.

Bretthauer, D. (2001). "Open source software: A history." UConn Libraries Published Works. Paper #7. http://digitalcommons.uconn.edu/libr_pubs/7.

Colaianni, A. and Cook-Deegan, R. (2009). Columbia University's axel patents: Technology transfer and implications for the Bayh-Dole Act. *Milbank Quarterly*, 87 (3): 683–715.

Colyvas, J., Crow, M., Gelijns, A., Mazzoleni, R., Nelson, R., Rosenberg, N. and Sampat, B. (2002). How do university inventions get into practice? *Management Science*, 48 (1): 61–72.

Greenstein, S. and Nagle, F. (2014). Digital dark matter and the economic contribution of Apache. *Research Policy*, 43 (4): 623–631.

Heller, M. and Eisenberg, R. (1998). Can patents deter innovation? The anticommons in biomedical research. *Science*, 280 (5364): 698–701.

Hicks, D., Breitzman, T., Olivastro, D. and Hamilton, K. (2001). The changing composition of innovative activity in the US — a portrait based on patent analysis. *Research Policy*, 30 (4): 681–703.

Higgins, M. and Rodriguez, D. (2006). The outsourcing of R&D through acquisitions in the pharmaceutical industry. *Journal of Financial Economics*, 80 (2): 351–383.

Kenney, M. (1986). *Biotechnology*. New Haven: Yale University Press.

Kenney, M. and Patton, D. (2009). Reconsidering the Bayh-Dole Act and the current university invention ownership model. *Research Policy*, 38 (9): 1407–1422.

Kenney, M. and Patton, D. (2011). Does inventor ownership encourage university research-derived entrepreneurship? A six university comparison. *Research Policy*, 40 (8): 1100–1112.

Kenney, M., Mowery, D. and Patton, D. (2014). Electrical engineering and computer science at UC Berkeley and Silicon Valley: Modes of regional engagement. In: M. Kenney and D. Mowery (eds) *Public Universities and Regional Development: Insights from the University of California*, 1st edn. Stanford: Stanford University Press.

Lécuyer, C. (2014). Semiconductor innovation and entrepreneurship at three University of California campuses. In: M. Kenney and D. Mowery (eds) *Public Universities and Regional Growth: Insights from the University of California*, 1st edn. Stanford: Stanford University Press.

Lenoir, T. and Lécuyer, C. (1995). Instrument makers and discipline builders: The case of nuclear magnetic resonance. *Perspectives on Science*, 3, 276–345.

Mody, C. (2014). University in a garage: Instrumentation and innovation in and around UC Santa Barbara. In: M. Kenney and D. Mowery (eds) *Public Universities and Regional Development: Insights from the University of California*, 1st edn. Stanford: Stanford University Press.

Moore, G. and Davis, K. (2004). Learning the Silicon Valley way. In: T. Bresnahan and A. Gambardella (eds) *Building High-Tech Clusters: Silicon Valley and Beyond*, 1st edn. Cambridge: Cambridge University Press, pp. 7–39.

Mowery, D. (2008). Plus ca change: Industrial R&D in the "third industrial revolution". *Industrial and Corporate Change*, 18 (1): 1–50.

Mowery, D., Nelson, R., Sampat, B. and Zedonis, A. (2004). *Ivory Tower and Industrial Innovation*. Stanford: Stanford Business Books.

Narin, F., Hamilton, K. and Olivastro, D. (1997). The increasing linkage between U.S. technology and public science. *Research Policy*, 26 (3): 317–330.

National Research Council (1999). *Committee on Innovations in Computing, Communications, & Lessons from History*. Funding a Revolution: Government Support for Computing Research. Washington D.C.: The National Academies Press.

National Research Council (2012). *Continuing Innovation in Information Technology*. Washington D.C.: The National Academies Press.

Nelson, A. (2012). Putting university research in context: Assessing alternative measures of production and diffusion at Stanford. *Research Policy*, 41 (4): 678–691.

Noble, D. (1977). *America By Design: Science, Technology, and the Rise of Corporate Capitalism*. Oxford: Oxford University Press.

Padgett, J. and Powell, W. (2012). *The Emergence of Organizations and Markets*. Princeton: Princeton University Press.

Perkmann, M., Tartari, V., McKelvey, M., Autio, E., Broström, A., D'Este, P., Fini, R., Geuna, A., Grimaldi, R., Hughes, A., Krabel, S., Kitson, M., Llerena, P., Lissoni, F., Salter, A. and Sobrero, M. (2013). Academic engagement and commercialisation: A review of the literature on university–industry relations. *Research Policy*, 42 (2): 423–442.

Popp Berman, E. (2008). Why did universities start patenting?: Institution-building and the road to the Bayh-Dole Act. *Social Studies of Science*, 38 (6): 835–871.

Riggs, W. and von Hippel, E. (1994). Incentives to innovate and the sources of innovation: The case of scientific instruments. *Research Policy*, 23 (4): 459–469.

Rosenberg, N. (1992). Scientific instrumentation and university research. *Research Policy*, 21 (4): 381–390.

Rosenberg, N. and Nelson, R.R. (1994). American universities and technical advance in industry. *Research Policy*, 23 (3): 323–348.

Siegel, D., Waldman, D., Atwater, L. and Link, A. (2004). Toward a model of the effective transfer of scientific knowledge from academicians to practitioners: qualitative evidence from the commercialization of university technologies. *Journal of Engineering and Technology Management*, 21 (1–2): 115–142.

Statista (2014). *Packaged Software: Worldwide Revenue 2010–2015 | Forecast*. Available online at: www.statista.com/statistics/208652/global-packaged-software-revenue-since-2010/ (accessed 24 August 2014).

Thursby, J. G. and Thursby, M. C. (2003). Industry/university licensing: Characteristics, concerns and issues from the perspective of the buyer. *Journal of Technology Transfer*, 28 (3–4): 207–213.

World Health Organization (2014). *WHO | Pharmaceutical Industry*. Available online at: www.who.int/trade/glossary/story073/en/ (accessed 24 August 2014).

19 International comparison of technology transfer data

The devil is in the details

Frank J.M. Zwetsloot, Lodewijk L. Gelauff and Robert J.W. Tijssen

Introduction

In the summer of 2013, a political debate raged in the Netherlands, even though most politicians were on holiday. *Times Higher Education* (*THE*) ranked the Netherlands as the country with the highest business investments per researcher of Europe – three times higher than that of the USA and even six times higher than the UK (Grove, 2013).

These numbers could not be matched with other recent findings on these issues in the Netherlands. Science watchers and analysts could not believe that the Netherlands had such a high standard of public-private cooperation in the field of academic research. Was it not Michael Porter who argued to the Dutch government that the Dutch needed better technology transfer if they wanted to improve their poor national innovation performance compared to the UK and the USA? It seems unlikely that the Dutch could have been such fast learners. ScienceWorks concluded in June 2013 that the average income in the Netherlands from business partners was less than 20 per cent of the number given in THE (Van Leeuwen, 2013). For this article, we have re-investigated this issue in an attempt to understand what might have been the cause for these remarkable differences.

Over the past years, several institutions have published numbers in relation to business investments which do not always seem to be on par with each other. In this article we compare the numbers published in THE with those found through U-Multirank, AUTM, ASTP[1] and ScienceWorks. We will look into the data collection methods used by these organizations and suggest how data harmonization improvements could be made.

Times Higher Education[2]

THE published the average "business funding" per academic researcher in its *2013 World Academic Summit Innovation Index*. The average business funding per researcher in the Netherlands was reported to be $72,800 (converted €50,900).[3] The business funding in the USA and the UK were much lower: $25,800 (€18,000) and $13,300 (€9,300) respectively. *THE* used the data from the Global Institutional

Profiles Project by Thomson Reuters, in which universities gather and sign off the data themselves.

Thomson Reuters defined business funding as "research income from industry and commerce, excluding income from general funding for the institution, income from teaching and income generated from public source, like government and charities", and used "FTE staff that is employed for an academic post" as their definition for academic staff. Academic posts are lecturers, readers, assistant/associate professors and professors. Predominantly, this includes permanent staff and staff employed on a long-term contract basis. Thomson Reuters excluded non-teaching fellows, researchers, post-doctoral researchers, research assistants, clinicians of all types (unless they also have an academic post), technicians and staff supporting the general infrastructure of the institution or students. They indicated that the number of researchers for Dutch universities was surprisingly low compared to others; it seems that the Dutch research system relies much more heavily on PhD students and post-doctoral researchers than other countries.

ScienceWorks

ScienceWorks published a "valorisatie" (Dutch for knowledge transfer/impact of science) ranking of the Dutch universities in *Elsevier Magazine* in June 2013 (Van Leeuwen, 2013). In this publication, the total "contract earnings per researcher" for the Netherlands was found to be on average €39,700 ($56,800); including income from contract education, international organizations, European Union (EU), private investments, charities, government and other non-profit organizations. These numbers are directly derived from officially published annual reports of the universities and include academic hospitals.

The business income per academic staff member for the Dutch universities was found to be much lower: €9,000 ($12,900). These numbers were based on the common Dutch definition of what a scientific researcher is: "all faculty members, including post-doctoral researchers and PhD students". The corresponding personnel statistics were published in the university annual reports.

U-Multirank[4]

U-Multirank (UMR) is a new multi-dimensional approach to international ranking of higher education institutions, funded by the European Commission. UMR measures several aspects of the university performance: research, teaching and learning, knowledge transfer, international orientation and regional engagement. Based on specific interests, universities can be benchmarked and compared to one another.

UMR published data in 2014 from 850 higher education institutions in 74 countries; it used self-reported data of the universities as well as data from independent sources. Based on this data, UMR calculated that the external investment per FTE academic staff of 74 large higher education institutions was on average €30,000 ($42,900). The seven Dutch universities in this sample scored substantially higher, bringing the numbers closer to those of *THE* (€50,000).

UMR uses a wider definition than "business funding", and includes revenue from research-related contracts and services, consultancies and other project funds from private business, from licensing, charities, private foundations, trusts and other non-profit organizations. The research taking place in academic hospitals is included in this calculation. UMR excluded revenues from contract related education, which is described as "continuous professional development". Academic staff are defined as the personnel holding an "academic rank" (up to post-doctoral researchers) and excludes PhD students. Academic staff in academic hospitals are only included when they carry out teaching and/or research tasks.

AUTM and ASTP[5]

The Association of University Technology Managers (AUTM) and the Association of European Science and Technology Transfer Professionals (ASTP) also collect data annually regarding technology transfer activities, which includes public–private contract research. AUTM and ASTP are the world's leading technology transfer organizations, respectively in the United States and Canada and in Europe. They share a database with information derived from similar survey methods and definitions of key concepts. From this data, it is possible to extract numbers on "research expenditures from industrial sources" for some 200 universities. However, this is on an individual university basis, and it is not normalized for the number of academic staff members. AUTM and ASTP define the investments of industrial sources in scientific research as "funding by for-profit corporations, excluding other sources such as nonprofit organizations".

Combining these numbers with the numbers of academic staff found in the annual reports results in €10,200 ($14,600) per researcher in expenditures from industrial sources for universities in the Netherlands; this includes post-doctoral researchers and PhD students. Excluding those post-doctoral researchers and students increases the average expenditures to €16,800 ($24,000) per researcher.

For the US, the number of faculty members per university is published by the Higher Education Data Center of the American Federation of Teachers, with associated research expenditures from industrial sources per faculty member being $19,200 (€13,400). Post-doctoral researchers and PhD students are excluded in the faculty counts.

However, if income from licensing is included, significant changes were found: in the USA business income doubles to $40,500 (€28.300). In the Netherlands we find a small increase to €11,800 ($16,900) when including post-doctoral researchers and PhD students and to €19,500 ($27,900) if we exclude them. However, it should be noted that this data is based on a relatively low number of universities: only three in the Netherlands and eighty in the USA.

Putting data together

When comparing data from these different sources, it is immediately clear that business income per capita varies: from a low €9,000 ($12,900; ScienceWorks) and

€10,800 ($15,500; ASTP) to a high $72,800 (€50,900; *THE* and U-Multirank). But similarly striking are the large differences between the USA and the Netherlands: where ASTP and AUTM found that researchers in the USA received around 2.5 times more business funding than their Dutch counterparts, *THE* found that US researchers only collected a third of the business income compared to the Dutch.

The disparities cannot be explained by a single, simple explanation. The following causes are likely to contribute to the large variety.

The difference among Dutch universities may arise due to the fact that the university administrations and management information systems may not always separate business funding from other external funding sources, such as the income from charities, the EU, or consortia. The ultimate source of the "other external funding" is also not always traceable or appropriately classified.

Data collection methodologies could be a cause: the information gathered by Thomson Reuters and U-Multirank were self-reported by the universities following a request submitted to the university management. ASTP and AUTM relied mostly on self-reporting by a smaller subset of universities through their members, who usually worked at the technology transfer offices (TTOs) of the institution rather than central administration. The income statistics published by ScienceWorks were based on annual reports, which were vetted by several departments in the institution such as accountancy, research, communication and general management. This may have led to a more thorough quality control and nuance in the final numbers. Sources vetted by a single department may not always do justice to the complex organization a university often is.

Another perspective is derived from national statistics. Looking at the data from the USA, UK and the Netherlands of 2011, comparable percentages of business funding as part of the total funding in scientific R&D were found. According to Statistics Netherlands (CBS) and the US National Science Foundation (NSF), respectively 8 per cent and 5 per cent of the total R&D expenditures of higher education institutes is derived from business. In the UK, 6 per cent of the total higher education income and grants for research is derived from industry (Breznitz, 2014). These relatively low percentages indicate that the lower reported amounts of business investments in research per researcher may be much closer to reality than the higher amounts.

The most obvious reason for the large differences, however, is the variety of definitions used by governments, rankings and universities. For example, there is no clear description or definition of what exactly constitutes a "researcher" – a highly critical information item when numbers of universities have to be normalized and compared. In some higher education systems, post-doctoral researchers or even PhD students are counted as researchers; on other occasions, only (assistant) professors are considered. Often, there is no consistent separation between the universities and the affiliated university hospitals and medical centers – leading to the question of which medical staff members should be considered to be researchers and which should not. But also on the funding side university hospitals and clinics might distort the larger picture, as they often receive more business income than universities.

For international comparisons across universities, normalizing their income data is a crucial step. Using (almost) identical definitions of a "researcher" is no guarantee for producing reliable and useful comparisons, as can be concluded from some of the analyses presented earlier. For example, using the number of research staff holding a certain academic job title (professor, assistant professor) as an indicator for the size of an institution is only useful when comparing similar institutions within the same scientific system. While PhD students are considered to be students in most countries, in the Netherlands they hold employee status, and conducting research is seen as their primary task. If excluded from the statistics (as happened in the *THE* publication), a very small pool of researchers remain.

The national legislation regarding what and how external funding has to be registered, accounted and published, and in what detail, differs widely from country to country. "Licensing income" may be added to the external funding or not – in Europe this amount is, in most cases, so small that it will not significantly influence the overall picture. However, at some American universities the investments into a patent is such that the numbers of business income per researcher are significantly influenced; several universities in the USA welcome over $100 million (€69.9 million) annually. Data from 2007 showed that the mean number of licenses for European universities was only 7.8, whereas US universities had an average of 26.4 licenses in the same year (Conti and Gaule, 2011).

But even within a country, the differences between universities and how they are organized and defined can have significant impacts on measurement; whether they have an academic hospital, have more or less affiliated research institutes or affiliations with companies delivering in-kind contributions. Even if a generally adopted user manual explaining the definitions exists, it could still be impossible for universities to fill in the data requested according to specific definitions, and they ultimately might fill in the next best thing or leave a blank. With the best of faith, a self-reporting system always relies on the interpretation and explanation by the person responsible for data collection at the university in question.

Business investments in universities are not always as transparent as one would like – increasingly more business investments into scientific research are made through university spin-off companies, with shares in the company being held by the university. Those investments could only become visible if the increased value of the university spin-offs would be appreciated thoroughly and administered. It is unlikely that these incomes are consistently added to the annual business income. The same holds for shares that are being "cashed" by the university holding company or the university seed fund. Often, however, the results of these seed funds are not always transparently included in annual financial reports when disclosing the external investments into the university research.

From economic to societal impact

The "contract research" income streams in Europe have many faces: most external funding for university research does not come from the industrial or business sector, but from governmental investments schemes (regional, national and international) and non-profit organizations.

The concepts of "knowledge economy" and "knowledge region" have evolved in the past decades, with more governmental partners taking an active role in this arena. This extended collaboration between universities and other (publicly funded) partners is visible in the way regional science parks and clusters develop, where regional and local governments are involved as active development partners. Governmental partners try to get more of a grip on university research agendas, and – with growing success –- direct them towards societal issues such as social cohesion, smart grids and clean technology. The role of the European Union as a funding source of university research increased substantially while having an increased focus on "grand societal challenges", like in their current *Horizon 2020* program.

As the focus towards income sources shifts, it becomes increasingly relevant for universities to demonstrate their broader societal impact, and not just whether or not they interact with the business sector. Generating societal impact is now often also a pre-condition for obtaining government research funds. The UK's Research Excellence Framework (REF) is a clear example of an innovative implementation: the lump sum funding for universities and research institutes has been made dependent not only on the scientific excellence of their research (65 per cent of the score), but also on the extent of their societal impact through qualitative case studies (20 per cent of the score). This trend in funding and government oversight requires new indicators for measuring and demonstrating societal impact beyond economic impact and benchmarks, both for the government bodies as for the university management.

Conclusions

The analytical relevance and strategic values of numbers increases when properly contextualized; for understanding the meaning of business income of universities it is relevant to compare those income statistics with those from other institutions and other countries. Internationally usable definitions are important to high-quality comparative information. Every ranking, evaluation, assessment, and survey provides a building block to create such a framework and context, and by doing so this enables stakeholders and other experts to compare and benchmark universities and to test hypotheses.

Ranking experts should engage more directly with major stakeholders (notably government, university management and funding organizations). Such interactions and dialogue offer opportunities to identify relevant managerial issues and policy questions, while providing a platform to develop commonly acceptable definitions of key concepts.

From the descriptions above, it becomes clear that different definitions are being used and that comparable definitions may, nonetheless, produce divergent results in different national university systems. If the experts working on these building blocks cooperate to find a "harmonized" set of definitions that scale internationally, quick progress could be made. A more consistent manner of presenting the data would give better insight into the interaction between universities and companies. Being able to make a fair comparison between countries in Europe, Asia and North America could trigger science policy makers to change their approaches, strategies and policies. Not only should the various university ranking systems play an important role in such a concerted effort, but also supranational organizations such as the European Commission and the Organisation for Economic Co-operation and Development (OECD), each providing expertise and acting as an international platform for dissemination.

A strategy that could be considered is to make more use of multiple indicators in a broad system rather than focusing at a single, unified ranking. While a single ranking might be more attractive for publicity reasons and perceived public understanding, a transparent system of definitions and values could improve the debate and would allow multiple approaches at once towards comparing institutions and countries with each other. U-Multirank already uses this approach to a large extent and this example might be worthwhile to follow, since U-Multirank collected a diverse data set in 2014 from multiple universities and other higher education institutes inside and outside Europe.

Being able to make fair comparisons across universities, countries and regions – especially with leading nations such as the USA – may better inform European science policy makers and assist in the exchange of university management strategies. International interaction between policy makers, university data providers, data analyses and scientometrists, will help obtain a more consistent view on the investments from – and outcome for – societal partners and business in university research.

Acknowledgements

We acknowledge Karen van den Nieuwendijk, of ScienceWorks, for her assistance. The data for this article is provided by Thomson Reuters, ASTP, AUTM, and U-Multirank. We acknowledge them for their assistance.

Notes

1 As of January 2014 ASTP has changed its name into 'ASTP-Proton'.
2 Definitions of THE are derived from: Data collection process – guidebook. Thomson Reuters. Available online: http://ip-science.thomsonreuters.com/m/pdfs/DataCollect_Guidebook_3.pdf (accessed January 2015).
3 USD is converted to euro using the exchange rate 0.699 of July 2011.
4 Definitions of UMR are derived from: Indicator book: Ranking indicators. U-Multirank. Available online: http://pre.umultirank.org/cms/wp-content/uploads/2014/10/Indicator book_ranking-indicators.pdf (accessed January 2015).
5 Definitions of AUTM and ASTP are derived from: STATT Database. AUTM. Available online: www.autm.net/source/STATT/index.cfm?section=STATT (accessed January 2015).

References

Breznitz, S. (2014) *The Fountain of Knowledge: The Role of Universities in Economic Development*. Stanford, CA: Stanford University Press.

Conti, A. and Gaule, P. (2011) Is the US outperforming Europe in university technology licensing? A new perspective on the European Paradox. *Research Policy* 40 (1): 123–135.

Grove, J. (2013) East Asia leads the world in business funding, *Times Higher Education*. Available online: www.timeshighereducation.co.uk/news/east-asia-leads-the-world-in-business-funding/2006387.article (accessed January 2015).

van Leeuwen, A. (15 June 2013) 'Munt slaan uit kennis: de Universiteit Twente voert de nieuwe valorisatie-ranking aan van Elsevier/ScienceWorks, Utrecht haalt weer het meest geld binnen'. Available online: http://scienceworks.nl/wp-content/uploads/2014/02/Artikel-Elsevier-final.pdf

20 University technology transfer in Brazil

A comprehensive picture

Guilherme Ary Plonski

Introduction

This chapter details the triple fragmentation of the academic technology transfer process in Brazil. One part of the fragmentation is due to *scope reduction*, by equating technology transfer to licensing deals. The second part is the *unaccounted for technology transfer*, led by foundations that are substantively connected albeit formally outside the university. A third rupture is *systemic*, by downplaying the historic virtuous partnerships between universities and research institutes.

The consequences of the partial depiction of academic technology transfer include the insufficient metrification, poor image of universities in society at large, and incomplete public policies. Positive tendencies are foreseen, especially in light of recent major changes in the Brazilian science and technology (S&T) legal framework. There is space for strategic involvement of TTOs in providing a holistic picture of university technology transfer in Brazil. With the necessary *caveats*, they may inspire their correspondents in other national innovation systems.

The need to broad-gauge university technology transfer

Fast diffusion of University Technology Transfer Offices (TTOs) occurred in Brazil since 2004, as this was required by the so-called Innovation Law.[1] Their activities are contributing to the development of new products, processes, applications, materials or services by enterprises. In parallel, although unwillingly, TTOs reinforce the public image of *technology transfer* as equivalent to protecting and commercializing academic Intellectual Property (IP). This is an undesirable *capitis diminutio* of the technology transfer concept, as Brazilian TTOs' focus on IP management covers only part of the actual conduits of knowledge from academia to other segments of society interested in innovation, such as businesses, public service providers, and non-governmental organizations.

Main channels for technology transfer also include: human mobility (graduates and faculty), continuing education (open courses and in-company training), publications (in academic journals, trade journals, technical standards and other media), entrepreneurship (academic spin-offs and spin-outs), and extension (especially to non-high-tech small and medium companies).

A consequence of the lack of consideration of the broad bandwidth mentioned is the focus on patenting as the key metrics for university technology transfer. This led to a somewhat unhealthy competition among Brazilian TTOs, as the number of patents is a component in many national and international academic rankings. A more serious consequence of the reductionist metrification is the opacity of the whole gamut of contributions of university-generated knowledge to society in general and to economy in particular.

A dynamic evolutionary approach may help to enrich the technology transfer process. In a sound Triple Helix environment, business looks at academy as a suitable potential source of the technology (or technologies) needed to take a product to market when the required knowledge is not internally available. TTOs are a useful point of entry, more so for companies that are not familiar with the academic milieu. In case a specific technology has been formally protected by the university, TTOs become a mandatory channel, in addition to the scientists involved, as the licensing negotiation demands specialized professionals in diverse aspects of IP management, particularly in sensitive areas, such as bioeconomy. This model allows clear-cut accounting related to each deal, including, in future instances, the resultant income. This is a positive attribute, as long as metrification does not become the aim.

The pursuit to impact society by transferring technology becomes multifarious if seen as a *strategic Triple Helix process* rather than a collection of individual deals. In accordance with this approach, a basic means of increasing the amount, effectivity, and sophistication of technology transfer is having scientists and professionals with symmetric knowledge repertoires on the two sides – academy and business. As relatively few companies in the Brazilian context, even large ones, employ researchers,[2] establishing permanent and qualified technological dialogues between university and industry is frequently a difficult or even impossible task.

Therefore, promoting human mobility is gradually being understood as an indispensable quest. It involves mainly students who have completed masters or doctoral degrees, and, in less frequent cases, also faculty that moves on to become part of or manage industrial technology centers. Government intermittently tries to entice such mobility by softening industry's costs related to the salaries of the high level newcomers during a definite period – usually one to three years – through grants, tax incentives and other forms of subsidy.

An opposite flow brings company technical professionals, mainly engineers, back to university for continuing education programs. Most come to get acquainted with specific technical themes, mainly new technologies, attending short-term courses; a smaller proportion has the drive and resources to get an advanced degree. Among the latter, the majority seeks an MBA-type program as preparation for a managerial career. Nevertheless, some do come back to the academic benches and laboratories searching for an advanced degree in the so-called STEM disciplines (Science, Technology, Engineering, and Mathematics).

The quantity of the latter increased substantially in Brazil since guidelines for the Professional Master's degree were published in 2009 by the Federal education authorities. They adopt identical scientific rigor and provide status equal to the traditional Academic Master's – for example, enabling access to doctoral programs. The main differences are teleological (focus on organizational versus academic challenges) and practical (timetable easing participation by people already working on a full-time basis).

The expected net result of the combination of human mobility and continuing education is a gradually higher intensity and level of technology transfer. It is therefore of interest to Brazilian TTOs to become involved with the above-mentioned mechanisms as part of the broad legal mandate to manage the university policy of innovation. This has to be done chiefly by combining actions among academic bodies, without the TTO taking on additional administrative responsibilities.

The university as a constellation

An institutional aspect specific to the Brazilian S&T ecosystem increases the detachment between the image and the reality of academic technology transfer. It derives from the fact that most research universities belong to the Federal or to a State Government. In spite of the constitutional provision of wide autonomy – didactic, scientific, administrative, and managerial – the rigid legal constraints for a dynamic operation of the technology transfer mechanisms led university faculties to create private non-for-profit foundations that are somehow connected to the respective university, school, or department of the institutors. A major role of these foundations is to facilitate technology transfer, by a private style management of R&D and consulting contracts with Triple Helix parties external to the university – companies, governmental S&T funding agencies, and others – that are of interest to a particular faculty member or research group. These foundations also offer and manage a vast array of continuing education programs.

Such institutions are now widespread and relevant agents in the Brazilian academic scene. For example, the University of São Paulo's (USP) faculty has created more than 30 foundations since this phenomenon began in the 1960s. One of the foundations[3] connected to the Rio de Janeiro Federal University (UFRJ) has been in charge of more than 1000 R&D and engineering consulting projects with Petrobras, the major Brazilian oil and gas concern, a world leader in offshore technology and the most important operator of the Triple Helix model in the country.[4] However, information related to foundation-managed projects seldom appears in university reports.

The main reason for this lack of integrated information has to do with internal academic politics. Combative faculty associations, which have been essential in helping academic authorities to advance the position of major research universities in society for several decades, including better government funding, were progressively taken over by organized groups related to national trade unions connected to political parties, some of them radical splinters.

In spite of maintaining former slogans such as the defense of high quality universities in the interest of society, the agenda of these associations changed sharply since the 1990s. Suddenly, the foundations, which were seen as a highly positive instrument for helping academic research groups to manage innovative projects (such as building the first Brazilian computer) and transferring knowledge to industry through continuing education and consulting, were portrayed by the faculty unions as private intruders in public institutions. Faculties involved in projects managed by foundations were singled out as motivated by greed and not by core academic values, as they received direct payments by the foundations for their participation in projects or courses. This was exposed as a threat to the general faculty interest of improving working conditions, as that external addition to the full-time university salary weakened union actions, such as strikes.

An emblematic case is USP. A clear definition was achieved during the discussion of new by-laws in 1989: after strong clashes, an MIT-inspired 80–20 rule was approved. However, this did not reduce the assault – verbal, legal, and sometimes physical – against the foundations by the unionized faculty association, which joined forces with equally radical students and non-faculty workers' associations for this purpose. This conflictual climate, which sometimes contaminates university authorities, explains the struggle of the foundation leadership to accommodate the desire for transparency and the reluctance to expose figures that may fuel further attacks. Nowadays, each foundation provides USP authorities with a yearly report, but these data are not included in the university databank nor published as part of the university report.

The presence of private foundations is publically acknowledged mostly in specific segments of the university, such as Business, Medicine, and Engineering. There is an active interest of the leadership to present their schools as a "mini-constellation" that includes the foundations with which they are connected. Just recently, the deputy dean of the Polytechnic Engineering School asked the three connected foundations to provide detailed information about their activities, including data on grants, proceeds from specialized services, and incomes from other sources, "enabling a more complete picture of the School's magnitude" in presentations to stakeholders and peer institutions. A similar attitude in favor of obliterating the formal borders between the public and the private academic faces is also present, for example, in the UFRJ's Graduate School and Research in Engineering reports.

The dual system tends to perpetuate itself, albeit with adjustments. For example, a new law concerning the relations between Federal universities and the connected private foundations was enacted in 2013.[5] A key change is the abolition of the previous requisite to deposit the money collected by a foundation on behalf of the university in the National Treasury. This was never a problem for State universities, such as USP, and their connected foundations.

There have generally been no relations between TTOs and private foundations, as the former concentrate on IP protection and commercialization. As a public asset, IP is subject to particularly stringent rules. Fierce legal and cultural resistance meets any attempt to have it privately managed by foundations (a few cases happened before the enactment of the Innovation Law requirement for TTOs).

A roadway to foster the depiction of public universities as an institutional constellation in the eyes of society – including foundations, business incubators and accelerators, science and technology parks, and other related organizations, can be paved by increasing and exposing joint projects between TTOs and the foundations. As continuing education programs – although not Professional Master's programs – are often managed by foundations, the earlier recommendation of involvement of TTOs in order to achieve a more symmetric cognitive platform between academy and industry is applicable.

Repairing the university: research institution bridges

A third aspect to be considered in a broad picture of academic technology transfer is the complementary roles of universities and non-academic industrial and technological research institutions. Once considered in Brazil as natural translators of academic knowledge to industrial practices, these institutes have been undervalued since the 1980s, both in public discourse and governmental funding. A key reason was their smaller contribution to the unidimensional metric of S&T favored at the time – the country's position in the international ranking of papers in peer-reviewed journals.[6]

The internalization of this measure in institutional evaluations had a perverse effect on the previous harmonic cooperation between universities and research institutions. A main reason was the requirement to allocate a published paper in only one institution – university *or* research institution, both for statistical purposes and advancement of the researchers' career. The progression rules in the university increasingly took into account almost exclusively the quantity of peer-reviewed publications; the research institution had other metrics, such as the direct effects of its staff in developing and transferring industry relevant technologies. As a practical consequence, the main identity of a double appointment researcher rapidly shifted toward academy.

As volumes of publications by the proponents became a dominant criterion for government-funding agencies to decide the allocation of resources in competitive bids for research facilities and projects, the academic identity became a natural preference. The two institutions, once synergic, became estranged. The shared day of a doubly appointed researcher – teaching in the morning at the university and doing industry-relevant work afternoon at the adjacent research institution – was gradually relegated to happy memories of those who are older.

Government woke up to this downturn only recently. Actions are being taken to revert the described situation. One of them is an innovative mechanism,[7] formally instituted in 2014, inspired in the German Fraunhofer-Gesellschaft funding model.

As TTOs and research institutions have a common interest in technology transfer, they might be facilitators for an inter-institutional dialogue conducive to new ways of joining forces. This would help boost industrial innovation, chiefly to medium and small business.

A new legal frame

A change in the Federal Constitution, enacted on February 26, 2015, includes *technology research* and *innovation* as national priorities. The main expected benefit is appeasing the public legal and control authorities, who have frequently placed obstacles in the way of the involvement of public universities in such initiatives, as they were not prescribed constitutionally. They will be treated in a similar way to education activities and basic science – as already provided in the Constitution.

This will surely increase the technology transfer movement and, therefore, TTOs' duties. In order to embrace the mandate to manage the university innovation policy, including the three depicted realms, TTOs will have to be upgraded in terms of talents. Staffing TTOs is one of the items included in the proposal for a new Innovation Law under consideration by Congress, as a continuation of the ongoing efforts to improve the Triple Helix environment in Brazil.

Notes

1 Federal Law 10973, signed on December 2, 2004, establishes the legal frame for incentives for innovation and scientific and technological research in the production environment. Most of its dispositions are permissive. Article 16, one of the few that are compulsory, requires public scientific and technological institutions to have an office in charge of *managing their innovation policy*.

2 In 2010, only 26% of Brazilian researchers worked in industry, compared to 61% in China and 77% in South Korea.

3 Fundação COPPETEC, created in 1970, has already managed more than 12,000 contracts and agreements with national and international, private and State-owned companies and governmental and non-governmental agencies for UFRJ's Graduate School and Research in Engineering.

4 Petrobras partners with more than 100 Brazilian universities and research institutes, organized in 49 thematic networks. In 2013, the company applied US$ 266 million in activities with these partners.

5 Federal Law 12863, signed on September 24, 2013.

6 The participation of Brazilian authors in the scientific journals indexed by Thomson/ISI tripled between 1996 and 2009; Brazil is today ranked 13th in the volume of papers.

7 The mechanism is embodied in the new Brazilian Company for Research and Industrial Innovation (the acronym in Portuguese is EMBRAPII).

21 The ethos of university technology transfer

Aligning transactional and humanistic values in a Bayh-Dole regime

Henry Etzkowitz

The rise of university technology transfer is a manifestation of the restructuring of the late nineteenth century dual mission Humboldtian academic model to a triadic format, encompassing economic and social development as well as research and education, with entrepreneurial endeavors based upon scientific knowledge discovered and humanistic knowledge conserved (Etzkowitz 2014). What is new is the universalization of a utilitarian academic mission; heretofore the province of a special class of tertiary education institutions, typically of lesser status than "Ivory Tower" schools in parallel with spreading a basic research mission, a task that is itself increasingly evaluated by social and economic impact measures.

There is a convergence between academic institutions that began with a practical orientation and industrial mission, like MIT with its original "land grant" focus on raising the technical level of local textile and mechanical firms, and theoretically oriented institutions, like the University of Chicago, that eschewed engineering until its quite recent bioengineering initiative and now views itself as an "entrepreneurial hub." Specialized precursors of the Entrepreneurial University, the Polytechnic and Land Grant academic movements in Europe and the US, anticipated a 2nd Academic Revolution paralleling the one that made research an explicit academic task (Jencks and Riesman 1968).

The rise of MIT and Stanford to status as contemporary innovation icons signals a reconfiguration of academic ideals, integrating transactional and humanistic objectives in degree and research programs. Harvard was the peerless icon of an earlier era, when to be called the Harvard of the Wabash, or whatever local geographical attribute at hand, was the highest academic compliment. The passing of the academic icon torch signifies the movement of universities away from being eleemosynary, or charitable, institutions that primarily gain their support from other sectors of society, on an idealistic basis, to a pragmatic justification that broadens their legitimation framework to include contribution to regional knowledge economies.

Impetuses to university technology transfer

The traditional academic knowledge transfer process takes place through conference presentations and proceedings, working paper series and peer-reviewed journals, in an ascending order of quality control. Non-academics typically access this arcane world through an overlay of popular media that occasionally precedes the academic process when scientific knowledge claims become newsworthy. Non-specialists are alerted via news stories, blog mentions and tweets, with the scientific and social media tracked most extensively by Google Scholar and Altmetrics, respectively. Formerly the two communications systems operated as separate worlds in relative isolation but in the Internet era of blogs, Facebook, Skype, Twitter and ResearchGate, they overlap and intermingle.

Transfer of knowledge to industry was theoretically freely available through professional and popular literature. But in practice industry needs relationships with academic scientists, both formal and informal, to translate this knowledge into a usable form. An oft cited impetus to disclosure by heretofore uninvolved faculty members and motivation to pursue non-conventional means of research support, ranging from individual philanthropic donation to crowd-funding, is that academic researchers are under increasing pressure to diversify their sources of funding in the face of traditional sources tightening budgets.

There is also the dream that a successful start-up could support a research group, despite conflict of interest policies that would make such a course of action difficult if not impossible in the US but not in Brazil! The Brazilian Innovation Law of 2004 allows academic research groups and start-ups, based upon them, to maintain a co-terminus existence, sharing research, personnel, space and equipment, virtually eliding the university industry boundary. A more fundamental impetus is the closing gap between the achievement of significant findings and the possibilities for their utilization. As the gap has closed between knowledge and technology, especially in emerging interdisciplinary fields, a tertiary overlay of university technology transfer has emerged.

The external impetus to technology transfer arises in part from "a deepening conviction on the part of society that basic knowledge should be put into human service wherever it can be, and as soon as possible" (Kennedy 1997: 241). Herz's discoveries had to wait decades before they were made the basis of a radio industry and his primary reward was the eponymization of the wave phenomena that he identified. Molecular biology pioneers have seen their fundamental discoveries made into an industry during their own lifetime and have participated in financial and industrial as well as recognition and scientific rewards (Kornberg 1995).

Reaping a harvest at the endless frontier

Short-term practical uses were hardly expected but eventual utility was part of the post-war "Endless Frontier" implicit "social contract" between science and government (Bush 1945, Guston 2003). Beginning in the 1970s, members of Congress began to call attention to underutilized intellectual property rights generated by federally funded research. A 1968 study had identified exceedingly few instances of this research being put to use (Stevens et al. 2015, this volume). Well in advance of public recognition of an innovation gap, a few patent attorneys in US research agencies became concerned about the problem.

Acting on their own initiative, patent lawyers at NIH and NSF established administrative procedures to allow universities to acquire patent rights to federally funded research on the condition that universities create professional in house technology transfer capacities to arrange patenting and licensing. These federal civil servants formed a network among themselves and congressional staffers who had also become concerned about the issue. Some of these congressional staffers were themselves academics on temporary leave from universities. As the number of universities with patenting staff grew, the pro-patenting network extended from government to the universities, culminating in the formation of a Society of University Patent Administrators, predecessor of the Association of University Technology Managers (Latker 1998).

The confluence of the Secretary of Health, Education and Welfare (HEW) in the Carter administration, an opponent of academic patenting, blocking new university patent agreements, coincided with the emergence of an innovation gap as a political issue in context of mid-1970s industrial decline. A lobbying campaign culminated in a new legal framework for the translation into use of the fruits of federally funded research. Its proponents view the Bayh-Dole Act as the "Magna Carta" of academic technology transfer in recognition of its transformational impact. The act provided an impetus for virtually all research universities, and those aspiring to the status, to become involved in technology transfer, beyond the few that, early on, had identified it as a significant task.

The amendment to US patent law also had broader implications for disposition of academically generated intellectual property rights, inspiring a host of imitators, (e.g. Denmark, Brazil, Japan) that, more or less, took account of local academic and innovation contexts in structuring their variations of Bayh-Dole (Kneller 2007). The outcome was also a balance between traditional professorial rights and the institutional interests of the university that, in one institutional sphere at least, partially returned intellectual property rights to the individual inventors, a Constitutional intention that had increasingly been subverted by industrial employment contracts.

In the universities at least, innovators, by tradition, and then by law, were guaranteed a significant proportion of the returns on their invention. For some a de facto right of first refusal to license their technology and control its diffusion and development was even more important. Inventors who had lost control of their intellectual property rights as part of corporate employment contracts typically found that they were precluded from further developing their original ideas after leaving the firm, and, if allowed, often having to pay their former employer a license fee. However, as industrial labs downsized and some former industrial scientists assumed professorships, they found they could explore the future implications of intellectual property that they generated as an auxiliary of academic freedom, in the context of an academic post and its attendant technology transfer regime.

Bayh-Dole as industrial and academic policy

Bay-Dole may be viewed as an indirect industrial policy rather than intervention in the sense of specific government measures requiring targeting of particular areas of research and development for support or, as occurs in Japan, requiring enterprises and research institutes to make contracts with each other, as occurred formally in the Soviet socialist model and somewhat less so in Brazil and Mexico. Instead, incentives were built into the US research funding system, in a precursor of the "nudge" model of social change (Sunstein 2014) to move academia closer to industry in its motivation and structure. This occurred in a context in which government was unable to take more direct measures, as it had in response to the 1950s' Sputnik crisis and the onset of the Second World War.

Bayh-Dole closed the gap that had opened up post-war when Vannevar Bush abruptly closed down OSRD at the close of hostilities, unraveling networks of cooperation developed in war-time triple helix collaborations, that were acceptable to Bush and many others, only in context of national emergency. A purpose of this book is to recognize the key role that university technology transfer plays in knitting together webs of collaboration at the institutional interface, expanding its purview from cross-border negotiation to Innovation Organizer.

Legitimization codification and incremental innovation of technology transfer practice ensued rather than invention of something entirely new. Nevertheless, the intervention of the federal government was crucial to resolving ambiguity in the status of intellectual property rights of federally funded research at universities that was impeding utilization of these rights due to perception of a "free rider effect" in which a potential licensee would hold off out of concern that access to any successful development would be requested for free by competitors since the original research had been paid for by taxpayers monies. Indeed, public provenance of university sourced intellectual property appears as an argument against university licensing to this day.

Patenting federally funded academic research was questioned by some legislators and members of the executive branch who believed that it was poor public policy, and even immoral, for research paid for by the taxpayers to be put up for sale to private industry rather than freely published and disseminated through traditional academic procedures. In other words, they believed the journal system, supplemented by the industrial lab hiring process that regularly brought newly minted PhDs to industry, along with potential links to their mentors, sufficed (Mowery et al. 2004).

Perhaps the traditional large-firm-based technology transfer model sufficed in the past, along with a subordinate industrially related academic regime largely confined to engineering schools and land-grant institutions, but by 1980, it was "all hands on deck", with the "Ivory Tower" subject to call, as well. In an era of industrial turbulence and firm belt tightening, in the 1970s and 1980s labs were being downsized if not eliminated from corporate budgets, opening up not only a knowledge but a transitional research and development gap, requiring new modes of technology transfer. Moreover, the transition from industrial to a knowledge-based society made start-ups, often based on intellectual property, a more salient innovation mechanism. The Bayh-Dole Act provided a stable ground for university technology transfer and a framework for resolving some issues.

From a minor interest of relatively few universities, such as MIT in the early 20th century, technology transfer became a significant element in an industrial policy, through which government indirectly incentivized universities to enhance industrial performance, while maintaining a discrete distance between government and industry. The Bayh-Dole Act altered the regulatory infrastructure that determined how the results of federally funded research, which would have been funded by government any way, could be used. Although no funds were appropriated for implementation, universities were able to charge some of the costs of their patent-licensing offices to their administrative overhead rates for federal grants, thus receiving an indirect subsidy.

University technology transfer

Technology transfer offices (TTOs) view themselves as part of the service mission of the university to provide public benefits by putting research to use. Moreover, they view themselves as promoting core academic values such as dissemination of knowledge through publication and expansion of research (Hatakenaka 2004). They advise on management of conflict-of-interest issues and general university policy on technology transfer. Earning money is important; especially to reach the break-even point of earning enough to pay for the costs of the office and justify its efficacy to the administration, but it is by no means the only objective. The balance between financial and other objectives was exemplified by the decision at Stanford not to integrate the TTO with the university's endowment-management organization, a unit highly oriented to financial maximizations (Sandelin 2004).

Financial goals rarely predominate; most TTOs see their role as providing a range of services for assisting their clients and view profit maximization from technology transfer as one objective to be balanced against assisting academics to put their technology to use, even when the financial rewards are not large. As one technology transfer officer said in reply to a query about return on investment (ROI), "Financial ROI is only one aspect that drives most academic institution's tech transfer offices",[1] and often not stronger than other key aspects. Indeed, in recent years the Association of University Technology Managers (AUTM, 2015)[2] has broadened its metrics from quantitative indicators, primarily focusing on licensing income and salary scales, to include qualitative data on social and economic impact through the Better World Project.[3]

As TTOs secure their financial base, still often a hoped for objective even by MIT and Stanford that are still dependent on "blockbusters" for temporary financial security, they will be more easily able to operate according to a long-range timeframe. Such a luxury is currently mainly confined to TTOs in countries such as Germany and Japan, with well-funded government initiatives to support university technology transfer but even in these countries it is an open question whether funders patience will wear thin in the face of the long-term struggle to build a successful technology transfer superstructure, that requires a massive research funded research substructure. Indeed, there is a rubric, akin to Moore's law, but without its exponential increase factor, of how much transfer earnings may be expected from how many dollars or euros of research funds input.

There is a divergence between elite and non-elite institutions exemplified by the statement of a technology transfer professional who said that, "We see tech transfer as a byproduct of basic research. Tech transfer is adding to the mission (getting others to invest in developing what we discover); not changing our purpose to discover."[4] On the other hand, non-elite institutions move up the academic food chain by capturing mission-oriented funding, such as anti-missile Star Wars' projects, and trim their sails to whatever funding wind blows as they develop the capacity to compete for basic research funding (Lanier 1989).

Conclusion: the prospect of university technology transfer

In the above, we have discussed some of the impetuses to the rise of university technology transfer and its role in a US national innovation system that is characterized by an undervaluing and under crediting of the role of government in innovation due to ideological strictures. The positive role of government in the US innovation system has been noted as an explanation of the strength and diversity of the American Knowledge economy (Etzkowitz et al. 2000, Mazzucatto 2013). Less noted than the creative role of firm entrepreneurship (Christensen 1997, Chesborough 2003), but now coming to increased attention (e.g. Berman 2012, Tournatzky and Rideout 2014) is the fundamental and increasing role of the university in the US innovation system.

Given an increasingly strategic position in a knowledge-based society, we can predict that external resources committed to universities will rise, even though the cast of supporters may change in relative importance. Private donors are currently taking a larger role in US public universities, indicated by the funding campaign banners flying on the Berkeley campus of the University of California, even as public financing became a significant part of the budget of private research universities in the post-war. Universities will also generate significantly larger numbers of entrepreneurial ventures through enhanced translational, mentoring and investment schemes on the assumption that only a small proportion of the academic capacity for translating knowledge into the economy and society is currently utilized even at a highly entrepreneurial university (Etzkowitz 2013). Nevertheless, the state of the art is changing rapidly as initiatives arise bottom up, top down and laterally, re-working the TTO into an innovation regime or de-facto subsuming it into a more or less articulated innovation system with accelerators, incubators, project-based entrepreneurship courses and mentoring programs.

Moving in ever closer contiguity to the polity and the economy, academic scientists and universities have retained their autonomy by increasing their salience to these institutional a significant driver of innovation in increasingly knowledge-based societies spheres. In an earlier era science was a relatively small institution defined by sharp boundary lines around a tightly knit community and this social structure was reflected in the norms of science. Under contemporary conditions scientific norms take the form of institutional imperatives to capitalize knowledge, thus creating entrepreneurial science. Eschewing the ideal of knowledge for its own sake, in practice if not in ideology, academic scientists and universities are becoming more central as drivers of innovation in increasingly knowledge-based societies. This is the premise of the Triple Helix Thesis, that universities are moving from secondary supporting roles, as contributors to industrial society through research and education, to equal status as an institutional sphere with industry and government through their emerging "third mission."

The Morill Act of 1861 donated federal land to support the development of higher education for the improvement of agricultural and industrial practice. The laws of 1980 turned over intangible property of scientific and technological knowledge to the universities with similar intentions. This legislation encouraged individual academics to include commercial activities in their roles and for universities to experiment with a variety of arrangements such as research parks, "incubator" facilities and offices for the transfer of technology to develop fruitful relations with industry. The "meandering stream" of basic research persists in an academic context increasingly characterized by interdisciplinary collaborations, like Stanford's BioX, where new basic research questions arise, as well, from projects to develop medical devices, based on close observation of medical practice, with a new topic selected each year.

The possibility opens up that academic institutions will become, at least in part, financially self-generating—obtaining revenues from their knowledge resources through equity in spin-offs, held from inception, or later philanthropic subventions emanating from them. Although income from licensing agreements cannot be expected to be a reliable stream as it is overly dependent upon anomalous "blockbusters" that inevitably run their course; nevertheless, it has grown significantly in recent decades from just over $100 million to $3.8 billion in 2008 (Stevens 2015, this volume). US academic institutions, exemplified by Stanford's decision, on the one hand, to take equity, after abjuring such opportunities until the mid-1990s, sold its equity holdings in Google at point of IPO, maintaining a shifting boundary between university and industry that also differs by country. For example, Chinese university holding companies own a significant share of some of the country's leading firms that originated as spin-offs and grew up within the university (Zhou 2015, this volume).

These developments represent a potentially fundamental modification of the traditional view of universities as institutions supported by governmental, ecclesiastical and lay patronage. The new arrangements open the possibility that universities will become, at least in part, financially self-supporting institutions, entities obtaining revenues through licensing agreements and other financial arrangements for the industrial use of new knowledge discovered at the universities. At present, this possibility is little more than that, but it certainly represents a novel idea in the history of universities—at least on the scale on which it is envisaged.

Acknowledgements

The author wishes to express appreciation to Lita Nelson, MIT TLO, for insightful comments and suggestions.

Notes

1 Techno-L. (2005) Listserve, accessed on 14 January 2005.
2 AUTM. (2015) Available online: www.betterworldproject.org//AM/Template. cfm?Section=Home (accessed 22 February 2015).
3 The author's suggestion for qualitative metrics, as a member of the AUTM statistics committee in the mid-1990s, was not taken up at the time. Nevertheless, a member of the committee, Gene Schuler, Director of Technology Transfer at Stony Brook University, commissioned the author to carry out an organizational analysis of the university's TTO, incubator, Center for Biotechnology and a related regional initiative, the Long Island Research Institute (LIRI). The project developed into an NSF sponsored study of US state science policy (Dougherty and Etzkowitz 1996).
4 Lita Nelsen, Director, Technology Licensing Office, Massachusetts Institute of Technology, communication to the author, 21 February 2015.

References

Berman, E. (2012) *Creating the Market University*, Princeton: Princeton University Press.
Bush, V. (1945) *The Endless Frontier*, Washington DC: US Government Printing Office.
Chesborough, C. (2003) *Open Innovation*, Cambridge, MA: Harvard University Press.
Christensen, C. (1997) *The Innovator's Dilemma*, New York: Harper.
Dougherty, K. and Etzkowitz, H. (1996) The States and Science: The Politics of High-Technology Industrial Policy at the State Level, a report to the NSF, January.
Etzkowitz, H. (2013) StartX and the Paradox of Success: Filling the Gap in Stanford's Entrepreneurial Culture, *Social Science Information*, 52 (4): 605–627.
Etzkowitz, H. (2014) Making a Humanities Town: Knowledge-infused Clusters, Civic Entrepreneurship and Civil Society in Local Innovation Systems, *Triple Helix*, vol. 1, published online.
Etzkowitz, H, Gulbrandsen, M. and Levitt, J. (2000) *Public Venture Capital*, New York: Harcourt.
Guston, D. (2003) Principal-Agent Theory and the Structure of Science Policy, Revisited: "Science in Policy" and the US Report on Carcinogens, *Science & Public Policy*, 30 (5): 347–357.
Hatakenaka, S. (2004) *University–Industry Partnerships in MIT, Cambridge, and Tokyo: Storytelling Across Boundaries*, London: Routledge.
Jencks, C. and Riesman, D. (1968) *The Academic Revolution*, New York: Doubleday.
Kennedy, D. (1997) *Academic Duty*, Cambridge, MA: Harvard University Press.
Kneller, R. (2007). *Bridging Islands: Venture Companies and the Future of Japanese and American Industry,* Oxford: Oxford University Press.
Kornberg, A. (1995) *The Golden Helix Inside Biotech Ventures*, Sausalito: University Science Books.
Lanier, A. (1989) *Star Wars PhD Dissertation, Department of Sociology*, Boulder: University of Colorado.
Latker, N. (1998) Attorney, former NIH Technology Transfer Official, interview with the author.

Mazzucatto, M. (2013) *The Entrepreneurial State: Debunking Public vs. Private Sector Myths*, London: Anthem Press.

Mowery, D. Nelson, R. Sampat, B. and Ziedonis, A. (2004) *Ivory Tower and Industrial Innovation: University–Industry Technology Transfer Before and After the Bayh-Dole Act.* Stanford: Stanford University Press.

Sandelin, J. (2004) Retired Technology Transfer Officer, Stanford OTL, interview with the author

Stevens, A. et al. (2015), this volume (Chapter 6).

Sunstein, C. (2014) *Why Nudge? The Politics of Libertarian Paternalism*, New Haven: Yale University Press.

Tournatzky, L. and Rideout, E. (2014) *Innovation U 2.0: Reinventing University Roles*, Self-published.

Zhou, C. (2015), this volume (Chapter 16).

22 Technology transfer in US universities and research institutions

Lita Nelsen

There are many routes through which the findings of university[1] science and engineering research are transferred to industrial utilization, increase productivity and bring new medicines and other important products to the public. These include scientific publication, faculty consulting seminars for industry, etc., and perhaps most importantly, the graduating student, educated at the state of the art, going to work in industry; all contribute to dissemination. But for the purpose of this chapter we will use the more formal, limited definition of "technology transfer" as the protection of inventions arising from the research via patents and other forms of intellectual property (IP) and the licensing of that IP to industry. Sponsored research by industry, where IP is often an important consideration, is a closely related activity, and startup companies formed around licenses to university IP are now a very visible contribution to the US economy, particularly with the formation of regional technology clusters in biotechnology, robotics and software.

This chapter first covers, in brief, a history of university technology transfer; then follows a discussion of the Bayh-Dole Act, legislation critical to the growth of the activity in the US. Then follows statistics on recent technology transfer activities in the US and their contribution to the economy, and an analysis of financial returns to the university. The next section covers startup company formation based on university licenses, and then finally, a discussion of threats to the current US university technology transfer enterprise.

A brief history of university technology transfer

Beginning in the 1920s, US universities slowly began to adopt formal patent policies, and a few significant (and remunerative) licenses were granted. By 1950, many research universities had some sort of patent policy, but there was little consensus as to ownership of patents, royalty sharing, and conflict of interest management. Few had "technology transfer offices" (TTOs) and patenting and licensing was mostly done on an ad hoc basis or through agencies such as Research Corporation, a situation that remained even into the 1970s. A few of the larger research institutions were able to negotiate "Institutional Patent Agreements" with one or another of the Federal agencies supporting some of their research. These IPAs allowed the universities to elect title to patents arising from their federally funded research, and led to more of these universities managing their own inventions and thereby developing technology transfer competence.[2]

A major inflection point in technology transfer occurred in 1980, when Congress passed the Bayh-Dole Act (which followed the provisions of the IPA plus other requirements) This law allowed any university to elect title to inventions arising from its federally funded research, and to grant licenses. (Details of the Bayh-Dole Act will be discussed further in a later section.)

In the decade following passage of the Bayh-Dole Act, university TTOs proliferated in the US, and licensing competence increased. To a large extent, competence was built by "learning from others," since there was no formal education for the field. The Association of University Technology Managers (AUTM), an organization of university technology transfer professionals, was highly influential in this endeavor, offering conferences, short courses, networking opportunities and other events in which the more experienced professionals taught the newcomers. By 1990, AUTM had over 1,000 members including about a third from industry.

Another inflection point occurred in the mid-1990s, when licensing to startup companies reached a critical mass, and the impact of these startups on local economic development became recognized by the states and even the Federal government. Other countries also began to take note of the impact of university patenting and licensing, primarily in the cause of economic development and industrial competitiveness.

In the UK, where some university technology transfer had begun fairly early, the government began several programs to try to encourage university startups (or "spinouts" as they are referred to in Great Britain.) By the late 1990s, Japan and Taiwan passed laws intended to follow the lead of the Bayh-Dole Act (although differing in important ways), and their governments encouraged the development of TTOs in their universities.

Singapore, Hong Kong, Germany, Finland, Brazil, China, South Africa and many other countries began programs to strengthen their systems for technology transfer from their universities and research institutes. And by 2000, the interest in technology transfer—and particularly in startups—was almost universal as countries began to look for new technologies transferred from their universities for economic development in the global Knowledge Economy.

National and regional professional technology transfer organizations modeled on AUTM have developed (along with a large international membership in AUTM itself.) These include, for example, PraxisUnico in the UK, FORTEC in Brazil, ASTP in Europe, swiTT in Switzerland, and many others. These organizations provide not only peer-to-peer training, but data, benchmarking of best practices, and also representation to governments concerning legislation and regulation of patenting and technology transfer. These organizations are remarkably, if unofficially, connected with each other through personal contact, exchanging best practices and learning from each other. These relationships have led to broadly similar approaches, worldwide, to university technology transfer—although with strong regional differences.

The Bayh-Dole Act

The Bayh-Dole Act originated with a concern for US economic competitiveness. In the 1970s, although the US was a leader in fundamental research in its universities, too little of the research results were being taken up by industry. An important issue (still dominating technology transfer) is that university research results are at a very early stage—nowhere near a product. Companies must therefore invest large amounts of money in further research and development to bring the technology to market. And the investments are often risky; neither the manufacturability nor market acceptance being certain at the time of investment.

Patent rights were seen as an important incentive for companies to assume such risks. If the "first mover" company was willing to invest, then—if the investment: succeeded—a strong university patent would protect the licensed company from competition for a period of time, allowing the company to recoup their investment.

Other incentives are also built into the Bayh-Dole Act, as follows.

- Allowing the university to own the inventions means that technology transfer can take place at the local level. Licensing officers can work with investigators to encourage them to identify new inventions and file patents; and they can work collaboratively with the inventors to identify licensees or to start new companies to develop the technology.
- The law also allowed universities to take royalties from licenses, mandating that the royalties be shared with inventors, while the institutional share of royalties must be used only for "research and education."
    - The percentage of royalties given to inventors is not mandated, but the majority of US universities give between 25 and 35% to inventors; others share on a sliding scale.

Safeguards are also built into the law.

- The US government must be granted an irrevocable, royalty-free license for government purposes for any invention that is funded in whole or in part by Federal funds.
    - Since the Federal government does not engage in manufacturing for the market, this license does not interfere with the grant of exclusive commercial rights to a company, but does allow the government to use the technology in research, and to procure products from non-licensees for military and other government use.
- Although there is no prohibition on licensing to foreign companies, the law mandates that if an exclusive license is given to a company, the licensee has to commit to "substantial manufacture in the US" for those products sold to the US market.
- If the university does not file a patent on the disclosed invention within a reasonable period of time, or if the university abandons the patent, the invention reverts to the US government.

- The US government retains a "march-in" right to grant another license (or even multiple licenses) if an exclusive licensee is not diligently pursuing commercialization or is unable to service an important market.
  - Fortunately, Federal agencies have recognized that frequent, or politically motivated, use of such march-in rights would be a serious deterrent to investment in early stage technology, since timelines for success are unpredictable. Requests for march-in under Bayh-Dole are very carefully evaluated by the agencies and to date, all have ultimately been rejected.

Development of technology transfer after passage of the Bayh-Dole Act

As hundreds of US universities established TTOs in the decade following passage of the Bayh-Dole Act, skills and policies developed. Most universities adopted uniform policies for institutional ownership of inventions arising from their research that used their facilities, regardless of whether the research was funded by the Federal government. The leading universities put forth strong policies, soon adopted throughout the academic community, to ensure that "academic values" took priority over commercial interests. One core principle was that their research had to be "open"—discussable within the university without confidentiality concerns, and publishable in academic journals without undue delay. Thus, TTOs, constrained from asking investigators to delay publication in order to preserve patent rights, instead had to develop procedures to rapidly evaluate inventions to decide whether to patent. Ideally, that decision would occur prior to the first public disclosure, but for US patents, the TTOs could take advantage of US patent law's "grace period" and file within a year after public disclosure—though at the cost of losing most foreign patent rights.

US technology transfer is now a mature field, 35 years after passage of the Bayh-Dole Act. A recent survey by the Association of University Technology Managers polled approximately 200 of the US research universities, hospitals and research institutes for activity in Fiscal Year 2012. The results show impressive activity:

- Newly Issued US Patents: 5145
- New License/Option Agreements: 6372
- New Startup Companies: 705
- Total Active License Agreements: 40,008.

Royalty returns and expectations

The AUTM survey also gives the total revenue from these activities in fiscal year 2012 (royalties, fees, and any cash-in of equity from startup companies): $2.6 billion.

Although this total seems large, it is important to note that the reported research expenditures for the responding institutions was $63.7 billion. Thus, the technology licensing returns were only 4.1% of the research base (and the net after inventors' shares were distributed was about three percent of the research base).

And the returns were highly skewed: 50% of the nationwide returns were received by only 12 institutions, with each of these "winning" institutions having 80–90% of their revenue due to only a single technology; in the majority of these cases, the technology is a pharmaceutical drug which will cease paying royalties when the institution's patent expires.

There is an undeniable conclusion from these statistics that is not widely recognized by university administrations: technology licensing cannot—and should not—be expected to be a reliable contributor to the university's financial health. The benefits from technology licensing need to be understood in a wider context. Society benefits through new medicines and other useful products, and through increased productivity of its industries. Jobs are created both in licensees' research and development, and ultimately in product manufacture and sale. A recent report funded by AUTM estimated that between 900,000 and 3 million employment years were attributable to such activities in the fifteen year period between 1995 and 2010, are attributable to these activities, with a contribution to US GDP of several hundred billion dollars. The government profits directly through employment and product tax revenues.

Startup companies

New companies started to develop university inventions are an increasingly important part of technology licensing. An unfortunate fact in technology transfer is that "university stage" technology is, in the vast majority of cases, not licensable directly to large companies. The inventions are simply "too early." They will often require tens of millions of dollars (or, in the case of pharmaceuticals, hundreds of millions) to even establish whether the final product is commercially viable. The risk is high, the product may or may not fit into existing product lines and distribution systems—and the time to market is longer than the strategic time horizons of established companies. The more "innovative" (i.e., radically different) the ultimate product, the less likely it will directly find a home in these companies.

As a consequence, the most innovative inventions arising from university research often must be licensed first to a startup company that can attract high risk capital to advance the technology to the point where its risk and time to market are reduced sufficiently to attract the attention of the larger companies. A large company can then acquire the product line, or the startup company at, it is hoped, a price that rewards the startup entrepreneurs and investors. Although some startup companies progress to a fully integrated company that profitably manufactures and distributes its own products, most ultimately sell off at least their first products or themselves to larger companies.

The startup company strategy for licensing of university inventions has proliferated in the last decade. As shown in the AUTM surveys, more than 500 new companies are licensed to university inventions every year. Studies have recognized the role of startup companies in net job creation in the country and government agencies supporting university research have become interested in advancing startups.

Student and faculty interest in entrepreneurship is high and growing, based in part on successful faculty and student startups, providing role models for new entrepreneurs within the university. Universities are responding to this interest with a variety of support mechanisms, including, among others:

- entrepreneurship and innovation courses in both schools of engineering and schools of business
- incubators that provide space for new companies at reasonable prices
- "mentoring services" providing advice to faculty, students, and alumnus starting companies
- community networking and educational events (such as are provided by the chapters of the MIT Enterprise Forum throughout the US and in many countries)
- business plan contests that provide mentoring to students throughout the process and provide visibility to potential startups
- "step up funds" to further develop patented research inventions within the universities to make them more attractive to investors
- and even university-owned venture capital funds to seed early stage companies.

The more successful of these entities draw heavily on volunteer mentors and advisors from the business and investment communities. These volunteers bring real world experiences and specific industry knowledge into the university, and provide realistic perspectives that both moderate and encourage the ambitions of faculty and students. On the other hand, these business people bring knowledge of new university technologies back to their companies and investors, making it easier for the nascent companies to get financial support when they spin out of the university.

The future of US technology licensing: some concerns

The US model of university technology transfer relies on three fundamental factors, each of which is currently under threat:

- Federal support of discovery research from which the inventions arise
- strong and predictable patents, assuring that investments in development can be protected
- availability of patient venture capital for early stage investment.

Support for basic research: Federal and industrial

Budget deficit problems and Congressional deadlock over many issues have contributed to a substantial decline in Federal funding for basic research. NIH support, for example, which almost doubled during the period 1999 to 2003, has now declined in real dollar terms in the past few years. Other Federal agencies have followed suit. Belief in the value of basic research is not universal among legislators, and many call for more "practical" or "outcome driven" research. Even cries for more Federal support of "translational research" or direct Federal support for technology transfer become a zero-sum game threatening long range discovery research. There is a danger of selling off the future.

The decline in Federal funding has led many universities to look toward industry to make up the shortfall in research support. Usually the funders will be large companies, since few small ones can support much research. And although working with industry in research brings many positive benefits to the university beyond just funding, it can also add encumbrances to intellectual property that limit technology licensing and development.

Most US university research agreements with industry insist that the university own inventions made by university employees, but offer options to the sponsors to negotiate licenses for these inventions, including royalty-bearing exclusive licenses. Some also offer royalty-free nonexclusive licenses. Statistics show that few options for exclusive licenses are exercised by sponsoring companies—simply because the inventions are too early for the large companies. But the encumbrances of long-term options or free nonexclusive licenses to the sponsors inhibit third party investment in development. The universities must make very difficult trade-offs between attracting needed funds for research and preserving IP rights to encourage development.

Changes in patent law

Technology transfer is dependent on strong, predictably valid patents to attract investment for development of university inventions. But since 1995, both legislative changes and Supreme Court rulings have chipped away at the strength, duration and scope of US patents. In 1995, in a desire to harmonize US patent law with that of most of the rest of the world, Congress changed the duration of patents from 17 years after issuance to 20 years from the priority filing date. Continuations in part dated from the same initial filing. The net effect, on average, was to shorten the period of patent life. This has a significant impact on university technology transfer. University patents are inevitably filed very early after initial reports of invention because of upcoming academic publication. And the commercial development of "university stage" inventions may take a decade or more in such fields as biotechnology or new materials; consequently, there may be only a few years of patent life left by the time the product reaches the market.

The recent American Invents Act changed the basis of awarding patents from "first to invent" to "first to disclose," eliminating the potential confusion and expense of interferences in patent disputes, but introducing a different potential confusion in derivation of invention, and weakening the protection of the grace period after disclosure. It also allowed an increased number of methods for challenging patents before going to court, weakening the presumption of validity.

Universities and licensees may have to defend against multiple challenges to their patents, a particularly heavy burden for non-profit entities and startup companies who do not have the funds to defend against multiple patent challenges.

Legislation currently under discussion in Congress threatens to further weaken patents and the ability of non-profit and small companies to defend their patents against challenges. Potential changes that lessen damages for infringement by narrowing the basis for awarding damages will offer far less protection—and will be a disincentive for investment in early stage university inventions.

While these legislative changes have been happening, Supreme Court rulings have significantly narrowed patentable subject matter in the biotechnology and diagnostic fields and in software—areas of major importance in university research and technology transfer.

The ultimate impact of all these changes is yet to be seen.

Availability of capital for early stage investment

The difficulty in obtaining capital for investment in early stage inventions is a major barrier to development of university technology. Public companies with stock prices sensitive to short term earnings often cannot risk investing in early stage technology that, even if successful, will not come to market for many years. Only a very small fraction of the hundreds of venture capital firms in the US invest in seed or A-rounds of new companies; and even those who do are often overly reactive to short-term stock market conditions and technology fads, with enthusiasm for biotechnology, for example, waxing and waning over roughly five-to-six-year cycles. And most wealthy individuals and family foundations do not have the domain knowledge to invest wisely in new technology.

Nonetheless, there are some important players in the field who understand the technologies and can both invest in the technologies and contribute to wise board management for new companies. Among them are "angel" investors who have made their fortunes in the technology fields in which they invest. In addition to seed capital, they bring knowledge of the market, introduction to industrial partners, and ultimately connections to venture investors. "Angel networks" (entities in which a dozen or more individual angels band together to explore opportunities to invest) provide potentially larger sums to startup companies, and are becoming increasingly important in regional "entrepreneurial ecosystems" surrounding large research universities.

The relatively small number of venture funds experienced in early stage investing is a critical element in the technology transfer system. They are characterized by partners who have deep technical knowledge and substantial business backgrounds in the fields in which they invest. Many of them have personal connections with one or more major research universities; they know the faculty and the TTOs and are aware of new technologies arising. Often, instead of investing in startups once they are formed, they will work with the inventors to put the company together, sometimes bringing in related technologies from other universities and attracting professional management with domain expertise.

Some large manufacturing companies are now also investing in university startups. Most frequently this is done through wholly owned investment funds, which invest "strategically", that is in technologies which may ultimately be of interest for the parent company to acquire. This trend has accelerated in the pharmaceutical industry, where startup biotechnology companies are an important part of the pharmaceutical companies' pipelines for new products.

Conclusions

Technology transfer from universities through protection and licensing of intellectual property, is a robust enterprise. It benefits from the autonomy granted by the Bayh-Dole Act to the universities to manage their own intellectual property, and by the university policies and TTO skills that have developed in the decades following the Act. Over 200 universities, research hospitals and research institutes in the US are actively engaged in the activity.

Job creation and economic development arising from this activity have been well documented, and both regional and national government encourage it.

Attracting investment in early stage ("university stage") inventions by established companies continues to be difficult, and universities have responded by putting more resources into encouraging startup companies based on these inventions. This has benefits not only to the startup entrepreneurs and universities, but also to established companies who will have access to more mature new products from the startups.

Direct financial return to the universities from technology licensing is, on the average, fairly small, with the occasional "blockbuster" patent arising that can yield hundreds of millions of dollars during the life of the patent. These blockbuster events are sufficiently rare that no university can count on their TTO being highly profitable. The benefits to be emphasized instead include, among others, new medicines and other important products for the public; industrial collaborations based on university-owned IP; job creation; and the development of entrepreneurial skills by faculty and students.

The future of technology transfer in the US continues to look promising, but certain threats should be understood by legislators and university administrators, including a decline in Federal funding of basic research, and changes in patent law that are tending to weaken the protection that patents offer as incentives to invest in development of inventions based on university research.

Notes

1 For brevity, "universities" will also include research hospitals and other non-government non-profit institutions primarily devoted to fundamental research and public dissemination of results.
2 Much of the information in this paragraph was derived from "American University Patent Policies: A Brief History" authored by the American Association of University Professors; downloaded from the internet on February 5, 2015.

Part VI

Conclusion

23 Making sense of university technology commercialization

Diversity and adaptation

Shiri M. Breznitz and Henry Etzkowitz

This edited volume has had two purposes. One, to expand our understanding of the need to diversify and adapt when it comes to university technology commercialization models. In particular, the chapters presented in this book demonstrate the necessity for more regional and national input in models of university technology commercialization. Universities are regional and national players. They do not exist in a void. Hence, all of their activities, be their teaching, research, or technology commercialization, need to adapt to the university's environment and they, in turn, recursively adapt to a broader environment, including but not limited to industry, government and Civil Society, to various degrees in different societies.

In this volume we used "developed" and "developing" to describe the level of university technology commercialization in each country. Interestingly, we can see that we have more "developing" vs. "developed" countries represented in this volume. This was not a conscious decision. However, we believe that this reflects the problems that arise in many countries when attempting to adopt a more U.S.-centric model. We find that even countries such as Spain and Italy, which on any economic scale will be considered as developed countries, find it difficult to move their university model of research and teaching to focus on technology transfer. One must understand the history and commercialization environment in these countries in order to understand these difficulties. It is ever more so in poorer countries.

The second purpose of this volume was to show the drawbacks, as well as the strong points, of the U.S. model, which is constantly used as a role model for university technology transfer. The U.S. model itself is variegated and sensitive to different academic and regional contexts, beyond the purview of leading university technology transfer regimes, like MIT and Stanford that have their distinctive features. Studies that focus on the US model tend to show the successful cases of commercialization, while ignoring the negative impacts and complications this model has created. The section on the U.S.A. in this book presents chapters that discuss the advantages and positive effects and disadvantages as well as the negative effects of this model. The issues presented in these chapters vary from litigations, to emphasis on output and metrics that require supplement with qualitative, as well as more complex quantitative measures. It is necessary to show impact on local, regional, national and multi-national knowledge economies, beyond disclosures, patents and licensing income to properly evaluate technology transfer, and its contribution to the renovation of drug development.

Importantly, the chapters and review pieces presented in this volume highlight significant issues in the current perspective on university technology commercialization. One, what is the meaning of university technology commercialization? In many countries and regions university technology commercialization has a different meaning. In many it includes the basic features of patents, licenses, and spinout companies. In others it represents a wider perspective that includes such things as publication, teaching, basic research, and university industry research collaboration. Second, How? What is the process by which university technology is commercialized? The chapters presented here have shown that in many countries inventions belong to the inventor and not the university, and hence, the process of commercialization at the university is minimal. In others, the state is dominant, with industry and university operating as integrated actors in a top-down managed system of technology commercialization. In still others, the system of commercialization is so highly structured, yet open to divergent interpretations, that any deviation or innovation, leads to conflicts, litigation, negotiation and compromise: the lifeblood of an open society. Last, in what way does university technology commercialization contribute to society? The academic view regarding the impact universities have through commercialization is as highly debatable and debated. Proponents see the glass half full, view it with great expectations, noting the increasing salience of universities, and their technology transfer regimes, to innovation entrepreneurship and regional development. Opponents note that most technology transfer offices (TTOs) are money-losing propositions for their universities, and agree with the large corporation perspective that views university TTOs as a hindrance to effect transfer and at heart feel that it is a distraction form the university's "true" missions of education and research. That said, it is very clear that some universities, regions, and countries have embraced the process of university technology commercialization on its faults, viewing the benefits as exponentially higher than its deficiencies, while attending to issues of equity, conflict of interest and obligation.

It is evident in the U.SA., where we can see the growth of university technology transfer offices, the renewal of the Bayh-Dole Act, and the constant demand of universities to show their contribution via quantifiable commercialized measurements. On the other hand, there has also been pushback from the thought leaders of the university technology transfer profession, through the Association of University Technology Managers, originally an almost entirely U.S. group that has become increasingly global in recent years, through initiatives like the Better World Project, setting forth role models of the contribution of university technology transfer to sustainability and social innovation as well as economic development, (Etzkowitz, this volume).

The idea of university technology commercialization is not a bad one. It may even be a quite good one, in evolved formats more closely integrated with education and research. Especially when considering the amounts of public funding invested in universities' research. However, we must remember that the technology transfer process requires multiple interactions and constant feedback. Beyond the traditional notion of tapping the "meandering stream of basic research" without dipping into its waters, or heaven forfend, attempting to divert its flow, is the informal interaction of researcher and technology transfer professional in which ideas for research extension, and the opening up of new tributaries and accessing alternative funding streams, are batted about. New applications are conceived, beyond those mentioned in the original disclosure statement that may also suggest promising new research directions.

When we think about technology commercialization at university we need to realize how much of this process is done beyond the bureaucratic structured process of the technology licensing office. Much takes place within the research group, the dormitory suite and the accelerator, that may be located just off campus beyond the reach of the university's intellectual property regime. Commercialization is about people, knowledge, and relationships. It's about promoting knowledge developed within higher education and research institutes to benefit society. The current model that has been promoted by university administrators and government representatives alike, has shown that there are many barriers, as well as incentives, to transferring university knowledge and technology to the general public. Even worse, by commercializing technology we may create obstacles to life saving medications and technologies. The case of the AIDS drug cocktail and its distribution in Africa provides just one example in many.[1] On the other hand, not protecting and commercializing drug discoveries can lead to lack of development or mis-development, as the Universities of Wisconsin and Toronto decided early on in patenting and licensing the milk purity test and insulin discoveries made on their respective campuses. These early 20th-century decisions provided an impetus to the development and growth of formal university technology transfer modalities, within or closely linked to the university, like the Wisconsin Alumni Research Foundation (WARF). Their efflorescence, detailed in the chapters of this volume, has occurred globally in recent decades. This is the Scylla and Charybdis of transfer that the university technology transfer office, at leading U.S. universities, is tasked with advising how to maneuver and balance without capsizing: the faculty in its deliberative bodies, the university administration, especially its Dean of Research and Vice President for Innovation, as well as the university's Board of Trustees, which may provide its own instruction.

Moreover, even the attempt to use the specific measurements of commercialization (patents, licenses, spinouts) is extremely chaotic. Different bodies in different countries measure different factors. Even within the same universities we find different definitions to certain technologies. This problem with the measurements has more profound impacts when we think about the representation of these figures and how they are used by politicians and policy makers, academic metrics researchers and public policy think tanks. Most universities are now required to show how "well" they are doing in commercialization. Hence, university reports have become focused on commercialization measurements and less on their two most important tasks: teaching and research. On the other hand, the rise of highly publicized university ranking schemes that privilege research, narrowly measured by citation and impact factors, has been found to draw attention away from the university's emerging entrepreneurial role since its outputs are seldom captured in these reports. Even worse, much of the grander work of universities—such as being a public place of knowledge sharing—is lost.

The race for commercialization may have negative impacts on society if we don't pay attention to some basic features of universities: their purpose and their contribution. Yet the very purpose and extent of university contribution to society is in flux in the transition from an industrial to a knowledge-based society. Pressing societal challenges: climate change, rising inequality and seemingly irreconcilable value conflicts among faiths and world views call upon the humanities, social and natural sciences for analysis and innovation. Technology commercialization is an epiphenomenon, albeit a significant one, on a broader role that the university has in influencing the course and direction of societal evolution.

Universities were created to expand societal knowledge. In time, universities began to offer more practical subjects, such as law and accounting, and training students for professions like medicine and engineering. Importantly, universities have become recognized as regional and national engines of growth, an institution from which new knowledge and innovations are delivered. Today's model of the university has a public service component, offering a wider base for research and teaching—both of which have the power to promote social change. It is vital to remember these features and understand that by diverting the role of universities from knowledge production and teaching we are compromising potential benefits.

Many of the world's most used products and our progress in human development have originated from basic research done in the name of science. Those research projects were not looking for a specific technology or a cure. On the contrary, these developments were discovered while conducting basic research with a very different agenda. It is true, universities brought us new technologies and platforms—from the recombinant DNA of the Boyer and Cohen patent, insulin, and giant companies such as Google. These are important discoveries that should not be missed. Especially since much of the research on these project was publicly funded.

That said, universities are much more than the sum of the technologies and companies they produce. They are a world of knowledge and ideas, these cannot be quantified nor can they be replaced. If the chapters of this volume teach us anything it is that we need to find ways to balance the knowledge creation at universities with our need to commercialize and produce new technologies. Pushing specific agendas onto universities will not result in better societies. However, allowing universities to produce knowledge using specific models and systems that fit their environments and abilities will maximize their capacity to positively contribute to society.

Note

1 See the case of Yale University and Bristol-Myers Squibb, www.theguardian.com/world/2001/mar/13/education.highereducation.

Index

'n' refers to end of chapter notes.

For Product Safety Concerns and Information please contact our EU
representative GPSR@taylorandfrancis.com
Taylor & Francis Verlag GmbH, Kaufingerstraße 24, 80331 München, Germany